INNSBRUCKER GEOGRAPHISCHE STUDIEN

Herausgeber: A. Borsdorf u. G. Patzelt   Schriftleitung W. Keller   Band 26

Human Geography in North America

New Perspectives and Trends in Research

Edited by Klaus Frantz

Selbstverlag
des Instituts für Geographie der Universität Innsbruck
1996

This publication was sponsored by:

Bundesministerium für Wissenschaft und Forschung
Casino Austria AG
Cultural Affairs Office of the Embassy of the United States of America
Fröschl Bau AG & Co.KG
Landes-Hypothekenbank Tirol
Raiffeisenkasse Alpbach
Raiffeisen Zentralkasse
Rektor der Universität Innsbruck
Restaurant-Pizza "Die Geisterburg"
Österreichische Hochschülerschaft
Stadtgemeinde Hall i. T.
Tiroler Landesregierung
Tiroler Loden
Tiroler Sparkasse
Tiroler Tageszeitung
Tirol Werbung
Tourismusverband Hall i. T.
United States Information Agency, Washington D.C.
Universität Innsbruck
Zillertaler Gletscherbahnen

All rights, especially for translation into other languages, reserved.

Cover picture:
Rancho de Taos, New Mexico (Klaus Frantz, January 1976)
Westin Bonaventure Hotel, Downtown Los Angeles (Thomas Mösl, September 1992)

1996, Department of Geography, University of Innsbruck

Printed by: Druck- und Verlagshaus, 6065 Thaur, Austria

ISBN 3-901182-26-8

Table of Contents

Introduction 5

Part I

Malcom Comeaux:
Cajuns and their Adaptation to a Modern World 7

Christoph Stadel:
Cultural Minorities in the Canadian Prairies; their Impact on
the Rural Landscape 17

Volker Albrecht:
Multiculturalism and Pluralism in the United States.
Perspectives from the Mexican American Experiences. 41

Hans Dieter Laux and Günter Thieme:
Model Minority or Scapegoat? The Experience of Korean Immigrants
in Los Angeles 65

Günter Thieme and Hans Dieter Laux:
Los Angeles - A Multi-Ethnic Metropolis Spatial Patterns and
Socio-Economic Problems as a Result of Recent Migration Processes 81

Ines M. Miyares:
To Be Hmong in America: Settlement Patterns and Early Adaptation
of Hmong Refugees in the United States 97

Barbara Hahn:
Poverty and Affordable Housing in New York City 115

Friedrich M. Zimmermann and Gert Krautbauer:
Aspects of Economic and Social Integration of African Americans -
The Case of New York City 129

Part II

Roland Vogelsang:
Internal Migration in Canada: Trends, Causes, and Consequences 151

Tibor Frank:
Via Berlin to New York:
The Human Geography of Hungarian Migrations after World War I 169

Part III

David J. Wishart:
Indian Dispossession and Land Claims: The Issue of Fairness 181

Dorothy M. Hallock:
Second Contact: Redefining Indian Country 195

Dick Winchell:
*The Consolidation of Tribal Planning in American Indian Tribal
Government and Culture* 209

Part IV

Joachim Vossen:
*The Amish Migration of Lancaster County and its Relevance for
the Amish Culture of the Northeastern United States* 225

George Cathcart:
Religion and Land Use: Mormon Ranchers of the Little Colorado 241

Gisbert Rinschede:
Geographical Aspects of Religious Broadcasting in the United States 253

Part V

Burkhard Hofmeister:
From Log Cabin to Edge City 267

Michael Conzen:
The Moral Tenets of American Urban form 275

Lutz Holzner:
*American Ideologies and the Building of Compromise-Landscapes
in Urban America* 289

Axel Borsdorf:
Cities of the Americas: Urban Development in Different Cultural Landscapes 301

Part VI

D.W. Meinig:
*Forging a National Axis
Problems of Geographical Decision-Making in a Federal State* 313

John Fraser Hart:
The Great American Deserted 337

Alvar W. Carlson:
Sources of Overseas Tourists (Pleasure Arrivals) to the United States, 1950-1989 357

Introduction

From the 17th to the 21st of May 1994 a symposium of the *USA-Speciality Group (Arbeitskreis USA)* took place in Hall in Tyrol. This group forms part of the *Central Association of German Geographers (Zentralverband der Deutschen Geographen)* and has existed since 1984. This was its fourth meeting to take place outside the German-speaking Geographers' Convention which is held every two years. The general theme of the conference *"Human Geography in North America – New Perspectives and Trends in Research"* was intended to be broad in scope in order to give as many geographers as possible the opportunity to present some aspects of their most recent research. Physical Geography was, however, not included this time, thus making it easier to focus on certain topics and give a more uniform structure to the conference.

In order to secure a larger number of participants, it was necessary to invite many geographers who were not members of the Speciality Group. These included colleagues from non-German-speaking countries, above all from the USA and Eastern Europe. This was also the reason why English was chosen as the language of the conference and why it was to be held in the second half of May rather than in fall as had been customary up till then. At this time of the year American geographers do not, as a rule, have to hold lectures at their universities, thus those interested would be able to attend the Hall symposium. For the first time emphasis was also placed on integrating one Canadian session with the intention of comparing the USA and Canada as this promised to open up new perspectives.

Hall in Tyrol was chosen as the site for this conference, also designed as a kind of secret lure. This attractive medieval town, far from the hustle and bustle of university life, yet easily accessible from Innsbruck, was to serve the participants as a tranquil setting for discussions before and after the sessions. A twofold connection links Hall to America. For more than 300 years after 1485 a great many *"Silbertaler"* (silver Thalers) were produced in the *Münzturm* (Mint Tower). This currency happened to be one of the forerunners of the U.S. American dollar. Also Father Eusebio KINO once attended the former Jesuit School in Hall. In Arizona and the adjoining Mexican state Sonora he is known as probably the most famous Indian missionary at the turn of the 17th and beginning of the 18th century. Both of these places served as festive settings for two special events that took place in the evening during the course of the symposium.

It was a matter of particular concern to me that the conference be accessible to young geographers. So that not only students from the University of Innsbruck would be able to attend the conference I wrote to many Austrian and German geography departments asking them to send students who were working on an American topic for their diploma or doctorate at that time. Students who came to Hall from further afield were given a grant to cover most of their travelling expenses and costs of accommodation. All in all eleven students from the universities in Bonn, Heidelberg, Saarbrücken, Salzburg, Trier and Vienna made use of this offer.

At first registrations for the symposium just trickled in but they accumulated and in the end a considerable number of participants had registered so that, in retrospect, the time and energy invested was undoubtedly well worth it. Finally one hundred and fifty people from thirty different universities took part in the conference, a third of whom were students. Twenty-eight people came all the way from the USA and five from Canada, just to be in Hall. Twenty-six were from Germany and one person came from Hungary. Unfortunately my effort to invite colleagues from Eastern European countries was not as successful as I had hoped. The rest of the participants were from Austria.

During part of the conference lasting four days in which talks were held in six sessions, including two key note lectures, altogether twenty-five papers were presented, seventeen of which are published in this volume. Some speakers, however, did not hand in the written version of their paper (Rudi HARTMANN/*Denver*, Michael MARCHAND/*Spokane*) and two geographers, namely Rainer VOLLMAR/*Berlin* and Alvar CARLSON/*Bowling Green* had already requested in advance that their papers be published elsewhere. Alvar CARLSON handed in a paper on tourism instead of the written version of his talk on migration for this publication. Hans Dieter LAUX and David WISHART, who were not able to attend the symposium, presented their topics only in written form.

Thus this volume consists of twenty-three articles which can be roughly divided into six thematic blocks. These essentially deal with aspects of ethnic diversity and multiculturalism (1), social and economic problems amongst minorities in urban environments (2), migration issues (3), land issues as well as perspectives and effects of the new way Native Americans see themselves (4), the spatial effects of religiously determined behavior (5) and urban development as an expression of social, economic and cultural change (6). The last three contributions to this publication do not fit into any of these thematic blocks and therefore form a category of their own.

Although the authors made a great effort to keep to the deadlines, several papers, which the editor by no means wished to exclude, were not completed in time. As a result the printing also had to be postponed more than once. Delays are, however, to be expected when a symposium volume of this size is published and, in this case, the topicality of this publication was not really effected. My thanks go to Dr. Willfried KELLER, the editor of the *Innsbrucker Geographische Studien (Innsbruck Geographical Studies)*, for waiting patiently. The publishers of this series, who had kindly agreed to print the scientific results of the conference, also showed great patience in this respect.

A conference of this size necessarily involves a considerable amount of work which cannot be done by the organizer alone. I am therefore especially grateful to the many students of the Geography Department at Innsbruck University who lent me a helping hand before, during and after the conference. I would like to particularly mention Mag. Irmgard HUTER, Margreth KEILER, and Christine OSL. I am also grateful to the University of Chicago Press and Yale University Press as well as to Dr. Roswitha HALLER of the Amerikahaus in Vienna who kindly agreed to set up a book and map exhibition at the venue. I also wish to express my special thanks to the twenty sponsors that are listed separately on one page of this volume. Without their financial assistence this conference would not have been possible.

Finally I wish to express the hope that this symposium will further narrow the information gap that still exists between the U.S. American geography and the geography in German-speaking countries, that it might widen the platform for future cooperation and that is has encouraged German-speaking geographers to become more interested in doing research on North American topics.

Innsbruck, February 1996 • Klaus Frantz

MALCOLM L. COMEAUX

Cajuns and Their Adaptation to a Modern World

The Cajuns of Louisiana, by European-American standards, have a long and tortured history. Their ancestors came to America from France primarily in the seventeenth century. They settled around the Bay of Fundy in what is now eastern Canada, and with the tradition of large families, their numbers grew very rapidly, reaching between 11,000 and 13,000 by 1755 (*Roy 1982, 152*). By this time they were known as "Acadians." They were unique and separate from the French-speakers of Quebec, a people with whom they never cooperated, and with whom they had few relations or connections. The year 1755 was particularly momentous for the Acadians. This was at the height of the *French and Indian War*, the American phase of a general struggle known in Europe as the Seven Years War, and at that time the English governor of Nova Scotia decided to rid the area of the Acadians, as they were considered a threat to English domination of the region. About 8,000 were deported, and the rest fled in order to avoid persecution and exile (*Clark 1968, 344-352; LeBlanc 1970*). Many of those deported were sent to English colonies to the south,[1] but others spent years in prisoner of war camps.
With cessation of hostilities and signing of the *Paris Treaty* of 1763 the Acadians were allowed to go wherever they wished. Many returned to Canada, but found their former lands now in the hands of English-speaking Protestants from New England. They were not welcomed, and many returning to that area were imprisoned. As a result, returning Acadians were forced to settle in areas not desired by English-speakers. Most were farmers, but there was little agricultural land available, and they generally settled in rocky coastal regions. Others, meanwhile, looked to Louisiana as a new homeland. The first group of Acadian refugees arrived in Louisiana in 1765, and the last and largest group came from France in 1785.
The Acadians found an environment in Louisiana that was very different from the one to which they had become accustomed in Canada. Much of their material culture had to change in order for them to survive, such things as house types, barns, crops, clothes, boat types, and the like. Within 100 years they had changed and adjusted their culture to this environment, and by this time were different from their cousins who had returned to eastern Canada. By the 1870s and 1880s they were referring to themselves as "Cajuns."[2] A person calling himself or herself an "Acadian" today in south Louisiana would be considered by others as "putting on airs." Meanwhile, the Acadians of Canada have always considered themselves as being "Acadians," and the word Cajun would never be used to describe them.
When the first Acadians, whose descendants were to become Cajuns, arrived in Louisiana, other persons of European descent were already living there. There were Americans who had drifted westward and southward along the Mississippi River system. New Orleans was a thriving town occupied mostly by French-speakers, though many of other nationalities lived there as well. Living up-river from New Orleans was a group of Germans who had migrated to Louisiana two generations earlier. They were remnants of the Company of the Indies, formed by John LAW. About 250 Germans settled an area along the Mississippi River in an area known as *Cote des Allemands* (German Coast) (*Kondert 1985, 386*) (*Fig. 1*). They were very successful farmers, supplying New Orleans with much of its food. These early German settlers had adjusted to this sub-tropical region before the first Acadians arrived, and undoubtedly had a great and beneficial influence on the earliest Acadian arrivals. There was much intermarriage, and the newcomers surely learned many traits that allowed them to survive in this environment. For example, the Cajuns adopted the house style used by the Germans - a house-type widely found in the Caribbean area - and the barns of the Cajuns evolved from an early German model (*Comeaux*

Fig. 1: Cajun Settlement in Southern Louisiana

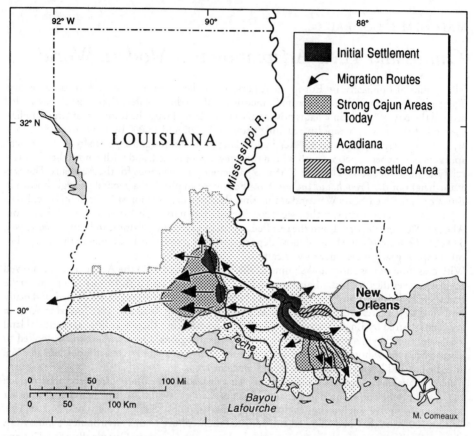

1989, 53). Nothing survives from this early German colony, and today there are many people with surnames such as *Toups* (once *Dubs*), *Zeringue* (once *Zehringer*), *Wiltz, Hymel, Schexnayder* (spelled many different ways), *Lambert* and *Heidel*, who consider themselves to be "Cajun," and while they may have more Cajun blood than German, they still carry the German name - though some had their names completely gallicized, as *Zweig* to *Labranche* (*Deiler 1909*).

The People of South Louisiana

There are people from many different backgrounds living in south Louisiana, and it is dominated by no one particular group. Cajuns are perhaps the most unique and visible, and certainly those to have received most attention. But, there are many others of French descent who are not Cajun, there are many blacks - some gallicized, others not, many Anglos and descendants of many foreigners who migrated directly to Louisiana.

It is very popular today to be a Cajun, and many persons without Cajun ancestors will claim to be Cajun. This is not unusual, as being Cajun is based more on cultural attributes than on descent (*Gibson and Del Sesto 1975, 3*). Cajun culture was not brought to Louisiana from Canada. Rather the first generation of Acadians in Louisiana were still "Acadians," but within a generation or two,

Cajun culture and Cajuns had evolved. In the 230 or so years since the first Acadians arrived in Louisiana there has been much mixing and assimilation of others into Cajun culture. Today there are many people with English, German and other surnames who claim to be Cajun, with or without Cajun ancestors. There are even some blacks, again with or without Cajun ancestors, who claim to be Cajun (*Tentchoff 1975, 89-90*), though most white Cajuns would argue otherwise.

Popular literature implies that the ancestors of the Cajuns were primarily from Brittany and Normandy, but this is not the case (*Fig. 2*). The majority of Cajun surnames originate in the central Loire Valley and along the coastal area in the La Rochelle region. The large number of Cajun names coming from the Loire valley can easily be explained. Charles DE MENOU, Sieur d'Aulnay, was governor of Acadia from 1635 to 1650, and he had a large estate in this region of France. During his tenure of office he recruited workers to come to Acadia, and he was successful in getting many from his estate to migrate to Acadia. There are fourteen Cajun surnames that have

Fig. 2: The Origins of Cajun Surnames in France.

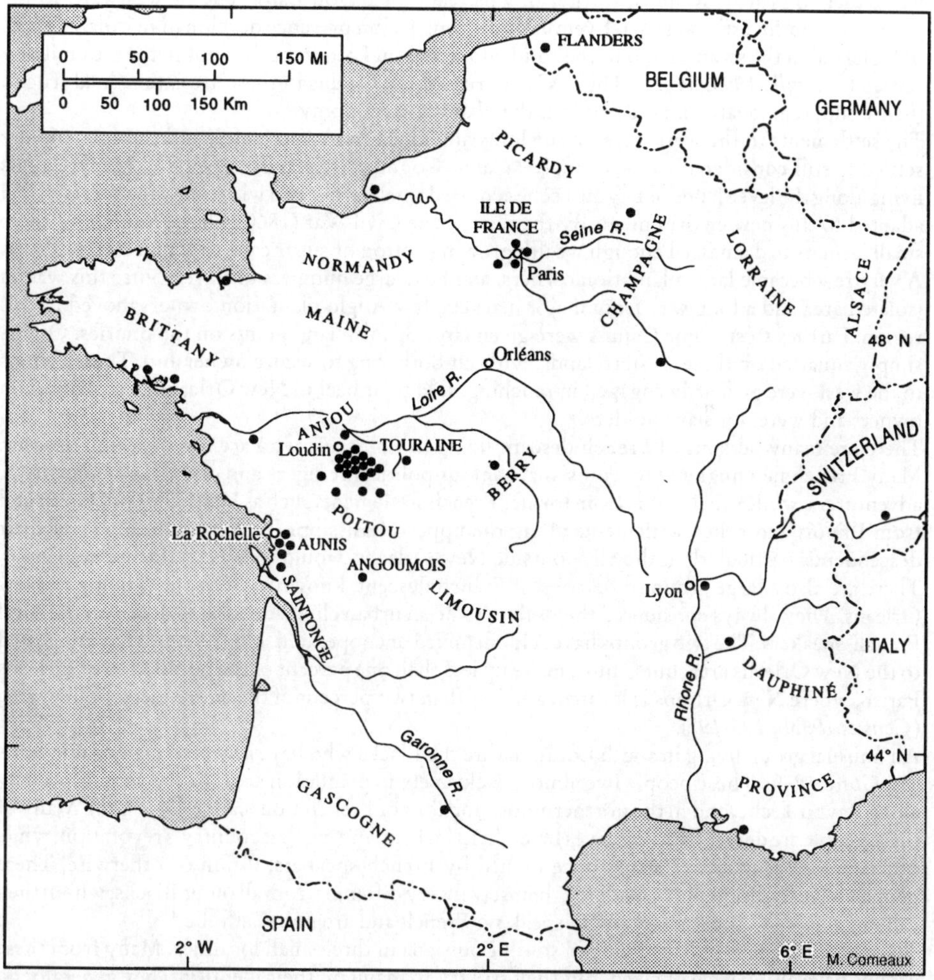

Source: after West 1986, 9 – 11.

their origin in three small villages near the town of Loudun (*West 1986, 9-12*). Other families from the surrounding area and the Poitou region in general, as well as the coastal area near LaRochelle, also migrated, most arriving near the middle of the seventeenth century. Other Frenchmen migrated to eastern Canada from scattered areas in France and nearby countries. Many of these were military personnel who were discharged in Canada and remained, while others were fishermen, adventurers or merchants.

The Cajuns who came to Louisiana were settled in two distinct regions - upriver along the Mississippi River and along the neighboring Bayou Lafourche, and secondly to the west, along the Bayou Teche and on the prairies of southwest Louisiana (*Fig. 1*). Those who acquired the rich levee lands upriver from New Orleans generally lost their lands when a plantation economy developed after the Louisiana Purchase in 1803. Many wealthy Americans migrated westward with their slaves from other Southern states, and they purchased the lands of the Cajuns. Today when one travels this area there is no evidence of the small French farmers, the *petit habitant*, as they generally migrated elsewhere when the plantation economy engulfed this area. Migration was either to nearby swamps, further downstream on Bayou Lafourche or westward to the prairies of southwest Louisiana. Eventually a strong Cajun presence developed in isolated spots of high land in the swamps and to the south along Bayou Lafourche, but not in the area initially settled (*Estaville 1993, 34-41*). The vast majority of the Cajuns in these areas remained true to their egalitarian ideals, and did not join the plantation economy.[3]

The settlements to the west were, in the long run, much more successful, and the area initially settled is still considered to be strongly "Cajun Country" (*Estaville 1993, 41*). Many Cajuns living along the levee lands of Bayou Teche acquired small farms, and with time they survived and adapted to this new environment. By the time of the Civil War (1860) a large number of these small farmers had amassed enough wealth growing cotton or sugar cane to acquire a few slaves. A very few became large plantation owners, and held large numbers of slaves. Since this was an isolated area and a long way from major markets, few Anglo plantation owners moved to this region. Farther west, some Cajuns were given large Spanish land grants on the prairies. Others simply squatted on these western lands, without bothering to secure ownership. These Cajuns to the west were primarily engaged in ranching, sold their beef in New Orleans or to plantation owners and were not slave holders.

There are many persons of French descent living in Louisiana who are not of Cajun descent. Many Frenchmen migrated to Louisiana, some as political refugees and others as merchants or adventurers, while others came from former French settlements such as Haiti, the Gulf Coast and from Illinois and other settlements along the upper Mississippi River system. Many of their descendants, particularly if they live outside New Orleans, would today call themselves Cajun. There are also a large group of persons of French descent, known as "Creoles", living in New Orleans. They always considered themselves to be an urban elite who looked down on the rural French-speakers. The two groups have seldom mixed or cooperated. Many Cajuns have migrated to the New Orleans area, but Cajuns make up less than one percent of the population of Orleans Parish, where New Orleans is located, and less than two percent of the entire metropolitan area (*Census 1993b, 195-197*).

An unusual group living in south Louisiana are the Blacks who have accepted many gallic traits (*MaGuire 1979*). These people live almost exclusively in plantation areas to the west, especially along Bayou Teche, and in the northernmost portions of French Louisiana (*Allen n.d.*). Many of these people are descendants of slaves brought from Haiti during that country's revolution, while others are descendants of slaves once owned by French-speakers, Cajun or otherwise. These peoples have traditionally considered themselves very different from all other Blacks, whom they call *neg merican* - those Blacks who speak no French and are non-Catholic.[4]

There are also a few Indians living in south Louisiana in three small localities. Many from these groups have also been gallicized, but they still try to maintain their identity. They generally do not identify themselves as Cajuns, but prefer to be known as Indians.

The single largest group in Louisiana, and in south Louisiana, are the "Americans" or *mericain* as pronounced in French (this writer's grandfather always called them *Methodist*, as those he knew were from that religion). These are the white, mostly Protestant, English-speaking persons of European descent who do not consider themselves as Cajuns. These people have traditionally controlled Louisiana politically since Civil War days. Some from this group, especially if they are Catholic and of the second or third generation to live in South Louisiana, would consider themselves as Cajuns.

English-speakers from north Louisiana offer a striking difference when compared to the Cajuns. They are Protestant - usually Baptist - are very conservative, and do not have the *joie de vivre* so commonly associated with French Louisiana. As a rule, the economy of south Louisiana has been strong when compared to the north, and that has always encouraged migration southward. Large numbers of white English-speakers moved to south Louisiana over the years, with particularly large numbers coming during the boom years of the 1970s when oil prices were very high.

Cajuns Today

The census in the past never attempted to identify Cajuns, but in the 1990 census a question concerning Cajun identity was included. And, the word "Cajun" was specifically mentioned as a possibility on the census form. This fact certainly encouraged many to put down Cajun as their ancestry. About 10% of the population in Louisiana (432,549 persons) said they considered themselves Cajuns (*Census 1993b, 56*). In the entire USA there were almost 600,000 persons who considered themselves as "Acadian/Cajun" (*Census 1993a, 2*). Most of the Cajuns live in Louisiana and in the neighboring state of Texas, while many Acadians migrated from Canada to New England, resulting in a large number of Acadians in that area. A total of 550,440 Louisianans listed their ancestry as French (excluding Basque) and another 86,569 listed themselves as of French Canadian ancestry (*Census 1993b, 56*). This answer is self-ascriptive, and is what the individual thinks of him or herself. Nevertheless, a very large number of people claim French heritage.

Since it is popular today to be a Cajun, these numbers are considerably larger, percentage-wise, than if they had been collected twenty or thirty years ago. The term "Cajun" was once used disparagingly by others to designate a backward, rural, poorly educated and French-speaking population. Cajuns referred to themselves as such, but did not appreciate others using this term - it was associated with a way of life looked down upon by others. They resented the word and when talking to outsiders preferred to call themselves "French" or "Creole." This has all changed. Today, all of French Louisiana has been "cajunized," at least in name, and all are proud to label themselves as "Cajun."

No one reason can be given for the recent rise in pride in being Cajun. Certainly, the recent search for roots so popular in America, and the recognition given to minority groups has gone a long way toward advancing pride in being Cajun. Playing along with this has been general acceptance of Cajun foods in America, as well as Cajun music gaining a wide acceptance outside the state. Cajun music is found at most folk festivals around the country and in many other parts of the world, and it has gained acceptance by the young at music festivals in south Louisiana. It also crept into popular American music, especially country and western. It is a major unifying force for all of French-speaking Louisiana. In the past, few would admit to playing or enjoying such music. In a derogatory way, it was called "chanky chank" music, but today, since it is so well recognized and received outside the state, it is something of which many young Cajuns are proud, and something they proclaim as "their" music.

Another unifying cultural factor among the rural French of Louisiana is food. Cajun cuisine is national news, and a fad that has swept the country. Local foods play a role in unifying the generations, and large festive family meals are very common. Foods also go a long way toward uniting the various French subcultures, as they all eat the same foods. The foods have always been unique, and were often an identifier used to distinguish French Louisiana from the rest of the South. In an earlier era, however, it was a cause for shame. The poor French-speaking folk ate such things as crawfish, frogs - and not only the legs - alligator, and the like, and rice was served at least once a day. It was the food of the lower classes, and one did not admit that he or she ate it, as it formed an ethnic and class boundary. Foods are now a positive reflection of Cajun identity, and Cajun food has become an acceptable cuisine across America. There are syndicated Cajun cooking television shows, and any large town in America now would have at least one "Cajun" restaurant, though many are not truly authentic.

The use of the French language is another unifying force. The French spoken by the Cajuns is quite different from standard French. Standard French was codified in the seventeenth century, the time when ancestors of the Cajuns were migrating to America. They brought with them an archaic *patois*, and it changed little over the years. This French spoken in the Canadian Maritimes and Louisiana, where it remains mutually intelligible, is very different from the French spoken in Quebec. The white Creoles of New Orleans spoke another variety of French, but today it is largely forgotten. The Black Creoles speak yet another variety of French - referred to as *gumbo*, *francais neg* or *couri-mo-vini* - one that is almost unintelligible to a Cajun French speaker. It is a variety of French closely resembling that spoken in Haiti. In some places, however, white Cajuns are to be found speaking the Black French, and in other areas there are Blacks speaking Cajun French. The Census of 1990 counted 261,678 persons speaking French in Louisiana, a figure this author considers much too high (*Census 1993b, 57*).[5]

The Cajun French spoken in Louisiana is a language that is greatly simplified and much shortened (*Phillips 1978, 177-79*). For example, most Cajun adjectives have only a masculine form - whereas the language of Black Creoles uses the feminine article *la* almost exclusively - the familiar *tu* is used almost universally for "you," and the formal *vous* is seldom heard - it is used to mock the "uppity," and will be used sometimes to an outsider or to a priest. Most Cajun French verbs have been regularized, and tenses have been greatly simplified (*Daigle 1984, XXI-XXV*). Cajun French also retains many nautical terms. Another factor that makes Cajun French very different is the borrowing of words. Many words were added to the language after the first Acadians arrived in Louisiana simply because new environmental situations were met, while other words were just adopted into the language. Many Spanish, Indian, African, and especially English words and phrases are found in Cajun French. Except for addition of these new words, it remains very similar to the French spoken by their cousins in eastern Canada. Unfortunately, it is considered a second-rate French, and not only by the intelligentsia, but by the Cajun speakers themselves. People are ashamed of their tongue, and this has hurt the survival of the language.

The French language of the Cajuns is dying out in Louisiana. Language is no longer at the heart of Cajun culture. Loss of the language was a gradual process. There was a time, from the 1920s through the 1950s, when it was a formal policy of school systems to discourage French being spoken on school grounds. French is now encouraged, but the battle has been lost. One researcher in the 1980s found that 98% of her senior informants were bilingual, and while 66% of their children could speak French, only 9% of their grandchildren could do so (*Trepanier 1990, 6*). It is not unusual for minority peoples in America to lose their mother tongue, as has happened to almost all those who have moved to the United States. Perhaps it is a wonder that the Cajuns were able to maintain their language in Louisiana for 240 years.

Cajun French is almost entirely oral. The first book written in the language spoken by Cajuns appeared in 1976 (*Reed 1976*), and the first grammar book, describing the language in one small area in southwest Louisiana, was published in 1977 (*Faulk 1977*). These books were great successes, but caused much controversy in Louisiana, as many thought only proper French should be used and taught to children.

The strongest supporter for use of "proper" French was CODOFIL (the Council for the Development of French in Louisiana). This government-funded agency, sponsored by federal and state money, plus support from Quebec, France and Belgium, was established in 1968, and had as its goal the renewing of pride in ethnic differences and in reinforcement of traditional values. Unfortunately, this group insisted that only proper French be used and taught in Louisiana. To this end, they brought in French-speaking teachers from around the world, and by 1978 they were reaching 43,000 elementary and secondary school students (*Rushton 1979, 291*). It did not take long, however, before hostility toward these foreign teachers developed. They were teaching a variety of French that could not be used when speaking to a Cajun. Even children wondered why they should be learning this French when they could not use it to speak to grandparents. Worse, many of these teachers looked down on Cajun French, and considered it an inferior tongue. These teachers were teaching throughout Louisiana, and after a few years it was most successful in north Louisiana, were there were few if any persons of French descent, as these Louisianians had no aversion to learning this language.

CODOFIL, however, did much good, and it was particularly important in leading the French renaissance in Louisiana. It was also politically powerful enough to have a portion of south Louisiana declared as "Acadiana," which today even has an official flag. Most people think Acadiana, which appears as a different color on state maps, has little significance, but it gives legitimacy to the idea that this is a different region - a "French Louisiana" (*Fig. 1*). CODOFIL was also significant in raising awareness and consciousness among Cajuns. In the end, however, CODOFIL was a failure, as it was considered too elitist, and its focus was too much on language - a battle that had already been lost. It was the creation of one man, James Domengeaux, a charismatic and politically powerful person. With his death in 1988 CODOFIL slowly began to grind to a halt. Today it has little funding, and has changed its focus to the promotion of local Francophone interests.

French Louisiana is a Catholic island in a Protestant South. The Louisiana French, of Cajun descent or otherwise, will often use religion to distinguish themselves from others. They are surrounded by Southern Protestants who have a strict and moral lifestyle that precludes them from truly enjoying life - they do not have the *joie de vivre* that is such a marker among the Cajuns (*Hill 1966; Peacock 1971*). Thus surrounded, their religion and resulting lifestyle is a source of strong cultural pride and identity.

The Catholic church, however, does not act as an ethnic institution, and has played no role in unifying the Cajuns of Louisiana. The Catholic church is "catholic" in the broader sense of the word, and also is concerned about others who are perhaps of Irish, German, or Italian Catholic descent. Very few young Cajuns have entered the priesthood, as the French of Louisiana are not very earnest Catholics. Traditionally, a large number of priests serving south Louisiana were foreigners, especially from France, Ireland, Belgium and Quebec. They used English, and played little or no role in local politics. There has never been an "activist" priest fighting for the rights of the Cajuns or the French-speakers in general. Today, one would have to look long and hard to find a mass in French, and if one were found, it would probably be offered very early in the morning when only the elderly would attend. Religion has simply played no role in the recent Cajun revival that swept south Louisiana.

Education has had a major impact on Cajun culture. For many years the agrarian masses of the Cajuns rejected the Anglo-American educational system. Only the elite among the Cajuns, those who had entered the planter class, believed in a good educational system, and many sent their sons to colleges in Northern cities to receive an education in English. The vast majority of Cajuns, however, viewed formal education as having no practical value to their children. They lived in a rich land, and they saw education as of little importance toward survival. Cajuns also viewed education as the function of the church, not the state, and they were not enthusiastic toward the public school system that began in Louisiana in 1845 (*Brasseaux, 1978*). Although they paid taxes into the public system of education, it was not until the twentieth century that young Cajun children began to get a formal education. This lack of education went a long way toward perpetuating Cajun culture and the French language.

Public schools were always taught in English. French was usually forbidden on school grounds, and children caught speaking French were punished. It was believed that only through English could children adapt and adjust to living in America. School teachers, many of whom were Cajuns, accepted this idea, and they too insisted on English use. This was a major factor in the decline of French, as it was perceived that a French-speaker had little chance to survive economically in an English-speaking America. This was true, but there was never an attempt at bilingual education. There was never a Cajun educator who stepped forward and fought for education in French, or for acceptance of French on school grounds.

By the 1920s and 1930s modern forces had begun to impinge upon rural French Louisiana- modern roads and automobiles made travel easier, radio, movies and other technological advancements began to alter Cajun values and lifestyles. Later, World War II forever changed the Cajuns. Young men returning from war realized the significance of education, and since that time almost all Cajuns have received a formal education. This education was entirely in English, and Cajuns have more and more been drawn into the mainstream of America as they accepted Anglo-American educational values.

Strong family ties were always an important feature of French Louisiana society. Until the later half of the twentieth century families were traditionally large, and many marriages were between distant cousins. These marriages established bonds between families that existed for generations. Selection of godparents also established bonds that lasted lifetimes between those involved, and provided bonds between extended families (*Brasseaux 1992, 38-44*). The strong feeling of closeness and cooperation between and within families was always an important feature of Cajun life, and an explanation as to why so few migrated beyond the narrow confines of rural Louisiana. This feeling of close ties between family members extended beyond life. Funerals were important social occasions, and the memory of deceased family members was kept alive by frequent visits to the cemetery, as was the tradition, adopted from New Orleans, of placing many family members in the same tomb.

The landscape is also very different in Cajun country when compared to the rest of the South. The houses, barns, fences, and outbuildings of the Cajuns are unique to the area (*Comeaux 1992*). They give a distinctive look to the land. Also different when compared to the rest of the South is the settlement pattern and the survey system. The survey system is typical of that used by the French wherever they settled in North America - in long narrow strips back from a stream or road. Settlement patterns tend to reflect this, and settlements are often in long narrow ribbons along a road. Much has changed over time, but it is still common to find young Cajuns building modern homes to resemble the traditional home of their ancestors, as they try to maintain the look of the land in Cajun country, and as they flaunt their Cajun identity.

Conclusions

There is considerable ambiguity in the definition of peoples in south Louisiana. It is a very complex situation, as there are many peoples within various ethnic, racial and linguistic groups, as well as blendings between groups. The Cajuns make up one identifiable group, and they are very visible, unique and the one here under study.

It is hard to define a Cajun, and it cannot be done to everyone's satisfaction. Some define it narrowly, claiming a Cajun must be of Acadian descent, but there are few "pure" Cajuns, and many would exclude those with any black ancestry. Others are willing to accept anyone as Cajun, with or without Cajun ancestors, if they "act" and choose to call themselves Cajun. The author would fit into the latter category, believing that Cajun culture evolved in south Louisiana, is unique to that region, and thus not based strictly on descent.

A Cajun would thus be one who considers himself/herself as such, is so perceived by others, and participates in Cajun culture. This person would be typically Roman Catholic - though many are nominal Catholics,[6] would have rural roots, would emphasize kinship relations over others types of associations, would speak English but also would probably speak or understand some Cajun French or would have relatives who do so, would eat Cajun foods, would enjoy life, having a *joie de vivre* that would be absent elsewhere in the South, and would occupy a distinctive landscape. Cajuns of the 1990s cannot be visually separated from others. Walking down a street, one could not separate out the Cajuns from the non-Cajuns simply by sight. They wear no distinctive clothes, and have no outwardly distinctive cultural traits. The vast majority today are town and city dwellers, speak good English - often with a distinctive accent, and have jobs that are like any others in America. They are a part of the American mainstream. They are, however, unique, and they consider themselves as being different.

Zusammenfassung

Im südlichen Louisiana gibt es eine beachtliche Vieldeutigkeit in der Bestimmung der Völker. Die Situation ist sehr kompliziert, da es viele Völker innerhalb verschiedener ethnischer, rassischer und linguistischer Gruppen und natürlich auch Mischungen zwischen diesen Gruppen gibt. Die Cajuns, die in dieser Arbeit näher untersucht werden, sind eine solche klar erkennbare und nicht verwechselbare Gruppe.

Es ist nicht leicht einen Cajun zu definieren und eine solche Definition kann auch nie völlig befriedigend ausfallen. Manche benützen eine enge Definition und fordern, daß ein Cajun von Acadia abstammen muß, aber so gesehen gäbe es wenige "reine" Cajuns. Viele würden Cajuns mit schwarzen Vorfahren ausschließen. Andere sind bereit, jeden als Cajun zu akzeptieren, mit oder ohne Cajun-Vorfahren, wenn sie sich wie Cajuns "benehmen" und sich selber als Cajun bezeichnen. Der Autor gehört zu letzteren Gruppe und glaubt, daß sich die Cajun-Kultur im Süden Louisianas entwickelt hat, nur in dieser Region auftritt und daher nicht strikt an Abstammung gebunden ist.

Ein Cajun ist daher eine Person, die sich selbst als Cajun sieht, von anderen so gesehen wird und an der Cajun-Kultur teilnimmt. Ein typischer Cajun wäre römisch-katholisch (obwohl viele nur nominale Katholiken sind), würde ländlicher Herkunft sein und verwandtschaftliche Beziehungen über alle anderen Beziehungen stellen. Er/Sie würde englisch im wesentlichen, aber wahrscheinlich auch etwas Cajun-französisch sprechen oder verstehen oder würde Verwandte haben, die dieses beherrschen. Er/Sie würde Cajun-Speisen essen, das Leben genießen und sich durch eine Lebensfreude (joie de vivre) auszeichnen, welche in den Südstaaten sonst so nicht anzutreffen ist. Weiters würde er/sie eine unverwechselbare Landschaft beanspruchen. Cajuns der 90er Jahre dieses Jahrhunderts können durch ihr Äußeres nicht von anderen unterschieden werden. Sie tragen keine besondere Kleidung und haben keine äußerlich auffälligen kulturellen Merkmale. Die überwiegende Mehrheit sind heute Stadtbewohner, sprechen gutes Englisch - wenn auch oft mit einem Akzent - und haben Berufe wie andere Amerikaner auch. Sie sind Teil des amerikanischen Mehrheitsgesellschaft. Sie sind jedoch unverwechselbar und sie sehen sich selber als andersartig.

References

Allen, J.P. (n.d.): French Mother Tongue: U.S.-Born Black Population, Southern Louisiana 1970. Cartography Lab, Department of Geography, California State University, Northridge.
Brasseaux, C. (1978): Acadian Education: From Cultural Isolation to Mainstream America. In: G. Conrad (ed.), The Cajuns: Essays on Their History and Culture. Lafayette, LA, 212-224.
Brasseaux, C. (1992): Acadian to Cajun: Transformation of a People, 1803-1877. Jackson, MS.
Clark, A.H. (1968): Acadia: The Geography of Early Nova Scotia to 1760. Madison.
Census of the Population. (1993a): Census of the Population, 1990, Ancestry of the Population in the United States. Washington, D.C.
Census of the Population. (1993b): Census of the Population, 1990, Social and Economic Characteristics, Louisiana. Washington, D.C.
Comeaux, M.L. (1989): The Cajun Barn. In: Geographical Review, 79, 47-62.

Comeaux, M.L. (1992): Cajuns in Louisiana. In: A. G. Noble (ed.), To Build in a New Land. Baltimore, 177-192.
Daigle, J.O. (1984): A Dictionary of the Cajun Language. Ville Platte, LA.
Deiler, J.H. (1909): The Settlement of the German Coast of Louisiana and the Creoles of German Descent. In: Americana Germanica (New Series) 8, Philadelphia.
Estaville, L.E. Jr. (1993): The Louisiana-French Homeland. In: Journal of Cultural Geography, 13, 31-46.
Faulk, J.D. (1977): Cajun French 1. Abbeville, LA.
Gibson, J.L. and Del Sesto, S. (1975): The Culture of Acadiana: An Anthropological Perspective. In: J.L. Gibson and Del Sesto, S. (ed.), The Culture of Acadiana. Lafayette, LA, 1-14.
Hill, S.S. Jr. (1966): Southern Churches in Crisis. New York.
Kondert, R. (1985): The German Involvement in the Rebellion of 1768. Louisiana History 26, 385-397.
LeBlanc, R. (1970): The Acadian Migrations. In: Canadian Geographical Journal, 81, 10-19.
MaGuire, R. (1979): Creoles and Creole Language Use in St. Martin Parish, Louisiana. In: Cahiers de Geographie du Quebec, 23, 281-302.
Peacock, J.L. (1971): The Southern Protestant Ethic Disease. In: J. K. Morland (ed.), The Not So Solid South, Southern Anthropological Society, Proceedings No. 4, 108-113.
Phillips, H. (1978): The Spoken French of Louisiana. In: G. R. Conrad (ed.), The Cajuns: Essays on Their History and Culture. Lafayette, LA, 173-184.
Reed, R. (1976): Lache pas la Patate: Portraits des Acadiens de la Louisiane. Montreal.
Roy, M. (1982): Settlement and Population Growth in Acadia. In: J. Daigle (ed.), The Acadians of the Maritimes. Moncton, NB, 125-196.
Rushton, W.F. (1979): The Cajuns: From Acadia to Louisiana. New York.
Tentchoff, D. (1975): Cajun French and French Creole; Their Speakers and the Question of Identities. In: J. L. Gibson and Del Sesto, S. The Culture of Acadiana. Lafayette, LA, 87-109.
Trepanier, C. (1990): Le Project Louisiane: The First Step Toward French Louisiana at the Threshold of the 21st Century. Paper presented at the Association of American Geographers Annual Meeting, Toronto.
West, R.C. (1986): An Atlas of Louisiana Surnames of French and Spanish Origin. Baton Rouge, LA.

Notes

[1] The largest forced migration to the United States were Blacks brought from Africa, and this movement of Acadians was the second largest forced migration.
[2] The word "Cajun" is a corruption of "Acadian", the name for these people when they lived in Canada, and the name used by their cousins who still live in the Maritime Provinces of Canada. The word Acadian is simplified by dropping the first "A", and by changing the "d" to a "j", as in "Indian" being changed to "Injun", and "would you" into "wouja". Cajun is spelled the same in English and French, but the pronunciation is different, depending on the language spoken. The derogatory word for Cajuns today is "Coonass". The origin of this word is unknown, but it was already in wide use by the 1930s.
[3] Very few of the Cajuns in this area owned slaves. To this day most of the Blacks living in this region are not Catholic, and do not speak French, indicating the Anglo-American ownership of slaves in this region in pre-Civil War days.
[4] The dioscese in this part of Louisiana has more Blacks than any other dioscese in the United States.
[5] According to the census, "In households where one or more persons speak a language other than English, the household language assigned to all household members is the non-English language..." (Census 1993b, B24). Thus, only one person in the family speaking French may result in all in the family tabulated as speaking that language, when in many cases that is not true.
[6] This author knows one professor at a major Midwestern college who was brought up as a Cajun in southwest Louisiana. This person no longer wants to be a Cajun, and to prove his point told this writer that he was now an Episcopalian. That ended all discussion.

Address of the Author

Malcolm L. Comeaux
Department of Geography
Arizona State University
Box 870104
Tempe, AZ 85287-0104
USA

CHRISTOPH STADEL

Cultural Minorities in the Canadian Prairies; their Impact on the Rural Landscape

Introduction

Ethnic themes and the impact of distinct cultural groups on the landscape and the settlement pattern, as well as their influence on the national culture and the economy of the Canadian Prairies have attracted the interest of geographers for quite some time *(Dawson, 1936; Schlichtmann 1977; Todd and Brierley 1977; Vogelsang 1985)*. This paper attempts to provide an overview of the impact of distinct minority groups on the rural landscape of the Prairies between the onset of the major settlement period in the early 1870s and the petering out of the agricultural pioneer period in the 1920s.

After 1870, the Canadian Prairies emerged as a major new agricultural frontier of North America. In a series of immigration booms, diverse ethnic and religious groups contributed to the colonization of the new land and shaped the basic settlement pattern *(Lenz 1965)*, although until the election of a Liberal administration in 1896, considerable restrictions existed for 'alien' population groups *(Lehr and Davies 1993, 139-141; Stadel 1994)*. Most settlers, whether driven out of their homeland by economic hardship or political turmoil, or lured to the new 'virgin lands' by the hopes of prosperity or freedom, faced major problems of how to make a home out of the new strange land of Prairie grasslands and partially wooded parkland regions. Few of the immigrants did anticipate the reality of the lonely plains and of the harsh climate: "It was probably stranger than they could have imagined" *(Rees, 1988, 35)*.

For most, the image of the Canadian West was initially framed by subjective assessments or by propaganda produced by the government, the railway companies, explorers, journalists, promoters, or the leaders of ethnic or religious communities.

In addition to the immediate problem of physical control of the new environment, most settlers faced the hardship of a sometimes painful spiritual adjustment: for many, the Prairies were "a new and naked land" *(Rees 1988)*. Early descriptions of newly arriving people often depicted the Prairies as a land that was flat, desolate, dry, sparsely treed and, by old world standards, lonely and empty of people, a land "from which the hand of God was withdrawn before the act of creation was complete" *(Rees 1988, 35)*. Americans described Western Canada as a land of ice, snow, drought and disillusionment while for some English settlers it represented the 'Siberia of the British Empire'. Others though praised their new homeland as invigorating, picturesque and prosperous: "Before us was the most beautiful landscape I had ever seen.... Luxuriant prairie untouched and unspoiled by the hands of man; ...an endless ocean of fertility" (Norwegian settler, *quoted in Rees 1988, 39)*. For others, who wanted to escape the taint of the world, isolation was precisely what they appreciated.

Some settlers felt almost immediately at home and adapted themselves easily to their new environment. Others, especially those from Central and Eastern Europe, would find the adjustment process an uphill struggle and were determined to preserve their cultural heritage, their beliefs and traditional ways of life. To these people, the maintenance of social ties in the form of closely knit communities was the logical response to coping with the new, unfamiliar environment.

Migration Pattern and the Settlement Process of the Cultural Minorities

Between the 1870s and World War I, a set of conditions existed both in the homeland of specific cultural groups and in the pioneer realm of the Prairies which triggered off large scale migrations. In some cases, environmental hardships forced the population to seek new destinations. An example of this type of push force were the Icelanders who in the 1870s escaped volcanic eruptions and heavy sea ice to migrate to the Interlake district of Manitoba *(Lenz 1965, 36)*.

Others were poor, disprivileged or oppressed and eagerly seized the opportunity to begin a new life. For the Ukrainians living in the Austrian Western Ukraine in the Provinces of Galicia and Bukowyna, social and political repression exacerbated the economic woes of the peasantry *(Lehr 1991, 31)*.

For a third group of immigrants, it was the threat to their religious freedom and integrity which forced them out of their homelands. The Mennonites, who were originally attracted to the steppe regions north of the Black Sea by promises of land and religious freedom under Empress CATHERINE the Great, found their existence threatened some hundred years later by new government policies of Russification, a threat of military conscription, but also by an increasing scarcity of available farmland *(Lehr 1985a)*. Similar reasons enticed the Hutterites to leave the Ukraine and migrate to North America between 1874 and 1879 *(Hostetler 1974)*. The determined pacifism and the rejection of the authority of the established Russian Orthodox Church in the Crimea and the Caucasus resulted in a repression and persecution of the Doukhobors who, through the mediation of American and British Quakers, were allowed to move to the Canadian Prairies in 1899 *(Lehr 1985f)*. The threat to religious principles by the passage of American legislation against polygamy was also the principal reason for a group of Mormons to leave their colonies in Utah, Arizona, Idaho and Nevada and to seek shelter in the frontier region of southwestern Alberta between 1886 and 1890 *(Lehr 1985d)*.

The Canadian Prairies promised to offer to these different cultural groups foremost land, prosperity and freedom. Following the establishment of the sectional survey system after 1869 and the granting of free homesteads after 1872, huge tracts of land became available for prospective settlers and a number of ethnic and religious groups wishing to maintain their cultural affinities by spatial proximity established distinct group settlements in the Prairies *(see Fig. 1)*.

The first one of the organized cultural groups arriving in the Prairies were about 7,000 Mennonites *(see Fig. 2)* who moved to Manitoba between 1874 and 1880 *(Hostetler 1983b; Friesen 1985)*. Both the United States and Canada were eager to attract the skilled and industrious settlers. Initially, Kansas and Nebraska with their milder climates were more attractive, whereas Manitoba rather disappointed the Mennonite delegates. They were disturbed by the threat of Indians and Métis, by the absence of railways, by the possibility of drought and by the aggressive mosquitoes whose "forwardness surpassed all limits of decency and moderation". Nevertheless, a few of the delegates opted for Manitoba. The Canadian government responded favourably to the Mennonite requests for freedom of religion, an exemption from military service, the right to operate their own schools, and the possibility for establishing group settlements.

The Dominion of Canada set aside two 'Reserves' for exclusive Mennonite settlement in 1873: the 'East Reserve' east of the Red River consisting of eight townships, and in 1876, the 17 townships of the 'West Reserve' located between the Red River and the Pembina Hills *(see Fig. 3)*. For the first time in the settlement process of the Canadian Prairies, a group of agricultural pioneers ventured into the open grassland region, away from the major rivers. However, initially many Mennonites were distressed by the treeless, flat openess of the land, by the scarcity of water and wood and by the poor quality of the soil in some areas. But it was the experience of the Mennonites with a steppe environment, their determination and hard work which prevented an early failure of this settlement experiment.

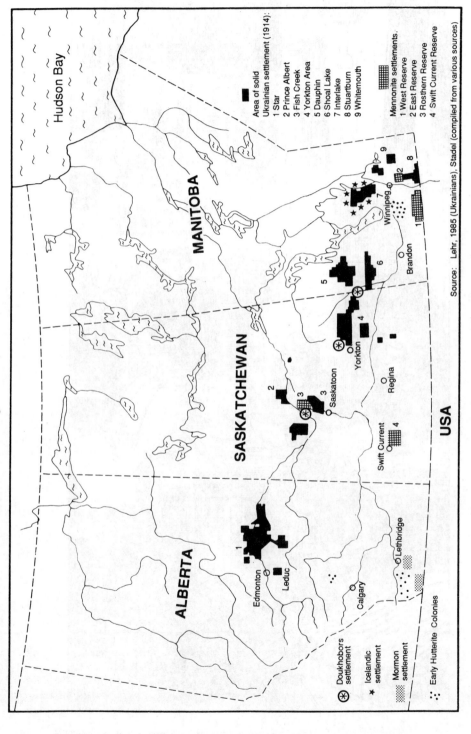

Fig. 1: Early Group Settlements in the Prairie Provinces (generalized)

Fig. 2: Early Mennonite Immigrants

Source: Mennonite Village Museum, Steinbach, Manitoba, 1982

Fig. 3: Settlements in the Mennonite 'West Reserve' (Manitoba)

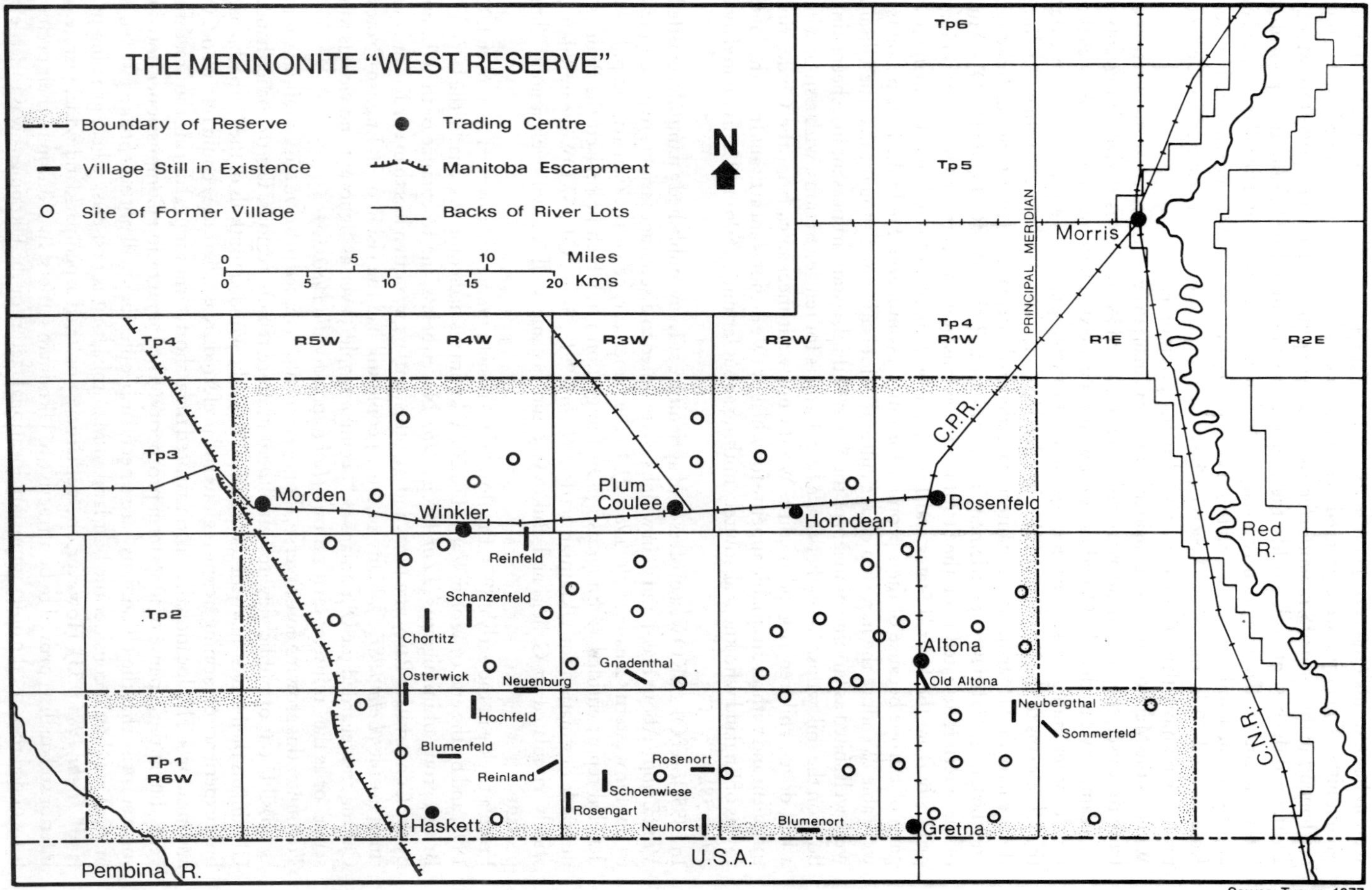

Source: Tyman, 1977

The regulations of the 'Homestead Act' which required holders of titles to live on the quarter section homesteads (160 acres) conflicted with the traditional village settlement system of the Mennonites. Thus they were granted an exemption which permitted them to establish group settlements in the form of *Straßendörfer*. According to John WARKETIN *(1959)*, the Mennonite *Dörfer* had the best of both worlds, the social advantages of village life and the opportunity to farm efficiently and independently on large, consolidated tracts of land. The villages varied in size and also in their ability to grow and to survive. Altogether, 59 villages were founded in the 'East Reserve' and 70 in the 'West Reserve', but frequent abandonment resulted in the fact that probably no more than 95 villages existed at any given time.

Whereas the Mennonites were considered by the Canadian authorities as excellent settlers right from the onset, the Ukrainians were only later regarded as good prospective immigrants when it became obvious that the Canadian West was still in need of farming pioneers. As was the case for the other immigrants, Canadian government officials played a very active role in attracting the Ukrainians to the Prairies and also in selecting contiguous land areas for them. In doing so, the agents of the Department of the Interior acceded to the demands of the Orthodox Bukovynians and the Uniate Galicians for settlement in separate areas *(Lehr 1987)*. Clifford SIFTON, Minister of the Interior, deviated from the attitude of previous governments which sought immigrants primarily from the United States and England as well as from French and German speaking parts of Europe because of their promise for quick assimilation. He looked for peasants who were able to endure the hardship of agricultural colonisation and thought that the Ukrainians were well suited as farming pioneers of the West: "I think a stalwart peasant in a sheepskin coat, born on the soil, whose forefathers have been farmers for ten generations, with a stout wife and a half dozen children is good quality. We do not want mechanics from the Clyde, riotous, turbulent and with an unsatiable appetite for whiskey. We do not want artisans from the southern towns of England who know absolutely nothing about farming" *(Sifton 1922, as quoted by Lehr 1991, 38)*.

In 1895, Josef OLESKOW, a professor of agriculture at Lvov, published a pamphlet entitled *Pro Vilni Zemli* ('About Free Lands') in which he attempted to discourage farmers to go to Brazil but to opt for western Canada *(Lehr 1983, 2)*. In the same year, he visited Canada and published a detailed report entitled *O Emigratsii* ('On Emigration') in which he praised the Prairies as a desirable destination for Ukrainian settlers *(Lehr 1991, 35-36)*. OLESKOW's pamphlets were widely circulated in Galicia and Bukovyna and became well known even among illiterate peasants.

From a trickle in the early 1890s, the flow of Ukrainian immigrants swelled to almost 4,000 in 1897, and by the end of World War I, 170,000 Ukrainians had come to Canada, the largest non-British group of immigrants *(Lehr 1985c, 875)*. Nevertheless, the acceptance of the Ukrainians by the Conservative Party and press and by other settlers was often less than cordial and even at times hostile *(Lehr 1987, 3)*. Many of these people still had the vision of an English-Protestant Canada and regarded the Ukrainians as "peculiar people", even as "ignorant and vicious foreign scum" or as the "refuse of civilization" *(Lehr and Moodie 1980, 93)*.

To counter this growing controversy, the government attempted to move the Ukrainians as much as possible out of public view to settle them in more remote regions. On the other hand, the Ukrainians themselves, many of them hailing from the wooded foothills of the Carpathians, had little experience of farming steppe regions and preferred areas where they could find wood, water and meadows. This locational decision assured them short-term survival during the first difficult years, but at the expense of long-term prosperity. The Immigration Commissioner noted with some surprise that the Ukrainians "are a peculiar people; they will not accept as a gift 160 acres of what we should consider the best land in Manitoba, that is first class wheat growing prairie land" *(Lehr 1985e, 33)*. However, the yet largely unsettled aspen parkland zone, inspite of its inferior soil quality, proved to be attractive to Ukrainian settlers. In addition to their preference for wooded regions, the other important locational factor for the Ukrainians was to settle close

Fig. 4: District of Origin of Ukrainian Settlers in the Stuartburn Area of Manitoba

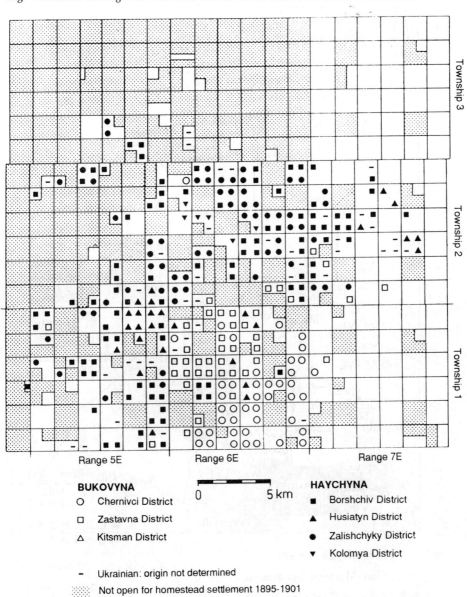

Fig. 5: Mormon Settlements and their Expansion in Southern Alberta

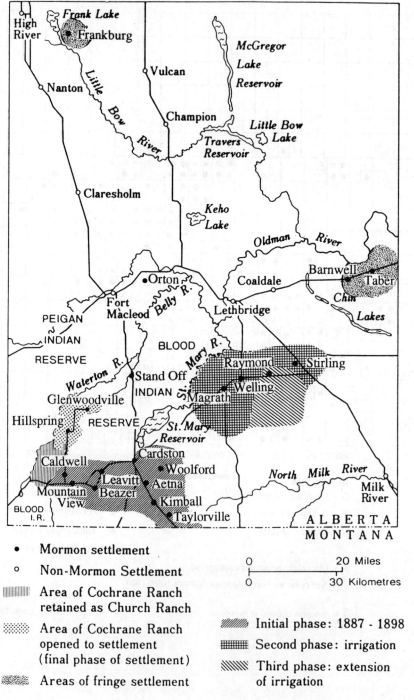

Source: Lehr 1974, 22.

to familiar neighbors. The first immigrants established homesteads at Star in Alberta near the farms of ethnic Germans who came from Western Ukraine and could also speak Ukrainian. Later, the settlers headed for the already existing Ukrainian blocks of land attracted by the familiar social, religious and linguistic milieu *(see Fig. 4)*. Efforts by the government to break up the clusters of Ukrainian settlement in the parkland belt of the Prairie provinces largely failed as proved the Fish Creek incident of 1898. In that year, an attempt was made to locate newly arriving Ukrainians at Fish Creek, Saskatchewan instead of taking them to their desired destinations of the Edmonton and Dauphin, Manitoba regions. After a fierce reaction of the immigrants, the government was forced to yield to the wishes of the settlers. Only a few families decided to stay at Fish Creek to form yet another nucleus of Ukrainian settlement.

Whereas the Ukrainians settled in the bush country of the parkland belt, another group, that of the Mormons, ventured into the dry grassland regions of southern Alberta *(Lehr and Katz 1991)*. Although the Mormon immigration had a slow start and initially involved only a rather small number of families, this religious minority had a major impact on the development of the cultural landscape in southern Alberta. LEHR *(1974, 20 - 28)* distinguishes five phases in the sequence of Mormon settlement between 1887 and 1910 *(see Fig. 5)*. The initial motive for the Mormons to leave Utah and to come to Canada was the anti-poligamy legislation of the United States. Under the leadership of Charles Ora CARD, 41 families settled in 1887 on Lee's Creek (later named Cardston) close to the International boundary. They chose this location as they initially intended to return to the United States as soon as the controversy over the polygamy issue was settled. In order to establish closely knit village communities, the Mormons occupied contiguous homesteads and also purchased adjacent railway land in order to become the dominant group within their settlement area. When a new Manifest of the Mormon Church suspended the practice of polygamy in 1890, the major impetus for leaving the United States had disappeared, and the Mormon migration to Canada slowed to a trickle *(Lehr 1988)*.

In contrast to the first stage, the second phase of Mormon immigration to Alberta, between 1896 and the turn of the century, was based primarily on economic motives. The experience and skills of the Mormons in irrigation, attracted the attention of the Alberta Railway and Coal Company. This led to a contract between the Company and the Mormon Church. The Church was to provide labour for the project and settlers for the irrigated lands, while the Company supplied the land for two townsites. The greater interest of the Mormon Church in Canada was a response to mounting economic pressures in Utah and a religiously motivated desire to extend Mormon frontiers.

The third phase between 1901 and 1903 was motivated primarily by the philantropic attitudes of a Utah businessman who acquired some 100,000 ha of land in Alberta for the cultivation of sugar beets and established a sugar refinery in the village of Raymond. However, the cultivation of sugar beets proved not to be too successful, and the immigration of additional Mormons did not reach the anticipated levels.

The fourth phase at the beginning of the 20th century was triggered by the opening up of new areas for colonization by the Canadian Pacific Railway. In these more peripheral areas further to the north, the Mormons never constituted a majority of the population, but nonetheless they had a major impact on the economy and the settlements of the area.

The final phase of Mormon colonization took place between 1906 and 1910. It resulted from the only incidence of a direct involvement of the Mormon Church in providing land for its members. The Church acquired the 24,000 ha large Cochrane Farm to the northwest of Cardston, which led to the foundation of two additional villages. Thus, different causal factors were responsible for each phase of settlement. In this process, the Mormon Church became progressively more involved in the settlement endeavours of its members. It is somewhat paradoxical that the Mormon Church should become more involved in the colonization process at a time when the theological motivations for migration and settlement declined in importance.

Fig. 6: Arrival of Hutterites in Canada

Source: Calgary Eye Opener, 21. 09. 1918 (after Evans, 1987)

The last one of the arriving cultural minorities being involved in a rural group settlement process in the Canadian Prairies were the Hutterites *(Anderson and Engelhart 1974; Hostetler and Huntington 1980).* As was the case with the Mennonites, the Doukhobors and the Mormons, a combination of religious and economic reasons motivated their settlement in the Prairies. Between 1874 and 1879, over 1,200 Hutterites arrived from the Ukraine and settled in South Dakota. About half of them decided to live on individual homesteads rather than in communal colonies. These so-called *Prairieleut* tended to affiliate with nearby Mennonite groups. On the basis of the three founding colonies in Dakota, three culturally slightly distinct groups of Hutterites evolved: the *Schmiedeleut,* the *Dariusleut* and the *Lehrerleut.* Because of considerable harassment in the United States during World War I, many Hutterites left for the Canadian Prairie provinces in 1918: *(see Fig. 6)* the *Schmiedeleut* settled in Manitoba, while the *Dariusleut* and *Lehrerleut* established themselves in Alberta and later in Saskatchewan *(Lenz 1977; Ryan 1977, 1985; Evans 1973, 1974; Pirker 1981).*

The basic form of settlement and the essential unit of Hutterite culture is the *Bruderhof*, a social unit as well as an economic entity where up to 130 persons live and work on a communal basis *(Hostetler 1983a).* When a *Bruderhof* reaches its threshold size, a new colony is founded, with half of the population of the parent colony moving to the new community. In this way, the traditional demographic vitality of the Hutterites turns into a source of strength in the expansion of their culture across the rural Prairies.

At the same time though, the rapid spread of the colonies and the ability of Hutterites to purchase new agricultural land was met by other farmers and by adjacent villages with suspicion and even hostility. Thus, at certain times, provincial governments and municipalities introduced a number of legislative measures to regulate the location of new colonies or to prevent the selling or even leasing of farmland to Hutterites.

In the selection of potential settlement sites, the Hutterites are guided by a number of cultural and economic considerations. An important aspect has always been a careful scrutiny of the land in terms of its agricultural potential and access to water. On the other hand, an attempt was made to be isolated to a certain extent from the outside world in order to be able to preserve the cultural identity and integrity of the colonies. This was vital to the survival of the Hutterite religion and culture as both are intimately linked to the *Bruderhof* and to agriculture as an economic activity and way of life. Thus, the Hutterites were able, in spite of an adoption of modern farming methods and technologies, to resist more than other cultural minorites cultural assimilation into the mainstream of Canadian society. The other locational consideration in the establishment of new colonies centered around the question whether the propinquity to other *Bruderhöfe* was desirable. Especially during the earlier period of difficult rural transportation and under-capitalization, economic advantages existed for locating daughter colonies close to the parent colonies. Spatial proximity also facilitated social interactions and strengthened the *Gemeinschaftssinn* among Hutterites. These considerations, when aided by the absence of legislative controls, accounted for the trend towards spatial clustering of early Hutterite settlements. On the other hand, some Hutterite leaders were of the opinion that the location of new colonies at considerable distances from each other allowed the communities a great deal of independence. Furthermore, the more dispersed settlement pattern was also the result of legislative restriction or voluntary concessions by the Hutterites to counter the popular perceptions that they were aiming at establishing large contiguous Hutterite enclaves within the provinces. As a result of these aspects, a dualisitc spatial pattern of Hutterite settlement tended to emerge. In Alberta for instance, a more clustered arrangement of the conservative *Lehrerleut* in the southernmost parts of the province; and a more widely dispersed spatial distribution of *Dariusleut* colonies extending to the region between Calgary and Edmonton and even into the Peace River district *(Evans 1987)*. Finally, the increasing difficulty of finding large tracts of suitable agricultural land forced the Hutterites to establish new colonies at the fringes of the agricultural realm of the provinces, e. g. the Interlake District of Manitoba.

Today, close to 400 Hutterite colonies exist across the Canadian Prairies, and both the number of Hutterites and that of their colonies is still increasing, although no longer at the hectic pace of earlier decades *(Evans 1987, 165; and oral information from the James Valley Colony, Manitoba)*. The economic significance of the Hutterites within Prairie agriculture, especially in the area of hog and poultry production, is much greater than the number of colonies or their share in the total farmland would suggest. In Manitoba, Hutterite colonies owned in 1991 25% of the laying hens, 25% of the turkeys, and 35% of the hogs in Manitoba *(ibid.)*

The Secular and the Sacred Landscape of Cultural Minorities

Landscapes in the Canadian West derive their diversity from the cultural impress rather than from topographic variations. The settlers who flocked to the vast territory of the Prairies which was opened up for colonization brought with them their cultural heritage which became manifested in the built environment. Yet, the immigrants also faced a number of constraints which tended to hinder or preclude the transfer of cultural elements to the new land *(Schlichtmann 1976)*.

Although the pioneers were quite free to create an environment of their own choice, they were nevertheless bound by the requirements of the land survey system and the homestead regulations. Only on the basis of exemptions granted were some cultural groups allowed to establish group settlements. The prospect of the creation of a number of distinct ethnically and religiously motivated concentrations of immigrants in the Canadian West alarmed many Anglo-Canadians, political parties and the mainstream press: "If they are put in colonies by themselves, they will be still less susceptible to progressive influences, and the districts where the colonies are located will be shunned by desirable immigrants" *(Nor'Western July 20, 1897, quoted by Lehr and Moodie 1980, 97).*

Even the Pro-Sifton *Manitoba Free Press* criticized the tendency to recreate traditional ethnic homelands and expressed the need for rapid assimilation of the immigrants: "These nationalities who dream of building up in this country an exact replica of conditions which prevail in the countries, from which they come, should be repudiated" (*Manitoba Free Press'*, February 24, 1913, quoted by Lehr and Moodie 1980, 98).

Apart from the Prairies' exceptional village or colony settlement forms, the cultural heritage of the pioneer groups was expressed in a particular secular and sacred vernacular architecture and in distinct ways of life. But from the inception, the particular traits of the distinct ethnic or religious landscapes which had the best chance to survive with some measure of integrity were generally found in the more isolated and marginal areas. Also, where a determined attachment to old cultural traditions and a strong sense of group identity prevailed, the onrush of assimilation was weakened. In many instances, when certain buildings or other expressions of the material culture of the minority groups had become victims of new economic circumstances, new social tastes or new forms of affluence or progress, they were either put to a lower-order functional use (e.g. from home to storage), or they were abandoned which generally meant dereliction and eventual dilapidation.

One of the most distinct secular and sacred landscapes to emerge in the Canadian Prairies was that created by the Ukrainians. Initially, the Ukrainians attempted to recreate a cultural landscape patterned on that of their homeland. They were accustomed to village settlement and to a tightly knit society, in both physical and social senses. Since the establishment of villages was impossible within the terms of the Homestead Act, Ukrainian pioneers sought at least to live together in contiguous blocks of land. They also attempted to achieve a greater population density by petitioning to settle on both odd-and even-numbered sections; they also resorted to an illegal subdivision of homesteads and to squatting. Although the Ukrainians were able to achieve greater settlement densities, the authorities were not prepared to make the same concessions as they had made previously for the Mennonites who were allowed to establish villages.

Since the Ukrainians were unable to transfer the basic element of their cultural landscape, the village settlement, to the Prairies, many elements of their material culture proved to be ephemeral or transient. However, during the first two decades of their pioneering settlement, the Ukrainian landscape of the Prairies resembled that of their homeland. Vernacular forms of architecture, farm layouts, and cemeteries were tranferred, but there was also the return to more simple, earlier forms of houses and churches, because in the new pioneer environment few settlers could initially afford to replicate the more elaborate forms of their homeland.

To build quickly and cheaply effective shelter was the immediate concern on the frontier. The first home of many immigrants was a small one-room hut called a *zemlyanka* or *borday*. These first shelters were built as temporary dwellings, although some were occupied for several years. When the second, more substantial house was built, the first shelter was used as a store house or summer kitchen. The second house, still built in the traditional style, constituted the major element in the domestic cultural landscape of the Ukrainian settlers. Despite some variations in appearance, initially reflecting the different regions of origin of the settlers, most of these houses exhibited some common features. They were single-storey, south oriented houses with two or three rooms, a central chimney, and a gable. Almost all of these homes were initially made of logs, with horizontal log building as the most commonly used form. Frequently, the Ukrainians plastered the log walls with mud and lime-washed the exteriors of their houses. During the frontier period, most homes had thatched roofs made of slough grass. In the popular perception of Anglo-Canadians, the domestic cultural landscape was "typically Russian", but it was rather typical of the Carpathian mountains and foothills of the western Ukraine *(Lehr 1980)*.

During the pioneer period, the farm layout, fencing, water-drawing devices,(especially the well sweep) and even the type of crops grown (with a preference for rye and hemp growing), reflected the Ukrainian tradition. In many early homesteads, farm buildings were arranged in the form of a square enclosing a central yard, which was subsequently abandoned, when the introduction of farm machinery made the central yard inconvenient. Also, the original fences of woven willows, of logs or sawn boards, were replaced by barbed wire, well sweeps gradually disappeared in most regions, and rye and hemp were largely replaced by early maturing wheat.

Thus, the pioneers adapted themselves often quite quickly to the new economic circumstances and to the tastes and preferences of Anglo-Canadians. Traditions survived the longest in the more remote and marginal regions, whereas traditional forms disappeared most rapidly in the more prosperous districts. The assimilation of many Ukrainians was not only a response to a new environment and to changing economic and technological conditions, but also an expression of status and of a desire to appear modern and progressive.

Religious architecture usually appeared in the pioneer landscape after a few years of settlement. The most apparent form of churches were seldom the traditional styles of the Carpathian mountains, but rather a Russified Byzantine architecture which was then replacing the older forms in the Western Ukraine. The most obvious features of the churches were the pear-shaped domes and the separate bell towers. Although the first churches were modest in size and decor, later churches had become a prominent element in the rural cultural landscape of the Prairies. The

Fig. 7: A Ukrainian Church (near Yorkton, Saskatchewan)

Fig. 8: A Mennonite Straßendorf (Gnadenthal, Manitoba)

Fig. 9: Original Village Layout and Field Pattern of Neuhorst, Manitoba

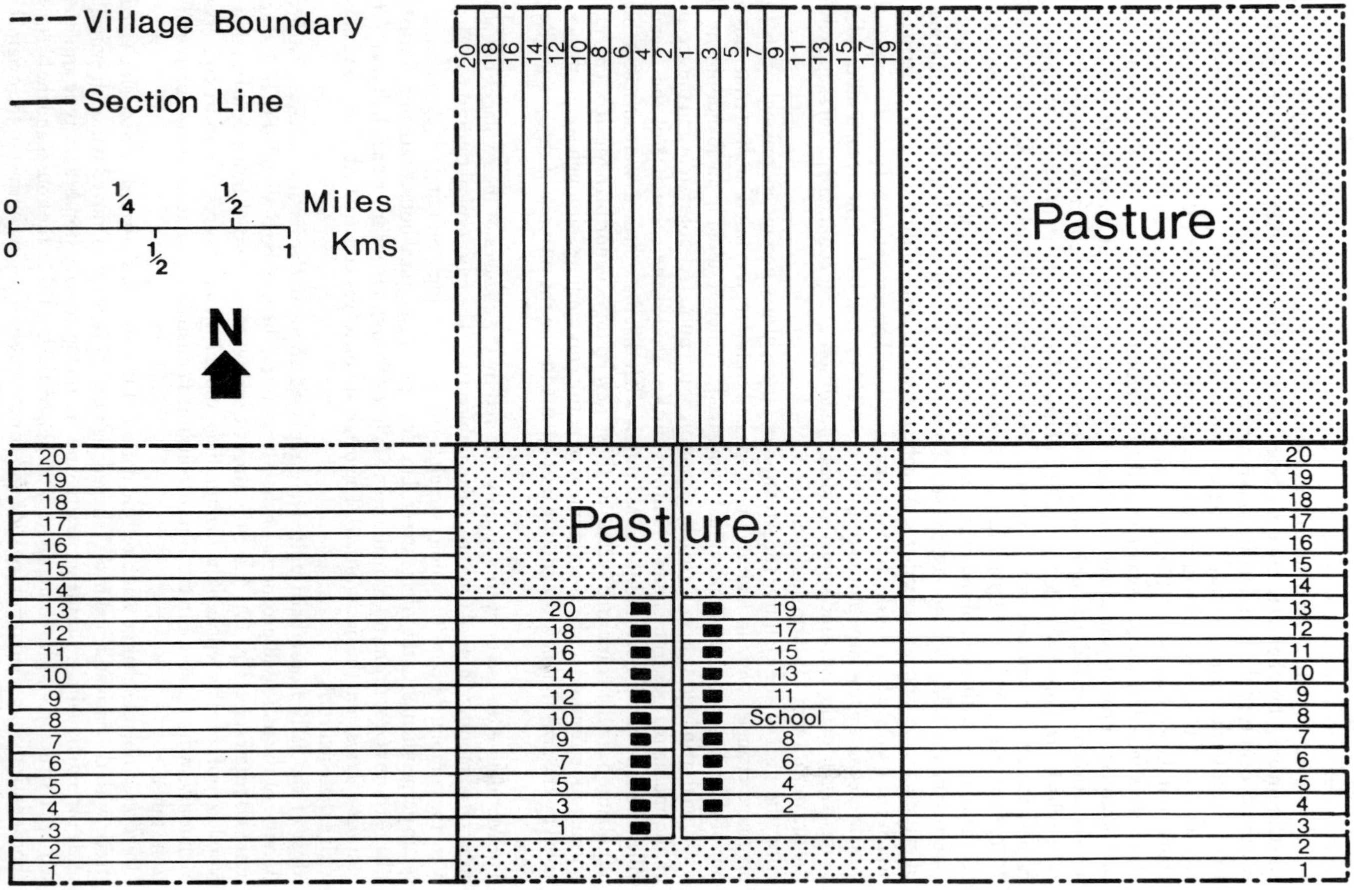

- - - - Village Boundary
——— Section Line

Source: Tyman. 1977 (after Warketin)

split of the Ukrainians into two groups on the basis of their home regions and religious affiliation contributed to a proliferation of churches. Most immigrants from Galicia were adherents to the Greek Uniate Church; those from Bukowyna to the Greek or Russian Orthodox Church. For the Ukrainians, churches were not only expressions of spiritual beliefs, but also manifestations of ethnic identity, culture and national aspiration.

In contrast to the rather quickly fading Ukrainian secular landscape, the sacred landscape has remained an "icon of identity in the Ukrainian landscape" *(Lehr 1984, 4)* and a highly visible element of the Prairies *(see Fig. 7)*. However, the churches and even more so the cemeteries have also been affected by the process of assimilation and modernization. Thus the sacred landscape of Ukrainians provides an excellent record for the progress of change and the process of acculturation during the last one hundred years of ethnic settlement in the Prairies *(Lehr 1989)*. While the Ukrainians had failed to establish farm villages in the Prairies, the Mennonites had earlier succeeded in transferring this cultural element from their homeland to Manitoba *(Sawatzky 1976; Lehr 1985a; Noble 1992)*. In their *Straßendörfer* the houses were laid out on both sides of the main street, with a school and usually also a church in the centre of the village *(see Fig. 8)*. The land around the village was pooled and subdivided in a way to give each family an equal measure of garden, arable land, and meadows. Attached to each farm building was a small strip of land which was used as a farm yard, garden or small pasture. The rest of the land (usually five sections) was divided into a few large blocks of arable land *(Gewanne)*, each of them being subdivided into strips *(Kagel)* for the use of individual families. In addition, a large communal pasture supplemented the organization of the farm land *(see Fig. 9)*.

After the turn of the century, the Mennonite farm villages became increasingly affected by profound changes. New agricultural methods and technologies enticed many farmers to move out of the villages to live on individual homesteads, which resulted in an abandonment of the traditional strip field system. Also, the adoption of the public school system and the acceptance of the municipal government in Manitoba further eroded the coherence of the Mennonite villages. Many of the more traditional Mennonites felt that these changes were unacceptable and left Manitoba in the years after 1920 to establish new colonies in northern Mexico. This massive outmigration resulted in the abandonment of entire communities, although some villages were saved by the arrival of new Mennonite immigrants fleeing the turmoils of the Russian Revolution.

The Mennonite 'Reserves' were not only affected by the changes of their villages but also by substantial modifications of the vernacular architecture. The most typical traditional structures were the combined house/barn units which formed a long single building which was originally set up perpendicular to the village street. The floor plan of a typical house/barn unit consisted of a large room *(Groote Shtov)*, a small room *(Tyleene Shtov)*, a front and a back hall *(Fae T'Hues and Alt T'Huis)* and the barn *(Shtall)*. The original house was constructed of logs and covered with a thatched roof.

Most of the early house/barn units were replaced about ten years after their construction. Because of the increased prosperity of the Mennonites, the new homes tended to be larger and more elaborate *(see Fig. 10)*. After the turn of the century, a wood frame construction and wooden roof shingles replaced the log buildings and the thatched roofs. The more conservative Mennonites who remained in the village, continued constructing attached house/barn units for some time.

However, a notable change was a re-orientation of the houses, so that their wide side faced the street, with the barn attached in a T-shaped fashion. Families who moved out of the villages to settle on individual farmsteads generally gave up the customary house/barn type and erected separated structures with a contemporary design. By the late 1920s, the houses and the barns were almost entirely of a contemporary style and construction. Also, in contrast to the original self-contained farm building, the newer farmstead was characterized by a variety of separate buildings for different purposes.

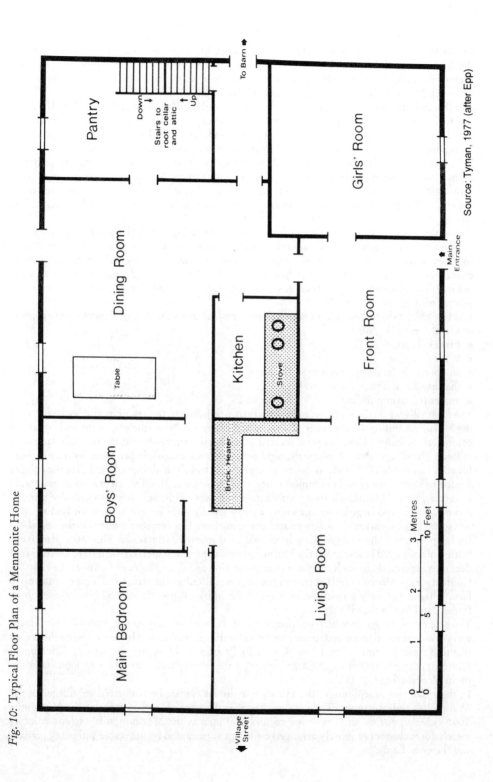

Fig. 10: Typical Floor Plan of a Mennonite Home

In contrast to the prominent sacred landscape of the Ukrainians, the churches and cemeteries of the Mennonites did not become outstanding landmarks of the cultural landscape. For the Mennonites, the churches, although they were the centre of the religious and cultural life, were simple and were often similar in appearance to Mennonite houses.

Another cultural landscape inspired by religion is that of the Mormons in Alberta. LEHR *(1973, 25)* distinguishes between the Mormon religious landscape and the Mormon cultural landscape. He defines the former as a "pristine religious landscape", and the latter as a "landscape incorporating many elements peripheral to Mormonism", but "religiously inspired".

In contrast to the Ukrainians and the Mennonites, the Mormon settlers lacked any common ethnic origin. They were, however, united in a religious conviction and in the theocratic socio-economic organization of the Mormon church. The cultural landscape which they created in Alberta reflected therefore their religious as well as socio-economic needs which tended to change over time *(Lehr 1973, 26)*.

As was the case with all new settlers on the Prairies, the evolving cultural landscape was a response to the immediate needs of an agricultural pioneer group which faced the challenge of adjustment to a new environment. In a rather pragmatic fashion, the Mormons only transferred those elements of the cultural landscape of their hearth in the United States *(Meinig, 1965)* which were feasible and relevant to the pioneer environment of Alberta, and were considered essential to Mormonism *(Rosenvall 1987)*.

LEHR *(1973, 28)* lists the following five elements which are indicative of the cultural landscape of the Mormons in Alberta:
- Farm villages;
- Ward Chapels;
- an open field landscape around settlements;
- the absence of liquor stores and bars;
- unpainted farm buildings

The farm villages can be interpreted as a pragmatic response to the religious and social needs of the Mormons and to the demands of an agrarian economy. Nevertheless, in the early years of colonization, many Mormons were located on isolated farmsteads and moved only later into villages. The villages did not follow the rigid design that was originally proposed by the Mormon founder Joseph SMITH in his so-called 'Plat of the City of Zion' design of 1833. But the villages tended to share a number of common traits, for instance a cardinally oriented system of wide streets; evidence of farming activity within the settlements, although they also included artisans and merchants; and large lots occupied by a single dwelling. This gave to these villages an open and sprawling appearance. Closely related to the nucleated settlement pattern was the open field landscape around the villages, largely devoid of dispersed farmsteads. The most prominent feature of the sacred landscape of the Mormons were the ward chapels characterized by their thin decorative spires, their brick or masonry construction and their absence of crosses *(Lehr 1978)*. Contemporary Mormon settlements in the region still reflect the structural legacy of the early farm villages, but only a small proportion of the Mormon population today continues to be farmers and live in the villages.

The sole minority group which continues to adhere in its entirety to the nucleated settlement form of colonies and to the economic pursuit of farming is that of the Hutterites. Since the arrival of this religious community in the Canadian Prairies in 1918, the spectacular diffusion of Hutterite colonies has left a significant imprint on the cultural landscape of the agricultural realm of the Prairies *(see Fig. 11)*.

In their size and morphology, the Hutterite colonies cannot be compared to villages of the Mennonites and Mormons. They are neither oriented towards a road spine as the Mennonite *Straßendörfer*, nor do they exhibit a regular grid plan as the Mormon villages. The colonies merely form clusters of loosely arranged buildings surrounded by vegetable and berry gardens and the open fields.

Fig. 11: Hutterite Settlement Areas and their Expansion in Alberta, Saskatchewan and Montana, 1973 - 1983

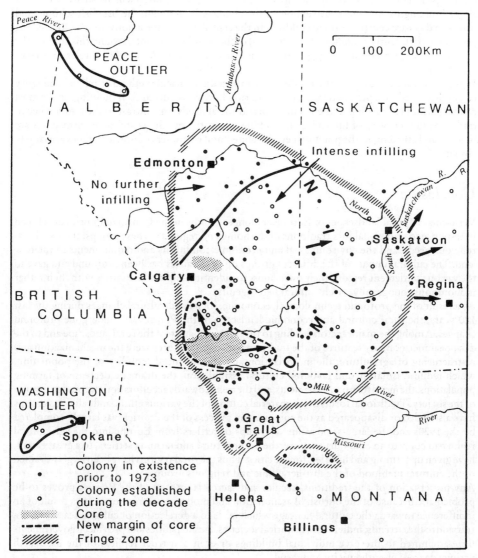

Source Evans 1987

In the center of the colonies, the kitchen/dining room unit forms the core of the communal buildings. The other major communal structures are the simple church which usually also serves as the building for religious instruction of the children in German, the 'English school', and usually a day care centre for small children. In the central part of the colony are also located the residences (frequently a number of row houses) of the families. Grouped around this core are the workshops, implement buildings, granaries and barns, as well as the small featureless cemetery (see Fig. 12).

In the architectural design of the *Bruderhöfe*, no specific vernacular ethnic or religious identity can be discerned. In a pragmatic way, the Hutterites have constructed their buildings in the most rational fashion according to their economic and social needs. In contrast to their adherence to traditions in their way of life and their clothing styles, the buildings and their furnishings are modern and efficient,to the point that even architectural reminders of previous times are largely absent.

Conclusion

Vernacular cultural landscapes of European pioneer groups in the Canadian Prairies developed in response to traditional folk traditions of the homeland regions of these groups, their social or religious needs, and the environmental and economic conditions and requirements in the new land. The cultural impact of the different groups on the Prairies has been profound and gave to the various settlement regions their own landscape identity, and to the Prairies with their rather monotonous topography a rich cultural heterogeneity.

As a result of the profound technological, economic, social and cultural changes during the last 120 years, the rural cultural and economic landscape of the Prairies has undergone profound changes. Among the major factors leading to the transformation of the rural landscape and to the disappearance of many features of the traditional material cultures were the mechanization and restructuring of agriculture, the motorization and the enhanced mobility of the population, which reduced isolation and favoured cultural assimilation, the dramatic decrease of farming populations, the move to urban settlements, and the trend towards acculturation and modernization of the society. Traditional forms of the material culture of the various ethnic and religious groups have also faded or disappeared as the colonization process of the Prairies was largely completed by the 1920s and the large-scale influx of groups of settlers from Europe into the agricultural realm had come to an end. Furthermore, the original rural and farming settlers, to a great extent, have given up farming and have left for the cities. Thus the rural regions have been largely drained of the cultural lifeblood of the distinct ethnic and religious groups.

Any preservation of the traditional secular and sacred landscape of the Prairies proves to be problematic because of the onrush of assimilation and modernization, and also as a result of an indifference towards the cultural heritage which leads to a dereliction of cultural features. As a reaction to these trends, individuals, historical societies, municipalities and provincial governments have attempted to preserve individual buildings or even construct replicas of the past, with various degrees of authenticity and taste!

The most visible expressions of this renewed interest in the history of Prairie settlement and the contributing cultural groups are the outdoor museums or heritage villages. LEHR *(1990, 269)* considers this approach as "a poor vehicle of heritage conservation in western Canada" as this does not represent an "authentic replication of landscape but only the preservation of single elements". In the case of some ethnic groups, for instance the Ukrainians, their presence in the railway villages and towns occurred often only decades after the immigration, and by that time, the traditional architecture had already changed considerably. Thus for LEHR *(1990, 270),* many so-called "heritage villages" represent not only a "temporal distortion" but also a "geographic misrepresentation". He therefore rejects the concept of pioneer villages and advocates a new

Fig. 12: Layout of the Crystal Spring Hutterite Colony, Manitoba

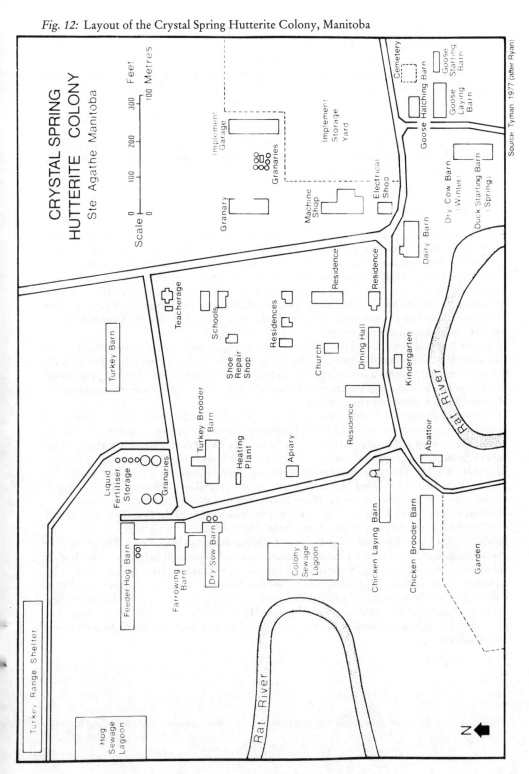

strategy to preserve the integrity of the ethnic landscapes of western Canada by efforts to save the aesthetic attributes of the cultural landscapes and to retain a sense of place, without arresting the process of landscape evolution at one particular time:
"Preservation of the ethnic landscape will be best served not by the almost antihistorical pioneer village with life arrested at a certain point, not by the ethnic kitsch of old houses bashed into new lives as 'authentic ethnic restaurants or souvenir stalls', nor by the establishment of entire districts within which the local population cooperates with heritage agencies to nurture a growing, evolving, living landscape. Only within a wide geographic area can the heritage of our past be successfully integrated within a modern technologically advanced agricultural system, and only within a wide geographic area may a unity of environment be achieved whereby buildings are seen in their true setting" *(Lehr 1990, 274).*

Zusammenfassung

Nach der 1879 erfolgten Eingliederung des weiträumigen "Rupert's Land" der "Hudson's Bay Company" in das "Dominion of Canada" wanderten verschiedene ethnische und religiöse Gruppen in das "new and naked land" (Rees) der kanadischen Prärie. Die Wanderung dieser Siedler, die sich als Einzelpersonen oder als Gruppen in der Prärie niederließen, wurde durch eine Reihe von "Push" - und "Pull"-Kräften ausgelöst. Das "Great Lone Land" der Prärie, das den Neuankommenden zunächst vielfach fremd und feindlich erschienen haben mag, wurde für diese Menschen schließlich zu einer neuen Heimat, die durch wesentliche kulturelle Merkmale dieser Bevölkerungsgruppen geprägt wurde.
Dieser Beitrag soll einen Überblick über die Einwirkungen einer Reihe von ethnischen und religiösen Minoritäten auf die ländlichen Regionen der kanadischen Prärie geben; ein Einfluß, der sich bis heute, wenn auch in abgeschwächter Form, erhalten hat. Zur Prägung dieser ländlichen Kulturräume eigener Identität haben besonders die Ukrainer, die Mennoniten, die Hutterer und die Mormonen beigetragen.
Die Mennoniten waren die erste religiöse Gruppe, die in den 1870er Jahren ein zusammenhängendes Territorium in der östlichen Prärie besiedelten. In der Folge kam es in diesen Gebieten zu einer Masseneinwanderung von Europäern die von einer Vielfalt von Menschen unterschiedlicher ethnischer, religiöser, kultureller oder "nationaler" Herkunft getragen wurde, und die im Zeitraum zwischen 1890 und dem Ersten Weltkrieg ihren Höhepunkt erreichte. Obwohl die Mehrzahl der Siedler britischer Herkunft waren, haben besonders die Bauern aus Mittel- und Osteuropa ihr kulturelles Erbe in die Prärie übertragen und diese grundlegend geprägt.
Die kulturelle und soziale Verbundenheit der einzelnen Gruppen, die Zahl der Einwanderer und der Zeitpunkt ihrer Ankunft in der Prärie, sowie das Verhältnis der Gruppe mit staatlichen Behörden haben wesentlich zur Prägung dieser Kulturlandschaften beigetragen. Trotz verschiedener Hindernisse ist es diesen Menschen gelungen, eine eigenständige regionale Identität zu entwickeln. Während viele materielle Zeugnisse der Kulturlandschaft aufgrund von Akkulturations- und Modernisierungsprozessen verschwunden sind, sind dennoch eine Reihe von kulturellen Merkmalen dieser Minoritäten in der Prärie erhalten geblieben. Die Erhaltung der Kulturlandschaft der ethnischen und religiösen Minoritäten ist durch moderne Entwicklungen und Schwierigkeiten bedroht und heute trotz verschiedener Bemühungen als problematisch zu betrachten.

References

Anderson, L.C. and Engelhart, M. (1974): A Geographical Appraisal of the North American Hutterian Brethren. In: Geographical Survey, 3(1), 53-71.
Dawson, C.A. (1936): Group settlement: Ethnic Communities in Western Canada. In: Mackintosh, W.A. and Joerg, W.L.G.(eds.): Canadian Frontiers of Settlement, Vol.7, Toronto, MacMillan.
Evans, S.M. (1973): The Dispersal of Hutterite Colonies in Alberta, 1918-1971: The Spatial Expression of Cultural Identity. M.A. (Geography), University of Calgary.
Evans, S.M. (1974): The Spatial Expression of Cultural Identity: The Hutterites in Alberta In: Occasional Papers in Geography, B.C. Geographical Series 18, Vancouver, Tantalus Research Ltd.
Evans, S.M. (1987): The Hutterites in Alberta. Past and Present Settlement Patterns. In: Rosenvall, L.A. and Evans, S.M., eds. (1987): Essays on the Historical Geography of the Canadian West. Calgary, Department of Geography, University of Calgary, 145-171.
Friesen, J. (1985): Mennonites through the Centuries. From the Netherlands to Canada. Steinbach, Mennonite Village Museum.
Hostetler, J.A. (1974): Hutterite Society. Baltimore/London, The John Hopkins University Press.
Hostetler, J.A. (1983a): Hutterite Life. Scottdale, Pennsylvania/Kitchener, Ontario, Herald Press.
Hostetler, J.A. (1983b): Mennonite Life. Scottdale, Pennsylvania/Kitchener, Ontario, Herald Press.
Hostetler, J.A, and Huntington, G.E. (1980): The Hutterites in North America. New York, Holt, Rinehart & Winston.
Katz, Y. and Lehr, J.C. (1991). Jewish and Mormon Agricultural Settlement in Western Canada: A Comparative Analysis. In: The Canadian Geographer, 35(2), 128-142.
Laatsch, W.G. (1971): Hutterite Colonization in Alberta. In: The Journal of Geography, 70, 347-359.
Lehr, J.C. (1972): Mormon Settlement Morphology in Southern Alberta. In: The Albertan Geographer, 8, 6-13.
Lehr, J.C. (1973): The Mormon Cultural Landscape in Alberta. In: Leigh, R.(ed.): Malaspina Papers: Studies in Human and Physical Geography (B.C. Geographical Series, 17), Vancouver, Tantalus Research, 25-33.
Lehr, J.C. (1974): The Sequence of Mormon Settlement in Southern Alberta. In: The Albertan Geographer, 10, 20-29.
Lehr, J.C. (1978): Mormon Settlement Morphology in Southern Alberta. In: The Albertan Geographer, 8, 6-13.
Lehr, J.C. (1980): The Log Buildings of Ukrainian Settlers in Western Canada. In: Prairie Forum, 5(2), 183-196.
Lehr, J.C. (1982): The Landscape of Ukrainian Settlement in the Canadian West. In: Great Plains Quarterly, 2(2), 94-105.
Lehr, J.C. (1983): Propaganda and Belief: Ukrainian Emigrant Views of the Canadian West. In: Rozumnyj, J. (ed.): New Soil-Old Roots: The Ukrainian Experience in Canada. Winnipeg, Ukrainian Academy of Arts and Sciences in Canada, 1-17.
Lehr, J.C. (1985a): From Russia with Faith. In: Horizon Canada, 2(17), 398-403.
Lehr, J.C. (1985b): Kinship and Society in the Ukrainian Pioneer Settlement of the Canadian West. In: Canadian Geographer, 29(3), 207-219.
Lehr, J.C. (1985c): Land's Sake. In: Horizon Canada, 3(36), 854-859.
Lehr, J.C. (1985d): The Mormons. In: Horizon Canada, 3(32), 752-757.
Lehr, J.C. (1985e): The Peculiar People: Ukrainian Settlement of Marginal Lands in Southeastern Manitoba. In: Jones, D.C. and MacPherson, I. (eds.): Building Beyond the Homestead: Rural History on the Prairies. Calgary, University of Calgary Press, 29-46.
Lehr, J.C. (1985f): Wrestlers of the Spirit. In: Horizon Canada, 6(64), 1526-1531.
Lehr, J.C. (1987): Government Perceptions of Ukrainian Immigrants to Western Canada 1896-1902. In: Canadian Ethnic Studies, 19(2), 1-12.
Lehr, J.C. (1989): The Ukrainian Sacred Landscape: A Metaphor of Survival and Acculturation. In: Material History Bulletin, 29, 3-11.
Lehr, J.C. (1990): Preservation of the Ethnic Landscape in Western Canada. In: Prairie Forum, 15(2), 263-276.
Lehr, J.C. (1991): Peopling the Prairies with Ukrainians. In: Luciuk, L. and Hryniuk, S. (eds.): Canada's Ukrainians: Negotiating an Identity. Toronto, University of Toronto Press, 30-51.

Lehr, J.C. and Davies, W.K.D. (1993): Canada's Ethnic Diversity: An Introduction to Old Problems and New Patterns. In: Davies, W.K.D. (eds.): Canadian Transformations: Perspectives on a Human Geography, Swansea, The University of Wales, Canadian Studies Group.

Lehr, J.C. and Moodie, W. (1980): The Polemics of Pioneer Settlement: Ukrainian Immigration and the Winnipeg Free Press. In: Canadian Ethnic Studies, 12(2), 88-101.

Lenz, K. (1965): Die Prärieprovinzen Kanadas. Der Wandel der Kulturlandschaft von der Kolonisation bis zur Gegenwart unter dem Einfluß der Industrie. In: Marburger Geographische Schriften, 21.

Lenz, K. (1977): Die Siedlungen der Hutterer in Nordamerika. In: Geographische Zeitschrift, 65(3), 216-238.

Meinig, D.W. (1965): The Mormon Culture Region: Strategies and Patterns in the Geography of the American West, 1847-1964. In: Annals of the Association of American Geographers, 55, 191-220.

Mennonite Village Museum (1982): Mennonite Village Museum. Steinbach, Derksen Printers Ltd.

Noble, A.G. (1992): German-Russian Mennonites in Manitoba. In: Noble, A.G. (ed.): To Build in a New Land: Ethnic Landscapes in North America. Baltimore/London, The John Hopkins University Press, 268-284.

Pirker, W. (1981): Gemeinschaftssiedlungen in der kanadischen Prärie: Eine sozialgeographische Untersuchung der Hutterer von Manitoba. Diss. (Geographie) Universität Salzburg.

Rees, R. (1988): New and naked land. Making the Prairies Home. Saskatoon, Western Producer Prairie Books.

Rosenvall, L.A. (1987): The Transfer of Mormon Culture to Alberta. In: Rosenvall, L.A. and Evans, S.M. (eds.): Essays on the Historical Geography of the Canadian West. Calgary, Department of Geography, University of Calgary, 122-144.

Ryan, J. (1977): The Agricultural Economy of the Manitoba Hutterite Colonies. Toronto, Mc Clelland and Stewart.

Ryan, J. (1985): Hutterites: Refugees from Persecution-Out of this World. In: Horizon Canada, 2(21), 494-499.

Ryan, J. (1994): Hutterites in Manitoba. Unpublished Manuscript, Winnipeg.

Sawatzky, H.L. (1976): Die Lebensfähigkeit geschlossener Volksgruppen am Beispiel der Mennoniten in Manitoba/Westkanada. In: Schott, C.(ed.): Beiträge zur Geographie Nordamerikas (Marburger Geographische Schriften, 66), 111-132.

Schlichtmann, H. (1976): The 'Ethnic Architecture in the Prairies' Conference: A Report and a Geographer's Reflection. In: Prairie Forum, 1, 69-75.

Schlichtmann, H, (1977): Ethnic Themes in Geographical Research on Western Canada. In: Canadian Ethnic Studies, 9(2), 9-41.

Simpson-Housley, P. (1974): Ideology and Environmental Perceptions-The Hutterite View of the World. In: Otago Geographer, 6, 1-11.

Stadel, C. (1994): Phasen der kulturlandschaftlichen Entwicklung in der kanadischen Prärie. Unpublished Manuscript, Salzburg.

Todd, D. and Brierley, J.S. (1977): Ethnicity and the Rural Economy: Illustrations from Southern Manitoba, 1961-1971. In: The Canadian Geographer, 21(3), 237-249.

Tyman, J.L. and Tyman, D. (1978): Where on Earth? Mid-latitude grasslands. Library Edition. Brisbane, Atham Educational.

Vogelsang, R. (1985): Ein Schema zur Untersuchung und Darstellung ethnischer Minoritäten-erläutert am Beispiel Kanadas. In: Geographische Zeitschrift, 73(3), 145-162.

Warketin, J. (1959): Mennonite Agricultural Settlement of Southern Manitoba. In: Geographical Review, 49(3), 342-368.

Address of the Author

Christoph Stadel
Institut für Geographie
Universität Salzburg
5020 Salzburg
AUSTRIA

"...daß wir nicht sehr verläßlich
zu Hause sind in der gedeuteten Welt"

(R.M. Rilke, 1980²)

VOLKER ALBRECHT

Multiculturalism and Pluralism in the United States

Perspectives from the Mexican American Experiences

Placing the Mexican Americans into the Multicultural Discourse.

The issue of multiculturalism has a long-standing history in the political debates and public rhetoric of the United States and is a central element for past and current battles that attempt to define a common U.S.-American identity. The slogan "*E Pluribus Unum*" signalizes a consciousness of National Identity that has traditionally been linked to the "American Creed" (*see Myrdal 1944*) which proposes that all different immigrant groups in the United States eventually emerge as a unity with a mutually accepted understanding of U.S.-citizenship. The main value-system of the American Creed and the strive for the American Dream refers to a set of ideological values which are closely related to the European Enlightenment and the Protestant-puritan ethic.

The emphasis on individual equality and equal rights for everybody, as expressed in the 14th Amendment to the Constitution, was constitutionally integrated after the Civil War, though not implemented into the social realities of the United States. It took nearly a century and the power of the Civil Rights Movement to make the idea of equal opportunity a part of the social and economic life of the United States.

The time of arrival, the region of origin, different cultural attributes, physical appearance were among the factors as to how one was treated and how the diversity of the stock that came, is coming or will be coming and living in the United States might be treated as a part of, or to be apart from the mainstream that embraces the American dream.

One segment of this dream was the concept of cultural pluralism that was formulated as early as 1915 (*Kallen 1915, 190-194*) emphasizing the strength of diversity. This concept was mainly related to white ethnic groups and did not necessarily include the black and Mexican population. The notion of cultural pluralism was not only bound to explicit forms of Americanization, but especially to the acceptance and the adaptation of the language and the life-style of the hegemonial WASP - middle class. A relic of this type of concept of a multicultural society are the many hyphenated Americans (German-American, Irish-American, Mexican-American, etc.).

This traditional concept of multiculturality was not firmly questioned until the "Black Power Movement" and, with a lesser impact, the "Chicano Movement" set a different tone in the argumentation of the multicultural discourse. Both movements were characterized by a strong affirmation of Non-WASP, Non-U.S.-American roots questioning the traditional values of individual rights and the Protestant work ethics.

The different arguments that form part of the discourse on multiculturalism and pluralism are closely related to the question to what extent cultural/ethnic/racial diversity and national identity exclude each other or are two sides of the same coin.

Among the multifaceted, outspoken or covered discourse on the new multiculturalism and the revival of the notion of ethnicity, two questions seem to determine the political debate and scholarly writing on the subject.

First, is equality a question of individual rights or group rights; and second, interrelated with this question, is it constitutional to distinguish citizens according to their membership to ethnic or racial groups, and is it justified to derive specific governmental action programs (e.g. Affirmative Action) from group-related characteristica?

Traditionally, judicial solutions were drawn from a universalistic and individualistic frame of reference (especially to the equal protection clause of the 14th Amendment to the constitution) that united American society around a strong procedural commitment to treat people with equal respect (*Taylor 1994, 56*). The social realities of inequality and injustice however - which undeniably ran and still run along ethnic and racial lines - present arguments to question the universalistic procedural approach as the only appropriate one of coping with social inequality, which often coincides with different forms of spatial segregation and negative living circumstances of individuals and groups.

The individualistic position of defining freedom and equality has led to a distinction between private and public, which confines socialization processes and the evolution of the self as well as the realities of cultural pluralism to the private sphere. "The cultural pluralism of American society is one of its greatest assets, but such pluralism is a private matter of local choice, and not a proper responsibility of the federal government .... it is clearly the intent of Congress that the goal of federally-funded capacity building programs in bilingual education be to assist children of limited or non-English speaking ability to gain competence in English so that they may enjoy equal educational opportunity and not require cultural pluralism" (*Epstein 1977, 21*). This kind of perception of cultural socialization, and the clear goal of Americanization as expressed by Under Secretary Frank CARLUCCI in 1974 was questioned since the New Deal, the Civil-Rights-Movement and culminated in efforts of institutionalizing multiculturalism in the late sixties and the seventies to prevent the distinctness of individuals or groups to be ignored and be assimilated by the majority identity.

In the dramatic debates on the meaning and value of public and common life the battle runs around the dichotomy of culturally and politically acceptable differences and nationally shared values and the foundation of a common ideological consensus. The majority of the Republicans in both Houses of Congress, and the acceptance of Proposition 187 in California 1994, which denies social security, schooling and medical care to illegals (undocumented) and their children, signalizes a strong recovery of an exclusive traditional value-system that focuses on the individualistic and local government interpretation of the Declaration of Independence: "We hold these truths to be self-evident, that all men are created equal, that they are endowed by their creator with certain unalienable Rights, that among these are Life, Liberty, and the pursuit of Happiness".

Bound to these more judicial questions is another perspective:

what are the identifying processes, ideals, values, set of frames of references that build the U.S. American nation, and how can and do the different cultural, ethnic and racial groups refer to the different offerings and rituals of national identity?

In asking these kind of questions I confine myself to a discussion on the elements of collective social identities that generally function as social categories. I do not touch the personal level of identity formation, where the loss of dignity and the effects of inequality are strongly felt. The construction of collective social identities are the outcome of discourses in the arena of the public sphere where the politics of recognition (*see Taylor 1994*) is shaped.

Putting the Mexican Americans, or Chicanos, or Mexicans, who are the largest part of the growing tide of Spanish-speaking people in the United States, into the multicultural discourse, I want to focus on the following questions:

- what does pluralism mean from the Mexican, and Mexican American experience in the USA,
- what are the battlegrounds between the traditional mainstream of U.S. America and the Mexican American, and
- what are the elements of the rhetoric for Mexican and Mexican American identity and how far have these elements a chance to function as a culturally unifying force in public space?

The last question is strongly related to what is generally labelled the social production of ethnic identity. Following the line that "ethnicity" in general, or belonging to a cultural group is a provisional, historically conditioned social construct that might be reinvented generationally, dependent on changing material conditions, semiotic codes and power relations at specific times and places (*Smith 1992, 512*), one has to ask of what kind were and are the elements, the changing material conditions, the semiotic codes, the power relations that conditioned the social construct "Mexican" and "Mexican American"?

I want to approach these questions from three different perspectives:

- to give a short overview of the main socio-cultural and socio-spatial characteristics of the Mexican /Mexican American,
- to describe the formative forces and construction of the label "Mexican", the effects of this label and its relevance for today's living situations of the Mexican Americans with special reference to Arizona/Sonora,
- to open up the nation-state perspective of the concept of the label Mexican American to a transboundary multi-centric worldview.

The method used to answer these questions will be a more hermeneutical one, specifically applied to the second perspective. It implies critical reading, decoding and interpretation of historical, territorial and structural facts. It refers to R.M. RILKE's line from the *Duineser Elegien* that is quoted at the beginning of this paper that there is insecurity to be felt at home in an interpreted and constructed world.

The scale of analysis will be regional. The core-periphery perspectives (Central Mexico, North-East United States and Virginia as the main core areas) as an explanatory frame for the cultural and socio-spatial processes in a semi-desert area will be neglected.

It is obvious - but I want at least to mention it - that the overall perspective I can only offer is an outside - inside one which even might be biased by a German-European point of view.

Immigration, migration, barrio, cultural and spatial connectivity to Mexico as key variables of past and present living situations of Mexicans in the U.S.

The concentration of 81 % of the Mexican American population at the Border States, California, Arizona, New Mexico and Texas, as well as the high proportion of Mexican Americans living in cities (*Tab.1*) refer to the main determinants that have shaped the living situations historically and geographically, the cultural and political situations of the Mexicans in the West and Southwest of the United States:

- the pull-factors of a highly developed country and the push factors of underdevelopment and poverty in Mexico,
- the life in spatially segregated areas, now mainly in urban barrios, and
- the spatial and cultural connections to Mexico.

I will treat the Mexican American experiences mainly from a Californian and Arizonian perspective. The situation in New Mexico is too different and unique. There the Spanish-speaking population identifies itself very much as Hispanos with the perception of a clearly defined concept of a homeland (*Nostrand, 1970*). This attitude also explains the low rate of

Tab. 1: Cities in the USA with more than 100,000 Inhabitants of Hispanic and/or Mexican Origin, 1990

	Total Hispanic Population	% Of total Population	% Mexican of Hispanic Pop.
New York City	1,783,511	24.4	03.2
Los Angeles (CA)	1,391,411	39.9	67.5
Chicago (IL)	545,852	19.6	65.0
San Antonio (TX)	520,282	55.6	93.3
Houston (TX)	450,483	27.6	80.7
El Paso (TX)	355,669	69.0	95.9
San Diego (CA)	229,519	20.7	86.3
Miami (FL)	223,964	62.5	00.9
Dallas (TX)	210,240	20.9	89.6
San Jose (CA)	208,388	26.6	83.9
Phoenix (AZ)	197,103	20.0	91.5
Santa Ana (CA)	191,385	65.2	92.0
Hialeah (FL)	164,652	87.6	00.6
Albuquerque (NM)	132,706	34.5	53.4
Corpus Christi (TX)	129,708	50.4	93.1
Tuscon (AZ)	118,595	29.3	92.0
Laredo (TX)	115,360	93.9	96.6
Austin (TX)	106,865	23.0	88.5
Fresno (CA)	105,787	29.9	93.4
Long Beach (CA)	101,419	23.6	81.6
San Francisco (CA)	100,717	13.9	39.7
Santa Fe (NM)	26,372	47.5	32.4

Source: Hispanic Databook of U.S. Cities and Counties, 1994

Hispanics declaring themselves as Mexicans in Albuquerque and Santa Fe (*Tab. 2*). Texas, again, is also different and here I lack any authentic regional knowlege.
The living situation of the Mexican Americans, their past and present labelling from the outside such as *Beaner, Wetback, Greaser, Chilibelly, Frito-bandito, Illegal* are closely connected with the different phases of immigration. The amount of immigrants were and are dependent of the catering of cheap labor force (e.g. the Bracero-Program 1942-64) and the attempts to stop Mexican immigration or to repatriate Mexican Workers (*Operation Wetback 1954, see Garcia, J.R. 1977*). The labor force was and still is mainly needed in mining (copper industry), in agro-business, the garment industry (sweatshops), and the growing service sector. The hope for a better economic life in the United States and the need for a labor force in the growing maquiladora industry at the Mexican border (mainly women in special sectors, *see also Tab. 7*) has intensified the migration to the north. The effect is an uncontrolled growth of the population and an urbanization of the Mexican border cities (*Tab. 2*) with spillover effects to the United States.
A continuing topic of public discourse in the USA is the question and problem of illegal immigration. The main gateways are Ciudad Juarez/El Paso, Nogales/Nogales and Tijuana/San Diego. The 450,000 arrests by the Border Patrol in San Diego during 1994 (*Los Angeles Times 30.1.1995, A14*) and the strengthening of the border fence (*Fig. 1*) are signs of the intensifying

Tab. 2: Population Development in Selected Cities of Mexican America, 1880-1990

	Tucson	Phoenix	El Paso	Tijuana	Ciudad Juarez
1880	7,007	1,708	736	-	-
1890	5,150	3,152	10,338	-	-
1900	7,531	5,544	15,906	350	-
1910	13,193	11,134	39,297	969	-
1920	10,292	29,053	77,560	1,228	-
1930	32,506	48,118	102,420	11,271	43,183
1940	36,818	65,414	96,810	21,977	55,024
1950	45,954	106,818	130,485	65,364	131,108
1960	212,892	439,170	276,678	165,690	276,995
1970	262,933	584,303	322,261	340,583	424,135
1980	330,537	789,704	425,259	709,340	590,809
1990	405,390	515,342	515,342	1,129,000	880,270

Source: Tuscon, Phoenix, El Paso for 1880-1970 Historical Statistics of the United States, Colonial Times to 1970. Washington D.C., U.S. Bureau of the Census, 1980, 1990, The U.S. Census of Population 1980, 1990, Arizona, California, Texas, U.S. Dept. of Commerce, Bureau of Census, 1982, 1992: for Tijuana and Juarez, INEGI, Censo del Poblacion Y Vivienda 1980, 1990 and Arreola, (1993)

mood related to immigration from Mexico. It has again led to measures to seal off the border and block off undocumented workers via newly introduced law enforcement operations "Gatekeeper" (San Diego CA, 1994) and "Hold the Line" (1993 in El Paso, TX). This has without any doubt an effect on the continuing overall negative stereotyping of the Mexicans.

Although the new Immigration Law 1986 opened a legal space for a number of so-called illegals to receive amnesty and legalize their status in the U.S. without repercussions, the battle regarding the "Illegal Issue" has been intensified since Proposition 187 in California was confirmed by the voters during the elections in November 1994.

The issue of illegal immigration is paramount when a public discourse deals with the Mexican or Mexican American population. This has a long tradition and creates a distorted picture. But what is the right picture and what kind of sources are available to draw some facets that might match the reality?

The first problem in dealing with Mexican Americans as a group is the difficulty to identify them by a continuous label through time in the U.S. census and official statistics: i.e., Spanish-speaking (1960) Spanish Heritage (1970), and since 1980 the more general term "Hispanic" is applied to all with a Latino or Spanish-speaking heritage. Instead of Hispanic, often the term Latino is used in public discourse, in avoiding the Spanish connotations and the supposedly inherited colonial meaning of the term Hispanic. Nowadays the hyphenated term Mexican-American does not exist in official publications:

only the term "Mexican" is used, grouped with Cubans, Puertoricans, Dominicans, Central Americans, South Americans and Other Hispanics under the label of "Hispanic Population". If the term Mexican American is used, however, generally it appears without a hyphen as it was still in use in the sixties. In the following pages I will apply the term Mexican as THERNSTROM *(1980)* does, whenever I discuss the people of Mexican descent living in the United States that has also been labelled Mexican American.

Fig. 1: The Boarder Fence between the USA and Mexico

To be Mexican in the United States embraces different experiences in time and space. This space is not confined to the West or Southwest of the United States. Taking the national boundary into consideration it is a transboundary space which I want to call Mexican America (*see also Garreau 1982* who introduced MexAmerica).
For the United States there are not only regional differences in the labelling of the Mexicans as Tejanos, Californios or Hispanos (New Mexico) whose families have a long tradition of residence in these areas and do not see themselves as immigrants. There are differences of time of arrival, and it makes a difference whether a Mexican is a newcomer or belongs to the first, second, third generation in the area. Bound to experiences in time and space are different kinds of acculturation and assimilation processes, which not only produce conflicts with the mainstream society, but have also evoked and still evoke inner-group conflicts and special labelling. For example, Cholo was primarily used in Northwestern Mexico and California as a term for lower-class people which was diffused from Peru during the 19th century characterizing a Mestizo with lower-class implications (*see Gamio 1971*). After the first World War, for the Native-born Mexican in the United States the newly arrived lower-class immigrant was called a chicano, and the first generation Mexican a pocho (*Villareal 1970*). During the years of the Depression and during World War II, young, usually underprivileged Mexicans were called pachucos. A pachuco was a stereotypical label for a Los Angeles born member of a neighborhood gang who was often identified by a special clothing (zoot-suiter). Today's use of the label Chicano is predominantly tied to the ideologically fixed Chicano Movement from the sixties. The main elements of the Chicano selfconcept, which held and holds its strongholds in California includes an affiliation with mestizo history, underclass and colonized people.
Politically the Mexicans are by no means a homogeneous group, although it is often taken for granted that most of them feel affiliated with the Democratic Party.
On the federal level different organizations take the cause of the Mexicans, as well as of Latinos in general (NCLR - National Council of La Raza, NALEO - National Association of Latino

Elected and Appointed Officials, LULAC - League of United Latin American Citizens, and MALDEF - Mexican American Legal Defense and Education Fund and the Congressional Hispanic Caucus).

The different experiences in time and space are primarily bound to living experiences in colonias and barrios. Colonias are a kind of workcamp for residential purposes in the mining industry or agro-business. They can have a stable development, often, however, life is disrupted according to the needs and the economy of the company that runs the mine or the agro-business. Related to the segregated life in camps is the reality and image of the migrant worker (migrants, campesinos, migrant pickers) and his family, whose rhythm of life was described by ESCALANTE (*1983*) from a personal experience. Most of the migrant pickers have their home in Texas and they follow the time of harvest in different areas up to Illinois. For the children moving with the migrant picker's family, migrant education programs have been developed to cope with the educational needs of this nomadic lifestyle.

The barrio is an urban institution that has the meaning of neighborhood. The Spanish derived the original meaning from the Aztecs. For them barrio in the original sense was a spatial living unity. Since the Chicano Movement, the term "barrio" also received a political connotation, as a source of political activism with murals as signals and territorial markers. A fine example are the murals of Barrio Logan in San Diego (*Fig.2*) drawn by artists who lived inside and outside the barrio. Another authentic expression of barrio life might be the graffiti that have grown out of Los Angeles first graffiti "crew", the L.A. Bomb Squad, whose members consisted of Latino youth from the barrios of Pico-Union and East L.A. (*see Martinez 1992*).

Living in a barrio or a colonia meant, and still implies, living in a segregated world, segregated from mainstream America. But the living situations differ very much from barrio to barrio, or from neighborhood to neighborhood. Some examples from California might help to illustrate the heterogeneity of what is labelled the Mexicans in California. *Tab. 3* shows that the Mexicans are either very segregated as a group as in East Los Angeles, or are a part of a certain portion of a larger Hispanic community as in Los Angeles City, or a larger proportion of a small Hispanic fraction in one neighborhood, as in El Segundo or in Los Angeles (Zip Code 90024).

Calexico, as a border city, has the highest ratio of Hispanics which are more or less all Mexicans. Taking into consideration some parameters by which one can distinguish the socio-economic level and socio-cultural integration, the listed neighborhoods differ very much according to the ratio of people speaking only Spanish, ratio of high school graduates and average yearly income per capita. It appears that there is a correlation between intensity of segregation, high ratio of people speaking only Spanish, low ratio of high school graduates, and very low yearly per capita income. The high ratio of people only speaking Spanish might hint to not yet assimilated new immigrants (Calexico) or to a long traditional Spanish-speaking area (East Los Angeles) or a mixture of both. The comparison of two neighborhoods in Los Angeles (Zip Code 90023, and Zip Code 90024) reveal that there are sharp spatial boundaries between the different socio-economic levels of multicultural living situations of the Mexicans in Los Angeles.

The dynamics that shape the urban barrio and influence the identifying process of a community-feeling can differ very much. Often the barrios located in the traditional city centers were destroyed or deformed by urban renewal projects, or the immigration of Asians change the contextuality of a Mexican barrio. Besides the concentration and segregation, a patchwork-like distribution in urban areas is part of the living realities of Mexicans.

Territoriality and Mexican Identity in the United States

This section attempts to elaborate on a specific hidden agenda that is bound to the Mexican experience in the United States, as well as in the rhetoric of the Chicano Movement. The main hypothesis that will carry my arguments through the following paragraph will be that there is a

Fig. 2: A Mural on a Column of the Coronado Bridge in San Diego

kind of territorial imperative in the hidden or openly presented identification rhetoric of the Mexicans.

The idea that Mexicans have been rooted in space, that they were annexed by conquest and that a specific set of historical and geographical factors are very much a part of the "Mexican problem" was articulated by Carey MC WILLIAMS: "The Spanish-speaking have an identification with the Southwest which can never be broken. They are not interloopers or immigrants but an indigenous people. They resent any designation which implies a hyphenated relationship to their native environment" *(1968, 7)*, and "Geographically the Southwest is one with the northern portions of Mexico and wars do not alter the facts of geography" *(1968, 207 f)*. He built in part his perspective of the class and social structure of the Mexican group in the United States on the work of some earlier social scientists such as the sociologist Emory BOGARDUS *(1928)*. BOGARDUS refers partly to the first larger official description of the Mexicans, the Reports of

Tab. 3: Socio-Cultural Parameters for Mexicans in Selected Californian Cities, 1990

City	Total Population	% Hispanics	% Mexican of Hispanic Population	% Speaking only Spanish	% Hispanics High School Graduate	Per Capita Income Hispanic	Overall
Los Angeles County	8,863,164	37.3	76.2	11.2	39.2	8,066	16,149
East L.A.	126,379	94.5	94.0	32.6	27.5	6,454	6,636
El Segundo	15,223	8.6	50.0	1.1	71.0	20,132	23,583
Florence-Graham	57,147	75.8	88.6	31.2	13.0	4,781	5,407
La Canada Flintridge City	19,378	4.6	57.7	0.3	79.3	21,999	38,132
L.A. City	3,485,398	39.3	67.5	14.3	33.0	7,111	16,188
Zip Code 90023	47,270	97.5	92.6	35.9	22.9	5,946	6,177
Zip Code 90024	38,319	7.0	57.5	0.5	72.1	12,109	33,073
Fresno County	667,490	34.7	94.4	7.8	40.4	6,593	11,824
Fresno City	354,202	29.1	93.4	4.7	48.1	7,044	11,528
Zip Code 93701	15,301	55.3	94.6	20.0	18.6	3,818	3,931
Zip Code 93722	33,274	30.1	93.1	3.6	50.3	8,401	12,587
Imperial County	109,303	65.3	97.4	17.2	37.7	6,260	9,208
Calexico City	18,633	95.2	98.8	31.8	33.6	6,194	6,595
El Centro City	31,384	64.7	97.1	14.5	43.4	6,357	9,898

Source: Hispanic Databook of U.S. Cities and Counties, Milpitas, 1994; derived from the Census of Population and Housing, 1990: Summary Tape Files 3B and 3C

the Immigration Commission (*Dillingham 1911*). In this report the Mexicans were identified as one of the problem immigrant groups. The institutionalizing of the "Problem image" was started.

The Chicano Movement was the strongest proponent for the idea of indigenous land and indigenous people. In trying to reassess the Treaty of Guadalupe Hidalgo (1848), which was the main Treaty to alineate the international boundary between Mexico and the United States, and in which the rights of the Mexican inhabitants were guaranteed, in 1987 a Chicano delegation spoke to the Geneva U.N.Commission on Human Rights, which was part of the International Indian Treaty Council:

"That same Treaty ... is continually being violated by injustices toward the Chicano indigenous people by the United States. These people have suffered since the military conquest of their indigenous land of AZTLAN. The Treaty right to maintain their language and culture have been denied to chicanos: their human rights and dignity have been subverted through racism, intended to undermine the cultural ethnicity of indigenous people" (*see Griswold de Castillo 1990*).

The notion that the Mexicans in the Southwest of the USA are rooted in space or the idea of an indigenous land is absolutely unacceptable for the mainstream idea of the USA being a nation of immigrants and characterized by an "absence of strong territorially based minorities (*Walzer 1994, 101*). "The United States is not most importantly a union of States but of nations, races, and regions, all of them dispersed and intermixed, without ground of their own", and "we might think of it as a contrast between territorially grounded ("tribal") and groundless ("multicultural") difference" (*Walzer 1992, 15*).

The United States ideology of nation-building and of the permanent confirmation of national unity - even under the headlines of multiculturalism - reflects a nation-state-centric world position with the rhetoric of a common language, common symbols of collective self descriptions and common myths (e.g. the frontier). The position of the Chicanos is by no means compatible with any of the mainstream arguments regarding multiculturalism. The strong Mestizo affiliation with their Indian heritage and the holistic enfranchisement of racial heritage and rights of indigenous land, imbued with the mythological idea of ATZLAN in the Southwest of the USA, where the Aztecs originated, has been totally marginalized (or worse: simply disregarded as a serious argument).

Taking into consideration the overall socio-economic status of the Mexicans in the United States and the territorially biased appeal of being Mexican by the Chicano Movement, one has to ask what kind of historical knowledge is available that might nurse some kind of distinctive sense of Mexican history in the United States? What kind of common and material culture can be found that appeals and transmits values for the social reproduction of being Mexican in the United States? It is understandable that I can cope with this question only on a very superficial and descriptive way. The method I use is a comparative analysis of two figures that describe some socio-spatial elements of the changing material conditions that represent economic and political power relations as well as the semiotic codes that are related to the term "Mexican".

To make some statements on the myths and realities of the Mexican experience in Arizona and Sonora the spatially presented facts will be analysed under the following headlines:

- the historical events and aspects of continuity,
- the continuity of socio-economic status and stereotypes,
- processes of deterritorialization,
- the development of a new make-up of the ethnic setting, and
- an increasing Mexicanization.

The theoretical framework into which the description is placed, is strongly bound to ideas of territoriality with the notion of security and accessibility. These terms were introduced by Jean GOTTMAN (1973), who also used categories such as continuity, extension and diversity of spatial patterns in his political geographical analysis. These aspects are often interchangeable and interdependent, and have ritual, symbolic, as well as functional, economic connotations, partly dependent on past experiences and memories.

Although the Social Geography of 1910/20 (*Fig. 3*) and 1990 (*Fig. 4*) is made up of different scopes of urbanization and population composition, the space-related processes, which shaped and are shaping this area, are very similar 1910/20 and 1990:

an interference of migration patterns that show interregional migration from different parts of Mexico, as well as from different parts in the United States. The direction of migration flows are similar, but especially as far as the U.S. is concerned the composition of the migrants has changed drastically. To analyse the multicultural settings in which the Mexicans lived and live today it is

Fig. 3: Socio-Spatial Elements of Historical and Economic Relevance for the Mexicans in Sonora and Arizona, 1910/20

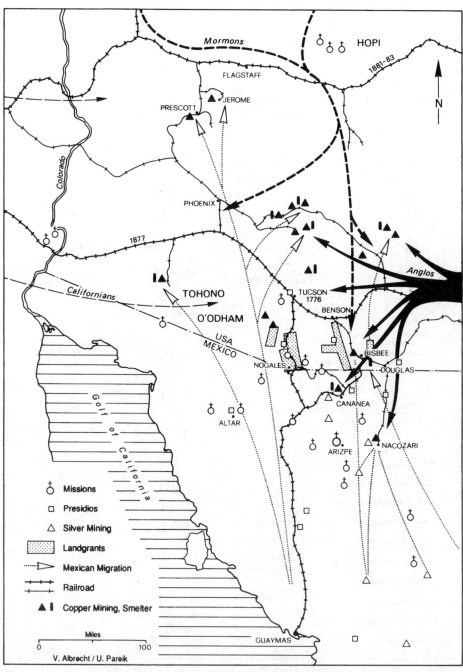

Source: based on Meinig 1971, 54 and 127; Walker and Bufkin (1986).

Fig. 4: Main Socio-Spatial Elements and Processes in Sonora and Arizona, 1990

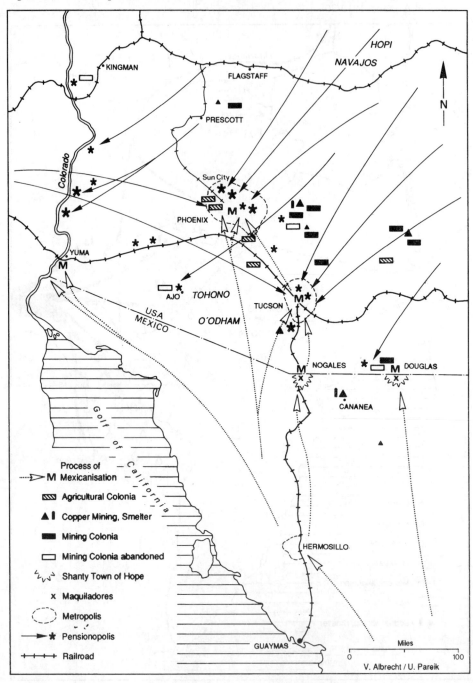

necessary to look at the spatial patterns and the locations in which the Mexicans lived and worked.

The social and spatial setting of 1910 (*see also Meinig 1971*) is crucial for the understanding of the evolution of the heterogeneous settings of the Mexicans. These were formed by the spatially organized settings of work, housing and education in a demographically and economically booming frontier society.

The opening up of the northern (1881-1883) and southern (1877) railways intensified the influx of people from the East, Texas and Chicago (The term Anglos in Fig. 3 covers these different Anglo immigrant groups from the East, Middle West, and Texas to the Southwest of the United States). The lure for gold and silver (Tombstone) drew a lot of people to a desert and semi-desert area, then sparsely populated. The many ghost towns in Arizona and elsewhere tell the story of this booming and unstable time. With the development of the copper industry since the end of the last century larger settlements evolved with clearly segregated living situations. The Mexicans were separated, they were living in barrios, their children went to segregated schools, and the salaries for Mexican workers for the same work were definitively lower than those of Anglo workers, although most of the mining experiences were derived from the long-standing silver mining experiences from Spanish and Mexican times. Bisbee, AZ developed as the Queen of the Copper towns with luxury housing and hotels that are a magnet for tourism today. Larger companies evolved (Phelps Dodge) which, besides Cananea and Bisbee, integrated other coppermining areas into their imperium. Parallel to the mining industry cattle barons accumulated large tracts of land for cattle-rearing in part by expropriating Spanish-Mexican land grants, not only to supply the growing mining communities, but mainly for export. Mining (copper) and cattle-rearing, as well as the later development of agro-business (cotton), laid the foundations of the economic development in northern Sonora and Arizona (with the exception of copper this also shaped California and Texas) and, as a result the living conditions of the Mexicans. They became associated with the image of an excellent stoop-laborer, who did not aspire landownership, and they also became bound to the image of being of "Indian descent" lawless and violent. The stereotyping of Mexicans as low-paid, uneducated, shiftless, improvident were in large part based on the social realities. This negative image that became fixed during the days of copper mining and the beginning of agro-business, had been shaped earlier primarily during the frontier period. These labels were so common that they had already passed into international literature. As early as 1877, RATZEL, the founder of Political Geography, wrote in an article on California "Es hat sich in diesem Kampf gezeigt, [der Kalifornier gegen die Spanisch-Mexikaner], daß die spanisch-amerikanische Kultur doch nichts als eine Halbkultur war.....", and referring to Mexicans he writes " für eine Familie betäubter, beschränkter, weltunkundiger Menschen..." (*1877, 10 f*). The restriction of the notion "Californians" to the Anglo side as well as the image of a demi-culture for the Spanish-American one and the concept of illiterate, dumb people for the Mexicans seems to have an irritating continuity if one looks at today's social realities of the Mexicans with the highest dropout rates in the U.S. and the lowest per capita income (with the exception of the Puerto Ricans).

Returning to the situation in 1910 as previously described, the colonia, lower-class situation describes a dominant situation of the Mexicans in Sonora and Arizona, yet it covers only a part of the social and historical realities which were formed over a longer time of Spanish and Mexican impact on the northern frontera. Silver mining, missions, presidios, land grants, and pueblos were the institutions that shaped the cultural landscape before 1848. Influential ranching and merchant families evolved and established strong territorial bonds to the territory. In Tucson these families developed strong traditions and did not fit into the overall image of uprooted and uneducated immigrants from central Mexico (*Sheridan 1986*). However, the cultural symbols that made up the historical landscape that might have functioned as identifying markers were funneled into the mainstream acquisition of the Anglo-market world at the end of last century.

As early as 1880, when Carleton E. WATSON photographed the missions in California, the relics, or in other words, the material culture of the past was aesthetized and valued for a growing tourist industry (*Weber 1994, 73 f*). The nature experience of the Southwest and the material culture of its past as symbols of a Catholic Spanish heritage were advertised to stimulate the tourist industry. A fantasy heritage was therefore created (*McWilliams 1968, 35-41*) with numerous institutions to keep this fantasy heritage alive. It seems to be that since that time the Anglo-Mexican relationship has "consisted of this amazing dichotomy between the Spanish and the Mexican Indian heritage" (*Mc Williams 1968, 40*). But, this dichotomy might be also true for the relationship between the traditional upper-class of Mexicans and the newly-arrived landless migrant workers.

The deterritorialization of land grants, the dispossession from land that came with migration, the aestheticization of cultural artifacts as an ideal Hispanic past and the spatial segregation of a socio-economic underclass in the mining towns, colonias and barrios were the settings that caused the schism for the Mexican reality at the beginning of this century. Nevertheless, the strongest constraints on Mexican identity and the effects of institutionalizing the racial minority perspective on Mexicans was the fight against the Spanish language. Schoolchildren were forbidden to speak Spanish in the schoolhouse or in the schoolyard. After the immigration law of 1924, and the quota regulation for immigrant groups, the growing labor market in the Southwest and West was in need of the cheap labor that came from Mexico. The growth of not only the copper industry but also of the agro-business sector increased the demand for Mexican laborers to Texas, Arizona and California. Under the ideological coverage of an exclusively defined multiculturalism, Spanish was forbidden in the workplace as well, and as an ultimate solution, repatriation was thought to be an appropiate response. The English-Only Movement (*Baron 1990*) is a post-World War II version of this fight. In 14 states amendments to state constitutions declare English as the only official language.

If we enter the analysis of *Fig. 4*, we see that some elements of 1910 remain. For instance, there are copper mines still in existence, but the decrease of smelters signalizes that copper is no longer the central focus of the economy, especially in Arizona. Nevertheless the continuity of copper colonias form part of the living situation. The best example is Pirtleville (close to Douglas - Cochise County), which has the highest concentration of Mexican population in Arizona (97%), yet it retains no relation to its former economic activities because the great smelter, in which copper from Bisbee as well as from Cananea was smelted, closed down in 1987. There are other instances, however, where the shut down of copper mines and smelters had caused a total territorial disruption and evacuation of the Mexican colonia. A fine example can be found in Ajo or in Tintown south of Bisbee, where still some remaining tinboxed huts hint of the life of a Mexican colonia that existed during the 1930s. From that time a number of agricultural colonias have evolved, especially in the Phoenix valley (El Mirage, Guadelupe) and around Safford where the Mexicans work on fields owned by Mormons. Often undocumented, they represent the lowest socio-economic strata of the Mexicans in Arizona. Compared with those, the Mexicans in the copper colonias with active copper production are better off, because the effects of unionization of the Mexicans working in copper mines provided them with higher income and access to better and high-skilled jobs.

Living in mining or agricultural colonias is only one aspect of the living situation of the Mexicans, and concerning their number in the area not the prevalent one. But the image that is bound to the term Mexican in the United States is very strongly related to migrant workers and colonias. Maybe this distorted image is also partly due to the Chicano Movement which emphasized the rural, exploited existence of Mexicans, as was very strongly expressed in the political activism of Cesar CHAVEZ, who placed the fight for equal rights of the farmworkers in California into the media of mainstream U.S. America. The "rural peasant" image still prevails, though most of the Mexicans live in urban or urbanized environments. The question is, how far this image also was promoted by academic writing (*Lewis 1959 and 1966*), and how far a small group of nation-wide acting Mexicans are unwillingly reinforcing the racially biased "rural peasant" image of being Mexican in the United States.

The description presented this far reveals a heterogeneous picture of past experiences which makes it difficult to refer to some kind of script that Mexicans can use in developing a collective identity, in as much the social conditions and the semiotic codes were centrally shaped - and generally negatively - by the American mainstream society and institutions. Two experiences seem to have a strong continuity: the unstable, nomadic, partly disruptive realities and the fixed, immobile living situations in barrios and colonias. The latter were often disentangled from their economic bases because of the closing down of the mining camps or companies.

The first spatial situation lacks security, as well as accessibility to the main infrastructures. The inner city barrio provides a closed superficial security without the necessary accessibility to the main institutions of society (high dropout rates).

The change of ethnic settings and regional and transboundary transformations

The Mexicans living in these traditional settings have to cope with new regional and transboundary transformations. They are characterized by new types of immigrants into the Southwest and the evolution of a multicentric transboundary network (*Rosenau 1993*).

Fig. 4 and *Tab. 4* demonstrate the setting and the ethnic break down of the population for selected mining towns in Arizona and highlights the different situations between mining towns which are still active and those which have undergone a phase of transition. There are mining towns with a balanced proportion of White and Hispanics in the population, even the age structure is balanced in this respect (Miami); others - like Clifton - have a high proportion of Hispanics (=Mexicans). Clifton and Miami seem to have developed sound Mexican communities in which all age structures are represented. Another trend is visible in Ajo and Surprise Town - a former agricultural colonia (*Tab. 5*).

The discrepancy of age structure in these two communities is obvious. In both Ajo and Surprise Town, the rate of Mexicans younger than 18 and the Anglos older than 65 is reversed and shows, at the microlevel, a dominant trend of spatial population development: the clash of elderly, looking for a decent place for retirement (the term Pensionopolis in Fig.4 refers to Retirement

Tab. 4: Population of Mining Towns in Arizona, 1980/90

	Total Persons		Hispanic in %		Age Structure 1990 in %			
					White	Hispanic	White	Hispanic
	1980	1990	1980	1990	<18	<18	>65	>65
Bagdad	2,331	1858	16.9	17.7	35.9	41.5	2.5	3.4
Morenci	2,736	1799	51.8	44.8	34.0	48.0	1.6	1.2
Claypool	2,365	1942	36.0	39.5	25.6	40.4	19.6	10.0
Miami	2,716	2018	56.4	59.1	27.9	32.0	17.0	16.3
Clifton	4,245	2840	60.3	61.4	31.0	35.4	8.7	13.7
Globe City	6,708	6062	28.1	33.1	22.1	31.3	21.4	14.3
Superior Town	4,600	3468	69.8	70.1	20.4	32.9	20.9	13.1
Bisbee	7,154	6288	32.3	36.5	18.2	34.7	25.8	12.7
Ajo	5,189	2919	44.7	43.0	11.1	30.7	38.2	17.8

Source: U.S. Census 1980, 1990

Tab. 5: The Structural Change of Surprise Town, AZ - an Agricultural Colonia, 1980 and 1990

	1980	1990
Total Persons	3,723	7,122
% Hispanic	71.2	55.0
White < 18	34.5%	12.5%
Hispanic < 18	46.6	44.0%
White > 65	9.7	36.8%
Hispanic > 65	2.2	3.9%

Source: U.S.Census 1980 and 1990

Communities) and young Mexican families with children under 18 striving to survive in the United States economy. This phenomenon is also exemplified at the meso-level, relating to the counties in California (*see Fig. 5 and Fig. 6*). Counties with a high degree of elderly and a low proportion of Hispanics can be distinguished from counties with a high degree of Hispanics and a high proportion of inhabitants younger than 18. The latter can be clearly related to the main areas of agro-business in the Imperial Valley, the San Joaquin Valley, and Los Angeles. Taking into consideration that property taxes are partly the source for school finances, one can imagine the potential conflict when the question arises about who is going to pay for the education of Mexican children who constitute, in some school districts, the majority of the students whereas the property owners expected to pay property taxes for schools are elderly white retired people (from a more general viewpoint *see Hayes-Bautisto 1988*).

But this is not the only new facet that has changed the multicultural environment for Mexicans in the Southwest and West. Since the 1970s the Asians have come, especially to California, and have caused a new ethnic environment for the Mexicans. The Asians not only immigrate into the big cities, but also into areas which traditionally were viewed as predominantly Mexican (San Joaquin Valley, *see Tab. 6*) and where the rate of Asians has increased very much beween 1980 and 1990. Some of the Asians, such as the Hmong, came from very peripheral regions in Southeast Asia. Their arrival has had an impact on all sectors of public and business life. As one representative example, the changing ethnic composition of the Merced City School District can be considered: between 1986 and 1992, the student ethnic count revealed a relative decrease of the White not of Hispanic Origin student population (from 3,584 = 40.3% to 3,553 = 31.1%) a relative equal situation for the Hispanic student body (2,757 = 31.1% to 3,843 = 33.7%) and an increase for the Asian student population (1,866 = 21,0% to 3,183 = 27.9%) (unpublished data from the *City School Office in Merced*). Asians and Mexicans are mixing and competing in the traditional Mexican-Anglo settings. Not all, but many Asians do achieve very fast social and educational standards that most Mexicans have not reached. An indicator is the proportionaly high rate of Asians in the University of California system. On average more than 30% of the student body is of Asian descent, compared with approximately 10% that are Latinos, though the latter constitutes 25 % of the total population in California.

The Process of Mexicanization

The growing numbers of immigrants from Mexico to the United States, as well as the development of different transboundary networks have caused an increased presence of Mexicans in the areas north of the international boundary that might be called a process of Mexicanization. The

Fig. 5: Population Under 18 and Older than 65 in the Counties of California, 1990

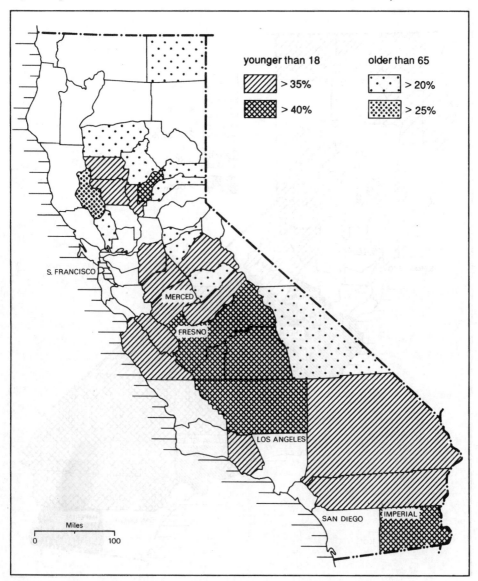

Source: U.S. Census 1990

immigrants generally head for urban areas, where the opportunities for work are the greatest. In the case of Arizona, they head to South Tucson south of 22nd Street - a politically independent part of Tucson -, and downtown Phoenix. Very often these are single mother families. In California, Los Angeles is without any doubt the key migration area. This Mexicanization process is due to interregional and international labor interdependence. But there is another transboundary process going on which is very obvious at the border, that also has far-reaching

Fig. 6: The Ratio of Hispanic Population in the Counties of California, 1990

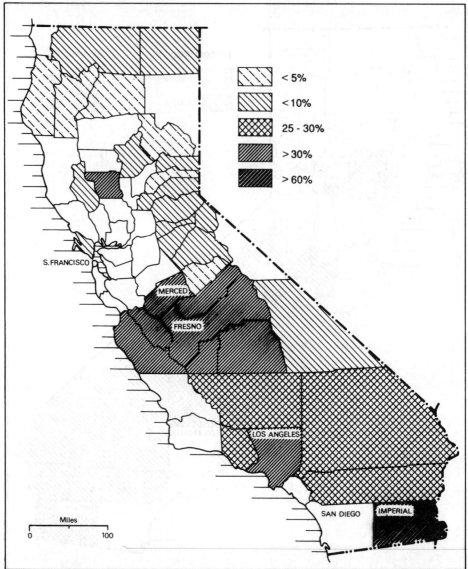

Source: U.S. Census 1990

effects. Douglas, a 14,000 inhabitants community in Cochise County, located in the Southeast corner of Arizona had, up to the early 1980s, one of the most segregated school system in Arizona. In 1976 out of 563 students in Douglas Junior High School 226 students were so-called English Only-students, and 290 spoke a language at home other than English, usually Spanish. Due to the border, in 1992, at the same school, out of 559 students, 539 were classified as Hispanic and 12 as White (School archive Douglas School District). Though the labelling of the students

Tab. 6: Percentage of Asians in Selected Cities in the Joaquin Valley, 1990

City	Population	Asians	% Asian	Increase % Asian 1980-90
Fresno	354,202	42,211	12	+591
Stockton	210,943	45,239	21	+225
Bakersfield	174,820	5,800	3	+176
Modesto	164,730	12,384	8	+431
Visalia	75,636	4,646	6	+592
Merced	56,216	8,001	14	+1,306
Lodi	51,874	2,327	4	+102

Source: U.S. Census 1990

is different for 1976 and 1992, the general tendency is obvious: Douglas Junior High School has become a Mexican school. This is partly due to the increase in the rate of Hispanics in Douglas from 75% in 1980 to 84% in 1990. But more and more children from the Mexican side attend American schools. This is especially true for the private Catholic school in Douglas to which middle-class parents from Agua Prieta send their children.

The transboundary linkages are not confined to the work, shopping or the use of the better infrastructure in the USA. The middle class of Agua Prieta organizes concerts and meetings for the Mexicans of Pirtleville, who seem to be locked into a legacy without hope and work since the smelter of Douglas has been closed down.

The transboundary networks and crossings shape and influence the social realities at the border areas and cause the evolution of a bi-national community at work, education and leisure time. In the San Diego/Tijuana metropolitan area, 5 to 6 million legal crossings are made monthly by approximately 521,000 individuals. The single most frequently-given reason for crossing the border is shopping (42%), as opposed to work (24%). The purpose for crossing the border to visit Mexico is primarily for social visits (40%), tourism (23%), shopping (9%) and work (4%) (all data taken from: Regents from the University of California, 1994).

There is another element that must be mentioned and has an impact on the Mexican experience: the growth of the maquiladora industry and an increasing number of employees (*Tab. 7*).

Since the beginning of the border industrialization program in 1965, the number of plants has risen from 12 (1965) to 2,089 (1994). 563,954 employees are working in the Maquiladora industry who spend a great deal of their income in the U.S. border cities.

Thus one can say that the U.S. Mexican border region clearly demonstrates the unique combination of two cultures that has evolved "demographically, economocally, linguistically, and culturally, the U.S. border is functionally an extension of Mexico, and in a similar fashion, the Mexican border zone is an extension of economic, social, and cultural influences from the United States" (*Martinez 1988, 145, also Martinez 1994*).

Summary and Conclusion:

In a world of globalization and regional as well as local differentiation there seems to be a special need for identification. The differentiations on the regional level have put new elements into the ethnic and socio-economic mosaic in the United States. Many older Anglo retired people live close to the increasing numbers of younger Mexicans. The latter have to cope with the immigration from different parts of Asia. The question that is bound to it is how identification

Tab. 7: The Evolution of the Maquiladora Industry

Year	Number of Plants	Total Employment	% Female Operatives
1965	12	3,000	-
1970	120	20,327	-
1975	454	67,213	78.3
1980	620	119,546	77.3
1985	760	211,968	69.0
1990	1,708	447,606	60.6
1994	2,089	563,954	-

Source: for 1965/1970 Weintraub, S., (1990), 159; for 1975 ff Carlos Salinas de Gortari (1994): Sexto Informe de Gobierno 1994., Anexo.; Mexico. D.F., 580; for female operatives: Skair, L. (1993), 167 and 241.

processes might work and what are the constituent elements for the Mexicans? Because of the heterogeneous settings and experiences in time and space it is difficult to define one unifying strata that might funnel the Mexicans in the United States into one culturally defined identity. It seems obvious that the regional differentiations and the complex socio-spatial behaviors of many Mexicans with its transboundary elements make the search for a unifying identity even more difficult. The competing ideologies for Americaness or Mexicaness are territorially orientated with a holistic approach. The slogans refer to 19th century nation-state-building ideologies. The most powerful will win. The extreme clash between the two forces driven by a similar territorial ideology is the border fence (*Fig.1*) and the murals in the Chicano-Park below the Coronado Bridge in San Diego (*Fig. 2*). These representations are contradictory to the reality of transboundary socio-spatial activities. In what ways the more national orientated ideologies will shape the fate of the increasing number of Mexicans or the transboundary realities with the possibility of equal access to the infrastructure of a democratic country will have an effect for all people living in the Americas.

Zusammenfassung

Die Auseinandersetzungen um die Interpretationen von Multikulturalismus und Pluralismus berühren zentrale Fragen des nationalen Selbstverständnisses der USA. Eine der Kernfragen ist, inwieweit kulturelle/ethnische/rassische Vielfalt und nationale Einheit sich gegenseitig ausschließen oder bedingen, und inwieweit die Gleichheitsidee primär an Individualrechte oder auf Gruppen bezogene Rechte gebunden ist.

Die Lebenssituationen der "Mexican Americans", die in Anlehnung an THERNSTROM (*1980*) Mexicans genannt werden, werden anhand folgender Fragen erörtert:

- was bedeutet Pluralismus aus der Perspektive der in den USA lebenden Mexikaner,
- welches sind die tradierten Konflikte zwischen den Anglo-Amerikanern und den Mexikanern in den USA,
- gibt es historisch und räumlich identifizierbare Elemente, die ein Zusammengehörigkeitsgefühl der Mexikaner in den USA bewirken könnten?

Einwanderung, Arbeitsmigrationen, Leben in Barrios und Colonias sowie die räumliche Nähe und Verbundenheit zu Mexiko werden als die wesentlichen Faktoren angesehen, die vergangene und gegenwärtige Lebenssituationen der Mexikaner in den USA bestimmen.

Die räumlich-sozialen Lebensrealitäten der Mexikaner in Sonora und Arizona der Jahre 1910/ 1920 und 1990 werden daraufhin überprüft, ob sie als eine Grundlage der sozialen Reproduktion einer mexikanischen Identität in den USA dienen können. Dies geschieht in Anlehnung an ein von GOTTMAN (*1973*) entwickeltes Konzept der Territorialität, das Aspekte der Sicherheit und Zugänglichkeit besonders betont.

Versuche, einheits- und identitätsstiftende Elemente für die Mexikaner in den USA zu definieren, sind mit großen Schwierigkeiten verbunden. Dies liegt unter anderem
an den räumlich vielfältigen Lebenssituationen, der Kontinuität eines niedrigen sozio-ökonomischen Status, den damit verbundenen negativen Stereotypen, und der Entwicklung neuer multikultureller Gegebenheiten durch Zuwanderung von Pensionären sowie durch Einwanderung von Asiaten.

References

Acuno, R. (1988³): Occupied America. A History of Chicanos. New York.
Albrecht, V. (1990): Nationale Einheit und kulturelle Vielfalt in den USA - aufgezeigt am Beispiel der Hispanics im Südwesten. In: Geographische Rundschau, 42, 488-496.
Arreola, D.D. (1993): The Mexican Border Cities. Anatomy and Place Personality. Tucson, The University of Arizona Press.
Baron, D. (1990): The English-Only Question. An Official Language for America? New Haven and London, Yale University Press.
Bogardus, E.S. (1928): Immigration and race attitudes. Boston, New York.
Bogardus, E.S. (1934): The Mexican in the United States. Los Angeles, University of Southern California Press.
Bayor, R.H. (1993): Historical Encounters: Intergroup Relations in a "Nation of Nations". In: The Annals of The American Acadamy, 530, 14-27.
Connor, W. (1985): Who are the Mexican-Americans? A Note on Comparability. In: Connor, W. ed.: Mexican-Americans in Comparative Perspective, Washington, D.C., 3-28.
Campa, A.L. (1979): Hispanic Culture in the Southwest. Norman, University of Oklahoma Press.
Dillingham, W.P. (1911): Reports of the Immigration Commission (41 volumes); especially volume 1 and 2: Abstracts of the Reports; Volume 5: Dictionary of Races and Peoples; Vol 23-25: Japanese and other Immigrant Races in the Pacific Coast and Rocky Mountain States. Washington, D.C.
Conzen, K.N. et al. (1990): The Invention of Ethnicity: A Perspective from the USA. In: Altreitalia, Aprile 1990, 37-62.
Dinnerstein, L. and Reimers, D.M. (1988³): Ethnic Americans. A History of Immigration, 107-133.
Elschenbroich, D. (1986): Eine Nation von Einwanderern. Ethnisches Bewußtsein und Integrationspolitik in den USA. Frankfurt.
Epstein, N. (1977): Language, Ethnicity, and the Schools. Policy Alternatives for Bilingual - Bicultural Education. Washington, D.C., The George Washington University Press.
Escalante, V. (1983): Migrant Pickers. Latinos in the Fields of Hardship. In: Los Angeles Times, August 10th.
Fad, L.R., Griffin, E. (1982): Chicano Park. Personalizing an Institutional Landscape. In: Landscape, 42-48.
Gamio, M. (1971): The life story of the Mexican immigrant; autobiographic documents. New York.
Garcia, J.R. (1977): Operation Wetback: 1954. PhD., (History), University of Notre Dame.
Garcia, M.T. (1981): Desert Immigrants. The Mexicans of El Paso,1880-1920.
Garreau, J. (1982): The Nine Nations of North America. NewYork, 207-244.
Gottman, J. (1973): The Significance of Territory. Charlottesville.
Grebler, L. et al. (1970): The Mexican American People: The Nation's Second Largest Minority. New York.
Griswold del Castillo, R. (1990): The Treaty of Guadalupe Hidalgo: A Legacy of Conflict. Norman, University of Oklahoma Press.
Hayes-Bautista, D.E. et al. (1988): The Burden of Support Young Latinos in an Ageing Society. Stanford, Stanford University Press.

Herzog, L.A. (1990): Where North meets South. Cities, Space, and Politics on the U.S.-Mexico Border. Center for Mexican American Studies. Austin, University of Texas Press.
Hispanic Databook of U.S. Cities and Counties (1994): Compiled by the Research Staff of Toucan Valley Publications, Milpitas, CA.
Hoffman, A. (1979[3]): Unwanted Mexican Americans in the Great Depression. Repatriation Pressures 1929-1939. Tucson, The University of Arizona Press.
Instituto Nacional de Estatistica Geografica e Informatica, INEGI (1982): X Censo General de Poblacion y Vivienda, 1980, Baja California, Chihuahua, Sonora. Mexico D.F.
Instituto Nacional de Estatistica Geografica e Informatica, INEGI (1991): XI Censo General de Poblacion y Vivienda, 1990, Baja California, Chihuahua, Sonora. Mexico D.F.
Kallen, H. (1915): Democracy Versus the Melting Pot. In: Nation, 18 Feb. 190-194; ibid., 25 Feb. 217-220.
Lewis, O. (1959): Five Families. Mexican Case Studies in the Culture of Poverty. New York.
Lewis, O. (1966): La Vida. A Puerto Rican family in the culture of poverty. San Juan and New York.
Martinez, O.J. (1994): Border People. Life and Society in the U.S.-Mexico Borderlands. Tucson, The University of Arizona Press.
Martinez, R. (1992): The Other Side. Notes from The New L.A., Mexico City, and Beyond. NewYork.
McWilliams, C. (1968): North from Mexico. The Spanish-Speaking People of the United States. New York.
Meinig, D.W. (1971): Southwest. Three Peoples in Geographical Change, 1600-1970. New York & London, Oxford University Press.
Myrdal, G. (1944): An American Dilemma; the Negro Problem and Modern Democracy. New York, London.
Nostrand, R.L. (1970): The Hispanic-American Borderland: Delimitation of American Culture Region. In: Annals of the Association of American Geographers, 60, 638-661.
Nostrand, R.L. (1973): "Mexican American" and "Chicano": Emerging Terms for a People Coming of Age. In: Pacific Historical Review, 42/3, 389-406.
Parsons, T. (1975): Some Theoretical Considerations on the Nature and Trends of Change of Ethnicity. In: Glazer, N., and Moynihan, D.P. (Eds.): Ethnicty. Theory and Experience. Cambridge, MA and London, Harvard University Press.
Pike, F.B. (1992): The United States and Latin America. Myths and Stereotypes of Civilization and Nature. Austin, University of Texas Press.
Ratzel, F. (1906): Über Kalifornien. In: Ratzel, F., Kleine Schriften, Bd. 2, ausgewählt von H. Helmholt. München, Berlin, 1-18.
Ravitch, D. (1976): Integration, Segregation, Pluralism. In: The American Scholar, 206-217.
Regents of the University of California (1994): Who Crosses the Border: A View of the San Diego/Tijuana Metropolitan Region. A Report of San Diego Dialogue. La Jolla, CA.
Rilke, R.M. (1980[2]): Duineser Elegien. Die Erste Elegie. In: Rainer Maria Rilke Werke, Bd. I, 2, Frankfurt am Main, Insel-Verlag.
Rios-Bustamante, A. (1985): Los Angeles, Pueblo and Region, 1781-1850: Continuity and Adaptation on the North Mexican Periphery. PhD. (History), UCLA.
Rose, P.I. (1993): "Of Every Hue and Caste": Race, Immigration, and Perceptions of Pluralism. In: The Annals of The American Acadamy, 530, 187-202.
Rosenau, J.N. (1993): Coherent Connection or Commonplace Contiguity? Theorizing about the California-Mexico Overlap. In: Lowenthal, A.F. and Burgess (Eds.): The California-Mexico Connection. Stanford, Stanford University Press.
Ruiz, L.V. (1987): Cannery Women, Cannery Lives, Mexican Women, Unionization and the Californian Food Processing Industry, 1930-1950. Albuquerque, University of New Mexico Press.
Salinas, C. (1994): Sexto Informe de Gobierno, Anexo. Mexico D.F.
Schlesinger, Jr. A.M. (1993): The Disuniting of America. Reflections on a Multicultural Society. New York, London.
Sheridan, Th.E. (1986): Los Tucsonenses. The Mexican Community in Tucson 1854-1941. Tucson, The University of Arizona Press.
Shorris, E. (1992): Latinos. A Biography of the People. New York and London.
Seller, M. (1977): America. A History of Ethnic Life in the United States.
Sklair, L. (1993): Assembling for Development. The Maquila Industry in Mexico and the United States. Center for U.S.-Mexican Studies. San Diego, UCSD.

Smith, M.P. (1992): Postmodernism, urban ethnography, and the new social space of ethnic identity. In: Theory and Society, 493-531.
Somora, J., ed. (1966): La Raza: Forgotten Americans. Notre Dame, University of Notre Dame Press.
Taylor, Ch. (1994): The Politics of Recognition. In: Taylor, Ch., (ed.): Multiculturalism. Princeton, Princeton University Press, 25-73.
Thernstrom, St., ed. (1980): Harvard Encyclopedia of American Ethnic Groups. Cambridge, MA, Harvard University Press.
Tomas Rivera Center (1986): The Changing Profile of Mexican America. A Sourcebook for Policy Making. Claremont, CA.
Trueba, H.T., et al., eds. (1993): Healing Multicultural America: Mexican Immigrants Rise to Power in Rural California. Washington, D.C.
U.S. Dept. of Commerce, Bureau of the Census (1975): Historical Statistics of the United States, Colonial Times to 1970. Washington, D.C.
U.S. Dept. of Commerce, Bureau of the Census (1982):1980 General Population Characteristics. Arizona and California. Washington, D.C.
U.S. Dept. of Commerce. Bureau of the Census (1982): Census of Population and Housing. Summary Social, Economic, and Housing Characteristics Arizona, California. Washington, D.C.
U.S. Dept. of Commerce. Bureau of the Census (1992): 1990 Census of Population. General Population Characteristics. Arizona, California. Washington, D.C.
U.S. Dept. of Commerce. Bureau of the Census (1992): 1990 Census of Population and Housing. Summary Social, Economic, and Housing Characteristics, Arizona, California. Washington, D.C.
Villareal, J.A. (1970) : Pocho. Garden City, New York.
Walker,H.P. and Bufkin,D. (1986^2): Historical Atlas of Arizona. Norman, University of Oklahoma Press.
Walzer,M. (1992): What it means to be an American. New York.
Walzer,M. (1994): Comment. In: Taylor, Ch., ed.: Multiculturalism. Princeton, Princeton University Press, 99-103.
Weber, D. (1973): Foreigners in their Native Land. Albuquerque, The University of New Mexico Press.
Weber, D. (1994): The Spanish-Mexican Rim. In: Millner, C.A. et al., (eds): The Oxford History of the American West. New York, Oxford University Press, 45-77.
Weintraub, S. (1990): A Marriage of Convenience. Relations between Mexico and the United States. New York, Oxford.

Acknowledgement

I thank Gabriela Lemus, visiting researcher at the U.S. Mexican Center at UCSD 1994/95, Dr. Antonio Rios-Bustamante, Assoc. Prof. at the Mexican American Studies and Research Center at the University of Arizona in Tucson for their critical reading and recommendations of the paper.

Address of the Author

Volker Albrecht
Institut für Didaktik der Geographie
Universität Frankfurt
Schumannstr.58
60054 Frankfurt a. M
GERMANY

HANS DIETER LAUX and GÜNTER THIEME

Model Minority or Scapegoat? The Experience of Korean Immigrants in Los Angeles

Introduction

The riots which occurred in Los Angeles between March 29 and May 1, 1992 can be considered as the severest case of civil unrest in recent American history. After the not-guilty verdict for four white policemen who were accused of brutally beating the black motorist Rodney KING a spontaneous outbreak of violence swept through Los Angeles. Large parts of the city went up in flames. Although the riots were concentrated in the inner-city neighborhoods of Los Angeles city, which are economically depressed and mostly inhabited by ethnic and racial minorities, looting and violence spread over a large territory ranging from the San Fernando Valley in the north to Long Beach City in the south. According to ONG et al. *(1993, 354)* the upheaval left in its wake 43 deaths, 2,383 injured persons, over 16,000 arrests, and estimated property damages and losses of about $ 1 billion.

Undoubtedly, this rebellion of 1992 shared similar features with the notorious Watts riots of 1965. But in contrast to this event and similar urban disturbances of the 1960s, the recent upheaval in Los Angeles had a distinct multi-ethnic character because both the rioters and their victims included whites, blacks, Latinos and Asians (see *Oliver et al. 1993, 118; Chang 1994, 104f.*). Thus, for example, the majority of the arrested persons were of Hispanic origin. It has widely been reported in the American and the international media that the Asian Americans in general and the Koreans in particular were the ethnic group most severely hit and affected by the riots. According to various sources (*Koch and Schockman 1993, 9; Ong and Hee 1993; Ong et al. 1993*) more than 2,000 Korean-owned businesses were burned, damaged or looted, creating an estimated loss of about $ 400 million, nearly 40% of the total property losses attributable to the riots.

As Elaine KIM argues, the psychic and material violence Korean Americans suffered during the Los Angeles riots can be considered as a "'wake-up call' about what the 'American dream' means in the 1990s", questioning the belief "that we could survive and flourish by working hard, minding our own business, and putting our faith in institutions like the police and politicians who are charged with protecting and representing us" (*Kim 1994, 73*). From these points of view the *sa-i-ku p'ok-dong*, as the 1992 riots are called by the Koreans, can be considered as a turning point in the history of the Korean minority in the United States similar to the internment of Japanese Americans during World War II (see *Chang 1994, 113*).

The purpose of the following essay is to give an overview on the history, the living conditions and the socio-economic situation of the Koreans in Los Angeles and to discuss the impact of the 1992 riots on how this minority defines its identity and place within the American society. Within this context two closely related questions have to be adressed: (1) Why did the Koreans become the most prominent targets of collective violence, and (2) how did the Koreans perceive, explain and overcome this unexpected and traumatic experience of victimization? Methodically the paper is characterized by a multi-level approach, combining and confronting the data of the latest population census (1990) and the results of various macroanalytical analyses with the individual experiences, views and judgements extracted from detailed qualitative interviews with selected members of the Korean community in Los Angeles in August 1993.

Susan Han - A Korean Immigrant

We will start with the biography of Susan HAN, a young Korean woman living in Los Angeles (here as in the following cases the name of the interviewed person was changed):
Susan HAN was born in Seoul, the capital of South Korea, in 1964 as the third of five children. Her parents came from North Korea where the families belonged to the wealthy upper class of civil servants. After the communists came to power the family had to flee to the south of the country and lost all their fortune. Because of the bad living conditions at home Susan HAN's parents decided to emigrate to the USA.
In 1970 the family went to Los Angeles. After a short stay with Korean friends the family moved to Oxnard, about 120 km away from Los Angeles. They bought two sewing-machines and started producing babies' and children's clothes at home. All the family used to work until late at night, sometimes 24 hours at a time because there were deadlines to meet. Even the children regularly helped after school. After a few months the family was able to buy a house and to enlarge the business.
In order to secure their children a good education at both school and college and to prevent them from having to stay in a university dormitory the parents moved to Los Angeles in 1983 where they acquired a small garment factory. For a long time the parents had intended to return to Korea eventually. In the end, however, they decided to stay in the USA and to become American citizens together with their children.
In 1988 Susan HAN graduated in business administration. She is now working as a corporate consultant in downtown Los Angeles. At the age of 29 she is still single. She lives in her own house in a Long Beach suburb mostly inhabited by whites and drives a BMW. Just like her, all her brothers and sisters have graduated from prestigious colleges and are working in managerial or professional occupations. She continues to be in close contact with her parents. During the visits to her parents' house she speaks Korean, but increasingly experiences her mother tongue as some kind of foreign language. She talks English to her brothers and sisters as well as to the Korean friends of her age. The majority of her closest friends are white (*Interview with the authors, 24 August 1993*).
Several questions can be derived from Susan HAN's biography: (1) Does this story lend itself to generalization? (2) How can the alleged success of Asian Americans in general and the Koreans in particular be empirically measured? Which are the main dimensions of this success in American society? (3) To what degree is the popular image of the Koreans as a part of an Asian American *model minority* valid? How is this widespread labeling perceived and criticized by the members of the Korean community? Before these questions are discussed in more detail, some basic information about Korean immigration to the United States shall be given.

Korean Americans in Los Angeles - A Growing Minority

The Koreans are among the fastest growing ethnic groups in the United States. Except for a handful of laborers and students who came to the United States in the late 19th century there was no significant Korean immigration to the U.S. mainland prior to the 1950s. Emigration from Korea only slightly increased after the Korean War (1950 - 53), when some 8,000 refugees, war brides and orphans were admitted between 1952 and 1960 (*see Kim 1980, 601*). Largely due to the liberalization of the immigration policy in 1965 (Immigration and Nationality Act), Koreans, like many of their Asian neighbors, began to migrate to America in strongly growing numbers. Korean immigration increased from an average of less than 3,500 per year in the 1960s to about 26,000 in the 70s, and to more than 33,000 per year between 1981 and 1990. In 1987 the Korean immigration reached its peak value with 35,397 persons admitted. Since this year, however, the number of immigrants has strongly declined to less than 19,000 in 1992, thus falling to the level of 1972 (*see Cheng and Espiritu 1989, 522f.; U.S. Immigration and Naturalization Service 1993, 27f.*).

Due to both immigration and an additional natural increase the total number of Koreans living in the United States rose from 69,150 in 1970 to 357,393 in 1980 and 798,849 in 1990 (*Gardner et al. 1989, 8; We the American Asians 1993, 8*). The majority of them have settled in large metropolitan areas such as New York, Washington, Philadelphia or Chicago, but especially in California where they are highly concentrated in the Los Angeles urban area. Thus, the 181,350 Koreans living in the counties of Los Angeles and Orange in 1990 comprise 22.7% of the total Korean population in the United States.

Within the Los Angeles area the Koreans show a very distinct residential pattern. The highest concentration can be found in the inner-city area of Koreatown located some kilometers west of downtown Los Angeles. During the last twenty years this area developed into the most important concentration of Korean businesses in the USA, serving as a focus of communication and ethnic identification as well as the center of economic activities for the Korean community in Southern California (*see Laux and Thieme 1992*). In contrast to this dominant social and economic function, however, large parts of Koreatown are residentially mixed areas with a growing population majority of Hispanic origin (*see Thieme and Laux in this volume*).

Outside Koreatown an increasing number of Koreans have settled in more suburban and wealthy areas of metropolitan Los Angeles mostly dominated by a white majority. Some parts of the San Fernando Valley, the Palos Verdes Peninsula or places like Glendale, Torrance and Cerritos within Los Angeles County (*see Fig. 2, Thieme and Laux in this volume*) as well as the city of Garden Grove in Orange County, which is developing into a new concentration of Korean businesses, can serve as examples for the trend towards suburbanization of the Korean minority.

Korean Americans as a Model Minority - Myth or Reality?

There are several aspects in the biography of Susan HAN that are considered as typical of the life stories of a large number of recent immigrants from Korea and other Asian countries. Among those elements are the high educational motivation and achievement, the devotion to the family, the readiness to integrate into the mainstream of society and to become an American citizen as soon as possible, the willingness to work hard - in numerous cases close to self-exploitation -, a high occupational status and a personal income significantly above average. All these characteristics of individual success stories, together with the collective posture of self-effacing accomodation, gave support to the image of Asian Americans as a *model minority*, which evolved in the American public since the mid-1960s.

How can we define and measure "success" or "model", terms that are often used interchangeably to characterize the social and economic achievement of Asian Americans? We will try to gather relevant information on major dimensions of these concepts mainly from the 1990 census results for Los Angeles County.

Family and Household Structures

Among the reasons for the socio-economic success of Asian immigrants the strong family ties are often emphasized. These family ties are considered to be rooted in the cultural traditions of Confucianism still dominating the value system of East and Southeast Asian populations to a great extent. Therefore it seems useful to have a closer look at the recent differentiation of household types by racial and ethnic groups (*see Fig 1*). If we concentrate on the Asians in general and the Koreans in particular we first see that there is a very high proportion of married couple families, many of them with children under 18, which is a sign of a comparatively young immigrant population. In contrast, the percentage of non-family households (singles, unrelated

Fig. 1: Los Angeles County - Household Types, 1990

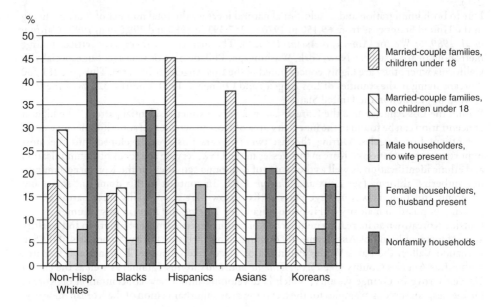

Source: Census of Population and Housing, 1990

persons etc.), which can also be considered typical of an immigrant situation, is still very low as compared to whites and African Americans. Another major aspect of the diagram is the number of shattered families, especially the proportion of female-headed households with no husband present, which is probably one of the main causes for many of the severe problems of the black population. This variable has a very low value among Asian Americans even though recent immigrants do not always come with all family members at a time. It must be emphasized that all these household and family characteristics are even more clearly recognizable among the Koreans than among the Asians in total.

Educational Attainment

Family cohesion undoubtedly is a primary source of the amazingly high educational achievement, which is commonly considered as the most obvious feature of Asian American success stories. During the last two decades numerous reports and studies have given evidence of the various aspects of extraordinary educational attainment such as enrolment in institutions of higher education, number of years of completed schooling, classroom behavior, and test scores (*see* Hirschman and Wong 1986; Hsia and Hirano-Nakanishi 1989). Indeed Asian Americans have frequently exceeded whites in educational attainment, above all in fields such as engineering, computer science and natural sciences (*see Nee and Sanders 1985, 82*). Obviously, these facts and trends have led to widespread feelings of admiration but also of fear and resentment of Asians among the general public.

Considering the situation in Los Angeles in 1990 (*see Fig. 2*) it becomes evident that the Asian population group in general has the highest percentage of college graduates among persons aged 25 years and over (37%). This is all the more obvious compared to Hispanics and blacks, but also

Fig. 2: Los Angeles County - Educational Attainment, 1990 (Persons 25 years and over)

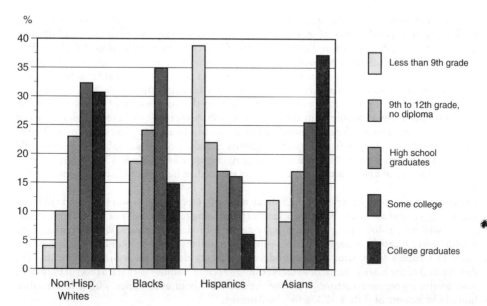

Source: Census of Population and Housing, 1990

to non-Hispanic whites. It must be noticed, however, that there is at the same time an above average number of Asians with a very low educational attainment (less than 9th grade), indicating a significant variability among and within the various Asian nationalities. No such detailed figures are available for the Koreans, except the percentage of college graduates, which is 34%. The deep respect for education among Asian Americans becomes even more apparent when the school enrolment of the younger generation is considered. Thus, in 1990 59% of the Asian population of Los Angeles aged 18 to 24 years were enrolled in college, compared to only 43% for whites, 30% for blacks, and 20% for Hispanics. Among the Asians the Koreans had a percentage of 62%, which was only surpassed by the Chinese and Japanese with 66%.

There is an intensive scientific discussion on the origins and causes of the high educational attainment among Asian Americans (*see Hirschman and Wong 1986, 3f.*). Regardless of whether this success is primarily explained by the cultural heritage of the immigrants, their social structure or the specific socio-economic situation of immigrants as *middleman minorities*, there is general agreement that education is perceived to be the primary means of social mobility and success in a competitive environment. Consequently, parents invest heavily in their children's education even at a disproportionate sacrifice to family returns. This corresponds with the judgement of Bong Hwan KIM, a prominent Korean community leader in Los Angeles:

"Immigrant Korean parents" KIM states "often view themselves as sacrificial lambs, believing that even though they go to their graves deaf, dumb, and blind, they are doing it so that their children can achieve the so-called American dream. Their kids work incredibly hard, knowing that only they can vindicate their parents for their sacrifice" (*Kim 1994, 90f.*).

Income and Occupation

Facing these experiences, the question arises whether and to what extent the educational attainment and qualification of Asian minority groups correspond with the level of their economic returns. Numerous studies (*see Kim and Hurh 1983; Nee and Sanders 1985; East-West Center 1990*) have shown that the majority of Asian ethnic groups in the USA have reached parity with whites and have surpassed the national average since the 1980 census as far as the mean or median household income is concerned. These findings are supported by the Los Angeles case as well (*see Fig. 3*). There is a very close resemblance of the distribution of household income groups between non-Hispanic whites and Asians in 1989. About 40% of these households earned $ 50,000 or more whereas the corresponding figures for blacks and Hispanics were only close to 20%. These figures are confirmed by the aggregate indicator of the annual median household income. The figures for non-Hispanic whites and Asians were $ 41,222 and $ 39,296 respectively, while the income of blacks was only $ 25,827 and the median income of Hispanics amounted to $ 27,361.

Looking at the income situation of the Korean minority (*see Fig. 3*), however, the data indicate that the aggregate values for all the Asians are far from being representative of the different ethnic groups which are subsumed under the broad category of Asian Americans. Within that category wealthy and educated groups like Japanese and Asian Indians are to be found as well as virtually illiterate refugees from Laos or Cambodia who largely depend on welfare payments. The distribution of the Korean household income in 1989 is more similar to the situation of the blacks than to the aggregate structure of all the Asians. This is in accordance with a low median household income of only $ 30,436 for the Koreans.

Irrespective of these facts, particularly Asian American scholars have argued that income figures should be interpreted with great caution. They emphasize that high incomes may be the result

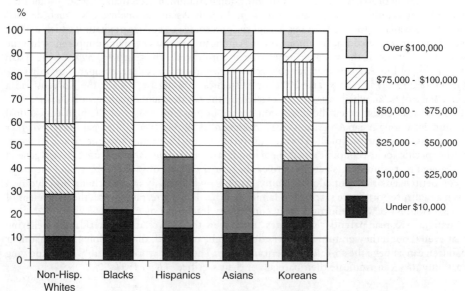

Fig. 3: Los Angeles County - Household Income, 1989

Source: Census of Population and Housing, 1990

of longer work hours or sacrificed weekends as well as of a larger number of workers per household or family. Above all, the numerous self-employed Asian Americans make use of the unpaid labor of wives, sometimes of children and other relatives, as became apparent in Susan HAN's biography (*see also Kim and Hurh 1983, 8; Bonacich 1987, 454*). From this point of view the per capita income could be a better indicator of economic success. If this variable is used the Asian Americans in general and the Koreans in particular are in an even less favorable situation with per capita incomes of only $ 14,690 and $ 13,003 resp. compared to $ 25,372 of the non-Hispanic whites. These data indicate a rather precarious economic situation of a considerable number of Korean households: in 1989 13.7% of all Korean families in Los Angeles had an income level below poverty.

Moreover, it is argued that minority groups can be considered successful "only if they have paid a price equal to that of whites for the same [income], social status and privileges" (*Kim and Hurh 1983, 7*). Following these arguments Asian Americans still experience a serious disadvantage in transforming their high educational achievement into income and occupation. Since the educational background of Asian Americans is generally higher than that of whites even parity of earnings would be an indicator of economic discrimination.

Occupational status is closely connected with income. According to the 1990 census 31.6% of all Asians in Los Angeles County were in the highest job classification, i.e. managerial and professional speciality occupations, compared to 39.3% of the non-Hispanic whites and 24.5% of the African Americans. Again there was a remarkable variability among the different Asian groups with Asian Indians in the top position (43.4%) followed by the Japanese (38.7%), the Chinese (35.7%) and the Koreans with a rather moderate share of 27.6%. These data indicate that the Koreans are far from having achieved an occupational status adequate to their level of education.

Self-Employment

Considerable attention has been given to one specific aspect of occupation among the Koreans, i.e. self-employment. Particularly the Korean community in Los Angeles has emerged as an ethnic community engaged in small businesses. According to the census figures 23.3% of the employed Koreans aged 16 years and over are self-employed and run a business of their own, a percentage much higher than the comparative figures for all other racial and ethnic groups in Los Angeles (*see Razin 1988*). The majority of the Korean – owned businesses is to be found in retail trade, where 30.6% of all employed persons are concentrated.

There is an extensive and controversial discussion on the origins and reasons for this propensity to self-employment among Koreans which cannot be presented here in detail (*see Min 1984; Bonacich 1987; Winnick 1990, 26f.; Lee 1992; Koch and Schockman 1993, 15f.*). Suffice it to say that there are two broad sets of explanations, one of them emphasizing the disadvantaged position and limited opportunities of the recent and well educated immigrant group facing the barriers of the U.S. labor market, and the other stressing the cultural basis of entrepreneurship and the ability to mobilize specific ethnic resources.

The first set of hypotheses refers to the theory of the *split labor market* (*Bonacich 1972*) or segmented labor market. According to this theory a primary segment with large companies and highly-qualified, well-paid and comparatively secure jobs is contrasted with the secondary segment of the labor market. The latter is characterized by fiercely competing labor-intensive firms with low wages and bad working-conditions, the notorious *sweatshops*, as well as by more or less informal and insecure jobs mainly in the service sector. As newly arriving immigrants have great difficulties finding access to the occupations in the primary segment of the labor market, which are adequate to their previous investment in human capital, they can only avoid the little attractive secondary segment by turning to small business. From this point of view self-employment can be interpreted as an avenue to economic and social mobility for a minority disadvantaged in the regular job market: "Korean immigrants seem to enter business not because they have advantages in it but because they have disadvantages in non-business occupations" (*Min 1984, 339*).

This theory, however, cannot fully explain the differential inclination of immigrant or minority groups to establish businesses. So the second set of arguments emphasizes the cultural heritage, value systems, ambitions, motivations, and the creation of specific institutional structures. For the Koreans in Los Angeles it is argued that they were able to mobilize specific ethnic resources, such as social solidarity, nepotistic hiring, formal and informal support networks to establish themselves in the business sector (*see Light 1984, 204; Winnick 1990, 26*).

There are two different types of Korean businesses according to their location and the customers served. The first category is mainly located in Koreatown which has developed into a business district characterized by a wide range of Korean-owned enterprises predominantly serving members of the Korean community (*see Laux and Thieme 1992; Lee 1992*). These areas of concentrated immigrant entrepreneurship are generally described as *ethnic enclaves* (*see Portes and Rumbaut 1990, 21*). The second type of Korean-owned businesses is located in predominantly black and Hispanic neighborhoods, virtually free of Korean residential population. South Central Los Angeles is a typical example of this locational behavior which can be explained by the theory of *middleman minorities* (*Bonacich 1973*).

According to this theory a minority, in our case the Koreans, takes over business functions and acts as some sort of mediator or middleman between the majority group of population and other less privileged minorities. It is evident that businesses of this type, such as gas stations, groceries, liquor shops and small markets, can only be founded in less attractive, poor and crime-ridden neighborhoods where there is little serious competition from native-born white American merchants or large companies. Moreover, it must be emphasized that such a middleman minority is frequently exposed to latent and open conflicts with the residents of the respective neighborhood.

To sum up, it can be concluded that the widespread ethnic entrepreneurship among the Korean community is an ambiguous thing. On the one hand it can serve as a vehicle of social and economic advancement, on the other hand self-employment entails severe risks and problems for the respective population. According to MIN (*1990*) those problems for Korean immigrant entrepreneurs are (1) long hours of work detrimental to their physical and psychological well-being, (2) exposure to physical danger in low-income and crime-ridden areas, (3) rejection and hostility by minority clients, (4) economic exploitation by suppliers and landlords, (5) status inconsistency, and (6) a slowing of assimilation. Some additional comments must be made to the last two points.

Concerning the pace of assimilation it has been argued that the concentration of an immigrant minority in small ethnic businesses, while enhancing ethnic attachment and solidarity, has a rather negative influence on its assimilation and integration into the host society. Taking the frequency of speaking English at home as an indicator of cultural assimilation, there is some evidence that both self-employed Koreans and those employed in Korean firms are less assimilated than Korean workers who are employed in American enterprises (*see Min 1990, 449*). In this context it has to be noted that according to the census data 53,0% of the Korean households in Los Angeles County are classified as "linguistically isolated households", a figure which is significantly above the percentages for the Asian Indians (10,7%), Japanese (21,9%), Chinese (41,0%), and even the Vietnamese minority (50,7%).

Another major problem Korean immigrant entrepreneurs are facing is *status inconsistency*. This sociological concept refers to the situation that any two of the three major status dimensions - education, occupation and income - are unbalanced. Taking into consideration the comparatively high level of both education and pre-immigrant occupation many Korean immigrants face three kinds of status inconsistency: one between education and income, another between education and the post-immigration occupation and the third between pre-immigrant and post-immigrant occupations (*Min 1990, 444*). From this point of view self-employment in a small business must be considered as a sign of downward social mobility and as a source of frustration and dissatisfaction. This seems especially true for the Korean community where traditionally the businessman has a very low rank in society compared with the scholar, the farmer and the state officer or engineer. The results of several surveys show that the experience of status inconsistency is at least typical of the first generation of Korean immigrants who graduated from a Korean college, whereas the American-college graduates of the 1.5 or second generation are increasingly successful as professionals or semi-professionals in the primary sector of the labor market (*see Kim and Hurh 1983, 9f.; Min 1990; Koch and Schockman 1993, 38f*).

Asian Americans - From Pariahs to Paragons?

At this point a closer examination of the popular image of Asian Americans as *model minorities* and its implications must be given. In the 19th and 20th centuries immigrants from Asia were discriminated and rejected as virtually no other immigrant group. The notorious "Chinese Exclusion Act" of 1882, the most ungentlemanly "Gentlemen's Agreement" of 1907/08 or the "Immigration Act" of 1917 with its establishment of an Asiatic Barred Zone can serve as evidence of the general agreement that "America was not to be a haven for the yellow race" (*Winnick 1990, 23*). Since the end of World War II, however, the negative perception of Asian Americans progressively changed via a benign tolerance and acceptance to an increasing admiration (*see Hata and Hata 1990, 80f.*). Originally coined by the social demographer William PETERSEN in order to characterize the societal advancement of two formerly marginalized populations, i.e. the American Asians and the Jews (*see Winnick 1990, 23*), the label "model minority" has been increasingly promoted since the mid-1960s by both the mass media and scholarly works.
There has been a lot of criticism and opposition against the model minority thesis, predominantly from scholars of Asian ancestry (*see Kim and Hurh 1983; Hata and Hata 1990; Winnick 1990; Worsnop 1991; Cho 1993*). The most striking argument is that the model minority stereotype is an incorrect oversimplification which does not take into consideration the large variety of Asian minorities in the USA as well as the socio-economic differences within the various ethnic groups. This means that "those Asians who don't conform to the model minority stereotype are invisible in mainstream society" (*Kim 1994, 91*). Moreover, it has been argued that the model minority thesis has been constructed to impress and discipline economically less successful and politically rebellious minorities (*Cho 1993, 203*).
Considering the situation of the Korean immigrants in Los Angeles, there is much evidence that the terms "success" or "model minority" are far from being an adequate description of the prevailing living conditions of the Korean Americans. Moreover, facing the experience of the 1992 riots, some Korean authors argue that this label has been unmasked as a meaningless and cynical stereotype without any consequences for the Korean minority: "One hard lesson to be learned from the aftermath of the King verdict and the Korean-American experience is that a model minority is expediently forgotten and dismissed if white dominance or security is threatened" (*Cho 1993, 202*).
In the following section we will discuss in more detail how the Koreans reacted to the traumatic experience of the civil disaster of spring 1992.

The Los Angeles Riots - A Traumatic Experience for the Korean Minority

As has already been pointed out in the introduction of this paper the riots which occurred in Los Angeles between March 29 and May 1, 1992 were the severest case of civil unrest in recent U.S. history. Among the victims the Koreans were the most severely affected group. In summer 1993, only 28% of more than 2,000 Korean-owned businesses burned, damaged or looted during the riots had been reopened (*Ong et al. 1993, 355*), thus leaving a large number of Korean families in an economically disastrous and hopeless situation.

This can be confirmed by the experience of Mrs. Kumja PARK, one of the Koreans we interviewed in August 1993. In 1970, Mrs. PARK, a 51-year-old childless widow, came to Los Angeles with her husband. In 1988, they bought a liquor store and supermarket from their savings accumulated during years of hard work in several jobs including her own occupation as a nurse. One year later Mrs. PARK's husband died. On April 29, 1992 her market, located in a predominantly black neighborhood, was looted and burned to the ground. With only a small insurance on her property and without additional savings, Mrs. PARK is facing the danger of losing her house in Hancock Park, a rather wealthy residential area west of Koreatown, which serves as a place of refuge for her within an environment perceived as increasingly hostile and unsafe. Concerning her future, she appears to have lost all hope although she is still looking for a new business.

> "I wish I were 30 years now. You know, in a few years I have to retire. How can I pay? It's just like a start from zero in this country".

In February 1994, Mrs. PARK opened a small restaurant with a 30-year loan from the SBA (Small Business Administration). She is again facing an indefinite period of hard work:

> "All I have is a 30-year SBA loan to pay off. I won't live another 30 years. But I have nothing left, so I have to try - just to survive. The last thing I want is to lose my home. I want to die in my house. I have so many memories with my late husband in that home" (*Los Angeles Times, April 30, 1994*).

Looking at such an experience it is easily understood why the precarious economic situation as well as the general perception of being the most conspicuous and unprotected victims of the massive outbreak of collective violence have led to widespread feelings of pessimism, despair and helplessness among the members of the Korean community. In many cases those feelings have developed into symptoms of depressions and stress-related illnesses culminating in an increasing number of suicides (*Los Angeles Times, July 23, 1993; April 30, 1994*). It must be emphasized, however, that the feelings of anguish and despair were not restricted to those members of the Korean community who were immediately affected by the riots, as the example of Bong Hwan KIM, the director of the Korean Youth and Community Center (KYCC) shows:

> "For several months, I suffered from serious depression. I would wake up in the middle of the night, overwhelmed by fear. I could neither sleep nor eat; I lost ten pounds and became haggard and gaunt... I know that many other Korean Americans, not only in Los Angeles but in other cities across the United States, are still so deeply wounded that a year later they cannot speak about what happened without weeping" (*Kim 1994, 96f.*)

Facing these outcomes of the riots, two related questions have to be addressed: (1) Why did the Koreans become the most prominent targets and victims of the collective violence and destruction, and (2) how did the Koreans perceive and explain this unexpected experience of victimization? In this paper only some aspects of these questions can be discussed in more detail. We have to neglect the broader political and economic context of race relations in the USA as well the consequences of the process of *economic restructuring* on the development of the American inner cities and the living conditions of the African American minority (*see Soja 1989; Cho 1993; Oliver et al. 1993; Ong et al. 1993; Chang 1994; Thieme and Laux* in this volume). We mainly focus on the economic and cultural tensions between the Afro-Americans and the Koreans and the perception and interpretation of these tensions by members of the Korean American community. Needless to say, these aspects are only some facets of the complex picture of the 1992 riots.

Korean Immigrants as Scapegoats

At first glance it seems incomprehensible that in response to the "Rodney King verdict" the anger and rage of the Afro-Americans was predominantly directed against the members of the Korean community who were in no way involved in the trial and its outcome. This observation gives support to the widespread *scapegoating hypothesis*. According to this social-psychological explanation "less-powerful groups [of a society] assuage their powerlessness by scapegoating their problems upon an identifiable but relatively helpless object" (*Cheng and Espiritu 1989, 526; see Heckmann 1992, 131f.*) It has been argued that within this context middleman minorities are in a particularly precarious and ambiguous situation. According to BONACICH *(1987, 462)* middleman minorities can be utilized as scapegoats to the underprivileged, by the elite; and at the same time these immigrant entrepreneurs are presented to other minorities as "model minorities" who show that the American Dream is valid for all who are willing to work hard (*see Koch and Schockman 1993, 16*).

Applied to the riots this theory means that the Koreans served as scapegoats for black deprivations. Trapped in their ghetto existence the blacks could not immediately direct their anger to the powerful white society. Instead, the Koreans became easy targets for black aggression and hostility and were blamed for the societal oppression of blacks that had become evident in the outcome of the "Rodney King trial". Moreover, this scapegoating argument is in line with the thesis that during the riots Koreatown, widely unprotected by the police, was sacrificed and used as a buffer zone to ensure the safety of wealthier and whiter communities (*Cho 1993, 197; Kim 1993, 220*). Not surprisingly, the self-assessment as scapegoats was frequently given by the Koreans we interviewed, as for example by Mrs. PARK.

> "To me the black people came as slaves and I think many black people have a feeling of frustration and anger, generation after generation... Every time they get blamed for nothing. So I have a lot of understanding. Even after the riots I visited many times to my neighbors and we had a lot of talks. And they complain about Korean people for nothing... They try to avoid that they are in problems making us scapegoats... We didn't do anything wrong. Our fault was just working hard... Black people try to get their rights through destroying minorities."

Black-Korean Conflicts and Prejudices

This interpretation is characterized by a deep bitterness and at the same time a remarkable empathy for the situation of the black minority. However, it only gives an incomplete explanation for the hostility against the Korean population. There is evidence that this violence must also be considered as an outbreak of deep-rooted and long lasting conflicts between the black and Korean communities. A perusal of the relevant information sources shows that numerous latent indications as well as open manifestations of these tensions could be observed throughout Los Angeles for more than a decade (*see Cheng and Espiritu 1989; Ong et al. 1993; Koch and Schockman 1993*). Since 1 January 1990, at least 25 Korean merchants have been killed by non-Korean gunmen (*Cho 1993, 199*). The tensions escalated after Latasha HARLINS, a 15-year-old African American girl, was shot by a Korean shop-owner in March 1991.

The causes of these severe conflicts can widely be connected with the specific role and position of Korean business owners as a middleman minority within predominantly black neighborhoods. As can be seen from a map which shows the Korean owned businesses burned or looted during the riots (*see Thieme 1994, 30*), there are two more ore less distinct clusters of destruction. One is Koreatown, the social and economic center of Korean community life. The second concentration is in South Central Los Angeles, predominantly inhabited by African Americans and an increasing number of Hispanics, but with virtually no Korean residential population.

In this part of the city Korean merchants have held a large percentage of the total retail trade, mainly in form of small markets, groceries, liquor stores, and gas stations. The interaction and communication between the black residents and the Koreans was largely restricted to the contacts between shop-owners and their customers. These antagonistic economic roles and the sharp cultural differences of the two minorities have produced a host of mutual misconceptions and prejudices (see Cheng and Espiritu 1989, 523f.; Cho 1993, 198f.; Ong et al. 1993, 346f.; Chang 1994, 110f.).

From the blacks' point of view the Korean shop-owners, who rarely had a good command of English, were considered as exploitative outsiders, playing the game of the white majority, and draining the money from the economically distressed neighborhood without paying anything back. These common prejudices widely originated from the residential absenteeism of Koreans and their failure to employ local black residents and to contribute to the community's social and economic well-being. Moreover, the blacks complained about Korean Americans as being rude and racially prejudiced, treating them as if they were prospective robbers and shoplifters. It is interesting to see how some of these judgements have been critically reflected by the interviewed persons, partly blaming their own fellow countrymen for the anti-Korean feelings of the blacks. In the words of Mrs. PARK:

> "But in South Central we are foreigners. And most of the Korean merchants don't speak good English. So one major problem is mis-communication, you know... But when I look at the many other victims, they were not prepared for the business in South Central or anywhere."

Yoon-Hui LEE, a 58-year-old unmarried man, who came to the United States in 1964 and who is working for several community organisations, is even more critical of his Korean compatriots when he says:

> "All they do they work here, work there, save money and they have no concept of what the American society is made of. They don't, since they cannot speak the language... Those guys are not accustomed to make a donation. So they never did... but those are the people who have never felt social obligations... They don't care what their neighbors, what black people want."

As shown by these self-critical remarks, especially by those Koreans who have lived in the USA for a long time, the behavior of some parts of the Korean American population is by no means free of misconceptions and cultural prejudices against the Afro-Americans. It has been argued that these prejudices stem from the ethnic and cultural homogeneity of Korean society which did not prepare Korean immigrants to live in a multiracial and multicultural society (see Cheng and Espiritu 1989, 525). Another cause may be the negative stereotypes of blacks transferred to Korea by American movies and TV shows. Moreover, those misconceptions about African Americans as lazy, complaining and criminal are partly reinforced in real-life encounters, no matter how selective they may be. Thus, the daily exposure to physical danger and potential crime are among the most common experiences of Korean merchants in the black neighborhoods, causing feelings of helplessness and making them react defensively towards their black customers (see Min 1990, 441). In the words of Mrs. PARK:

> "They steal a lot. I cannot deny that. They steal a lot. Even if we watched them... Many innocent Korean people have been killed in the past few years and nobody mentioned [it] in the black community. We have no defenses, there is no help for us as we need it. We see a lot of discriminations."

Finally, a second set of prejudices and misconceptions must be mentioned, which refer to the economic role of small businesses in deteriorating ghetto areas like South Central Los Angeles. Members of the black community often see the Korean shop-owners as callous, unfair competitors and mercenary exploiters. Koreans have been accused of being almost a barrier to African American development and of being responsible for the creation of a black underclass (see Kim

1994, 81). These arguments are strongly rejected by the Koreans who emphasize that their small businesses are of vital importance serving the basic needs of the economically backward ghetto neighborhoods and filling economic niches natives have missed or shunned. According to Yoon-Hui LEE:

> "Why did they dare going to such a dangerous place? But actually the Koreans made some substantial contribution there. They brighten up the place... But the blacks don't see it that way."

Moreover, from the Koreans' point of view their modest economic success is the outcome of the typical organisation of labor in their family businesses. An extreme devotion to work and a thrifty way of life must be considered as well as the widespread use of financial resources based on ethnic solidarity (*Cheng and Espiritu 1989, 527*). All these aspects are perceived by the Koreans as some kind of a specific "work ethic" unknown to the African Americans. As Mrs. PARK says:

> "The Koreans are hard working people. We were up from 6.30 in the morning and then we close at midnight, eleven or twelve... And we are very close with the family and we will do anything to support the family... And then we succeeded. Now black people are telling us that we are only concerned about money."

Conclusion

As already pointed out in the beginning of this paper, the 1992 riots or *sa-i-ku* can be considered as a turning point in the history of the Korean minority in the United States. These events clearly revealed the precarious and ambiguous situation of the Koreans as an economically respected and admired minority and, at the same time, as a discriminated and politically rather powerless segment of the American society. Considering such a collective experience several questions arise concerning the future of the Korean American minority. Two of these questions are the further development of immigration from Korea and the preferred destinations within the USA. Will the riots accelerate the already existing trend of a declining immigration from Korea thereby making it a short-term phenomenon within the U.S. immigration history? Will the Los Angeles area lose its role as the most prominent concentration of Korean Americans to other places in the country? Apart from these quantitative aspects the riots may have significant impacts on the future race relations and the political activity of Asian minorities. Above all, a stronger political consciousness and the development of a new kind of Asian American identity and solidarity, largely absent during and after the riots, have been demanded by representatives of the Korean community. Finally, the challenge remains to build new and solid bridges between the Korean and Afro-American population, a task which may not be without any chance considering the tolerance and historical vision of one of our Korean interview partners:

> "I think we have to thank the black people for fighting for the civil rights... It's the black people who opened the door for Asian people to come in."

Zusammenfassung

Die Unruhen in Los Angeles vom Frühjahr 1992 können als die schwersten ihrer Art in der jüngeren amerikanischen Geschichte betrachtet werden. Nach dem Freispruch von vier weißen Polizisten, die der Mißhandlung eines Schwarzen angeklagt waren, gingen weite Teil der Stadt in Flammen auf. Eine der bemerkenswertesten Aspekte dieser Unruhen ist, daß die Koreaner, obwohl sie nur etwa 2% der Gesamtbevölkerung von Los Angeles stellen, von allen ethnischen Gruppen mit Abstand am stärksten unter diesem Gewaltausbruch zu leiden hatten.

Der Aufsatz soll einen Überblick über die Geschichte, die Lebensbedingungen sowie die sozioökonomische Lage der koreanischen Minorität in Los Angeles geben und die Frage diskutieren, wie die Unruhen vom Frühjahr 1992 das Identitätsgefühl der Koreaner und ihr Rollenverständnis innerhalb der amerikanischen Gesellschaft beeinflußt haben. Dabei ist zu klären, warum vor allem die Koreaner zu Opfern der Gewalt wurden und wie diese Minderheit die erlittenen materiellen Schäden und psychischen Verletzungen wahrgenommen und bewältigt hat. Auf der Basis von Zensusdaten und Interviews wird zunächst geprüft, ob und in welchem Umfang das in der amerikanischen Öffentlichkeit verbreitete Image der Asiaten und damit auch der Koreaner als einer *model minority* berechtigt ist. Dieses Image basiert u.a. auf dem überdurchschnittlichen Ausbildungsstand und dem hohen Maß beruflicher Selbständigkeit unter den Koreanern. Es kann gezeigt werden, daß nicht zuletzt die Rolle der koreanischen Geschäftsleute als sog. *middleman minority* innerhalb der Wohngebiete der Afro-Amerikaner eine Quelle von ökonomischen, sozialen und kulturellen Konflikten sowie wechselseitigen Mißverständnissen und Vorurteilen darstellt. Wie die Auswertung von ausführlichen Interviews mit Vertretern der koreanischen Bevölkerungsgruppe im Sommer 1993 deutlich macht, wird die Bewertung der Unruhen und das Rollenverständnis der Koreaner nach den traumatischen Gewalterfahrungen des Frühjahrs 1992 sehr stark durch die Vorstellung geprägt, als weitgehend unschuldige Sündenböcke für die politischen Versäumnisse und strukturellen Mißstände der amerikanischen Gesellschaft gedient zu haben.

Acknowledgement

This research work was supported by a generous grant of the German Research Foundation (DFG).

References

Bonacich, E. (1972): A Theory of Ethnic Antagonism: The Split Labor Market. In: American Sociological Review, 37 (5), 547-559.

Bonacich, E. (1973): A Theory of Middleman Minorities. In: American Sociological Review, 38 (5), 583-594.

Bonacich, E. (1987): "Making it" in America. A Social Evaluation of the Ethics of Immigrant Entrepreneurship. In: Sociological Perspectives, 30 (4), 446-466.

Chang, E.T. (1994): America's First Multiethnic 'Riots'. In: Aguilar-San Juan, K., ed.: The State of Asian America. Activism and Resistence in the 1990s. Boston, South End Press, 101-117.

Cheng, L. and Espiritu, Y. (1989): Korean Businesses in Black and Hispanic Neighborhoods: A Study of Intergroup Relations. In: Sociological Perspectives, 32 (4), 521-534.

Cho, S.K. (1993): Korean Americans vs. African Americans: Conflict and Construction. In: Gooding-Williams, R., ed.: Reading Rodney King - Reading Urban Uprising. New York and London, Routledge, 196-211.

East-West Center (1990): Recent Korean Immigration to the United States: A Profile. Honolulu, HI.
Gardner, R.W., Robey, B. and Smith, P.M. (1989): Asian Americans: Growth, Change, and Diversity. Population Bulletin, 40 (4), Reprint.
Hata Jr., D.T. and Hata, N.I. (1990): Asian-Pacific Angelinos: Model Minority and Indispensable Scapegoats. In: Klein, N.M. and Schiesl, M.J., eds.: 20th Century Los Angeles. Power, Promotion and Social Conflict. Claremont, CA, 61-99.
Heckmann, F. (1992): Ethnische Minderheiten, Volk und Nation. Soziologie inter-ethnischer Beziehungen. Stuttgart, Ferdinand Enke Verlag.
Hirschman, Ch. and Wong, M.G. (1986): The Extraordinary Attainment of Asian-Americans: A Search for Historical Evidence and Explanations. In: Social Forces, 65 (1), 1-27.
Hsia, J. and Hirano-Nakanishi, M. (1989): The Demographics of Diversity. Asian Americans and Higher Education. In: Change, The Magazine of Higher Learning, November/December, 20-27.
Kim, E.H. (1993): Home is Where the *Han* is: A Korean American Perspective on the Los Angeles Upheavals. In: Gooding-Williams, R., ed.: Reading Rodney King - Reading Urban Uprising. New York and London, Routledge, 215-235.
Kim, E.H. (1994): Between Black and White. An Interview with Bong Hwan Kim. In: Aguilar-San Juan, K., ed.: The State of Asian America. Activism and Resistence in the 1990s. Boston, South End Press, 71-100.
Kim, H.-Ch. (1980): Koreans. In: Thernstrom, St., ed.: Harvard Encyclopedia of American Ethnic Groups. Cambridge, MA, and London, Harvard University Press, 601-606.
Kim, K.Ch. and Hurh, W.M. (1983): Korean Americans and the "Success" Image: A Critique. In: Amerasia Jornal, 10 (2), 3-21.
Kitano, H.H.L. and Daniels, R. (1988): Asian Americans. Emerging Minorities. Englewood Cliffs, NJ, Prentice Hall.
Koch, N. and Schockman, H.E. (1993): Riot, Rebellion or Civil Unrest? Perspectives of the Korean-American and African-American Korean Business Communities in Los Angeles. Unpublished Paper, Los Angeles.
Laux, H.D. und Thieme, G. (1992): Jenseits des Schmelztiegels: Die asiatische Einwanderung in die USA und das Beispiel der Koreaner in Los Angeles. In: Die Erde, 123, 191-205.
Lee, D.O. (1992): Commodification of Ethnicity. The Sociospatial Reproduction of Immigrant Entrepreneurs. In: Urban Affairs Quarterly, 28 (2), 258-275.
Light, I. (1984): Immigrant and Ethnic Enterprise in North America. In: Ethnic and Racial Studies, 7, 195-216.
Min, P.G. (1984): From White-Collar Occupations to Small Business: Korean Immigrants' Occupational Adjustment. In: The Sociological Quarterly, 25, 333-352.
Min, P.G. (1990): Problems of Korean Immigrant Entrepreneurs. In: International Migration Review, 24 (3), 436-455.
Nee, V. and Sanders, J. (1985): The Road to Parity: Determinants of the Socioeconomic Achievements of Asian Americans. In: Ethnic and Racial Studies, 8 (1), 75-93.
Oliver, M.L., Johnson Jr., J.H. and Farrell Jr., W.C. (1993): Anatomy of a Rebellion: A Political-Economic Analysis. In: Gooding-Williams, R., ed.: Reading Rodney King - Reading Urban Uprising. New York and London, Routledge, 117-141.
Ong, P. and Hee, S. (1993): Losses in the Los Angeles Civil Unrest, April 29 - May 1, 1992. Los Angeles.
Ong, P., Park, Y.K. and Tong, Y. (1993): The Korean-Black Conflict and the State. Unpublished Paper, Los Angeles.
Portes, A. and Rumbaut, R.G. (1990): Immigrant America. A Portrait. Berkeley, University of California Press.
Razin, E. (1988): Entrepreneurship Among Foreign Immigrants in the Los Angeles and San Francisco Metropolitan Regions. In: Urban Geography, 9 (3), 283-310.
Soja, E. (1989): Postmodern Geographies. The Reassertion of Space in Critical Social Theory. London and New York, Verso.
Suzuki, B.H.(1989): Asian Americans as the "Model Minority". Outdoing Whites? Or Media Hype? In: Change, The Magazine of Higher Learning, November/December, 13-19.
Thieme, G. (1994): Das Ende eines Traums? Die Unruhen von Los Angeles 1992 - das Ende der multikulturellen Gesellschaft? In: Geographie Heute, 119, 28-31.

U.S. Immigration and Naturalization Service (1993): Statistical Yearbook of the Immigration and Naturalization Service, 1992. Washington, D.C.
We the American Asians (1993): U.S. Department of Commerce, Bureau of the Census. Washington, D.C.
Winnick, L. (1990): America's "Model Minority". In: Commentary, August, 22-29.
Worsnop, R.L. (1991): Asian Americans. In: Congress Quarterly Researcher, 1 (30), 947-963.

Addresses of the Authors

Hans Dieter Laux
Geographisches Institut
Universität Bonn
Meckenheimer Allee 166
53115 Bonn
GERMANY

Günter Thieme
Institut für Geographie
Universität Dortmund
Emil-Figge-Str. 50
44227 Dortmund
GERMANY

GÜNTER THIEME and HANS DIETER LAUX

Los Angeles - A Multi-Ethnic Metropolis
Spatial Patterns and Socio-Economic Problems as a Result of Recent Migration Processes

Introduction

For the last three decades the ethnic and socio-economic patterns of immigration to the United States have changed dramatically. Especially in California and, within this state, the Los Angeles agglomeration area, these immigration processes have resulted in a substantial shift of the ethnic composition of the population. This process can be seen as a step away from the traditional idea of the *melting pot* towards a *mosaic* of cultures and ethnic groups. Los Angeles has become the prototype of an EthniCity *(see Roseman, Laux and Thieme 1995)*, but many of the initial hopes and expectations for a harmonious and peaceful living together of different racial and cultural groups were shattered during and after the riots of 1992 and an increasingly anti-immigrant mood has developed among the U.S. American population. It therefore seems most rewarding to analyze the interplay of immigration, economic and social forces in the Los Angeles urban area.

The purpose of this paper is (1) to summarize the recent trends of immigration to the USA, (2) to describe and explain the newly emerging spatial pattern of the main racial and ethnic groups in the Los Angeles area, and (3) to discuss the problems and tensions between these groups in the context of the processes of urban restructuring and its socio-economic consequences.

Recent Trends of Immigration to the United States

In 1992 almost one million immigrants were admitted to the United States. This figure was hardly lower than the record numbers of the years in the decade from 1901 to 1910 and marked at least the temporary climax of a completely new era that had begun after the Immigration Act of 1965. This new law abolished the national origins system and discrimination against Asians *(see Bouvier and Gardner 1986, 13ff.).* Another important consequence was the change in the preference system: family reunification replaced labor qualifications as the primary criterion rationing immigration.

After the reform of immigration legislation, which was carried on in the 1980s, a dramatic change of the regional origins of immigrants occurred. In the period from 1961 to 1970 North and Central American countries had already been dominant with over 40 % of the total number of immigrants (particularly from Mexico, Canada and Cuba), the "classical" European immigration countries, however, still had a share of more than one third. In the past decades European immigration has lost most of its importance while the volume of immigration has generally been increasing. In contrast, Asians have made good use of the new preference system as well as people from Mexico and other Latin American countries. A significant number of immigrants among the latter group had come as illegal immigrants but they were granted an amnesty and given the chance of legalizing their status and applying for permanent residence (Immigration Control and Reform Act of 1986).

These recent immigration processes have had a noticeable effect on the population composition of the USA *(see O'Hare 1992, 10ff.)*. Of the 255 million Americans in 1992 less than 75 % were non-Hispanic whites. They were followed by 11.9 % African Americans and by the strongly growing number of Latinos or Hispanics with 9.5 %. Although the percentage of Asians among the American population has only reached 3.1 % or 7.9 million this is the group with the highest relative increase since the 1980 census.

As shown not only by the number of academic publications but, particularly, by intensive public discussion, this development has added a new dimension to the question of how the American nation defines itself. "E pluribus unum", this device that has always been open to interpretation, has gained fresh significance as hardly ever before in the history of this "unfinished society", no matter whether it is seen as a claim or as a question. Among the more recent contributions to this controversial debate, Arthur SCHLESINGER *(1992)* in his book "The Disuniting of America" has warned that the American society might increasingly drift apart, and Andrew HACKER *(1992)* speaks of "Two Nations" that are separate, hostile, and unequal.

Two adverse concepts dominate the arguments over the American society in the future. On the one hand, this is the classic idea of the *melting pot of nations*, an extensive assimilation and integration of all groups of immigrants into a more or less homogeneous American society. In contrast, the idea of *cultural pluralism* favors a multicultural society, in which a basic assimilation has to be realized, but where a mosaic of ethnic groups and cultures continues to exist and is considered as an asset, a benefit for society as a whole (for a middle way between these concepts see Kim and Hurh 1993).

It is impossible to discuss these questions in detail here. One thing seems sure, however: if the metaphor of the melting pot has ever been anything more than a myth it was useful to describe the coalescence of European flows of immigrants characterized by very similar cultural traditions. In contrast, there are good reasons to expect that the new immigrants from Latin America and Asia are less willing than their European predecessors to give up their cultural heritage and identity in favor of a more or less complete assimilation into the mainstream of American society. Among the Latinos the close connections and short distances to their countries of origin are considered obstacles for rapid assimilation. Among Asian ethnic groups the marked cultural distance to the Anglo-American world obviously is of considerable influence (for a discussion of the *model minority* role frequently ascribed to Asian immigrants see the contribution of *Laux and Thieme* in this volume).

Los Angeles - Spatial Patterns in a Multiethnic Metropolis

California in general and metropolitan Los Angeles in particular appear to be most appropriate places to study these topics and problems. Here at the Pacific rim of the USA and in close proximity to the Third World is the arena where the ethnic and social transformation of American society is most clearly visible, with all its problems and its massive tensions and conflicts, as the spring riots of 1992 have demonstrated.

Some basic data on population development in Los Angeles County reveal the dramatic changes taking place in the population composition of this largest agglomeration area in the west of the USA. As can be seen in *Fig. 1* the total population grew from 2.8 to 8.9 million people within the time period 1940 - 1990. The most significant increases happened in the two decades from 1950 to 1960 and 1980 to 1990. To what extent migratory movements have contributed to this growth is shown by the fact that in 1990 almost 60 % of the total population was born outside the state of California and one third even outside the USA.

Even more impressive than the total growth of population in Los Angeles County is the change of ethnic composition happening at the same time. Non-Hispanic whites made up 80 % of the population in 1960, but their share was almost cut by half until 1990. This implied an absolute

Fig. 1: Major Racial and Ethnic Groups in Los Angeles County, 1940-1990

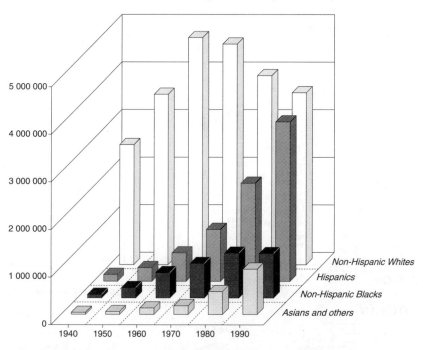

Sources: Clark 1987, Census of Population and Housing 1990

decrease of more than 1.1 million people who mainly settled in the suburban areas of neighboring counties like Orange, Ventura, San Bernardino or Riverside, in recent years also in other Western states of the USA, particularly Arizona, Oregon, Washington and Nevada.

This *white flight* is in contrast to growth processes for all the other groups, although the rates are much different. Most rapidly growing in absolute numbers are the Hispanics or Latinos whose population figures almost equalled those of the whites in 1990. As to relative growth, the Hispanics are even surpassed by the Asian Americans. This group, comprising a multitude of nationalities, increased its number to 900,000 (10.2 % of the total population) in Los Angeles County. Only moderate growth, almost stagnation, has been typical of black population development since the 1970s. In recent years there have not only been distinct flows of outmigration of African Americans to suburban areas but also return migration to Southern States, the traditional origins of black population in the USA *(see Johnson a. Roseman 1990, 209ff.).*

In the light of these processes it appears fully justified to call Los Angeles, as Zena PEARLSTONE put it in her book "Ethnic L.A.", "the first multiracial and multiethnic metropolis in the continental United States" *(Pearlstone 1990, 25).* This hypothesis is supported by several important characteristics of the population in Los Angeles County. Almost one third of the total population was foreign born at the time of the latest census in 1990, among those over eighteen years the proportion was almost 40 %. In addition, more than 45 % of all persons over five years did not speak English at home - in the City of Los Angeles the corresponding figure was even 48 %!

Fig. 2: Orientation Map, Los Angeles County

A Short Typology of Immigrants

Let us now take a closer look at some of the immigrant groups, emphasizing the situation in Los Angeles. In their book "Immigrant America" PORTES and RUMBAUT *(1990, 14ff.)* classify contemporary immigrants to the USA into four basic categories: labor migrants, professional immigrants, entrepreneurial immigrants, and refugees and asylees.

Labor migration has always tended to represent the bulk of migration, both legal and undocumented. This is true for Los Angeles as well: garment contractors, electronic components firms or employers in menial service jobs argue that they have to rely on the willingness of the immigrants to work hard for low pay. It is particularly the Mexican and other Central American immigrants who are applying for these modest entry jobs with tough competition, low wages and bad working conditions. This potential of a cheap labor force is permanently supplemented by means of illegal immigration across the Mexican border.

The second group may be called *professional immigrants.* They come legally, on the basis of the third preference category of the immigration law. The main motive of this type of immigrants is to improve their careers, and so they try to compete in the primary segment of the labor market. In Los Angeles, as in most other big American cities, the proportion of Asians in this group is very high - main contributors are the Philippines, India or Taiwan. This type of immigrants tends to be much less visible than the labor migrants - they do not form tightly knit ethnic communities and therefore are spatially more dispersed.

Refugees and *asylees* were not given formal status until the 1965 immigration reform. For a long time U.S. policy had been to grant refugee status primarily to people escaping from communist countries, mainly Southeast Asia, Cuba and Eastern Europe - after the collapse of the communist system almost worldwide this practice may have to be changed. In the Los Angeles area there are scattered communities of Indochinese refugees, above all Vietnamese in Orange County ("Little Saigon") and Cambodians in some parts of Long Beach where they are engaged in the arch-American doughnut business.

Among the fourth category of *entrepreneurial immigrants* the Koreans in Los Angeles have attracted both public and academic attention because of their alleged economic success but also because they were extremely hard hit by the riots in 1992 *(Light and Bonacich 1988, Laux and Thieme 1992, Chang 1994)*. Their high degree of self-employment, which by far exceeds the comparative figures of other immigrant minorities, appears especially remarkable. Almost 26 % of employed Koreans over 16 years were self-employed or worked in these businesses as unpaid family members at the time of the 1990 census. These figures are more or less in line with earlier studies by LIGHT and BONACICH *(1988)*, RAZIN *(1988)* and MIN *(1990)*. In order to start a small business, a grocery shop, a liquor store, a gas station or a real estate office Koreans even accepted a temporary social decline - many Korean businesspeople in L.A. used to be academics in their home country!

Spatial Patterns of Ethnic Segregation in the Los Angeles Area

The question how the different ethnic groups are distributed across a city or an urban area has been one of the classical themes of sociology and social geography since the days of the Chicago school of social ecology. Do the various groups live in ethnically homogeneous residential areas with distinct regional patterns or are the ethnic groups more or less evenly distributed? A first answer to this question may be given by the *Index of Segregation* measuring the similarity between the spatial distribution of one group and the rest of the population. The calculation *(Tab. 1)* based on the tracts of the 1990 census in Los Angeles County presents a rather clear picture concentrating on the principal groups of population: African Americans are most strongly segregated, i.e. separated from the other population groups, followed by the non-Hispanic whites in second place. Asians have the lowest degree of segregation. It seems remarkable that the extent of spatial segregation is largely independent of the size of the different groups. Blacks and Asians who have similar population shares are characterized by quite different index values. The various ethnic groups summed up under the collective term Asians live more segregated, however. Even if we leave apart the rather small group of Cambodians in Los Angeles County, the segregation indices of Chinese and Korean Americans are at the same, or nearly the same, level compared to non-Hispanic whites. Obviously, most Asian ethnic groups (Asian Indians and Filipinos are exceptions to the rule, possibly because of their good command of the English language) live in rather distinct neighborhoods and tend to form clear spatial concentrations within the metropolitan areas of Los Angeles and Orange Counties (see also map "Percent Asian Population" in *Turner and Allen 1991*).

A second aspect of segregation concerns the similarity of settlement patterns between the different ethnic groups. This question is answered by means of the *Index of Dissimilarity* calculated on the basis of the census tracts in Los Angeles County *(Tab. 2)*. As expected, there is a strong segregation between the white population and the African Americans *(see also Allen and Turner 1995)*. The distance between most of the Asian groups and the blacks, however, is hardly smaller, in some cases (Chinese and Koreans) even greater. Much less distinct is the spatial

Tab. 1: Index of Segregation, Los Angeles County: 1990

Non-Hispanic Whites	57	
Non-Hispanic Blacks	64	
Hispanics	50	
Asians (total)	42	
Chinese		57
Filipinos		44
Japanese		48
Indians		41
Koreans		55
Vietnamese		51
Cambodians		81

Source: Census of Population and Housing 1990

separation between the residential areas of the Hispanics and the other groups, whereas the Asians tend to live in closer connection with both whites and Latinos. Perhaps surprisingly for some, the segregation between the individual Asian American groups is by no means low, and it is increasing *(see Allen and Turner 1995)*.

What are the effects of such a behavior for the spatial fabric of Los Angeles? The first map *(Fig. 3)* shows the distribution of the predominant ethnic population in metropolitan Los Angeles County 1990. It can easily be seen that the old stereotype of "chocolate city and vanilla

Tab. 2: Index of Dissimilarity, Los Angeles County: 1990

	Non-Hispanic Whites	Non-Hispanic Blacks	Hispanics	Asians	Chinese	Filipinos	Japanese	Indians	Koreans	Vietnamese	Cambodians
Non-Hispanic Whites	–										
Non-Hispanic Blacks	73	–									
Hispanics	61	59	–								
Asians	46	68	50	–							
Chinese	60	80	65	–	–						
Filipinos	52	70	50	–	58	–					
Japanese	49	73	63	–	49	56	–				
Indians	39	70	58	–	55	47	51	–			
Koreans	54	78	65	–	58	49	51	46	–		
Vietnamese	60	71	53	–	44	50	61	55	63	–	
Cambodians	86	86	79	–	81	80	87	85	89	73	–

Source: Census of Population and Housing 1990

Fig. 3: Predominant Ethnic Populations, Metropolitan Los Angeles County: 1990

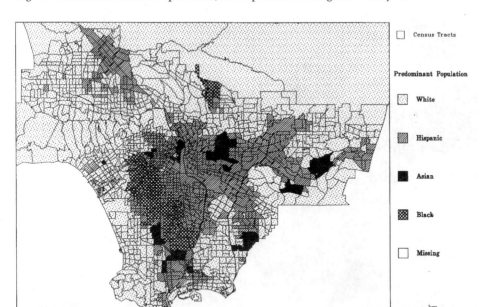

Source: Census of Population and Housing 1990

suburb" is no longer valid in a much more complex ethnic environment, as is the case in Los Angeles County. Non-Hispanic whites who make up less than half of the county's population continue to be the predominant ethnic group in the more attractive areas along the Pacific coast, along the slopes of the Santa Monica Mountains and in parts of the San Fernando Valley as well as in recently developed suburbs along the northern border of the map. As expected, the area with a predominance of African Americans is rather compact: Blacks are concentrated in Southern Los Angeles and some neighboring cities such as Compton or Inglewood.

Latinos or Hispanics are the most expansive group in the Los Angeles area. Particularly in East and Southeast Los Angeles there are numerous tracts that are almost exclusively inhabited by this ethnic group now but used to be solidly white working-class areas until twenty years ago (e.g. the city of Huntington Park). Latinos have also been spreading to the San Fernando Valley, the San Pedro Harbor area and to some eastern suburbs (Pomona, Duarte). They are by no means an ethnically homogeneous group - Salvadorans and Guatemalans have formed autonomous neighborhoods that are visibly different from those of the Mexican Americans. Not only white neighborhoods have increasingly been taken over by Latinos very much according to the invasion and succession model of the Chicago school. Hispanics also penetrate into traditional black areas. As shown in the map, the main residential area of African Americans which in vast parts has a ghetto character extends along a 20 kilometer strip south and southwest of downtown. The Watts neighborhood, famous or rather infamous for the riots of the 1960s, used to be almost 100% black. Now it is a good example of the "battle zone" between the expansive Latino population and the African Americans *(see Fig. 9.1* in: *Oliver, Johnson and Farrell 1993, 123).*

Fig. 4: Second Leading Ethnic Populations, Metropolitan Los Angeles County: 1990

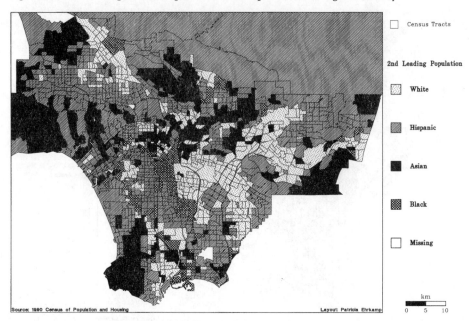

Source: Census of Population and Housing 1990

A totally different pattern is characteristic of neighborhoods with Asian predominance in Los Angeles County. They form something like a broken ring around the black and Latino areas. The multi-nuclei structure of their settlements is striking - these are the concentrations of single Asian ethnic groups: the Koreans in Koreatown, the Japanese in Gardena, the Cambodians in Long Beach or the Chinese in Chinatown, Monterey Park or in the eastern suburb of Walnut.

While there is a rather distinct pattern of the predominant ethnic populations the spatial fabric of the second leading ethnic populations *(Fig. 4)* is more complex and fragmented and cannot be discussed in detail here. Suffice it to say that Asians are the second leading group mostly in those areas where non-Hispanic whites are dominant, e.g. in many of the privileged and most attractive neighborhoods along the sea coast (Malibu, Pacific Palisades, Palos Verdes etc.), in the San Fernando Valley and the Burbank, Glendale and Pasadena areas. In contrast, blacks in most cases are second in numbers to Latinos, which is indicative of the invasion-succession process mentioned above. Finally, by their sheer numbers alone Latinos are the second leading ethnic group almost everywhere except in the most exclusive neighborhoods as well as in those areas where they are in first place anyway.

Economic Restructuring in a Multi-Ethnic Context

So far, we have largely described the spatial patterns of ethnic groups in Los Angeles. Fascinating as these maps tend to be for a geographer, they want some theoretical underpinning. What are the forces that have made so many people come to this place? What chances do the immigrants have to enter the labor market and, possibly, to move up the social ladder? How far do these efforts affect the position of other ethnic groups? These are some of the questions to be asked about the motives of immigration, the socio-economic status and progress of recent immigrants in Los Angeles.

"It all comes together in Los Angeles" - with this chapter of his book on "Postmodern Geographies" UCLA geographer Edward SOJA *(1989)* wants to express that for him Los Angeles is a *prototype*, a *paradigmatic place*, a *mesocosm* where numerous, sometimes conflicting economic, social and cultural processes and movements are blended. Often, Los Angeles is considered a most exceptional case among the cities of the world, as being bizarre and incomparable. This is not wrong, but it is only half the truth.

In close connection with international migration flows and the resulting ethnic and socio-cultural diversity it will be necessary to focus the attention on the process of *economic restructuring* manifesting itself in Los Angeles in a most typical way. In contrast to the popular idea of Los Angeles being a typical post-industrial metropolis, the urban region of Los Angeles has developed into one of the largest centers of manufacturing, not only in the United States *(see Soja 1989, 191f.)*. During the last decades, Los Angeles was continuously among those regions of the USA with the highest growth rates in the secondary sector of the economy. In recent years, however, Los Angeles, as the state of California in general, was particularly hard hit by the economic recession.

The economic development of the Los Angeles urban area is characterized by four restructuring trends underlying the transition: deindustrialization, reindustrialization, public-sector contraction, and service-sector expansion *(see Wolch and Dear 1993, 52)*. In the years 1978 - 1982 alone, the agglomeration lost more than 75,000 manufacturing jobs because of plant closures and indefinite layoffs *(see Soja 1989, 200ff.)*. Most of these jobs were lost in the traditional core branches of U.S. manufacturing industry: steel, automobile assembly, tyre manufacturing, electrical engineering, and aircraft construction.

Despite these massive job losses in the classical branches of manufacturing which, moreover, had a distinct regional and ethnic component, the job balance in the manufacturing sector was positive until the late eighties. This development was mostly due to an extraordinarily strong expansion at the two extremes of the labor market and resulted in a clear polarization by qualification and income. On the one extreme we find a considerable accumulation of highly qualified jobs e.g. in microelectronics and the space industry. Admittedly, after the end of the cold war a large number of jobs was cut in different sectors of the defense industry, but still Los Angeles and Orange Counties are major nuclei of high technology in the USA *(see Scott 1993, 12ff.)*.

On the other extreme there are expansive branches which normally could not be expected to prosper in a technologically advanced industrial country such as the USA. The model example is the garment industry experiencing a remarkable period of growth in Southern California which has recently surpassed New York as the major center of production in the USA *(see Scott 1993, 11)*. Official statistical data for 1990 give a number of almost 100,000 employees in the garment industry of Los Angeles County. The true figures, however, are supposed to be significantly higher since it is well known that a large part of the jobs in this branch have been held by undocumented workers, about 90 % by women *(see Soja 1989, 207)*. In these businesses any union membership is almost inconceivable, infringements of minimum wages, working hours, child labor or safety laws are endemic. The working conditions of such *sweatshops* recall the situation of the Industrial Revolution and appear to justify David RIEFF's *(1991)* thesis of Los Angeles as "capital of the third world".

The different areas of the Los Angeles agglomeration as well as the various ethnic groups are diversely affected by these polarization processes of the labor market. Undoubtedly, the black population of Los Angeles suffered most. African Americans used to hold many of the solid blue collar jobs in manufacturing activity which was concentrated in aircraft, automobiles, steel, glass, and rubber. Most of these jobs were located in the areas south of downtown to the harbor districts of San Pedro and Long Beach, close to the major concentration of black population in Los Angeles. The workforce in the traditional branches of manufacturing was severely affected, however, by the restructuring process: tens of thousands of jobs were lost, the deskilling of the labor force led to a decline in pay scales, and unionized labor was drastically weakened *(see Storper and Scott 1989)*. As a consequence, increasing numbers of workers no longer earn adequate wages, others have dropped out of the labor force altogether. So large parts of the black ghetto of Los Angeles have become places of hopelessness, despair and neglect.

The whites still hold the majority of the highly qualified and well-paid jobs in the *primary segment* of the labor market, i.e. in the prosperous branches of e.g. microelectronics or biotechnology. Only recently they have been severely affected by the plant closures of the military industrial complex as a consequence of cuts in the defense budget after the end of the cold war. In contrast to the spatial pattern of the traditional manufacturing industry, only few enterprises of high technology are to be found in the central parts of Los Angeles (mostly close to Los Angeles International Airport), but rather in the suburban areas of Burbank and Glendale, the San Fernando Valley or in neighboring Orange County *(see Soja 1989, 206; Scott 1993, 13)*. The Latinos, especially the newly arrived and frequently undocumented labor migrants, find their place in the *secondary segment* of the labor market where both foreign- and native-born workers face stiff competition for low-skill jobs. These jobs, in branches of manufacturing such as the garment industry or in a multitude of service-related industries, are most insecure, extremely low-paid and often without job-related benefits such as old age pensions and health care coverage *(see Wolch and Dear 1993, 48)*. It is mainly due to the presence of multiple wage-earners in Latino households that the median household income of this group with $ 27,361 in 1989 slightly exceeds the comparative figure of African Americans ($ 25,827).

How do Asian Americans cope with the various processes of economic restructuring in the Los Angeles area? There cannot be an easy answer to that question because Asians have a share in all the different types of migration to the USA: Chinese or Korean immigrants often start as labor migrants and compete with Mexicans or other Central American nationalities for the sweatshop jobs in the secondary labor market. On the other hand, Filipinos, Asian Indians or Chinese from Taiwan or Hong Kong frequently arrive as university-educated professionals who do not accept menial jobs although they often have to enter the labor market at the bottom of their respective occupational ladders *(see Portes and Rumbaut 1990, 19)*. In contrast, many Southeast Asian refugees continue to be dependent on welfare payments even after several years in the USA, others enter the lower segments of the labor market. Asian entrepreneurial immigrants try to escape the various difficulties and hardships of the secondary labor market by establishing small family businesses either in their own ethnic enclave or in the neighborhoods of other ethnic minorities less willing or prepared to run the economic risk of self-employment. Diverse as the economic strategies and opportunities of Asian Americans may be in the Los Angeles urban area, there is one common characteristic for almost all members of these ethnic groups: they try to gather and combine all their resources to secure a better future for their children. This high educational motivation, together with the devotion to family and the willingness to work hard, have led many experts in the field of immigration studies to call Asian Americans a "model minority" (a critical assessment of this concept is given in the contribution of *Laux and Thieme* in this volume).

Socio-Economic Disparities and Inter-Ethnic Conflicts

To sum up the socio-economic and ethnic anatomy of the Los Angeles area some maps for indicators of social well-being are presented from three different dimensions: family and household structures, education, and income.

The stability of families is one of the major prerequisites for socio-economic success. Therefore, a high proportion of single-parent families must be considered as an alarm signal for the prospects not only of the young generation. *Fig. 5* shows the percentage of female-headed households in metropolitan Los Angeles County. There is a very distinct cluster of high values in the black ghetto of South Central Los Angeles where there are many census tracts with more than 30 % of all the households in this category. Minor concentrations of female-headed households can be found in some areas with a majority of Hispanic population groups. Wherever Asians or non-Hispanic whites are the predominant ethnic group the figures tend to be well below average.

Another major dimension of socio-economic status is education. The spatial mosaic of the proportion of persons with low educational attainment *(Fig. 6)* closely resembles the main concentrations of Hispanic population groups. Indeed, the level of formal education is by far lowest among the Latinos: In Los Angeles County less than 40% of the adult members of this group had a high school diploma or any higher qualification. Low levels of educational attainment, even illiteracy, are particularly common among recent immigrants from Central America (Guatemala, El Salvador, Honduras), but also among people of Mexican origin. Together with their limited command of English this prevents many Latinos from competing in the more qualified segments of the labor market and keeps them in their ethnic enclaves. All other

Fig. 5: Female-Headed Households, Metropolitan Los Angeles County: 1990

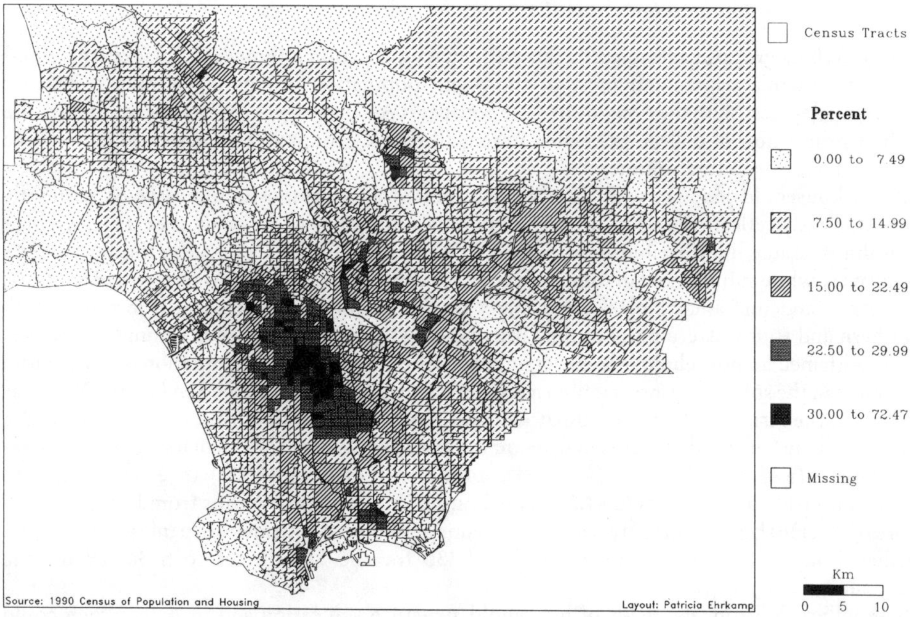

Source: Census of Population and Housing 1990

Fig. 6: Persons with Low Educational Attainment, Metropolitan Los Angeles County: 1990

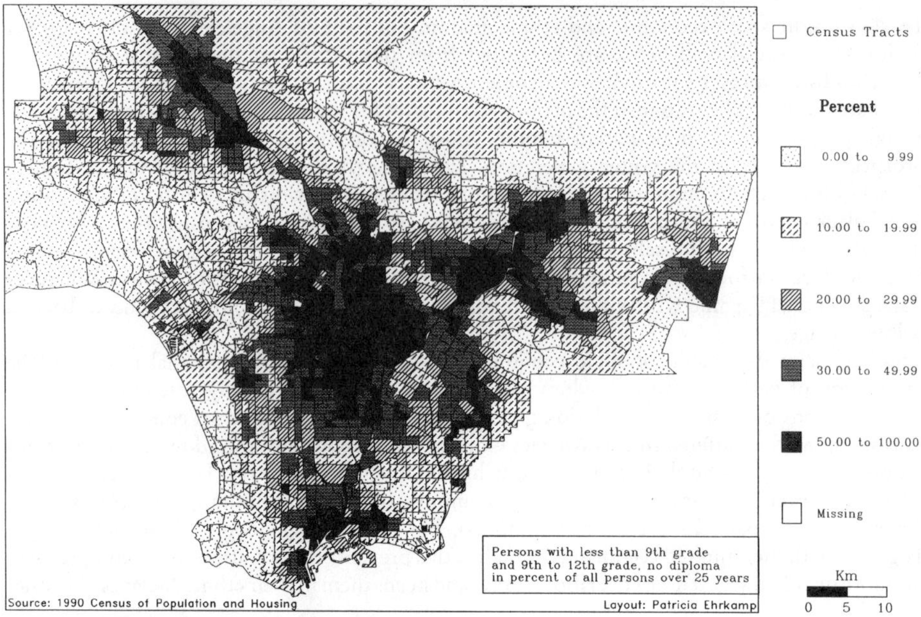

Source: Census of Population and Housing 1990

racial or ethnic groups have at least a fair elementary education although the blacks lag behind the non-Hispanic whites and most of the Asian population groups concerning college or university degrees. With the exception of the Southeast Asian refugees Asian Americans have the highest proportion of college graduates among all ethnic groups in Los Angeles County (see *Laux and Thieme* in this volume).

Median household income, which can be interpreted as a composite indicator of economic success, clearly reflects the ethnic pattern of population groups in the study area *(Fig. 7)*. There is an almost crater-like distribution with median incomes well above $ 50,000 in the more or less exclusively white suburbs and in some suburban concentrations of Asian Americans. In contrast, poverty is endemic among blacks and many of the recently arrived Latinos in the central, southern and southeastern parts of the City of Los Angeles where there are numerous census tracts with median household incomes significantly below $ 20,000. The situation is a little more favorable in the solidly Latino neighborhoods in East Los Angeles and the San Gabriel Valley as well as in the Asian enclaves of Chinatown and Koreatown. Both within the different Asian groups and the Latinos there are strong income disparities: While the median household incomes of Filipinos ($ 46,497), Japanese ($ 44,433), and Asian Indians ($ 46,912) are even higher than those of non-Hispanic whites ($ 41,222), the household incomes of Asians from Indochina and Korea ($ 30,436) lag considerably behind. The same applies to the various Hispanic groups whose median household incomes range from $ 21,330 for the Hondurans to $ 36,779 for the Dominicans.

These indicators from the fields of household structure, education and income, which could easily be supplemented by a large number of similar variables, clearly demonstrate the complex

Fig. 7: Median Household Income, Metropolitan Los Angeles County: 1989

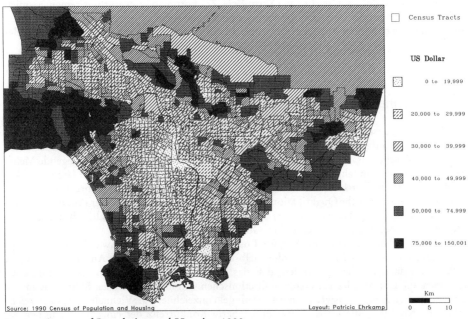

Source: Census of Population and Housing 1990

interrelation between socio-economic disparities and racial and ethnic structures. On the one end of the social ladder there are the highly segregated neighborhoods of affluent whites and, sometimes, Asian Americans. On the other end there is a syndrome of poverty, unemployment and a multitude of social pathologies such as shattered families, crime and drug addiction which has made large parts of South Central and Southeastern Los Angeles into a declining and derelict area with very few signs of revitalization and hope. These socio-economic problems have been intensified by the arrival of new immigrants from Latin America and Asia. Especially lower income blacks have increasingly found themselves in conflict and competition with these immigrant groups over jobs, housing, and scarce public resources *(see Oliver, Johnson and Farrell 1993, 121)*. There are, however, also conflicts between old-resident white Americans and Asian immigrants over economic development in an affluent suburban setting *(see Horton 1989)*. The social explosion in Los Angeles on 29 April 1992 was a shock for the American public. It can be interpreted as a mixture of democratic protest against a verdict perceived as unjust, a bread riot of the poor in a time of severe recession, and an interethnic conflict *(see Davis 1993, 142f.)*, but also as an outbreak of aggression and violence caused by frustration and fury bottled up. In fact, the Los Angeles riots did not come as a surprise. There were many signs of tension between blacks and Latinos along the "battle zone" of invasion and succession in South Central Los Angeles, or between African American residents and Korean shopowners in the same district *(see Laux and Thieme* in this volume). In November 1994 59 % of the Californian voters passed Proposition 187 denying illegal aliens public education and health-care services *(see Hornblower 1994, 56)*. In the city of Compton situated just south of Los Angeles's Watts all schools were closed the day after Prop. 187 had been passed. The city used to be overwhelmingly black but now has a Latino majority, and therefore the black officials were afraid that riots might break out after that political decision *(see Lee and Sloan 1994, 27)*. Fortunately, everything remained quiet, but this incident is a clear sign that the complex mixture of socio-economic problems and interethnic tensions continues to be a great danger for the future development in the Los Angeles urban region.

Zusammenfassung

Seit der 1965 verabschiedeten Reform der Einwanderungsgesetzgebung hat sich die Zahl der pro Jahr in die USA aufgenommenen Immigranten wesentlich erhöht. Gleichzeitig veränderte sich auch die ethnische Zusammensetzung der Einwanderer grundlegend: Die überwiegende Mehrzahl der in den letzten Jahren in die USA eingewanderten Personen ist entweder lateinamerikanischer oder asiatischer Herkunft. Diese Migranten sind zudem, auch was ihre Wanderungsmotive und ihre berufliche Qualifikation angeht, keineswegs homogen. Dieser Prozeß hat in den USA eine kontroverse Diskussion über Assimilation, Integration und Multikulturalismus als Modelle der zukünftigen amerikanischen Gesellschaft ausgelöst.

Kalifornien und besonders die Stadtregion Los Angeles sind für diese Einwanderer neuen Typs geradezu ein neues *Ellis Island* geworden. Selbst vor den Unruhen in Los Angeles im Frühjahr 1992 war jedoch deutlich geworden, daß das Zusammenleben der zahlreichen ethnischen Gruppen, die Los Angeles zur ersten multiethnischen und multikulturellen Metropole in den USA gemacht haben, keineswegs von Harmonie gekennzeichnet war. Vielmehr gab es zahlreiche ethnische Konflikte, die nicht zuletzt durch harte Konkurrenz der einzelnen Gruppen am Arbeits- und Wohnungsmarkt ausgelöst wurden.

Auf der Basis der Zensusergebnisse von 1990 setzt sich dieser Aufsatz zum Ziel, aktuelle Bevölkerungsprozesse und sozio-ökonomische Entwicklungen in der Stadtregion Los Angeles zu analysieren. Im Zuge der ökonomischen Restrukturierung hat sich eine deutliche Segmentierung des Arbeitsmarktes entwickelt. Der Zugang zu den vergleichsweise sicheren und gut bezahlten Arbeitsplätzen im primären Segment des Arbeitsmarktes oder, im Gegensatz hierzu, die Beschränkung auf die Arbeitsplätze des sekundären Segments mit niedrigen Löhnen und sehr problematischen Arbeitsbedingungen hat eine deutliche ethnische Komponente und führt zu klaren räumlichen Disparitäten.

Insbesondere die schwarze Bevölkerung von South Central Los Angeles leidet an einem Syndrom von wirtschaftlicher Vernachlässigung, Arbeitslosigkeit, Armut, zerbrochenen Familienstrukturen und, in Abhängigkeit hiervon, einer Vielzahl von Sozialpathologien. Zusätzlich hat der wachsende Zuwanderungsdruck von Latinos sowie das Eindringen asiatischer, insbesondere koreanischer Geschäftsinhaber weitere Spannungen erzeugt, die auch nach den Unruhen von 1992 kaum nachgelassen haben.

References

Allen, J.P. and Turner, E. (1995): Ethnic Diversity and Segregation in the New Los Angeles. In: Roseman, C.C., Laux, H.D. and Thieme, G. (eds.): EthniCity. Geographical Perspectives on Ethnic Change in Modern Cities. Totowa, N.J., Rowman & Littlefield. (forthcoming).

Bouvier, L.F. and Gardner, R.W. (1986): Immigration to the U.S.: The Unfinished Story. Population Bulletin, 41(4).

Chang, E.T. (1994): America's First Multi-Ethnic 'Riots'. In: Aguilar-San Juan, K. (ed.): The State of Asian America. Activism and Resistance in the 1990s, 101-117. Boston, MA, South End Press.

Clark, W.A.V. (1987): The Roepke Lecture in Economic Geography. Urban Restructuring from a Demographic Perspective. In: Economic Geography, 63, 103-124.

Davis, M. (1993): Uprising and Repression in L.A. In: Gooding-Williams, R. (ed.): Reading Rodney King. Reading Urban Uprising, 142-154. New York and London, Routledge.

Hacker, A. (1992): Two Nations. Black and White, Separate, Hostile, Unequal. New York, Charles Scribner's Sons.

Hornblower, M. (1994): Lashing out at Illegals. In: Time, 144, No. 47, 21 November, 56-57.

Horton, J. (1989): The Politics of Ethnic Change: Grass-Roots Responses to Economic and Demographic Restructuring in Monterey Park, California. In: Urban Geography, 10, 578-582.

Johnson, J.H. jr., Oliver, M.L. and Roseman, C.C. (1989): Introduction: Ethnic Dilemmas in Comparative Perspective. In: Urban Geography, 10, 425-433.

Johnson, J.H. jr. and Oliver, M.L. (1989): Interethnic Minority Conflict in Urban America: The Effects of Economic and Social Dislocations. In: Urban Geography, 10, 449-463.

Johnson, J.H. jr. and Roseman, C.C. (1990): Increasing Black Outmigration from Los Angeles: The Role of Household Dynamics and Kinship Systems. In: Annals of the Association of American Geographers, 80, 205-222.

Keil, R. (1993): Weltstadt - Stadt der Welt. Internationalisierung und lokale Politik in Los Angeles. Münster, Westfälisches Dampfboot.

Kim, K.C. and Hurh, W.M. (1983): Korean Americans and the "Success Image": A Critique. In: Amerasia Journal, 10(2), 3-21.

Kim, K.C. and Hurh, W.M. (1993): Beyond Assimilation and Pluralism; Syncretic Sociocultural Adaptation of Korean Immigrants in the US. In: Ethnic and Racial Studies, 16, 696-713.

Laux, H.D. und Thieme, G. (1992): Jenseits des Schmelztiegels: Die asiatische Einwanderung in die USA und das Beispiel der Koreaner in Los Angeles. In: Die Erde, 123, 191-205.

Lee, C.S. and Sloan, L. (1994): 'It's Our Turn Now'. Prop 187: As California cracks down on illegals, blacks and Hispanics fight a deeper ethnic war. In: Newsweek, 124, No. 21, 21 November, 27.

Light, I. and Bonacich, E. (1988): Immigrant Entrepreneurs. Koreans in Los Angeles 1965-1982. Berkeley, Los Angeles and Oxford, University of California Press.

Martin, Ph. and Midgley, E. (1994): Immigration to the United States: Journey to an Uncertain Destination. Population Bulletin, 49(2).

Min, P.G. (1990): Problems of Korean Immigrant Entrepreneurs. In: International Migration Review, 24, 436-455.

O'Hare, W.P. (1992): America's Minorities - The Demographics of Diversity. Population Bulletin, 47(4).

Oliver, M.L., Johnson, J.H. jr. and Farrell, W.C. jr. (1993): Anatomy of a Rebellion: A Political-Economic Analysis. In: Gooding-Williams, R. (ed.): Reading Rodney King. Reading Urban Uprising, 117-141. New York and London, Routledge.

Pearlstone, Z. (1990): Ethnic L.A. Beverly Hills, CA, Hillcrest Press.

Portes, A. and Rumbaut, R.G. (1990): Immigrant America. A Portrait. Berkeley, Los Angeles and Oxford, University of California Press.

Razin, E. (1988): Entrepreneurship Among Foreign Immigrants in the Los Angeles and San Francisco Metropolitan Regions. In: Urban Geography, 9, 283-301.

Rieff, D. (1991): Los Angeles: Capital of the Third World. New York et al., Simon & Schuster.

Roseman, C.C., Laux, H.D. and Thieme, G. (1995): Modern EthniCities. In: Roseman, C.C., Laux, H.D. and Thieme, G. (eds.): EthniCity. Geographical Perspectives on Ethnic Change in Modern Cities. Totowa, N.J., Rowman & Littlefield. (forthcoming).

Schlesinger, A.M. jr. (1992): The Disuniting of America. Reflections on a Multicultural Society. New York and London, W.W. Norton & Company.

Scott, A.J. (1988): Metropolis. From the Division of Labor to Urban Form. Berkeley, Los Angeles and London, University of California Press.

Scott, A.J. (1993): Technopolis. High Technology Industry and Regional Development in Southern California. Berkeley, Los Angeles and Oxford, University of California Press.

Soja, E.W. (1989): Postmodern Geographies. The Reassertion of Space in Critical Social Theory. London and New York, Verso.

Storper, M. and Scott, A.J. (1989): The Geographical Foundations and Social Regulation of Flexible Production Complexes. In: Wolch, J. and Dear, M. (eds.): The Power of Geography. How Territory Shapes Social Life, 21-40. Boston, MA, Unwin.

Turner, E. and Allen, J.P. (1991): An Atlas of Population Patterns in Metropolitan Los Angeles and Orange Counties. Northridge, CA.
Wolch, J. and Dear, M. (1993): Malign Neglect. Homelessness in an American City. San Francisco, CA, Jossey-Bass Publishers.

Acknowledgement

This research work was supported by a generous grant of the German Research Foundation (DFG)

Addresses of the Authors

Günter Thieme
Institut für Geographie
Universität Dortmund
Emil-Figge-Str. 50
44227 Dortmund
GERMANY

Hans Dieter Laux
Geographisches Institut
Universität Bonn
Meckenheimer Allee 166
53115 Bonn
GERMANY

INES M. MIYARES

To Be Hmong in America: Settlement Patterns and Early Adaptation of Hmong Refugees in the United States

Introduction

Between 1975 and 1989, nearly nine hundred thousand Southeast Asian refugees were resettled in the United States through a series of "scatter" policies designed to disperse the refugees throughout the nation.[1] The goal of these policies was to inhibit the development of enclaves in order to bring about rapid assimilation into the host communities. The scattering of refugees failed to prevent the development of Southeast Asian ethnic communities. Family reunification and secondary migration led to a concentration of Southeast Asians in nine states; as early as 1981 sixty percent resided in 40 counties (*Mortland and Ledgerwood 1987, 297*).

Prior to the Vietnam War era, there were no significant pre-existing Vietnamese, Cambodian (Khmer), Hmong, or other Lao national communities in the United States. The initial geographic settlement patterns were determined by differential responses by local communities to requests for sponsors. Later waves were sponsored either by family members who had been part of the first wave or by volunteer sponsors from within host communities. Certain communities that responded to the initial call for sponsors retained refugees and ultimately developed large enclaves through family reunification and secondary migration. However, nearly 1,000 communities that were involved in the primary resettlement process saw a complete outmigration of refugees to other locations (*Miyares 1994*). A third set of communities were only moderately or minimally involved in the primary resettlement process, but experienced the development of large refugee communities through secondary migration.

This study examines the experience of the Hmong who have been resettled in the United States. Anthropologists and archeologists have traced the origins of the Hmong to the Yellow River region of China (*Quincy 1988, 13; D. Yang 1992, 253*). Hmong culture developed as an adaptation to a long history of a migratory people without a homeland. Hmong share a strong cultural identity although dispersed throughout southern China, northern Vietnam, northern Thailand, northern Myanmar, northern Laos, and since the fall of the Royal Lao government in 1975, in Australia, France, Canada, Argentina, and the United States (*D. Yang 1992, 253*).

The highland region of northern Laos is the primary source area for Hmong refugees resettled in the U.S. Their refugee status results from involvement in covert operations in Laos during the Vietnam conflict. Participation in the French/Lao resistance of the Japanese occupation of Laos during World War II led the Hmong to develop the reputation of being fierce guerrilla fighters. During the 1970s, Hmong guerrillas, under the command of General VANG Pao and clan leaders, and with the assistance of the American military, organized a temporarily effective deterrence of the Pathet Lao. However, with the fall of the Royal Lao government in 1975, thousands of Hmong were killed for their cooperation with the American military and for their guerrilla activities. Those that were able fled across the Mekong River to Ban Vinai refugee camp in Thailand. If qualified for refugee status, sponsors were found to facilitate resettlement in third countries.

The evolution of the ethnic geography of the Hmong in the U.S. is unique in several aspects. There were no pre-existing enclaves prior to 1975 that would have influenced settlement patterns.

The most significant Hmong enclave in terms of population and sociopolitical influence in the U.S. and possibly in the world - Fresno, California - formed as a result of secondary migration, not as a result of the federal resettlement program.

Southeast Asian refugee enclaves have formed through a combination of two processes. The first is primary resettlement in locations where large numbers of sponsors assumed the responsibility for a refugee individual or household. The second is through secondary migration. In the context of this study, a secondary migrant is a refugee who is primarily resettled in a location determined by the sponsoring agency, and then chooses to migrate elsewhere within the destination country. From the time the refugee enters a country of first asylum (the location of refugee camps) until he or she is resettled, migration decisions are determined by policy. Once resettled, the refugee is then faced with the decision of whether to remain in the original location determined by the sponsoring agency or to secondarily migrate to another location.

National Geographic Patterns of Resettlement

Between 1975 and 1989, 197,538 primary refugees from Laos were resettled in the United States. The first year of Southeast Asian refugee resettlement, 1975, was dominated by refugees from Vietnam. Of the 130,400 refugees resettled, 425 were from Laos. That year, the primary voluntary sponsoring agency or "volag" responsible for Lao resettlement was the Iowa Refugee Service Center. Three hundred and thirty-five or 78.8% of those from Laos were resettled in Iowa, with most in Des Moines.

During the following year, the cohort of Lao primary refugees was 7.5 times larger and the resettlement patterns began to reflect the scatter policy. Sponsors came forward in urban centers throughout the South, West, and Midwest. Many of the communities involved had either no or very small pre-existing Asian communities. Patterns reflect the willingness of host community members to sponsor families through the recruitment processes of the various volags.

In 1977, only 360 primary Lao refugees arrived in the U.S. Unlike in 1975, these were scattered as individuals and households throughout the country. The patterns over the next several years begin to reflect the tension between the scatter method of resettlement and the development of incipient enclaves.

The first visible Hmong enclave was in St. Paul.[2] The benefits perceived by other Hmong of being near key leaders resettled in St. Paul led many to remain. The same process began to occur in communities across Wisconsin. Through secondary migration, refugees resettled as dispersed families joined fellow clan members in the upper Midwest. As earlier refugees converted their residency status to resident alien, they were able to become sponsors of family members remaining in countries of first asylum. From 1978 to 1989, St. Paul (Ramsey County) maintained a dominant role in the relative distribution of primary refugees from Laos as former refugees continued to welcome family members.

In 1978, the Hmong population in the San Joaquin Valley was still relatively small. With few exceptions, refugees were being resettled in the major population centers in the San Francisco Bay Area and Southern California. General VANG Pao had chosen Santa Ana as his "base of operation" as both the continuing figurehead of Hmong national unity and politics and of Lao Family Community Inc. This drew and retained Lao refugees in Southern California. However, few were being resettled in San Joaquin Valley communities. Those that were resettled in the valley were placed in Stockton, an urban center that has retained primary refugees and drawn secondary migrants from Vietnam, Cambodia, and numerous ethnic groups from Laos.

The new decade brought continuing waves of refugees from Southeast Asia. Twice as many Lao refugees (54,502) arrived in 1980 as had in 1979. While many were resettled as "free cases" as individuals or families, much of the resettlement occurred in urban centers that had been active participants in resettlement in earlier years. The most important primary resettlement node was St. Paul.

By 1980, the United States Catholic Conference (USCC), the dominant "volag" in Lao refugee resettlement, sought out key leaders within the refugee communities to facilitate the resettlement process. While the "scatter method" was still national policy, USCC began resettling refugees in clusters, attempting to pre-empt the secondary migration process. USCC recognized the importance of resettling *communities* as opposed to *individuals* in facilitating the adjustment process.

One of those employed by USCC was VANG Chou,[3] nephew of General VANG Pao and leader of the VANG clan. He and his family were originally resettled in Santa Ana in 1976. VANG had received about nine years of education in Laos and was multilingual, speaking Hmong, Lao, Thai, English, and French. During the war, he was the first Hmong to be trained as a fighter pilot. Despite exposure to education and western technology while still in Laos and a very brief stay in refugee camps, VANG felt overwhelmed by the size and pace of Southern California's urban centers. He learned about Merced, a small city in the San Joaquin Valley, an agricultural region with a similar climate and diversity of crops to his native Laos. In May 1977, he moved his family to Merced, the first Hmong family to arrive.

The San Joaquin Valley Hmong communities remained small for several years. In 1977, there were only thirteen families in Merced, one in Fresno, and several in Stockton. VANG Chou and General VANG Pao perceived the Valley to be a good location for the Hmong as the agricultural component of the region would decrease the stress of social and economic adjustment to American culture. Many of the crops grown in the region were the same as those grown by Hmong farmers in Laos, and the climate allowed for the introduction of new crops from their native Lao highlands.

While maintaining his base in Santa Ana, General VANG Pao initiated a plan to purchase the Del Monte Farm near Planada in rural Merced County. He hoped to build a self-sufficient Hmong community on this 3,500 acre farm. Although the plan did not materialize, the area's Hmong population peaked and waned as families came to the area to be part of the proposed community and then returned to locations of resettlement or to where other kin resided. By the end of the decade of the 1970s, there were again only thirteen families in Merced. VANG Pao returned to Montana where he owned a ranch, and was joined by VANG Chou and his family, the latter having found employment in the region.

In 1980, VANG Chou commenced working for USCC in Spokane, Washington. His responsibilities were to help locate sponsors, housing, and employment for new refugees. He worked closely with local farmers who would employ large numbers of Hmong as field laborers, particularly during the harvest season. When he returned to Merced in 1982 to rejoin family members who had remained there, he was followed by Hmong he had helped resettle in Spokane. Clan loyalties and the perceived benefits of being near the clan leader resulted in traditional Hmong chain migration patterns.

By the early 1980s, clan leaders were becoming concerned with their loss of authority resulting from the dispersal of the community. This was compounded by new leadership emerging among younger clan members who had learned English. The influence of American culture was perceived to be destroying the traditional roles of women and to be negatively influencing the youth. Active steps were taken to reunite the clans. The San Joaquin Valley was again selected, this time by leaders of several clans, as the new focus for the Hmong community.

Initial warm receptions by sponsoring families and agencies and by the communities at-large of Fresno and Merced strongly influenced the selection of these two locations as sites to reunite dispersed Hmong. The Mediterranean climate of the valley was perceived as sufficiently similar to the monsoon climate of Laos. Unable to adjust to urban industrial settings of primary resettlement, many Hmong were drawn to the smaller cities in Central California. The Hmong came to the valley expecting to farm, but had difficulty purchasing land or even finding employment in agriculture.

There is a Hmong saying that "rumors travel faster by word of mouth than by telephone wire." Word concerning the establishment of Hmong enclaves in the valley passed quickly through informal kin communication networks. Despite difficulties in obtaining employment, rapid secondary migration commenced soon after clan leaders selected Merced and Fresno as destinations. Smaller "satellite" enclaves emerged in the cities of Porterville and Visalia in Tulare County and in Stockton in San Joaquin County. However, the primary city for the Hmong became Fresno. As secondary migrants established themselves in Fresno, they became sponsors of new refugees. Fresno emerged as the "port-of-entry" enclave for growing numbers of primary refugees, with Merced attaining importance in the relative distribution of new refugees from Laos by 1982.

Beginning in 1983, Fresno began a gradual movement toward dominating the national patterns. Between 1985 and 1989, Fresno was the key resettlement node for primary refugees from Laos, with most being Hmong. Growing numbers of Hmong moved to Fresno and became sponsors of family members remaining in Thai refugee camps. By the end of the decade, even St. Paul was drawfed by Fresno's dominance in primary resettlement.

Several counties in Southern states involved in resettling refugees from Laos did develop and retain ethnic Lao enclaves. Many of these such as New Orleans and Atlanta have viable Vietnamese and Cambodian communities as well. However, the largest communities are in the San Joaquin Valley of California.

The Hmong are much more concentrated than the ethnic Lao, with two dominant subregions: the San Joaquin Valley and Minnesota/Wisconsin. Secondary migration has been *important* in the growth of enclaves in both regions as shown in *Tab. 1*, but it *dominates* the growth patterns in the Central California communities.

As of 1990, the ethnic Lao reside in 1,003 counties, with the largest number (8,174) in Fresno, and the Hmong reside in only 300 counties, with the largest community also in Fresno (18,321).[4] These observations reinforce the continuing centrality of the clan to the Hmong and the emergence of Fresno as the national "Hmong capital" or primary city. Merced, with 6,458 Hmong, and St. Paul, with 11,798 Hmong, continue to serve as key power centers in the national network of Hmong enclaves (*Fig. 1 and 2*).

The determination of Fresno as the "Hmong capital" results from several factors. The perception of Fresno as "home" among the Hmong goes beyond solely the numeric concentrations in the city. The role of the various Hmong clan leaders which reside in Fresno is such that the city is perceived by Hmong elsewhere as "home" whether or not they themselves have ever lived in Fresno. Cultural festivals such as the national Hmong New Year celebration in Fresno attract Hmong from throughout the U.S. and the world. Numerous Hmong organizations such as the Hmong Council and the United Hmong Foundation are headquartered in Fresno. The word *tsev* (pronounced "chae") meaning *home* in Hmong does not refer to a geographical location but to one's relationship to extended family and clan leadership. Traditional Hmong culture is semi-nomadic, based on slash and burn agriculture. Homes and villages change location regularly, but the clan relationships are permanent. Thus, if the clan leader calls Fresno "home", then Fresno becomes *tsev* for those who follow his leadership.

The greatest concentrations of Hmong in Merced County are found in the poorest sections of the county seat of Merced, with large numbers also residing in the co-central city of Atwater. Merced County is much smaller in population and in economic strength than Fresno and has had a more difficult time meeting the needs of the Hmong. In response, the Hmong in Merced have tended to be more activist in addressing the needs of their community. Many of the community-based and university student organizations which have emerged in the Hmong community have their roots in Merced. This enclave serves as a regional political capital and seedbed for local and national leaders.

Not all has gone as well as originally hoped. Agricultural land has been difficult to obtain. Lack of adequate English skills, coupled with high unemployment rates in the valley has hindered the

Tab. 1: Primary Resettlement and Net Secondary Migration for Selected States and Counties[a]: 1975 – 1989, 1990

	Total Primary Refugees from Laos 1975–1989	1990 Hmong Population	1990 Ethnic Lao Population	Total Enumerated Lao and Hmong Populations	Net Secondary Migrants	Primary Refugees as Percent of Population	Net Secondary Migrants as Percent of Population
California	*52,395*	*46,945*	*58,892*	*105,837*	*53,442*	*49.5*	*50.5*
Butte	327	1,294	676	1,970	1,643	16.6	83.4
Fresno	6,040	18,321	8,174	26,493	20,453	22.8	77.2
Merced	2,340	6,458	2,052	8,5120	6,170	27.5	72.5
Sacramento	2,891	5,470	6,935	12,405	9,514	23.3	76.7
San Diego	7,774	1,585	7,025	8,610	836	90.3	9.7
San Joaquin	3,418	4,628	4,236	8,864	5,446	38.6	61.4
Tulare	942	1,874	3,033	4,907	3,965	19.2	80.8
Yuba	518	2,162	625	2,787	2,269	18.6	81.4
Michigan	*3,001*	*2,257*	*2,190*	*4,447*	*1,446*	*67.5*	*32.5*
Wayne	578	1,122	585	1,707	1,129	33,9	66.1
Minnesota	*15,020*	*17,215*	*6,379*	*23,594*	*8,574*	*63.7*	*36.3*
Hennepin	3,569	4,357	3,484	7,841	4,272	45.5	54.5
Ramsey	8,355	11,798	765	12,593	4,238	66.3	33.7
Wisconsin	*9.066*	*16,359*	*3,629*	*19,998*	*10,922*	*45.4*	*54.6*
Brown	961	1,410	295	1,705	744	56.4	43.6
Eau Claire	575	1,485	50	1,535	960	37.5	62.5
La Crosse	869	1,933	85	2,018	1,149	43.1	56,9
Marathon	821	1,968	115	2,083	1,262	39.4	60.6
Milwaukee	2,135	3,354	1,858	5,212	3,077	41.0	59.0
Outagamie	538	1,254	91	1,345	807	40.0	60.0
Sheboygan	508	1,255	109	1,364	856	37.2	62.8

Source: Office of Refugee Resettlement Primary Resettlement Records, 1975 – 1989; 1990 Census of Population and Housing Summary Tape File 3a.
[a] Includes all U.S. counties with enumerated Hmong poplations greater than 1,000.

ability of sixty to seventy percent of Hmong in Merced and up to ninety percent of Hmong in Fresno to come off public assistance (*D. Yang 1992, 255*). Many Hmong are taking advantage of federally funded tertiary migration programs to states such as Texas and North Carolina where there seem to be job opportunities in host communities open to the development of Hmong enclaves.[5] Members of the VANG clan have purchased land in North Carolina and have founded the first Hmong-named town in the U.S., Sam Thong. The incipient poultry enterprises in Sam Thong are attracting growing numbers of San Joaquin Valley Hmong, as are opportunities in manufacturing in Morganton and Charlotte, North Carolina. The Hmong have a long history of being a gypsy-like people that have clearly reaffirmed their commitment to the clan structure. If the leaders residing in Merced or Fresno were to move, at least a large proportion of the enclave would follow.

Fig. 1: Enumerated Hmong Population by County, 1990

Source: Census Bureau STF-1a, 1990

Fig. 2: Enumerated Ethnic Lao Population by County, 1990

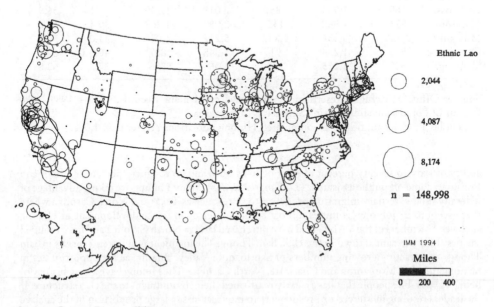

Source: Census Bureau STF-1a, 1990

Redefining Perceptions of Space and Place

Laos is a landlocked underdeveloped political state on the mainland of Southeast Asia. It has only one city of any magnitude, the capital city of Vientiane, with an estimated population of 377,440 or 8.5% of the country's total population. It is one of the least populated states in Asia (4,440,000) and has one of the lowest population densities at about 19 persons/km^2. The neighboring countries of Vietnam and Cambodia have population densities of 210 persons/km^2 and 50 persons/km^2 respectively. Thus, with the exception of Vientiane, the various Lao ethnic groups, including the Hmong, resided in dispersed patterns throughout the bounded territory.

The low density allowed slash-and-burn or *rai* agriculture of Hmong traditional life. In this century, the Hmong in Laos resided in small villages ranging in size from 10 to 20 houses. It was rare to find villages of greater than 50 houses. Most houses were small temporary structures with bamboo walls, dirt floors, and palm frond roofs. In accordance with traditional geomantic practices, main entrances faced the north, determined by the position of the sun. Often with the assistance of the shaman, heads of households would divine the best location, position, and size for the structure that would shelter their families (*Monzel 1994*).

The semi-nomadic lifestyle required simple and portable "furniture", typically woven mats for sleeping and for preparing food. Although there was little physical differentiation of space within Hmong houses, there was an *understood* sense of gender-based use of space. Men occupied the central areas for conversation, teaching sons, weaving mats and baskets, and making and maintaining farming and hunting implements. Cooking areas were "female space" where mothers instructed daughters in food preparation, sewing, and traditional crafts such as *pa ndau*. Hmong villagers were primarily self-sufficient subsistence farmers, sometimes cultivating opium for medicine and as a cash crop in exchange for salt and MSG. There was little exposure to wage labor unless one moved to Vientiane or entered the Royal Lao Army. The most highly respected professions were the farmer, the soldier, and the teacher. Nearly everyone was a farmer, very few were teachers, and most "soldiers" were organized in informal militias which defended local areas (*Hamilton-Merritt 1993, Quincy 1988, H. Yang 1993*).

World War II, the Lao involvement in the Vietnam Conflict, and the Lao Civil War resulted in major changes in settlement patterns among the Hmong residing in the highlands of Laos. Prior to this prolonged period of conflict (1941 to the present), Hmong villages were concentrated in the highlands of northern Laos, particularly in the provinces of Xieng Khoung and Luang Prabang. The greatest number were on the *Plaine des Jarres* or Plain of Jars in central Xieng Khoung Province. During the 1960s, this plain became one of the most contested regions of Laos (*Hamilton-Merritt 1993, Quincy 1988 H. Yang 1993*). The result was mass migration from smaller villages to military bases such as those at Sam Thong, Long Cheng, and Pha Khao. The populations of these bases grew to approximately 15,000, 30,000, and 7,000 respectively (*D. Yang 1993, 18*). The prolonged conflict also drove many to combine villages with other Lao ethnic minorities or to seek safe haven in the jungles.

Ban Vinai refugee camp was the second and became the most important refugee camp for the Hmong. Ban Vinai opened in November 1975, and within a month, housed a refugee population of 12,700. While there were other camps housing Hmong refugees, Ban Vinai became the lead camp for the Hmong and other Lao highlanders. By 1986, Ban Vinai's population exceeded 42,000 and was "home" to 80% of the Hmong in Thailand (*Conroy 1990, 4*). As of January 1994, there are still 25,600 refugees and asylum seekers in Ban Vinai eligible for resettlement, most of whom are Hmong. Of these, 11,500 are in the resettlement process and will most likely go to the United States. An additional 13,300 have refused resettlement for a variety of reasons. Many of these have resided in Ban Vinai for over a decade.[6]

Hmong were provided with minimal food rations by camp officials, resulting in overt and covert (usually theft or intimidation) activities to increase supply. A new overt method for obtaining supplemental food developed in Ban Vinai. Although *rai* cultivation practiced in Laos was *extensive* slash-and-burn farming, the Hmong in Ban Vinai began *intensive* cultivation of vegetables and spices, making small plots near the entrance of family living quarters very productive as seeds became available. Surpluses could be sold or traded to other refugees or via local Thai markets.

Enclave culture in the U.S., especially in Fresno, resembles patterns which emerged in either the three military base refugee camps within Laos or the culture which evolved from survival mechanisms in Ban Vinai refugee camp in Thailand. Nearly all Hmong refugees were processed through Ban Vinai, and their current behavior patterns and landscape signatures have been strongly influenced by that experience.

Most residents of the Hmong communities of Merced and Fresno are former residents of the refugee camp of Ban Vinai in Thailand. The city of Fresno serves as a "port-of-entry" for new refugees and a redistributor of earlier refugees taking advantage of government-sponsored tertiary migration programs to North Carolina and Texas.

Merced County's Hmong community is divided between two cities, Merced and Atwater. The greatest concentration of Hmong are in South Merced adjacent to the fairgrounds in a neighborhood which also houses large concentrations of ethnic Lao, Mexican nationals, Mexican-Americans, and African-Americans. This area serves as a local "port-of-entry" for several immigrant groups and does not hold the regional and national importance of Fresno's "port-of-entry" Hmong neighborhood.

Fresno has received the greatest proportion of *recent* refugees who experienced *long-term* residence in the refugee camps. "Freedom", manifested through self-sufficiency, independence, and a geomantic world view has been replaced by patterns of behavior and economic practices dependent on government provision. Unemployment and dependence on public assistance are evident in all refugee enclaves, but impacts of this are magnified in Fresno since a large proportion of Hmong residents were in Ban Vinai for at least ten to fifteen years.

Within Fresno, there are patterns of Hmong neighborhood succession, with a regional and national "port-of-entry" neighborhood commonly referred to as "Ban Vinai" (*Fig. 3*). The "Ban Vinai" neighborhood is a large apartment complex located in southeast Fresno proximate to the fairgrounds.[7] Most of the residents were formerly in the Thai refugee camp and have recreated a similar landscape and social structure. The use of the term "Ban Vinai" reflects the similarities between the culture which developed in the camps and that which has emerged in a neighborhood dependent on various forms of public assistance for survival.[8]

Residents are not permitted to cultivate the lawn areas which surround the apartments. However, most units have small window boxes or other plots near entrances in which residents are free to garden. The Hmong tend to intensively cultivate these plots, raising fruits, vegetables, and spices native to Southeast Asia. This practice, initiated at Ban Vinai in Thailand, has become a dominant "Hmong signature" on Fresno's landscape. Additionally, the "Asian Village" shopping center which borders the complex hosts several Hmong specialty shops and service agencies.

From there, Hmong move northward to central Fresno, the northeastern suburb of Pinedale, or the northwestern suburb of Clovis. These areas have numerous apartment complexes in which the majority, if not all, of the residents are Hmong. The residential patterns are not necessarily contiguous as nearly all Hmong reside in "Section 8" or federally supported housing. Fresno's planning policies require that "Section 8" housing be dispersed throughout the city. Apartments in these complexes are made available to qualified applicants of any national origin, but those rented by Hmong households are readily identifiable through the form of gardening. Preferred complexes appear to be those with courtyards or open areas. Much of Hmong community life occurs outdoors and it is very common to see large numbers of Hmong engaging in conversation, work, meals, and play in the open areas between apartment buildings. As in "Ban Vinai", the central Fresno Hmong neighborhood has developed its own small shopping center.

Fig. 3: Hmong Residents of Fresno and Immediate Suburbs by Block Group, 1990

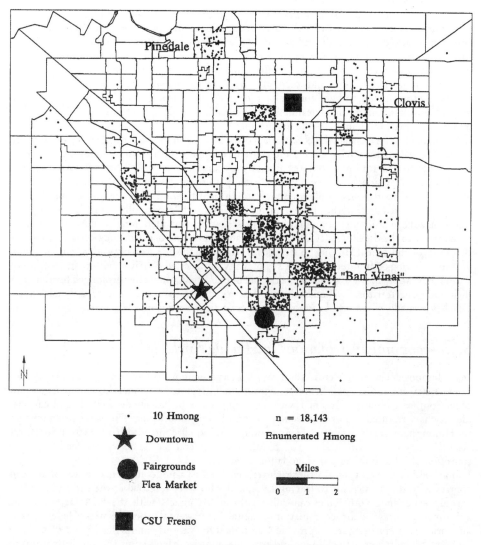

Source: Census Bureau STF-1a, 1990

Within apartments, there is also a cultural signature which suggests the duration of residence in the United States. As traditional Hmong life was based on a semi-nomadic slash-and-burn economy, permanent structures were rare in villages. Families seldom became truly settled, and this was reflected in the patterning of furniture within the dwelling place. Typical shared living areas had only essential items. Those unnecessary for daily life remained packed and stacked along walls of the dwelling, prepared for the next move. Family members slept on bamboo mats brought out in the evenings and stored in the mornings. Other furniture items such as mats on which food was served or seats were also brought out only as necessary. The semi-nomadic lifestyle inhibited the development of permanent dwellings, creating living quarters reflecting "unsettledness" or preparation for the next move.

This pattern continues among many Hmong adults whose socialization experience was predominantly in either Laos or Ban Vinai refugee camp. Living rooms reflect an "unsettledness" with boxes stacked against walls and only utilitarian furniture and household items in the shared space. Couches, if present, are among the few permanently placed furniture items, probably due to the awkwardness of moving. Chairs, tables, and other more portable pieces of furniture are brought out only as necessary and stored after use. The activity space for women in such homes is typically the kitchen, utilized for cooking, *pa dnau*, and conversation. The activity space for men for conversation, business dealings, and the making or repairs of tools, baskets, and other traditionally male implements is the living room.

In homes of Hmong raised in the U.S., there is often little difference in the patterning of furniture in central areas such as living rooms and those of members of the host community. Furniture styles range from simple to elaborate based on the economic status of the individual household, but there is a greater degree of "settledness" in the patterning of furniture placement. The shared living space of apartments of older or more traditional Hmong gives the impression that the family is prepared for another imminent move. Younger Hmong, other than more typically transient college students, communicate a message through their interior design a sense of permanence to the dwelling place. Beyond the landscape signatures, the long-term influence of Ban Vinai on individual Hmong households is relative to the duration of residence in the camp. Fresno's Hmong community is comprised of many refugees who arrived within the past five to seven years. Many of these spent over a decade in Ban Vinai, often after prolonged hostilities in their traditional territories. Thousands are at least a generation removed from traditional culture. This has created a situation of economic and social diversity within the enclaves.

Socio-economic Adaptations in Hmong Enclaves

In the Hmong enclaves of Merced and Fresno, internal economies have emerged but have yet to become as strong as those of other refugee groups in the region. Long-standing animosity toward other Southeast Asians, combined with a growing sense of independent ethnic and national identity have resulted in a firm resistance to non-Hmong middlemen. This is the first time that the Hmong perceive themselves as having a unique and equal identity with others from Southeast Asia. Hmong are entering the role of middleman in several economic sectors, facilitating the transition of other Hmong to a wage-labor economy.

Hmong middlemen are typically those who received at least a moderate formal education and had contact with the West prior to leaving Laos, and who were resettled in the early years. Pre-existing experience with American culture through contacts with the CIA facilitated the adjustment process and the accumulation of capital. Many were also beneficiaries of federal, state, and local programs designed to provide seed capital for various enterprises (*Fass 1986*). These serve as a bridge between the Hmong and host communities in facilitating the transition from the welfare economy to various wage-labor sectors.

The majority of the Hmong in Fresno and Merced have had a very difficult time entering the wage-labor economy. Sixty to seventy percent depend on some form of public assistance as a primary income (*D. Yang 1992, 255*). While this places most households below the poverty level according to American standards, incomes are higher than they ever were in Laos. It is common to find extended families sharing dwelling places, pooling their incomes to meet the needs of the total household. The Hmong are very conservative in their spending habits. The uncertainty of a farming economy and the stark poverty during the war and refugee camp experiences have resulted in a fragile economic culture. Major expenditures are typically limited to automobiles, televisions, VCRs, and traditional costumes.

Although economic needs are met by public assistance, there is great frustration at the perceived inability to enter the wage-labor market. Few Hmong had been exposed to wage-labor as most were subsistence level slash-and-burn or *rai* agriculturists. In Laos, the entire family would labor together to make farms successful. As young children were able, they assumed responsibilities for simpler tasks such as feeding chickens. Fathers maintained a central role in parenting, especially of sons, as the family spent the workday as a unit. Most employment in an American context is individual, requiring workers to leave the household for the day. Making that adjustment has been very difficult for many Hmong men. This is compounded by a lack of English language skills, literacy, and numeracy.

While seasonal agricultural employment opportunities are prevalent in the San Joaquin Valley, Hmong are in competition with Mexican and other Spanish-speaking laborers. As the latter have a long-standing presence in the region, many labor contractors are fluent in Spanish and give preference in hiring to Spanish or English speakers.

Growing numbers of Hmong are becoming labor contractors either in agriculture or reforestation projects which require leaving the home for extended periods of time. This removes the barriers caused by lack of English and formal education. The barrier caused by the need to work as an individual as opposed to a family has been equally difficult to overcome. Mexican immigrants and others previously experienced in individually-based temporary or migrant employment have been more active in seeking jobs from Hmong contractors than have the Hmong themselves.

Hmong who have accumulated sufficient capital are purchasing strawberry farms in the San Joaquin Valley. Farm owners hire members of their clans as field laborers. As in Laos, families work together in the fields. In the Merced area, Hmong farmers have over 400 acres of strawberries in year-round production. Fresno Hmong also have hundreds of acres of strawberries. Using labor-intensive family-based techniques, there are now two strawberry seasons - the traditional April harvest and a new November harvest. As a result, Hmong farmers are acquiring a growing percentage of the market.[9]

The 1993 growing season saw a significant setback to many of the Fresno area strawberry farmers. Hmong farm owners hired clan members who would labor as households in the fields, following traditional patterns. However, many of those employed in these farms were either receiving forms of public assistance that would be lost if wage employment were reported, or were younger than the minimum age defined by child labor laws in California. Fresno County Department of Social Services investigators had difficulty proving the first violation, but were convinced it was more prevalent than the second. Using the vehicle of child labor violation penalties, stiff fines were imposed on numerous Hmong farmers. Unable to pay the fines, and unable to run economically viable farms without clan labor, many Hmong farmers are considering taking their farms out of production.[10]

Several Hmong farmers are among those introducing a new crop to California consumers - the Asian pear. This fleshy fruit is gaining popularity among Californians who enjoy exotic new products. Common to Southeast Asia, this fruit also allows Hmong farmers to utilize familiar production techniques while adjusting to the western economic system. Asian pear farms are at much lower levels of production than are strawberries as demand is still small and trees take several years to reach maturity.

Another agricultural sector into which the Hmong are entering in growing numbers is vegetable garden truck farming. This involves smaller capital investments to be economically viable. As with the strawberry and Asian pear farms, truck farmers hire clan members as field laborers and to assist in sales at flea markets and farmers markets. More successful truck farmers are traveling to several major markets throughout California each week. As Mexican-origin residents of San Joaquin Valley cities also frequent these markets, many Hmong truck farmers have learned Spanish and can be heard hawking vegetables in both languages.

The flea markets are becoming major economic centers of Hmong enclaves. The open market atmosphere and freedom to barter for prices parallels Hmong traditional experience. In addition to fresh produce, household items, clothing, crafts, and electronic equipment are available at highly discounted prices. The flea markets in Fresno and Merced also have booths that specifically target unique Hmong needs. There are certain clothing styles preferred by older Hmong women that are produced by women in the enclave and sold at the flea market. Bolts of brightly colored Hmong traditional material are sold at numerous booths as are traditional holiday outfits, often imported from Thailand or China and hand-sewn *pa ndau* ("flowery cloth" and storycloth) accessories.

Pa ndau or "flowery cloths" are highly detailed handsewn patterns combining appliqué and cross-stitch techniques. These have traditionally been used to embellish Hmong ceremonial outfits. However, the popularity of *pa ndau* among host community members has led to products such as purses, eyeglass cases, pillow covers, and wall hangings. Storycloths, embroidered records of Hmong legends and family histories, have also become very popular and valuable in the host as well as enclave communities (*Livo and Cha 1991, 11-12*). While flea market booths may not specialize in these craft items, it is not unusual to find several for sale at booths selling other products.

Hmong ceremonial outfits are also commonly available at flea markets. They are comprised of multiple pieces of intricately designed needlework, silver jewelry, and hats. Hmong tradition calls for new outfits to celebrate each New Year and in courting. Wearing old clothes at New Year is believed to bring bad luck. As courting continues to be prevalent at the New Year celebration, there is high seasonal demand for traditional outfits. The deceased are traditionally buried in ceremonial outfits in order to be recognized as Hmong in the afterlife (*Livo and Cha 1991, 10*). This results in a year-round demand for these products.

Chickens and pigs hold important roles in both the Hmong diet and shamanist practices and are now raised as forms of income. Live chickens and pigs are sacrificed to commemorate important events such as births, deaths, marriages, and holidays such as New Year. Live chickens are available at particular booths at flea markets operated by women whose products are seen as appropriate for ceremonial offerings. While not commonly sold at flea markets, several large pig farms have emerged in the Fresno and Merced areas, providing ceremonial pigs raised in traditional ways. Sacrificed animals are eaten and comprise an important component of Hmong dietary protein. Traditional Hmong prefer fresh chicken and pork to that available in host community grocery stores or butcher shops, resulting in economically viable enterprises.

Clothing produced for older Hmong women, *pa ndau*, storycloths, and traditional ceremonial outfits are also sold door to door. Since "rumors go faster by word of mouth than by telephone wire," marketing of these items goes by word of mouth, supplementing public assistance incomes. Known also in the Hmong communities are the women who informally raise ceremonial chickens and pigs. Small numbers of hens and sows are kept for eggs, piglets, and ceremonies, providing for both the needs of the community and "therapeutic" occupations for older women experiencing difficulty in adjusting to American society.

Video and audio cassettes have become important vehicles for reinforcing the Hmong language, music, poetry, and dance. While most are imported and marketed in the formal economy, there is an unknown amount of private production and marketing. Again, sales are door-to-door within the enclave and through word of mouth.

In the early 1980s, bartered labor was prevalent among unemployed Hmong. This has decreased as Hmong have moved into wage-labor employment in agriculture and other sectors or have opened small businesses. The informal economy has instead focused on the production and marketing of items that meet unique needs of the enclaves.

Although they comprise an estimated 3 - 5% of Fresno's population,[11] the Hmong are highly underrepresented in sales employment in host community businesses. Additionally, there is limited availability of Hmong food items and cultural media in mainstream stores. Meeting this demand has provided a niche for Hmong entrepreneurs, but in a way that is economically rational only if understood within the context of culture.

The clan structure as the organizing element of Hmong culture is as evident in small businesses as it is in agricultural labor. There are more Hmong grocery stores than can be efficiently supported by the community. Each clan represented in Merced and Fresno operates its own store. Clan members are expected to support operations owned by their family members, whether or not desired items might be available at another clan's store. It is seen as an offense to shop at a store owned by Hmong with whom one does not have genealogical or marital connections. This is magnified by centuries-old feuds between clans. Despite clan support, though, most Hmong grocery stores are only marginally successful economic ventures.

A similar pattern is seen in shops specializing in cultural media - video and audio cassettes of Hmong language, songs, poetry, and dance. However, as this is a more specialized sector, the expectation to support clan-held stores is less. Part of the supply is created locally as Hmong artists partner with enclave-based production studios. Locally produced video and audio cassettes range from traditional dance, songs, and poetry to performances by the growing number of Hmong rock groups and balladeers. Most of these tapes are produced in Hunan Province in China, the region with the largest number of dispersed Hmong, and in Thailand, either in Bangkok or in areas near Ban Vinai refugee camp along the Thai-Lao border. These account for a large proportion of the international trade linked to Fresno's internal Hmong economy.

As many of the products desired by the Hmong community are not readily available in the United States, businesses such as the "Fresno Import and Export Company" have developed to meet this need. Food items such as sticky rice and traditional spices are imported from Thailand and marketed through the Hmong grocery stores. Cultural media and video cassettes of movies dubbed in Hmong are also imported in large numbers.

Import-export companies are also "formalizing" the informal economies of Ban Vinai refugee camp. *Pa ndau* and storycloths have become chic artistic collector's items in the U.S. because of the intricacy of the needlework and the deep symbolism in the patterns. Younger Hmong women raised in the enclaves are often not trained in the skills of traditional crafts as were their mothers and grandmothers. Thus the demand for *pa ndau* and storycloths at American craft fairs is often met by importing items produced in Ban Vinai in Thailand. Profits are remitted to the camp, resulting in improved standards of living for refugees still awaiting resettlement.

As education increases among the Hmong and as the communities develop a sense of permanence, a Hmong professional class is developing, providing services never before needed in the culture. The first major expenditure for most Hmong households after a television is a car. As the number of automobiles owned by Hmong increases, so does the demand for insurance. Economically successful Hmong become able to purchase homes and other property but are hesitant to approach non-Hmong brokers. Also, employed Hmong often have difficulty understanding tax codes and tax return forms. Thus a growing number of bilingual Hmong adults with at least a moderate education are entering professions which provide these services. Hmong, as well as other area refugees, are more likely to trust members of their own national group for these services before they would trust members of the host community. By capturing this otherwise untapped market, many entrepreneurs are becoming economically successful in trades previously unknown among the Hmong.

One of the roles played by community-based organizations identified by TREUDLEY (*1949, 45*) was to help immigrants adjust to American business organization. This included training in skills as well as work values and practices such as time schedules, tax laws, "paperwork", and importance of professional organizations. The *organizations* serve as middlemen, linking the immigrant community with formal sectors of the economy.

Numerous organizations serve in this middleman role for the Hmong in the San Joaquin Valley. The most important are the various local offices of Lao Family Community. The primary function of the Fresno and Merced Lao Family Community organizations is to facilitate economic self-reliance through education, job training, and English language instruction. Other

training has included "American survival skills" such as drivers' training, essential for negotiating in "suburban-style" cities with limited public transportation systems.
Staff members at Lao Family also serve as "cultural brokers" and middlemen in the provision of social services such as medical and mental health care. The refugee experience has been such that medical and mental health care are essential in the adjustment process. If these needs are not met, it is unlikely that refugees will move out of the welfare economy into any form of wage-labor or entrepreneurial sectors. The staffs at Lao Family in Merced and Fresno are predominantly Hmong who arrived early in the resettlement process and have strong links to both the enclave community and the host community. They are the best positioned to stand in the gap, bridging two very different cultures and facilitating the mutual adjustment process.

To Be Hmong in America

When Hmong adults are asked what it means to be Hmong in America, to a person they list cultural values and practices they hope the younger generation passes on to their children. The most frequently cited are language; commitment to family and clan; New Year celebrations, especially the gifts to elders; a sense of self-awareness as Hmong; traditional songs, dances, and poetry; and traditional Hmong arts and crafts. When Hmong college students are asked the same question, they struggle to respond. They realize that their generation will be responsible for redefining Hmong culture for their children. Many are concerned, though, that they do not sufficiently understand their traditions. So much has changed that it becomes difficult to know what is "traditional" and what has already been redefined.

As the Hmong have never had their own homeland, they have experienced numerous migrations prior to coming to the United States. This most recent migration has completely redefined numerous aspects of Hmong culture, but cultural dynamism has also become central to the Hmong way of life. The following is a Hmong proverb which expresses a predisposition to adaptability (D. Yang 1992, 255):

| *Hla dej yuav hle khau* | [Cross the river, you'll take off your shoes; |
| *Tsiv teb tsaws chaw yuav hle hau* | Flee from your country, you'll take off your status] |

Many traditional Hmong practices are either prohibited in the U.S. or are inhibited by the national settlement patterns. While many Hmong traditional practices seem unusual or even absurd to those whose world view has been formed in a western technological society, it can be difficult to convince adults socialized in Third World settings to abandon known behavior. Among these are slash-and-burn agriculture, public animal sacrifices, and adolescent marriages, all of which come into direct conflict with the laws and values of American society. Adjusting to American laws and values is resulting in a redefinition of Hmong culture as certain practices are adapted to an American context and as Hmong are exposed to ideas and opportunities never anticipated in their former home. The culture emerging in the various Hmong enclaves reflects this culture change process. Thus the enclaves serve adaptational settlements, manifesting the dynamism of culture.

In a welcoming speech at the Hmong Culture Night at CSU Stanislaus in April 1994, Thae XIONG, president of the Hmong Student Association, included the following comments concerning the relationship between Hmong culture and the process of acculturation to dominant American culture.[12]

> "Here at CSU Stanislaus, we have many different cultures from all over the world. One of the goals that our club tries to achieve is to share our cultures with others and at the same time learn something from their culture. After all, the Hmong have migrated to many lands in the course

of our history and have borrowed many good things from many other cultures. In Hmong we have a proverb: *Nyob luag ntug yuav tsum yoog luag txuj; nyob luag teb yuav tsum yoog luag ci.* It literally translates into English as "Live in their world, you have to follow their rules. Live in their land you have to obey their ways." This proverb reflects our realization that we must be adaptable and changeable when living among other cultures.

But acculturation is a complex and interesting matter. For some, changes are quick and easy and in less than 20 years, some Hmong have undergone changes that have historically taken other people centuries. While for others it may take many more generations. Some Hmong have been here in the USA for almost 20 years now and have already obtained the American Dream. Others have been here a mere few months or years and are still facing many difficulties in the acculturation process, mainly because of language barriers and the different American lifestyle. Many of our elders still hold on to our traditional culture, while our young brothers and sisters are slowly losing much of our valuable knowledges and values. Those of us that are of college age have now realized that there is nothing wrong with *some* of us clinging to our own culture and have begun the road to rediscover some our people's lost knowledges and values. Yet, many of us still find ourselves in two worlds. One is in Hmong society where we try to live up to the expectations of our elders. The other is in American society where we try to learn new ways to survive in this complex and high tech society. As a young Hmong American, I would ask all people to change and adapt to the conditions and demands of one's environment, but not to be ashamed of one's own cultural heritage... for these are the very fabrics of who we are."

Summary

This study examines the evolution of the Hmong ethnic geography in the United States and the role of Hmong enclaves as adaptational settlements for first-generation residents. The relationship between the federal resettlement program and subsequent volitional migration patterns is examined utilizing data provided by the Office of Refugee Resettlement and from the 1990 Census of Population and Housing. In-depth interviews with key informants from the Hmong enclaves of Merced and Fresno in California provide a description of changes in Hmong culture which have occurred at each step of the resettlement process. The Hmong have a cultural propensity toward adaptation, raising the question of what it will mean to be Hmong in America.

Keywords: Hmong, refugees, resettlement, adaptation

Zusammenfassung

Diese Studie untersucht die Entwicklung der geographischen Verteilung der Hmongs in den Vereinigten Staaten und die Rolle ihrer Enklaven als einen Mechanismus für Siedlungen der ersten Einwanderungsgeneration. Die Beziehung zwischen dem bundesstaatlichen Siedlungsprogramm und dem darauffolgenden Aussiedlungsverhalten ist untersucht, und belegt mit Daten, welche vom Büro für Flüchtlingsaussiedlung und aus der 1990 durchgeführten Volkszählung zur Verfügung gestellt wurden. Gründliche Befragungen von Schlüsselinformanten aus den hmongischen Enklaven von Merced und Fresno in Kalifornien beschreiben die Veränderung in der Hmong-Kultur, welche auf jeder Stufe des Wiederaussiedlungsprozesses stattgefunden haben. Die Hmong haben eine kulturelle Neigung zur Anpassung, die die Frage aufwirft, was es bedeuten wird, Hmong in Amerika zu sein.

Acknowledgement

This research was funded by National Science Foundation Dissertation Grant SBR-9304124. The author would also like to thank Dr. Kevin E. MC HUGH, Department of Geography, Arizona State University, for his input throughout the development and completion of the project.

Notes

[1] The Office of Refugee Resettlement data records show a total of 891,059 Southeast Asian Refugees were resettled in the United States during this period.
[2] Personal interviews: VANG Chou, Maykou VANG, Ze XIONG, Dr. Tony VANG, Pa Lai VUE, Thae XIONG.
[3] Descriptions of the formation of the valley enclaves developed primarily from personal interviews with VANG Chou, Dr. Tony VANG, Ze XIONG, with further information provided by Pa Lai VUE, Yang HER, Thae XIONG, Maymou LEE.
[4] A total of 1,687 counties received primary refugees from Laos between 1975 and 1989. There was complete outmigration from 801 counties by the 1990 census.
[5] Actual numbers are difficult to estimate or cite as a large proportion of these are "failed migrations" - migrants who return to Merced or Fresno within a few months of moving to Texas or North Carolina.
[6] These data were cited by Werner BLADDER, Regional Director for Asia, United Nations High Commissioner for Refugees at a public hearing in Fresno, CA on January 13, 1994 concerning the desire of the Royal Thai Government to close Ban Vinai refugee camp.
[7] The census block group containing "Ban Vinai" had over 2,000 enumerated Hmong in 1990.
[8] Stockton, CA's "port-of-entry" neighborhood is also known as "Ban Vinai". None of my informants were aware of a Hmong neighborhood utilizing a Hmong toponym other than Sam Thong, North Carolina. They attribute the use of "Ban Vinai" to the sense of dependency and lack of self-determination originating in the camp.
[9] Actual numbers of Hmong involved in these ventures were impossible to obtain. California data on acreage in production are not disaggregated by the national origin of the farmer. Most farms are owned by several families; labor is seasonal and fluid in nature.
[10] Personal interviews: Staff of Fresno County Department of Social Services, VANG Chou, Ze XIONG, Dr. Tony VANG.
[11] According to the census, the Hmong comprise 2.7% of Fresno's population, the ethnic Lao 1.2%, Vietnamese 0.3%, and Cambodians 0.6%. The range suggested here incorporates concerns of a possible undercount.
[12] Portions of this speech, presented on April 16, 1994 at CSU Stanislaus in Turlock, CA, are included as written with permission of its author, Thae XIONG, a fourth-year university student (sociology). Thae is the first in his family to attend college. His parents had no formal education, yet he intends to pursue a graduate degree after completion of his teaching credential.

References

Bureau of the Census (1990): 1990 Census of Population and Housing STF 1A, 3A, CD-ROM.
Conroy, T. P. (1990): Highland Lao Refugees. Bangkok, Thailand, UNHCR, Royal Thai Government MOI.
Fass, S. (1986) Innovations in the struggle for self-reliance: The Hmong experience in the United States. In: International Migration Review, 20(2), 351-379.
Hamilton-Merritt, J. (1993): Tragic Mountains: The Hmong, the Americans, and the Secret Wars for Laos, 1942-1992. Bloomington, IN, Indiana University Press.
Livo, N. J., Cha, D. (1991): Folk Stories of the Hmong. Englewood, CO, Libraries Unlimited, Inc.
Miyares, I. M. (1994): Ethnic Enclave Formation and Function: A Study of Hmong Refugees in the United States. Ph.D. (Geography), Arizona State University.
Monzel, K. L. (1994): Divining the landscape: Use of geomancy by Hmong refugees from Laos. Unpublished manuscript, 1994 meeting of the Association of American Geographers, March 29-April 2, 1994, San Francisco, CA.
Mortland, C. A., and Ledgerwood, J. (1987): Secondary migration among Southeast Asian refugees in the United States. In: Urban Anthropology, 16, 291-326.
Quincy, K. (1988): Hmong: History of a People. Cheney, WA, Eastern Washington University Press.
Treudley, M. B. (1949) Formal organization and the americanization process, with special reference to the Greeks of Boston. In: American Sociological Review, 14(1), 44-53.
Yang, D. (1992): The Hmong: Enduring traditions. In: Lewis, J., ed. Minority Cultures in Laos: Kammu, Lua', Lahu, Hmong, and Mien. Rancho Cordova, CA, Southeast Asia Community Resource Center, 252-324.
Yang, D. (1993): Hmong at the Turning Point. Minneapolis, MN, WorldBridge Associates, Ltd.
Yang, H. (1993): Through the Spirit's Door: A True Story of the Hmong People at War: 1975-1980. Arlington, VA, HYCO International.

Address of the Author

Ines M. Miyares
Department of Geology and Geography
Hunter College-CUNY
695 Park Avenue
New York, NY 10021
USA

BARBARA HAHN

Poverty and Affordable Housing in New York City

From 1980 to 1990 the population of New York City grew from 7,1 million to 7,3 million or by 3.5 percent. Even though the proportion of households whose incomes were below the poverty line was relatively stable during the 80s, the number of people living in poverty is very impressive. The official poverty definition is based on pre-tax money income only, excluding capital gains, and does not include the value of noncash benefits such as employer-provided health insurance, food stamps, or *Medicaid* (*Bureau of the Census 1992, 11*). Opposed to a national rate of about 13 percent, one in four or about 1,8 million New Yorkers lived below the poverty line in 1991. At that time the poverty line for a family of three was $ 11,400 (*New York City Coalition for the Homeless 1993*).

Due to several factors it is becoming more and more difficult for many New Yorkers to find an affordable place to live. Whether housing is affordable depends on the relationship between housing costs and incomes. New York City is a city of tenants. Only 30 percent of the households own their home, whereas 70 percent rent their home (*City of New York, Department of City Planning 1991a, 6*).

Until the end of the 70s, national housing policy guidelines indicated that housing expenses should not exceed 25 percent of family income. The REAGAN administration revised these guidelines, establishing an allocation of 30 percent of income as acceptable for tenants (*De Giovanni and Minnite 1992, 271; Felstein and Stegman 1987, 5*). At the end of the 80s, 50 percent of all tenants in New York City spent at least 30 percent of their income on rent, almost one third spent at least 40 percent and nearly one quarter of all tenants were paying at least 50 percent of their income for rent (*City of New York, Department of City Planning 1991a, 8*). Especially low income households, defined as households with 80% or less than the area median income, had to pay a high proportion of their income for rent. Additionally, many of these households had to live in substandard houses. Nearly 50 percent of the New York City housing stock was built before 1939, and another 16 percent was built before 1949. Many of these houses did not receive sufficient maintenance. Families living from welfare in New York City are twice as likely to live in housing units with multiple maintenance deficiencies than others (*Wolkoff 1990, 29; Fellstein and Stegman 1987, V*).

Due to the loss of many housing units and the lack of new construction over the last two decades (*see Fig. 1*), New York City suffers from a severe housing shortage today. Between 1981 and 1991 only 113,000 dwelling units have been completed (*City of New York, Department of City Planning 1992, 11*). At the end of the 80s it was estimated that there was a shortfall of 231,000 dwelling units and a need to bring another 447,000 deteriorated units up to a minimum standard. The housing gap, defined as the total of these two measures, was an alarming 678,000 units (*Felstein and Stegman 1987, 6*). This supply gap primarily affects lower income households. The vacancy rate for units renting below $ 300 per month is less than 1 percent.

As a result of this situation, many families are not able to find a place to live and they have doubled up with friends and relatives. In the *Public Housing Projects* alone about 100,000 people doubled up (*Main 1993, 35*). Even though it has to be admitted that homelessness is not purely a housing problem, more and more people live in the streets or are sheltered by the city because they cannot find a place to stay. It is estimated that New York City has about 90,000 homeless people today.

Fig. 1: New Dwelling Units Completed in New York City, 1921-1991

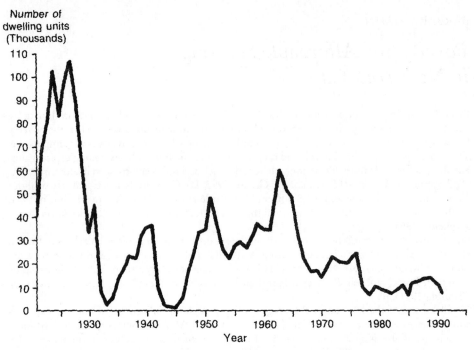

Source: New York City, Department of City Planning, New York 1992, 10.

Rents in New York City

Everybody moving to New York City complains about high rents. Available studio apartments rent for $ 600 to $ 900 a month, one bedroom apartments in a safe neighborhood rent for $ 1,000 and it is hard to find two bedrooms for under $ 1,500 (*Salins and Mildner 1991, 42*). However, the average rent in New York City is only $ 504 (1991). Average rents are highest in Manhattan ($ 664), followed by Queens ($ 456), while rents in Brooklyn ($ 405) and the Bronx ($ 387) lag behind (*see Fig. 2*). The figure for Staten Island is not available (*New York City Rent Guidelines Board 1992, 31*).

The complicated composition of the New York housing market is the reason for the difference between the rent for apartments that are being offered in the newspapers and the average rent. The New York housing market splits into four: there are rent-controlled units, rent-stabilized units and there is the unregulated sector and last not least there is public housing. Today there are about 1,9 million rental units in New York City. 155,000 of these units are rent-controlled and another 900,000 are rent-stabilized (*see Fig. 3*). New York City introduced rent control in 1943. All apartments that were built before 1947 were affected by rent control. Over the next 25 years there was only one rent increase for these apartments. In 1969 rent-stabilization was introduced in order to regulate rents in buildings that were built after 1946. Rent stabilization is a milder form of regulation and allows annual rent increases at a rate determined by the *Rent Stabilization Board*. In 1974 it was decided that all rent-controlled apartments that are voluntarily vacated become subject to rent stabilization. This way, eventually all controlled units will fall under the stabilization laws (*Wollkoff 1990, 45; Tucker 1991*).

Fig. 2: Average Rent per Unit per Month by Borough and Building Size, 1991

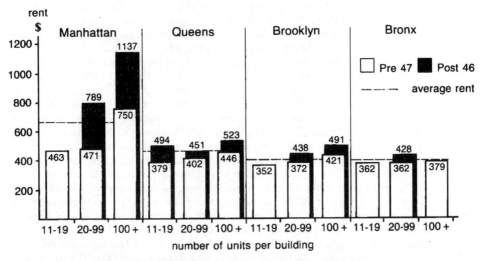

Note: Data on post 46 buildings in Brooklyn and the Bronx are insufficient

Source: New York City Rent Guidelines Board, New York 1992, 31.

Fig. 3: Rental Units in New York City, 1991

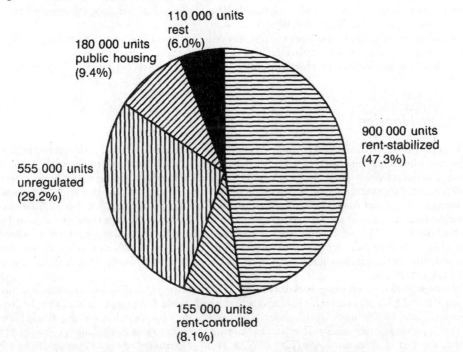

Source: Tucker 1991, 49 and City of New York, Department of City Planning, 1991 (a), 10.

Rent-controlled tenants pay between 50 to 90 percent below market, whereas tenants of rent-stabilized apartments pay from 10 to 40 percent below market. On the other hand, most tenants who live in the unregulated sector are paying above market prices because unregulated apartments are the only units that ever come to the market. Rent-controlled and rent-stabilized apartments are usually passed on to friends and relatives (*Tucker 1991, 49*).

Many critics argue that rent-regulation is the reason for many of the problems of the New York housing market. First of all, often the wrong people such as actress Mia FARROW and ex-mayor Edward KOCH live in the cheap housing, while many others are stuck in housing they cannot really afford. A study conducted by Harvard University in 1989 (*cited in Salins and Mildner 1991, 41 and in Crowitz 1991, 44*) found out, that the average New Yorker saves $ 44 per month when living in a rent-regulated apartment. But in the better neighborhoods of Manhattan the rent-control discount averages up to $ 432. Also, due to rent-regulations, tenants tend to stay in apartments even if the family becomes smaller and the apartments too large. The median age for people living in rent-controlled apartments is over 65 and most are living in apartments that are too large for them (*Tucker 1991, 49*). The overconsuming of housing also restricts tenant mobility. Each year, only about 200,000 tenants or 11 percent move from one apartment to another. This is about one-third the number of units which turn over in Chicago and Los Angeles annually (*New York City Rent Guidelines Board 1992, 57*).

It is also argued that rent-regulation also limits the construction of new housing units. The City of New York denies this because rent-regulation does not apply to new units. However, the city has to agree that potential investors might be afraid of changes in the regulation laws. This actually happened in the 80s when buildings constructed in the 70s became rent-stabilized as a result of receiving tax abatements and exemptions (*Tucker 1990, 24; Tucker 1991, 20; Felstein and Stegman 1987, 102*).

Additionally, there seems to be no doubt that rent-regulations have a negative impact on building maintenance because landlords who upgrade their buildings cannot pass along maintenance costs by increasing rents (*Wolkoff 1990, 48*).

Even though the City of New York realizes that rent regulation has many disadvantages, it still does not plan to abolish rent regulations, because too many families have too little income to pay the rents that landlords could charge in a fully deregulated market (*Felstein and Stegman 1987, 136*).

Public Housing

Since the passage of the Federal Housing Act in 1937, the United States invested about $ 75 billion in public housing. Once targeted to the working poor, public housing has increasingly become home to the extremely poor. Whereas in 1963, the median family income in public housing was 47 percent of the average annual U. S. income, in 1988 it was only about 22 percent of the national average (*Dreier and Atlas 1992, 393; Hartmann 1980, 122*). Today there are about 1,2 million public housing units in the United States or less than 3 percent of the nation's total housing stock (*see Fig. 4*). Most of these units have been built until the 70s. Federal support for low income housing was drastically reduced by President REAGAN. In the 80s new construction was mainly limited to units for the elderly (*Dreier and Atlas 1992, 387; Kivisto 1986, 1; Sternlieb and Listokin 1987, 30*).

The *New York City Housing Authority (NYCHA)* administers 180,000 units in public housing projects and has a reputation for having one of the best public housing programs in the United States. These 180,000 units are more than 10 percent of the nation's public housing stock. New York's public housing stock is four times as large as the next largest stock (Chicago) and larger than the next 10 cities combined (*City of New York, Department of City Planning 1991a, 10; Tucker 1990, 20; Bratt 1989, 66*). 48 percent of the units in New York City have two bedrooms,

Fig. 4: Public Housing in New York City

26 percent three or more bedrooms and another 26 percent one bedroom (*City of New York, Department of City Planning 1991a, 47*).
Even though New York City has by far the largest public housing stock in the country, there were 92,967 families on the waiting list for an apartment in May 1991. Three quarters of these families were living in substandard housing when they applied for public housing (*see Tab. 1*). Hispanics and blacks were clearly over-represented on this waiting list (*see Tab. 2*).
87 percent of the city's housing stock are federally subsidized, while the remainder has been financed by the state or the city (*City of New York, Department of City Planning 1991a, 47*). Due to the cutbacks in federal subsidies in the eighties, hardly any new units have been built in the last few years. In 1993 *NYCHA* added only 250 apartments through new construction and building renovations. At the same time more and more families are seeking public housing. This reflects the impact of severe cuts in housing development funds, the city's growing homeless population and the economic downturn of the early 90s. At the end of 1993 nearly 150,000 families were on the waiting list. Each day more people are joining the list than units are being added in a year (*New York Times, 6.2.94*). At the same time, annual turnover is averaging less than 4 percent and it is estimated that people joining the waiting list have to wait 18 to 20 years for an apartment (*Felstein and Stegman 1987, 24; Filer 1990, 36*).
Tenants of public housing pay only 30 percent of their income for rent. In the case of very large families, which are defined by having six or more members, the percentage of income can drop to 15 percent (*Kivisto 1986, 6 - 11*).

The Section 8 Program

In 1974 Congress created another possibility for low income households to find affordable housing. The *Section 8 Program* and its predecessor the *Section 23 Leased Housing Program,*

Tab. 1: Waiting List by Priority for Public Housing in New York City, May 1991

Priority	Total	Percent
Homeless	3,486	3.7
Other Emergency	5,050	5.4
Doubled up/Severe	178	0.2
Other Doubled up	166	0.2
Health Hardship	12,786	13.8
Substandard Housing	70,209	75.5
Extreme Rent Hardship	928	1.0
Standard Housing	164	0.2
Total	92,967	100.0

Source: City of New York, Department of City Planning, New York 1991 (a), 12.

Tab. 2: Ethnicity of People on the Waiting List, 1990

Ethnicity	Waiting List (%)	New York City (%)
Hispanics	42.0	24.4
Black Non-Hispanics	40.9	25.2
White Non-Hispanics	7.9	43.2
Asians and others, unknown	9.2	7.2
Total	100.0	100.0

Source: City of New York, Department of City Planning, New York 1991 (a), 12.

which was authorized in 1965, enables low income families to rent units in privately owned housing. The Section 8 Program not only offered various financial incentives like mortgages to interested landlords to rehabilitate and to construct new units (*Kivisto 1986, 11*), it was supposed to assimilate the poor into society and shelter at the same time by limiting Section 8 subsidized apartments to 20 percent of a project total. This idea more or less failed, because the program rapidly became a relief measure to rescue financially insecure projects under earlier programs (*Sternlieb and Listokin 1987, 32*).

Applicants are required to find housing within a rental range known as the Fair Market Rent. As in public housing, they are expected to pay only 30 percent of their income (*Back 1988, 9*). The local housing authority enters into long-term contracts with landlords and pays the difference between the unit's market rent and the 30 percent of the tenant's income with federal subsidies (*Bratt 1989, 6*).

New York City's inventory of privately-owned, federally-subsidized low and moderate income housing consists of over 76,500 rental units in about 500 projects. The 10 community districts with the largest concentrations of privately-held, federally subsidized units are East Harlem, the West Bronx, Central Harlem, East Tremont, The South Bronx, Bedford-Stuyvesant, Hunts Point, Coney Island, Bronxville and Roosevelt Island. A major problem is that most of this housing inventory was built before 1985 and is now at risk as a result of expiring federal subsidies until the year 2005. The prepay long-term mortgages expire after 15 to 20 years of ownership (*Back 1988*). The reduction of this stock means that low income New Yorkers will lose another major resource of affordable housing.

The Abandonment of Housing

For many reasons, New York City has more abandoned buildings than any other city in the country. A survey of property tax rates in 22 U. S. cities found out that New York City has the highest tax rate on apartment buildings. Additionally, New York City seems to overestimate the market value of properties in poor neighborhoods, which in turn increases property taxes (*Mildner 1991, 21 - 23*). Another problem is that due to rent-regulations, many landlords hardly make any profit. In reaction to several simultaneous events, the peak period of disinvestment came between 1968 and 1976. At that time there was a sequence of national and local recessions, New York City went bankrupt, energy costs rose and social indicators worsened. Thousands of landlords could not pay their taxes any more and eventually just walked away from their buildings or set their buildings on fire to claim the insurance money. From 1974 to 1984, more than 300,000 rental units were abandoned. Most of these rental units housed low income New Yorkers. Abandonments slowed during the early 80s, but were on the rise again in the late 80s, largely because property taxes for buildings had gone up drastically (*Harloe, Marcuse and Smith 1992, 182; Mildner 1991, 24 - 26*).

The *Department of Housing Preservation and Development (HPD)* of New York City seized most of the abandoned buildings for unpaid taxes (*see Tab. 3*). In the 80s the so-called in-rem housing inventory numbered more than 9,000 buildings with more than 100,000 units (*see Fig. 5*). About half of these buildings were vacant. New York City pays over $ 180 million

Tab. 3: HPD's In Rem - Inventory

Fiscal Year	Occup. Bldgs.	Vacant Bldgs.	Total Bldgs.	Units
1985	4,102	5,732	9,834	95,035
1987	4,629	4,638	9,267	100,911
1990	4,008	3,110	7,118	86,602
1992*	3,260	2,590	5,850	n.a.

* First Quarter only

Source: City of New York, New York 1991 (b) and New York Guidelines Board, New York 1992, 84.

Fig. 5: In-rem Housing in Northern Manhattan

each year for the operation and maintance of the *in-rem housing inventory* (*Mildner 1991, 24; City of New York, Department of City Planning 1991b, 150*).

The *HPD* rehabilitates most of the buildings itself and sells them afterwards for a nominal fee to tenants and no-profit organizations. This way the city became not only New York's biggest landlord but also its largest developer. But the city loses a lot of money by rehabilitating the buildings itself. It spends an average of $ 27,000 to renovate apartments and sells the apartments for as little as $ 250 a unit, or as little as 2 percent of their renovated market value. The city does not sell the units to private developers because it is afraid that these might sell the apartments in a few years at a higher price (*Riebling 1991, 14 - 19*). Due to limited funds it takes a long time for the city to rehabilitate vacant buildings. These units are not available for low income households for many years.

In some of the at-risk or abandoned buildings the tenants organized themselves to fight for their homes. First they fought against landlord neglect and abandonment and later against the city's inability to cope with its role as the largest landlord of New York City. This way some tenants with good records managed to control and manage their apartments themselves through several programs. These tenants were usually given between $ 3,000 to $ 5,000 to rehabilitate their apartments themselves. However, even though the programs were quite successful, only a comparatively small number of tenants in abandoned houses were given the opportunity to manage their houses themselves (*Leavitt and Saegert 1990; Leavitt 1980*).

The J-51 Program

In 1956 the city established the *J-51 Program* which provided tax incentives for developers to upgrade deteriorating warehouses and factories into middle income rental housing. Eventually more and more developers used J-51 to subsidize the conversion of low rent apartments into luxury apartments. Between 1978 and 1985, J-51 financed the upgrading of more than 500,000 units and in the early 90s more than 100,000 units benefited from the programm each year (*Hock and Slayton 1989, 39; New York City Rent Guidelines Board 1992, 82*). The improvement made the apartments unaffordable for low income tenants. In the 1970s J-51 tax abatements were mainly used to upgrade apartments in midtown Manhattan and thus contributed significantly to its gentrification. Since 1982 the program has been restricted to upper Manhattan and the outer boroughs (*Tucker 1990, 82*).

J-51 also encouraged the renovation of *Single Room Occupancy Hotels (SROs)* into more expensive studios and one bedroom apartments. SROs had always provided shelter for the single poor. In the mid 70s these "hotels" usually charged less than fifty dollars per week for a room and a 1979 survey found out that 85 percent of the residents had incomes below $ 3,000. Most of the SROs were concentrated on the Upper West Side and in Midtown Manhattan. Between 1970 and 1982 87 percent of the city's SROs or about 100,000 units were either upgraded or abandoned. In the mid 80s New York City realized that by upgrading SROs many single poor citizens had lost their only possibility to find affordable housing. Landlords who wanted to upgrade their SRO hotels from 1987 onwards had to make a payment of between $ 35,000 and $ 45,000 to a *Single Room Housing Occupancy Development Fund*. Landlords who upgrade their SROs without permission have to pay a penalty of $ 150,000 per unit. Even though the buy-out fees and the penalties are very high they do not help very much because there are only a few thousand SRO units left in New York City (*The Coalition for the Homeless 1992, 14; Hoch and Slayton 1989, 238 and 249; Blau 1992, 139*).

Homeownership Programs

Two homeownership programs are trying today to increase the housing supply for low und middle income New Yorkers. In 1987 the U. S. government established the *Nehemiah Housing Opportunity Grant*. The Grants were supposed to be made to no-profit organizations that, in turn, will provide loans of no more than $ 15,000 to low income home-buyers. Until spring 1993 in New York City a consortium of East Brooklyn churches had constructed about 2,300 single-familiy homes in the poorest neighborhoods in Brooklyn and was planning to build 600 more units in the South Bronx. The developer receives a grant of $ 10,000 per housing unit and free land of no great value from the city. The houses are sold to families with incomes as low as $ 20,000. When the first owner sells the home, he has to pay back the $ 10,000 loan to the city. In 1993 Nehemiah single-family homes sold for $ 63,000. The family had to pay a down payment between $ 5,000 and $ 14,000 and a monthly payment between $ 300 to $ 600 (*Bratt 1989, 31 and 181*).

Similar to the Nehemiah programm, the *New York City Housing Partnership*, an organization representing the city's financial, corporate, and service industries, sponsors the development of 4,000 affordable housing units, usually in two family row houses. The two-family houses sell for about $ 140,000. In spring 1993 4,500 units were completed and another 8,500 units were planned (*Husock 1993, 76 - 79*).

Both the Nehemiah and the Partnership program are a way to provide low income or at least middle income families with their own home. A Study found out that 48 percent of the new home-buyers had been tenants in public housing before. The city knows that Nehemiah and Partnership Houses are not really affordable to very low income New Yorkers, but hopes that now poorer households can move into the housing left behind (trickle down effect) (*Felstein and Stegman 1987, 7 f.*).

Homelessness

Even though there is no exact information on the number of homeless people in the United States, there is no doubt that the homeless population grew considerably over the last 20 years. The *National Coalition for the Homeless* estimates that there were at least 3 million homeless people in the United States in the early 90s. The most important characteristic of homeless people is that they have no fixed residence. This includes people who spend the nights in shelters or emergency housing placement like motels or hotels that are paid for by local welfare agencies, people who live in abandoned buildings, as well as people living on streets or in parks. Additionally there is an "invisible" homeless population. These are for example people who double up with friends or relatives (*National Coalition for the Homeless 1992, 2*).

A survey of 26 cities that was taken in 1989 found out that New York City had the highest number of homeless people. At that time about 70,000 to 90,000 people were homeless in the city (2. rank: Los Angeles with 50,000 homeless people) (*National Coaltion for the Homeless 1992, 3*). Based on the number of people who used the city's shelter system, the City of New York estimated that there were at least 90,000 homeless persons (without "invisible" homelessness) in summer 1993 (*Department of Housing Services of New York City 1993, unpublished data*).

It is generally acknowledged that New York City does more for its homeless population and each individual homeless person than any other city in the United States. As a result of the *Callaghan case* which went to trial in 1981 and the *McLain case* which went to trial in 1986, the City of New York has a legal obligation to shelter any individual or family who claims to be homeless and requests such shelter (*Hirsch 1991, 18f.; Blau 1992, 141*). In 1988 New York City spent almost $ 25,000 to shelter each individual homeless person, compared with an avergae of $ 5,500 spent in Los Angeles, Chicago or Philadelphia (*Filer 1990, 39*).

New York City operates 22 shelters for single men with a total capacity of 6,618 beds and 14 shelters for single women with a total capacity of 1,587 beds. In 1992 these shelters were used by nearly 7,300 homeless people per night on average. The biggest of these shelters (Camp La Guardia) has more than 1,000 beds. In June 1993 the City of New York housed an additional 5,631 families or a total of 17,317 persons including nearly 10,000 children in hotels or special family shelters (*Department of Housing Services of New York City 1993*).

Two surveys taken in 1987 found out that 44 percent of the families seeking emergency shelter had never had an apartment of their own. Before requesting shelter they had usually doubled up with families for some time. Families including pregnant women or new borns were specially at risk of becoming homeless. Other major risk groups included families who had moved at least twice in the prior year, had experienced an eviction, had prior shelter use, and had one adult with a mental illness or a drug or alcohol problem (*Main 1993, 31; City of New York, Department of City Planning 1991a, 25*). But altogether homeless families did not suffer unusually high personal or behavioral problems that would impair their ability to maintain stable housing arangements. Thus family homelessness seems to be typically a housing and income problem. African Americans (54%) and young people (44% are under 25 years old) are more likely than other families to ask for emergency shelter (*Blau 1992, 158*).

Homelessness among families is twice as common in New York City as in most other large cities of the United States (*Filer 1990, 31 f.*). Many critics argue that New York City has more families seeking shelter than other cities as a result of the city's housing policy.

There are three different kinds of emergency housing for families in New York City: welfare hotels, congregate shelters with private rooms for each family (Tier I), and shelters offering private sleeping quarters but without shared bathrooms and dining areas (Tier II). Until 1988 most of the families seeking shelter were placed in welfare hotels. Because, since 1984, New York City has given priority to homeless families for public housing, many families choose to live in welfare hotels for some time, even though the conditions in these hotels were very bad. Whereas

Fig. 6: Number of Families in Temporary Housing, Fiscal Years 1986-1992

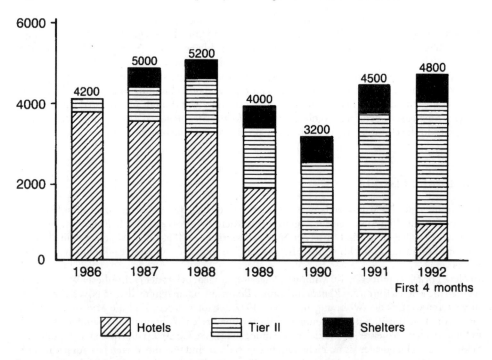

Source: New York City Rent Guidelines Board, New York 1992, 69.

a "normal" family applying for public housing had to wait up to 20 years, homeless families had to wait only about one year for a subsidized apartment (*Filer 1990, 35 f.*).
Welfare hotels could cost as much as $ 1,500 a month to shelter a family. Up to 1987 the *U. S. Department of Health and Human Services* reimbursed half of these costs. In 1987 the Department proposed limiting the reimbursement to $ 312 per family. For several reasons the implementation of this rule was delayed until the fall of 1991 (*Blau 1992, 161*). In response to these proposals, New York City stopped assigning new families to hotels in 1988. Instead, they were placed to the much cheaper shelters, mostly of the Tier II type. Because the families preferred welfare hotels to shelters, the number of homeless families went down from 5,200 in 1988 to 3,200 in 1990 (*see Fig. 6*). In 1990 New York City started a huge effort to end family homelessness by placing more families than ever in permanent housing. But unfortunately setting aside more permanent subsidized housing for homeless families did nor solve the problem. The number of families seeking shelter from the city increased again from 1990 because now homeless families were given more priority than ever before (*Blau 1992, 158 - 164; Filer 1990; Main 1993, 31 f.*).

Conclusion

A high proportion of people with low incomes, the absence of units renting for less than $ 300 or $ 400 per month, the inability of many households to afford the rent of availale units, a high rent burden and a housing need seem to be chronic problems of New York City. However, the situation has worsened over the last few years. Federal subsidies were drastically curtailed in the 80s, very few public housing units have been built, the waiting list for public housing is getting longer and longer, many houses have been abandoned and other buildings that provided units for low income families have been upgraded and gentrified. Even though an estimated 4 percent of the city's expense is dedicated to housing (*Felstein and Stegman 1987, 166*) - more than in any other city in the country - there seems to be no end to the housing crisis of New York City.

Zusammenfassung

1,8 Millionen der 7,3 Millionen New Yorker leben unterhalb der Armutsgrenze. Obwohl in den USA nach offiziellen Aussagen der Regierung die Miete 30% des verfügbaren Einkommens nicht übersteigen sollte, geben ein Drittel der New Yorker mehr als 40% und 25% sogar mehr als 50% ihres Einkommens für die Miete aus. Hiervon sind besonders die unteren Einkommensgruppen betroffen.

In New York City gibt es ca. 1,9 Millionen Mietwohnungen. In fast der Hälfte dieser Wohnungen werden die Mieten durch das *Rent Stabilization Board* auf einem sehr niedrigen Niveau gehalten, in weiteren ca. 8% der Wohnungen, die vor 1947 gebaut wurden, sind die Mieten fast völlig eingefroren, knapp 30% der Wohnungen gehören dem freien Wohnungsbau an und weitere 9% befinden sich in Projekten des sozialen Wohnungsbaus (*see Fig. 3*). Da die Mieten im regulierten Sektor sehr viel niedriger als im nicht-regulierten Sektor sind und die Mieten fast ausschließlich bei einem Mieterwechsel angehoben werden dürfen, ziehen die Mieter dieser Wohnungen nur selten um oder geben die Wohnungen unter der Hand weiter. Gleichzeitig ist es den Eigentümern der mietregulierten Wohnungen aufgrund der geringen Mieten kaum möglich, ihre Wohnungen zu pflegen. Viele Eigentümer geben sogar ihre Häuser ganz auf, da sie die Steuern nicht mehr zahlen können. Diese Häuser gehen in das Eigentum der Stadt New York über (*see Tab. 3*).

Ende 1993 standen 150,000 Familien auf der Warteliste für eine der 180,000 Sozialwohnungen. Viele der Familien lebten zu diesem Zeitpunkt in minderwertigen Häusern (*see Tab. 1*). Die Stadt New York berücksichtigt vorrangig obdachlose Familien bei der Vergabe von freien Sozialwohnungen. Diese Vergabepolitik sehen viele Kritiker als Grund dafür an, daß es in New York City mehr obdachlose Familien gibt als in jeder anderen Stadt der USA.

References

Bach, V. (1988): Housing at Risk: Expiring Federal Subsidies. Summary Characteristics of the At-Risk Inventory of the HUD-Subsidized Private Rental Projects in New York City. New York.
Blau, J. (1992): The Visible Poor. Homelessness in the United States. New York, Oxford.
Bratt, R. G.: Rebuilding a Low-Income Housing Policy. Philadelphia.
Bureau of the Census (1992): Income, Poverty and Wealth in the United States: A Chart Book. Washington D. C.
City of New York, Department of City Planning (1991 a): Proposed Comprehensive Housing Affordability Strategy. Federal Fiscal Year 1992. New York.
City of New York, Department of City Planning (1991 b): Annual Report on Social Indicators, New York.
City of New York, Department of City Planning (1992), New Housing in New York City 1990-91. New York.

Crowitz, L. G. (1991): Taking Rent Control to Court. In: The City Journal, Spring, 40-45.
De Giovanni, F. K. and L. C. Minnite (1992): Patterns of Neighborhood Change. In: Mollenkopf, J. H. and M. Castells (Ed.): Dual City, Restructuring New York. New York, 267-311.
Dreier, P. and J. Atlas (1992): Housing. In: Green, M. (Ed.): Changing America. Blueprints for the New Administration. (= The Citizens Transition Project). New York, 383-398.
Felstein, C. and M. A. Stegman (1987): Toward the 21st Century. Housing in New York City. New York.
Filer, R. (1990): What Really Causes Familiy Homelessness. In: The City Journal, Autumn, 31-40.
Harloe, M., P. Marcuse and N. Smith (1992): Housing for People, Housing for Profits. In: Fainstein, S. S., I. Gordon and M. Harloe: New York & London in the Contemporary Worlds, Cambridge, MA, 175-202.
Hartman, C. (1980): Realities of the Federal Housing Allowance. In: Plunz, R. (Ed.): Housing Form and Public Policy in the United States. New York, 121-128.
Hirsch, Dennis (1991): Workfare for the Homeless. In: The City Journal, Autumn, 17-19.
Hoch, C. and R. A. Slayton (1989): New Homeless and Old. Community and the Skid Row Hotel. Philadelphia.
Husock, H. (1993): New Frontiers in Affordable Housing. In: The City Journal, Spring, 76-84.
Kivisto, P. (1986): A Historical Review of Changes in Public Housing Policies and their Impact on Minorities. In: Momeni, J. (Ed.): Race, Ethnicity and Minority Housing in the United States. New York, Westport, London, 1-18.
Leavitt, J. (1980): Resident and Community Receivership Programs in New York City. In: Plunz, R.: Housing Form and Public Policy in the United States. New York, 97-106.
Leavitt, J. and S. Saegert (1990): From Abandonment to Hope. Community Households in Harlem. New York.
Main, T. (1993): Hard Lessons on Homelessness. The Education of David Dinkins. In: The City Journal, Summer, 30-39.
Mildner, G. C. S. (1991): New York's Most Unjust Tax. In: The City Journal, Summer, 21-27.
National Coalition for the Homeless (1992): Homelessness in America: A Summary. Washington D. C.
New York City Coalition for the Homeless (1993): Unpublished Statistics.
New York City Rent Guidelines Board (1992): Rent Stabilized Housing in New York City. A Summary of Rent Guidelines Board Research. New York.
New York Times, 6.2.94
Riebling, M.: Who's Warehousing Now ? In: The City Journal, Autumn, 14-19.
Salins, P. and G. Mildner (1991): Does Rent Control Help the Poor?. In: The City Journal, Winter, 39-45.
Sternlieb, G. and D. Listokin: A Review of National Housing Policy. In: Salins, P (Ed.): Housing America's Poor. Chapel Hill, London, 14-40.
The Coalition for the Homeless (1992): What is Government for ? The Surge of Homeless Persons with Mental Illness in New York City. New York.
Tucker, W. (1990): The Hidden Cost of Housing Madness. In: The City Journal, Autumn, 19-30.
Tucker, W. (1991): Zoning, Rent Control and Affordable Housing. Washington D. C.
Wolkoff, M. J. (1990): Housing New York. Policy Challenges and Opportunities. New York.

Address of the Author

Barbara Hahn
Wirtschafts- und Sozialgeographie
Universität Lüneburg
Wilschenbrucher Weg 84
21335 Lüneburg
GERMANY

FRIEDRICH M. ZIMMERMANN and GERT KRAUTBAUER

Aspects of Economic and Social Integration of African Americans - The Case of New York City

Some Theoretical Issues

Severe riots in Los Angeles and in other U.S. cities in April 1992 revealed that despite efforts put into the Civil Rights Movement in the 50s and 60s, race conflicts still exist.
Concerning the solution to the issues of minorities in the USA, the society seems to have reached its limits. In this context, the term *minority* cannot be seen in a quantitative sense as in some of the U.S. cities, the population is more than 50% black (e.g. Washington, D.C. 66%, Atlanta 67% and Detroit 76%). The belief that African Americans are socially discriminated against by the dominant white population is important for the following considerations (*see Hacker 1992, 228; Rose 1990, 7ff*):

Despite numerous attempts of integration, i. e.,
- the "Anglo Conformity" and "Americanization Movement" models of assimilation
- the democratic way of the "Melting Pot" concept for a social improvement by means of the mixture of various cultures or lately
- the pluralistic, multicultural ideology of society,

the economic and social conditions for African Americans are still very poor. The socio-economic differences seem to be a permanent phenomenon of the U.S. society. These tendencies are reinforced by the global economic development. One must consider that prejudice against African Americans brings about personal, family, social problems. The African Americans, being so hindered by the toll of these problems, are prevented from developing their full occupational/professional potential. Thus, there is a loss of human resources in the American job market, which results in competitive disadvantages in the national, as well as international economy. Political intervention and regulation would be necessary, but do not conform with the U.S. idea of a free economy.

According to THOMAS (*1993, 328ff*) research concerning race and class as an interpretation for disparities centers on three main perspectives:

- The "race perspective" (*based on Willie 1978*) insists on the persistance of discrimination of class levels, limiting the chances for all blacks.
- The "class perspective", stressed by WILSON's "The Declining Significance of Race" (*1980*) is based on the view that problems of blacks are due to their overrepresentation in lower classes. Racial problems are the effect of class-related phenomena.
- The "interactional perspective" (*Pettigrew 1981*) based on the hypothesis of racial effects varying across different class levels, e.g. discrimination for middle class blacks to move into jobs leading to political or economic power.

Integrating these perspectives into geography, one could find a connection to "welfare geography". This concept analyses socio-political developments in different local organization models, and applies to the resulting social, cultural and economic pressure, to stress local implications by means of a regional and social approach. Furthermore, it considers science as a prescribing and an intervening medium.

Big improvements are hardly conceivable, private and institutional initiatives may somewhat relieve the present misery but do not even touch the main reasons of the problem. Sustainable development and the use of endigenous potential are the main aims of the two projects "Youth Build" and "Harlem Urban Development Corporation". Both initiatives should guarantee a long-term improvement of African American's standard of life.

The Persistence of Discrimination

While the main part of immigrants was able to take advantage of equal rights, the basic principle of the U.S. society "All Men Are Equal", written in the Declaration of Independence; was not intended for black slaves (*Norton 1988, A5*). The abolition of slavery in 1863 guaranteed freedom but not equality in the American society. The discrimination of blacks was particularly strong in the South. The end of the occupation enabled the reconstruction of old power structures in the South, where about 90% of the population was black. "The Jim Crow Laws" in the 1890s split society into two classes. Segregation and discrimination laws prevented a mixture of races and made it impossible for blacks to join institutions run by the leading white class. The supplementary articles 14 and 15 in the Constitution conceded the citizenship and the right to vote to blacks. These provisions were ignored or circumvented by most of the Southern states. It should be noted, however, that discrimination was not only practised in the South. In the case *Plessy against Ferguson*, the Supreme Court decided on the practice: "Separate but Equal", as the valid principle of the American society (*Rose 1990, 24*).
Financial dependence of blacks on land-owners worsened their situation. "Share cropping" was the slogan. Blacks rented land from the farmers and had to pay in goods they produced. In case of a bad harvest the sharecroppers had to ask their land owners for a credit and thus became more and more financially dependent on them.
The bad conditions in the South provoked a big migration to the North-Eastern cities. This migration was motivated by the hope of getting a job in industry, better pay, better housing and less discrimination. During World War II numerous blacks found their hopes fulfilled. At the end of the war the tensions increased: The blacks did not only have to compete with the war veterans but also with a huge amount of refugees from Europe, who increased rapidly in numbers because of the war. Between 1915 and 1949 race riots were very common.
D. ROOSEVELT's policy of the "New Deal" was an important and progressive development. ROOSEVELT's social policy ensured workers minimum wages, unemployment support and included a job creation program from which also blacks profited. During World War II many blacks found a job in industry, replacing, in particular, the soldiers involved in the fighting in Europe and Asia.
A fundamental change concerning desegregation did not take place before 1954. The Supreme Court declared in a sentence that the "Separate but Equal" doctrine does not conform with the Constitution (*Rose 1990, 24*). The self-consciousness of blacks which increased after World War II accelerated the process which had already begun at the turn of the century. The fight for Civil Rights resulted in the declaration of the Civil Rights Acts of 1964, 1965 and 1968. In particular the Civil Rights Act of 1968 caused major changes for the black minority. Beside the prohibition of separating races in public institutions, it forbade any kind of discrimination against individuals because of their race, color, religious denomination, sex and origin at the labor market. Title VII includes the prohibition of discriminating people concerning their employment, payment, promotion, education or termination of their employment contract and assured blacks equal opportunities in many parts of the private economy (*Jaynes and Williams 1989, 315ff*). The Civil Rights Act of 1965 effectively ensured blacks the right to vote. The one of 1968 forbade discrimination in the housing market. In fact, there was a much higher acceptance of equal rights among races in various aspects of life, and an increasing number of the white population would

accept blacks as being equal and treat them according to the democratic ideals of the American Constitution.

After 1973 the Affirmative Action Program was permanently questioned by the white majority. Many of them thought that the program caused a reverse discrimination. This change in opinion was provoked by the deterioration of the global economic situation in the USA caused by the first oil crisis. The competition at the labor market increased and many whites felt disadvantaged, provoked by the improved socio-economic situation of the blacks. This debate will most likely continue as long as these programs exist (*see Norton et al. 1988, 14; Weatherspoon 1985, 23*).

To summarize, the majority of blacks did not really receive a chance to participate in the economic progress of the USA. Furthermore, the history of discrimination shaped a certain "black value system" which evidently has a very negative effect on the formation of a reasonable capital. This seems to be one of the plausible reasons that after about two centuries of legal equality, blacks were not able to catch up with the economic standard of the white population.

The Socio-Economic Situation of the Blacks at the Beginning of the 90s

Private Property/Capital

Since property is of particular significance in the American economic system, the distribution of private property, of firms and human resources is most important for the following considerations. On the one hand, capital should produce income, on the other, investors determine the production process and therefore influence the racial or ethnic composition of employees. Anticipating the result, this means that African Americans, because of their small property, may only get a very low income out of their assets and have fewer chances to get a job in a white domain.

The disparities concerning the distributions of private capital are significantly high (*Tidwell 1992, 64*). In 1988 the mean of wealth ownership (total net worth) of blacks amounted to $ 26,130 which is only 23% of that of whites ($ 111,950). The per capita rates of blacks ($ 8,981) is 20% of that of whites ($ 43,164). A discrepancy will be noticed concerning all existing assets. Just 44% of blacks owned interest-earning capital at financial institutions while the share of whites was 77%. A comparison of the black/white share of stock and mutual funds comes to 7/24%, the equity of homes to 43/67%, of automobiles 65/90% (*U.S. Department of Commerce 1992c, 9ff*).

Property of Firms

A similar situation occurs if one compares the property of firms (*see Tab.1*). Of approximately 17,5 million businesses only 424,000 were owned by blacks. The Black/White ratio of 0.198 shows the underrepresentation of blacks who in the case of parity should own more than 2,1 million firms; in all economic fields the presence of blacks is too small. The differences concerning the profits of firms are extremely high. The smaller businesses owned by blacks only produce 22,8 Mill $ which are 0.2% of the profits of all firms!

Two small examples should illustrate the situation: A survey of the wealthiest Americans in the *Forbes Magazine* only included three blacks; John Harold JOHNSON - the boss of Ebony and Jet, Berry GORDON - owner of Motown Records and Reginald LEWIS who bought Beatrice Foods recently. The survey of the 1,000 biggest U.S. firms in *Business Week* only mentioned one black managing director (quoted in: *Hacker 1992, 108*). Considering the fact that blacks amount to 12.5% of the American population, it is obvious that blacks are extremely underrepresented, especially in leading positions.

Tab. 1: Receipts (in Mill $) and Number of Firms (1,000's) by Industry, 1987

	Black Receipts	Total Receipts	B/T**	Black Firms	Total Firms
Total	22.8	11,413	0.016	424	17,526
Construction	2.6	591	0.037	37	560
Manufacturing	1.2	3,056	0.003	8	642
Transport and Public Utilities	1.8	872	0.017	37	735
Wholesale Trade	1.5	1,407	0.009	6	641
Retail Trade	6.7	1,729	0.032	66	2,658
F. I. R. E.	0.9	1,741	0.004	27	1,426
Selected Services	7.1	956	0.060	210	7,095
Other Industries*	0.9	1,060	0.007	34	3,769

Source: Tidwell 1992, 66; modified
Note: 1987 dollars were converted to 1990 dollars using CPI-U
* Includes Agriculture, Mining, and Industries not elsewhere classified.
** This is black receipts or firms per capita divided by the complement for total per capita.

Tab. 2: Years of School Completed by Persons 25 Years and Older, 1970 and 1990 (in %)

1990	Black male	White male	Black female	White female
8 yrs. Elementary school	17.0	10.3	13.8	9.5
1-3 yrs. High School	16.3	9.9	19.4	10.5
4 yrs. High School	38.3	36.1	37.2	41.8
1-3 yrs. College	16.9	18.4	17.9	18.8
4 and 4+ yrs. College	11.4	25.4	11.6	19.3
1970	Black male	White male	Black female	White female
8 yrs. Elementary school	44.0	25.5	38.7	23.6
1-3 yrs. High School	21.9	15.4	25.6	17.1
4 yrs. High School	23.3	31.6	25.2	39.5
1-3 yrs. College	6.0	11.8	6.2	10.9
4 and 4+ yrs. College	4.8	15.7	4.4	9.0

Source: Tidwell 1992, 68.

Human Resources

Social status and income are directly associated with education. Therefore, the education level is used as a qualitative criterium of human resources.

Tab. 2 shows that the level of education of both male and female blacks is much lower than that of whites. In 1990 14% of black females and 17% of black males reached the level of Elementary School (compared to 10% of whites). In contrast to this, about 12% blacks completed their study (which lasted at least 4 years), compared to 25% white males and 20% white females. In the last two decades blacks have made a notable gain as far as education is concerned. The percentage of black males without a High School degree decreased from 44% in 1970 to 17% in 1990. With black females the percentage decreased from 39% in 1970 to 14% in 1990. Improvements are also noticed in the completion of studies. Between 1970 and 1990 the percentage of black males who graduated from 4 yrs. College increased from 5% to 11%, whereas the percentage of whites changed from 16% to 25%.

There are some deficits in higher education in the USA which are gaining more and more importance. One explanation for this deficit may be that public schools in the USA are financed by taxes. Poor communities have less money available to finance schools and so the preconditions for education are worse than in other communities. In many cases African Americans have to stay away from renowned colleges since they cannot afford high tuitions or their level of education is not high enough to meet the requirements of the entrance examinations.

Another effect, increasing the problem of lower education, can be found in the post-Fordism developments within the American society: Segmentation of labor markets, industries leaving the inner cities, the decreasing number of low quality jobs and the increasing importance of the production of services perpetuates the bad economic and social situation of blacks with a low level of education (*Thomas 1993*).

Considering the influence of education on the experience at the job-market, people with a higher education level have better chances to find a job, both sexes and races compared. Whereas, for example, only 40% of the black females with Elementary School found a job in 1990, the percentage of black males was 55%. With a completed study the chance to find a job is over 90%. A higher education level also serves to reduce the disparities between the races concerning the possibility to find employment. Black females without a college degree have fewer chances to find a job than their white counterparts, whereas the opposite is the case when both white and black females completed college. The chances for well-educated black and white males are also about the same. To sum up, it is important to invest in human resources in order to give both races a similar chance at the labor market.

Labor Market

During the recession at the beginning of the 80s the employment rate of the blacks essentially decreased. After the recession the rate of 56% remained stable. Whereas the rate of black males declined, that of black females rose. A similar result shows the black/white relation which proves deterioration of the position of blacks in the 70s and stabilisation during the 80s. Black teenagers still have big problems in finding a job. Their employment rate had not reached 30% in the last two decades and therefore was on average half as high as that of white teenagers.

Since 1978 the unemployment rate (*Tab.3*) of blacks has always been over 11% which was twice as high as that of whites during the 70s and 80s. There are two main reasons for the extremely high unemployment rate in the urban ghettos of New York City (exemplifying all inner cities of the

Year	Total		Men (20 and over)		Women (20 and over)		Both Sexes (16 to 19 yrs)	
	Black	White	Black	White	Black	White	Black	White
1972	10.4	5.1	7.0	3.6	9.0	4.9	35.4	14.2
1982	18.9	8.6	17.8	7.8	15.4	7.3	34.7	14.4
1990	11.3	4.7	10.4	4.3	9.8	4.1	31.1	13.4

USA), which is also considered a main cause for the downfall of whole communities. First of all, the migration of firms causes a big loss of jobs and secondly, a structural change in the economy contributes to a high unemployment rate. The reinforcement of a service society caused a reduction of jobs in manufacturing industries from 38% to 16% (1970 - 1984). This again provoked a loss of 500,000 jobs which only required lower qualification, whereas the 240,000 newly created jobs asked for a much higher education level (*Tobier 1984, 66ff; Wilson 1987, 40*). In particular, the badly qualified poor and working-class blacks and Hispanics were affected by the structural unemployment and still are on the virtue of the economic crisis at the beginning of the 90s. Additionally, the official statistics of unemployment with a view to people who get registered regularly at the office of labor exchange, do not reflect the real situation sufficiently. Unofficial sources dealing with unemployment rates, which include all non-registered unemployed, estimate this rate to be twice as high as the official one. The official statistics of the unemployed consider only people who get registered regularly at the office of the labor exchange. A considerable number of blacks who are able to work have lost hope in finding a job and thus are not interested in being registered at the office of labor exchange anymore. This fact explains the big difference between the total number of employed plus unemployed people against the number of blacks who are able to work (labor force). Therefore, the average unemployment rate of black males is estimated to be more than 20% and that of black teenagers to be 60%. Judging these estimates the existence of a huge conflict potential in the American inner cities is understandable (*see U.S. Department of Commerce 1991, 108*).

Disparities in Income

Besides sex, age, marital status and regional effects, differences in capital, education and at the job market are mainly responsible for the imbalance of income and other socio-economic factors. Per capita and median income revealed essential differences between blacks and whites. In 1990 the per capita income for blacks amounted to $ 9,017 which is 59% of the average income of whites ($ 15,265). There is no evidence for a positive change in this racial gap (*Tab.4*). On the contrary, the situation is deteriorating. Since the end of the 70s the Black/White relation has been stagnating (1974 highest percentage 62% - now 59%). Comparing the figures of the average income (*Tab.5*) of black females ($8,328), it is 81% of the income of their white counterparts ($ 10,317). In opposition to this, black males are more discriminated against than white males: On average they get paid $ 12,868 which is 60% of what white males earn ($ 21,170). Considering the average values, only 65% of all black males are integrated in the working process compared to 74% of white males (*Hahn 1993*). Although women of both races were able to improve their income, the differences are still striking: In 1980 the average income of black females was 93% of that of white females, it decreased to 81% in 1990!

Tab. 4: Per Capita Income in Selected Years, 1970 - 1990 (in $)

	Per Capita Income - Black	Per Capita Income - White	Relation B/W in %
1970	6,296	11,298	55.7
1980	7,620	13,059	58.4
1990	9,017	15,265	59.1

Source: Tidwell 1992, 75; modified. Data is 1990 CPI-U adjusted dollars.

Tab. 5: Median Income of Persons With Income by Race and Sex, 1970 - 1990 (in $)

	Black Male	White Male	Black Female	White Female
1970	14,003	23,617	6,949	7,633
1980	12,704	21,140	7,265	7,847
1990	12,868	21,170	8,328	10,317

Source: Tidwell 1992, 77; modified. Data is 1990 CPI-U adjusted dollars.

Fig.1 shows that these facts are similar to the family income. The inflation-adjusted income of black families changed only from $ 21,151 in 1970 to $ 21,423 in 1990. Compared with this, the income of white families increased by 7% which caused a change in the difference of the medium income between the two races from $ 13,330 to $ 15,492. A distinction between income groups shows an obvious increase of well-earning white families. Whereas only 1.3% of black families earned more than $ 100,000 a year, 6% of white families earned that much. Very critical is the fact that the number of families with a lower income has been growing dramatically. The share of black families with an annual income under $ 5,000 increased from 7% in 1970 to 12% in 1990, whereas the category with an income of $ 10,000 to $ 25,000 decreased drastically from 41% to 30% (*see Barringer 1992, A12*). *Fig.1* shows another essential fact. White families are more and more afflicted by the polarisation of the income-distribution which can be explained by the economic policy of the REAGAN - BUSH era. Consequently certain black families with substantial income gains lead to the emergence of a black middle class. The percentage of families earning more than $ 35,000 rose from 24% to 30%.

Fig. 1: Distribution of Income - Selected Income Classes by Race, 1970 - 1990

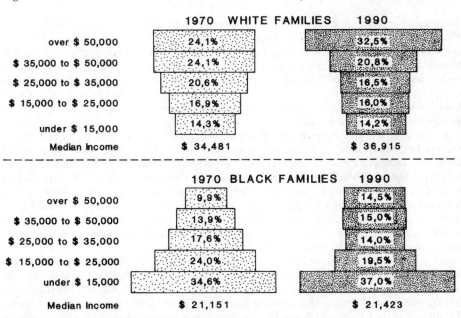

Source: Hacker 1992, 98. Data is 1990 CPI-U adjusted dollars.

In general, the income disparities between whites and blacks have been growing continuously, which shows that despite noticeable success in the education sector, these differences seem to be due to discrimination *(see Fig.1)*.

Poverty

Since there are major income disparities, poverty also must be taken into consideration. In 1990 32% of blacks lived below the poverty line, as defined by the state (9,8 million). This is true only of 11% of whites (total 22,3 million). Since 1970 the rates concerning blacks varied between 30% and 36%, the ones of whites varied between 9 and 12% with a rising tendency *(Pear 1992, A14)*. Within just one year (1990 - 1991) the total number of poor people increased by 2,1 million to 35,7 million.

Tab. 6: Households Headed by Women (in %) and Selected Poverty Rates, 1970 - 1990

Year	Black	White	Blacks in Poverty	Whites in Poverty
1970	34.5	9.6	58.7	28.4
1980	45.9	13.2	56.6	30.0
1990	56.2	17.3	50.6	29.8

Source: Hacker 1992, 68; Tidwell 1992, 89; modified.
Note: Figures focus on families that have no husband present and with children under 18.

The number of black children living in poverty was 45% in 1990, that of white children 16%. Thus, 4,5 million black children and 8,2 million white children live in poverty. A further specification turns out as the following: In 1990 over 50% of all persons living in female headed households lived below the poverty line. The corresponding share of whites is about 30% (in both cases 6 million people), which is a striking indicator for the family structure being an important factor for the economic well-being. In this respect the growth of single parent households (due to the increasing amount of missing black males) *(see Tab.6)* reduces hope for an improvement in the near future.

The consequence of this extreme poverty is a lack of medical care. In 1990 the share of blacks without health insurance was 50% higher than that of whites. (*U.S. Department of Commerce 1992a, 19*). Inadequate medical care may also contribute to the fact that whites, on average, live 5,7 years longer than blacks. In fact, the probability for a black male to reach 75 years of age is lower than for a man living in Bangladesh. A further consequence is that the mortality rate of black babies is twice as high compared with that of white babies. At the same time children of inner city families are much more prone to illnesses *(Hacker 1992, 46; 231)*. Apart from health problems, there are other social consequences of poverty, such as the high number of drug addicts and a striking crime rate in urban ghettos.

Social problems can not be reduced to race and minority conflicts. The difficulties of the American society can be explained by the impoverishment of whole urban districts. The increasing impoverishment of blacks is certainly a consequence of the historical development. Nevertheless, it is discernible that also the white majority is effected by the increasing poverty. The division of the society into rich and poor caused in many cases the formation of white ghettos in the USA.

New York City

New York City and the Harlem Community

New York City is the biggest city in the USA with 7,3 million inhabitants, compared with 7,1 million inhabitants in 1980, the increase in population has been about 3.5%. At first sight this increase does not express dynamism. Looking at the development of single ethnic and racial groups more carefully, a dramatic change may be recognized. In 1900 the number of colored people in New York City which consisted almost only of blacks was 60,000, in 1950 it was 776,000 and in 1960 it amounted to 1,141,000 (*Hall 1966*). Since the 40s there has been a big rush of Puerto Ricans to New York City. Between 1980 and 1990 the whites decreased by 12%, whereas the percentage of blacks (18%), of Hispanics (27%), of Asians (109%) and other minorities (27%) increased considerably. As a consequence 55% of the population of New York City belonged to a minority group (4,1 million) (*see Tab. 7*).

Tab. 7: New York City's Racial Composition, 1980 - 1990

Category	New York C. City	Bronx	Brooklyn	Man-hattan	Queens	Staten Island
Total Population						
1980	7,071,639	1,168,972	2,231,028	1,428,285	1,891,325	352,029
1990	7,322,564	1,203,789	2,300,664	1,487,536	1,951.598	378,977
difference in %	3.5	3.0	3.1	4.1	3.2	7.7
Whites						
1980	4,294,075	554,046	1,249,486	841,204	1,335,805	313,534
1990	3,827,088	430,077	1,078,549	867,227	1,129,192	322,043
difference in %	12.2	28.8	15.8	3.1	-18.3	2.7
African Americans						
1980	1,784,337	371,926	722,812	309,854	354,129	25,616
1990	2,102,512	449,399	872,305	326,967	423,211	30,630
difference in %	17.8	20.8	20.7	5.5	19.5	19.6
Asian/Pacific Groups						
1980	245,759	17,412	46,217	75,652	99,132	7,346
1990	512,719	35,562	111,251	110,629	238,336	16,941
difference in %	108.6	104.2	140.7	46.2	140.4	130.6
Other Groups*						
1980	688,898	227,763	227,763	175,412	85,631	4,890
1990	880,245	288,751	238,559	182,713	160,859	9,363
difference in %	27.8	26.8	4.7	4.2	87.9	91.5
Hispanic Origin**						
1980	1,406,044	396,353	392,118	336,247	262,442	18,884
1990	1,783,511	523,111	462,411	386,630	381,120	30,239
difference in %	26.8	32.0	17.9	15.0	45.2	60.1

Source: U.S. Bureau of the Census; author's own calculation.
* Includes American Indian, Eskimo, and Aleutian categories.
** People identifying themselves as Hispanics without checking a racial category on the census form. Hispanics can fall under white, black, or other categories, depending upon respondent.

Fig. 2: The Harlem Area

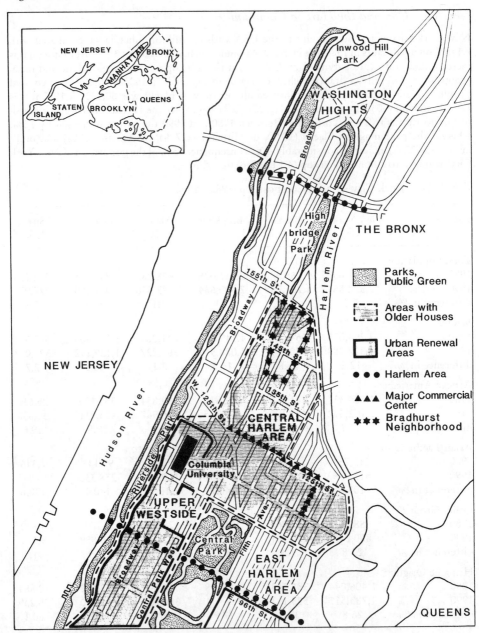

Source: Basic map: Diercke Weltatlas 1991, 196 (modified).

The migration movements continuously stabilise the formation of ghettos in the critical areas of Harlem, Brooklyn and the Bronx. The suburbanization of whites especially after World War II, the so-called White Flight, and the permanent immigration of the poor, working-class blacks and Hispanics caused the social descent of whole communities. The migration of middle-class and upper-middle-class blacks from inner-city ghettos and slums accelerated the decay. The filling up of inner-cities with socially weak and isolated strata of society as well as the loss of vertical integration not only provoked many social problems but also impaired the economic power and the urban functions of these communities.

Both projects explored within this study are situated in Harlem. The Harlem Community (*see Sherell 1991*) extends from 96th to 178th Street. In the western part it is limited by the Hudson River and in the East the Harlem River functions as a border (*see Fig.2*). In an area of about 3,829 acres lived 476,722 people in 1990. The ethnic composition of the Community did not change compared to that of 1980. The biggest ethnic group are the blacks with 42%, followed by 40% of Hispanics. The third group are the whites with a share of still 15%. Segregation is practised within the Community, its characteristic is also a mosaic of differently structured neighborhoods. Whereas blacks mainly settled in Central Harlem Areas (share of blacks over 90%), Hispanics (especially Puerto Ricans) generally dominate East Harlem, parts of Washington Heights and the area around Central Park West. Whites usually live in the outermost West, especially in the area of Columbia University as well as north of 155th Street.

Some main issues for the situation in Harlem:

- The population of Harlem is on average very young: about 23% of its inhabitants are younger than 18, only 14% are over 64 years old.
- Whereas in 1980 still 54% of all households earned under $ 10,000, today the percentage of households earning that much decreased to 43% but is still higher than the average figure of total Manhattan which is 27%. Since the share of Manhattan, also decreased by 11% since 1980, it is obvious that the improvement is only a statistical illusion due to a missing inflation adjustment. Furthermore, it is clear that Harlem was not able to improve its relative position. About 31% of the households in Harlem earn between $ 10,000 and $ 25,000 and only 26% earn more than $ 25,000. The comparative figures of Manhattan are 27% and 46%.
- About 1/3 of the inhabitants of Harlem are recipients of public assistance. The unemployment rate of some neighborhoods is mostly higher than 50%; the unemployment rate of juveniles is extremely high.
- The buildings of many areas of Central, East and West Harlem were constructed before 1900 and in many cases they are overcrowded and would badly need renovation. Graffiti indicate that gangs exist there as a consequence of social conflicts (*see Fig. 3 and 4*).
- A large number of apartments is vacant as a result of the suburbanisation of the black middle and upper class. Numerous buildings lack any minimum standard of sanitary facilities. In many characteristics Harlem corresponds with the prototype of an urban ghetto.
- Several blocks, especially in the West Side Area, have been renovated in the last few years which has resulted in higher rents and in a dislodging process of poor black tenants (*see Fig. 5*)
- Many institutions, organisations and private initiatives, which include Harlem Urban Development Corporation and that of Action YouthBuild, aim at redressing these grievances (*see Fig. 6*).

Fig. 3: Many buildings in Harlem, constructed before 1900, are in bad shape and either overcrowded or vacant, and would badly need renovation

Fig. 4: Graffiti indicate the existence of gangs as a consequence of social conflicts

Fig. 5: Blocks or parts thereof have been renovated already which has resulted in higher rents and dislodging processes of poor tenants

Fig. 6: Public and private institutions and organizations aim at reducing the grievances by a lot of measures and initiatives

Youth Action YouthBuild

The Emergence of YouthBuild

The idea of YouthBuild emerged at the end of the 70s from numerous initiatives taken by two non-profit community organisations: the *Youth Action Program* and the *Banana Kelly Community Improvement Association*. Both organisations aimed at combatting unemployment and crime on the one hand, renovating the buildings of the Community on the other. Instead of providing young people with already completed programs, the initiators preferred the process of an endogenic development. Beside the renovation program which is called *YouthBuild*, many other programs were developed to encourage juveniles to learn self-responsibility and guiding abilities. Initially, financial aids mainly consisted of donations by charity organisations, private persons and firms. Since 1984 single initiatives under the name of *Coalition for Ten Million* tried to get money from the city treasury. Beside Youth Action and Banana Kelly the Coalition comprised some other community organisations, churches, representatives of homeless people and several youth organisations. After having tried to get financial aid from the *Capital Jobs Program*, the Coalition for Ten Million received a new program called *Cityworks*. Although it received only $ 4,75 million instead of the required $ 10 million, it was still able to improve a lot. The characteristic of the education program consists in combining the education of juveniles and the construction of relatively inexpensive apartments to accommodate homeless people. This requires a good cooperation between the Department of Employment (DOE) and the Housing Preservation Department (HPD). In 1986 the Coalition changed its name into *Coalition for Twenty Million Dollars*. The assignment of the aid increased to $ 12,75 million. Economy measures required the reduction of a considerable part of the aid.

The Essential Parts of the YouthBuild Program

The YouthBuild program has two main goals: (1) The renovation of vacant, often dilapidated houses and (2) the education of young people. The education of young people is based on a theoretical (school lessons) as well as on a practical level (working in construction sites under instructions). The whole program lasts nine months. Half of the time the juveniles spend at school, the other half is used for the purpose of job training. Every education cycle consists of about 30 to 45 teenagers at the age of 17 to 21 years, 85 to 90% of them are males provided they can read (4th to 8th grade). The program invites all young persons to make use of it. It is most popular with the youth in the Harlem Community and therefore almost only blacks and Hispanics take part.

Each of the 15-23 trainees of a group spends two weeks in the construction site. Under instructions by YouthBuild cooperators and some specialists working on a voluntary basis, vacant buildings which are generally named by the New York City Housing Preservation Department (HPD) are renovated (about 65% of all vacant buildings are possessed by the municipality). The buildings on average comprise eight to ten dwelling units with three or four rooms each. In the construction site trainees work 35 hours a week. At the beginning they receive minimum wages of $ 4.25 an hour by the Department of Employment (DOE). From time to time, their pay increases if they are highly engaged in the job. The trainees work in a team, each consisting of five persons. To guarantee an all-round education, trainees work according to a rotation principle. To finish the renovation in time, further specialists are employed temporarily in critical phases. Of course, the specialists who are employed for this purpose work in firms which are situated in the Community. This is a further effect of YouthBuild for the local economy.

One of the biggest challenges for the organisation of the program was the provision of a working plan. On the one hand, the young people should learn as much as possible, on the other, the renovation had to be finished in time. One problem is the fact that the completion of a project lasts about 30 months. During each program which lasts nine months the trainees are not taught all operations which are necessary for the whole renovation. A possible solution would be to let them work at several projects in different stages of renovation at the same time. Thus, the trainees of one group would learn all operations and end up with the same experience of success.

An essential part of the YouthBuild program are school lessons given to the trainees in a warehouse prepared for this purpose. Its aim is to impart knowledge according to a High School standard to the teenagers, which is prescribed by the Department of Employment. In order to get financial aid from the Cityworks Program, public authorities are expected to present at least 20% of the trainees with a General Equivalency Degree (GED), which they acquire in class. In comparison to the job in the construction site, the teenagers consider the requirements on classroom education as a bigger challenge. The classroom education comprises 30 hours a week. For each lesson trainees receive a premium of $ 1. Since the achievement level varies, the lectures are given on an individual basis. About 10% of the groups acquire the GED.

One of the central elements of the Youth Action Program is the philosophy of *"Youth Leadership Development"* which should increase the self-consciousness and the identification of young people to make them responsible members of the Community.

Evaluation of the YouthBuild Program

The YouthBuild Program only educates high risk youth, i.e. young people without a school certificate. In many cases they have spent part of their lives in a detention center. Extreme personal and social circumstances of the young people make it impossible to use a strictly regulated education program. The extreme low success rates concerning the achievement of the GED or of the procurement of employment (about 50% are able to work) are the result of a very high expectation level by the bureaucrats. An extension of the education time and simultaneous work at several different projects to control the success rate of the trainees would be a proposal for the future.

The YouthBuild Program can be seen as a model, already twelve American cities with different organisation structures and different types of provision for financial aid are involved in this program. The Congress approved a YouthBuild Act which enabled YouthBuild to employ the education program all over the country.

The Harlem Urban Development Corporation (HUDC)

Aims and Basic Philosophy

Politicians stood up for the formation of the Harlem Urban Development Corporation. The basic philosophy of the HUDC does not concentrate on the advancement of individuals but concentrates on the improvement of basic conditions of the whole Harlem Community, whereby a local integration of blacks is not absolutely necessary to improve the socio-economic situation. This idea is opposed to the earlier social integration concept of the USA. The strategy of HUDC aims at stopping or reversing the trends of the continuing formation of ghettos, especially by means of increasing the attractiveness for moderate and middle income families. This results in higher taxes and as a consequence in improvement of public services, such as education and medical care. An economic and political vital community may finally combat discrimination.

The Harlem Urban Development Corporation (HUDC) was founded on a legal basis by the state of New York City in July 1971 and functions as a subsidiary company of the New York City State Urban Development Corporation (UDC). The head of the HUDC is the managing committee which consists of politicians (federal, state and city level), representatives of the most important institutions and organisations of the Harlem Community, firms and representatives of the church. This extremely wide spectrum guarantees an immediate feedback by the Community. The inclusion of important politicians makes it easier to obtain access to various resources. Thus, also ideas about changes in the zoning or economic advancement measures, e.g. tax relief for investments, etc. can be realized much faster.

The HUDC plans comprise a comprehensive revitalization of Harlem neighborhoods by means of a broad spectrum of development measures. Although a strict separation of different measures is neither possible nor wanted, three main goals should be mentioned:

- the procurement of housing facilities for low, moderate and middle income families
- the stabilisation or improvement of the economic situation by means of the support of existing firms and the advancement of the settlement of new businesses
- the cultivation and improvement of social and cultural life in the Harlem Community.

Problems of the HUDC

It is understandable that HUDC also gets bogged down with problems which delay or even prevent their success. For many years the New York City municipality deposited its numerous social problems in Harlem. They tried to solve the problem of homelessness by building housing silos to make homeless people disappear from the streets. Of course this increased the isolation of socially weak individuals and accelerated the descent of the Community.

Furthermore, the municipality had not yet developed an extensive revitalization concept for the Harlem Community. Measures are only patchwork, without long-term planning, and only meet the requirements of the actual policy.

- The municipality only builds rented apartments although HUDC made the conclusion that ownership increases the sense of responsibility.
- Instead of being adapted as a business street to renew the economy, Harlem's broadest boulevard served as a lodging place for homeless people.
- The space of most business places provided by the municipality is max. 400-500 sq. ft. For an appropriate catering of the population one would need much bigger spaces. The size of a pharmacy should be about 2,000 sq. ft., the size of a shop selling supplies about 3,500 sq. ft.
- One further problem of the Harlem Community is the real estate sector which has broken down. On the one hand side, numerous buildings are vacant on the virtue of suburbanisation of the black middle class (Black Flight), on the other, many families live in disgraceful conditions. The formation of ghettos provoked owners of vacant buildings to let them deteriorate, instead of investing in the Commuity.

The success of HUDC is badly disturbed by these deficiencies. Yet HUDC still tries to reach its ambitious aims by applying appropriate adaptive strategies.

Possibilities of Realization

Consequently, HUDC concentrated on the renovation of existing buildings and not on the construction of new ones. Carrying out the reconditioning measures did not change the basic structure of the buildings. The apartments are equipped with suitable standard furniture without any extras. Gentrification is not one of HUDC's goals. The Grass Roots Concept helps to identify and consider the needs of the population. Private firms are responsible for the building measures. These firms are situated in the Community, thus additional jobs are created and further income is guaranteed for the Community.

Besides the procurement of apartments to rent in the form of Co-ops (co-operative societies) or Condos, HUDC also supports initiatives of private persons and non-profit organisations in the form of consultation activities in the planning stage, financing, and providing technical knowhow. Finally, all these measures aim at improving the quality of life within the Community in order to attract families who left Harlem once, to return.

Structural improvements in the Harlem Community should be realized by means of a carefully calculated policy concerning the settlement of firms. The catering of the population and the creation of jobs with the view to income stabilisation are most important here. For this purpose, employers can make use of extensive consultation in the planning stage. HUDC procures credits and gives advice in finding open spaces or business premises suitable for the settlement of firms. The planning and provision of spaces and premises for commercial businesses and service industries is a special aim of the revitalization program. A good connection to charitable institutions make it possible to support social and cultural activities. On this occasion assistance to reduce the problems of homelessness and unemployment are provided. HUDC also helps public schools offer job consultation for students. Last but not least, HUDC supports the social and cultural life of the Community by sponsoring social and cultural events.

Success by HUDC

The HUDC has had considerable success in the revitalization of Harlem. Whereas, for example, at the beginning of the 80s, 125th Street was almost deserted, today it is a lively commercial street (*see Fig.6*). Beside numerous small shops and restaurants, a market, offering different African products exists. Despite the constant activity taking place on this major Harlem artery, one can still frequently find boarded-up houses, which remind us of the despair of the past.

Since it is absolutely impossible to renovate the total ghetto of the size of almost 4,000 acres, HUDC gave priority to some central neighborhoods which should enable a diffusion process. The renovation of the Bradhurst neighborhood is so far the biggest and most extensive revitalization program of HUDC (see Fig. 2). The Bradhurst neighborhood extends from 138th to 155th Street between Edgecombe Avenue and Adam Clayton Powell, Jr. Boulevard. During the Harlem Renaissance numerous famous people lived in Bradhurst. Since this time a permanent decay followed and Bradhurst developed into a low income neighborhood. 36% of the population left Bradhurst, 50% of the blocks are owned by the municipality of New York City. The share of persons with an income below $ 10,000 was 64%. The unemployment rate was 55%, about 33% of the inhabitants received public assistance.

The plan of HUDC comprised the following measures:

- The renovation of 2,841 dwelling units with estimated costs of $ 165 million. At least 50% of these dwelling units should be sold as cooperative apartments. Furthermore, it was also suggested that buildings owned by the municipality within the renovation program are to be modernized.
- The procurement of business premises of a size of 300,000 sq. ft. to improve the basic economic conditions and the creation of an industrial area.
- The creation of almost 500 new jobs which should guarantee an additional annual income of $ 9 million for inhabitants of the neighborhood.
- A vacant building was converted into an activity centre to strengthen the social and cultural life.
- Further building measures, such as the renovation of facades, the planting of traffic islands, parks, grass stripes, benches and fountains helped to create a pleasant atmosphere in the neighborhood.

To realize this project, HUDC put an effort into uniting different social powers of the Community, winning them for their plans. Thus, the Consortium for Central Harlem Development (CCHD) which was joined by many important organisations and institutions was founded (examples of various integrated groups are: Harlem Business Alliance, Greater Harlem Real Estate Board, Harlem Athletic Association, New York City Coalition of Black Architects, Uptown Chamber of Commerce etc.). Besides the creation of jobs by means of extensive building measures, HUDC made an important progress in 1989 concerning the economic stabilisation of the Bradhurst neighborhood. In cooperation with the urban authorities and other institutions HUDC was able to provide the Alexander Doll Company with a new business ground. Thus, HUDC succeeded in the resettlement of a firm within Harlem, in the preservation of 600 jobs (about 70% of the employees of Alexander DOLL live in the Harlem Community) and in transferring know-how.

All these initiatives seem to have changed a lot in Bradhurst. But, it will take a few more years to see whether the improvements will cause the return of middle class families, and not until then a long-term improvement of the socio-economic conditions can be guaranteed in the Bradhurst neighborhood.

Evaluation of the Work Done by HUDC

The concept-oriented projects of HUDC doubtlessly caused a considerable improvement of the living conditions in some of the Harlem neighborhoods. Since the revitalization process of the Harlem neighborhood has still been going on, the success cannot be quantified. Still, it is obvious that the stabilisation of the revitalization process must be invested in the communities in the long run. Furthermore, it is important that the described projects are not only concentrated on black ghettos, according to the existing dynamism of the population. This fact is necessary and future-oriented. There are numerous cities in the USA in which economic and social grievances, such as unemployment, crime and drug abuse etc. are similar to those in black ghettos. There is only one difference: the people of these ghettos are whites.

Conclusion

- Despite legal equality, the African Americans still face discrimination across class lines in many aspects.
- To guarantee an enduring socio-economic integration of African Americans, essential capital transfers would be necessary. Social problems provoke big losses for the national economy caused by the destruction of property and a loss of human resources due to drug abuse, etc. The imprisonment of young persons costs about $ 25,000 per person a year (including the costs for psychological training, education it is about $ 100,000). A place in the YouthBuild Program would only cost $ 20,000 (according to the Office of the Deputy Director of Parole, New York City State Penal System and to Andrew BAER, Director of the YouthBuild Program in East Harlem).
- The welfare system of the USA which offers little incentives for private initiatives, is urgently in need of reform. An example is the case of the 20 year old Sandra Rosado. She saved $ 4,900 to be able to attend college. Her family was asked by the authorities to either spend the money immediately or to renounce any payments by the welfare office in future (*Hays 1992, A1, B4*). A federal law allows families who receive public relief to have assets of max. $ 1,000. This makes it impossible for such families to escape from poverty.
- More participation of African Americans in public life in the form of grass root activities and cooperation in political decision-making would be desirable. A participation rate of 30% in voting is too low to reduce the political weakness of African Americans.
- In contrast to the social aid-programs, the presented projects are possibilities to improve the living conditions of African Americans on a long term perspective. The project-oriented

financial aid for YouthBuild and HUDC are not consumptive expenses but investments which guarantee a return on investment.

- Investments in human resources and in improvements of infrastructure may be a way out of the miserable situation of African Americans.
- In addition to financial aid, social and psychological measures for creating a value system for African Americans are important and would help to overcome the feeling of being second-class and to reduce fears concerning the future.
- Despite these arguments in favor of capital transfers, there are no signs at the moment that regulations and political interventions, which do not correspond with the American philosophy of a free economy, are planned or being discussed.

Zusammenfassung

Das Problem der Minderheiten hat die U.S.-amerikanische Gesellschaft an den Rand ihrer Lösungskompetenzen gebracht. Verbesserungen im großen Stile sind kaum vorstellbar, private und institutionelle Initiativen erscheinen wie ein Tropfen auf den heißen Stein. Sustainable development und das Ausschöpfen des endogenen Potentials stehen bei den Projekten *YouthBuild* und *Harlem Urban Development Corporation* auf die die folgenden Betrachtungen aufgebaut sind, im Mittelpunkt.

Trotz zahlreicher Integrationsversuche wie Assimilation in Form der "Anglo Conformity", der demokratische Weg des "Melting Pot" Konzeptes zur Verbesserung der Gesellschaft durch kulturelle Integration oder neuerdings die multikulturelle Gesellschaftsideologie, sind die ökonomischen und gesellschaftlichen Bedingungen der African Americans denkbar schlecht:

- Nur 12% der Schwarzen haben einen Bildungsabschluß auf College - Niveau (4- und mehrjährig), der Anteil bei den Weißen ist mit 25% mehr als doppelt so hoch.
- Das pro-Kopf-Einkommen der Schwarzen liegt mit $ 9,000 weit unter dem Durchschnitt der Weißen mit $ 15,300.
- Der Anteil der Personen, die unter der Armutsgrenze leben liegt bei den Schwarzen mit 32% (alleinerziehende Frauenhaushalte: 51%), wesentlich höher als bei den Weißen mit 11% (30%).
- Der Anteil der alleinerziehenden Frauenhaushalte beträgt bei den Schwarzen 56%, bei den Weißen 17%.
- Die Arbeitslosenrate (1991) ist bei Schwarzen mit 12% doppelt so hoch wie bei den Weißen.
- Das Durchschnittsvermögens der Schwarzen beträgt mit rund $ 26,000 weniger als ein Viertel desjenigen der Weißen ($ 112,000).
- Von rund 17,5 Millionen Firmen befinden sich nur 425,000 im Besitz von Schwarzen, die Einnahmen aus Industrie- und Gewerbeunternehmungen der Schwarzen betragen nur knapp 2% der Einnahmen der Weißen.

Folgen dieser ökonomischen und sozialen Disparitäten sind tiefe gesellschaftliche, persönliche und intrafamiliäre Krisen, wobei Wohlfahrtsinitiativen und Sozialprogramme nur die aktuelle Not lindern können, die eigentlichen Ursachen des Problems aber nicht erfassen. Im Gegensatz zu sozialen Hilfsprogrammen sollen mit Youth Action - YouthBuild und der Harlem Urban Development Corporation zwei alternative Projekte zur langfristigen Verbesserung der Lebensbedingungen der African Americans vorgestellt werden.

Bei den für YouthBuild und HUDC aufgewendeten finanziellen Mitteln wird in Produktionsfaktoren wie Humankapital und Infrastrukturen investiert, die langfristig ein return on investment erwarten lassen. Bedeutend sind die Investitionen flankierenden sozialen und psychosozialen

Maßnahmen, die die Wiederherstellung eines Wertesystems der African Americans zum Ziel haben und helfen sollen, das Gefühl der Zweitklassigkeit zu überwinden und Zukunftsängste abzubauen.

Die beträchtlichen sozio-ökonomischen Disparitäten scheinen dennoch ein dauerhafter Begleitumstand der U.S.-amerikanischen Gesellschaft zu sein, die Globalisierung der Wirtschaft verstärkt diese Tendenzen noch. Dennoch stellt sich die Frage, ob die Benachteiligung der African Americans nicht nur soziale Problem und damit verbundene volkswirtschaftliche Verluste erbringt, sondern auch eine Verschwendung von Humankapital bedeutet, was international Wettbewerbsnachteile bedingen kann. Regulative politische Eingriffe wären vonnöten, widersprechen allerdings der U.S.-amerikanischen Philosophie des freien Marktes.

References

Barringer, F. (Sept. 25,1992): Income Gap Thins Middle-Class Blacks. In: The New York Times, A12.
Blume, H.(1988^2): USA - Eine geographische Landeskunde, 2: Die Regionen der USA (=Wissenschaftliche Länderkunden 9), Darmstadt.
Diercke Weltatlas (1991): New York - Manhattan. Westermann, Braunschweig.
Dayment, T. N. (1980): Racial Equity or Racial Equality. In: Demography, 17, 379-393.
Farley, R. (1985): Three Steps Forward and Two Back? Recent Changes in the Social and Economic Status of Blacks. In: Alba, R. D. (ed.), Ethnicity and Race in the USA. London.
Freeman, R. B. (1976): Black Elite - The New Market for Highly Educated Black Americans. New York City.
Guinness, P. and Bradshaw M. (1985): North America - A Human Geography. New Jersey.
Hacker, A. (1992): Two Nations - Black and White, Separate, Hostile, Unequal. New York City.
Hahn, R. (1993^3): USA - Geographische Strukturen, Daten, Entwicklungen. Stuttgart.
Hall, P. (1966): Weltstädte. München.
Hays, C. L. (May 15, 1992): Welfare's Limit on Savings Foils One Bid to Break the Cycle. In: The New York Times, A1, B4.
HUDC (1991): HUDC Impact Area Fact Sheet - 1990 Statistics. New York City.
Jaynes, G. D. and Williams, R. M. Jr. (1989): A Common Destiny - Blacks and American Society. Washington, D.C.
Norton, M. et.al. (1988): A People and a Nation. Boston.
Pettigrew, T. F. (1979): The Changing but not Declining Significance of Race. In: Michigan Law Review, 77, 920.
Rinschede, G. (1985): Rassen- und Minderheitenprobleme - Ein weltweites Phänomen. In: Praxis Geographie, 2, 4-9.
Rose, P. I. (1990): They and We - Racial and Ethnic Relations in the United States. New York City.
Sherrell, M. (1991): Harlem Area - An Updated Report (1990 Statistics). New York City.
Thomas, M. E. (1993): Race, Class, and Personal Income: An Empirical Test of the Declining Significance of Race Thesis, 1968-1988. Social Problems, 40(3), 328-342.
Tidwell, B. J. (1992): The State of Black Amerika 1992. New York City.
Tobier, E. (1984): The Changing Face of Poverty: Trends in New York City City's Population in Poverty: 1960-1990. New York City.
U.S. Department of Commerce - Bureau of the Census (1991): The Black Population in the United States: March 1990 and 1989. Washington, D.C.
U.S. Department of Commerce - Bureau of the Census (1992a): Household Economic Studies, Health Insurance Coverage: 1987-1990. Washington, D.C.
U.S. Department of Commerce - Bureau of the Census (1992b): How We're Changing, Demographic State of the Nation: 1992. Washington, D.C.
U.S. Department of Commerce - Bureau of the Census (1992c): Housing In America: 1989/90. Washington, D.C.

Weatherspoon, F. D. (1985): Equal Employment Opportunity and Affirmative Action - A Sourcebook. New York City.
Willie, C. V. (1978): The Inclining Significance of Race. In: Society, 15(10), 12-15.
Wilson, W. J. (1980^2): The Declining Significance of Race: Blacks and Changing American Institutions. Chicago.
Wilson, W. J. (1987): The Truly Disadvantaged: The Inner City, the Underclass and Public Policy. Chicago.

Addresses of the Authors

Friedrich M. Zimmermann
Department of Geography
University of Klagenfurt
9020 Klagenfurt
AUSTRIA

Gert Krautbauer
Seehoferstraße 16
80686 München
GERMANY

ROLAND VOGELSANG

Internal Migration in Canada: Trends, Causes, and Consequences

Introduction

One of the outstanding characteristics of Canada is the country's unbalanced population distribution. It's large size is well known. Canada is the second largest country in the world, but its approximately 27 million inhabitants have settled this space and are using it in extremely different ways. Intensive, multifunctional land use in city cores with high rise buildings are but one extreme, the others are large areas in which very extensive land use is practised and in which population density is arithmetically calculated by figures such as 0.02 people per square mile for the Territories. With remarkable success, therefore, the core - hinterland concept was used by MC CANN (1982 and 1987) in his regional geography of Canada. Although heterogeneous distribution of population is a characteristic of many countries, Canada is an extreme example. There is a remarkable dynamic in all settlement systems. For a better understanding of processes, as background for policy makers, planners, business people as well as for personal purposes, trends in the distribution and redistribution of population are at least as important as the settlement system itself. In both cases, we need approaches, approaches which are appropriate for the specific aims of understanding problems and for making recommendations and taking decisions.

This paper will first discuss some general trends in population change and population redistribution. Second, it will investigate the role of migration in these observed processes. Two points are of particular interest: (a) the regional aspects of migration and (b) the age-specific nature of migration.

In trying to understand migration, we look for forces which influence the decision of people to migrate. A brief summary of this wide field of research, in relation to the Canadian situation, will lead to some basic questions of changes in preferences. Finally, rising from the observation of growing differentiation in migration patterns and growing specialization of areas and communities, some general conclusions are presented.

Trends in Canada's Population Distribution and Redistribution

Three approaches can be used to investigate population trends in Canada:
a) the concept of the rural-urban dichotomy,
b) the concept of Metropolitan regions
c) the urban hierarchy concept.

ad a) The number of people living in the urban areas of Canada has increased continuously since the middle of the last century, probably in contrast to the image of the development of the Canadian settlement system. The percentage of the population classified as urban increased from 13% in 1851 to 50% as early as 1921, and in 1991 it is 77% (Census 1961, Cat. 92 - 536; Census 1991, Cat. 93-339)[1]. We may see this as a clear trend towards urbanization. Clearly, Canada is a country with a highly urbanized society.

Rates are more interesting regarding trends. Urban growth rates exceeded rural growth rates during most periods of Canadian history, thus supporting the use of the term urbanization to describe this process[2]. Between 1971 and 1976, for the first time, the rural population grew faster than the urban population. Analysing this trend, PARENTEAU came to the conclusion that "increase in the rural proportion of the total population between 71 - 76 is a landmark in the evolution of Canada's population. It may signify the end of the increasing trend toward urbanization." Similar trends were observed earlier in the U. S. and were labelled as "Counterurbanization" (*Berry 1976*). For some Canadians this turnaround, "ruralization" or back-to-the-land phenomenon was assumed to take place in Canada as well.

However, this trend did not continue. Between 1976 and 1986, it looked as if Canada was going back to "normal" urbanization. The latest figures from 1986 to 1991 indicate another change. Consequently we may now speak of a "turnaround of the turnaround of the turnaround". In 1991 urban and rural population growth rates are approximately the same.

ad b) The general idea of Census Metropolitan Areas (CMAs) is one of a large urban core, together with adjacent "urban" and "rural" areas which have a high degree of economic and social integration with that core, thus overcoming a somewhat artificial rural-urban dichotomy[3].

The number of Canadians living in large urban complexes has grown over time. This was partly due to newly defined CMAs, 17 of which we counted in 1961, compared to 25 since 1981. Changes of boundaries, that means adjustments and enlargement of CMAs, were made in reaction to the continuing spread of suburbs and rural areas used by commuters. Since 1966, we count more people in Canada's CMAs than in the rest of the country. In 1991, just over 60% of the Canadian population live in big cities and their hinterlands.

Again, the growth rates present a more complicated picture. Notwithstanding the fact that, since 1951, the rates of the CMAs are above those from the "rest", the differences of both growth rates are not continuous and trends are sometimes converging, sometimes enlarging. ANDERSON and PAPAGEORGIOU who published a detailed analysis of Metropolitan and Non-Metropolitan Population trends in Canada between 1966 and 1982 remark: "Trends consistent with the shift from urbanization to counter-urbanization and back again ... were clearly reflected in the Canadian metropolitan system during the period of our study" (*Anderson and Papageorgiou 1992, 138*). During the latest intercensus period (1986 to 1991) the two growth rates came closer again.

ad c) Within the urban hierarchy, i.e. settlements classified by size of population, the growing dominance of the metropolitan centers is impressive[4]. Between 1951 and 1986, large urban growth rates exceeded rural and small town growth rates. However, small towns and rural population, more precisely the rural non-farm population, did not decline correspondingly. Since 1951, about the same number of people have lived in the medium sized (10,000 to 100,000) and in the small towns (1,000 to 10,000) category.

In addition, the growth rates as shown in the census indicate some interesting changes: Whereas during the period 1951 - 1961 there existed in general a statistically significant positive relationship between size and growth rates, meaning further concentration, in the following decades this "hierarchical" order was broken. Between 1961 and 1971, the medium sized group grew fastest, the small towns grew remarkably. In the following decade, the increase in rural population was second only to that of the big cities, and in the last decade, the growth rate for people living in medium and large cities has come close. Considering these patterns, FIELDING's (1983) methodological approach to judge urbanization and counterurbanization by the statistical relationship between size and growth rates becomes questionable. HODGE (1983) wondered if the "intellectual commotion" surrounding a perceived rural growth and regrowth was adequately captured by the term "counterurbanization". He decided to use small centers (settlements up to 10,000 inhabitants in 1971) to assess population growth trends in non-urban areas. He found that "for 1971 - 1976 among villages with fewer than 100 and 500 population, slightly less than one-half grew; and among those with more than 1,000 residents, over three-quarters added to their population" (*Hodge 1983, 22*). For the same time, small town growth did not only exceed the overall national growth rate in five provinces, but in the same number of provinces, small town

aggregate annual growth rates were greater than the growth rate of CMAs.
Here, as well as in the discussion of rural growth rates we may ask ourselves about spillover from large urban agglomerations. Proximity to the metropolis is a crucial point. HODGE (1983) pointed out that while the growth of about 800 small centers seemed to be accounted for by metro proximity, there were over 3,800 other growing small centers well beyond the metropolis[5].
Using different approaches one comes to the conclusion that there are no clear trends any more. As late as 1981, in a paper on Canadian urban growth trends, ROBINSON (1981) identified three spatial population trends in Canada:

- an increasing concentration of people in Central Canada (Quebec and Ontario);
- an increasing concentration of people in the upper level of the urban size hierarchy;
- a gradual abandonment of rural areas.

It looks as if these previously well-established population trends do not exist any more. Characteristic of more recent times are non-linear trends. At least for some time, the dominance of Central Canada declined, a deconcentration away from the upper levels of the urban hierarchy was obvious, and a population movement from urban areas toward rural areas could be identified (*see also: Anderson and Papageorgiou 1992, 126*).

The Role and Impact of Migration

Changes in population distribution are the complex result of different, sometimes overlapping and contradictory trends. However, migration is the most sensitive of the demographic components. Migration indicates, better than changes in fertility or mortality, recent trends in society. Furthermore, regional and temporal variations of natural demographic figures, which were significant in Canada in earlier times, diminished during recent decades and are almost marginal today (if we exclude the native peoples in the North). Our focus on migration is consistent with observations by POOLER (1987) and ANDERSON and PAPAGEORGIOU (1992) that migration is the dominant force behind the differential rates of population growth across regions of Canada.

Sources for Internal Migration Data in Canada

VANDERKAMP and GRANT (1988) analysed the major sources of existing internal migration data in Canada and provided some comparisons and evaluations of the various data sets available. They came to the conclusion that the Census micro data sets are the best currently available in Canada, but their usefulness is somewhat limited as it does not represent a longitudinal data base. Data have only been since the 1961 Census. Family Allowance Files and Revenue Canada Tax files are even more limited with regard to time series. The advantage is that these are available on a yearly basis, whereas the Census migration survey uses data derived from a question about the individual's residence location five years prior to the census date; hence it is a 5-year retrospective migration data set. The lack of a reliable longitudinal micro data base is the most serious problem in Canadian migration research. There is nothing comparable to the major U.S. micro data sources or to the data available in Germany.

General Trends in Migration in Canada

How mobile are Canadians, has the mobility and mobility status changed in the last decades? Almost half of the Canadian population recorded a move between the different censuses (*Fig. 1*). Going more into detail, we observe some surprising changes.
There is, in general, an increase in mobility from 1961 to 1976, a decrease in the following two periods and an upswing again for the latest period. This is the case not only for movers in total

Fig. 1: Percentage Distribution of Population ≥5 Years: Mobility Status for Canada, 1961 - 1991

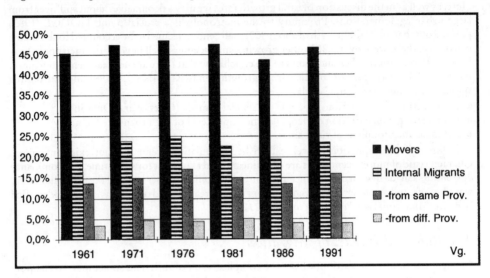

Sources: Statistics Canada: Census 1986 (Cat. 93 - 108); Census 1991 (Cat. 93 - 322)

Fig. 2: Interprovincial Migration Rates: Canada, 1970 - 1992

Sources: Revenue Canada Tax Files and Family Allowance Files; from Dumas/ Lavoie 1992, and Dumas 1994.

(including all persons who, on Census Day, were living at a different address than the one at which they resided one year earlier) but similar and somewhat clearer for internal migrants, movers who were residing in a different City or Census Subdivision five years earlier (i.e. at the previous Census). This increase and decline of migration rate was noticed by VANDERKAMP and GRANT (1988) as well. By comparing data from different sources they remark: "Two possible explanations come to mind. First, the incidence of repeat migration may have diminished over this period; but we have no data to support this. Second, the migration propensities of other members of the population (other than families), and particularly of unattached individuals, may have changed over time. The increase of young people entering the labor market during the seventies and early eighties is at least consistent with this" (*Vanderkamp and Grant 1988, 21*).
In detail, we find another surprising fact: whereas the intraprovincial migrants show a pattern similar to that just described, the interprovincial or long-distant migrants did have the highest migration rate for the period 1976 to 1981, followed by a more continuous decrease between 1981 and 1991.
Complimentarily, we can look at migration rates derived from Canadian Family Allowance files and Revenue Tax files which have been available since 1970 only, but on a yearly base.
The curve (*Fig. 2*) gives some support to the well known fact that the mobility of the population is linked to the economic dynamics of the country[6]. For example, we can clearly see the effects of the recession of the first half of the 1980s. Nevertheless, there has been a general trend towards lower mobility since 1973 which cannot be explained by economic factors alone. Changes in migration rates indicate ambiguous trends, they vary considerably.

Regional Aspects of Migration Trends in Canada

Main Regions and Provinces

Since Canada is a large country, there are substantial regional differences in resources, in the economic and social development and consequently in recent structure. In general the regional approach is very important in Canada. The easiest regional differentiation is that by provinces or by combined provinces ("main regions").
The interprovincial migration rates are calculated in comparison to the Canadian average, the regional divergences are obvious (*Tab. 1*). For all the Census results shown, Quebec is well below the average and the rest of Canada (a term often used today to summarize the cultural duality in Canada)[7]. At the same time, we see relatively low rates in Newfoundland which at first glance may be seen as a consequence of dominant out-migration. However, there are relatively low rates for Ontario, too, for all the different Censuses. The exceptionally high figures in the Territories are remarkable which have an extreme fluctuation of some people and where the migration rates are influenced by the small number of people living there. In general, the most western provinces (Alberta and British Columbia) have high migration rates as well, primarily due to immigration from other provinces. On the other hand, there are relative high rates for Prince Edward Island and the other two maritime provinces (Nova Scotia and New Brunswick), which supposedly are a result of substantial returning migration. As interesting as these figures might be, in our context they are first of all used to demonstrate the diversity of the internal migration structure in Canada. What are the overall results of the internal migration streams over the last decades?
From the early 60s until the early 80s, Quebec had an increasingly strong net out-migration while Ontario gained until about 1972, when out-migration from this province started to surpass in-migration as well (*Tab. 2*). But while Ontario turned back to positive net-migration figures, Quebec has been losing people up to the present. According to this data, Quebec had a net out-migration balance of about 340,000 people between 1956 to 1991.

Tab.1: Interprovincial Migration Rates by Provinces: Divergence from Canadian Average, 1971-1991

Region	Province	(Divergence from Canada =100)				
		1971	1976	1981	1986	1991
	Canada	100	100	100	100	100
Atlantic	Nfld	47	70	93	71	83
	P.E.I.	165	195	249	175	205
	N.S.	121	151	170	137	173
	N.B.	144	149	177	127	140
Quebec	Que.	44	33	33	20	28
Ontario	Ont.	82	79	63	63	85
Prairies	Man.	159	147	142	114	148
	Sask.	124	100	144	143	150
West	Alta	215	202	242	325	208
West	B.C.	188	226	200	182	143
North	Terr.s	685	624	624	501	510

Source: Statistics Canada: Census1986, 1991 (Cat. 93-108, -322)

Tab. 2: Net Internal Migration by Provinces of Canada, 1956-1991

Region	Province	5-years Net-Migration						
		1961	1971	1976	1981	1986	1991	1956 - 91
Atlantic	Nfld.	-4,673	-15,400	-6,880	-19,835	-16,555	-13,945	-77,288
	P.E.I.	-1,009	-1,005	2,385	-5	1,535	-850	1,901
	N.S.	-15,277	-7,770	5,395	-8,420	6,275	-4,885	-19,797
	N.B.	-5,270	-7,610	9,305	-8,505	-1,375	-6,060	-13,455
Quebec	Que.	-7,756	-70,715	-59,805	-141,725	-63,300	-25,560	-343,301
Ontario	Ont.	34,274	54,550	-52,505	-78,065	99,360	46,965	57,614
Prairies	Man.	-15,957	-29,900	-26,610	-43,585	-1,545	-35,260	-117,597
	Sask.	-33,577	-68,040	-30,150	-5,825	-2,815	-60,365	-140,407
West	Alta.	16,787	22,730	61,860	197,650	-27,665	-25,005	271,362
West	B.C.	33,230	120,035	95,885	110,935	9,500	125,870	369,585
North	Yukon*	-682	1,550	400	-550	-2,660	790	-1,942
	N.W.T.	-	1,575	710	-2,055	-750	-1,695	-520

*1961 N.W.T. included in Yukon
Source: Statistics Canada: Census 1986 (Cat. 93-108), T. 3; Census 1991 (Cat. 93-322), T. 2A.

If we look at the main gaining provinces, it seems clear that the most western Provinces, Alberta and British Columbia, are the destination of most Canadians. The net balance for British Columbia is almost 370,000, the second winner is Alberta. This population redistribution due to migration is sometimes interpreted as a westward movement, in contrast to the older migration pattern, which perpetuated and strengthened the dominance of central Canada.

However, the migration streams are not as clear as the balances might suggest. Even in the table showing net-migration only, we can observe inconsistent patterns. The Atlantic Provinces (Nfld., P.E.I., N.S., and N.B.) are well known for their predominant out-migration stream, but in the balance over more than 30 years, the little Prince Edward Island (with a population of only 130,000 in 1991) gained in total. Without discussing these figures in detail, what could be labeled "exceptions" should be pointed out, i.e. inter-censual deviations from the long-time results, as indicated by bold figures in *Tab. 2*.

Most striking are two periods in Ontario and Alberta. Anticipating part of the discussion on impacts of migration below, these outstanding shifts are first of all interpreted as a consequence of the boom and bust turnaround in the energy sector. But we will see that this is only one of a number of diverse determinants. So far it is important to realize the shifts over regions and over time.

The impact of net-migration on population distribution and redistribution plays an increasing role, since differences in natural demographic changes have diminished. However, if we are interested in migration as an expression of economic and social changes in a society, we have to look at migration streams rather than at net-migration.

In the last line of the *Tab. 3*, there are the net-migration figures for the different provinces, corresponding with those of the second last column in *Tab. 2*.

As an example, Newfoundland had a negative balance for the period 1986 to 1991 of about 14,000 in general consistence with predominant out-migration during the last decades. But this province counted for the period 1986 to 1991 almost 21,000 in-migrants. Or another example: Quebec registered 82,000 in-migrants, but had a negative balance of 25,500 people. It is therefore important to realize that there is in fact no such thing as net-migrants or net-migration streams outside of the statistical use in the calculation of population changes in space.

In every case, there are migration streams in both directions - which are several times as large as the net-migration figures, and this fact must be kept in mind during the discussion of factors which may influence people's decision to migrate.

Tab. 3: Interprovincial Migrants >5 years: Place of Residence, 1986 and 1991

Place of Residence 1991	Place of Residence 1986						In-Migrants
	Atl. Prov.	Que.	Ont.	Prair. Prov.	B.C.	Terr.n	
Atl. Prov.	-	12,220	43,335	17,590	7,335	1,180	81,660
Que.	12,330	-	51,430	12,265	5,530	440	81,995
Ont.	63,840	72,780	-	92,680	37,745	2,940	269,985
Prair. Prov.	17,960	10,410	58,245	-	57,865	5,750	150,230
B.C.	11,655	11,500	67,830	141,140	-	6,045	238,170
Terr.n	1,615	645	2,180	7,185	3,825	-	15,450
Out-Migrants	107,400	107,555	223,020	270,860	112,300	16,355	837,490
Net-Migration	-25,740	-25,560	46,965	-120,630	125,870	-905	

Quelle: Census 1991 (93-322), Tab. 2A.

CMAs and Rest

SIMMONS (1980) and FIELD (1988) found that the tendency of population to concentrate in the largest cities, at least temporarily, abated during the seventies. Both studies were based on migration flows among over 200 census divisions on five-year intervals 1966 - 1971 and 1971 - 1976. SIMMONS found that the net migration rates of the largest cities declined rapidly between

Tab. 4: International Migrants and Net Internal Migration, 1986-1991 by Census Metropolitan Areas (CMAs)

Region	CMA	Internat. Migrants [1]	(Canadian) Internal Migration			Total Net-Migration [2]	Total Pop. (1,000) 1991
			Net with Non-CMA	Net Between CMA	from outsinde the Province		
Atlantic	St.-John's	680	5,610	-3,975	67%	2,315	172
	Halifax	2,700	4,900	-4,145	73%	3,455	321
	St. John	470	435	-1,040	46%	-135	125
Què.	Chicoutimi	130	1,630	-5,655	19%	-3,895	161
	Québec	2,375	15,650	-6,915	14%	11,110	646
	Trois-Rivières	145	3,750	-2,175	4%	1,720	136
	Sherbrooke	1,025	2,870	-3,035	8%	860	139
	Montréal	80,115	-20,000	-10,625	29%	49,490	3,127
	Ottawa-Hull	23,095	7,385	17,625	52%	48,105	921
Ont.	Oshawa	3,665	-5,735	21,595	14%	19,525	240
	Toronto	250,950	-82,490	-32,500	44%	135,960	3,893
	Hamilton	12,910	-8,980	12,755	18%	16,685	600
	St. Catherine	3,535	55	6,885	18%	10,475	365
	London	10,835	2,575	3,105	17%	16,515	382
	Kitchener	10,770	-2,875	12,870	16%	20,765	356
	Windsor	6,120	-2,155	-3,445	25%	520	262
	Sudbury	330	2,660	-30	16%	2,960	158
	Thunder Bay	720	-1,075	-2,315	37%	-2,670	124
Prairies'	Winnipeg	15,240	-590	-18,565	66%	-3,915	652
	Regina	1,735	2,200	-9,985	45%	-6,050	192
	Saskatoon	1,680	3,485	-13,925	44%	-8,760	210
Alberta	Calgary	22,645	1,600	1,470	64%	25,715	754
	Edmonton	21,245	6,200	-17,940	56%	9,505	840
B.C.	Vancouver	87,410	-7,050	46,970	59%	127,330	1,603
	Victoria	3,055	6,640	12,890	48%	22,585	288
total		563,580	-63,305	(±136,165)		500,170	16,665

[1] Population >5years living outside Canada in 1986 and received as immigrants between 1986 and 1991.
[2] Canadians living 1986 abroad not included.

Source: Census 1991 (Cat. 93-222); s.a. Dumas 1994, 66-74.

the late sixties and the early seventies. Confirming this, FIELD found that the 23 largest cities, taken as a group, had negative net migration over the period 1971 - 1976. ANDERSON and PAPAGEORGIOU (1992) analysed a data series of annual income tax records and migration flows among 35 regions in Canada: 25 CMAs and the non-metropolitan components for each of the ten provinces. They found that internal migration trends indicate "that prior to 1970, the internal net migration rate is positive for metropolitan Canada and negative for non-metropolitan Canada. During the period from 1972 to 1979, the opposite is true. However, the reversal ended in the early eighties as both metropolitan and non-metropolitan internal net migration rates get close to zero" (*Anderson and Papageorgiou 1992, 128*).

In addition, ANDERSON and PAPAGIORGEIOU pointed out that the difference between total and internal net migration rates is greater for metropolitan than for non-metropolitan areas, which is consistent with the observation that most new immigrants (about 80%) first settle in large cities. Of the immigrants aged five years and over living outside Canada in 1986 and in Canada in 1991, about 70% still stayed in Census Metropolitan Areas in 1991 (calculated after: *Statistics Canada, 1991 Census (Cat. 93 - 222)*). In this respect Toronto is outstanding where about a quarter of a million people settled who immigrated between 1986 and 1991 (*see Tab. 4*). International migration is important for the large CMAs in particular.

Between 1986 and 1991 total population growth of CMAs was higher than for the country as a whole (10% compared to 6.2%, *see also: Vogelsang 1993, 202*). However, all CMAs together lost population to non-metropolitan areas due to Canadian internal migration (*see Tab. 4*). Looking at this kind of migration, of the 25 CMAs 16 gained and only 9 lost. The largest positive balance was in the Quebec City CMA (15, 650) and the big loser was Toronto which alone accounted for 63% of the total loss.

Since over 60% of the Canadian population lives in CMAs, it is not surprising that migration between them explains a substantial part of the differential growth. In general for the time period 1986 to 1991 in Ontario CMAs recruited a large percentage of their in-migrants from the other CMAs, in particular from within Ontario. It therefore exchanged population mainly with other CMAs and mainly with Toronto and Ottawa. The few CMAs in the Atlantic Provinces generate a special situation, in which the proportion of in-migrants from other provinces is fairly high. In Quebec, all CMAs lost population to other CMAs. The CMA in Quebec received a small proportions from other CMA in the province. In general, they received very little population from outside Quebec and recruited in-migrants from smaller towns or rural areas. With the exception of Montreal, no CMA recruited 20% of its immigrants outside the province. In contrast, in Western Canada a high proportion of in-migrants came from a province other than that in which the CMA is located. "Each of the western CMAs, of which there are few, recruited differently, both in the country's CMAs (30% in Saskatoon and 61% in Victoria) and in smaller cities" (*Dumas 1994, 69*).

In more recent time, migration streams between CMAs and CMAs, between CMAs and non-CMAs, between CMAs and census agglomerations, between CMAs and rural areas seem to be more complicated than 10 or 15 years ago.

Age Specific Aspects of Migration in Canada

Age Groups and Spatial Structures

It is often stated that migration is age specific. What does this mean? First of all, migration is most likely to occur at a particular age, as demonstrated by the status of migration by age groups for Canada, based on the 1991 Census (*Fig. 3*):

Clearly, the 25 - 34 age group is the most mobile. According to the Census this group is in fact the only one in which movers surpass non-movers. More remarkable is the fact that the number of internal migrants (migrants from the same and from different provinces) surpassed non-

Fig. 3: Canadian Population ≥5 Years by Age Groups and Mobility Status, 1991

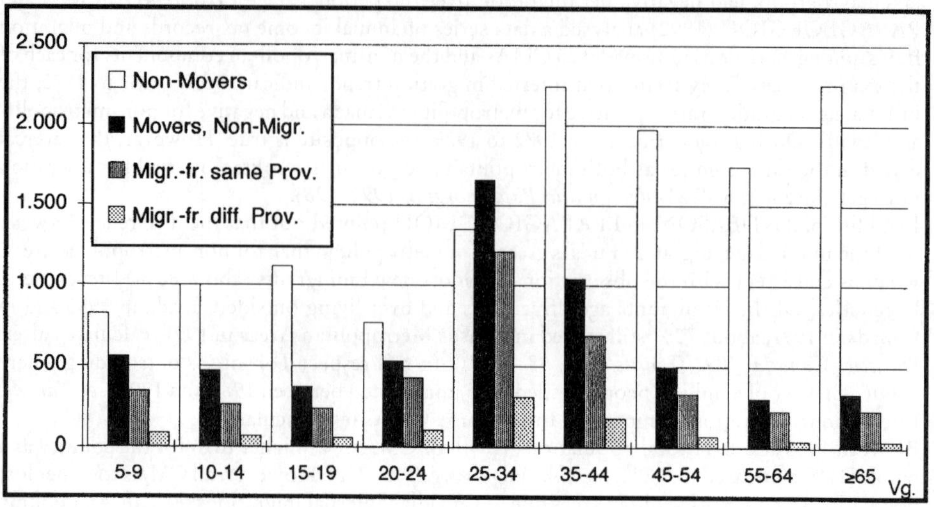

Source: Statistics Canada: Census 1991 (Cat. 93 - 322, Tab. 1A).

movers as well. But even though it is correct to say that from this group upwards with growing age, mobility is declining, there is no symmetry in this pattern with the downward age groups. Moreover, it is worth pointing out that in all age groups there are movers and migrants! One of the reasons is that while statistically it is often assumed that a move is made to a location in which the individual will stay for the remainder of his life, we have to realize that multiple moves occur. The growing literature on elderly migration is only one reaction to this fact. It seems more adequate to take the life cycle notion and expect that individuals make moves at various times to take advantage of location characteristics that they know will be attractive only during a particular life stage.

Consequently, MUESER et al. (1988) for example identify four phenomena in which settlements tend towards specialization in serving particular age groups, such as:

a) large teaching institutions,
b) labor market attraction (in a wider sense) for young adults, including diverse occupational opportunities, special job training in large corporations etc.,
c) residential amenities attractive to a disproportionate number of families with children (suburban areas of large metros) and
d) areas with the lowest costs of living and high levels of residential amenities which will be most attractive to retirees and are less attractive in terms of job opportunities (*Mueser, White and Tierney 1988,* 60).

As a result of the growing diversification in Canadian society, we observe a process of settlement differentiation during the last decades. Greater wealth and improvements in the technology of communications and transportation make migration easier, and the patterns of area specialization according to age-specific amenities and opportunities are increasing.

The Role of Elderly Migration and Elderly Settlements in Canada

Canada is experiencing a rapid aging of its population as is true in almost every highly developed country. The share of Canadians aged 65 and over grew from 7.6% of the total population in 1961 to 10.6 in 1991. But the growth of the elderly population is not occurring uniformly across space. Such a geographic redistribution of the elderly population is caused not only by regional mortality differentials and delayed effects of regional fertility and mortality differentials, but also by migration among elderly population as well as by migration among the non-elderly population. Given the somewhat uniform patterns of fertility and mortality within Canada, migration is therefore paramount in shaping spatial differentials in the growth of the elderly population. Although migration of the non-elderly population (which, after migrating, ages in place) is probably in the long run a more important factor than elderly migration, the latter makes the largest contribution to regional concentrations of elderly in the short term (*Ledent and Liaw 1989, 1093*).

As demonstrated already, the elderly are significantly less likely to migrate than the non-elderly. Nevertheless, elderly migration affects the population age structure at various levels. The impact of an increasingly mobile elderly population, coupled with particular migration destinations, concentrates the elderly in specific areas of Canada.

It has already been pointed out that the majority of moves undertaken by the elderly are of short rather than long distance. Despite this fact, similarities and differences in the migration streams of the older population give an impression of what can be called "age-specific" migration (*Tab. 5, Fig. 4*).

First of all we see that in the Atlantic Provinces there are positive net-migration figures, in contrast to the balances for all migrants. We may suspect that a great part of this is return-migration, a fact which unfortunately can be verified by data of the census only indirectly. On the other hand, there is a remarkable out-migration of elderly from the Atlantic Provinces into Ontario. This province attracted more than 40% of those ≥ 55 years leaving Newfoundland and Nova Scotia and about 72% of those leaving Quebec. The in-migrants into Ontario, however, are outnumbered by out-migrants. For elderly migrants out of Ontario and the Prairie Provinces, Alberta and in particular British Columbia were the most important destinations. Therefore, we can observe an east-west division of the migration pattern in Canada. - Again, we are confirming the importance of migration streams in contrast to net-migration.

Tab. 5: Interprovincial Migrants ≥ 55 years: Place of Residence 1986 and 1991

Place of Residence 1991	Place of Residence 1986						In-Migrants
	Atl. Prov.	Que.	Ont.	Prair. Prov.	B.C.	Terr.n	
Atl. Prov.	-	1,280	4,790	720	410	70	7,270
Que.	730	-	4,620	750	345	15	6,460
Ont.	2,765	8,115	-	4,780	2,760	115	18,535
Prair. Prov.	690	985	5,035	-	6,430	440	13,580
B.C.	465	820	5,435	9,035	-	205	15,960
Terr.n	65	10	55	220	145	-	495
Out-Migrants	4,715	11,210	19,935	15,505	10,090	845	62,300
Net-Migration	2,555	-4,750	-1,400	-1,925	5,870	-350	

Quelle: Census 1991 (93-322), Tab. 2A.

Fig. 4: In- and Out-migrants ≥55 Years for Ontario and Atlantic Provinces, 1986 - 1991

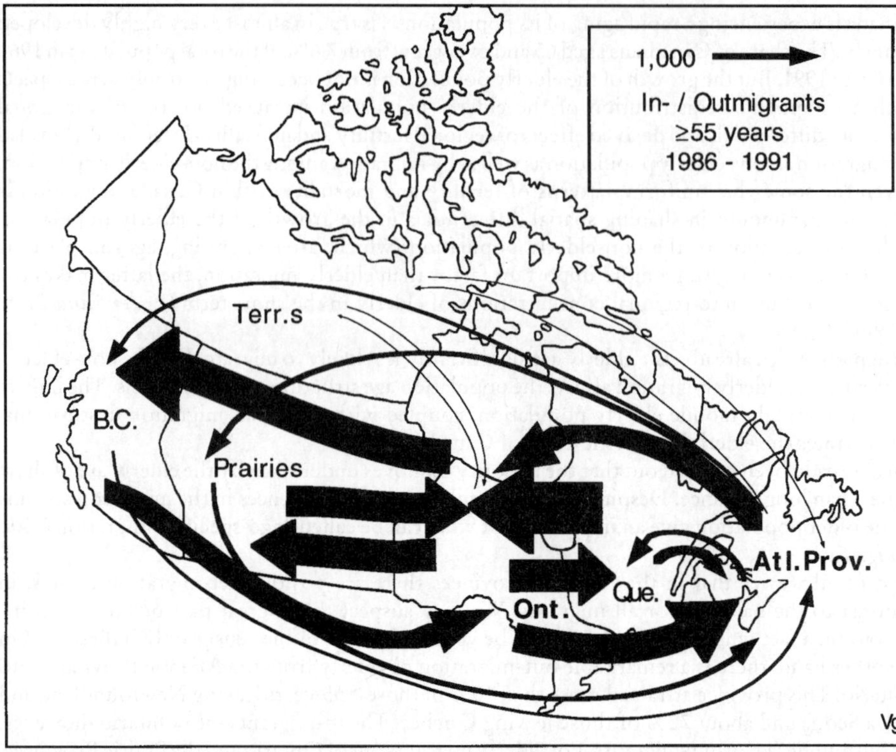

Source: Statistics Canada Census 1991 (Cat. 93 - 322)

In addition, LEE (*1980, 135*) found, that the long-distance migration of the older population tends to be "diffuse in origin" and "highly specific in destination". For example, older persons from all over the Prairie Provinces have a tendency to migrate to south-central and southwestern British Columbia. In other words, the migration of older persons has a tendency to lead to their concentrations in selected locations. Similar observations can be made for small towns in in Ontario. DAHMS found that "Retirees from cities were especially attracted to places with historic architecture, beaches, marinas or good housing stock. Retired farmers often made a short move from their farms to their local market town" (*Dahms 1987, 61*). This "graying of local or regional populations" implies both social and economic transformations.
This concentration of the elderly is most impressively illustrated by HODGE (1991) by showing the small towns in which the share of population • 65 is above average (*Fig. 5*).

Factors Influencing Migration

In view of our more or less descriptive results on migration patterns and their changes, it is hardly surprising that migration in Canada - as elsewhere - is viewed as an extremely complex process. Research by different disciplines, planners, and policy-makers has expressed a great deal of

Fig. 5: Towns with a High Percentage of Elderly in B.C.

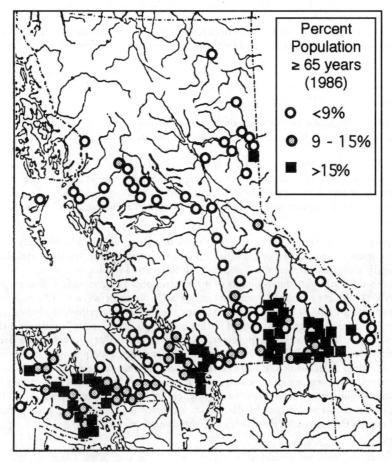

Source: from Hodge 1991, 3.

interest in monitoring patterns and changes of migration and the impact on the development of towns, cities or entire regions. Besides the studies already mentioned, in Canada most research during the last few decades has basically described spatial movements, whereas other studies were seeking to analyse rates of in- or out-migration in correlation with social and economic data available. Pioneering work in this respect has been undertaken by ANDERSON (1966) and STONE (1967, 1969, 1978, 1979), although their results were hampered by limited data. Typical for such findings were observations that short distance, intra-area moves make up the largest proportion of total mobility and that an east-west division of the migration field has been an important feature of Canada's demographic system (*Stone 1974*).

ANDERSON (1966) was probably the first to publish a wide ranged study on Internal Migration in Canada, covering the period 1921 -1961[8]. He basically confirmed the classical economic observation of a close relationship between migration and changes in economic activities, whether as "push" or as "pull" factors, but he nevertheless remarked: "a precise delineation of the causes is not a simple and straighforward task" (*Anderson 1966, 27*). In addition he noted that migration is selective with respect to age, education, occupation and physical capacity, as well as with respect to other characteristics such as marital status and the stage of family formation. ANDERSON found that rates of migration tend to be high for people in their twenties and, after the age of thirty, they decrease as age increases. He summarized: "internal migrants are typically young adults in the ages of greatest productivity and of greatest reproductivity" (*Anderson 1966, 30*).

During the following decades research concentrated more or less on testing these observations with increasingly better statistical methods. To take one example there follow some of COURCHENE's (1981) results:

- "Gross out-migration rates tend to decline with increasing age.
- "Migration rates are higher for the low-income class than they are for the middle-income class."
- "The all-provinces migration rate for interprovincial movers in the high-income group is greater than it is for the middle-income group, while intra-provincial high-income movers have a lower rate than the middle-income group."
- "Age is a more important determinant of migration than is income class." (*Courchene 1974, 142f*).

It is impossible here even to summarize the different analyses undertaken by many Canadians seeking a better understanding of (internal) migration, but it is clear that the methods became increasingly sophisticated with more and more differentiated results.

A comprehensive study on determinants of intermetropolitan migration in Canada is provided by SHAW (1985). He examined variations in migration flows between CMAs over four time periods spanning 1966 to 1981. As in other studies, the aim was to decipher the behaviour of the "average" or "typical" migrant in terms of his/her response to "objectively" measured differences between CMAs. Based on 29 hypotheses, he extensively analyzes the Census data using multivariate statistical techniques. He identifies what can be called plausible determinants of migration. Most interesting are his results concerning the changing nature of migration determinants, since we see these changes as an expression/indication of the more or less continuous evolution of society over time. Changes in production technologies, in the social system, in values and preferences in lifestyle are expressed in changing migration patterns.

SHAW divides the explanatory variables into three components:

- "traditional" market variables,
- "public sector" or fiscal variables
- a mélange of "additional" economic and non-pecuniary variables (*Shaw 1985, 143*).

His findings are consistent with the idea that "the influence of 'traditional' market variables such as wages, employment opportunities, and business activity, has diminished over time and that fiscal variables, involving unemployment insurance or federal equalization grants, have partially displaced 'traditional' market variables as influences of recent migration" (*Shaw 1985, 140*).

In detail, he for example "confirm[s] that both employment and unemployment contribute to our understanding of migration, independently of wages. ... this implies that high wages may exist side-by-side with unemployment. These results conform with expectations of segmented labor market theory" (*Shaw 1985, 145*).

This does not mean that economic variables and causes for migration are disappearing, but their relevance is changing - and may yet (theoretically) become more important again over time.

As "traditional" determinants we would include measures of distance, language/ ethnicity, and educational selectivity. SHAW concludes in this respect: "While distance always exhibits the expected negative effect, its significance as a cost/ information barrier to migration has been observed to decline over time" (*Shaw 1985, 146*). On the other hand, he sees language/ethnicity measures exerting a greater effect on migration after 1971. This variable seems most relevant to explaining lower rates of migration to and from Montreal and Quebec City. In addition, the pursuit of a separatist policy and the implementation of language Bill 101 increased the importance of this variable after 1971.

Finally it is interesting to note that regional disaggregation is changing the coefficients on several variables. For example, language/ethnicity are considerably more important to migration to and from CMAs in eastern than in western Canada. In contrast, distance emerges as a greater deterrent of migration to and from CMAs in western than in eastern Canada. - With respect to "traditional" components such as wages and unemployment, they are more relevant to understanding migration to and from western Canada than to eastern Canada. The explanation is seen in more generous unemployment insurance benefits and equalization grants in the east, which are working to displace "traditional" market influences (*Shaw 1985, 149*).

Conclusion

Migration decisions are motivated by a wide variety of factors which change over time, and individuals have different sets of tastes, talents and opportunities. The fact that people are moving in opposite directions may make perfectly good sense for each single person concerned. Even repeat and return migration, which affects the net-gross impact measures, may well be "rational". Modernization induces new patterns of mobility in which different personal preferences play an increasing role, and in which the character of locations may reflect such selecting processes.

My hypothethis is that differentiation in migration pattern and specialization of areas and communities have became more important during the last few decades. Generalizations based on aggregated population, economic and other data suggest statistical trends and are necessary, but they do not explain the diverse causes of migration, and consequently population change, for individual regions, cities, towns and rural areas.

Zusammenfassung

Zunächst werden einige allgemeine Tendenzen der Bevölkerungsverlagerung in Kanada diskutiert. Unter Anwendung verschiedener konzeptioneller Ansätze ergibt sich, daß die Konzentration der Bevölkerung ("Urbanisierung"), die bis in die 1960er Jahre hinein herrschte, in eine Phase (1970er Jahre) überging, in der sich dieser Trend umkehrte ("Counterurbanisation") und jüngst nochmals wendete. Dabei ist die interregionale Migration die wichtigste demographische Komponente. Sie ist gleichzeitig der beste Indikator für ökonomische und soziale Entwicklungen.

Zwei Aspekte sind besonders aufschlußreich: (1) verschiedene regionale Konzeptionen (Großregionen, Stadt-Land Gegensatz, Stadtagglomerationen etc.) und (2) altersspezifisches Wanderungsverhalten. Bei letzterem ist vor allem die Wanderung der Alten von Interesse, da die kanadische Gesellschaft - wie alle hochindustrialisierten Staaten - zunehmend altert.

Eine Durchsicht der Literatur, die die Gründe für Wanderungen in Kanada analysiert, belegt, daß die Migrationsursachen sehr vielschichtig und äußerst komplex sind. Jedes Individuum wägt ökonomische und nicht-ökonomische Vor- und Nachteile eines Wohnstandortwechsels nach seinen eigenen Vorstellungen ab. Diese ändern sich je nach persönlicher Situation und im Laufe des Lebens.

Es existiert keine Übereinstimmung darüber, welche Ursachen für die Veränderungen im Wanderungsverhalten der Kanadier verantwortlich zu machen sind. Zusätzlich zu den mehr traditionell untersuchten, ökonomischen Variablen sind fiskalische und zunehmend auch nichtmaterielle Präferenzen wichtig. Während sich die Erklärungsansätze früher auf Arbeitsmarktfragen konzentrierten, werden seit einiger Zeit Wohnortspräferenzen stärker beachtet. Wanderungsverhalten ist aber auch Ausdruck von Veränderungen der Verkehrs- und und

Kommunikationbedingungen, die insbesondere das Raumverhalten in dünn besiedelten, peripheren Regionen beeiflussen können.

Technische und gesellschaftliche Neuerungen erlauben neue Formen der Mobilität, bei denen verschiedene persönliche Präferenzen eine zunehmende Rolle spielen. Die unterschiedlichen Bevölkerungs- und Sozialstrukturen von Siedlungen spiegeln solche Selektionsprozesse wider. Es wird die Hypothese vertreten, daß die Verschiedenartigkeit der Wanderungsmuster und die Spezialisierung von Regionen und Siedlungen in Kanada während der letzten Dekaden an Bedeutung gewonnen haben. Generalisierungen und Modellbildungen, die auf aggregierten Bevölkerungsdaten, auf ökonomischen und anderen Durchschnittsdaten beruhen, mögen zwar der statistischen Analyse von generellen Trends dienen, sie können aber kaum die vielfältigen Gründe aufdecken, die zu den verschiedenartigen Migrationen und folglich zu Bevölkerungsveränderungen führen, wie sie in einzelnen Regionen, Städten oder kleineren Siedlungen und ländlicher Gebieten zu beobachten sind.

Notes

[1] Basically Statistics Canada classifies a settlement of 1,000 or more population as "urban" and the remaining population as "rural". For a brief overview of changes in definitions by Statistics Canada see BOLLMAN 1992, 4f.

[2] Here it is necessary to note that new definitions caused additional urban population growth. For example, a modification of the rural-urban definitions and extension of boundaries of cities between 1951 and 1956 resulted in an increase of almost 250,000 in urban population (*Dominion Bureau of Statistics. Census 1961 Cat. 99-512, 2f*).

[3] CMAs are defined as the main labor market of an urban area (the urban core) with a population of at least 100,000. Once an area becomes a CMA, it is retained as such even if its population subsequently declines. - CMAs comprise one or more Census Subdivisions which meet at least one of the following criteria: (1) The CSD falls completely or partly inside the urban core; (2) at least 50% of the employed labor force living in the CDS works in the urban core; (3) at least 25% of the employed labor force working in the CDS lives in the urban core (*Statistics Canada: 1991 Census Dictionary (Cat. 92-310E)*).

[4] For details see: BOLLMANN *1992, 1 Fig. 5*.

[5] The various changes in definition are seriously complicating the analysis of population data. For example: Rapid population growth in rural areas adjacent to urban areas leads to reclassification through a) urban boundary expansion, b) fringe population achieving urban density thresholds and c) rural communities attaining urban population levels. - One of the basic problems of investigating trends is how to compare census results. Apparently, a better comparison is possible if the rural/urban designation of one census is imposed on the data from previous censuses. However, reclassification is part of the inherent process of urban expansion and hence its effects are included in data of Statistics Canada.

[6] Analysing annual data, one should keep in mind that there is often a lag between the economic indicators and demographic reactions.

[7] It should be kept in mind, that these figures are based on the question: "where did you stay 5 years ago?" which means, that out-migrants are counted in the migration rate of destination, rather than in the province of orgin.

[8] Since no migration data existed at this time, the study based on estimates made by using one of the residual methods. The method derives figures for net-migration only, and past recorded data on population and on the flow of birth and deaths are required to make the estimates.

References

Anderson, I. B. (1966): Internal Migration in Canada: 1921-1961. In: Economic Council of Canada Staff Study 13. Ottawa, Queen's Printer.

Anderson, W. P. and Papageorgiou, Y. Y. (1992): Metropolitan and Non-metropolitan Population Trends in Canada: 1966-1982. In: The Canadian Geographer, 36 (2), 124-144.

Berry, B. J. L. (1976): The Counterurbanization Process: Urban America Since 1970. In: Berry, B. J. L. (ed): Urbanization and Counterurbanization. In: Urban Affairs Annual Review, 11, 17-30.
Bollman, R. D. ed., (1992): Rural and Small Town Canada. Lewiston, N.Y./Toronto, Ont., Thompson Educational Publications.
Champion, A. G. ed., (1989): Counterurbanization: The Changing Pace and Nature of Population Deconcentration. London, Edward Arnold.
Courchene, T. J. (1974): Migration, Income, and Employment: Canada: 1965-1968. Montreal, Howe Research Institute.
Courchene, T. J. (1981): A Market Perspective on Regional Disparities. In: Canadian Public Policy, 7, 506-518.
Dahms, F. (1987): Population, Migration and the Elderly. Guelph (= Occasional Papers in Geography 9).
Dominion Bureau of Statistics (1901-1961): Census of Canada. Ottawa, Statistics Canada.
Dumas, J. (1994): Report on the Demographic Situation in Canada 1993: Current Demographic Analysis. Ottawa, Statistics Canada.
Dumas, J. and Lavoie, Y. (1992): Report on the Demographic Situation in Canada 1992: Current Demographic Analysis. Ottawa, Statistics Canada.
Ellenwood, D. S. (1992): Population Redistribution and "Counterurbanization": A Study of Nine Urban Regions in Canada. MS (Geography) Simon Fraser University.
Field, N. C. (1988): Migration through the Rural-Urban Hierarchy: Canadian Patterns. In: Canadian Journal of Regional Science, 11 (1), 9-32.
Fielding, A. J. (1983): Counterurbanization in Western Europe: Recent Empirical and Theoretical Contributions to the Debate. Manusc. (Anglo-Dutch Migration Symposium, 14.-16. Sept. 1983, Soesterberg, Netherlands).
Grant, E. K. and Vanderkamp, J. (1976): The Economic Causes and Effects of Migration: Canada 1965-1971. Ottawa, Economic Council of Canada/Supply and Services Canada.
Hodge, G. (1983): Canadian Small Town Renaissance: Implications for Settlement System Concepts. In: Regional Studies, 17 (1), 19-28.
Hodge, G. (1991): Seniors in Small Town British Columbia: Demographic Tendencies and Trends, 1961-1986. Vancouver, UBC, Centre of Human Settlements.
Keddie, P. D. and Joseph, A. E. (1991a): The Turnaround of the Turnaround? Rural Population Change in Canada, 1976 to 1986. In: The Canadian Geographer, 35 (4), 367-379.
Keddie, P. D. and Joseph, A. E. (1991b): Reclassification and Rural-versus-Urban Population Change in Canada, 1976 to 1981: A Tale of two Definitions. In: The Canadian Geographer, 35 (4), 412-420.
Ledent, J. and Liaw, K. L. (1989): Provincial Out-Migration Patterns of Canadian Elderly: Characterization and Explanation. In: Environment and Planning A, 21 (8), 1093-1112.
Lee, E. S. (1980): Migration of the Aged. In: Research on Aging 2, 131-135.
McCann, L. D. ed., (1982 and 1987): Heartland and Hinterland: A Geography of Canada. (1st and 2nd Ed.). Scarborough, Prentice-Hall.
Mueser, P. R., White, M. J. and Tierney, J. P. (1988): Patterns of Net Migration by Age for U.S. Counties 1950-1980: In: The Impact of Increasing Spatial Differentiation by Life Cycle. Canadian Journal of Regional Science, 11 (1), 57-76.
Newbold, K. B. and Liaw, K. L. (1990): Characterization of Primary, Return, and Onward Interprovincial Migration in Canada: Overall and Age-Specific Patterns. In: Canadian Journal of Regional Science, 13 (1), 17-34.
Northcott, H. (1988): Changing Residence: The Geographic Mobility of Elderly Canadians. Toronto, Butterworths.
Parenteau, R. (1979): Is Canada Going back to the Land-Urban-Fringe? Canadian Perspectives. (= Statistics Canada: Working Paper, Geographical Series). Ottawa, Supply and Services.

Pooler, J. (1987): Modelling Interprovincial Migration Using Entropy-Maximizing Methods. In: The Canadian Geographer, 31 (1), 57-64.

Robinson, I. (1981): Canadian Urban Growth Trends: Implications for a National Settlement Policy. Vancouver, UBC Press.

Shaw, R. P. (1985): Intermetropolitan Migration in Canada: Changing Determinants over Three Decades. Toronto, NC Press.

Simmons, J. W. (1980): Changing Migration Patterns in Canada: 1966-71 to 1971-76. In: Canadian Journal of Regional Science, 3, 139-162.

Statistics Canada: Censuses (see detailed notes in text, tables, and figures).

Stone, L. O. (1967): Urban Canada. Ottawa, Queen's Printer.

Stone, L. O. (1969): Migration in Canada: Regional Aspects. (= 1961 Census Monograph). Ottawa, Statistics Canada.

Stone, L. O. (1974): What We Know about Migration in Canada: A Selective Review and Agenda for Future Research. In: International Migration Review, 8, 267-281.

Stone, L. O. (1978): The Frequency of Geographic Mobility in the Population of Canada. Ottawa, Statistics Canada.

Stone, L. O. and Fletcher, S. (1976): Migration in Canada: 1971 Profile Study. Ottawa, Statistics Canada.

Vanderkamp, J. and Grant, E. K. (1988): Canadian Internal Migration Statistics: Some Comparisons and Evaluations. In: Canadian Journal of Regional Science, 11 (1), 9-32.

Vogelsang, R. (1993): Kanada: Geographische Strukturen, Entwicklungen, Probleme. Gotha, Justus Perthes Verg laGotha. (= Perthes Länderprofile).

Address of the Author

Roland Vogelsang
Institut für Kanada-Studien
Universität Augsburg
86135 Augsburg
GERMANY

TIBOR FRANK

Via Berlin to New York

The Human Geography of Hungarian Migrations after World War I

The Austro-Hungarian Monarchy was among the top ten countries that sent emigrants to the USA between the 1880s and 1914 *(Puskás 1982, 15-44)*. The nature and patterns of emigration dramatically changed in Hungary as a result of World War I, the 1918-1919 revolutions, the Paris Peace Treaties, and the anti-Semitic legislation of 1920 on higher education. Just as Hungary was undergoing those radical changes, the United States introduced the Literacy Test in 1917 and the Quota Laws in 1921 and 1924. Within less than a decade, the combined effect of the momentous changes in both countries fundamentally transformed the geographic patterns as well as the cultural landscape of Hungarian migrations.

Typically illiterate and unskilled, pre-World War I migrants left for the United States for primarily economic reasons. Most of these people could be classified as migrant workers, *Gastarbeiter,* of peasant (rural, agricultural) background, who headed directly to the United States where a cheap labor force was needed and, indeed, welcome. They went to the USA mainly to make money, in many cases returning (repeatedly) to their native land to invest or spend what they had earned. It is safe to suggest that an estimated one-fourth of all Hungarian emigrants ultimately returned to Hungary. Many of them originated from regions in the Old Kingdom of Hungary that were particularly densely populated by ethnic minorities such as the Slovaks in Upper-Hungary (today Slovakia), the Romanians in Transylvania (today Romania) and Croatians in the South-West and the South-East (today Croatia and Serbia). Although together they represented some 50% of the total population of the country, they were severely handicapped in the increasingly nationalistic, chauvinistic political atmosphere of turn-of-the-century Hungary.

A mere half a century after the emancipation of the serfs in Hungary (1848), these groups particularly faced roadblocks to social mobility, as a consequence of the heavily feudal social composition of Hungarian society as well as the surviving system of large landed estates. Offering a complex explanation for late 19th-century emigration to the USA, historian John BODNAR concluded that all emigrants moved "toward industrial jobs and wages" *(Bodnar 1985, 19)*. The much delayed distribution of land, the hopeless rate of illiteracy, and increasing nationalistic political pressure held no promise for a large section of the population of Hungary: the lack of social and economic mobility quickly translated into a pattern of geographic mobility *(Frank 1995)*.

Contemporary Americans were sometimes struck by the "cosmopolitan make-up of Hungary," and "the assimilative powers of Hungarians," for them important points of resemblance between pre-World War I Hungary and the United States. Some observers offered these geographic similarities as an explanation for the challenging power of the United States drawing hundreds of thousands of Hungarians to America. "In the variety of its climate and its productions," noted American author and geographer Francis E. CLARK somewhat naively in 1913,

> "Hungary bears some relation to America. Though comparatively small when placed side by side with the nation that stretches from the Atlantic to the Pacific, it is larger than Great Britain, Italy, or Austria, and ranks seventh among the nations of Europe in the number of square miles. In the varieties of climate found within its borders, it resembles America more than in the extent

of its territory... Perhaps because of these similarities between the two countries, America of late years has proved to be a great magnet, drawing the Hungarian peoples from their Alföld, or prairies, to the virgin prairies of the new world." (Clark 1913, 170, 173f).

Subsequently, huge waves of "new" immigration in the United States created fear and furor among "old" immigrants. The influx of cheap labor and of "undesirable aliens" led to race riots. Racist policies and ideologies quickly emerged to oppose and, in effect, bar immigration: first from China, later from Russia, Austria-Hungary, and Southern Italy. Spanning over a long period of approximately 35 years, a series of anti-immigrant measures were instituted to check the tide of immigration. A decade after the Chinese Exclusion Act of 1882, the U.S. government started to resort to the secret "emigration surveillance" of several European countries (1892, 1903, 1906) where most people had come from before World War I *(Frank 1992)*. The late 1890s also saw the beginning of the fight for, and against, a Literacy Test that was to provide the U.S. government with a measure of "quality control" over the selection of immigrants. Though the idea of such a test was vetoed by subsequent Presidents such as Grover CLEVELAND, William Howard TAFT and Woodrow WILSON in 1897, 1913 and 1915, the literacy debate proved to be a permanent feature during 25 years of U.S. political discourse. The seemingly unstoppable flow of immigrants in the 1900s led President Theodore ROOSEVELT and the U.S. Congress to establish the Immigration Commission (1907-1911). The Commission, chaired by Senator William Paul DILLINGHAM, produced the 42 volume Dillingham Report (probably the single largest immigration survey), as well as the subsequent Dillingham Bill (1913), which paved the way towards the Literacy Test of 1917. This test was ultimately passed by Congress over the veto of President WILSON.

U.S. experiences in World War I, the ensuing isolationist foreign policy and restrictionist immigration legislation drastically reduced the number of "undesirable aliens." This included the people who used to arrive from the Austro-Hungarian Monarchy. In fact, the Quota Laws of 1921 and 1924 put an end to mass immigration to the USA from East-Central and South-Eastern Europe *(Handlin 1951, Higham 1955, 1988, Haller 1963, 1984, Divine 1957, Chase 1977, Gossett 1965)*.

Born after World War I, the new Hungary suddenly offered very limited opportunities for her people, particularly for the younger generation. The country lost over two thirds of her territories through the Peace Treaty of Trianon in 1920, becoming one of the politically independent but small and insignificant new countries of Europe. Just when most needed, mass emigration into the USA was made impossible by the Quota Laws. For a society that had used emigration as a regular outlet for some 30-35 years before 1914, the Quota Laws added considerably to the cumulative effects of the War, the Revolutions and the Peace Treaty. The new U.S. immigration laws of 1921 and 1924 preferred a small group of people joining their families as well as skilled agricultural laborers. The United States, however, became increasingly eager to receive specially gifted and/or highly educated people with particular skills, who were received on top of the quota as "non-quota immigrants" *(Jenks and Lauck 1926, 538f)*[1]. The non-quota provisions of the new law allowed professors and students to enter the United States, indicating a new commitment toward an educated workforce *(Jenks and Lauck 1926, 537f)*[2].

Losing their chances to go to the USA after the political changes of 1917-21, small groups of intellectually gifted Hungarians, very often of Jewish origin, started to migrate toward the German speaking countries of Europe. These included not only Germany, but also what was then called German-Austria and even Czechoslovakia, with her prestigious German universities in both Prague and Brno. Berlin and other cities of Weimar Germany provided a particularly attractive setting to young Hungarian scientists, scholars, musicians, artists, authors, and film-makers. The vibrant yet tolerant and inspiring intellectual atmosphere of pre-Nazi Germany, and particularly an increasingly "Americanized" Berlin, gave them a foretaste of the United States.

With the emergence of HITLER, Jewish-Hungarians had to leave Germany and a vast number of them continued to migrate, either directly or via some European country, into the USA. The majority of those immigrants never returned to Hungary or did so only in a largely symbolic way. Chain migration came to replace return migration as a characteristic pattern of the 1920s and 1930s. A characteristic change of direction appeared in the interwar period when Latin American countries also emerged as new destinations for masses of European emigrants, changing in yet another way the global patterns of 20th century Hungarian and international migrations *(Varga 1976, 3-21).*

In the 1920s, in what turned out to be a brief but shining moment, a splendid cultural life emerged in Berlin. It became the European center for film and theater, photography and literature, opera and the performing arts, architecture and the social sciences. The great German conductor Bruno WALTER remembered this creative splendor suggesting

> "that it seemed as if all the eminent artistic forces were shining forth once more, imparting to the last festive symposium of the minds a many-hued brilliance before the night of barbarism closed in" (Walter 1946, quoted by Gay 1970, 130). "Berlin aroused powerful emotions in everyone - delighted most, terrified some, but left no one indifferent,"

commented the biographer of piano virtuoso Vladimir HOROWITZ *(Plaskin 1983, 70).* Berlin was the center of Germany's cultural upheaval, "a magnet for every aspiring composer, writer, actor, and performing musician" *(Plaskin 1983, 69).* The playwright Carl ZUCKMEYER remembered it as a city that

> "gobbled up talents and human energies with unexampled appetite." He added, "one spoke of Berlin as one speaks of a highly desirable woman whose coldness, coquettishness are widely known. She was called arrogant, snobbish, parvenu, uncultivated, common, but she was the center of everyone's fantasies" (Plaskin 1983, 69).

After the War ended, the prospects for early arriving Hungarians, already in beaten Germany, naturally worsened. Well established in Germany since receiving his Ph.D. in Göttingen in 1908, University of Aachen Professor Theodore von KÁRMÁN described the 1920 situation in chilling terms to Michael POLANYI. An assistant to future Nobel Laureate Georg de HEVESY during the Hungarian Commune, POLANYI left Budapest at the end of 1919 and went to Karlsruhe where he had already studied chemistry from 1913-14. In the early 1920s he was still trying to decide about his future as a scientist and get his *Habilitation* or a job[3]. "The mood in the universities vis-à-vis foreigners is momentarily very bad but it may change in a few years...," Von KÁRMÁN wrote to POLANYI. "The inflation conditions are very unpleasant today and it is much more difficult to wait for a job."[4] From 1920 on, Von KÁRMÁN himself helped a number of Hungarians start their careers in Germany, readily sponsoring friends of his family, often under the most adverse circumstances[5]. Several years later, in 1923, American visiting scholar Eric R. JETTE described the German university scene in remarkably similar terms:

> "conditions in the universities were very bad, of course, in all places. The same story was heard everywhere, no money, no new professors or docents but laboratories filled with students who had almost nothing to live on. Yet the research goes on and the students still keep at their books."[6]

Nevertheless, Hungarians were difficult to turn down. Networking, using available contacts and relying on people already established in Germany, were among the most natural methods used to secure a place somewhere in Germany. Michael POLANYI had to turn to Von KÁRMÁN for help. In turn, the future engineering professor, Mihály FREUND asked for POLANYI's assistance for a young relative: Tibor BÁNYAI had just finished his high school in Budapest and wanted to become an engineer at the University of Karlsruhe, where POLANYI had been active for some time.

More importantly, in 1922, POLANYI paved the way for Leo SZILARD who tried to get an assistant's job at the Institute of Physical Chemistry at the University of Frankfurt am Main. SZILARD, of course, was well on his way to becoming a scientist in his own right. The degree he had just received in Berlin under Max von LAUE was the best letter of recommendation he could possibly present. Yet, under the circumstances, he needed POLANYI's letter to Frankfurt professor B. LORENZ which called him a "wonderfully smart man."[7] Of all the Hungarian scientists, however, Von KÁRMÁN proved to be the most active and successful contact person whose German and subsequent U.S. correspondence provides a wealth of information on half a century of Hungarian networking. A typical letter from his German period was sent in 1924, by a Hungarian friend in Vienna, asking for his assistance with Hungarian chemical engineering student Pál ACÉL to continue his studies "in Germany, preferably under you."[8] Correspondence on these matters sometimes had to be clandestine: in dangerous years such as 1920, such mail was better sent to Vienna, rather than Budapest, and picked up there personally.[9]

Though Germany was certainly the most tempting and promising emigrant destination after World War I, Hungarian step-migration to the United States did not lead through Germany alone. Persecuted in or barred from their homeland, many young Hungarians, usually equipped with a good working knowledge of German (and German alone), moved to a number of other, usually German-speaking, countries.

Unlike Berlin, Vienna was disillusioned, uninspiring and lacking substance. Though many Hungarians lived there, they did not necessarily like it. The ambiance in the city was particularly bad after the revolutions of 1918-19. Karl POLANYI, who lived there for many years serving as the editor of the economic paper *Der österreichische Volkswirt* compared it to a "salt desert, where not even through loneliness can one get rid of the aggressive atmosphere of barrenness."[10] Karl POLANYI bitterly complained in a letter to his mother: "The spiritual Vienna is so disappointing... To live here is just nonsensical: It is expensive(!!), bad (!!), plundering [raubig] (!!) hot (!!) dull, desolate, nervekilling... Everything escapes Vienna..."[11] Karl POLANYI became increasingly anxious to leave Vienna for Berlin and prepared to transfer his paper to the German capital.[12]

> "A hundred doubts, a thousand problems. This doubt and restlessness tortures everybody and as people exchange their Deutschmarks into [U.S.] dollars, their dollars into [Swiss] francs, their francs into [Russian] rubels, they change their beliefs accordingly."[13]

Many young people went to Czechoslovak universities. There were general and technical German universities both in Prague and in Brno, this combined with the shared cultural heritage within the Austro-Hungarian Monarchy, as well as the budding democracy of the new country proved to be very attractive. "There was an entire colony of Hungarian students in Brno," remembered engineer Marcel STEIN in an interview granted in New York in 1989.

> "I came from a Pozsony (today Bratislava, Slovakia) family where the mother tongue was German. Most of us in Brno were not Communists, but members of the Jewish middle-class. For the holidays, students [like Mr. STEIN] went to Pozsony rather than Budapest, but after graduation the majority returned to Hungary. Some of them continued their studies in Berlin-Charlottenburg and Karlsruhe in Germany, or, like the eminent engineer László HELLER, in Zürich, Switzerland. Coming home to anti-Semitic Hungary was a real shock after the experiences in democratic Czechoslovakia."[14]

The German universities of Czechoslovakia were very popular among the Hungarian-born citizens of that country, though several in the Hungarian community of Pozsony attempted to have their children educated in Germany. Some worked through Hungarian connections in Germany and, later, in the USA, and sent these often very gifted students to German or American universities.

The Hungarian intellectual diaspora was huge and not confined to German-speaking Europe: it was scattered all over the Continent of Europe and subsequently in the United States. The human geography of Hungarian intellectual migrations is truly astonishing. Mathematician György PÓLYA married his Swiss professor's daughter and settled in Switzerland during World War I. He became a citizen of Zürich in early 1918 and ultimately, in 1928, a full professor of the reputable *Eidgenössische Technische Hochschule* of that city. It was at the invitation of his friend and co-author Gábor SZEGΔ that he left Switzerland for Stanford shortly after the outbreak of World War II.[15]

Yet, not all the eminent Hungarians who wished to leave for Germany could go there. "There are enough physical chemists in Germany so it is hardly possible for me to get a job there. I don't even entertain such plans," prospective Nobel Laureate Georg de HEVESY (Chemistry 1943) wrote to Michael POLANYI in early 1920, and he settled in the institute of Nobel Laureate Niels BOHR in Copenhagen, Denmark.[16]

Music- and language psychologist Géza RÉVÉSZ worked at the Psychological Laboratory of the University of Amsterdam in the Netherlands. Mathematician Marcel RIESZ left for Sweden, taught in Stockholm and in Lund until 1952, when he went to teach in the United States at Princeton, Stanford, the University of Maryland and the University of Indiana *(Gårding 1970, Horváth 1975)*.

The international community of scientists and scholars showed a great deal of compassion for those being threatened by Hitler. They supported emigrating colleagues from Germany by providing the necessary organizational framework and material assistance *(Fermi 1968, 60-92)*, providing for some 6,000 highly qualified professionals to leave Germany in quick succession *(Strauss and Röder, eds., 1983)*. A number of parallel initiatives emerged to bring about an effective framework for rescuing the community of German-Jewish scientists. Headquartered in Zürich, Switzerland, the *Notgemeinschaft deutscher Wissenschaftler im Ausland* [Emergency Society of German Scholars Abroad] was founded largely as a result of the efforts of a Hungarian-born scientist. "Professor Philip SCHWARTZ," wrote Lord Beveridge in his *A Defence of Free Learning*,

> "Hungarian by birth but holding a Chair of General Pathology and Pathological Anatomy at Frankfurt-am-Main in Germany, was an immediate victim of HITLER's racial persecution and went in March 1933 to Zurich in Switzerland. There he founded at once the Notgemeinschaft and directed it for six months. ... For money it had to depend almost wholly on contributions from displaced scholars whom it had helped to re-establish. But by its personal knowledge of the scholars themselves and by using its contacts with universities everywhere, it rendered invaluable service" (Beveridge 1959).

The *Notgemeinschaft* provided a list of nearly 1,500 names of dismissed academics in Germany, which was published in 1936 with the assistance of the Rockefeller Foundation *(Fermi 1968, 62)*. The first major success of the *Notgemeinschaft* was an agreement with the Turkish government to place 33 German professors at the University of Istanbul. Similar arrangements were discussed with Australian, Indian, South African, Soviet and U.S. authorities as well as with the Committee for Intellectual Cooperation of the League of Nations.

In May 1933, scientists in Great Britain established the *Academic Assistance Council* (first conceived as the International Board of Scientists and Scholars) with Nobel Laureate Lord RUTHERFORD as President and Sir William [later Lord] BEVERIDGE and Professor C. S. GIBSON as Secretaries.[17] A few weeks later the *Emergency Committee in Aid of Displaced German* [later *Foreign*] *Scholars* was established as the American counterpart of the AAC to provide grants or fellowships to immigrant scientists and scholars *(Rider 1984, 116, 139)*.[18] The main contributions to the Emergency Committee funds came from Jewish foundations and individuals *(Rider 1984, 144)*.

Another support committee, the *Comité International pour la Placement des Intellectuels Réfugiés* was formed in Geneva, offering positions to refugee professors from Austria, Germany, and Italy *(Fermi 1968, 62f)*.
Jewish groups in Europe considered raising funds for a new university based on refugee faculty alone, an idea that originated in the mind of Albert EINSTEIN who envisaged a *Flüchtlings-universität*, a refugee or emigrant university somewhere in Europe.[19] A longtime and valued colleague, Leo SZILARD was able to convince EINSTEIN "that this would not be an easy task," and that he should "concentrate on one promising effort."[20] This is how EINSTEIN started to support the idea of the Academic Assistance Council. Another suggestion was to raise more money for the Palestine University.[21] Immediately after the recession, however, there was not enough money for any of these projects to materialize. Instead, several agencies provided relief of some sort, such as the *Jewish Relief Committee* in Amsterdam in the Netherlands.
The academic community in the United States was horrified to learn of what was happening in Germany. German-born Franz BOAS was one of the first to receive an authentic report from Benjamin LIEBOWITZ who travelled throughout Europe collecting information and helping plan relief operations. "It is impossible to describe the utter despair of all classes of Jews in Germany," he wrote in early May 1933 to BOAS.

> "The thoroughness with which they are being hunted out and stopped short in their careers is appalling. Unless help comes from the outside, there is no outlook for thousands, perhaps hundreds of thousands, except starvation... It is a gigantic 'cold' pogrom. And it is not only against Jews; Communists, of course, are included, but are not singled out racially; social democrats and liberals generally are ... coming under the ban, especially if they protest in the least against the Nazi movement. Please note that I am not speaking from hearsay: I know people, friends in many classes - scientists, scholars, doctors, lawyers, business men, economists, etc."[22]

Ultimately, some 6,000 displaced scholars and professional persons from Europe applied to the New York-based Emergency Committee, out of which 335 were granted assistance *(Fermi 1968, 76ff)*.[23] Hungarians eventually receiving grants or fellowships either left Germany in 1933-1934, or left Hungary after anti-Semitic legislation was introduced there in 1938-1939.[24]
Even the small sample of the people who turned to the Emergency Committee demonstrates that many who were registered as German when the 1933 exodus started were, in fact, immigrants to Germany from Hungary. Their list included scientists Leo SZILARD and Edward TELLER, as well as mathematicians Otto SZÁSZ and Gábor SZEGΔ *(Rider 1984, 172-176)*.[25]
Hungarians had a particular sensitivity to the emergency situation in Germany because of a strong sense of *déja-vu*. The rise of anti-Semitism and anti-foreignism as well as the persecution and threat that emerged in Germany was strongly reminiscent of the Hungarian ordeal of 1919-1920. Rather than become passive victims of HITLER's takeover, this sensitivity made some of the Hungarians in Germany extremely active and successful organizers, and leaders of the rescue operations that saved the lives and careers of several thousand scientists and scholars in Germany. Physicist Leo SZILARD took on the enormous task of volunteering to head these operations throughout 1933 and the subsequent period. SZILARD, who was generally recognized as a man of extraordinary abilities and completely without selfish motives, may have been induced to do this work because of his appreciation and gratitude to the German professors, colleagues, and friends who had helped him as a young Hungarian émigré throughout the 1920s and early 1930s. Perhaps more than anybody else, SZILARD contributed to the foundation of the Academic Assistance Council in 1933. "What I am concerned with at the present is to co-ordinate the foreign groups which are already in existence, and to stimulate the formation of groups in countries where there are no suitable groups as yet," SZILARD wrote to Dr. Max DELBRÜCK.[26]
In Belgium he met the Rectors of all four Belgian Universities, as well as Professor Jacques ERRERA of the University of Bruxelles and Hendrik de MAN who assisted him in mobilizing

Belgian colleagues to aid refugee scientists and scholars.[27] In Switzerland he talked to Dr. KULLMAN of the Committee for Intellectual Cooperation at the League of Nations and Dr. KOTSCHNIG of the International Student Service.[28] In Britain SZILARD met with university leaders and leading scientists such as Sir William BEVERIDGE, Director of the London School of Economics and Political Science. SZILARD persuaded BEVERIDGE to form a committee to aid refugee scientists and scholars. He also worked there with Professor F. G. DONNAN of University College, Professor Gilbert MURRAY of Oxford, Chairman of the League of Nations Committee for Intellectual Cooperation, Sir John RUSSELL, Professor G. H. HARDY (Cambridge), Nobel Laureates Niels BOHR (Physics 1922) and Archibald V. HILL (Physiology 1922), Lord MELCHETT, as well as Jewish leaders Neville LASKI, Claude Joseph GOLDSMID MONTEFIORE, Sir Philip HARTOG, Chairman of the Committee of the Jewish Board of Deputies and the Anglo-Jewish Association, and Dr. Chaim WEIZMANN, the future President of Israel.[29] He also worked in the office of the Academic Assistance Council headquartered in the Royal Society on the Piccadilly in London *(Fermi 1968, 64)*.[30]

The Academic Assistance Council helped several Hungarian scholars get to Britain, including Karl POLANYI[31] whose brother Michael also tried to help some of his own gifted students in Germany obtain a scholarship to Britain.[32] SZILARD also considered mobilizing the Nobel Laureates worldwide in aid of the refugee scientists and scholars, but the plan failed to receive general approval and was dropped.[33]

SZILARD soon realized that a fellowship granted by the Academic Assistance Council would not necessarily result in a permanent appointment in England.

> "It is therefore important to take up every case as soon as possible with America and other countries in order to get a more uniform distribution as far as permanent appointments are concerned. A certain number of American scientists and scholars should in view of this problem be asked to act as correspondent members of the Academic Assistance Council..."[34]

The relief operation enjoyed a good deal of support in the United States, where the academic community was "terribly concerned about the situation in Germany."[35]

"I have a letter this morning from an old friend", wrote Abraham FLEXNER, Director of the Institute for Advanced Study to John von NEUMANN, "telling me unspeakable things about the way in which HITLER is ruining the German Educational Ministry and other cultural activities. The whole thing seems to me the act of mad men. I cannot believe that it will endure."[36] In a few weeks he added:

> "The whole American nation is a unit that respects the crazy performances of the German Government. Göttingen has been absolutely ruined and the University students must all be mad. Nothing crazier has happened in human history since the days of the French Terror."[37]

Acting through Benjamin LIEBOWITZ, SZILARD was instrumental in securing the support of Franz BOAS, of Columbia University, who played a leading role in marshalling support for the refugee cause.[38] BOAS invited John DEWEY, Ezra POUND, [probably Frank William] TAUSSIG, Raymond PEARL, Walter CANNON and others to serve on a board that coordinated the Academic Assistance Council and U.S. universities and scientists.[39] Other Hungarians who contributed toward launching the support project included John von NEUMANN and Theodore von KÁRMÁN who played an active role in relief operations. Von NEUMANN, then Professor of Mathematics in the Institute for Advanced Study, was asked to provide information about scientists in trouble in Germany.

"It would be a good idea," Oswald VEBLEN wrote to John von NEUMANN, "to write me whatever you know in detail about the mathematicians and physicists who are in difficulties."[40] VEBLEN also reported that "there are a number of attempts being made to raise money to provide relief in this country for the Jews and Liberals who are being dispossessed in Germany."[41]

Von NEUMANN himself supported the *Notgemeinschaft deutscher Wissenschaftler im Ausland,* both in terms of supplying money and information.[42]

Oddly enough, despite all the relief work he did for others, Leo SZILARD was himself in trouble in regard to his own future. In June 1933 he requested the support of Eugene WIGNER: "Last, not least, someone must take care of myself, as I naturally can't do this myself and it would be incompatible with my current activities anyway."[43] At this point, fellow Hungarian scientists rated SZILARD rather poorly as a physicist. WIGNER gave him his "complete appreciation for his directness and trustworthiness. His unselfishness is almost unparalleled among my acquaintances. He has an imagination that would be of extraordinary use to him and to any institution for which he works. I don't know if a purely scientific job would be the best for him, although this should be also considered."[44] WIGNER thought of two possible jobs for SZILARD, though neither of them in academia. Likewise, Theodore von KÁRMÁN did "not think that the case of SZILARD is a very strong one,"[45] when asked for his comments on SZILARD as a prospective U.S. visiting professor in 1934.

Another important group of Hungarians who were forced to leave Germany by the Nazi takeover were the filmmakers. The exodus of 1,500 members of the German filmmaking community during the Nazi era, including about 100 producers, directors and performers originally from Hungary, was a dramatic turn in the history of the German film industry. Celebrities of the German screen along with film technicians and other artists left Germany after 1933 and moved to Vienna, Prague, Paris, London, Palestine, Mexico and the United States. We now have an almost complete list of all the "German" victims including the Hungarians: the best-known Hungarian filmmakers who left Germany for the USA after 1933 included Laslo (László) BENEDEK, the internationally celebrated hero of the psychopathic *M* (1931), actor Peter LORRE, director Andrew (Endre) MARTON, producer-director George PAL (PÁL), producer-director Gabriel PASCAL, actor S. Z. SAKALL ("Sz≈ke Szakál", b. SZAKÁLL Ger≈ Jen≈), as well as director Steve SEKELY *(Loewy 1987, Katz 1979, 103, 734, 783, 890, 898, 1011, 1036).* Several of the émigré directors and producers continued working successfully in the United States, though most actors had to be satisfied with minor roles of "foreigners" in Hollywood productions *(Varconi and Honeck 1976).*[46]

Once in the USA, immigrants from Hungary followed predominantly urban patterns of settlement: typically they tended to go to big cities where the universities, the symphonies, or the hospitals provided much needed jobs. Experiences in modernized and urbane Germany played a major role in their quick socialization.

Patterns of Central European emigration were fundamentally changed by the rise of Adolf HITLER and the Nazi Party in Germany. Émigré Hungarians, mostly Jewish in origin, either returned to Hungary or migrated towards Western Europe, the Soviet Union, or the United States. Together with many other East and Central European people they also continued to migrate to Latin America *(Varga 1976).* The geography of these repeated relocations was, however, often determined simply by accident and good or bad fortune: family and friends, influential patrons or colleagues, previous experience or roots in a particular country, emotional needs and professional inclinations all played a part in rerouting and resettling. For the lonely émigré it was networking, cohorting that proved to be perhaps the single most effective way to cope with the harsh political and psychological realities of the increasingly threatening world of the pre-World War II era. Hundreds of requests for letters of recommendation or affidavits have survived in the papers of the most well-established Hungarian-Americans, such as aviation pioneer Theodore von KÁRMÁN at Caltech, mathematician John von NEUMANN in Princeton, physicist Leo SZILARD, and violinist Joseph SZIGETI. These documents may help reconstruct not only individual destinies and the social history of the Central European academic and artistic élite, but also contribute to an emerging intellectual geography of the interwar decades.

Conclusion

The Austro-Hungarian Monarchy was among the top ten countries that sent emigrants to the USA. In Hungary, the nature and patterns of emigration were dramatically changed by World War I, the Paris Peace Treaties, the 1918-1919 revolutions, and the anti-Semitic legislation of 1920 on higher education. At the same time, the United States introduced the Literacy Test in 1917 and the Quota Laws in 1921 and 1924. These sudden and momentous changes transformed both the geographic and the cultural patterns of post-World War I Hungarian migrations entirely.

Pre-War emigrants were typically illiterate and unskilled laborers of peasant background who went to the USA primarily to make money and frequently returned to their native land to invest or spend what they earned. After the political changes of 1917-1921, small groups of intellectually gifted Hungarians, very often of Jewish origin, started to migrate toward the German speaking countries of Europe, including Czechoslovakia with her prestigious German universities. Berlin and other cities of Weimar Germany provided a particularly attractive setting to young Hungarian scientists, musicians, visual artists, and film-makers. The vibrant, yet tolerant intellectual atmosphere of pre-Nazi Germany, and particularly an increasingly "Americanized" Berlin, gave them a foretaste of the United States.

Those who went directly to post-War America showed remarkably different features. The new laws preferred people to join their families as well as skilled agricultural laborers. U.S. immigration authorities, however, became increasingly eager to receive specially gifted people with particular skills. With the emergence of HITLER, most Hungarians had to leave Germany and a vast number of them migrated, either directly or eventually via some European country, into the USA. The majority of these immigrants never returned to Hungary or did so only in a very symbolic way.

The paper assesses the impact of early 20th century Hungarian immigration on American social and cultural history.

Zusammenfassung

Die österreichisch-ungarische Monarchie war eines jener zehn Länder, von denen die USA die meisten Einwanderer erhielt. Sowohl der erste Weltkrieg und die Pariser Friedensverträge, als auch die Revolutionen von 1918-1919 und die antisemitischen Universitätsgesetze veränderten die Natur und die Zusammensetzung der Emigration in radikalem Maße. Zur selben Zeit wurden der Lesetest als Zulassungskriterium (1917) und die Quota-Gesetze (1921, 1924) in den USA eingeführt. Diese plötzlichen und einschneidenden Veränderungen führten zu einer völligen Umgestaltung der geographischen und kulturellen Züge der Migration in Nachkriegsungarn.

Die meisten Emigranten der Vorkriegszeit waren weder schriftkundig noch besaßen sie irgendeine Fachausbildung, hatten meistens einen bäuerlichen Hintergrund und gingen zumeist nach Amerika um Geld zu verdienen und damit wieder heimzukehren. Nach den gesellschaftlichen Veränderungen von 1917-1921 hingegen begannen kleinere Gruppen von intellektuell begabten Ungarn, häufig jüdischer Herkunft, in die deutschsprachigen Länder Europas zu übersiedeln, unter anderen auch in die Tschechoslowakei mit ihren hervorragenden deutschsprachigen Universitäten. Berlin und andere Städte der Weimarer Republik hatten eine besonders große Anziehungskraft für junge ungarische Wissenschaftler, Musiker, Künstler und Filmfachleute. Die vibrierende, zugleich tolerante intellektuelle Atmosphäre im Vorkriegsdeutschland und besonders im zunehmend "amerikanisierten" Berlin war für sie ein echter Vorgeschmack der USA.

Ganz anders war die Auswanderungsgruppe gestaltet, die nach dem Krieg unmittelbar nach Amerika emigrierte. Die neuen Einwanderungsgesetze begünstigten diejenigen, die sich ihren Familien anschließen wollten und Fachkräfte aus der Landwirtschaft. Die amerikanischen Einwanderungsbehörden entwickelten jedoch ein steigendes Interesse an besonders befähigten

Einwanderern mit Spezialkenntnissen. Die meisten Ungarn mußten, nachdem HITLER die Macht ergriffen hatte, Deutschland verlassen. Viele von ihnen flohen entweder direkt oder auf Umwegen über andere europäische Länder nach Amerika. Die meisten kehrten nie - oder höchstens als eine symbolische Geste - wieder nach Ungarn zurück.

Der Aufsatz schildert den Einfluß der ungarischen Auswanderer auf die amerikanische Gesellschafts- und Kulturgeschichte des zwanzigsten Jahrhunderts.

Notes

1. Cf. Immigration Act of 1924.
2. Cf. Immigration Act of 1924.
3. Michael Polanyi, "Curriculum vitae", June 14, 1933, Michael Polanyi Papers, Box 2, Folder 12, Department of Special Collections, University of Chicago Library, Chicago, IL.
4. Theodore von Kármán to Michael Polanyi, Department of Special Collections, University of Chicago Library, Chicago, IL.
5. Cf. e.g. the case of the son of his brother's friend Michael Becz, see Elemér Kármán to Theodore von Kármán, Budapest, May 9, 1920 (German), Theodore von Kármán Papers, File 139.1, California Institute of Technology Archives, Pasadena, CA.
6. Eric R. Jette to Michael Polanyi, Up[p]sala, February 10, 1923, Michael Polanyi Papers, Box 1, Folder 19, Department of Special Collections, University of Chicago Library, Chicago, IL.
7. Michael Polanyi to B. Lorenz, October 16, 1922. (German), Michael Polanyi Papers, Box 1, Folder 18, Department of Special Collections, University of Chicago Library, Chicago, IL.
8. Elemér Székely to Theodore von Kármán, Wien, April 29, 1924. (Hungarian), Theodore von Kármán Papers, File 29.14, California Institute of Technology Archives, Pasadena, CA.
9. Mihály Freund to Michael Polanyi, May 4, 1920. (Hungarian) Michael Polanyi Papers, Box 17, Department of Special Collections, University of Chicago Library, Chicago, IL.
10. Karl Polanyi to Michael Polanyi, Küb/Semmering, n.d. (Hungarian), Michael Polanyi Papers, Department of Special Collections, University of Chicago Library, Chicago, IL.
11. Karl Polanyi to Cecilia Polanyi, [Vienna,] April 24, 1920, (German), Michael Polanyi Papers, Box 17, Folder 2, Department of Special Collections, University of Chicago Library, Chicago, IL.
12. Karl Polanyi to Michael Polanyi, Vienna, October 7, 1925 (Hungarian), Michael Polanyi Papers, Box 17, Department of Special Collections, University of Chicago Library, Chicago, IL.
13. Unknown to Michael Polanyi, Vienna, March 11, 1920 (Hungarian), Michael Polanyi Papers, Box 1, Folder 7, Department of Special Collections, University of Chicago Library, Chicago, IL.
14. The author's interview with Marcel Stein, New York, Columbia University, November 29, 1989.
15. Georg Pólya, "Bürgerrechts-Urkunde, March 7, 1918; Appointment to the Eidgenössische Technische Hochschule, February 24, 1928, George Pólya Papers, SC 337, Box 87-034:3, Department of Special Collections and University Archives, Stanford University Libraries, Stanford, CA.
16. Georg de Hevesy to Michael Polanyi, [Budapest,] January 27, 1920 (Hungarian), Michael Polanyi Papers, Box 1, Folders 6, Department of Special Collections, University of Chicago Library, Chicago, IL.
17. Leo Szilard to Jacques Errera, London, June 4, 1933 (German), Leo Szilard Papers, Box 7, Folder 22; Benjamin Liebowitz to Ernst P. Boas, London, May 4, 1933, Leo Szilard Papers, Box 12, Folder 4, Mandeville Department of Special Collections, University of California, San Diego Library, La Jolla, CA.
18. Karl Brandt Circular, New York, February 1, 1934 (German), John von Neumann Papers, Box 7, "1933: Some very interesting letters to J. v. N.," Library of Congress, Washington, D.C.
19. Albert Einstein to Leo Szilard, Le Coq-sur-Mer, April 25 and May 1, 1933; Leo Szilard to Albert Einstein, London, May 4 and 9, 1933 (German), Leo Szilard Papers, Box 7, Folder 27, Mandeville Department of Special Collections, University of California, San Diego Library, La Jolla, CA.
20. Leo Szilard to Sir William Beveridge, Brussels, May 14, 1933, Leo Szilard Papers, Box 11, Folder 18, Mandeville Department of Special Collections, University of California, San Diego Library, La Jolla, CA.
21. Leo Szilard to Sir William Beveridge, London, May 4, 1933, Leo Szilard Papers, Box 4, Folder 30, Mandeville Department of Special Collections, University of California, San Diego Library, La Jolla, CA.
22. Benjamin Liebowitz to Ernst P. Boas, London, May 4, 1933, Leo Szilard Papers, Box 12, Folder 4, Mandeville Department of Special Collections, University of California, San Diego Library, La Jolla, CA.
23. Emergency Committee in Aid of Displaced Foreign Scholars, New York Public Library, Manuscripts and Archives Division, New York, N.Y.

24 Emergency Committee, 195 boxes of correspondence and papers.
25 This list is based on the documents of the Emergency Committee in Aid of Displaced Foreign Scholars kept in the Manuscripts and Archives Division of the New York Public Library, New York, N.Y. Robin E. RIDER compiled a list of mathematicians and physicists who emigrated to the USA or to Britain which appears in the appendix of her excellent paper. Compared to my list, she added a few more émigré Hungarian names such as physicists Gusztáv KÜRTI, Cornelius LÁNCZOS, and Elisabeth (Erzsébet) RÓNA, as well as mathematicians Paul ERDΔS, Tibor RADÓ, and Stefan (István) VAJDA. Yet, Ms RIDER made no distinction between Germans and Hungarians among the immigrant scientists and gave no attention to Leo SZILARD's activities or to other Hungarian contributions to the establishment of the Academic Assistance Council or the Emergency Committee.
26 Leo Szilard to Max Delbrück, London, May 7, 1933, Leo Szilard Papers, Box 7, Folder 9, Mandeville Department of Special Collections, University of California, San Diego Library, La Jolla, CA.
27 Jacques Errera to Leo Szilard, Bruxelles, June 5, 1933 (French), Leo Szilard Papers, Box 7, Folder 2; Leo Szilard to unknown, Brussels, May 14, 1933, Leo Szilard Papers, Box 12, Folder 21, Mandeville Department of Special Collections, University of California, San Diego Library, La Jolla, CA.
28 [Leo Szilard,] Report, May 23, 1933, Leo Szilard Papers, Box 4, Folder 30, Mandeville Department of Special Collections, University of California, San Diego Library, La Jolla, CA.
29 Leo Szilard to Dr. Delbrück, London, May 7, 1933, Leo Szilard Papers, Box 7, Folder 9, Mandeville Department of Special Collections, University of California, San Diego Library, La Jolla, CA.
30 Leo Szilard to Eugene Wigner, London, August 17, 1933, Michael Polanyi Papers, Box 2, Folder 12, Department of Special Collection, University of Chicago Library, Chicago, IL.
31 Karl Polanyi to Michael Polanyi, London, October 31, 1934 (Hungarian), Michael Polanyi Papers, Box 17, Folder 5, Department of Special Collection, University of Chicago Library, Chicago, IL.
32 [Sir Lawrence] Bragg to Michael Polanyi, Manchester, July 10, 1933, Michael Polanyi Papers, Box 2, Folder 12, Department of Special Collection, University of Chicago Library, Chicago, IL.
33 Leo Szilard to Maxwell Garnett, London, May 9, 1934, Leo Szilard Papers, Box 8, Folder 23, Julian Huxley to Leo Szilard, London, May 3, 1934, Leo Szilard Papers, Box 9, Folder 12, Mandeville Department of Special Collections, University of California, San Diego Library, La Jolla, CA.
34 Leo Szilard to C. S. Gibson, London, June 13, 1933, Leo Szilard Papers, Box 8. Folder 23, Mandeville Department of Special Collections, University of California, San Diego Library, La Jolla, CA.
35 Abraham Flexner to John von Neumann, New York, March 30, 1933, John von Neumann Papers, Box 7, "1933: Some very interesting letters to J. v. N.," Library of Congress, Washington, D.C.
36 *Ibid.*
37 Abraham Flexner to John von Neumann, New York, May 6, 1933, John von Neumann Papers, Box 7, "1933: Some very interesting letters to J. v. N.," Library of Congress, Washington, D.C.
38 Benjamin Liebowitz to Ernst P. Boas, London, May 4, 1933, Leo Szilard Papers, Box 12, Folder 4, Mandeville Department of Special Collections, University of California, San Diego Library, La Jolla, CA.
39 Leo Szilard to C. S. Gibson, London, June 13, 1933, Leo Szilard Papers, Box 8. Folder 23, Mandeville Department of Special Collections, University of California, San Diego Library, La Jolla, CA.
40 Oswald Veblen to John von Neumann, New York, May 22, 1933, John von Neumann Papers, Box 7, "1933: Some very interesting letters to J. v. N.," Library of Congress, Washington, D.C.
41 *Ibid.*
42 K. Brandt to John von Neumann, New York, March 19, 1934, John von Neumann Papers, Box 7, "1933: Some very interesting letters to J. v. N.," Library of Congress, Washington, D.C.
43 Leo Szilard quoted by Eugene Wigner to Michael Polanyi, [Budapest, n.d. (July 1933?)] Michael Polanyi Papers, Box. 2, Folder 12, Department of Special Collection, University of Chicago Library, Chicago, IL.
44 Eugene Wigner to Michael Polanyi, [Budapest, n.d. (July 1933?)] Michael Polanyi Papers, Box. 2, Folder 12, Department of Special Collection, University of Chicago Library, Chicago, IL.
45 Theodore von Kármán to Robert Oppenheimer, [Pasadena,] March 12, 1934, Theodore von Kármán Papers, File 22.10, California Institute of Technology Archives, Pasadena, CA.
46 Primary documentation on individual careers is available in the *Deutsches Film Museum* in Frankfurt am Main, Germany. Very little is preserved in U.S. public collections such as the Library of the Academy of Motion Picture Arts and Sciences in Los Angeles, CA. The *Deutsches Film Museum* organized a very rich exhibition on the exodus of the film people from Germany, "From Babelsberg to Hollywood: Film Emigrants from Nazi Germany," in Frankfurt am Main, 1987, and in Los Angeles, 1988 (cp. *Loewy 1987*, *Variety*, May 20, 1987; August 15, 1988).

References

Beveridge, Lord [W.] (1959): A Defence of Free Learning. Oxford, Oxford University Press.
Bodnar, J. (1985): The Transplanted. A History of Immigrants in Urban America. Bloomington, Indiana University Press.
Chase, A. (1977): The Legacy of Malthus. The Social Costs of the New Scientific Racism. New York, Alfred A. Knopf.
Clark, F. E. (1913): Old Homes of New Americans. The Country and the People of the Austro-Hungarian Monarchy and Their Contribution to the New World. Boston and New York, Houghton Mifflin.
Divine, R. A. (1957): American Immigration Policy, 1924-1952. New Haven, Yale University Press.
Fermi, L. (1968): Illustrious Immigrants. The Intellectual Migration from Europe 1930-41. Chicago & London, University of Chicago Press.
Frank, T. (1992): "Ellis Island követei. Az osztrák-magyar kivándorlás titkos amerikai megfigyelése (1906-1907) [The Emissaries of Ellis Island. The Secret American Surveillance of Austro-Hungarian Emigration, 1906-1907]," In: Valóság XXXV, No. 7, 77-90.
Frank, T. (1996): "From Austria-Hungary to the U.S.: The Exodus of National Minorities, 1880-1914," In: Nationalities Papers, Special Issue on The Hungarian Minorities.
Gårding, L. (1970): "Marcel Riesz in Memoriam," In: Acta Mathematica 124, I-XI.
Gay, P. (1970): Weimar Culture. The Outsider as Insider. New York, etc., Harper Torchbooks.
Gossett, T. F. (1965): Race. The History of an Idea in America. New York, Schocken Books.
Haller, M. H. (1963, 1984): Eugenics. Hereditarian Attitudes in American Thought. New Brunswick, N. J., Rutgers University Press.
Handlin, O. (1951): The Uprooted. The Epic Story of the Great Migrations that Made the American People. Boston, Little, Brown.
Higham, J. (1955, 1988): Strangers in the Land: Patterns of American Nativism 1860-1924. New Brunswick, N. J.-London, Rutgers University Press.
Horváth, J. (1975): "Riesz Marcel matematikai munkássága I" [The Mathematical Work of Marcel Riesz], In: Matematikai Lapok, Vol. 26, No. 1-2, 11-37.
Jenks, J. W. and Lauck, W. J. (1926): The Immigration Problem. A Study of American Immigration Conditions and Needs. New York and London, Funk & Wagnalls.
Katz, E. (1979): The Film Encyclopedia. New York: Thomas Y. Crowell.
Loewy, R. ed. (1987): Von Babelsberg nach Hollywood. Filmemigranten aus Nazideutschland. Exponatenverzeichnis. Frankfurt am Main, Deutsches Filmmuseum.
Plaskin, G. (1983): Horowitz. A Biography of Vladimir Horowitz. New York, William Morrow and Co.
Puskás, J. (1982): From Hungary to the United States (1880-1914). Budapest, Akadémiai Kiadó.
Robin, R. (1984): "Alarm and Opportunity: Emigration of Mathematicians and Physisists to Britain and the United States, 1933-1945," Historical Studies in the Physical Sciences, Vol. 15, Part I.
Strauss H. A. and Röder, W. eds. (1983): International Biographical Dictionary of Central European Émigrés 1933-1945. München-New York-London-Paris, K. G. Saur.
Varconi V. and Honeck, E. (1976): It's Not Enough To Be Hungarian. Graphic Impressions, Inc.
Varga, I. (1976): "A kivándorlás irányváltozása és a magyar kivándorlók beilleszkedése Latin-Amerikában a két világháború között" [Changes in the Direction of Emigration and the Adjustment of Hungarian Emigrants in Latin America Between the Two World Wars], Acta Universitatis Szegediensis de Attila József Nominatae, Acta Historica, Tomus LVI, Studia Latinoamericana VIII, Szeged.
Walter, B. (1946): Theme and Variations; An Autobiography.

Address of the Author

Tibor Frank
Department of American Studies
School of English and American Studies
Eötvös Loránd University
Ajtósi Dürer sor 19-21
1146 Budapest
HUNGARY

DAVID J. WISHART

Indian Dispossession and Land Claims: The Issue of Fairness

Introduction

The treatment of the original Americans, long the nation's poorest minority, is, along with slavery, the major blemish on the reputation of the United States. A long list of atrocities, running from Sand Creek to the Bear Paw battlefield and the snow-swept plains of Wounded Knee stands as testimony to the often brutal treatment of Native Americans (or Indians - the two designations will be used interchangeably here) by the colonizing forces. But in the long run, it was the routine and mundane effects of Federal policy which tore at the fabric of Native American life, leaving societies in tatters, from which pieces tribal life has since been sown back together.
In this study the focus is on the most crucial transaction that took place between the United States and Native Americans, namely the American takeover of Indian lands. This takeover was posed as a deal: an exchange of Indian lands for American civilization. The dynamics of this exchange have previously been cast in only the most general terms, and no issue in American history is more distorted by myth. The objective here is peel away the layers of myth by posing, and answering, the following questions: How much did the United States pay the Native Americans for their cessions of land in the nineteenth century? How was the Native Americans' money used? What did the Indian Claims Commission (which met from 1947 to 1978) conclude about the fairness of nineteenth century dispossession? And how fair were the actions of the Indian Claims Commission? In other words, how genuine was, and is, the United States' commitment to the deal that it has offered the Native Americans? First, however, the complexities of assessing fairness (meaning "justness" or "equitableness") must first be reviewed.

Complexities

A major difficulty in assessing the overall fairness of Federal Indian policy is, as the legal scholar Charles WILKINSON has pointed out, that it is a "time-warped field" (*Wilkinson 1987, 12*). An earlier legal scholar, Felix COHEN, made much the same point, though in more poetic language, when he wrote that, "Like the miner's canary, the Indian marks the shifts from fresh air to poison gas in our political atmosphere...." (*Cohen 1953, 390*). What these scholars are alluding to are the frenetic swings that have characterized Federal Indian policy: the same government that has, in some periods, eviscerated Native American societies has, at other times, attempted to revive them.
Take, for example, the pendulum swings in twentieth century Indian policy. The first thirty years of the century were a continuation of the forced acculturation that had intensified after the passage of the General Allotment Act in 1887. The imposition of allotments and the sale of remaining reservation lands ("surplus lands"), mandatory Americanization of Indian children in schools, and repressive Supreme Court rulings, such as *Lone Wolf v. Hitchcock (1903)*, which confirmed the unlimited power of Congress over Native American societies, characterized this "poisoned period" in Federal-Indian dealings. Then the pendulum swung, and in the 1930s, during the "Indian New Deal", Native American societies were revitalized and previous repressive policies, including the allotment policy, were repudiated. This was followed by

another "poisoned period", lasting from 1947 until the late 1960s, when more than 100 Native American societies were terminated, or abolished as separate entities in American life. American attitudes, and Federal policy, swung again after 1968 and a new era of Indian self-determination ensued. Terminated tribes and bands were restored and some protection was given to Native American religious freedoms. Then again, in the 1980s, there came new attacks on Native American sovereignty as Supreme Court decisions such as *Montana v. United States (1981)* and *Brendale v. Yakima Indian Nations (1989)* compromised the Indians' rights to exercise regulatory jurisdiction on their own reservations (Wunder 1994).

Given such swings, it is hardly surprising that there have been contradictory assessments of the fairness of the United States' dealings with Native Americans. It depends, at least in part, upon which section of the record is emphasized. WILKINSON, for example, concluded that, "For all its flaws, the policy of the United States towards its native people is one of the most progressive of any people" *(Wilkinson 1987, 5)*. WILKINSON based his assessment on the recognition of Indian sovereignty as inherent, not delegated, and the special status of Native American societies as extraterritorial to states, a status established by the Marshall Court in the 1820s and 1830s and upheld ever since. Other indigenous societies, in Canada, Australia, even in New Zealand, have not, at least until recently, had such unambiguous recognition of sovereign status.

Emphasize another part of the record, however, and the assessment might be very different. FLERAS and ELLIOT, for example, conclude that Native Americans are "still under the thumb of Washington; their treaty rights are still denied; their resources flow out of their communities to the benefit of non-Indians; and the government that rules them does so without their consent" (Fleras and Elliot 1992, 164). They came to this conclusion by pointing to Congress' plenary (or absolute power) over Native Americans, as well as to the continued condition of poverty on most reservations.

Contradiction is inherent in the United States' dealings with Native Americans, with vastly different motivations giving rise to the same policies. This was the case in the nineteenth century, when both humanitarians and exploiters of Native Americans supported the allotment policy. It was also the case in the 1930s and 1940s in the buildup to the creation of the Indian Claims Commission. Ostensibly this commission - or, more accurately, court, because that is how it functioned - was established to hear outstanding land claims and to "redress past injustices". But not far in the background was the idea that once these claims had been settled termination could proceed. In its final report, the Indian Claims Commission candidly admitted this dual purpose, stating that "The problem of giving the Indian his due had to be balanced somehow with giving him his walking papers...." *(Indian Claims Commission 1978, 14)*. Such multiplicity of motivations makes assessing fairness of dealings a complicated task.

Finally, among the complexities, is the fact that history writing itself is a "time-warped field". The British historian E. H. CARR, anticipating the postmodernists, put this well when he wrote, "The historian is part of history. The point in the procession at which he finds himself determines his angle of vision over the past" *(Carr 1947, 43)*. There will always be contradictory conclusions as to the fairness of the treatment of Native Americans because the art of historical representation is inherently subjective. In each age different questions will be asked, different "angles of vision" applied. Recognizing this, it becomes imperative to emphasize empirical data, to lay a foundation of fact as a firmer base for analysis than mere opinion. This paper attempts to do just that. The first question is: how much did the Native Americans receive for their lands?

Compensation

There have been previous attempts to estimate, in a general way, how much the United States paid the Native Americans for their lands. Cohen believed the figure was about $ 800 million, while Barsh calculated that the United States paid 75 cents an acre for one-half of the continental United

States and took another one billion acres for nothing (*Cohen 1947; Barsh 1982*). The findings of the Indian Claims Commission now allow a much more specific itemization.

The first two major steps in claims case proceedings are to establish, in acres, the size and location of each Indian nation's traditional homeland, and to calculate how much the United States paid for cessions from that homeland. These data, therefore, enable a cents per acre figure to be placed on each cession of land. Moreover, because the Indian Claims Commission was set up as advocacy proceedings, with the claimants (Native Americans) and defendant (United States) arguing against each other, a relatively accurate accounting is likely because neither side would allow the other to prevail with unsubstantiated conclusions.

According to the commission's findings, the Native Americans were paid $ 35,613,790 for 149 cessions of original territories[1]. This is an average payment of 9.4 cents an acre per cession. Payments ranged from nothing for vast areas of the western United States (including California) to $ 1.02 for the tiny (9,000 acres) Samish cession on the Puget Sound.

Even if all cessions of land, including those which did not become the subject of claims cases, are included, the average compensation is little different. All cessions on the northern Great Plains during the nineteenth century, for example, involving 290 million acres of original territories and reservation lands, brought $ 29,977,015, or an average of 10 cents an acre. Vast areas of original territories in Kansas and Nebraska in the 1820s and 1830s and on the western and northern Great Plains in the 1860s, 1870s, and 1880s passed to the United States for less than 10 cents an acre, and often for nothing at all. More substantial payments of over $ 1 an acre came from small cessions of reservation lands after 1860 (*Wishart 1990*).

How can the geographic variations in payments be explained? First, it is clear that the buying price had no relationship to the value that either the Native Americans or the United States placed on the land. The intense connection between Native Americans and their homelands was of no relevance. The fact that their histories and religions were place-specific, and that they lost their cultural bearings when they lost their homelands, was not taken into account when the United States set the purchase price. More surprisingly, perhaps, the buying price was not related to the American perception of the worth of the land. Fine agricultural land in Kansas and Nebraska, for example, was obtained for meager payments of a few cents an acre.

This is explained by the United States' buying policy, which was to obtain the land as cheaply as possible. The Indian Office was always underfunded by a Congress which regarded Indian affairs as a marginal issue. More than this, however, there were great profits to be made on the deal: obtain the land for a few cents an acre, then sell it to settlers, or speculators, for $ 1.25 an acre (the standard selling price for much of the nineteenth century) and swell the revenues of the Government. BARSH has already shown how bursts of Indian land purchases came when the Federal Government was particularly in need of money (*Barsh 1988*).

Payments for Indian lands were higher than average if the size of the cessions was small. The United States could afford to pay more than 50 cents an acre if only a few thousand acres were involved. This explains why the highest payments per acre for cessions of original lands occurred around the Puget Sound in the 1850s when the Samish and other nations sold their slivers of forested coastlands. Similarly, the highest prices paid for Indian lands on the northern Great Plains were for small cessions from reservations, or for the sale of entire small reservations when the residents were moved to Indian Territory (later Oklahoma).

Finally, payments for Indian lands were likely to be higher than average if the frontier of Euro-American settlement was close at hand. The availability of a local market for resales meant that there would be little time-lag between purchase and resale, so costs could be recouped quickly. Moreover, if the frontier was close to the cession it was also likely that the Native Americans would be aware of the market value of their lands and would argue more strenuously for a fairer price.

There is an important connection to be made at this point in the analysis. It goes right to the heart of the issue of fairness. The funds for the "civilization program" were derived from the proceeds that the Indians received for their lands. The Indians' own money would be used to prepare them for assimilation into American society. Clearly there is a contradiction here: because the United States endeavored to obtain the lands as cheaply as possible, there were never sufficient funds available to make a genuine commitment to helping the Native Americans adjust to the new world that was being thrust upon them. The second question, then, is how was the Native Americans' money used? The question is answered here by specific reference to the dispossession of the Nebraska Indians.

The Dispossession of the Nebraska Indians

The case-study of the Nebraska Indians (Ponca, Pawnee, Omaha, and Otoe-Missouria) sheds light on the circumstances surrounding Native American land sales and the way their own money was used by the United States as an instrument of social control.

In 1800 there were approximately 14,000 Native Americans in the eastern half of Nebraska, occupying about 30 million acres of land. A century later, of the original Nebraska Indians, only 1,203 Omahas and 229 Poncas remained in their homelands, and their combined estate was little more than 200,000 acres.

For the most part, the divestiture of the Indians' lands was in accordance with the laws set by the United States (only the Ponca cession of 1877 was an illegal taking). But every cession was made against a backdrop of poverty, which obliged the Indians to sell their only resource so that they could survive. The cessions were also made in an intensifying atmosphere of envelopment, as Euro-Americans crowded in, making the Indians feel like strangers in their own lands.

The Nebraska Indians sold their lands in three stages (*Fig. 1*). The first sales took place in the 1830s when, for example, the Pawnee and the Otoe-Missouria between them sold about 14 million acres at an average price of less than 2 cents an acre. The United States wanted these lands for the resettlement of nations like the Delaware who were being pressured out of the eastern half of the country by the westward movement of Euro-American settlers. Compensation was low partly because the Indian Office argued that the Nebraska Indians could still support themselves in traditional ways, an assumption that was not correct.

The second wave of sales came in the 1850s, following the Kansas-Nebraska Act of 1854, which opened the area to Euro-American settlement. The frontier had caught up with the once remote Nebraska Indians. From 1854 to 1858 they sold their remaining ancestral lands, retaining only small (but generally fertile) reservations. Indian leaders journeyed to Washington; treaties were negotiated; the Indians had their say; but in the end they were given no option but to sell, and it was the United States which set the terms of the purchase. Payments were higher than in the 1830s because the Indians could not support themselves in the old ways and because, with local demand for land high, the United States could quickly resell at a substantial profit to the settlers.

The final cessions were made from the 1860s to the 1880s, as first portions of reservations, and then entire reservations, were sold. Life on the reservations during the 1860s and 1870s was marked by a deepening poverty, recurring epidemics, unrelenting attacks by the still powerful Oglala and Brule Dakota (or Sioux), and demands from Nebraska settlers that Indians should not be allowed to impede the progress of the frontier. First the Pawnee, then the Ponca, and finally the Otoe-Missouria were excised from Nebraska and resettled in Indian Territory (*Fig. 1*). Only the Omaha were able to withstand the demands for removal, but even they had to sell parts of their reservation to survive (*Wishart 1995*).

The outlines of this story of dispossession can be traced on the graphs of population change (*Fig. 2*). During the first thirty years of the nineteenth century, epidemics, such as smallpox in 1800 - 1801, devastated Nebraska's Native American populations. But their homelands were still intact, their annual cycles still turned with the changing seasons, and their populations could rebound.

Fig. 1: Land Cessions of the Nebraska Indians, 1830 - 1881.

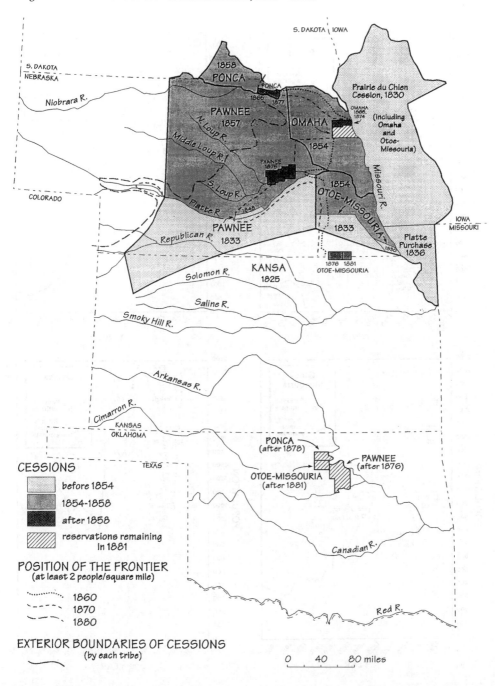

Source: Wishart 1994, 72-75.

Fig. 2: Total Population Change of the Nebraska Indians, 1780 - 1910.

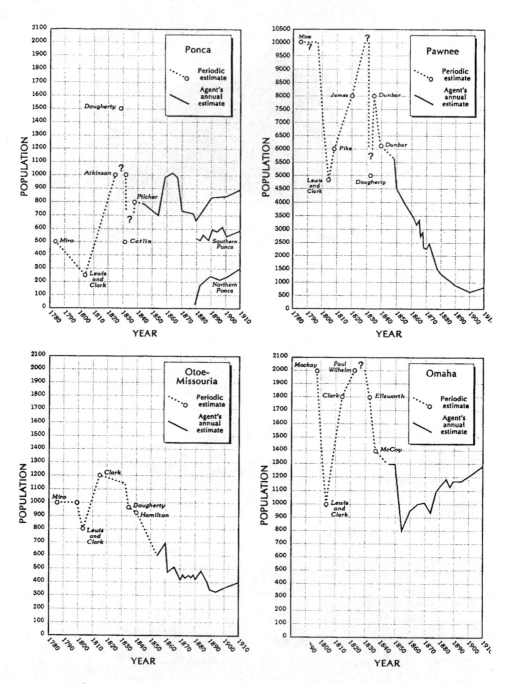

Source: Wishart 1994, 72-75.

This all changed after 1830. The bison herds were driven back to the western Great Plains and the Dakota stalked the range. Famine became the norm, and epidemics - cholera, measles, malaria, as well as smallpox - struck without respite. Entire generations, perishing when they were children and most vulnerable, were missing from the Indians' population structures[2]. The epidemics waned after 1850, but tuberculosis and other afflictions of poverty kept up the killing. Population totals plummeted. For the Pawnee and Otoe-Missouria the downward plunge was not reversed until after 1900; even the rebounding of the Omaha's population after 1855 was marked by periodic declines and was, overall, a hesitant recovery.

With the collapse of their traditional subsistence base, the Nebraska Indians became increasingly reliant on the proceeds from the sale of their lands for survival. By the terms of the treaties of the 1850s, they were given annual payments which would decline over the years as they, theoretically, became self-sufficient farmers. The Otoe-Missouria, for example, received $ 20,000 a year for the first three years, $ 13,000 a year for the next ten years, $ 9,000 a year for the next fifteen years, and $ 5,000 a year for the final twelve years (*Kappler 1904, Vol. 2, 608 - 614*). This was a total payment of $ 463,424 for 1,087,893 acres, or 42.6 cents an acre.

But this money was not the Indians' own to use. All the 1850s treaties stipulated that the President of the United States would control the allocation of the funds. Much of the Indians' money was spent on annuities - biannual deliveries of blankets, tools, provisions, and other "useful goods". Often the goods were not useful at all; sometimes the crates arrived empty, their contents having been stolen on the way from St. Louis or another supply point.

By the 1860s the Indians' money was being applied to the Government's increasingly mandatory "civilization" program. It was spent on wages and uniforms for Indian police forces, composed of the most "progressive" men from each nation. It was used to pay blacksmiths and farmers who were supposed to teach the Indians' "practical skills", or to fund schools where Indian children were taught English and ordered to leave their pasts behind. The Otoe-Missouria's money was even used to construct a jail, which was quickly filled with Indians. Annuities were withheld from parents who failed to put their children in school and from men who refused to work in the fields - a bizarre situation whereby they had to work to earn their own money. After all these expenditures, per capita payments to the Indians amounted to less than $ 10 a year. And this was not paid in coin, but in script which could only be used to purchase goods at inflated prices from the trader's store. The Indians were also prohibited from leaving their reservations unless they had a pass signed by the agent, which added a spatial dimension to these mechanisms of social control.

The fading traditional world of the Nebraska Indians can be glimpsed in the photographs of W. H. JACKSON, taken around 1870. Ga-hi-ge's tipi, for example, on the Omaha Reservation (*Fig. 3*), is made of Government-supplied canvas rather than the traditional and more effective cover of bison hides. Hides and skins - which can be seen drying next to the tipi - were so scarce and valuable by this time that they were dressed by the Indians and sold in nearby Nebraska towns. JACKSON's portrait of Pawnee women (*Fig. 4*) also shows how the traditional (the earth lodge) and the new (Government blankets) existed side by side in 1870. It was about this time that an old Pawnee chief told John WILLIAMSON, the farmer at the agency, that he was "neither white man or Indian now" (*Williamson 1871*).

A final view from the late nineteenth century is provided by population pyramids (*Fig. 5*), constructed from census counts of the Nebraska Indians in the 1880s. These pyramids are encapsulated histories, with all the traumas of a century of dispossession etched into their shapes. The smallpox epidemics of the 1830s, the Dakota raids, the ravages of tuberculosis, the measles epidemic which carried off one-quarter of the Omaha children in 1873 - 1874, are all in evidence. For the old people who had witnessed it all, the changes were almost inconceivable. As Joseph LAFLESCHE of the Omaha sorrowfully recalled in 1873,"the white men came like blackbirds and settled all around us" (*Sen. Misc. Doc. 1879-1880, 11*).

Fig. 3: Ga-hi-ge's Tipi, by W. H. Jackson, 1868-1869.

Source: Smithsonian Institution Anthropological Archives, No. 4044.

Fig. 4: Group of Pawnee Women, by W. H. Jackson, circa 1870.

Source: Nebraska State Historical Society, I396.

The Indian Claims Commission and the Issue of Fairness

The express purpose of the Indian Claims Commission was to judge the fairness of Indian dispossession and repay the nation's debts to it's original inhabitants. If the Commission decided that original payments for Indian lands had been "unconscionable", unfair, or illegal then a second payment would be given to remedy the situation. This was arrived at by assessing the "fair market value" of the original cessions.

The fair market value is an estimate of the price that an "informed purchaser" would have paid for the land at the time it was taken. No subsequent developments, such as the discovery of oil, for example, was included in the accounting, no adjustment for inflation was made, and no attention was paid to the value that the Indians themselves placed on the land. And no return of land was allowed, only a second payment calculated by subtracting the original compensation from the fair market value. In addition, "gratuitous offsets" (payments, such as rations, that had been made without treaty obligation) and lawyers' fees were deducted from the final award.

According to the decisions of the Indian Claims Commission the fair market value of the 149 cessions was $506,643,600, or $1.02 an acre per cession. So, according to this measure, the Native Americans had originally been paid only 10.7 percent of the fair price. Similarly, there was a wide gap between what the United States paid for original and subsequent cessions on the northern Great Plains and what a fair payment would have been. The Indian Claims Commission found that the fair market value for cessions from the northern Great Plains averaged 88 cents an acre, or almost nine times the original average payment (*Wishart 1990*).

The Indian Claims Commission, therefore, formally acknowledged that the United States' payments for Indian lands had been unfair. A close examination of one case, the Pawnee claims case, will serve to reveal that the fairness of the Indian Claims Commission itself is open to question. The Pawnee lodged their claims before the Indian Claims Commission in 1947. It would be seventeen years before they would get any satisfaction, and even then it was only a qualified victory.

Fig. 5: Population Pyramids of the Nebraska Indians, 1886 - 1887.

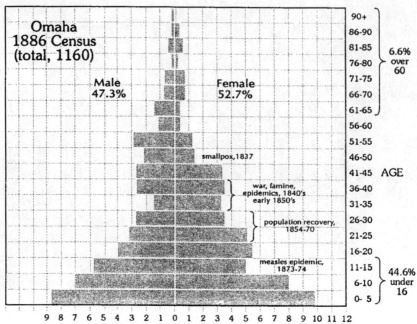

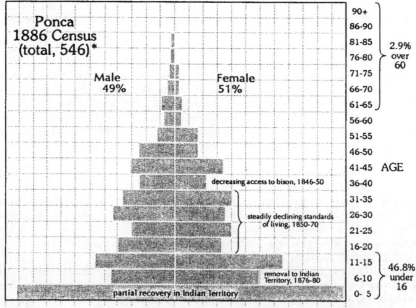

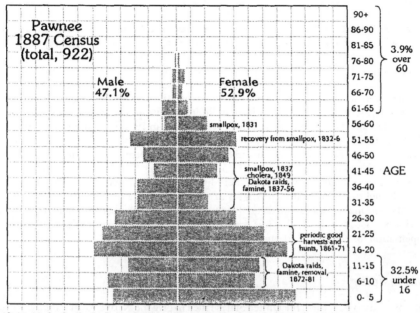

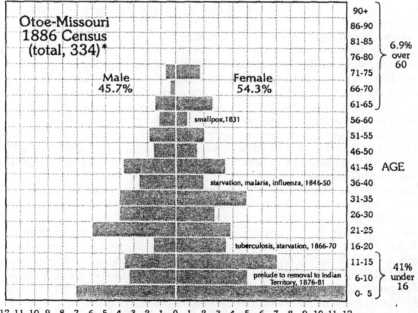

The Pawnee initially asked for an award or more than $ 30 million for about 40 million acres that they had ceded to the United States from 1829 to 1875. The grounds for the claims were fraud, duress, and unconscionably low payments. The Indian Claims Commission's response was to award the Pawnee $ 200 plus a small amount of interest. The Pawnee appealed the decision to the Court of Claims, which remanded the case back to the Commission along with a stern reprimand that it should do its job properly. In 1957 the Commission recognized that the Pawnee had valid title to 23 million acres of the land they had ceded, and the case advanced to the valuation stage.

The Pawnee's lawyers argued that the Pawnee were due an award of more than $ 33 million, that being the difference between the original payments and the fair market value. The Government's lawyers, interpreting the same record quite differently, proposed only a $ 2,5 million award. When the Indian Claims Commission made its decision, in 1960, its findings were much closer to the Government's figures. The Pawnee were awarded almost $ 8 million as a second payment for lands that had been sold to the United States in the nineteenth century for payments so low "as to shock the conscience".

But the case was not yet finished. There were appeals, and the lawyers' fees, totalling $ 876,897, were deducted from the award. In August of 1964 the Pawnee received their final award of $ 6,499,088. The money was divided equally among the 1,833 members of the tribe, each person receiving $ 3,530. No doubt this was a welcome relief in hard times, but it was hardly a just compensation for the loss of a homeland (Wishart 1986).

Conclusion

By it's own admission, then, the United States failed to give the Native Americans a fair price for their lands. If a fair price had been given then perhaps the Native Americans' distress might have been ameliorated, and certainly the gap between the Government's rhetoric and the harsh realities of Indian living conditions would have been narrowed. A fairer compensation in the nineteenth century would have reduced the intensity of the Native Americans' poverty. Reduced poverty would in turn have allowed Native Americans to delay the sale of their lands, and later cessions, with the frontier close at hand, would have brought higher payments.

But, of course, higher payments were not the heart of the issue. The retention of traditional lands and lifestyles was, and that option was never there. In this respect too, the Indian Claims Commission was more a continuation of the past than a break from it, because the Commission was expressly prohibited from returning land as an award. In a few instances - the Havasupai, Passamaquaddy, and Taos Pueblo - land has been returned, but these were through acts of Congress and were defined as unique cases which did not set a precedent for a more general return of homelands. The Dakota, for example, are still waiting for a return of the Black Hills, while their financial award from the Indian Claims Commission (subsequently modified to the Dakota's benefit by the Supreme Court in 1980) now stands at more than $ 300 million and accruing interest at 5 percent a year.

Perhaps Native Americans will be able to regain some of their lost estate through purchase with money earned in gaming or other economic enterprises. The Omaha, for example, made a $ 17 million profit from the first seventeen months' operation of their casino at Onawa, Iowa. Similarly, large profits have been made at the Oneida's Turning Stone casino near Syracuse, New York. Ray HALBRITTER, who manages the casino, sees "history coming full circle" for the Oneida as they plan to buy back homelands that were ceded in the nineteenth century. But HALBRITTER is not confident that this opportunity will last for long and he cautions that "Indian people can't have things too long before the white man starts coveting them" (Clines 1994). Already states are set to challenge the Indian Gaming Regulatory Act.

The end product of centuries of dispossession is manifest in the statistics of the 1990 census. Native American median family income is $ 8,248, compared to the United States average of $

14,420; 27.7 percent of Native Americans live below the poverty level, compared to 10 percent of all Americans; and 9.4 percent of Native Americans have bachelor's degrees, compared to the national average of 20.3 percent. Moreover, the poverty statistics show that poverty has only deepened for most Native Americans since 1980 *(U.S. Bureau of the Census, 1990)*.

Many Americans, including many now in power in Washington D.C., will look at these statistics and conclude that the Native Americans' situation is their own fault, that they lack a work ethic and have a welfare dependency. This writer looks at the statistics and, placing them in historical perspective, concludes that they are the result of the prevailing unfairness of the United States' treatment of the first Americans.

Zusammenfassung

Wie sie selber eingestehen, verabsäumten die Vereinigten Staaten im 19. Jahrhundert, den nordamerikanischen Indianern für ihr Land einen gerechten Preis zu geben. Wenn damals ein gerechter Preis gezahlt worden wäre, dann hätte das Elend der nordamerikanischen Indianer vielleicht gemindert werden können, und die Kluft zwischen den Aussagen der Regierung und der harten Realität der indianischen Lebensbedingungen wäre sicherlich verringert worden. Geringere Armut wiederum hätte den nordamerikanischen Indianern ermöglicht, den Verkauf ihres Landes hinauszuzögern, und spätere Abtretungen hätten aufgrund der nahe gelegenen Siedlungsgrenze höhere Zahlungen erbracht.

Höhere Zahlungen waren aber natürlich nicht der Kern der Sache. Vielmehr ging es um die Erhaltung des traditionellen Landes und Lebensstils, und diese Möglichkeit gab es nie. Auch in dieser Hinsicht bot die Indian Claims Commission eher eine Fortsetzung der Vergangenheit als einen Bruch mit ihr, da es der Commission ausdrücklich verboten war, Land als Entschädigung zurückzugeben. In einigen wenigen Fällen wie den Havasupai, den Passamaquaddy und den Taos Pueblo wurde Land zurückgegeben. Dies geschah aber aufgrund von Kongreßgesetzen und sie wurden als einmalige Fälle bezeichnet, welche keinen Präzedenzfall für eine generellere Rückgabe des ursprünglichen Indianerlandes bildeten. Die Dakota warten zum Beispiel immer noch auf die Rückgabe der Black Hills, während ihre finanzielle Entschädigung von der Indian Claims Commission (1980 erfolgte eine nachträgliche Abänderung zugunsten der Dakota vom Obersten Bundesgericht) derzeit bei mehr als $ 300 Millionen liegt, wobei jährlich 5 % Zinsen anfallen.

Vielleicht können die nordamerikanischen Indianer einen Teil ihres verlorenen Besitzes mit dem Geld, das sie mit dem Glücksspiel oder durch andere wirtschaftliche Unternehmungen verdienen, wiedererlangen. Die Omaha, zum Beispiel, erzielten in den ersten 17 Monaten nach der Inbetriebnahme ihres Kasinos in Onawa (Iowa) einen Gewinn von $ 17 Millionen. Ebenfalls große Gewinne wurden im Turning Stone Kasino der Oneidas in der Nähe von Syracuse (New York) erwirtschaftet. Ray HALBRITTER, der das Kasino führt, sieht, wie für die Oneidas "die Geschichte sich zu einem Kreis schließt", da sie vorhaben, ihr ursprüngliches Land, das im 19. Jahrhundert abgetreten wurde, zurückzukaufen. HALBRITTER ist aber nicht zuversichtlich, daß diese Gelegenheit lange bestehen wird und er warnt, daß "Indianer Dinge nicht sehr lange besitzen können, bevor nicht der weiße Mann beginnt, sie zu begehren" *(Clines 1994)*. Einige Staaten gehen bereits daran, Einwendungen gegen den Indian Gaming Regulatory Act zu erheben.

Das Endprodukt aus Jahrhunderten von Enteignungen ist in den Statistiken des U.S. Zensus von 1990 festgehalten. Das mittlere Familieneinkommen der nordamerikanischen Indianer beträgt $ 8,248 verglichen mit dem Durchschnitt der Vereinigten Staaten von $ 14,420; 27.7 % der nordamerikanischen Indianer im Vergleich zu 10 % aller Amerikaner leben unter der Armutsgrenze; und nur 9.4 % der nordamerikanischen Indianer haben einen Universitätsabschluß, verglichen mit dem nationalen Durchschnitt von 20.3 %. Darüber hinaus zeigt die Statistik, daß die Armut für die meisten nordamerikanischen Indianer seit 1980 ständig zugenommen hat *(U.S. Bureau of the Census, 1990)*.

Viele Amerikaner, auch jene, die nun in Washington D.C. an der Macht sind, werden sich diese Statistiken ansehen und daraus schließen, daß diese Situation die Schuld der nordamerikanischen Indianer ist, daß ihnen eine Arbeitsmoral fehlt und daß sie von der Wohlfahrt abhängig sind. Wenn der Autor dieser Arbeit sich die Statistiken ansieht, dann betrachtet er sie in ihrem historischen Zusammenhang und folgert daraus, daß sie das Ergebnis der vorherrschenden Ungerechtigkeit der Vereinigten Staaten gegenüber den sogenannten First Americans sind.

Notes

1 This represents about 38 percent of the land area of the United States. Not included is much of the area east of the Appalachians, where lands were previously ceded to the British, and other areas where Indian claimants were unable to prove title to a defined territory. The legal references for each case and details of the awards are itemized in Indian Claims Commission. (1978): Final Report. Washington D.C., G.P.O.
2 During situations of high mortality, as in nineteenth century Nebraska or parts of contemporary Africa, more than 50 percent of all deaths occur to children under the age of 5. See Mosley, W.H. and Cowly, P. (1991): The Challenge of World Health, Population Bulletin, 46 (4), 1 - 39.

References

Barsh, R.L. (1982): Indian Land Claims Policy in the United States. In: North Dakota Law Review, 58, 1-82.
Barsh, R.L. (1988): Indian Resources and the National Economy: Business Cycles and Policy Cycles. In: Policy Studies Journal, 16 (4), 799-825.
Carr, E.H. (1967): What is History? New York, Knopf.
Clines, F.X. (Aug. 2, 1994): Where Profit and Tradition Mix. In: New York Times, B1, B5.
Cohen, F.S. (1953): The Erosion of Indian Rights, 1950-53 : A Case Study in Bureaucracy. In: Yale Law Journal, 62, 348-90.
Fleras, A. and Elliot, J.L. (1992): The Nations Within: Aboriginal-State Relations in Canada, the United States, and New Zealand. Toronto, Oxford University Press.
Indian Claims Commission. (1978): Final Report. Washington D.C., G.P.O.
Kappler, C.J. (1903-1938): Indian Affairs: Laws and Treaties. 5 Vols. Washington D.C., G.P.O.
Senate Miscellaneous Document, (1879-80): 31, 47th Congress, 1st Session, SN 1993.
U.S. Bureau of the Census. (1990): Census of Population, Characteristics of American Indians by Tribe and Language. 1990 CP-3-7.
Wilkinson, C.F. (1987): American Indians, Time and the Law: Native Societies in a Modern Constitutional Democracy. New Haven, Yale University Press.
Wishart, D.J. (1986): The Pawnee Claims Case, 1947-64. In: Sutton, I: Irredeemable America: The Indians' Estate and Land Claims. Albuquerque, University of New Mexico Press, 157-86.
Wishart, D.J. (1990): Compensation for Dispossession: Payments to the Indians for their Lands on the Central and Northern Great Plains in the Nineteenth Century. In: National Geographic Research, 6, 94-109.
Wishart, D.J. (1994): An Unspeakable Sadness: The Dispossession of the Nebraska Indians. Lincoln, University of Nebraska Press.
Wunder, J. (1994): " Retained by the People": A History of American Indians and the Bill of Rights. New York, Oxford University Press.

Address of the Author

David J. Wishart
Department of Geography
University of Nebraska
Lincoln, NE 68588-0135
USA

DOROTHY M. HALLOCK

Second Contact: Redefining Indian Country

Introduction

First Contact is the term which anthropologists use to define the moment when interaction between North American Indians and European people began. During the five hundred years which have followed the process of interaction begun by COLUMBUS, it seems that fate has favored the European culture over that of indigenous American peoples. Indians lost their land, they lost great numbers of people to disease and warfare, and they lost political control until they faced near-extinction at the beginning of this century. Indian tribes throughout the USA were sunk in social, political, and economic ruin.

Indian tribes today are emerging from this seemingly hopeless situation through an amazing display of cultural resilience. The beginning of this resurgence occurred when tribes very cleverly began to take advantage of their individual geographic circumstances and of time-honored legal precedents. Tribes have initiated a period of Second Contact in which Indians are exercising their sovereign powers of political and economic self-determination in ways that redefine intercultural interaction.

The story of how some of America's poorest, least politicized people are growing rich and strong is a remarkable one. For example, the 307 member Pequot Tribe is the largest single taxpayer in the State of Connecticut. The Pequot Tribe pays the state over $ 100 million a year. This equals 30 percent of the state's tax revenues. Only monies paid to the state by the federal government exceed the amount paid by this tiny tribe (*Las Vegas Review-Journal 1994, D12*). Casino gambling is the source of this tribe's wealth.

Legal and Historical Foundations

Complex legal and historical foundations have made the Second Contact possible. The revitalization occurring throughout Indian country has roots that draw from deep in American culture. The Second Contact is not simply an Indian phenomenon. It is one more step in the evolution of the relationship between a dominant culture and a minority culture. The Second Contact cannot be understood without first understanding something of the convoluted cultural stratigraphy of America. A selective examination of American law as it has been applied to Indian tribes, and of key polarities in American intellectual and cultural history, are basic to this understanding. Once these ideas are explained, a clearer understanding of how they have shaped the Second Contact can be arrived at by looking in detail at the case study afforded by the Fort Mojave Indian Tribe in the lower Colorado River Valley.

"Indian country" is a term which dates back to the very beginnings of the American experience. The term has always had legal as well as geographic connotations. Tribes were treated as foreign nations, first by the colonies, and then by the independent United States. The U.S. Constitution codified the legal and geographic connotations of Indian country. Indian country is a phrase which appears in the Constitution under the Commerce Clause, which gives the Congress, not the individual state governments, the exclusive authority to regulate affairs with Indian tribes (*U.S. Constitution, at Article I, Section 8, Clause 3*). This explicit statement of the federal government's exclusive power over Indian tribes was the direct result of the ongoing threat to

American territory and polity presented by the alliances of European nations with various tribes. It would have been a recipe for disaster to allow each of the original thirteen states to deal directly with the tribes, in effect creating thirteen separate foreign policies.

This expedient solution to controlling foreign policy by assigning the federal government the responsibility for dealing with Indian tribes solved one problem, but created another which has not been resolved in the 200 years since Indian country became the exclusive territory of the federal government. That problem is the constant tension to find a workable balance between federal centralization of power, and states' rights. Although relations with tribes is the exclusive domain of the federal government, there is always pressure from those states in which tribes reside to exercise some degree of control over Indians living within their jurisdictional area. Having a unique class of citizens who occupy territory within a state, but who are not governed by the state, creates chronic friction among the tribes, the states, and the federal government.

This friction reached the U.S. Supreme Court in 1831 in a landmark case known as *Cherokee Nation v. State of Georgia*. In this case, Chief Justice John MARSHALL acknowledged the primordial rights of stone age people as being superior to, and separate from, those of the states in which they live. MARSHALL also acknowledged that the relationship of Indian tribes to the larger American society was unlike any other.

> "The condition of the Indians in relation to the United States is perhaps unlike that of any other two people in existence. In the general, nations not owing a common allegiance are foreign to each other. The term "foreign nation" is, with strict propriety, applicable by either to the other. But the relation of the Indians to the United States is marked by peculiar and cardinal distinctions which exist nowhere else. ...[I]t may well be doubted whether those tribes which reside within the acknowledged boundaries of the United States can, with strict accuracy, be denominated foreign nations" (*Washburn 1964, 120*).

Penning one of the most famous phrases in the history of American-tribal relations, MARSHALL went on to define the unique relationship of Indian tribes to the United States as that of "domestic dependent nations" (*Washburn 1964, 121*).

In a subsequent case, *Worcester v. Georgia*, he further clarified the status of tribes as political and geographic entities which are "extraterritorial" to the states in which they are located, and possessing "rights with which no State could interfere, and that the whole power of regulating the intercourse with them was vested in the United States" (*Washburn 1964, 123*). Thus, Marshall gave the force of law to the two most fundamental legal concepts which shape American relations with Indian tribes. One, they are sovereign nations. From this definition of tribes flowed the second, that only the federal government may regulate Indian affairs, to the total exclusion of the states. The effect of MARSHALL's interpretations was to place full authority over tribes with the legislative power of the U.S. Congress, with responsibility for defining broad policy toward tribes and some very limited power also placed with the President of the United States. The fact that the U.S. Congress - and Congress alone - may regulate Indian affairs is an idea absolutely central to understanding the resurgence of self determination that is spreading throughout Indian country.

The special legal status given all of Indian country is derived from the concept of limited sovereignty. Limited sovereignty is an old idea - the Romans continued a limited sovereignty in the Kingdom of Israel. Limited sovereignty is a very practical solution to the problem of governing far away and culturally diverse people, for it eliminates much of the day to day nuisance of having to govern by allowing local control over routine matters and customs, while keeping a tight grip on major matters such as making war and collecting taxes.

English common law, which is, of course, the basis for U.S. law, characterized sovereignty as inherent, acknowledging that sovereignty is something that aboriginal people have always had, not something that is granted to them by the conqueror. However, if it is not exercised, inherent sovereign power is, in effect, meaningless. This is a second idea to keep in mind in order to understand the Second Contact: sovereignty has no value if it is not used. For more than 200 years, and especially in the last years of the 19th century and the first half of the 20th century, Indian tribes possessed in theory a limited sovereignty which in practice they used so rarely that it atrophied as the tribes themselves withered into social and economic debility.

Indian country is more than just a phrase in the Constitution which refers to a uniquely American legal concept. It is also a uniquely American geography. Indian country is a geographic paradox: it is at once discontiguous, and unitized. Indian country is made up of more than 300 scattered remnants of aboriginal land which are given unity by the special status conveyed by the U.S. Constitution, and by centuries of case law. In addition to being unique legal and geographical concepts, Indian country is also a uniquely American historical concept. Indian country is a theater in which we can watch the ebb and flow of national morals and ethics. Thus, Indian country in all its meanings is tied intimately to American cultural history.

In the late 19th century, genocide was the U.S. government's de facto policy towards Indian people. General Philip SHERIDAN, who moved on to fight in the Indian Wars after the Union victory in the American Civil War, summed up a strong current of popular feeling in his chilling statement, "The only good Indian I ever saw was dead." This statement has become part of the American idiom, familiar to anyone who has watched movie Westerns: "The only good Indian is a dead Indian."

I do not minimize in any way the atrocities of the American holocaust. However, there is another part of the Indian story which has not been given as much attention. That story is the consistency with which the American Congress, and the American legal system, have upheld and protected the rights of Indian people over the entire span of American and tribal relations. When we look at the whole of that time, we see that periods of great excess, such as the Indian Wars of the 19th Century, are counterbalanced with corrective actions.

For example, after being defeated by the U.S. Army, many tribes almost ceased to exist as political entities when Congress passed the General Allotment Act of 1877. The General Allotment Act would have eliminated the tribes' limited sovereignty by breaking up the large, communally owned reservations into small parcels owned by individual Indians. Without their communally owned land base, Indian people would have become part of the population at large without special status under law. Indians would have ceased to be part of a tribal group, and would have been assimilated into society at large. Tribal geography was used as an instrument of the government policy known as "assimilation".

Indians understood the profound threat to tribal existence posed by the allotment system. On the Gila River Indian Reservation in Arizona, Indians barricaded the roads into the reservation by parking their horses and wagons across them to prevent the allotment agent and his crews from gaining entry to perform the land surveys which would define the individual allotments (Z. Simpson Cox[1], oral interview).

Polarities in Federal Indian Policy

The assimilation approach to tribalism dates to Enlightenment philosophy which was brought into American thought by the writings of Thomas JEFFERSON. In this line of thought, people with origins in European culture had a moral obligation to civilize Indians who, once civilized, would become indistinguishable from other American citizens. The tools most commonly employed to civilize Indians were Christian religion, and agricultural arts (*Sheehan 1974, 4f*). Sometimes simple bribery was employed, as in the example of the promise that any Indian man who would agree to cut his hair and learn farming would be given a wagon. When a water rights attorney asked one of his Indian clients why he was the only man on the Tribal Council who had long hair, the man replied, in a superb example of Indian humor, "I already had a wagon" (Z. Simpson Cox, *oral interview*).

If the civilizing forces of Christianity and farming did not bring speedy results, the civilizing process was accelerated by military force (*Sheehan 1974, 9*). The Civil War's most successful Union general, William Tecumseh[2] SHERMAN, continued his military career in campaigns against Indians. SHERMAN was blunt in his assessment of the prospects for successful assimilation:

> "If it be the policy of the government, as I believe it is, to save the remnant of these tribes, it can only be accomplished by and through military authority. Sooner or later these Indians... must be made self-supporting. Farming and the mechanic arts are so obnoxious to their nature and traditions, that any hope of their becoming an agricultural people can hardly be expected in our day..." *(Prucha 1990, 147)*.

Although SHERMAN showed considerable acumen in his prognostication about the success of turning hunter-warriors into JEFFERSON's ideal yeoman farmers, his recommendation to turn the entire civilizing mission over to the military was rejected. The efforts to civilize Indians remained in the hands of bureaucrats and missionaries, with the military as their occasional brutal instrument.

Swinging back to a government policy that reaffirmed the political integrity of tribes and the critical role that the tribal land base played in preserving that integrity, the break up of reservation land was halted by the Indian Reorganization Act of 1934. The Indian Reorganization Act renewed the federal government's commitment to the continued sovereign existence of Indian people in Indian country, and put in place organizational structures which were the beginnings of political self determination under American rule, such as establishment of federally recognized tribal governments with written constitutions. The Indian Reorganization Act has received its share of criticism, particularly for imposing a representational democracy on tribal people (*Prucha 1988, 65f*) who, in large measure, made decisions through the group in a consensual process[3].

Whatever the defects of the Indian Reorganization Act, it must be credited with reversing a policy which would have destroyed tribalism in America. From the Reorganization Act, tribes gained time in which to learn the "tricks of the trade" of using American institutions to further tribal ends. Although they were unfamiliar and culturally foreign means to further those ends, the institutions of imposed American governmental forms served a vital function by protecting tribalism so that it could find its own expression and renewed vitality at a later time.

The period of grace brought by the Indian Reorganization Act lasted barely a generation before another swing in government policy threatened to destroy all Indian tribes at once. President Dwight EISENHOWER made a dramatic shift back to the policy of assimilation when he initiated a policy known as termination. Like the General Allotment Act, termination attempted to employ geographic fragmentation to achieve political results. Termination was a vigorous move to destroy the special status of tribal people by eliminating their land holdings and by withdrawing federal recognition of tribal governments.

Termination's rhetoric is reactionary and assimilationist, and can be read as racism hiding under a cloak of patriotism. PRUCHA ascribes the motives for termination to the Cold War, and a nervousness on the part of Americans at continuing to allow in their midst foreign political bodies composed of ethnic minorities (*Prucha 1988, 69*), albeit minorities who were American citizens. This line of reasoning is close, in time and content, to the reasoning which forced removal of thousands of American citizens of Japanese descent into concentration camps during World War II[4]. Ironically, one of these camps was built, without tribal permission, or any compensation for the use of the land, on the Gila River Indian Reservation[5]. At the end of the internment, the camp housing was burned to the ground, while many Indians on this reservation still lived in deplorable shelters, and all the remaining food supplies were dumped into a trench and doused with gasoline and burned, rather than distributed to the hungry tribal members who watched the proceedings. More than 50 years after he witnessed these events, a tribal elder still vividly recalled the smell of bacon burning *(Nathan S. Thompson[6], oral interview)*. These events illustrate how easily government programs can become mindlessly compartmentalized.

The U.S. Congress passed a resolution in 1953 which established termination as the Indian policy of the day. The resolution states that tribes "...should be freed from Federal supervision and control and from all disabilities and limitations specifically applicable to Indians" *(Prucha 1990, 233)*. Congress was acting with the full authority over Indian affairs granted it by the Constitution, and, with this resolution, did terminate a number of tribes by dissolving their reservations, and by annulling federal recognition of these tribes' political status. Without either polity or geography, these tribes ceased to exist except as cultural and ethnic minorities within a pluralistic democracy[7]. The Jeffersonian policy of assimilation into society at large was completed, at least for the few tribes named in the Congressional resolution.

An advocate for termination, Senator Arthur V. WATKINS, made an imaginative attack on the two foundations of tribalism in the United States - the sovereignty and the geography which define Indian country. He argued that Indians should be freed "from special federal restrictions on the property and person of the tribes and their members" *(Prucha 1990, 238)*. This removal of "federal restrictions" was defined as essential to complete the "movement toward full freedom" which was "delayed for a time by the Indian Reorganization Act..." *(Prucha 1990, 238)*. The patriotic rhetoric reached full voice in the concluding argument which states:

> "In view of the historic policy of Congress favoring freedom for the Indians, we should end the status of Indians as wards of the government and grant them all the rights and prerogatives pertaining to American citizenship.
> With the aim of "equality before the law" in mind our course should rightly be no other. Firm and constant consideration for those of Indian ancestry should lead us all to work diligently and carefully for the full realization of their national citizenship with all other Americans. Following in the footsteps of the Emancipation Proclamation of ninety-four years ago, I see the following words emblazoned in letters of fire above the heads of the Indians - THESE PEOPLE SHALL BE FREE!" *(Prucha 1990, 238)*.

These statements are remarkable for several reasons. First, the author was from the state of Utah, a state which has hardly any reservations, and the few it has are very small. More important, Utah was, and still is, dominated by members of the Church of Jesus Christ of Latter Day Saints (LDS; commonly called Mormons[8]) whose membership sought refuge in the isolated western United States in order to escape the "federal restrictions" on polygamy, which was practiced by many church members. WATKINS, apparently, saw no hypocrisy in his arguments. Second, WATKINS calls for "equality before the law". In fact, Indians have enjoyed "all the rights and prerogatives" of citizenship since 1928. Third, the argument put forward rests on a factual error. Indians were not, and have never been, granted special status because of their "Indian ancestry". The sovereign status of tribes is wholly political, and not derived from racial status or ancestry. Finally, WATKINS artfully sets up a reaction based on emotion, not reason, by playing to American beliefs in freedom and equality, and by his implicit equation of Indians and the slaves set free by LINCOLN's Emancipation Proclamation. The cleverness of his emotional appeal becomes even more apparent when put in its contemporary context. The Negro civil rights movement had achieved a major victory on the national level just three years earlier when the U.S. Supreme Court handed down the ruling in *Brown v. Board of Education* which ended school segregation.

What were WATKINS' motives: Were his statements made in honest ignorance of the facts which confer special status to Indians? Termination was contemporaneous with the Congressional hearings on Communism in America led by Senator Joseph MC CARTHY, and which made a national figure out of Richard NIXON. Was fear of Communism - and, therefore, of any group which had a communal basis of organization - the motive, as PRUCHA suggests? Or was WATKINS taking advantage of the sea change in national policy marked by *Brown*, attempting to terminate the special status of Indians by launching them on the rising tide of Negro civil rights movement, hoping that no one would notice the fallacy of his comparison? Whatever the motives behind termination as argued by its most outspoken proponent, it proved to be a short swing in the pendulum of national Indian policy.

Very shortly after EISENHOWER's termination policy, President Richard NIXON ushered in the modern era of Indian affairs by reaffirming the concept of Indian self-determination. In a special address to Congress, NIXON repudiated the policy of termination. The address merits reading in its entirety. His language is eloquent, and his policy and its specific directives derive from "...the special relationship between the Indian tribes and the Federal government which continues to carry immense moral and legal force. To terminate this relationship would be no more appropriate than to terminate the citizenship rights of any other American" (Prucha 1990, 257). He summarizes his Indian self-determination policy by saying that it must "strengthen the Indian's sense of autonomy without threatening his sense of community" (Prucha 1990, 257). In an emphatic conclusion, he states, "But most importantly, we have turned from the question of *whether* the Federal government has a responsibility to the Indians to the question of *how* that responsibility can best be fulfilled" (Prucha 1990, 258).

In a subsequent demonstration of his commitment to these themes, NIXON signed Congressional legislation which returned sacred lands taken by the Federal government to the Taos Indians. His remarks at the signing ceremony further expand his self determination policy and its historical, legal, and moral ties. He states:

> "This is a bill that represents justice.... This bill also involves respect for religion. ...I can only say that in signing the bill I trust that this will mark one of those periods in American history where, after a very, very long time, and at times a very sad history of injustice, that we started on a new road - a road which leads us to justice in the treatment of those who were the first Americans, of our working together for the better nation that we want this great and good country of ours to become..." *(Prucha 1990, 260).*

n reading his words, there can be no question that NIXON sets his Indian policy in the context of national morality. His strong sense of history, and of law, are very apparent. He alludes skillfully to the destructiveness of the General Allotment Act on tribal community, and on the equally destructive policy of termination. Most noteworthy, however, is the strong moral tone of his remarks. It almost seems that NIXON is consciously aware of a peculiar function that Indians play in American life, which is to measure the moral health of the dominant society as it can be seen in treatment of its Indian minority.

NIXON's Indian policy gives a sense of the complex genius which drove one of America's most controversial political figures. Certainly his superb grounding in international law influenced his new policy of self determination. But what are the origins of its moral and historical content? It is possible that his upbringing in the Society of Friends (Quaker) religion, with its emphasis on non-violence and its history of special ministry to Indian tribes[9], also influenced his Indian policy. Whatever his reasons, NIXON's break with the termination policy of his mentor EISENHOWER could not be more complete. In rejecting termination, NIXON returned to the historical roots of American Indian policy, which is based on law, on geography, and on a sense of national morals - specifically, a morality of justice, of seeking to do what is right - which underlies "this great and good country of ours...."

Modern Tribal Sovereignty

From NIXON's self-determination policy to the present, tribes have continued to strengthen their sovereign status as a third sphere of government which is neither federal, nor state. President Ronald REAGAN recognized the unique governmental status of tribes, defining Federal-tribal relations as being relations between two sovereigns. He augmented NIXON's self-determination policy with his own policy of "government to government relations".

Although REAGAN's policy had centuries of precedent, it grated harshly on state governments, and reopened old tensions of states rights vis à vis the Federal government when it came to the special political status and geography of Indian tribes. The tribal exemption from state jurisdiction, and the strong presence of the federal government wherever there are Indian tribes, remains a source of conflict between tribal and state governments, which erupts from time to time in state assertions of jurisdictional authority. For example, states presently are mounting major assaults on Indian sovereignty in the arena of taxation, such as imposing taxes on non-Indians doing business on Indian reservations. These tribal-state contests inevitably end up in federal court, which again irritates the states because they must submit to federal authority. The proliferation of Indian casino gaming is a more publicized source of tribal-state conflict. Gaming on reservations is outside of state control except for recent accommodations of states' rights in which Congress has allowed very limited state involvement through mandatory tribal-state compacts[10] in which states must enter into agreements which allow gaming on reservations, but may negotiate particulars, such as the number of video poker machines which a tribe may install. Despite clear recognition of their sovereignty, it was not until the tumultuous 1960s that tribes finally began to exercise their sovereignty, which had lain dormant for so long. Although tribes' sovereignty was acknowledged, it was largely undefined. Tribes began to define their powers by testing the limits to their sovereignty in federal court. The first test was whether tribes controlled the natural resources in Indian country. Tribes, often, had been relocated to occupy what was perceived as worthless land. Ironically, this worthless land proved in some instances to be rich in resources such as coal, oil, natural gas, and uranium. In a series of cases[11], the U.S. Supreme Court upheld tribal rights to these resources[12]. Tribal sovereignty took on new dimensions when joined to control over economic resources. Paper political power now had the real power of wealth behind it. Clear legal definition of tribal rights to valuable natural resources marks the beginning of the present period of genuine self-determination.

The Fort Mojave Indian Tribe

The Fort Mojave Indian Tribe illustrates the importance of natural resources as the underpinnings of self-determination. The Fort Mojave Tribe's self-determination is based on water, and the unique advantages of Indian sovereignty and geography. Following the precedent of more than three centuries of court decisions which have upheld and reinforced the sovereign rights of Indian people and the unique legal status of Indian land, the U.S. Supreme Court awarded the 500 members of the Fort Mojave Tribe a right to 129,000 acre feet[13] of water from the Colorado River. This tribal water right supersedes the rights of the state of California, on which more than 18 million residents of urban Southern California depend for their water supply. It supersedes the rights which supply water to the politically powerful casino gaming industry in Las Vegas, Nevada, and the 2,5 million people of Phoenix, Arizona. This means that, if there is not enough water in the Colorado River to satisfy the rights of all water users, the Fort Mojave Tribe gets all of its water first, even if that means that Southern California cities get none.

The Indians' right to the water[14] was upheld because, in the water law of the western United States, the first person to use the water has the first right to the water. This is known as prior appropriation. The Mojave Indians have lived in the Mohave[15] Valley longer than any other water users (perhaps for more than 8,000 years), so they (and other tribes located in the area) have first right to the water of the lower Colorado River.

Ownership of such abundant water in one of the world's great deserts is an economic asset of enormous value. In the arid west, there is a market for water rights, which can be sold or leased. However, rather than becoming instantly wealthy by selling or leasing its water rights to urban users, the Fort Mojave Tribe has chosen a slower path to riches which will enable present and future tribal members to secure a stable and permanent economic self-determination. The Fort Mojave Tribe is using water to turn its piece of the uniquely American geography of Indian country into a strong, diversified economy based on agriculture, commercial ventures, large scale residential real estate development, and casino gaming.

The Fort Mojave Indian Reservation occupies some 33,000 acres along the lower Colorado River in the Mohave Desert. They are one of the tribes which was never relocated, and remain on a reservation created out of their original homeland. Part of what is now the reservation was a military post at a ford across the Colorado River where the U.S. Army guarded emigrants and gold seekers going to California. More land was added to the reservation when a railroad company went bankrupt and its land was given to the Indians by the federal government. The Fort Mojave Reservation is unusual because it lies in three states - Arizona, California, and Nevada. If states, rather than the federal government, had jurisdiction over reservation lands, one can imagine the chaos that would result for this tribe if its lands were governed by three wholly separate state governments. The sovereign status of the tribal government allows the Fort Mojave Tribe to govern all of its lands as a whole, regardless of which state they are located within.

The physical geography of the Mohave Valley is dominated by the Colorado River, its historic floodplain, vast alluvial fans called bajadas which were created before the last Ice Age, and parallel mountain ranges of igneous and metamorphic rock. The Mohave Desert landscape is starkly beautiful, with rich mineralization that creates a glorious array of mauves, seafoam greens, deep ochres, neon red-violets and purples that changes with the light and the seasons.

The lower Colorado River flows through extremely arid land. The economic significance of such a large river in such a desert is enormous. On the reach of the river flowing through the Fort Mojave Reservation, Davis Dam creates a reservoir used for recreation and to store water for irrigation and hydroelectric power generation. The electricity supplies the vast conurbation of Southern California. The river supplies drinking water to millions of people, and irrigates millions of acres of cropland in Arizona and California. The flow of the river is entirely regulated by a series of dams located between its headwaters in Wyoming and its final user, Mexico.

The Colorado is one of the most used and reused rivers in the world. However, the river is not the most important factor in the economic geography of the area. The backbone of the regional economy is casino gambling in Laughlin, Nevada, which is approximately fifteen miles upriver from the Fort Mojave Indian Reservation's northern boundary.

Laughlin is a gambling boomtown which grew from a few slot machines beside a gas station in the 1960s to a single-purpose recreation center with 11 casinos and 10,000 hotel rooms - which have a 93 percent occupancy rate. In 1993, 5,5 million visitors came to Laughlin. Eighty percent came by car from Southern California. These tourists spent $ 524 million - making Laughlin the third largest gambling center in America, behind only Las Vegas and Atlantic City. The Laughlin gaming industry employs 50,000 people (*Staff, Laughlin Convention and Visitors Bureau, oral interview*).

Laughlin has a unique clientele. The typical gambler is a 61 year old single female. These "gambling grannies" represent a huge blue collar retiree market which Laughlin has captured with great success.

However, Laughlin has reached its limits of growth because it is out of water. There is no source of water to buy, or acquire by legislative transfer from some other Nevada user. This fact has created an economic opportunity for the Fort Mojave Tribe.

The Tribe's development strategy is to provide all the things a water-rich landowner can offer in a water-poor environment, and build a diverse economic base for itself in the process. Key to its development is a 4,000 acre parcel in Nevada which will have 11 casino-resorts, three golf courses, a series of inland lakes, housing for 40,000 people, a civic center and commercial centers. The Tribe has named this new town "Aha Macav", which means "Place by the River" in the Mojave language.

Land uses in Aha Macav were determined by how many residents and visitors could be sustained by the 12,500 acre feet of water allocated to the tribe's Nevada lands, and how the water could be reclaimed and recycled to support lakes, golf courses, and landscaping. In the U.S., it is unusual to begin with the resource as the way to determine the land uses in a real estate development. Because the tribe owns the land and the water that goes with it, and has complete governing authority over land development, it has been able to apply rational planning that will avoid the problems of growth without regard to sustainability which have plagued so many other developments in the western United States.

Unlike Laughlin, Aha Macav will be a selfcontained new town with many recreational and civic amenities. Aha Macav is planned as a diverse community which can continue to prosper after the brief window of opportunity enjoyed by Indian gaming comes to an end when gaming is legal everywhere and tribes have lost their present advantage.

Gaming has been legal in Nevada for more than half a century, so the tribe had no major legal obstacles to Indian gaming even before the Indian Gaming Regulatory Act of 1988 forced even those states without legalized gaming to enter into compacts with tribes. Fort Mojave's water rights were settled in 1965. Yet it has taken the tribe 30 years to realize its dream of building a gambling center in the desert. One great obstacle was the cost of building a city out of raw desert. The Tribe now has a $ 37 million bank loan which is guaranteed against default by the federal government. This is the largest amount ever guaranteed against default for an Indian tribe. The money is being used to build telecommunications systems, water, sewer, roads, and other infrastructure, a new bridge across the Colorado River, a new beach and marina on the river, and its first 300 room casino, which will open in February, 1995. Other development will be financed by individuals who lease land on which to build their own projects within the structure provided by the tribe's master land use plan for Aha Macav. The end result will be a new town with 40,000 permanent residents and casino resort/hotel accommodations for 20,000 visitors.

Physical planning is only the beginning of a project of this scale. In addition to physical infrastructure, the tribe must build its administrative infrastructure. For example, there was the opportunity to write innovative land use ordinances which are tailored to fit the unique circumstances of Indian law, and of this tribe. They are not based on zoning, because all of the land is owned by single owner - the tribe - which is also land regulator, and land developer. The land development ordinances prohibit homeowners' associations because they would pose a clear threat to tribal control of non-Indian people living on Indian land. They also require that all physical plans must be submitted in a format compatible with the Tribe's Geographic Information System (GIS), which uses a Unix-based system with a SUN Sparcstation and ARC/INFO software. Because Aha Macav is a new project, there are no files full of "paper plans" which must be converted to digital format; digital technology will be in place from the start. GIS also allows the Tribe to operate a parcel-based system for tracking property taxes, utility billings, water use, and other urban management activities. Innovative land development ordinances and GIS are but two examples of the progressive approach to managing its resources the tribe is pursuing.

However, until the first casino begins to produce revenue for the tribe, the cost of the Aha Macav project is a great drain. Interest on the bank loan is over $ 1,000 a day. The tribe has spent almost $ 3 million on legal, financial, engineering, planning, and other "soft" costs to date. This money has come from successful tribal agricultural and commercial ventures, especially from its mini market with tax free cigarette sales, which grossed $ 10,2 million in 1993 and is thought to be the highest grossing such store in Arizona.

The scale of gaming activities planned by the Fort Mojave tribe sets it apart. Only tribes like the Pequot of Connecticut, which have a near-monopoly on the huge mid-Atlantic urban market, may rival it in potential gaming wealth. It is hard to imagine the amount of money that flows through even a modest Indian casino. The Tohono O'Odham Tribe's Desert Diamond Casino, near Tucson, Arizona, grosses approximately $ 50,000 every three hours in a small building crammed into the tribal industrial park. The Fort McDowell Reservation, east of Phoenix, Arizona, has had a casino for ten years. Profits from this single small building have allowed the tribe to set up trust funds for all its minor children, predicted to be worth more than $ 5 million each by the time a child turns 18. This same tribe offered to endow a new medical degree program and hospital at Arizona State University with profits from its casino; the offer was rejected. For many tribes which lack any kind of natural resource base or other means of generating income, Indian gaming has made possible levels of prosperity which would not otherwise be possible.

Tribes are aware that the sovereign advantage which allows them to offer gaming may not last long. As state governments continue to feel the pressure of shrinking revenues and mounting costs, they have one by one passed legislation which allows some form of gambling as a way to make money. Tribes are beginning to feel the pinch from this competition, as there is a finite market of gamblers to draw on. Expert opinion gives a window of opportunity of five to ten years for tribes to cash in on their gaming advantage. After that time, tribes will have to struggle to maintain their share of the gambling public in a saturated market.

Many people voice criticism of tribal dependence on gaming. This criticism has a distinctly racist tone in its paternalistic implications that Indians are not competent to manage their own affairs. One often-stated fear is that criminal elements will corrupt, or take advantage of, tribes, despite well-publicized findings from Congressional investigations which have found no connection between tribal gaming and criminal activities. Another concern is the effect of sudden wealth on tribal cultural integrity. This group of critics apparently does not consider the effect of chronic poverty on tribal cultural integrity. Finally, critics say that gaming will be a short-lived phenomenon, and that tribes will suffer when they become dependent on a revenue source that

Fig. 1: Indian gaming is controversial because it is outside of state control, and because of accusations that criminality and culture degradation will beset tribes which operate casinos on their reservations. *The Arizona Republic, February 13, 1992.*

will suddenly dry up. Would tribes be better off never to know wealth at all? One cannot help but wonder if these same critics would have advised tribes not to trap beaver because the fashion for felt hats might change.

Indians have their own humorous responses to such obviously condescending criticisms. One young man mused about the possibility that white people would spend all their money gambling in Indian casinos, and that wealthy tribes would then have to herd all the impoverished white folk onto reservations and provide food for them. *(Fig. 1)*

The Fort Mojave Tribe has taken precautions not to depend solely on gaming for its economic future. It has also positioned itself to remain highly competitive as the gaming market gets tighter. By offering gambling in a full-resort environment in a market characterized by no-frills casinos and lottery tickets, the tribe should be able to stay a strong player in the leisure services market. It also has broadened its market by appealing to families, rather than the more limited though large "gambling grannies" market which supports its neighbor, Laughlin.

Surrounding the casino core, Aha Macav will provide an on-going stream of lease and tax revenues from housing and commercial development. Additional housing and commercial development on reservation lands in Arizona will contribute to tribal income, as well.

Fort Mojave also has invested in its more traditional revenue source, agriculture. The tribal farming operation has some 3,000 acres in cultivation with crop yields significantly higher than regional averages. The tribal farming enterprise has zero indebtedness, and shows a profit - claims few farms in America can make. As old land leases to non-Indians farming on the reservation expire, the land will be returned to tribal control. Eventually, about 15,000 acres will be producing under tribal management.

Conclusion

The Fort Mojave Tribe illustrates the economic success that is redefining Indian country. Yet, Fort Mojave and other American Indian tribes also illustrate another kind of success which is worthy of study as a model with great relevance to the rest of the world. Tribalism and tribalization presently have very bad connotations as sources of conflict and fragmentation of political and social structures around the world, whether in the former Soviet Union, Rwanda, Somalia, Bosnia Herzogovnia, Chiapas, or the Middle East. The "peculiar and cardinal distinctions" which characterize the history of relations between the United States and Indian tribes are a unique example of persistent tribalism which has much to teach us about accommodating culturally diverse groups within a larger political structure.

Despite many sporadic actions to destroy them as separate political entities, American Indian tribes have survived, and even flourished, for more than 300 years after the First Contact. This can be accounted for by their own vitality and resilience, by the largely consistent protection of tribal rights under U.S. law, and by the counterbalancing forces inherent to democratic processes, which may careen from time to time into expressions of reprehensible excess, yet return again and again to a morally centered position with regard to Indian people. The bond is flawed, but no other example comes as close to fulfilling the moral imperative of human rights.

Zusammenfassung

Der Stamm der Fort Mojave zeigt den wirtschaftlichen Erfolg, der das Indianerland mit anderen Augen sehen läßt. Aber Fort Mojave und andere nordamerikanische Indianerstämme zeigen auch eine andere Art von Erfolg, welcher es wert ist, als ein Modell mit größter Bedeutung für den Rest der Welt untersucht zu werden. Mit Stammesstruktur und Stammesbildung werden zur Zeit schlechte Assoziationen verbunden, die an Quellen des Konflikts und der Zerrüttung von politischen und kulturellen Strukturen in der ganzen Welt, wie zum Beispiel die ehemalige Sowjetunion, Ruanda, Somalia, Bosnien-Herzegowina, Chiapas oder den Mittleren Osten erinnern. Die "besonderen und äußeren Unterschiede", welche die Geschichte der Beziehungen zwischen den Vereinigten Staaten und den Indianerstämmen charakterisieren, sind ein einmaliges Beispiel für eine beharrliche Stammesstruktur, welche uns darüber viel lehren kann. wie man kulturell unterschiedliche Gruppen innerhalb einer größeren politischen Struktur entgegenkommen kann.

Trotz vieler sporadischer Aktionen, die das Ziel hatten, die nordamerikanischen Indianerstämme als eigenständige politische Wesen zu zerstören, haben die Indianerkulturen während mehr als 300 Jahren nach dem ersten Kontakt überlebt und sich sogar weiterentwickelt. Dies kann ihrer eigenen Vitalität und ihrer Unverwüstlichkeit, aber auch dem größtenteils konsequenten Schutz der Stammesrechte unter dem amerikanischen Gesetz und den ausgleichenden Kräften, die demokratischen Prozessen innewohnen, zugeschrieben werden. In der Indianerpolitik der Mehrheitsgesellschaft treten von Zeit zu Zeit verwerfliche Ausschweifungen auf. Dennoch wird immer wieder eine moralische Mittelposition in Bezug auf die Indianer gefunden. Die Verbindung zwischen den Indianerstämmen und der weißen Mehrheitsgesellschaft ist voller Fehler, aber kein anderes Beispiel kommt so nahe, die moralischen Befehle der Menschenrechte auszuführen.

Notes

[1] Simpson COX, who died in 1993, represented the Gila River Indian Community in its water rights litigation for over 40 years. His two sons, who are also lawyers, continue the legal battle begun by their father.

[2] SHERMAM's father had no way of foreseeing the ironic twist that the future would bring to his decision to name his son after the famous Indian warrior, TECUMSEH, Chief of the Shawnee. The elder SHERMAM had fought in the French and Indian wars and admired TECUMSEH, who was made a general in the British army for his service against the French in Canada. The irony is that TECUMSEH was more than a soldier, he was a statesman who nearly succeeded in uniting tribes to fight together to protect their land from white settlement. His namesake William Tecumseh SHERMAM was instrumental in opening Indian lands to settlement.

[3] The old ways of decision-making give way slowly. During my work with the Gila River Indian Community, a group of elderly women told me that they merely tolerated the democratically elected middle aged men who thought they ran tribal government, and that if the men strayed much farther out of line, the women would resume control and make tribal decisions in the old way, restoring governmental power to the Tribe's elders.

[4] One of World War Two's best known soldiers, Ira HAYES, was a Pima Indian from the Gila River Reservation. He is immortalized in the photograph of U.S. Marines raising the flag on Mt. Suribachi.

[5] Internment of American citizens of Japanese descent was a reenactment in miniature of the displacement of Indians onto reservations some 60 years earlier. The irony of locating a Japanese internment camp on an Indian reservation did not escape the affected tribe, which has refused to allow a historical marker to be set on the site of the Japanese camp because it would monumentalize the federal government's double racism.

[6] Nathan S. THOMPSON was a Pima Indian who lived on the Gila River Indian Reservation. He shared memories of his eighty-plus years with me over many sociable cups of black coffee and cigarettes while I worked as a planner for that tribe. He died in 1994.

[7] Several terminated tribes later petitioned Congress to have their political status and land restored, and Congress reinstated them. Still other tribal groups have petitioned to be recognized as tribes, and have succeeded. Alaskan native groups also have acquired tribal status.

[8] The Church of Jesus Christ of Latter Day Saints doctrine assigns a special place to Native Americans, who are believed to be descendants of a lost tribe of Israel, the Lammanites. Converting a Native American to the LDS faith brings special spiritual rewards to the successful proselytizer. These beliefs color interactions between LDS members and Indians. A Pima woman told me that when she moved

to a new high school in a mostly-Mormon rural Arizona town she thought she was very popular because she was invited to all the LDS dances until she learned that LDS teenagers got into the dances free if they brought an Indian. Native protest about the Mormon practice of adopting Indian children, raising them in the LDS faith, and then returning them to their tribes of origin to proselytize was a major factor in passage of the Indian Child Welfare Act in 1978, which requires that ethnic considerations be given priority in placing Indian children with adoptive families. A majority of Indian children now are placed with Indian adoptive parents as a result of this legislative reform. Overall, the LDS missionary effort has been quite successful among some tribes, and the LDS faith has strong followings on a number of reservations.

[9] From their earliest presence in the American colonies, members of the Society of Friends began a history of fair dealings with native peoples. The founder of the Quaker colony in Pennsylvania, William PENN, purchased a town site from the local tribe which became the city of Philadelphia. This purchase was clearly eccentric for its time because it overtly recognized Indian title to the land. The purchase document, known as "Penn's Treaty," inspired the remark, attributed to VOLTAIR, that it was *"The only treaty never ratified by an oath and never broken"*(*Washburn 1964, 314*). Some two centuries later, the Quaker reputation for fair dealings with Indians served President Ulysses S. GRANT's need to reform the Indian Bureau, which has raised an outcry of public criticism because of its corruption and indifference to the welfare of Indians relocated to reservations. In a shrewd action, GRANT turned over management of Indian agencies on the newly formed chain of reservations to the Quakers as evidence of his "peace policy" towards tribes recently subdued by military action, and as a means of replacing corrupt and venal Indian agents - most of whom received their appointments as "plums" in reward for political favors - with Quaker agents who were not motivated by profit. The Quaker agents were appointed by Congress as "business agents of the government and zealous missionaries of civilization" as part of GRANT's "plan of bringing moral influences to bear on the conduct of Indian affairs..." (*Prucha 1990, 130*). Once again we can see the commingling of the themes of morality and civilization which came from Jefferson's Enlightenment ideas into the mainstream Indian policy of assimilation. Quakers were both moral influences, and strong proponents of assimilation, being convinced that assimilation was the only means by which Indians could escape from the wretched conditions which were so widespread at the close of the 19th century.

[10] Three states, including California, have refused to negotiate in good faith with tribes, and have brought the matter to the U.S. Supreme Court in a classic contest between states' rights and tribal sovereignty. The case will be heard by mid-1995, more than 160 years after John MARSHALL's opinion in *Worcester v. Georgia*.

[11] See Charles O. WILKINSON's legal history, Time, Indians and the Law, for insightful analysis of specific cases involving natural resources.

[12] This legal recognition of tribal rights to reservation resources is very different from treatment of aboriginal people by other nations with legal systems based on English common law, such as Australia or Canada, where rights to land resources - not just to land occupancy - are not so clearly defined.

[13] An acre foot is the amount of water required to cover one acre to the depth of one foot. If the Fort Mojave Tribe took all of its water at once, it would cover all of the 33,000 acre reservation to a depth of four feet.

[14] A number of Indian water rights claims remain unsettled; one of the largest is the Gila River Indian Community's claim to 1,5 million acre feet of water in Arizona, most of which is presently used by Arizona cities and irrigated farms.

[15] The Tribe chose to retain the old Spanish spelling of Mojave, which uses a "J," rather than the Anglicized version, which uses and "H". The name Mojave derives from "Aha Macave," which means "People by the River" in the Mojave language.

References

Las Vegas Review-Journal (April 27, 1994): Connecticut Signs Deal For Second Indian-run Casino. 12D.
Prucha, F. P. (1992²): Documents of United States Indian Policy. Lincoln, University of Nebraska Press.
Purcha F. P. (1985): The Indians in American Society From the Revolutionary War to the Present. Berkeley, University of California Press.

Sheehan, B. W. (1974): Seeds of Extinction: Jeffersonian Philanthropy and the American Indian. W. W. Norton Company.
Washburn, W. E. (1964): The Indian and the White Man. New York, New York University Press

Address of the Author

Dorothy M. Hallock
Sterzer Gross Hallock, Inc.
517 W. University Drive
Tempe, AZ 85281
USA

DICK WINCHELL

The Consolidation of Tribal Planning in American Indian Tribal Government and Culture

Introduction

It was a great pleasure to participate in this conference on Human Geography in North America, and I would like to thank the organizers for inviting me and my American colleagues and for allowing us to fully participate by holding the sessions in English. The stimulating papers on American geography during the conference have led me to serious reflection, and have caused a slight refocus of my paper. Although my topic of sovereignty as the basis for tribal government may seem an unlikely one for an attempt at synthesis, in light of the conference theme on new perspectives and trends in research for North American geography, I believe sovereignty as opposed to ethnicity offers such a new direction, and needs to be examined as such a new trend. As a result, the work I am reporting on in tribal planning has relevance in relation to a number of papers presented in the conference by providing a point of departure from a focus on ethnicity to a new focus on the process of sovereignty.

Human and social geography in North America has always had an emphasis on mobility and migration, and on changing land use patterns in relation to culture, community, and religion. The model to understand the social/cultural contexts of community, particularly when addressing unique cultural, ethnic, or racial aspects of North American cities, has been with a focus upon ethnicity. From David LEY's (*1974*) work *The Black Inner City as Frontier Outpost*, to his later co-edited collection (*Clarke, Ley and Peach 1984*), he has led North American geographers with regard to our understanding of the social aspects of spatial relations within communities. The clear necessity to depart from Positivist paradigms displayed in such works as Humanistic Geography (*Ley and Samuels 1978*), provide the notion of culture and community, particularly ethnicity, as defining forces in American cities and in our interpretation of the meaning and essence of spatial behavior. As demonstrated by many papers in this conference and publication (particularly ALBRECHT, BORSDORF, CARLSON, LAUX and THIEME, MIYARES and WISHART), the focus of current social and spatial community research in North America is on ethnicity, the definition of unique racial and ethnic community identity through ascription from within and recognition of unique ethnic and racial status from without.

Those of us who work with Native Americans, however, are forced to recognize that an alternative framework to ethnicity must be utilized for work with tribal groups, and that such an alternative offers considerable insight into spatial analysis and the meaning of space within all social contexts. That alternative framework is sovereignty, in which political rights and powers of government, community, and individual, are recognized and exerted by tribes. The source of identity for Native Americans within the United States lies not in their ethnicity, but instead in the fact that American Indian tribes held political and cultural powers which pre-existed the U.S. Constitution and the U.S. federal government. When those federal institutions were established in the United States, tribal "nations" were recognized as representing the political, social, and cultural integrity of aboriginal cultures, and therefore sovereignty was granted to those groups. It is that concept of sovereignty which can be examined through Native American geographic research, and which in fact may create a better framework than ethnicity for understanding the social geography of North America, which will be presented in this paper.

The purpose of this paper is to define sovereignty as the proper context for research on American Indian tribes, based on the legal frameworks of sovereignty as they have evolved between the United States federal government and each of the 500 independent tribal governments. The unique sovereign status of tribal governments goes beyond ethnicity into the realm of legal political powers and nationhood. These legal and political structures, with a basis on tribal specific local histories, actions, and responses to efforts at forced assimilation and genocide, have produced the reality of American Indian tribes today.

The significance of the fact that sovereignty is a more accurate context for community than ethnicity leads to an important conclusion for this paper, that: "American Indians are not an ethnic group." Although this statement is not totally true, because over 60% of all American Indians lived off reservations in 1990, and ethnicity does play a role in Indian identity, especially for urban, non-reservation Indians (*e.g. Weibel-Orlando 1991*), it is not ethnicity but sovereignty which creates the successful power and persistence of American Indian culture. Through a description of sovereignty and its application in tribal planning processes I hope to challenge the reader to reach the same conclusion, that "American Indians are not an ethnic group." The significance of this statement for research in Native American geography, and, at a broader level, for more appropriate constructs for social geographic research in North America, is that it opens a new framework for the human geographic research of North America.

Ethnicity

Ethnicity is a concept which has driven much thought and activity within social geographic research in North America. Because of the great diversity of populations of North America, particularly in cities, ethnicity, or the unique identity of groups within the larger community, has been a constant topic for geographic and sociological research. It is clear that this framework within geography shaped the way we understand North American cities through analysis of immigrant neighborhoods and ghettos which formed and remained or became dispersed, and the new racially and ethnically defined communities and ghettos which have replaced them. The dynamics of neighborhood change linked to ethnicity, and to the perception of issues like safety and well-being, has produced an extensive literature dating back to Ezra PARKS and the Chicago School of urban sociology in the early 1900s to the works of Gerald SUTTLES (*1968 and 1972*). The context of ethnicity and race in community were also recognized in geography (*e.g. Morrill 1965; Rose 1970 and 1972*), and is indicated most recently by the formation of an Ethnic Specialty Group in 1992 within the Association of American Geographers.

Despite its influence in North American geography, ethnicity as a process and concept is perhaps best defined within anthropology and sociology; the later providing models of assimilation and ethnic pluralism used to frame our understanding of the future prospects for community change, while the former providing a more clear definition of ethnicity as a process within community. Anthropologist Frederick BARTH (*1969*) described ethnicity as shared culture and values of a group which create a unique identity, establishing three criteria for ethnicity:

- the group is to some extent biologically self-perpetuating
- shared values existed within the group along with a common field or network of associations or references and
- a common self-identity is assigned by group members and outsiders.

BARTH suggested these traits are a function of the degree of group separation (physical and cultural) from other groups, but also that the maintenance of ethnic identity can be preserved even when such separation or isolation no longer occurs. Anthropologists recognize within ethnicity that:

"... boundaries persist despite a flow of personnel across them ... categorical ethnic distinctions do not depend on an absence of mobility, contact and information, but do entail social processes of exclusion and incorporation whereby discrete categories are maintained despite changing participation and membership in the course of individual life histories" (Barth 1969, 10).

Abner COHEN (1974 and 1976) further refined our understanding of the processes of ethnicity through the model of a continuum which recognizes both formal and informal activities which are used in ethnic identity. COHEN emphasized that the examination of ethnicity in contemporary culture relies most importantly on informal organization and symbolic activities within these communities. These processes demonstrate that ethnic community formation may be both formal and informal in character, but that ethnicity emphasizes the informal. In fact, it is the informal side of the scale, through symbolic actions, ritual, and kinship, in which ethnicity and ethnic identiy is created and preserved.

While anthropologists have defined the informal nature of ethnicity, we must turn toward sociologists to identify the dilemma this creates for understanding culture and society within North America. Indeed, based mostly on analysis of immigrant groups in American cities, sociologists at one time emphasized assimilation as the dominant pattern, where formal organizations and structures of community came to dominate and destroy unique cultures and ethnic identity, a "melting pot" society. GLAZER and MOYNIHAN's analysis of the "melting pot" (1963) became the first to challenge this notion, and as MOYNIHAN (1993, 22) refers to a quotation which summarizes these earlier findings:

The notion that the intense and unprecedented mixture of ethnic and religious groups in American life was soon to blend into a homogeneous end product has outlived its usefulness, and also its credibility ... The point about the melting pot ... is that it did not happen. (Sills and Merton 1991, 79).

In the re-examination of the processes of cultural change in American cities the concept of ethnicity as a focus of community dynamics was developed. Through ethnicity even though people worked and lived in non-ethnic settings, they could and did often choose to maintain and even strengthen their ethnic identity. Ethnicity, particularly when tied to race, became a more accurate reflection of the social realities of North American communities in which racial and ethnic groups were not "melting" together, but instead, were strengthening ethnic identity and distinction represented by cultural pluralism.

GLAZER and MOYNIHAN (1975) revisited the topic in Ethnicity, which again recognized that the "melting pot" in American cities was a myth, but also pointed out the dilemma of cultural pluralism. Without an all-embracing movement toward a single culture as presented in the melting pot, what would exist within American culture to bind it together? Cultural pluralism was perceived to lead ultimately toward disruption of American meta-culture, at least politically, and as a threat to the nation. This concept is expanded to a world-wide application in MOYNIHAN's latest work (1993) Pandemonium: Ethnicity in International Politics, which again points out the difficulties in lack of assimilation (cultural pluralism) of cultures into modern assemblages of nations and suggests it is the critical topic which will affect our world future.

Social geography, although addressing race, ethnicity, and ethnic identity in community through an extensive literature, has generally failed to address the political aspects of ethnicity, in part because they are not clear within the social context of community and have not been recognized as particularly relevant with regard to spatial aspects of community. The efforts of CLARKE, LEY, and PEACH (1984) to provide a context of ethnicity for research rely on a colonial model as the basis to describe plural societies (Furnivall 1939 and 1948) instead of the North American urban context of pluralism as the basis for social action policies (Glazer and Moynihan 1963, 1970; Moynihan 1993). Ethnicity in this geographic context results in pluralism such that:

"pluralism implied a colonial and inherently unstable society, where a dominant but alien minority exercised control over an indigenous majority" (Clarke et al. 1984, 2).

This notion of the renewal of ethnic movements around the world (*e.g. Smith 1980; Ra'anan 1981*) and more recently of the linkage of multi-ethnic communities to nationalism (*Brass 1991; Toland 1993*), fail to create a relationship between the processes of ethnic identity which include territorial elements and the notion of sovereignty as shall be defined in this paper which incorporate territory as part of legitimated political power through an emphasis on self-determination and political processes.

Another tradition within social geography is recognized in which:

> "Ethnicity is often the key ingredient of what may be essentially a voluntary form of cultural differentiation; ethnic and perhaps life-style identities may be assumed or not, largely at will" (*Clarke et al. 1984, 2*).

Although this later model better describes the notion of ethnicity most recognized in North American geography, it is not a model which describes the American Indian processes of community structure and power as will be described under the concept of sovereignty.

For research on Native Americans, it is the political aspects of identity which becomes the dominant framework for research. Despite over two centuries of genocide and forced assimilation, American Indian tribal governments and cultures have persisted (*e.g. McNickle 1968*), through a combination of the informal processes of symbolic behavior and defining the meanings of the actions of tribal members (ethnicity), and through the particular legal structures of sovereign tribal governments (sovereignty). The persistence of American Indians reflects processes at work involving more than ethnicity, and so the concept of sovereignty is presented as a new context to properly describe the geography of Native Americans and to offer a new insight into the dynamics of spatial and social identity within North American human geography.

Sovereignty

Sovereignty is a difficult concept, particularly because it has traditionally been defined as an all or nothing proposition, something one either does or does not have. Nationhood became the test for this old definition of sovereignty. Sovereignty meant freedom from external control, or "the supreme power over a political structure," and was often associated with an autonomous state and the power to make war against other nations.

Sovereignty, with this "all or nothing" context, is identified in political geography, when DE BLIJ (*1967, 579 - 582*) discusses sovereignty with reference to the Peace of Westphalia and the sovereign independence of princes who still owed allegiance to the Empire (*Leibniz 1864*). As DE BLIJ stated:

> "Thus some of the factually sovereign territorial rulers in Europe were somehow still under a higher authority. Were they now "sovereign" or not? What accounted for sovereignty?" (*1967, 579*)

Sovereignty in LEIBNIZ's notion included a minimum size of territory and ultimately some power which could be extended to war. This led to the present international order, described by DE BLIJ (*1967, 581*):

> "From territoriality resulted the concepts and institutions which characterized the interrelations of sovereign units, the modern state system. Modern international law, for instance, could now develop...Only to the extent that it reflected their territoriality and took into account their sovereignty could international law develop in modern times. For its general rules and principles deal primarily with the delimitation of the jurisdiction of countries."

For Native Americans in North America (both Canada and the United States), however, the evolving notion of sovereignty shifted from this original definition to concepts of "semi-sovereign nations" or "dependent domestic nations," as defined over time by the federal governments. Indeed, two notions of sovereignty exist today in Indian country, one which can be called constitutional sovereignty, and the second, known as inherent sovereignty. Many researchers within North America, particularly lawyers, but also geographers, have adopted the framework of constitutional sovereignty, suggesting that the rights of tribes are defined only under federal law and subsequent relations with tribes. This approach fails to recognize the inherent powers of tribal governments and tribal cultures today, and leaves tribal governments as remnant oddities within the American landscape, but also as institutions which will probably eventually fade away or become assimilated.

This is not the legacy and direction American Indian governments choose for themselves, nor is it a proper description of the condition of Native Americans. It is instead through the inherent sovereignty notion of the powers of tribal government and sovereignty that an appropriate definition and description of tribal governments and American Indians today occurs. Sovereignty exists not because it was identified in the constitution and subsequent legislative and judicial decisions, but these inherent powers of sovereignty exist because at the time the United States federal government was created or developed relationships with tribes, those tribes were sovereign nations, and they never relinquished the powers to define themselves. Sovereignty in this sense is a dynamic process which remains in place today.

Tribal governments and tribal cultures, through their inherent sovereign powers, are empowered to create and recreate the political, social, religious, and cultural structures necessary for their continued existence as defined from within. This notion of sovereignty has been elaborated by my colleague from American Indian Studies, Cecil JOSE (*1992*), and emphasizes a new context for understanding sovereignty. This new sovereignty includes different levels, from the individual or personal level where each tribal member defines his or her identity and powers related to that tribal identity, to group identity related to processes of ethnicity, and to the political identity and the legal identity of the tribal government.

Sovereignty in this complex and multi-faceted form, describes the central forces of American Indian tribes and tribal governments in the United States. American Indian tribal governments control lands directly under the federal government and are not subject to state or local regulations. Tribal governments have their own legal systems and court systems, and maintain the powers to operate as sovereign governments which control their own lands and identity. Tribes operate under constitutions or treaties with the federal government, and the powers to change these tribal constitutions to redefine proper political structures or to maintain and preserve tribal culture and community lie within the tribe subject to some federal review.

This new model of sovereignty exists in part in relation to ethnicity, with its emphasis on the informal processes of group identity, and the internal processes of symbolic action and recognition of common meanings for activities by members of the group. Under this new framework of sovereignty, when those processes of ethnicity seek to resolve formal legal and political issues in particular places, the process being described is no longer ethnicity, but sovereignty. The focus is not on internal definition or recognition of the group, or control from within, but specifically with the legal and political powers of the group. For American Indians, those political and legal powers of sovereignty go back to the recognition of sovereign powers of individual tribes through treaties, constitutions, and the establishment of reservations, and through the actual and inherent rights associated with that sovereignty. It is not an interactive process of identification (ethnicity) that in fact defines the status and structure of American Indian lands and peoples within the United States, but it is sovereignty, as exhibited at different levels, in a complex framework, which describes American Indians today.

Sovereignty in Native American Geography

Sovereignty as it has been addressed in Native American geography has often relied on the more standard definition of an all or nothing status. SUTTON (*1976*) identified the problem, stating:

> "When loosely identified both by layman and scholar as tribal lands held in trust and protected by federal immunities, Indian reservations present little definitional problem. However, all too often they are treated either as a portion of the public domain or as private property no different in legal or political status from land held by non-Indians" (*281*).

SUTTON sought clarification of the status of tribal lands and relevance of sovereignty, and further (*1976, 284*) stated:

> "If it were only necessary to recognize the Indian reservation as an ethnic place, a tribal homeland that is the locus of Indian identity in a cultural sense, few problems - interpersonal or intergovernmental - would persist ..."

SUTTON clearly recognizes the dilemma, that sovereignty creates a different and difficult process of land status which needs to be redefined and applied on reservations. The problem with such "neutral" statements was that tribal governments at the time continually sought to exert and clarify their sovereignty, and were successful in doing so in the courts, but there was generally no support for those tribal efforts by academic geographers. SUTTON relied on the old definition of sovereignty which led him to this conclusion:

> "No longer possessing the status of sovereigns, the tribes can only be described as semi-autonomous and their lands as a tertium quid, neither a civil division in American political institutions nor an administrative district or unit in our field service traditions" (*Sutton 1976, 286*).

SUTTON does recognize the unique status of tribal governments in his conclusions (*1976, 295*), and offers insight toward an alternative perspective by stating:

> "If this political-geographical status is unique, perhaps it is because no other modern nation has sought political equilibrium with its indigenous peoples or has given them the recourse of law and the courts to redress inequities".

The failure to define this unique case of Indian land tenure as a new form of sovereignty and proceed from there, which is what tribes have done, remains a problem for geographers (*Sutton 1975 and 1985*), who have failed to create the proper context of sovereignty or dispossession for describing American Indian land issues and reservation status. This failure was ultimately pointed out by Ward CHURCHILL's (*1992*) critique in a chapter of his recent book entitled facetiously "Friend to the Indian," in which he criticizes much of our geographic research on reservation status for its failure to recognize dispossession, sovereignty, and genocide as the basis of description of tribal issues.

Indeed, this new notion of sovereignty was not a notable component of a literature survey and overview of Native American geography (*Winchell et al. 1989*), but was stressed as a future research direction:

> "Sovereignty of Native American tribes over their lands is a major topic for geographic investigations. Spatial autonomy and government varies from tribe to tribe. The unraveling of these patterns is essential to an understanding of the geographic qualities of the Native American landscapes" (*247*).

This perspective is recognized in some research by geographer David WISHART (*1987, 1994*), historian Janet MC DONNELL (*1991*), and as presented by Native American authors CHUR-

CHILL (*1993*) and JAIMES (*1992*). Perhaps planner Jane JACOBS (*1980*), and more recently Menno BOLDT (*1993*) come closest to accurately assessing the new version and context of sovereignty as it has evolved in Canada and elsewhere in North America as being flexible, not an "all or nothing" proposition, and therefore representing the political and legal aspects of American Indian tribal governments.

Personal and Cultural Sovereignty Preserved

Two short examples will demonstrate the special nature of sovereignty based on personal and cultural contexts in Native American research, while the political and legal aspects of sovereignty will be discussed as part of tribal planning. As BARTH noted, it is often the symbolic nature of actions which provide the greatest insight into the processes of self identification as part of a group, and which link particular groups to particular places in their identity. It is the context of sovereignty, particularly for Native Americans, which provides the context for this identification to be recognized and established for those places, where not only the processes define the cultural meaning, but in fact tribal governments have the political power and authority for self-determination to determine how those values become manifest.
While conducting research on the Yavapai in Arizona, a group in which self-identity, group identity, and the legal and political structures of tribal government are very much related and linked to sovereignty, the subtle and often not so subtle relations of individuals within a culture and their space and place is critical (*Winchell 1982*).
For the Yavapai, who occupied most of central and western Arizona relatively undisturbed until the 1860s, their existence was in small bands of hunter-gatherers who moved from place to place to exploit particular ecological niches, and their knowledge of space to find the resources for survival was critical. Traditionally the Yavapai were given a personal name first for the place they were born. Later they could choose or be given a second name for a place they liked or felt a kinship with. Their names, then, were also the names of specific places upon the landscape. Repeating the names of the members of the group would promote the continued knowledge of places within each group.
When non-Indians first arrived in the 1860s, upon the discovery of gold near Prescott, Arizona, efforts were made to relocate the Indians. These were successful for a time, until in the 1900s Yavapai reservations were re-established in their traditional homelands near Prescott, Arizona. Almost immediately after the creation of the Prescott reservation, non-Indians tried to buy the reservation lands and again force the Yavapai to leave. When they asked the tribal elder if they would leave, his reply was simple:
"I am Wipukyipai. (I am this place). If you take this place, then I cannot exist."
It was not only the individual sovereignty expressed in that statement, but the political and legal aspects of sovereignty which created the structures of the Yavapai Prescott Indian reservation as a semi-sovereign nation, a political and legal structure which had the power to preserve the tribe's land and identity, in combination with the individual and group structures to preserve those places. The land was not taken.
In a similar manner of using space to create group identity, but in new forms, my dissertation research (*Winchell 1982*) found that Yavapai young people playing basketball used an area where they could be gatekeepers to their community. The location of the basketball court in the center of the community on a hill overlooked the only roads into or out of the community. This enabled these junior and senior high youth to track who was coming and going, to keep out unwanted visitors, to know where resources were, and where friends and enemies were. While playing basketball someone might say "There's Joe's aunt coming back from town. I bet she has some beer." For relatives of that family such knowledge would be valuable to find out who is partying or to exploit resources in the community. Even while playing the game people would comment

on who had gone for food, who for beer, so anyone there would know where to visit for a meal or party, and whom to avoid.

This spatial knowledge of community members functions the same way as traditional spatial knowledge of places to exploit resources and maintain knowledge about what bands would be at what place at any given time. The persistence of Yavapai culture, community, and identity is linked to the informal ability to adopt old processes, in this case the use of spatial information, to new forms within the group.

In a similar manner tribal governments will be shown to have evolved around the concepts of sovereignty and the powers not just to exist, but to re-create tribal culture and government in appropriate frameworks. The Department of Urban and Regional Planning and the American Indian Studies Program at Eastern Washington University have been active in assisting tribes in such efforts, as described in the next section.

The Tribal Planning Process

The main impetus for this paper was to describe sovereignty issues as part of the applied research being conducted by the planning and American Indian Studies programs at Eastern Washington University. Planning within a tribal context is best illustrated by a description of this model which has evolved in conjunction with the efforts of Cecil JOSE (*1992*), Director of American Indian Studies, Eastern Washington University. Our efforts in tribal planning involve three major phases:

- to develop a common acceptance and understanding of the principles of sovereignty and the purposes tribal government and tribal planning among the Tribal Council, the planning commission, the tribal planners and staff, and the members of the community as the basis for tribal planning within the community;
- to provide training in state of the art planning and management techniques including community decision-making; and
- to develop the frameworks for specific documents to be created in a tribal government's comprehensive plan.

Tribal planning programs need to be designed to strengthen tribal sovereignty and self-governance through the development of responsive leadership and informed decision-making under the planning function of tribal government. This process is cyclic and self-renewing, as it builds the capacity of the tribe to strategically plan for the optimal utilization of its natural, human, and other resources. This tribal planning process will help formalize and renew the planning efforts within the community under the direction of the community.

The Key Elements of Tribal Planning

There are essentially two processes of critical concern to the tribal planning process: first, that tribal governments must define for themselves the meaning of sovereignty through tribal specific definitions formally recognized by the federal government (such as a tribal constitution) which become the basis for tribal government and community decision-making, and second, that tribal planning has a function much different than standard non-Indian planning, so the tribal planning process needs to reflect appropriate processes and models. To the extent possible, this effort should be formalized into written documents of the tribe which clarify for the tribe and for other governments the role and function of each tribal government.

It is each tribe's responsibility to define and enact tribal sovereignty through establishing cultural competency which has both an internal and external component. Internally, tribal competency means that tribal members become competent in their own culture. Many tribes have made great progress in the last five years in such efforts to preserve language and culture, create museums and educational programs which link elders and youth, and in efforts to identify, protect and preserve tribal traditions and values. Some of these efforts are done within tribes, while some are more formal activities like college classes in language, history, culture, and traditions, involving outside institutions and resources.

The external component of cultural competency involves the provision of training or insight to persons from the outside so that non-Indians who work for tribes and others can be competent in their jobs and interact in appropriate manners for the tribal culture.

Planning to Build Tribal Capacities

Sovereignty in tribal planning is about building the capacity and competency of local tribal governments to enhance the ability of tribes to make good and appropriate decisions which reflect the community's culture and values. The capacity to make good decisions and the competency to act on those decisions is an on-going issue for tribal governments. The Indian Self-Determination and Education Act (*PL 93 - 638*) recognized the failure of the federal government to meet its trust responsibilities to tribes to provide support and training for them to take over their own affairs. Despite long-term historic efforts, it is only in recent years that efforts to redress this failure have led to programs which support tribal leaders and staff in becoming effective governments where such programs have been taken over by Indian people with great success. Tribes now form strong governments which preserve the sovereign rights and powers of each tribe, but also hold the skills and qualifications of self-determined governments to exert their sovereignty for self-determination.

Time Frameworks and Major Tools in Planning

There are a number of "tools" or standard planning practices and products which guide the implementation of any planning program. These are classified under three general headings: land use controls; comprehensive plans; and strategic or policy plans. The latter two, comprehensive plans and strategic or policy plans are usually longer term, looking five to thirty years into the future, while land use controls including zoning, subdivision regulations, environmental ordinances, are short-range, usually concerned with 1 - 3 years into the future.

In all cases, the ability to plan is dependent upon the development of a long-range goal direction which is based within the community. The importance of this in tribal communities has been stressed, and so although land use controls or development proposals will constantly need review and analysis, the implementation of an effective tribal planning program must also involve the revision of the Comprehensive Plan and the development of a Tribal Strategic Plan which links decision-making and management to overall tribal priorities and operations to include budgeting and land development.

The Elements of the Comprehensive Plan

Modern Comprehensive Plans have evolved into complex studies of a number of specific topics and issues with regard to their impact on land development and community development. Each topic is covered in an element or chapter of a report which forms the Comprehensive Plan. For local governments these "elements" are often mandated or required by state laws. In Washington, for example, state planning legislation mandates six Comprehensive Plan Elements including an Environmental Element (identification of environmentally sensitive areas), a Public Facilities and Services Element, a Transportation Element, a Housing Element, a Land Use Element and Map, and a Capital Improvement Plan for implementation. Other states have more requirements, such as California, which mandates over 15 different planning elements, including seismic safety, open space, and recreation.

Tribal governments, since they do not fall under state jurisdiction, have no mandated or even model frameworks for elements of the Comprehensive Plan. Often Comprehensive Plans have simply been patterned from non-Indian communities. This is generally not adequate to address critical tribal issues, particularly sovereignty concerns, and as a result, a more expansive framework for tribal planning is proposed.

The Tribal Comprehensive Plan

As stated earlier, the mission of tribal government is clearly different than local non-Indian governments, and include critical concerns with tribal culture, language, religions, and values; tribal history; and a broad range of community concerns such as health, social well-being, education, and employment which need to be addressed in manners which are culturally appropriate. These clearly extend beyond what most local non-Indian governments consider within their state-mandated comprehensive planning efforts. The Tribal Comprehensive Plan can be defined to include whatever issues each American Indian Community feels are most critical, but to include the following elements:

Tribal Cultural Element

The Cultural Element of a Tribal Specific Comprehensive Plan should be a report or series of studies and reports to document the major aspects of tribal culture and community, including a history of the community. This might include legends, stories, and histories as told by tribal elders in addition to ethnographic and historic records, publications, and documents.

The History of the Tribal Government

This element should describe the evolution of tribal leadership including descriptions of traditional decision-making and community leaders from the past (written if appropriate), the history of tribal treaties and decisions leading to the formation of the Tribal Council (full-manuscripts if possible), and the history of Tribal Council, including documentation of who served on the Council, their accomplishments, and perhaps interviews with tribal leaders. Where possible original documents such as speeches, the treaties, and official governing documents should be re-printed as a community resource for all tribal members to be able to trace back the foundations of tribal government and sovereignty.

Tribal Lands Element

This document should begin with the identification of traditional lands utilized before European contact, and the land areas (watersheds) which could impact this area. Historic documentation of the loss of this land, including treaties, and the changes in land use and land pattern from pre-contact to contemporary times should be documented. This document can serve as the basis for land claims and concerns regarding off-reservation destructive activities, and for consideration of strategies to impact land use and preserve areas which may have significance to the community. This document should also identify current land status, and include information on Indian/non-Indian ownership of reservation lands and heirship issues.

Growth Element

The Growth Element for tribes should reflect not only recent population trends, but seek early demographic information on the tribe, seeking to document estimates of population and settlement patterns in earlier time periods. Contemporary demographic information should include tribal members on- and off- reservation, and perhaps include some survey of members with regard to long-term residence preferences on- or off-reservation and their concerns and needs for the future. Three critical issues of population: size, rate, and distribution should all be addressed. The recent study of population provides an excellent resource for this type of information, but could be expanded by the addition of more historic demographic data and data on the off-reservation population. Most reservations have more than 50% of their populations under age 18. This excaberates all other tribal needs and issues, and must be recognized for effective long-range planning.

Tribal Specific Health Plan

The tribal specific health plan should identify health care facilities and services along with the need and demand for such services both at the present time and into the future. The tribal government should be actively involved in understanding health care issues and promoting the development of preventive care as well as assuring adequate health care facilities and services. This effort will need to be completed in conjunction with Indian Health Services staff.

Tribal Specific Housing Element

The physical conditions and the location of housing are essential components of the Comprehensive Plan. Housing needs are great, but must be developed with sensitivity to community culture, residential pattern preferences, and individual housing design desires. Part of the Housing Element should identify traditional settlement patterns and housing/structural design and construction. These traditional forms and spaces should be recognized and recommended where possible in the design of Appropriate Housing within the community. Housing is just one component of a wide range of Human and Social issues to be addressed in a related Human Services Element.

Social Well-Being Element

This report addresses the social and human resources of the community, the needs and concerns of residents including descriptions of programs and services now available, and strategies for self-sufficiency and community well-being. This project should involve human service providers and resources in and near the community.

Education Element

The Education Element to the Comprehensive Plan should identify levels of education, skills, and training, both with regard to non-Indian skills and educational attainment, as well as tribal skill attainment such as knowledge of community history, language, and culture. Programs should be developed in public schools and educational institutions as well as informally among community members to lead to cultural competency as well as competency within the larger community in job employment and life.

Because of the Tribal Council's special obligations and unique relation to its tribal membership, these elements reflect the efforts of the tribe through the Comprehensive Plan to address critical issues and set policy directions for all tribal staff, appointed and elected officials, and community members to work together toward a self-sufficient future in which sovereignty exists as the central component and strength of the Indian Community. These additional elements to the Comprehensive Plan can help coordinate efforts throughout the tribal government to move effectively and actively toward the future. The implementation of such plans will require considerable commitment in terms of time and resources to develop the plans, and in terms of cooperation and coordination among departments and divisions of the tribal government.

It should be noted that the responsibility to complete all of these elements may not lie with the tribal planning staff or planning commission, but planning staff and commissioners should guide these studies or offer initial direction. Several of the reports might best be carried out by local consultants including community college faculty, utilizing community elders, tribal members, and all other resources available.

For the development of a Tribal Comprehensive Plan, emphasis upon the cultural heritage and sovereignty concerns becomes the top priority for most tribes. The focus on sovereignty and the unique tribal heritage of the Indian Community should be an essential component of the Planning Program, with the planning program assisting in overall policy issues which affect the direction of the community. The purpose of such a planning effort is to create a Tribal Comprehensive Plan to guide the activities and future of the community while at the same time addressing critical issues of the environment, development concerns including economic and community development, program development, and deal with critical issues as they arise.

Sovereignty as a New Perspective

Sovereignty has evolved to form a new meaning as it has been applied and is understood by American Indian tribal governments. It is this new meaning of sovereignty, and not ethnicity, which provides the identity and basis of American Indian culture and community. This context of sovereignty for American Indians should respect the inherent powers and sovereignty of tribes as tribes define them, and as they in fact exist. American Indians are not bounded by the limitations of reservations, but many tribes have recognized legal as well as inherent sovereign powers over lands which they occupied aboriginally or which have been identified as "usual and accustomed" areas. Tribal history is not just a documentation of land losses and the current legal status of land as defined by federal courts, but the on-going history which creates and recreates the essential aspects of tribal lands, tribal cultures and their relevance in contemporary tribal government.

The purpose of tribal planning is to enhance the awareness and use of those sovereign powers in support of tribal governments who hold those powers in relationship to tribal traditional leadership within each culture and tribe. Applied research should be conducted for and with tribal governments, and both researchers and their research institutions need to state their initial recognition of tribal sovereignty, and in the case of institutions, their commitment to form of government to government or institutional relations which build on the recognition of sovereignty. Appropriate tribal research in such contexts is not focussed simply on individual projects, but in effective long term relationships in which both parties benefit, where the research activities are developmental in the sense of contributing to the knowledge and skills of the tribe.

American Indians are not an ethnic group. They are not defined by the processes of ethnicity. Instead, they are representatives of sovereign tribal cultures and governments which pre-existed the formation of the United States federal government, and which still exist today as sovereigns, albeit limited to some degree, in their powers.

American Indian reservations do not represent enclaves, places of forced isolation for American Indian people, but as given meaning by tribal governments and Indian people, they are the focal point of each tribe's culture, their community, and their future. Despite poverty on reservations, despite lack of housing and infrastructure, despite high unemployment, despite high levels of crime and difficult social problems, reservations exhibit a place that tribes control. They are the last symbol and stronghold of the sovereign powers of each tribe. The central place or places of reservations to Indian people, preserved and properly utilized within a context of each culture through tribal planning, represents the basis of tribal identity and culture. It is the significance and the meaning of this land, and of the sovereign powers exerted there, as defined by American Indian tribes and tribal governments, that forms the basis for an understanding of American Indian tribes, culture, and community today.

Finally, the significance found in this concept of sovereignty as it has evolved within the relationships between the United States federal government and American Indian tribal governments, represents a new and necessary construct to better define and distinguish the processes of ethnicity related to political power and legal power of other communities and groups. This concept of sovereignty offers a better understanding, not just of American Indian people, but is the element lacking in our use of ethnicity as the defining construct for ethnic cultures within the United States. As ethnic groups seek to respond, react, or recreate new frameworks of political power, or seek to legitimize political and legal powers of groups, it is in fact this new definition of sovereignty, rather than ethnicity, which more accurately reflects the processes on-going.

Sovereignty, as a concept which relates to political and legal powers of groups in specific places and historic contexts, is in fact the defining construct and the appropriate topic of human geographic research in many settings in the United States. Ethnicity remains important related to the processes of community identity and its on-going formation and persistence, yet when those activities seek legal or political recognition, sovereignty is a more accurate description of the process.

One new direction for human geography of the United States, therefore, is to distinguish between the processes of ethnicity, of community creation, preservation, and persistence of unique groups; and the processes of sovereignty which seek political and legal recognition or powers for those groups, particularly within specific geographical areas. The result of such applications of this form of sovereignty should be a more enlightened description of the complex dynamics of human behavior within the United States, and contributions toward better understanding of community dynamics within world systems.

Zusammenfassung

Der Begriff Souveränität hat, so wie er von den Stammesverwaltungen der nordamerikanischen Indianer verstanden und verwendet wird, eine neue Bedeutung gewonnen. Es ist diese neue Bedeutung von Souveränität, und nicht so sehr die Ethnizität, welche die Identität und Grundlage für die Kultur und Gemeinschaft der nordamerikanischen Indianer liefert. Dieser Zusammenhang in Bezug auf Souveränität für die nordamerikanischen Indianer sollte die den Stämmen innewohnende Macht und Souveränität so respektieren, wie sie die Stämme selbst definieren und wie sie eigentlich in Wirklichkeit existieren. Die nordamerikanischen Indianer werden nicht durch die Einschränkungen der Reservationen eingeengt, sondern viele Stämme üben anerkannte gesetzliche wie auch eigene souveräne Macht über Land aus, das sie als Ureinwohner besaßen oder das als "gewöhnliches und gewohntes" Gebiet erklärt worden ist. Die Stammesgeschichte ist nicht nur eine Dokumentation des Landverlustes und der derzeitigen gesetzlichen Stellung des Landes, wie sie die Gerichte der einzelnen Staaten definieren, sondern sie ist die laufende Geschichte, welche die notwendigen Aspekte des Stammeslandes und der Stammeskulturen und ihre Bedeutung für die moderne Stammesverwaltung schafft und neu hervorbringt. Die Stammesplanung hat den Zweck, das Bewußtsein und den Einsatz dieser souveränen Kräfte zu verbessern, um Stammesverwaltungen zu unterstützen, die diese Mächte in Beziehung zur traditionellen Stammesführung innerhalb jeder Kultur und jedes Stammes besitzen. Angewandte Forschung sollte für und mit Stammesverwaltungen durchgeführt werden. Sowohl Forscher als auch ihre Forschungseinrichtungen müssen ihre anfängliche Anerkennung der Stammessouveränität darlegen. Im Falle der Institutionen müssen diese eine Verpflich-

tung eingehen, Beziehungen von der Verwaltung zur Regierung oder Institution aufzubauen, welche sich auf die Anerkennung der Souveränität stützen. Passende Stammesforschung ist in diesem Zusammenhang nicht einfach auf einzelne Projekte beschränkt, sondern bezieht sich auf effektive Langzeitbeziehungen, von denen beide Teile profitieren, wo die Forschungsaktivitäten gleichzeitig auch Entwicklungsaktivitäten sind, so daß sie zum Wissen und zu den Fähigkeiten des Stammes beitragen.
Die nordamerikanischen Indianer sind nicht nur ethnische Gruppe. Sie werden nicht allein durch den Prozeß von Ethnizität definiert, sondern sind Vertreter von souveränen Stammeskulturen und -verwaltungen, welche vor der Bildung der Bundesverwaltung der Vereinigten Staaten bestanden und welche heute noch als Souveräne bestehen, wenn sie auch teilweise in ihrer Macht beschnitten sind.
Die Reservationen der nordamerikanischen Indianer sind nicht nur Enklaven bzw. Plätze erzwungener Isolation für die Völker der nordamerikanischen Indianer, sondern indem ihnen von den Stammesregierungen und den Indianern eine Bedeutung zuerkannt wird, sind sie Brennpunkt der Kultur, der Gemeinschaft und der Zukunft jedes Stammes. Trotz der Armut auf den Reservationen, trotz des Mangels an Unterkünften und Infrastruktur, trotz der hohen Arbeitslosigkeit, trotz der hohen Kriminalitätsrate und den schwierigen sozialen Problemen, stellen die Reservationen einen Ort dar, den der Stamm kontrolliert. Sie sind das letzte Symbol und die Hochburg der souveränen Mächte eines jeden Stammes. Der zentrale Platz oder die zentralen Plätze der Reservationen, welche im Zusammenhang mit jeder Kultur durch die Stammesplanung erhalten und entsprechend genutzt werden, stellen für das indianische Volk die Grundlage der Stammesidentität und -kultur dar. Wie es die Stämme und Stammesregierungen der nordamerikanischen Indianer selbst definieren, ist es die Wichtigkeit und Bedeutung dieses Landes und der souveränen Mächte, die dort ausgeübt werden, welche heute die Grundlage für ein Verständnis der Stämme, Kultur und Gemeinschaft der nordamerikanischen Indianer bildet.
Die Bedeutung schließlich, die in diesem Konzept der Souveränität innewohnt, das sich als Teil der Beziehung zwischen der Bundesregierung der Vereinigten Staaten und den Stammesverwaltungen der nordamerikanischen Indianer entwickelt hat, vertritt ein neues und notwendiges Gedankengebäude, um die Prozesse der Ethnizität, die mit politischer und rechtlicher Macht anderer Gemeinschaften und Gruppen zusammenhängen, besser zu definieren und unterscheiden zu können. Dieses Konzept der Souveränität bietet ein besseres Verständnis nicht nur von den nordamerikanischen Indianern, sondern es ist jenes Element, das in unserem herkömmlichen Gebrauch von Ethnizität als erklärendes Konstrukt für ethnische Kulturen innerhalb der Vereinigten Staaten fehlt. Da ethnische Gruppen danach suchen, auf neue Rahmenbedingungen der politischen Macht zu antworten, zu reagieren und diese neue zu erschaffen, oder bestrebt sind, die politischen und rechtlichen Kräfte von Gruppen zu legitimieren, ist es in Wirklichkeit nicht die Ethnizität, sondern vielmehr diese neue Definition von Souveränität, welche die laufenden Prozesse genauer widerzuspiegeln vermag.
Souveränität als Konzept, welche sich auf politische und rechtliche Kräfte von Gruppen in bestimmten Orten und geschichtlichen Zusammenhängen bezieht, ist eigentlich das definierende Konstrukt und das passende Thema der humangeographischen Forschung in vielen Regionen der Vereinigten Staaten. Ethnizität bleibt in Bezug auf die Prozesse der Identität einer Gemeinschaft und ihrer laufenden Entwicklung und Beharrlichkeit von Bedeutung, wenn jedoch diese Aktivitäten rechtliche und politische Anerkennung suchen, ist Souveränität eine passendere Beschreibung des Vorgangs.
Für die Humangeographie der USA ergibt sich daraus eine neue Richtung. Sie beruht auf der Unterscheidung zwischen den Prozessen der Ethnizität, der Gemeinschaftsbildung und der Erhaltung sowie Persistenz von individuellen Gruppen einerseits, und den Prozessen der Souveränität andererseits. Letztere streben die politische und rechtliche Anerkennung sowie die Zuteilung von Machtbefugnissen für diese Gruppen an, vor allem Gruppen in bestimmten geographischen Gebieten. Das Ergebnis dieses Gebrauchs der Souveränität sollte eine aufgeklär-

tere Beschreibung der komplexen Dynamik des menschlichen Verhaltens in den Vereinigten Staaten und einen Beitrag zu einem besseren Verständnis der Dynamik der Gemeinschaft innerhalb des Weltsystems sein.

References

Barth, F. (1969): Ethnic Groups and Boundaries: the Social Organization of Culture Difference. Boston, Little, Brown and Company.
Boldt, M. (1993): Surviving as Indians: The Challenge of Self-Government. Toronto, University of Toronto Press.
Brass, P. R. (1991): Ethnicity and Nationalism: Theory and Comparison. Newbury Park, CA, Sage Publications Inc.
Churchill, W. (1992): Fantasies of the Master Race: Literature, Cinema and the Colonization of American Indians. Monroe, ME, Common Courage Press.
Churchill, W. (1993): Struggle for the Land: Indigenous Resistance to Genocide, Ecocide and Expropriation in Contemporary North America. Monroe, ME, Common Courage Press.
Clarke, C., Ley, D. and Peach, C., eds. (1984): Geography and Ethnic Pluralism. London, George Allen & Unwin.
Cohen, A. (1974): Urban Ethnicity. London, Tavistock.
Cohen, A. (1976): Two Dimensional Man: an Essay on the Anthology of Power and Symbolism in Complex Society. Berkeley, CA, University of California Press.
de Blij, H. J. (1967): Systematic Political Geography. New York, NY, John Wiley and Sons.
Furnivall, J. S., (1939): Netherlands India. Cambridge, Cambridge University Press.
Furnivall, J. S. (1948, 1956): Colonial Policy and Practice. New York, New York University Press.
Glazer, N. and Moynihan, D. P. (1963, 1970): Beyond the Melting Pot; the Negroes, Puerto Ricans, Jews, Italians, and Irish of New York City. Cambridge, MA, M.I.T. Press.
Glazer, N. and Moynihan, D. P. eds. (1975): Ethnicity: Theory and Experience. Cambridge, MA, Harvard University Press.
Jacobs, J. (1980): Canadian Cities and Sovereignty: 1979 Massey Lectures (Sound recording). Toronto, Radio Canada International.
Jaimes, M. A., ed. (1992): The State of Native America: Genocide, Colonization, and Resistance. Boston, MA, South End Press.
Jose, C. (1992): Tribal Sovereignty Workshop, Unpublished Lecture Notes from Introduction to Tribal Planning. Cheney, WA, Eastern Washington University, Department of Urban and Regional Planning Summer Institute.
Leibniz (1864): Entretiens de Philarete et d'Eugene sur le droit d'Ambassade. from Werke, First Series, III, Havover. 331ff.
Ley, D. (1974): The Black Inner City as Frontier Outpost; Images and Behavior of a Philadelphia Neighborhood. Washington, D.C., Association of American Geographers (Monograph Series 7).
Ley, D. and Samuels, M., eds. (1978): Humanistic Geography: Prospects and Problems. Chicago, Maaroufa Press, Inc.
McDonald, J. A. (1991): The Dispossession of the American Indian, 1887-1934. Bloomington, IN, Indiana University Press.
McNickle, D'A. (1968): Native American Tribalism: Indian Survivals and Renewals. New York, NY, Oxford University Press.
Morrill, R. L. (1965): The Negro Ghetto: Problems and Alternatives. In: The Geographical Review, 55, 339-361.
Moynihan, D. P. (1993): Pandaemonium: Ethnicity in International Politics. Oxford, Oxford University Press.
Ra'anan, U. (1980): Ethnic Resurgence in Modern, Democratic States: A Multidisciplinary Approach to Human Resources and Conflict. New York, Pergamon Press.
Rose, H. M. (1970): The Development of an Urban Subsystem: the Case of the Negro Ghetto. In: Annals of the Association of American Geographers, 60, 1-17.

Rose, H. M. (1972): The Spatial Development of Black Residential Subsystems. In: Economic Geography, 48, 43-65.
Sills, D. L., and Merton, R. K., eds. (1991): International Encyclopedia of the Social Sciences. Volume 19. New York, NY, Macmillan, 79.
Smith, A. D. (1981): The Ethnic Revival. Cambridge, Cambridge University Press.
Suttles, G. D. (1968): The Social Order of the Slum: Ethnicity and Territory in the Inner City. Chicago, University of Chicago Press.
Suttles, G. D. (1972): The Social Construction of Communities. Chicago, University of Chicago Press.
Sutton, I. (1975): Indian Land Tenure: Bibliographical Essays and a Guide to the Literature. New York, NY, Clearwater Publishing.
Sutton, I. (1976): Sovereign States and the Changing Definition of the Indian Reservation. In: The Geographical Review, 66, 281-295.
Sutton, I. (1985): Irredeemable America: The Indians' Estate and Land Claims. Albuquerque, NM, University of New Mexico Press.
Toland, J. D. (1993): Ethnicity and the State. New Brunswick, NJ, Transaction Publishers.
Weibel-Orlando, J. (1991): Indian Country, L.A.: Maintaining Ethnic Community in Complex Society. Urbana, IL, University of Illinois Press.
Winchell, D. G. (1982): Space and Place of the Yavapai. Unpublished Ph.D. diss. Department of Geography, Arizona State University.
Winchell, D. G. et al. (1989): Geographical Research on Native Americans. In: Gaile, G. and Willmott, C., eds., Geography in America. Columbus, OH, Merrill Publishing Company, 239-255.

Address of the Author

Dick Winchell
Department of Urban and Regional Planning
Eastern Washington University
Cheney, WA 99004
USA

JOACHIM VOSSEN

The Amish Migration of Lancaster County and its Relevance for the Amish Culture of the Northeastern United States

Introduction

With the generous assistance of the German Research Foundation, the author spent the summer of 1993 studying several younger settlements of the Lancaster County Amish in Pennsylvania. This research can be divided into two parts. The first part consists of Amish migration behavior. Questions about amount and distance, the consideration of push- and pull factors, or questions about the religious influenced evaluation of migrations, establish direct preconditions for an adequate understanding of the new regions. The second part deals with the structure and analysis of the new settlements.[1] It became clear that in the face of increasing cultural and economic threats to the traditional settlement area, the founding of new settlements is becoming more important for the maintenance of the Amish culture in southeastern Pennsylvania. This raises the question as to how far, due to the continuing modernization of the Amish of Lancaster County, the new settlements can be considered as "retreat or surviving areas" where a traditional Amish culture will continue.

This study will concentrate on the first part of the research i.e. on questions about Amish migration behavior. After a short introduction the situation of the Old Order Amish within Lancaster County as "mother area" of the migrants will be discussed. Then the dimensions and directions of Amish migration as well as the motives and characteristics will be taken into consideration. Finally the different functions of Amish migration will be described.

In contrast to other groups of immigrants the religious group of the Old Order Amish, who originated in Anabaptism in 1693 in Europe, resisted a rapid integration into the Anglo-American mainstream culture. Still today the Old Order Amish, whose members number over 130,000 in the USA, are a striking phenomenon within the American population mosaic and their lives differ considerably from the lifestyle of the dominant culture. Separation from the "unbelieving world" is one of the basic demands of Amish faith, visible, for example, through patterns of dress, a special school system and a distinctive language. The almost complete rejection of modern technological means - for example, their decision to remain aloof from the public distribution network and their rejection of phone, TV, electric lighting, electrical appliances, as well as their retention of the use of horses for transport and fieldwork - has led to the marked economic, social and religious features which determine Amish identity.

The Settlement Lancaster County

To understand the basis and motives of Amish migrations and the situation of the younger "daughter settlements", it is necessary to know the initial situation of Lancaster County as the region of origin.

Lancaster County is located in southeastern Pennsylvania, west of the Atlantic Megalopolis. The access to the northeast- and middle Atlantic markets gives them a strong economic advantage. Lancaster is 158 miles from New York City, 112 miles from Washington D.C. and 72 miles from

Fig. 1: Distance of Lancaster County from the Large Eastern Seaboard Agglomerations

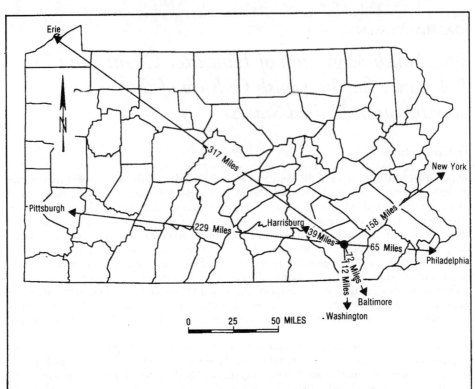

Source: Vossen 1994, 56

Baltimore (*Fig. 1*). Within a radius of 150 miles, one finds one-sixth of the nation's population, one-eight of the nation's homes, one-fifth of the nation's retail outlets and one-third of the nation's income. More than 30 million people live within a day's automobile journey of Lancaster County. A well developed traffic network and transportation system put these tremendous markets within easy reach (*The Lancaster Chamber of Commerce and Industry 1990, VII*).
Today the County is a prosperous, economically well-established area and one of the most highly populated counties of Pennsylvania, characterized by a continuous urbanization. A population growth of approximately 16 percent between 1980 and 1990 makes the County the fastest growing area within the state (*Pennsylvania State Data Center 1992, 6*). This growth is linked with a continuous demand for land. Most of this land has been developed into new residential areas, industrial parks, shopping centers, parking lots, roads etc.
Mainly this process has taken place to the disadvantage of agricultural land. Farmland which formerly covered 90 percent of the County's land area now covers approximately 60 percent. By 2010 it is predicted that the agricultural land will decrease from 416,000 to 400,400 acres (*Tab. 1*).

Tab. 1: Current and Projected Land Cover

Land Use	1978 (acres)	2010 (acres)	Difference 1978-2010
Residential	50,700	73,100	+ 22,400
Commercial	5,000	6,920	+ 1,920
Industrial	5,400	8,280	+ 1,680
Institutional	4,400	6,800	+ 2,400
Utilities	5,300	6,260	+ 960
Other Urban	4,100	–	–
Public Parks	8,900	10,340	+ 1,140
Woodland	86,700	78,700	- 8,000
Brush	6,200	0	0
Agricultural Land	424,500	400,400	- 24,100
Wetlands	500	00	0
Other	2,100		0
Total Land	603,800		
Total Water	20,800		
Grand Total	624,600		

Source: Vossen 1994, 225; 1984, II-16

Despite this reduction in agricultural land, Lancaster can still be characterized as a favorable agricultural region. As part of the Piedmont Physiographic Province the County consists of some of the most productive agricultural land nationally and internationally, and leads all other non-irrigated counties in the value of agricultural goods produced (*The Lancaster Chamber of Commerce and Industry 1993, G.1*). Under these conditions a productive Amish farm is economically viable on only thirty acres. Agriculture, and herewith the traditional family farm, remains a strong factor within the economic structure of the County, but is declining compared to manufacturing, wholesale, retail trades and services.

At present a diversified economy with a wide spectrum of products and services creates a strong and balanced economic base. As a result the County has a low unemployment rate and a high standard of living. Also responsible for this situation is tourism which is one of the important economic factors in the County. In 1989, over three million visitors spent in excess of 772 million dollars on goods and services in the County. The Old Order Amish culture and the rural environment, create a recreation area in the immediate vicinity of the large cities of the east coast which draws a large number of tourists. In fact, Lancaster County has one of the strongest economies in the State. Between 1980 and 1987, the Mellon Bank's Economic Performance Index indicated that Lancaster County's economy grew faster than any other region in Pennsylvania (*Lancaster Planning Commission 1993, 1-9*). For this reason the area attracts more visitors, new residents, industries and employees and is expected to continue to prosper.

Lancaster County is one of the largest and oldest Amish settlement areas in North America. In 1988 the County had approximately 3,000 households, with a population of around 14,000 Amish. The large families which are promoted by their religion - they have an average of seven children - are responsible for the fast growth of the Amish population. Under these circumstances the group is becoming an increasingly visible element within the region. In 1988 Amish families were settled in most of the townships of the County. The highest population density can be found in the traditional eastern settlement area. Here the Amish make up to 30% of the total Township population. Their high birthrate ensures that the trend will continue. The growing space requirements of the Amish population, as well as the requirements of the total County, lead to problems which endanger the traditional Amish social and economic structure. This is one of the main reasons for Amish migrations.

The Amish Migration

The migration of Amish families out of Lancaster County is a characteristic part of their culture which has continued up to the present. The migrations dealt with here are all migrations across the boundaries of the County. Movements within the County are not taken into consideration. Therefore, the change of the domicile is at the same time accompanied by a shift of jobs, schools, supplies etc.

Fig. 2: Amish Migrations of Lancaster County, 1978 - 1992

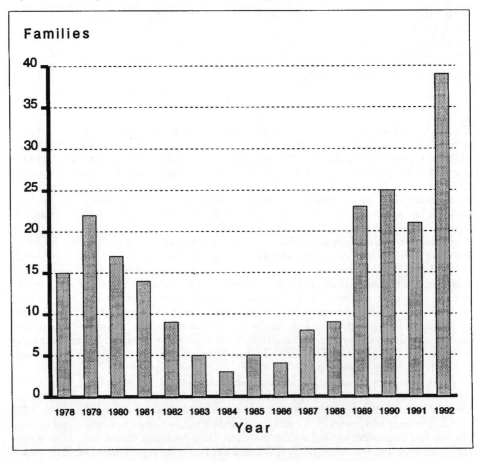

Source: Vossen 1994, 169 and author's investigation of The Diary, Vol. 24 (1992), Vol. 25 (1993)

Within the 15 years between 1978 and 1992, 219 Amish households left the County. While at the end of the seventies high migration rates took place, a drastic decrease could be observed at the beginning of the eighties. Only at the beginning of the nineties do the migration rates increase. In 1992 the Amish migration peaked at 39 Amish households or 206 persons which was the highest migration rate for the last twenty years (Fig. 2).

The obvious decline of the migration rate in the eighties has to do with developments within the State. Between 1981 and 1986 Pennsylvania had experienced an economic depression. The availability of farmland at this time, one of the most important reasons for migration, had been reduced because of low farmland prices. Only in 1986 when a stronger economic growth took place and the prices for farmland increased, were more farms again on the market. At this time Amish migration rose accordingly.

The destination of most Amish migrations are the Amish settlements which have already been established. Because of similar religious and social behavior and practices, settlement areas are preferred which are founded and mainly settled by Lancaster County Amish and not other Amish groups. Some of the oldest "daughter settlements" of Lancaster County are St. Marys County (Maryland 1940), Lebanon County (Pennsylvania 1941), Adams County (Pennsylvania 1964) and Centre County (Pennsylvania 1967). All new settlements are in within a short distance of the initial settlement, so that Lancaster County can be reached with the help of a driver, in one

Fig. 3: New Settlements Founded by Lancaster County Amish in Pennsylvania

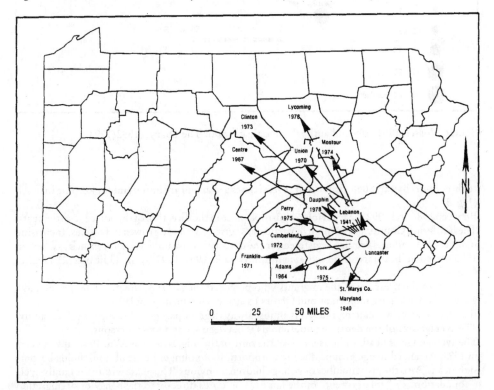

Source: Drawn after Hostetler 1981[3], 135

Fig. 4: Amish Migrations between 1986 and 1992

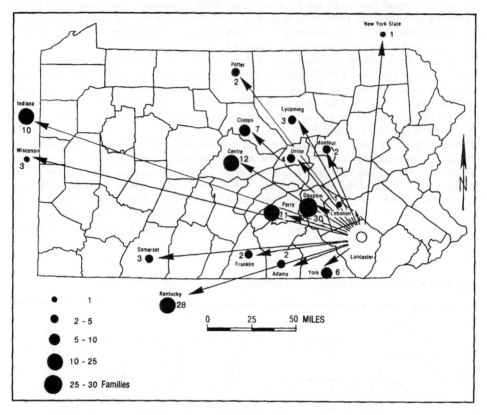

Source: Vossen 1994, 169 and author's investigations of The Diary, (1992/1993)

to three hours by car. Such visits occur several times a year and are important for keeping in touch (*Fig. 3*).
Between 1986 and 1992 the main migration took place in the direction of the adjacent settlements. The bordering County of Dauphin in particular registered a large growth in families. Increasing numbers of families were also registered for the destination area of western Kentucky, where in 1990 three families started the settlement, followed in 1991/1992 by an additional 23 families (*Fig. 4*).
Apart from the presence of the migrants who preceded them, very attractive land prices and a good milk market are important pull factors to attract an Amish population.
If a single man or woman migrates, it is almost always a grandparent following his or her family. The average size of the departing households is between six and seven persons.
The average age of heads of households at the time of the migration was 33 in 1991 and 38 years in 1992. Arranged in age groups, the high proportion of younger heads of households become significant. Also the great number of young children is obvious. The phase within the family cycle ("foundation" or "enlargement" of the family) correlates directly to the behavior of migration (*Fig. 5*).

Fig. 5: Age Groups of Amish Migrants between 1991 and 1992

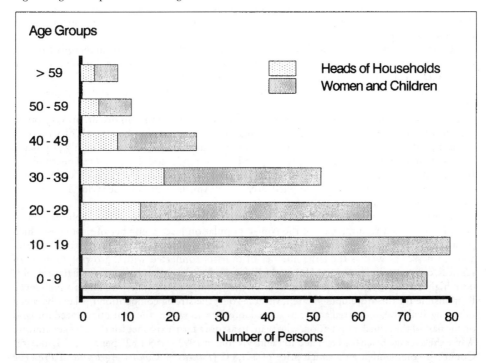

Source: Author's investigations and Amish Directory 1988 and The Diary 1992, 13-18; 1993, 32-35

Most of the households are young married couples. Before the children reach the age to establish their own social contacts which would make it difficult to migrate, the parents make the decision for migration.

Motives and Characteristics of Amish Migration

Although the Old Order Amish show strong social ties, migrations are a permanent phenomenon of the cultural and religious lifestyle. Emigration caused by religious persecution, which can be classified as forced migration, is deeply rooted in today's Amish consciousness of religious tradition and is frequently an important and permanent element of hymns and sermons during the Sunday service. The "Martyrs Mirror" an account of Christian martyrdom first printed in 1660 is part of every small Amish library. The Amish songbook "Ausbund", the only book used during the long-lasting periods of chants in the church service, consists of over 50 hymns which were written by Anabaptists at the time of their imprisonment in the 16th century. These hymns express sorrowness, loneliness and especially protest against the persecution of the sinful world. They help to keep alive the readiness to migrate in the face of a modern threat to the Amish faith. Beside these specifically Amish precedents, Amish migrations also have Biblical models. The separation from the world, one of the primary Amish principles, which is responsible for the special socio-cultural structure of the group, is also one of the most important motives for the migration. The demand, "and be not conformed to this world" (*Roman 12,2*) or "love not the world, neither the things that are in the world" (*1. Joh. 2, 15-17*) is in many cases the reason to leave a settlement area in which an Amish lifestyle is hard to realize. Furthermore, migration and the foundation of new settlements has its parallels to the Exodus of the Israelites from the fleshpots of Egypt.

Alone these links make it obvious that Amish migrations are characterized by numerous different factors (*Fig. 6*). A simple push and pull pattern alone, which is based only on objective and intersubjective, reconstructible factors is not a sufficient basis for analyzing Amish migration behavior. Subjective factors are also important: the motives, wishes, needs and purposes of the migrants.

In general, spatial and here especially economic factors belong to the important, or, very often, even to the basic reasons of migrations. In this case, migrations can be a result of structural disparities of two different regions. Rural areas and small cities, in contrast to highly populated areas and large agglomerations, supply only limited economic, social and cultural possibilities. Because of these significant disparities between such regions, a huge migration difference is existing in favor of the better supplied area. The Amish migration behavior however, is characterized by an inverse regularity.

As mentioned above, Lancaster County is currently experiencing a favorable economic development. As a result, a part of the Amish population faces a number of problems which promote the readiness to migrate. The rapid growth of the population, the increase of industries and businesses as well as the large number of tourists connected with a growing number of services, create a dramatic demand for land (*see Fig. 7*). As a result, land prices, which have always been higher in Lancaster County than in any other county of the state, remain on a high level. Responsible for this development are favorable soils, the strong competition for land between urban, agricultural, industrial and recreational interests, as well as the continuous need for land on the part of the Amish population, who want to assure a farm existence for the next generation. While the average price for farmland in Pennsylvania in 1992 was $ 1,820 per acre, in Lancaster County it commanded an average price of $ 4,855 (*Lancaster County Agricultural Preserve Board 1992, 9 and 15*). Furthermore it is nearly impossible to buy farmland in the central parts of the Amish settlement region. 70 to 90% of the farmland in some townships is owned by Amish. For this reason farmland is only sold within the family and is not available on the open market. In light of this, it is increasingly difficult to establish a farm within Lancaster County. The religiously determined ideal of farming is therefore endangered. Consequently, a growing number of Amish households have to work in non-agricultural occupations, or, if they want to farm, to migrate into other areas of the state. Migration in order to live on a farm is one of the most important motives of Amish migration. Within the new settlements approximately 70 to 80% of the households live on the farm.

Another problem caused by the growing population within the County is the lack of sufficient building sites for the Amish. Because of the strong social and family ties, a large number of younger households, not working within agriculture, try to settle near to their relatives and friends. Especially within the eastern part of the County the Amish population density is growing fast. For several years, especially in the face of high land prices, a small part of farmland has been subdivided to build a new home for a young family or a retired couple. This practice is meeting growing opposition from the planning institutions because of the increasing damage to the landscape by unplanned settlements of low density. The Lancaster County planning Commission states that: "A limited amount of new residential development will be permitted in our rural areas, but this development will reflect its traditional pattern of growth. Rural residents will live primarily in villages or in cluster developments." (*Lancaster County Planning Commission 1991, 7*) The special demands of the Old Order Amish, who, because of their numerous children, as well as horse and buggy transportation, need a greater amount of floor and property space, cannot easily be satisfied under these circumstances. In addition, a mixture of Amish and non-Amish dwellings within a modern American settlement area will cause an abundance of problems

Fig. 6: Pattern of Amish Migration

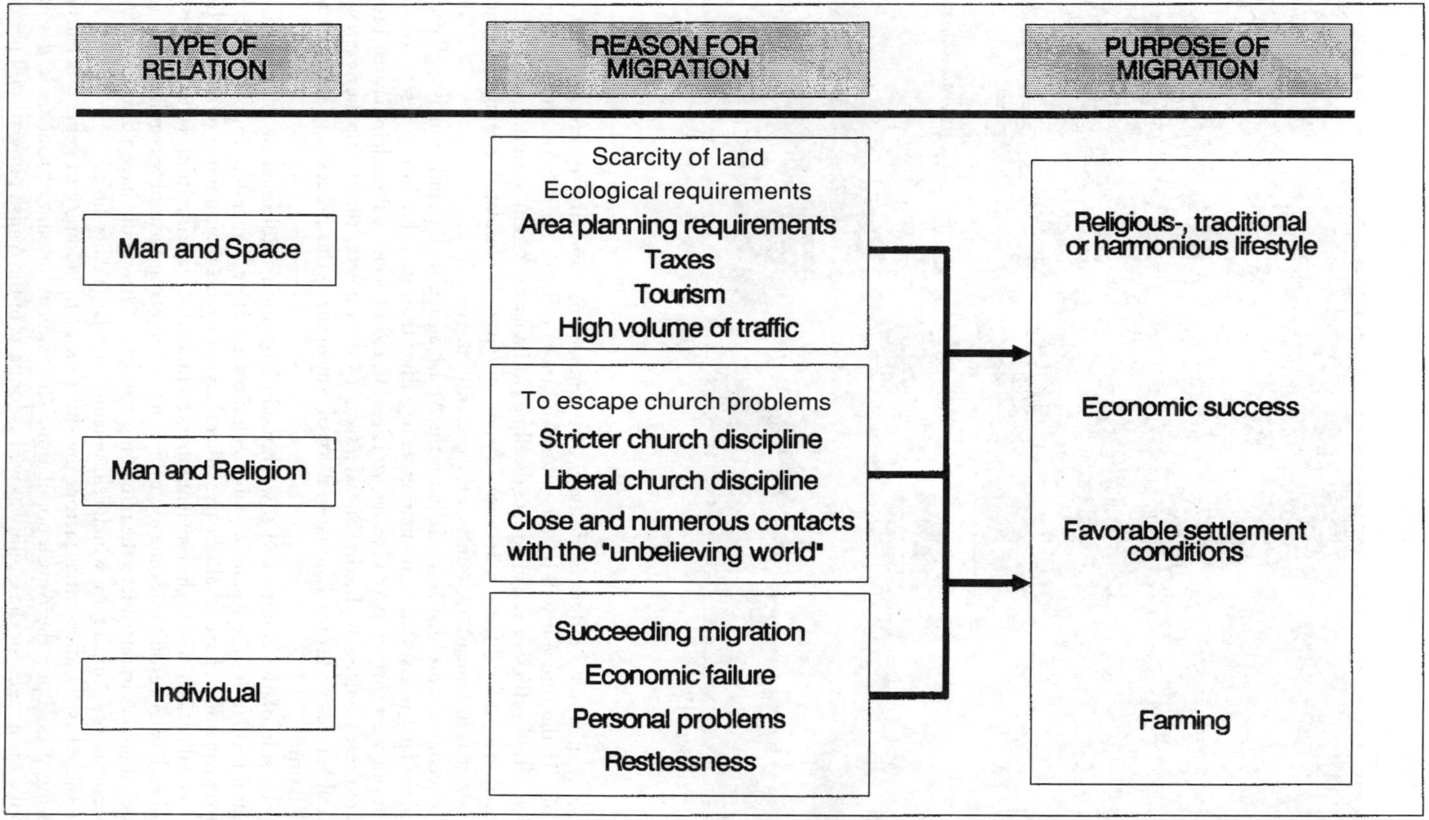

TYPE OF RELATION	REASON FOR MIGRATION	PURPOSE OF MIGRATION
Man and Space	Scarcity of land Ecological requirements Area planning requirements Taxes Tourism High volume of traffic	Religious-, traditional or harmonious lifestyle Economic success Favorable settlement conditions Farming
Man and Religion	To escape church problems Stricter church discipline Liberal church discipline Close and numerous contacts with the "unbelieving world"	
Individual	Succeeding migration Economic failure Personal problems Restlessness	

Source: Author's investigation

Fig. 7: Tourism in Lancaster County. Symbolic for the Amish Situation is the Forlorn Buggy in the Center.

Source: Vossen, 1993

because of the totally different lifestyles of the inhabitants and distinct construction of the buildings. In the future it will become more and more difficult for the Amish and their large families to find sufficient and adequate dwellings in Lancaster County. In the new settlements the situation is totally different. Because they are only sparsely populated, zoning ordinances are not as strict as in Lancaster County at the present time (*see Fig. 8*).

Another economic problem, especially for the Amish agricultural population, is high property taxes since land is assessed at its market value rather than its value in its present use. In the neighboring western county of Chester, which is located adjacent to Philadelphia area, property taxes are already twice as high as in Lancaster County. It is expected that within the next few years comparable taxes will reach Lancaster. A lot of Amish see in this process a growing danger to Amish farms.

From the side of the county and township administration, additional problems caused by ecological regulations are becoming more and more concrete. Lancaster County farmers who wish to expand often have no alternative other than to increase their number of animals. But the trend to smaller farms and high animal numbers on limited acreage is putting a tremendous strain on land and water resources. Some townships in the County are planning regulations to reduce livestock numbers in relation to the remaining farmland. This would have a direct impact upon the income of the Amish farm which relies mainly on a large dairy herd.

Beside these basic and essential factors the situation of the County in general is causing an increasing stress upon the Amish population. The eminent amount of tourists is, despite the economic advantages for the County as well as for parts of the Amish population, a permanent

Fig. 8: Amish Farm in Center County. Within the Young Settlements the Amish Find Sufficient Space and Seclusion.

Source: Vossen, 1993

burden. A high volume of traffic with overcrowded roads, especially in the summer, is a continuous source of danger for horse-drawn vehicles. At the same time curious, nosy tourists disturb Amish privacy. Moreover, especially for the younger generation, touristic establishments can be considered as a permanent temptation to unorthodox behavior.

Besides spatial and economic factors, social and religious reasons have an important connection with Amish migration. However, here it is much more difficult to acquire useful and abundant information, because of its sensitive character. Motives such as the avoidance of church problems, or the search for a more liberal or even plainer church discipline can be named. Another reason can be the introduction of technical innovation. A strong emphasis is very often placed upon the necessity of living within an environment which supports the Amish values. In a slightly developed region far from tourist resorts Amish can be reared with little "worldly temptation". In addition, within these young church districts one can find an intact and intensified church and social life. Parents and children are dependent upon each other during their free time. For these reasons, even in Lancaster County, very successful Amish businessmen leave their flourishing businesses to live a plain and traditional life within the circle of their family.

Migration is not only caused by rational factors, but very often through irrational motives. Especially for individual or personal reasons one can find a large number of different and in part unexplainable motives. They vary from differences with neighbors, personal economic failure, to love of adventure, or personal restlessness. In many cases it has been simple succeeding migration. Once traced "migration roads" encourage and attract additional households. Family ties to "daughter settlements" have the function of migration bridges. Detailed and authentic information about the new settlements through members of the family furthermore reduce the risk uncertainty and elevate the readiness to migrate.

The decision for or against migration is, however, not only a process of personal decision. The social environment is also an important factor of influence. While the basic decision must always be considered as an individual procedure, the evaluations by the religious group directly influence the behavior of the Amish migrants. In principle, from the religious point of view, there are no restrictions connected with migrations. In fact, as mentioned above, there are religious and traditional precedents for migration. Even so, in the sixties and seventies, emigrants received a condescending smile. An obvious improvement of the social and economic situation through migration did not exist at that time.

Today the wish for migration has become, in view of the growing negative agricultural circumstances within the county, a continuous and accepted phenomenon within the Amish society, supported by recognized, mostly older persons of the group. Even an active and intensive promotion is taking place. It has gone so far that a promoter of Amish migrations bought farms in another county of Pennsylvania and sold these farms at a low profit to young Amish families. To raise the large sum of money for this project, he even put a mortgage on his home farm in Lancaster County. Today still he considers it his duty to help Amish families in starting a farm in a new settlement area. In the youngest settlement area in Kentucky he is presently active as a type of consultant and attendant to help farm-willing Amish families who want to move there with their families to set up their farm. The motive for his engagement is the preservation of the traditional Amish culture, which he sees endangered in Lancaster County.

Functions of Amish Migrations

Which functions do migrations have for the Amish? The stability of the Amish society is tied to the satisfaction of the economic, social and religious needs of the majority of their members. Disappointment in the conditions within the County can possibly lead to an endangerment of the total group, or to a division of more liberal fractions, especially considering the growing number of younger families. Migrations create an outlet for these problems. The following functions can be listed:

- Migrations relieve the Amish population pressure somewhat. In 1992 39 families left the County, while 118 new households were set up. The problem of the strong Amish demand for farmland cannot be solved by migration alone but it can be lessened.
- Regional mobility is an instrument of cultural expansion.
- Migrations help preserve the traditional Amish economic, social and religious system
- Migrations form "retreat areas" for Amish culture. This becomes increasingly important in view of the threats to the culture in its "mother settlement".

This last is especially important because of the limited growing conditions of the religious group. The problem finds a parallel in MALTHUS. According to MALTHUS a population must exceed its potential to feed itself because of its exponential growth. The production of food however, despite modern and innovative agricultural methods, grows at a constant rate. If this principle is applied to the cultural situation of the Amish in Lancaster County, it would mean that the group, because of its exponential growth, must in the long term exceed its traditional economic possibilities. This is true because the existence of abundant and inexpensive farmland, necessary for a traditional religio-cultural character of the group, grows at a slower pace than the need. At the same time, in addition, the general situation of the County is being tightened by mainstream society. Even considering the introduction of innovations into Amish agriculture and the intensification of agricultural production based on smaller farm units, Lancaster County has no further capacity for a traditional structured Amish culture. Only a continuous cultural adaptation, especially within the economy, can guarantee the survival of the group. The danger of a growing assimilation does not need to be emphasized and can be easily observed today within the County. To evade this situation, a migration into sparsely populated areas stabilizes the traditional Amish culture.

This is why Amish migration is characterized through a movement from an economically prospering area into slightly developed, rural regions. Responsibility for this type of migration rests with the fundamental system of values, which evaluates spatial factors in a different manner as, for example, the mainstream culture. Underdeveloped social and cultural facilities, limited education chances and traditional economic conditions with a focus on agriculture are a spatial pattern which pulls Amish migrants. This enables the group to keep their system of values, their social structure and their distinctive lifestyle. In this sense Amish migrations have to be considered conservative, because the purpose of the migration is to continue their previous lifestyle or, even better, acquire a more traditional lifestyle than before. The spatial situation of the "daughter settlement" meets these expectations. In agricultural regions away from large agglomeration areas in agricultural regions, the Amish are offered a traditional economic base. Therefore it can be predicted that the Amish as a traditional culture will have a greater chance to survive within the younger settlements.

Summary

The religious group of the Old Order Amish is a striking phenomenon within the American population mosaic. The oldest and one of the largest settlement areas of the Amish culture is Lancaster County located in southeastern Pennsylvania. For various reasons an increasing number of Amish families are moving out of Lancaster County. In 1992 the Amish migration peaked at 39 Households or 206 persons which marked the highest migration for the last twenty years. Destination of most Amish migrations of Lancaster County are the Amish settlements which have already been established in the more westerly counties of Pennsylvania.

Amish migrations are motivated by many different factors. A simple push and pull pattern alone is not a sufficient basis for analyzing the migration behavior. Not only economic but also social and especially religious motives belong to the important reasons of migration.

In contrast to non-religiously motivated population groups the Amish migration is characterized by a movement from an economically prospering area into slightly developed, rural regions. Underdeveloped social and cultural facilities, limited education chances and traditional economic conditions with a focus on agriculture are a spatial pattern which serve to attract Amish migrants. The functions of Amish migration can be summarized as follows:

- Migrations help relieve the Amish population pressure somewhat.
- Regional mobility is an instrument of cultural expansion.
- Migrations help preserve the traditional Amish economic, social and religious system
- Migrations form "retreat areas" for Amish culture. This becomes increasingly important in view of the threats to the culture in its "mother settlement".

Zusammenfassung

Die religiöse Gruppe der Old Order Amish oder Amischen Alter Ordnung gehört aufgrund ihrer religiösen Grundsätze zu den signifikanten Bevölkerungserscheinungen Nordamerikas. Zu einem ihrer ältesten und größten Siedlungsgebiete gehört die Region von Lancaster County im südöstlichen Pennsylvania. In dieser Region sind in den letzten Jahren zunehmend amische Abwanderungsbewegungen festzustellen. Die Abwanderung aus der County fand ihren vorläufigen Höhepunkt 1992 mit 39 Haushalten oder 206 Personen. Zielort dieser Migration sind in vielen Fällen die schon von Amischen besiedelten Counties des westlichen Pennsylvania.

Amische Migrationen sind durch eine Vielzahl unterschiedlicher Faktoren charakterisiert. Ein einfaches Push- oder Pullmuster reicht als alleinige Erklärungsbasis nicht aus, um amisches Wanderungsverhalten zu analysieren. Wirtschaftliche als auch soziale und besonders religiöse Motive gehören zu den wichtigen Beweggründen.

Im Gegensatz zu Migrationsbewegungen nicht religiös motivierter Bevölkerungsgruppen findet daher die amische Migration Lancaster County's von einer wirtschaftlich prosperierenden - in eine wirtschaftlich schwach strukturierte Region statt. Regionen mit begrenzten sozialen, kulturellen Möglichkeiten, eingeschränkten Bildungseinrichtungen sowie traditionellen wirtschaftlichen Strukturen und einem größeren Gewicht innerhalb der Landwirtschaft, verfügen über räumliche Muster, die amische Migration anziehen. Zusammenfassend lassen sich die nachfolgenden Funktionen amischer Migration nennen:

- amische Migration entschärft die große amische Landnachfrage innerhalb Lancaster County's
- regionale Mobilität ist ein Instrument der kulturellen Expansion
- Migrationen unterstützten und erhalten das traditionelle amische Wirtschafts- und Sozialsystem
- amische Migration schafft Rückzugsinseln amischer Kultur. Dies wird vor dem Hintergrund der gefährdenen Situation in der "Muttersiedlung" zunehmend wichtiger.

Notes

[1] The second part will be published in Geographia Religionum Vol. 10: Vossen, J.: Die Wirtschaftliche und soziale Entwicklung von jungen Siedlungsgebieten der Amischen Alter Ordnung im zentralen Pennsylvania (Centre - und Dauphin County) unter Berücksichtigung der Sondergruppe der Old School Amish (Snyder County, Pa.). In: Rinschede, G., Vossen, J., Hrsg.: Geographia Religionum 10.

References

Bähr, J., Jentsch, C., Kuls, W., eds. (1992): Bevölkerungsgeographie. Berlin, New York, De Gruyter.
Franz, P. (1984): Soziologie der räumlichen Mobilität. Frankfurt, New York, Campus Verlag.
Fuller, Th. and Smith, St. M. (1993): Road to Rennaissance VII. PennState.
Hostetler, J.A. (1981[3]): Amish Society. Baltimore and London, John Hopkins University Press.
Kuls, W. (1980): Bevölkerungsgeographie. Eine Einführung. Stuttgart, B.G. Teubner.
Luthy, D. (1985): Amish Settlements Across America. Ontario, Pathway Publishers.
Pennsylvania State Data Center (1992): 1992 Pennsylvania Abstract. A Statistical Fact Book. Harrisburg.
The Diary. A Church Newsletter Serving The Old Order Society. Vol. 11 (1978) - Vol. 23 (1991), Gordonville, PA.
The Lancaster County Agricultural Preserve Board (1992): Farm Sales Analysis with background data 1984-1991. Lancaster County, PA.
The Lancaster Chamber of Commerce and Industry (1993): The Lancaster Marketplace. Lancaster, PA.
The Lancaster County Planning Commission (1993): Lancaster County Comprehensive Plan. Growth Management Plan. Lancaster, PA.
The Lancaster County Planning Commission (1991): Lancaster County Comprehensive Plan. Policy Plan. Lancaster, PA.
The Lancaster Chamber of Commerce and Industry (1990): The Lancaster Marketplace. Lancaster, PA.
Vossen, J. (1989): Eine religiöse Minorität im Kräftefeld der Amerikanischen Gesellschaft. Die Old Order Amish in Lancaster County, Pennsylvania. In: Rinschede, G., Rudolph, K., eds.: Beiträge zur Religion/ Umwelt-Forschung II. Berlin, Dietrich Reimer Verlag (= Geographia Religionum 7),187-203.

Vossen, J. (1994): Die Amischen Alter Ordnung in Lancaster County, Pennsylvania. Religions- und wirtschaftsgeographische Signifikanz einer religiösen Minorität im Kräftefeld der amerikanischen Gesellschaft. Berlin, Dietrich Reimer Verlag (= Geographia Religionum 9).

Vossen, J. and Beiler, A. (1992): Modernität und Identität - die Old Order Amish in den USA. In: Geographie heute, 106, 23-31.

Address of the Author

Joachim Vossen
Institut für Geographie
Universität Regensburg
93040 Regensburg
GERMANY

GEORGE CATHCART

Religion and Land Use: Mormon Ranchers of the Little Colorado

Introduction

This paper addresses the role of religious belief as a cultural value affecting land-use practices among Mormon cattle ranchers in the Little Colorado River region of east-central Arizona. The study aims at understanding how these cultural values helped Mormons adapt to harsh environmental conditions and dominate the region as cattle ranchers. Early western Mormons - from 1847 to about 1890 - predominantly practiced self-sufficient irrigated agriculture as part of their effort to prepare for the second coming of Jesus Christ. The establishment of irrigated agriculture and the cooperative, interdependent social structure of early Mormonism largely precluded market-scale cattle ranching, which requires wide land areas and highly independent people *(Peplow 1958, 140)*. Mormons in the Little Colorado region made remarkable adaptations to harsh environmental and social conditions *(Abruzzi 1987)*. These adaptations enabled some Mormons to succeed and ultimately dominate the region, many of them as cattle ranchers grazing on public-land allotments *(Schauss undated)*. I have looked at the relationship between adaptive strategies and core religious beliefs, concentrating on historical events from 1876 into the 1890s within the framework of cultural ecology and the geography of religion, as well as the practices and perceptions of contemporary Mormon ranchers in the region.

Mormons and the Geography of Religion

Geographers have generally treated religion either as a cultural trait among many, or, in some cases, they have looked at religious groups as culture groups *(Meinig 1965)* but without closely studying belief systems and how those beliefs impact the cultural landscape.
SOPHER *(1967, 10)* urged geographers to look beyond superficial values and seek the underlying meaning of religion. He described two major belief paradigms: ethnic religions, characterized by isolation and parochialism; and universalizing systems *(Sopher 1967, 16)*. He specifically identified Mormonism as a universalizing system, meaning:

- Mormons believe their tenets can work for all people;
- they proselytize;
- they have broken through spatial and social constraints; and
- they have established a significant regional dominance *(Sopher 1967, 7 and 10)*.

While contemporary Mormonism clearly fits SOPHER's definition of a universalizing system, Mormon history includes a period of severe isolationism characteristic of ethnic religion. Ethnic religions derive from a special relationship between God and the religious group, a relationship "expressed through a special act of creation, a special revelation, or a special favor" *(Sopher 1967, 16)*. The Mormons, whose formal name, Church of Jesus Christ of Latter Day Saints, even suggests a belief in a special status, believe their founder, Joseph SMITH, received a special revelation from God in the form of a set of golden tablets and the unique and temporary ability to translate a portion of those tablets. The Book of Mormon, equal to the Bible in Mormon dogma, resulted from that revelation. The early history of the Mormons includes a hegira across the Great Plains to escape persecution after the murder of Joseph SMITH in Nauvoo, Illinois, followed by the establishment of a powerful theocracy in Utah, based on policies of economic and political isolation.

Erich ISAAC in more general terms defined two types of religious beliefs, which he regarded as dichotomous: those in which the creation of the world provides the meaning of human existence, and those in which meaning derives from a divine charter granted to a people. In the first, adherents will try to reproduce the cosmic plan in the landscape, as 19th century Mormons did in trying to create the city of Zion *(Sopher 1967, 32 f, 45; Nelson 1952, 25)*. In the latter, ritual practice reproduces the covenant between God and the chosen people *(Isaac 1962)*.

The Mormon geographer Richard JACKSON scoffs at the contention that the pioneer Mormon village represented religious values *(Sopher 1967, 32 f, 45; Francaviglia 1978b)*, contending that its form followed pioneer function, not scriptural mandate *(Jackson 1977; Jackson and Layton 1976)*. In another context, though, JACKSON and HENRIE *(1983)* found that contemporary Mormons everywhere generally ascribe great religious value to Utah, the center of the Mormon Culture Region as defined in MEINIG's landmark 1965 paper. JACKSON and HENRIE concluded that the perception of sacred space follows successful settlement.

Historian Jan SHIPPS detected a perception of sacred space among 19th century Mormons, a perception that she says ended in 1890, when the Mormon church officially abandoned polygamy and made other political and economic concessions *(Shipps 1985, 125 f)*. Those events profoundly altered the Mormons' view of themselves and the world. Prior to 1890, the Mormons viewed Mormondom as sacred space, a place apart, where polygamy, the "order of patriarchal marriage," defined the difference between Mormons and non-Mormons *(Shipps 1985, 125)*. In response to the manifesto that ended sanctioned polygamy, the Mormons began to rely more heavily on ritual to express their "chosen status" *(Shipps 1985, 128)*, a status that had always existed in their doctrine but had taken a subordinate role to the immediate work of gathering the Saints in Utah and preparing for the Second Coming and the building of Zion. Hence, Mormons embraced both poles of the fundamental religious dichotomy identified by ISAAC *(1962)*. In Sopherian terms, they evolved from ethnic religion to universalizing system, while clinging to their core theology and objectives, their belief in the nature of humans' relationship with God as a process of continuing improvement and redemption. Zion has become an attitude, not a place *(Francaviglia, 1978a, 101)*.

History

Mormon colonists from Utah began to settle the lower valley of the Little Colorado River in 1876. Under the direction of Lot SMITH, the Mormons established four communities along the river, at Joseph City, Sunset Crossing, Brigham City and Obed as part of church president Brigham YOUNG's efforts to extend the Mormon realm *(Tanner and Richards 1977, 16)*. In spite of fiercely hostile environmental conditions, these Mormons stubbornly persisted in trying to install communities consistent with the prevailing Mormon concept of self-sufficient agrarianism, centered on village life, communal fields and home industry *(Tanner and Richards 1977, 75-80; Arrington 1958, 354)*.

The settlers first tried to dam the Little Colorado River to irrigate their crops, but flash floods repeatedly washed out dams. Crop failure followed crop failure. The settlers established a saw mill, a dairy farm and a woolen mill, all at some distance from the riverside villages, but these could not make up for the effects of crop failures. Discouraged, many of the settlers returned to Utah within a few years *(Fish 1936, 24)*. Others moved upstream (to the south) on the Little Colorado and its principal tributary, Silver Creek *(Fish 1936, 46)*. By 1884, all four of the original lower river settlements had failed *(Fish 1936, 8)*. Today, only the town of Joseph City still exists, just west of Holbrook *(Tanner and Richards 1977, 10)*.

The settlers who moved upstream also had a hard time keeping dams in place *(Udall 1959, 175)*, but floods had a less devastating effect closer to the headwaters and in the more permeable soil of higher elevation valleys *(Abruzzi 1987)*. Successful farming communities arose at Snowflake and Taylor on Silver Creek *(Fish 1936, 83)*, and at Eagar and Springerville in Round Valley on the Little Colorado itself *(Winn 1969; Abruzzi 1987)*. The settlers in these towns faced a different challenge from their downstream brethren - competition from non-Mormons *(Peterson 1973, 17; Winn 1969)*.

The Mormon settlers on the lower river encountered only Indians, and part of the mission included converting the Indians *(Tanner and Richards 1977, 64)*, who play a key role in Mormon theology. But for the nearly 30 years since arriving in Utah and trying to establish the prototype for the Kingdom of Zion, the Mormons had avoided contact with other non-Mormons, with good reason. Mormons had encountered chronic persecutions and violence in previous settlements in Ohio, Missouri and Illinois before Brigham YOUNG brought the Mormons west in 1847 to establish a self-sufficient society isolated from hostile Gentiles *(Peterson 1973, 8; Meinig 1965)*. The Arizona colonies represented part of an effort to expand that society and develop a Mormon-dominated corridor to Mexico as overpopulation stretched the resources of Utah, and federal authorities stepped up pressure on Mormons to abandon polygamy, block voting and exclusive business dealings *(Arrington 1958, 354; Peterson 1973, 8 f)*.

But others also had their eyes on northern Arizona by the 1870s. The Atlantic and Pacific Railroad rapidly approached from the east, encouraging cattle operations in Texas to seek new grazing grounds on Arizona rangeland *(Peterson 1973, 168)*. Other settlers also began arriving, shortly before the Mormons, along the Little Colorado and Silver Creek. So the Mormons who moved from the initial settlements on the lower river had to establish their Mormon-style agrarian villages on land already occupied by ranchers *(Peterson 1973, 17)*.

William J. FLAKE acquired the village sites of Snowflake, Nutrioso, Springerville and Showlow, paying for the land in cattle *(O. Flake, 67, 71, 86, 88f)*. FLAKE made numerous trips back to Utah to get church-owned cattle and drive them back to Arizona to pay off the land *(O. Flake, 78 f)*. Mormon settlers quickly arrived in these new sites to build villages and dams, dig irrigation ditches and grow crops *(Smith 1970, 233 ff)*. The Mormons had cattle, but they did not run them on open range. Instead, they herded them in common pasture and kept them in barns in the villages *(Arrington 1958, 310, 354; Nelson 1952, 25)*. Livestock are still a common feature of the Mormon village landscape.

Through the 1870s and 1880s, the Mormons faced considerable internal and external pressures. Even the relatively successful farm villages sometimes failed to produce sufficient food to take care of all the settlers *(Peterson 1973, 143; Udall 1959, 161)*, and many Mormons had to go to work for the railroad and the cattle outfits. Some Mormon leaders organized work teams and contracted with the railroad *(Peterson 1973, 124, 128)* while others, in accordance with church doctrine of the time, warned against any business dealings with non-Mormons, especially in cattle and freighting *(Smith 269, 1970)*. Meanwhile, federal and territorial authorities increased the pressure on Mormon families to abandon polygamy, and many Arizona Mormon leaders, including FLAKE, served prison terms for plural marriage *(O. Flake, 104-109; Udall 1959, 97-112)*. Others fled to Mexico and established Mormon settlements in northern Sonora and Chihuahua *(Standiford undated, 239)*. In addition, the Aztec Land and Cattle Company bought thousands of acres of checkerboard pattern railroad grant land between Flagstaff and Holbrook and brought in about 60,000 head of cattle, which severely overgrazed not only the Aztec land but adjoining lands as well, including, of course, the land on which the Mormons had settled. *(Peterson 1973, 169 f; Fish 1936, 22)*. Aztec open-range cattle also attracted rustlers and other outlaws from Texas, resulting in frequent outbreaks of violence *(O. Flake, 113; Flake 1976, 111; Peterson 1973, 170 f)*. Eventually, the Mormon church had to purchase from Aztec the land Mormons in Snowflake and Taylor had settled and irrigated years earlier *(Peterson 1973, 174 f)*. In 1890, the Mormon church capitulated to government pressure. Church president Wilford

WOODRUFF announced he had received a revelation from God that spelled the end of sanctioned polygamy. In addition, church leaders agreed to abandon church policies on block voting restrictions and on trade with non-Mormons *(Arrington 1958, 380)*. These events brought about a reconciliation with the federal government and led eventually to the admission of Utah as a state in 1896 *(Arrington 1958, 378 f)*. Other effects included de-centralization of the church's economic role, manifested in Arizona when the well-subsidized Arizona Cooperative Mercantile Association gave way to joint-stock corporations and a new emphasis on private property *(Arrington 1958, 384)*. Farming continued to dominate Mormon activity, but individuals became more mobile and more unfettered in their business and personal activities *(Arrington 1958, 384; Peterson 1973, 267)*.

Religion and Mormon Values

Sociologists, historians and anthropologists who have studied Mormonism have all remarked on the strong Mormon cultural traits of cooperativeness, organization, dedication and adaptability *(O'Dea 1957, 187 f; Vogt and Albert 1966, 27 ff; Winn 1969; Nelson 1952, 50; Barnes 1913, 84, 87)*. These cultural traits derive from religious values and beliefs, and these values contributed to the Mormons' adaptive advantages in the Little Colorado region. Religious belief, practice and doctrine have always played a strong role in the lives of Mormons at individual and community levels *(Vogt and Albert 1966, 263; Tanner and Richards 1977, 99; O'Dea 1957, 261)*. Many observers note that early Mormons, and some even today, made no distinction between religious belief and secular activity; the latter, for all practical purposes, simply did not exist *(O'Dea 1957, 154)*. Through most of its pre-statehood history, Utah functioned as a theocracy. Church leaders at the highest levels directed land occupance and settlement patterns, and Mormon villages developed a distinctive landscape based on the plat for the City of Zion that church founder Joseph SMITH published in 1833 *(Francaviglia 1978a, 80)*. As more and more settlers arrived in Utah, the church directed them to new settlements and "called" leaders to organize such settlements *(Meinig 1965; Francaviglia 1978a, 91)*. By design, the new settlements, including those in Arizona, followed distinctive Mormon patterns: nucleated villages of large square lots with houses and barns, whence villagers commuted to their irrigated fields outside the village *(Arrington 1958, 354)*. Central church leaders also directed the economic activities of those settlements *(Arrington 1958, 355 f)*. Settlement leaders gathered locally every quarter and twice a year at church headquarters in Salt Lake City for religious conferences that also served to exchange economic information from throughout Mormondom *(Abruzzi 1987)*.

Some writers contend that in the early days the church had a greater impact as an organizing force than as a source of religious doctrine *(Tanner and Richards 1977, 99)*. But others *(Francaviglia 1978a, 91-97; Nelson 1952, 27 f)* have noted that the church's strong interest in local economic and developmental affairs clearly derives from religious doctrine, notably:

- The Mormons believed they had a divine destiny to fulfill.
- Their destiny included redeeming the Earth for the second coming of Christ.
- The work of the early Mormons aimed at preparing for The City of Zion, where the Latter-Day Saints would gather and whence Christ would rule *(Nelson 1952, 28)*.

Note that these characteristics conform with SOPHER's description of ethnic religions. In historical terms, O'DEA has asserted that the Mormons took then-prevailing American attitudes about land use, agriculture and economic development and made them religious doctrine *(O'Dea 1958, 86; O'Dea 1954)*. In other words, the church had a central theological reason for directing the economic and social activities of its followers, who believed their work fulfilled their own individual destinies, as well. The first settlers on the lower Little Colorado clearly considered their own destinies tied to the church's *(Tanner and Richards 1977, 12; Flake 1976, 54, 111)*. They followed the leadership of Lot SMITH, who established the communal United Order organization in the four settlements and insisted on following the Mormon agrarian principle to the letter. Indeed, some have argued that if Smith and his followers had given up on irrigated agriculture and taken up cattle ranching in 1876 they would have succeeded *(Tanner and Richards 1977, 34)*. Instead, the communities perished as dams washed away and crops failed *(Peterson 1973, 120)*. By many accounts, SMITH ruled the settlements tyrannically *(e.g. Peterson 1973, 102 f, 114; Woodruff 1882)*, and many Mormons left to seek better land and more pleasant company upstream.

SMITH denounced those who left, including William J. FLAKE, who, after incurring ostracism from SMITH and his followers for trading a community-owned cow to a hungry family traveling through, in 1878 bought a ranch on Silver Creek from James STINSON. SMITH said that FLAKE violated Mormon principles by striking out and buying property on his own, even though he intended to establish a new Mormon community. The Mormon apostle Erastus SNOW visited the area, heard FLAKE's account and not only approved of the purchase but helped build and gave his name to the resulting town of Snowflake *(Peterson 1973, 30)*.

SNOW's willingness to assist this new venture demonstrates the organizational flexibility of Mormonism, perhaps the sect's most important trait in its struggle to gain a foothold and survive on the fringes of its territory *(O'Dea 1958, 215)*. The Mormons' successful adoption of cattle ranching as a commercial enterprise in the 1910s reflects this adaptability as well.

Mormons and Cattle

The Mormons never eschewed cattle. Cattle accompanied them through all their migrations westward and played a part in the effort to develop a self-sufficient agrarian society into a holy land. William FLAKE had established a cattle ranch near Beaver, Utah, before he received the call to join the Arizona pioneers in 1876 *(O. Flake, 55)*. The Mormons used their cattle for beef and for dairy, but they kept them in the context of the self-sufficient society they tried so hard to establish throughout their domain. Individuals owned individual animals, but they grazed them on communal fields and herded them back to their barns in the farm villages at night *(Arrington 1958, 310)*.

In Arizona, the lower Little Colorado settlers established a dairy at Mormon Lake, some distance from the settlements on the river, in spite of excellent range conditions near the river *(Tanner and Richards 1977, 34)*. FLAKE devoted a lot of time to driving cattle, but mostly he brought herds of high-quality Utah cattle into Arizona to pay for his land purchases at Snowflake, Nutrioso, Springerville and Concho *(O. Flake, 120)*. A newspaper writer in the 1930s suggested an appropriate epitaph for FLAKE: "He bought ranches; he made them towns" *(O. Flake, 121)*. Clearly, while FLAKE knew cattle well and spent much of his life driving and herding them, he acted more as a land agent, with cattle for currency, than as a rancher.

On Silver Creek and the Upper Little Colorado River, cattle ranchers had already established themselves when the Mormons arrived *(Peplow 1958, 126)*. Except for a few in the Round Valley area *(Apache County Centennial Commission 1980, 174, 176 ff)*, the Mormon settlers who bought the ranches immediately began building dams, digging irrigation ditches and surveying town plots and small fields *(O. Flake, 86; Smith 1970, 233; Standiford undated, 95; Udall 1959, 76-77)*, obviously striving to extend the Mormon agrarian theocracy into Eastern Arizona. Towns like Snowflake had small co-op herds, which boys and young men tended on church-assigned rotations *(Fish 1936, 50)*. The herds provided the towns' beef and dairy needs, and in hard times, they provided occasional cash with the sale of a few head to the Army and to railroad crews at Holbrook *(Nielson 1886, 32)*. More often, cash-poor Mormons took jobs with the railroads or the cattle outfits *(Peterson 1973, 128)*.

But church leaders like Jesse N. SMITH, who had an early hand in the effort to provide contract Mormon laborers for the railroads *(Smith 1970, 249 f)*, recoiled from the effects of such work on the men, who "are profane and uncouth like those of our people who live by freighting" *(Smith 1970, 251)*. SMITH preached far and wide throughout the 1880s in support of agrarian values and self-sufficiency through home industry *(Smith 1970, 255, 269)*. Clearly SMITH delivered his message in the face of dwindling confidence that agrarian self-sufficiency could succeed. Mormons had already begun leaving their families on their marginal farms and taking more lucrative employment where they could find it *(Peterson 1973, 190)*. Church influence on land use had begun to diminish in Arizona even before 1890 *(Peterson 1973, 267)*. Then came the cataclysmic no-more-polygamy Manifesto of 1890. Most Mormon diaries and memoirs don't even mention it, which may indicate a high degree of spiritual confusion. To use SHIPPS' words, "it was such a disconfirming event that it thrust the Saints into the modern age. Interpreted in a phenomenological context, the very ambiguity of the historical accounts reflects an ambiguity that infects society as the natural and inevitable consequence of passage out of sacred into profane, linear, historical time" *(Shipps 1985, 126)*.

To use SOPHER's definitions again, the Manifesto marked the most significant moment in the Mormons' transformation from ethnic to universalizing religion. The Mormons' reaction to the Manifesto both demonstrated and strengthened the adaptability that has impressed most observers of Mormon culture and history. Even the Mormons themselves recognized that trait in the Manifesto, and for some at least, it has the effect of a religious principle. Writing 50 years later, William J. FLAKE's son defended the concept of polygamy as "a saving principle," but recognized that Mormons also must "obey the laws of the country in which we live, and when prohibitory laws were passed, God relieved His people of the requirement" *(O. Flake, 48 f)*.

After Polygamy

When the economy of eastern Arizona collapsed in the drought and national economic setbacks of the 1890s, the Arizona Mormons adapted, just as the church hierarchy had adapted to political realities a few years earlier. They became the dominant culture group throughout the Little Colorado and Silver Creek valleys. They dominated because they adapted to economic conditions, perhaps because they had persisted through poverty throughout their early settlement days. When beef prices rose before and during World War I, many engaged in profitable ranching. They even found ways to maintain their herds during economic downturns in the 1920s and '30s, by establishing dude ranches in the White Mountains *(Schauss undated)*, and Mormons continue to dominate ranching activity in the Silver Creek and Upper Little Colorado regions, grazing their herds on public land allotments and leased private land in the area *(Ericksen ed. 1987, 177)*. Just as the Mormon pioneers in Arizona faced the challenge of having to deal with non-Mormons, Mormon ranchers today face challenges to their livelihood and way of life that their immediate ancestors did not have. Concerns over the quality of public land used for grazing, demands for higher grazing fees for using public lands, and competition from other public land users all contribute to a growing sense of impending doom for the ranchers. For those Mormons whose fathers and grandfathers adapted by ranching and passed the ranch lands and grazing allotments on to them, these threats aim at the core values of the religious communities that persist in the small towns of Snowflake, Taylor, Springerville and Eagar. The field portion of my research took place in those towns in the form of interviews with and observations of some of the ranchers who trace their roots to the first Mormon pioneers in the Little Colorado region.

The purpose of this field research was to gain an understanding of personal religious beliefs and the perception the ranchers have of the role of religion in their livelihoods and in their attitudes toward land use, including public land policy. The field interviews also aimed at determining whether the Mormons persist today in ranching for economic reasons or because of the way of life ranching offers, as suggested by some researchers *(Smith and Martin 1970)*, and what value ranchers place on religion as a factor in the cowboy way of life.

Contemporary Mormon Values

The interviews with ranchers and their families revealed a number of strong values held in common that derive from the central role played by the church in their lives. These values influence social life, family life, economic behavior and perceptions of the land, for those who have or work large land areas. The key values include: family, work, devotion to God and a fear of losing their connection with God. The church stands as the source and center of Mormon values, and Mormons feel strongly that their elected church leaders represent the will of God for them. While some variations in personal beliefs occur among Mormons, several values emerge consistently and strongly among all of them.

First, all good Mormons place the highest value on the family. The family represents the nucleus of the community. Mormon doctrine encourages bringing children into the world to provide earthly bodies for spirits on their journey toward perfection. Some contemporary Mormons insist they do not feel a theological obligation to raise a lot of children, but children in some numbers play a significant role in the economic life of the family and the social life of the community for all. Most Mormons regard as their first priority, their highest obligation, the support and maintenance of the family.

Contemporary Mormon family values raise the question of the role of polygamy in Mormon doctrine. Many contemporary Mormons, like rancher Voigt LESUEUR of Eagar, Arizona, regard polygamy as a relic of the past, a frontier necessity to protect the widows and orphans who flourished in those pioneer days. He is delighted with the one wife he has. Rancher Dick UDALL, also of Eagar, believes his grandfather's nine wives were a real asset, producing not just children for him, but a ready and willing labor force in his far-flung freighting operations.

Other Mormon ranchers, though, like Sank FLAKE, still believe strongly that God's will includes polygamy, and that God gave the Mormons permission to abandon the practice in order to get along with the powers of the United States government. In the life to come - in the city of Zion - polygamy will be restored, FLAKE believes, and other Mormons quietly agree.

Second, Mormons place a very high value on work. This value also has theological roots. Mormons believe their role on Earth is to improve themselves by work as part of their own journey toward spiritual perfection in this and the life to come. Mormons believe that their spiritual destiny is to become gods themselves, and they believe they have an obligation on this Earth to work to improve the planet and the people in order to become worthy of that destiny. The ranchers all mentioned work and learning to work as among the most important values associated with their ranching activities. Shea FLAKE, a great-great grandson of William J. FLAKE, hopes to inherit his father's ranch near Snowflake so his children can learn the value of work as he did, by milking cows, driving cattle, branding and castrating calves. Although he hopes to become a Certified Public Accountant, Shea believes he learned his work ethic working on the land and with the animals.

The Mormon work ethic also appears strongly in the need to redeem the earth to the glory of God. Mormon doctrine stresses the importance of improvement in members' personal and spiritual lives, and the idea projects into views of the land as well. Land that does not work, such as wilderness areas locked up to development, is worthless land, according to rancher Dick UDALL whose cousin Morris was a vocal champion of vast wilderness areas during his long-time membership in the U.S. House of Representatives. Every Mormon rancher I spoke with, including the younger ones, agreed that the idea of a little wilderness is okay, as long as it doesn't interfere with the productivity of the land. Land, like people, should work and produce. That is doctrine. Voigt FLAKE says that every day he has in the back of his mind that he has to get something accomplished that day or he could lose it all.

Third, the Church represents the center of not only the Mormons' spiritual lives, but also their social lives in the small towns where the church dominates. Although the Mormons place a high value on free will, the dominant role of the church in community life gives the church enormous power to affect behavior. The most important tool in this regard is the threat of ostracism, or ultimately, excommunication from the church. William J. FLAKE departed the United Order colonies when his fellow settlers subjected his family to ostracism. FLAKE, of course, later redeemed himself in the eyes of the larger church. Even non-Mormons talk of suffering the ostracism of their Mormon friends in Snowflake when their behavior deviated from the norm. Connected with the power of the church is a common fear of loss - loss of connection with church and community, loss of connection with God.

One of the most important connections Mormons have with their church is the mission. Mormons proselytize heavily. The church calls people to serve missions at all stages of their lives, but especially young people. Missionaries pay their own way, often by raising money in their home communities, and they spend up to two years carrying the Mormon gospel throughout the world and converting people to latter-day sainthood. Missions have an extraordinary impact on the lives of ranchers, who often have to leave their ranch operations behind while spreading the gospel. Sanford J. (Sank) FLAKE learned much of what he knows about his cattle ranch by running his father's ranch while his father served a mission late in life. Sank left last spring with his wife to serve an 18-month mission in New Zealand; his son Shea has had to temporarily abandon the pursuit of his college degree in order to operate the ranch.

Also important in the life of the church and the community is the ritual importance of Sunday as a day of worship, fellowship and rest. Harold LESUEUR, a Mormon rancher who runs a herd of more than 300 cattle in the White Mountains of Arizona, once believed he could not ranch and be a good Mormon, because he felt he would have to miss too much church. So he did not take his own inheritance of cattle land when his father passed it on. He ranched in another state until he met his wife, a non-Mormon, and moved back to Eagar, Arizona, to take over her family's ranch operations near Mt. Baldy in the White Mountains. But Harold's son Voigt, who now does most of the ranching, has no difficulty meeting his obligations to his ranch, his church or his family. No other Mormon ranchers expressed any difficulty doing the same.

That may result partly from the nature of ranch operations in this part of Arizona. Mostly small, the pastures can all be reached by pickup truck within an hour or two from the ranchers' homes. Only if a cow is literally bogged in the mire should a rancher have to miss church because of ranch operations.

Fourth, the value of pioneer heritage stands out particularly strongly among the Little Colorado Mormon ranchers, who all trace their lineage directly to one or more of those first settlers with Lot SMITH or in one of William J. FLAKE's communities. Aldrice BURK raises the hay he uses for winter feed for his cattle on 130 of the 160 acres his great grandfather homesteaded in Springerville in 1880 when he arrived from Farmington, Utah. Sank FLAKE literally chokes up when he recalls the story of his great grandfather William J. FLAKE returning from his buying expedition just an hour after the death of his infant son. Dick UDALL recalls the persecutions and violence directed at Mormons that led to their crossing the plains to their ultimate home in Utah and the Great Basin.

Family histories are passed down in journals and in oral history, and even the younger FLAKES - Sank's son and daughter, Shea and Lily - know the legends of William J. FLAKE and his family's encounters with winter hardships, Indians and outlaws. These legends add a spiritual value to the land that matches its value as cattle forage. On the FLAKE's grazing allotments north of Snowflake, Sank and Shea often ride their horses into the country to find spiritual guidance to the daily questions in their lives: whether to marry, whether to borrow money to expand the ranch, what to say to a wayward child. Sank FLAKE recalls with tears in his eyes his mother's worries about his father when he had not returned from riding with the cows before dark.

FLAKE's father often returned late from riding with the cows because he could not begin riding with them until late in the day. Like nearly all the Mormon cattle ranchers in the region then and now, FLAKE's father had to work at a "regular" job each day to keep food on the table and clothing on his family's backs, not to mention to pay tithing to the church. Not only do the ranchers need other sources of income to survive, all of them must incur debts to operate their ranches, borrowing money against future beef prices to pay grazing fees and make improvements on the land. The Mormon church discourages its members from going into debt, but all the ranchers quickly point out that the church recognizes that members have to carry some indebtedness, as long as they have means to pay it off.

Nevertheless, the issue of debt prompts the serious question of why the ranchers stay in business. Ranching for most amounts to a second job, a job which usually forces them to go into debt. In addition, public land policies that affect the cattle industry, such as grazing fees on public lands and regulations to protect environmental quality make it harder and more expensive still for the ranchers to continue to put their cows on the land. Harold and Voigt LESUEUR had to move their 300 cows and their calves from the grazing allotment they have had for nearly 50 years so government officials could study a endangered willow tree in 1992. They don't know if they will ever get the old allotment back.

Other challenges for ranchers with summer grazing allotment in the White Mountains include competition with wildlife. They don't generally have problems with predators like wolves, coyotes, bears and mountin lions, as ranchers in other parts of the state do, but the absence of predators aggravates another kind of competition for those with grazing permits in the White Mountains: elk. The Arizona Game and Fish Department has allowed elk herds in the mountains to grow to what the ranchers believe to be oversized herds, and the elk compete strongly with the cows for forage.

Why, then, do the ranchers stay on the land? That question haunts them. Sank FLAKE points to his pioneer heritage. He believes that Mormon leader Brigham YOUNG called his ancestors to settle in Arizona and to stay, and he feels an obligation to do so. Yet, he left his family home in Snowflake to serve as a policeman in Phoenix for a number of years, before returning as sherrif of Snowflake in the early 1960s.

None of the other ranchers expressed any sense of obligation to Brigham YOUNG to stay on the land, and most wonder what will happen to their ranches when they die or retire. Dick UDALL's five sons all live far away, and only one has much interest in the ranch. Aldrice BURK has two daughters living in the Phoenix area, 200 miles away, and neither of them has any interest in taking over the operation, though Aldrice is ready to retire. Jake FLAKE and his brother have too many children and not enough ranch between them to divide up and leave working ranches to any of them.

Both Shea and Lily FLAKE, Sank's children, have an interest in the ranch and hope it will always be there, but their professions and their spouses' professions may make that impossible. Of all the ranchers' children studied in this research, only Voigt LESUEUR, Harold's 33-year old son, seems certain to continue in what he calls the cowboy business, and only Voigt makes almost all of his family's living by ranching.

What will happen if the Mormon ranchers fade from the landscape? The landscape will surely change. The family-owned ranches that have dominated the region for nearly a century have already begun to give way to subdivisions and to the big business operations of absentee, non-Mormon ranches. The towns themselves still boast barns and gardens and livestock in the big plots divided by the wide roads of the quintessential Mormon landscape. But non-Mormon newcomers have already begun to change that landscape as well, arriving for jobs in power plants and saw mills. In Springerville and Eagar, nestled at the base of the White Mountains, urban-based hunters and fishermen seeking recreation have begun to change the economies and will likely change the landscape as well.

The Mormons do not necessarily mind all the new activity. Power plants and saw mills, and even recreationists bring jobs, as long as they stay open. But non-Mormons come for those jobs, too, and they have recreational interests that the Mormon church, long the center of social activity, does not provide, from bars and pool halls to parties and dances not sponsored by the church. Voigt LESUEUR worries aloud about the "different type of people moving in, with lesser values or whatever." And Jake FLAKE, full-time rancher and bishop of the Snowflake Stake of the Mormon Church, thinks his community lost something valuable when the newly liberal school board abandoned the conservative dress code for the local high school.

The ranchers sense that change is inevitable, and a geographer knows that cultural changes will bring changes to the landscape. But the history of the Mormons includes a mass hegira across the Great Plains to escape persecution and the establishment of a powerful theocracy in Utah in spite of both human and natural oppression. The Mormons have always found ways to adapt, whether by giving up the practice of polygamy as a church or adopting cattle ranching as a survival strategy in Arizona. The Mormons have dominated their region in large part because of the powerful organizing force of the church, a force that is organized around deep religious conviction. This conviction has kept them successfully on the land and will probably continue to do so.

References

Abruzzi, W. S. (1987): Ecological Stability and Community Diversity During Mormon Colonization of the Little Colorado River Basin. In: Human Ecology 15(3); 317-338.

Apache County Centennial Commission (1980): Lest Ye Forget. Compiled by E. Wiltbank and Z. Whiting. Apache County Centennial Commission.

Arrington, L. J. (1958): Great Basin Kingdom: An Economic History of the Latter Day Saints, 1830-1900. Cambridge, Mass.: Harvard University Press.

Barnes, W. C. (1913): Western Grazing Grounds and Forest Ranges. Chicago: The Breeders' Gazette.

Ericksen, B., ed. (1987): Snowflake Stake Centennial, 1887-1987: A Story of Faith. Snowflake, AZ: Snowflake State President's Office.

Fish, J. (1936): History of the Eastern Arizona Stake of Zion and the Establishment of the Snowflake Stake. Typescript in collection of Arizona Historical Foundation, Arizona State University Library, Tempe.

Flake, O. D. (n.d.): William J. Flake: Pioneer, Colonizer. Title page missing.

Flake, Lucy Hannah White (1976): To The Last Frontier: Autobiography of Lucy Hannah White Flake. ed. by Roberta Flake Clayton (daughter). Mesa, AZ, by the editor.

Francaviglia, R. V. (1978a): The Mormon Landscape. New York: AMS Press.

Francaviglia, R. V. (1978b): The Passing Mormon Village. In: Landscape. 22(2): 40-47.

Isaac, E. (1962): The Art and the Covenant: The Impact of Religion on the Landscape. In: Landscape, 11 (Winter), 12-17.

Jackson, R. (1977): Religion and Landscape in the Mormon Cultural Region. In: Butzer, K. (ed.): Dimensions of Human Geography: Essays on Familiar and Neglected Themes. Chicago: University of Chicago Press.

Jackson, R. H., and Henrie, R. (1983): Perception of Sacred Space. In: Journal of Cultural Geography, 3, 94-107.

Jackson, R. H. and Layton, R. L. (1976): The Mormon Village: Analysis of a Settlement Type. In: The Professional Geographer, 28(2), 136-141.

Meinig, D. W. (1965): The Mormon Culture Region: Strategies and Patterns in the Geography of the American West, 1847-1964. In: Annals of the Association of American Geographers, 55(2), 191-220.

Nelson, L. (1952): The Mormon Village: A Pattern and Technique of Land Settlement. Salt Lake City: University of Utah Press.

Nielson, F. G. (1886): Diary of F.G. Nielson. Typescript in George S. Tanner Collection, Arizona Historical Foundation, Arizona State University Library.

O'Dea, Th. F. (1954): Mormonism and the American Experience of Time. In: Western Humanities Review, 8, 181-190.

O'Dea, Th. F. (1957): The Mormons. Chicago: University of Chicago Press.
Peplow, E. H. (1958): History of Arizona, vol 2. New York: Lewis Historical Publishing Co.
Peterson, C.S. (1973): Take Up Your Mission: Mormon Colonizing Along the Little Colorado River, 1870-1900. Tucson: University of Arizona Press.
Schauss, R. (No Date): Unpublished typescript. Richard Schauss Papers, Arizona Historical Foundation, Arizona State University Library.
Shipps, J. (1985): Mormonism: The Story of a New Religious Tradition. Urbana: University of Illinois Press.
Smith, J. N. (1970): Six Decades in the Early West: The Journal of Jesse N. Smith, 1834-1906. Provo, UT, Jesse N. Smith Family Association.
Smith, A. H., and Martin, W. E. (1970): Cattle Ranching - A Business or a Way of Life? Unpublished paper delivered at meeting of Arizona Cattle Growers Association, Aug. 7, 1970, Springerville, AZ.
Sopher, D. (1967): Geography of Religions. Englewood Cliffs, NJ: Prentice-Hall.
Standiford, J. H. (no date): The Journals of John Henry Standiford. Typescript on microfilm. Arizona Historical Foundation.
Tanner, G. S. and Richards, J. M. (1977): Colonization Along the Little Colorado: The Joseph City Region. Flagstaff, AZ: Northland Press.
Udall, D. K. (1959): Arizona Pioneer Mormon: David King Udall, 1851-1938, in collaboration with his daughter, Pearl Udall Nelson. Tucson: Arizona Silhouettes.
Vogt, E. Z. and Albert, E. M. eds. (1966): People of Rimrock: A Study of Values in Five Cultures. Cambridge, MA: Harvard University Press.
Winn, F. (1969): The Story of Lee Valley and Greer. In: Arizona Cattlelog. July 4-20.
Woodruff, W. (1882): Letter to Lot Smith. 23 Oct. 1882. Lot Smith Correspondence. Arizona Collection. Arizona State University Library.

Address of the Author

George Cathcart
News Bureau
Arizona State University
Box 871803
Tempe, AZ 85287-1803
USA

GISBERT RINSCHEDE

Geographical Aspects of Religious Broadcasting in the United States

Religion and telecommunication are both of significant importance in the United States. So it is not astonishing that both are closely connected with each other, closer than in any other country of the world.

As the American culture expands worldwide and within a few years different innovations are transferred to other cultural regions of the world, it is very interesting for me as a non-American to study this phenomenon a little bit closer. As a geographer I will, of course, try to emphasize the geographical aspects of religious broadcasting, especially of the religious TVevangelism. I propose to touch upon the history of religious broadcasting, current structure of TV evangelism, facilities at religious TV ministries and satellite networks, their regional distribution and their outreach, effects of religious television and the future of religious television.

Geographers have not dealt with this phenomenon so far. I became interested in this area when I did field research on pilgrimage in the United States at the end of the 1980s. Then in 1991 after the AAG-Meeting in Miami I visited most of the religious TVstations in the United States.

History of Religious Broadcasting

Religious Radio Broadcasting

On January 2, 1921, only two months after the first licensed radio station came on the air, a church worship service was broadcast in Pittsburgh, PA (KDKA). This was probably the beginning of religious broadcasting worldwide. The first regular religious broadcast was aired in Chicago in 1922 on WJBT. From these beginnings, religious radio grew quickly to become a small but solid portion of the early broadcasting industry.

In 1925 63 of a total of 600 stations on the air were owned by churches or other religious groups. In these early days, few regulations governed the broadcasting process and licenses were easily obtained, but not so easy to hold on to. Commercial broadcasting became the mainstay by the mid 1920s, and religious broadcasters were among the first to fall to this new competition, as religious stations were bought out by commercial concerns or failed financially during the Depression. Also contributing to religious radio's initial decline was the Radio Act of 1927 which favored commercial stations over religious ones, defining the latter as "propaganda" stations. In addition, their frequent lack of the necessary funds, equipment, and personnel made it difficult for many religious stations to survive.

In the 30s the model of religious broadcasting became largely one of mainline church services because the major networks (NBC, CBS and ABC) refused to sell time for religious broadcasting but at the same time donated time only to mainline church groups.

The more conservative evangelical broadcasters responded by purchasing time on commercial stations and paying the bill with contributions from listeners. Their association with commercial radio stations helped religious broadcasts to quickly become professional. Independent evangelicals were understandably concerned over the dominance of large organized religious broadcasting and formed the National Association of Evangelicals in 1942 and the National Religious Broadcasters in 1944 (NRB). This latter group is very active today and represents nearly all religious broadcasters in the United States.

Religious TV Broadcasting

By the early 1950s, television had replaced radio as the most popular mass medium. At first the religious community was slow to adapt to this change. A majority of the ministers did not even own a TV set.

It was the 57-year old Roman Catholic bishop, Fulton SHEEN, whose success convinced religious practitioners that TV could be a dramatically effective medium for "spreading the word and increasing the flock".

Through the mid-1960s, religious television continued to develop, but primarily as a forum for established mainline churches. Most of the time allocated to religion was still provided free of charge by TV stations and networks as part of their public service responsibility. The non-mainline evangelists were largely excluded. Most prestigious stations had a policy against "commercial religion" and refused to sell them time.

Beginning in the 1970s, however, there has been a trend toward a wider variety in religious broadcasting. Since then paid time programming has virtually taken over the religious broadcasting field as it was discovered that on-air request for donations virtually pay for all the costs of program production and distribution.

The Current Structure of Religious Television

Today the theological background of the "electronic church" or "electric church" - as it is called - is mainly charismatic and fundamentalistic, which means a return to basics: the Bible, the family, hard work, clean living and simple belief in God. They attack alcohol, sloth, swearing, crime, adultery, and communism, as well as religious liberalism and to some degree Roman Catholicism. In terms of style and technique we have seen five generations of electronic preachers:

- Billy GRAHAM represented the first generation. He used TVcameras in a relatively simple way in his mass meetings.
- In the second generation was Oral ROBERTS, originally a so-called tent evangelist and who later bought radio time. Later he brought the cameras into the tent, and finally moved out of the tent into a formal TV studio setting. Here ROBERTS offered to heal people right in their homes, if they would listen and place their hands on the TV set.
- The third generation developed in the 1960s with Rex HUMBARD, another tent evangelist, who built the first church studio in Akron, OH. His church services were basically TV productions.
- The fourth generation of the electric ministries is best exemplified by Pat ROBERTSON. He originally bought a UHF station and later became famous with his 700 Club with an applauding and laughing studio audience.
- The fifth generation of TV evangelists has recently emerged. They own TV networks feeding cable systems nation-wide via satellite like e.g. Paul CROUCH and his TBN-Network in Santa Ana, CA and Forth Worth, TX.

To this new generation of religious TV shows and TV evangelists belong:

- "The Hour of Power" with Robert SCHULLER, Garden Grove, Los Angeles, CA;
- "The World Tomorrow" from the World Wide Church of God, Pasadena, CA;
- "Oral and Richard Roberts", Tulsa, OK;
- "In Touch" by Dr. Charles STANLEY, Atlanta, GA;
- "Dr. James Kennedy", Fort Lauderdale, FL;
- "700 Club" with Pat ROBERTSON, Virginia Beach, VA;
- "It is written" with George VANDEMANN, Thousand Oaks, CA;
- "Mother Angelica", Birmingham, AL;
- and until recently "The Jerry Falwell Show", Lynchburgh, VA.

They all own a complete TV studio complex and church facilities which range from a small chapel to a monumental cathedral. Three of them (Oral ROBERTS, Pat ROBERTSON, and Jerry FALWELL) own a university each. Pat ROBERTSON manages a complete radio and TV satellite network (CBN) that, together with Family Channel, broadcasts on nearly 10,000 cable systems with a total of 45 million subscribers in the United States.

Altogether there are at least eight religious satellite networks, so-called inspirational networks:

- CBN / (The Family Channel): Pat ROBERTSON, Virginia Beach, VA (also with family programming)
- Family Net: Fort Worth, TX (till 1991 in Lynchburgh with Jerry FALWELL)
- ACTS: American Christian Television System, Fort Worth, TX
- EWTN: Eternal Word Television Network, Birmingham, AL (Roman Catholic/Mother ANGELICA)
- TNIN: The New Inspirational Network, Fort Mill, SC (David CERULLO) (formerly in Charlotte, NC)
- TBN: Trinity Broadcasting Network, Santa Ana, CA (Paul CROUCH)
- VISN: Vision Interfaith Satellite Network, New York City, NY
- CTNA: Catholic Telecommunications Network of America, Washington, DC

Three networks are strictly mainline (Roman Catholic/Presbyterian/Protestant). The rest are interdenominational or fundamentalistic.

They all send their programs partly via scrambled satellite signals to about eleven satellites such as: Anik E 1 (VISIN); Anik E 2 (The Family Channel); Galaxy I; Galaxy III (ACTS, EWTN); Galaxy VI (Family Net, Oral and Richard Roberts Ministries); Galaxy V (TBN since Febr. 1992); Satcom IV; Satcom F 1 R (TBN, VISN, The Family Channel, TNIN); Weststar 5 (CTNA); Spacenet 1 (Keystone) and Spacenet 3 (IN TOUCH).

Facilities at Religious TV Ministry Centers and Satellite Networks, their Distribution and Regional Outreach

Facilities at Religious TV Ministry Centers

The facilities of typical TV ministries do not differ too much. They all have a church like the "First Baptist Church of Atlanta" owned by the "In Touch Ministry" of Dr. Charles STANLEY on Peach Tree Street, or the "Coral Ridge Presbyterian Church" in Fort Lauderdale of Dr. James KENNEDY, or the "Crystal Cathedral" of Robert SCHULLER in Garden Grove, CA close to Disneyland *(see Fig. 1).*

Besides these churches or cathedrals they sometimes have smaller chapels. Directly adjacent to their facilities are the TV studio complex, choir rehearsal, concert facilities, assembly halls, a visitor center, kindergarten and a nursery complex *(see Fig. 2).* Schools of theology and music for training pastors, missionaries and church musicians are to be found there, too, like the "Knox Theological Seminar" in the Coral Ridge Ministry in Fort Lauderdale and the "Robert Schuller Institute for Successful Church Leadership" in Garden Grove. Since 1991 Robert SCHULLER has even built an open-air mausoleum with individual, companion and family crypts.

Facilities at Religious TV Satellite Networks

Some religious TV satellite networks originated in local churches that expanded to radio broadcasting ministries and finally to TV ministries and even TV networks.

One of the evangelists who began in this manner is Jerry FALWELL in Lynchburgh, VA with his Thomas Road Baptist Church, his "Old Time Gospel Hour", and The Liberty Broadcasting Network (later called Family Net) that now has been sold to ACTS in Fort Worth.

Fig. 1: Crystal Cathedral (Garden Grove, CA)

Source: Rinschede 1989

Fig. 2: Facilities of Coral Ridge Ministries (Ft. Lauderdale, FL)

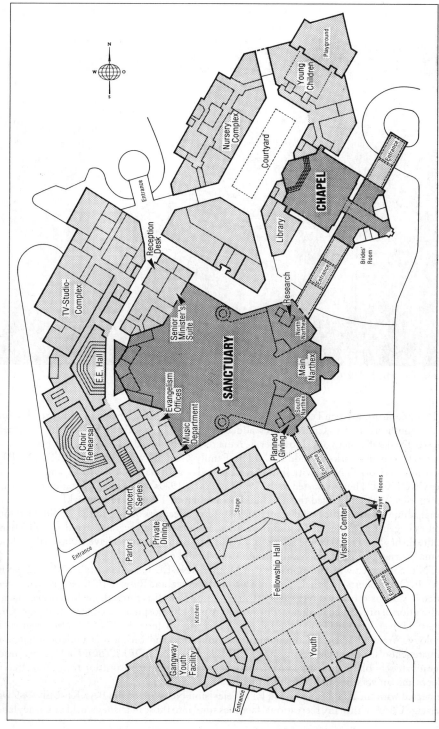

Source: Information from "Coral Ridge Ministries 1989"

Fig. 3: TV Studio and Satellite Dishes at Oral Roberts University /Oral Roberts Evangelistic Association (Tulsa, Oklahoma)

Source: Rinschede 1989

ACTS (American Christian Television System) in Fort Worth, TX started with radio broadcasting from a Southern Baptist Church, later added television broadcasting and finally became a national TV satellite network. However, it remains closely linked with local churches.
Other religious networks include CBN/The Family Channel with Pat ROBERTSON, PTL Television Network (TNIN) with Jim BAKKER (today with David CERULLO) and TBN with Peter CROUCH. They all started in the 1960s and early 1970s with single TV stations or at least TV experience which enabled them to build up a religious TV satellite network.
Special administrative offices and sometimes conference centers belong to the satellite network facilities in general besides all TVstudio facilities, and, of course, several C-Band and KU-Band satellite dishes *(see Fig. 3)*. Some religious TV ministries and networks have additional facilities like monastries, hospitals, universities and Disneylandlike recreational parks.
EWTN is connected with the monastery of Mother ANGELICA, the so-called "Broadcasting Nun". In Oral Roberts' hospital, "City of Faith and Medical and Research Center", patients were treated in various ways by direct spiritual intervention as well as through medical procedures, a combination of prayer and medicine. For various reasons his hospital closed a few years ago. Oral Roberts University (ORU) and the Liberty University of Jerry FALWELL offer degrees in Theology, Arts and Science, Communication, Education and Business at undergraduate and graduate schools. Regent University at the CBN Center of Pat ROBERTSON in Virginia Beach is a graduate school. Its students come to this evangelical Christian institution from 200 different colleges and universities after finishing their graduate degrees.
Connected with the PTL Ministry and PTL Television Network of Jim BAKKER till 1989 was "Heritage USA" with many recreational facilities similar to those in Disneyworld or Disneyland.

"Heritage USA", located not by chance halfway between Canada and Florida, was a major tourist attraction and all TV ministries are visited by a certain number of partly religiously motivated tourists. Oral Roberts University and his ministry, as the largest tourist attraction in Tulsa, are visited by about 250,000 persons a year. Other ministries are visited by up to 20,000 persons each year, partly in order to take part as the audience in religious TV shows.

Depending on the size of the TV ministry or network, up to 500 people work there e.g. 300 at EWTN in Birmingham, AL; 300 at Oral Roberts Ev. Assoc. in Tulsa and even 500 at TBN in Santa Ana, CA.

TV evangelists in general buy time on TV stations, cable systems, or networks. Sometimes TV evangelists like Pat ROBERTSON or Jerry FALWELL have their own networks. The Trinity Broadcasting Network also has a policy of directly buying low and medium power TV stations all over the USA in order to take part in the local cable system, too. The religious TV shows (with or without audience) produced in TV studios, are sent from the network via scrambled signals to the satellite transponder and received at their local self-owned TV stations and are finally distributed via cable systems or TV antennas to the households. But now Paul CROUCH is even renting new Ku-Band satellites and transponders, and reaches homes worldwide directly by satellite.

Regional Distribution of TV Programs and Networks

The regional distribution of certain TV programs and their networks in different TV and cable systems all over the country depends, of course, on the acceptance of the TV viewers. So the religious programs of ACTS - a satellite network of the Southern Baptist Convention in Fort Worth - are mostly concentrated in cable systems of the Bible Belt *(see Fig. 4)*. TBN, with a greater variety of programs from various TV evangelists, is concentrated in cable systems of the Northeast, Midwest, Southwest and California, where the network facilities are located. But in order to be closer to their audience in the Bible Belt they have moved part of their operation from California to the Dallas/Fort Worth area.

Mainline TV ministries like Robert SCHULLER or Dr. James KENNEDY are equally distributed in all parts of the USA The 745 cable systems of the Catholic EWTN, the fastest growing religious network in the USA, are concentrated in the most Catholic states of the Northeast, Midwest and Southwest and California although its TV facilities and monastery are located in Alabama, the center of the Bible Belt. VISN (Vision Interfaith Network), located in downtown Manhattan, is a non-charismatic and non-fundamentalist network that has been founded by cable systems of the USA in order to promote religious TV programming of mainline churches, especially of the Roman Catholic Church. Therefore its viewers are more or less concentrated in regions with a dominance of the Catholic Church, but also of the LDS Church in Utah *(see Fig. 5)*.

Nevertheless, the origin of the top 50 religious TV shows lies mainly in the southern parts of the United States. In the future the Dallas-Fort Worth area should achieve more prominence because TBN and Family Net already moved there a few years ago *(see Fig. 6)*.

The Effects of Religious Television

In general there are three major effects of religious television: these concern church attendance, money contribution and politics.

All studies that have examined the issue of "church attendance" have noted that piety and religious TV viewing tend to go hand in hand. On the other hand, the more time people spend watching secular network television programming, the less likely they are to read the Bible, to attend religious services or to identify themselves as evangelicals.

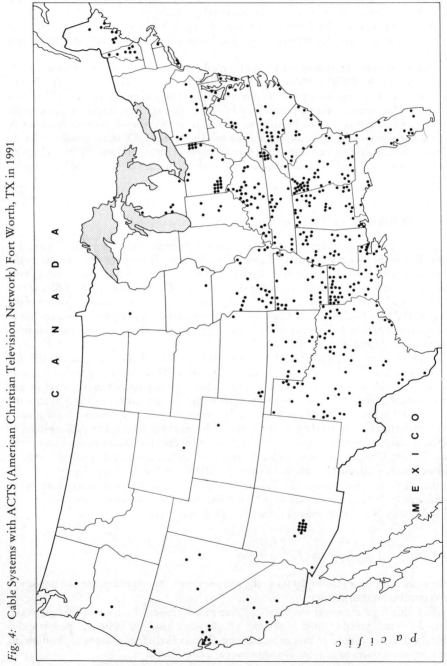

Fig. 4: Cable Systems with ACTS (American Christian Television Network) Fort Worth, TX in 1991

Source: Information from the Acts Affiliate Report 1991

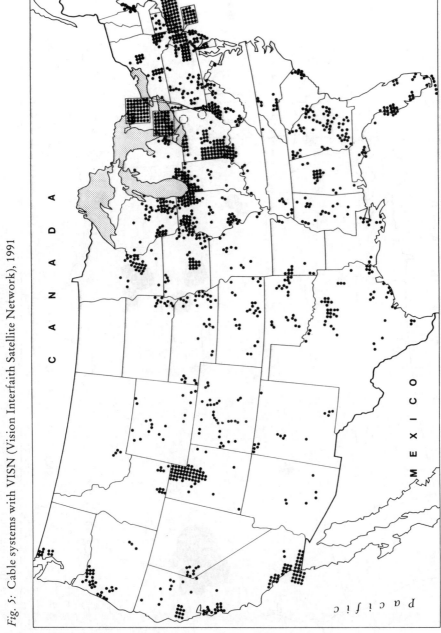

Fig. 5: Cable systems with VISN (Vision Interfaith Satellite Network), 1991

Source: Information from VISN, New York, 1991

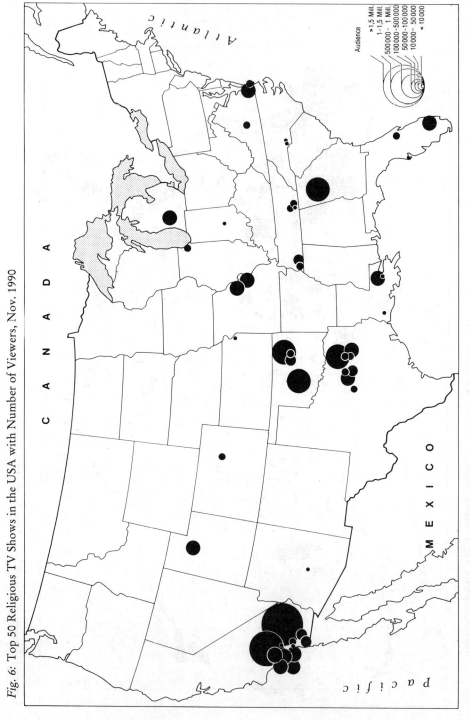

Fig. 6: Top 50 Religious TV Shows in the USA with Number of Viewers, Nov. 1990

Source: Information from "The Arbitron Company" and "Nielsen Research"

Fig. 7: Religious Broadcasting in the USA, 1972 - 1992

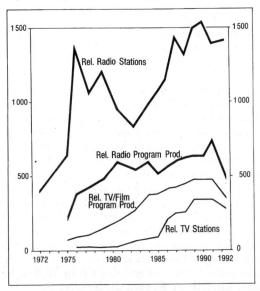

Source: Information in the "Directory of Religious Broadcasting 1992/93"

Fig. 8: Oral Roberts Weekly and Richard Roberts Live Audience, Nov. 1971 - Nov. 1990

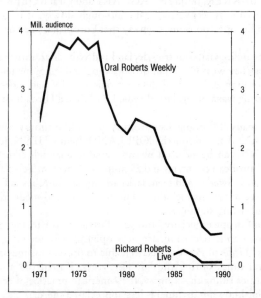

Source: Information from "Oral Roberts Evangelistic Assoc.," Tulsa, OK

The level of contributions to the TV preachers is, of course, a closely guarded secret. Especially the PTL scandal (the revelation that Jim BAKKER of the PTL Club had committed adultery and received a million dollar salary) brought to public attention the fact that television ministries were multi million dollar organizations depending on viewers for their existence. Later Jimmy SWAGGERT's confessions to moral lapses added new fuel to an already raging fire. Oral ROBERTS told his audience that God was going to take him "home" to Heaven if he did not gather eight million dollars for his hospital services by a certain date. In the following years after these scandals in 1987 the audience and the donations to many of the major television ministries quickly declined. To critics it appeared that tele-evangelism was more a business than a ministry. Even the number of religious TV stations and TV program producers dropped *(see Fig. 7 and 8)*. A couple of surveys have attempted to quantify and explain contributions of viewership. They found that one third of the respondents usually had made individual contributions averaging $ 30 (1984). Others found that the average donor is characterized as being "born again", being non-Catholic, being older and having little education.

Some television evangelists addressed current political issues and established specific political agendas on their programs. For example, Jerry FALWELL talks about evolution, prayer in the public schools, sex education and textbook censorship. During most of the 80s FALWELL led the "Moral Majority", a political organization espousing conservative causes.

Pat ROBERTSON speaks out on abortion, separation of church and state, and he left the 700 Club in 1987 to run for the Republican nomination for President of the United States. In the 1992 campaign he again became active for the re-election of George BUSH. At the same time Jerry FALWELL and Dr. James KENNEDY attacked CLINTON.

The Future of Religious Television

Religious TV broadcasting in the United States grew steadily until the late 80s, when it was halted by problems with Jim BAKKER, Jimmy SWAGGART and Oral ROBERTS. But after all these setbacks religious television is recovering again, although slowly. It is expanding in Western Europe and in Eastern Europe, too. Some even say that Europe has been or still is going through another Reformation.

The Netherlands, the Scandinavian countries, Iceland and Switzerland are the European countries with the longest experience with Christian broadcasting and religious television. In the more Catholic countries like France, Italy and Belgium religious TV had more difficulties because there private broadcasting was not legal until 1984. Until then all broadcasting had been strictly regulated.

Since then, however, many TV evangelists from America like Jimmy SWAGGART, Robert SCHULLER, Ernest ANGLEY, Kenneth COPELAND, Benny HINN, John OSBORNE and George VANDEMANN can be seen on private satellite channels like Superchannel (as of December 1993 in 22 European countries and 25 million homes) on Tele 5 (Munich), or Nordic Channel (only in Norway, Sweden and Denmark). Mainline Churches in Europe (Catholic and Protestant) also produce programs including church services and meditations, which are then shown on public broadcasting stations.

The nations of Eastern Europe especially Hungary, Poland or the former Soviet Union, which had state-controlled or public television, are now open to new media influences. So Robert SCHULLER with his "Hour of Power" has been able to present his message about Christmas on Russian TV several times during the last few years. But in the aftermath of so many authoritarian personalities ruling the country, the American practice of centering religious TV programs around a well-known individual is less appreciated there.

The changes in Europe will be more rapid than in the past because of the deregulation of public broadcasting in most of the countries in Europe, because of the direct reception of satellite programs by the cheap, modern small rooftop Ku-band satellite dishes (in contrast to the old expensive three-foot C-Band dishes in America), and, of course, because of the rapidly expanding cable systems all over Europe.

Summary

Religion and telecommunication are increasingly linked in the United States. This relationship is extremely obvious in the religious TV shows of the so-called "electronic churches". Their theological background is mainly charismatic and fundamentalistic. In terms of style and technique we have seen five generations of electronic preachers: Billy GRAHAM, Oral ROBERTS, Rex HUMBARD, Pat ROBERTSON and Paul CROUCH/Robert SCHULLER. Altogether there are at least eight satellite networks which send inspirational programs: CBN/ The Family Channel, Family Net, ACTS, EWTN, TNIN, VISN and CTNA. Besides the usual TV studios and satellite dishes, American religious TV ministries and satellite networks also own churches, chapels, assembly halls, administrative offices and sometimes theological seminaries, universities, hospitals, monasteries and even Disneyland-type recreational parks. Some ministries are large tourist attractions which are visited by up to several 100,000 persons each year, many of whom join the audience in the religious TV shows.
The regional distribution of religious TV programs and networks depends, of course, on the acceptance of TV viewers. So the more fundamentalistic and charismatic programs are mostly distributed in the Bible Belt. Programs of the Catholic church are concentrated in the Catholic states of the Northeast, Midwest and Southwest.
Religious TV strongly influences donations to the TV preachers, regular church attendance and even American politics. During the recent years its influence has been curtailed by various problems. But after weathering all these setbacks, religious television in the United States is slowly recovering again, is expanding worldwide, especially in Western and Eastern Europe.

Zusammenfassung

Religion und Fernsehen sind in den USA von besonderer Bedeutung. Insbesondere zeigt sich diese Verbindung in den religiösen Fernsehsendungen der sog. "Fernsehkirchen". Der theologische Hintergrund der "elektronischen Kirche" (electronic church) ist im wesentlichen charismatisch und fundamentalistisch. In stilistischer und technischer Hinsicht lassen sich fünf verschiedene Generationen von Fernsehpredigern unterscheiden, die durch folgende Persönlichkeiten charakterisiert werden:
Billy GRAHAM, Oral ROBERTS, Rex HUMBARD, Pat ROBERTSON und Paul CROUCH/ Robert SCHULLER.
Insgesamt gibt es mindestens sieben religiöse Satelliten-Gesellschaften (inspirational networks): CBN/The Family Channel, Family Net, ACTS, EWTN, TNIN, TBN, VISN und CTNA.
Zu den Einrichtungen der religiösen Fernsehzentren und Satelliten-Networks gehören in der Regel zusätzlich zu den Fernsehstudios und Satelliten-Sendeanlagen vor allem Kapellen, Kirchen, Versammlungs- und Verwaltungsgebäude, z.T. auch Theologische Seminare, Universitäten, Krankenhäuser, Klöster und Freizeitparks. Einige Fernsehkirchen sind größere Touristenattraktionen, die alljährlich von bis zu mehreren 100.000 Touristen aufgesucht werden, um in den religiösen Fernsehshows als Zuschauer teilzunehmen.
Die regionale Verbreitung religiöser Fernsehprogramme und Networks in verschiedenen Kabelsystemen hängt natürlich von der Akzeptanz der Zuschauer ab. So sind die mehr fundamentalistischen und charismatischen Programme im wesentlichen im sog. Bible Belt verbreitet. Programme der katholischen Kirche konzentrieren sich in den katholischen Staaten des Nordostens, Mittleren Westens, Südwestens und in Kalifornien.

Das religiöse Fernsehen hat in unterschiedlichem Maße auch einen großen Einfluß auf den Kirchenbesuch, das Spendenaufkommen der Fernsehprediger und auf die aktuelle Politik genommen. In den letzten Jahren ist der Einfluß jedoch nach verschiedenen Skandalen dramatisch zurückgegangen. Seitdem erholt es sich wieder, wenn auch langsam. Heute breitet es sich weltweit aus, vor allem auch in West- und Osteuropa.

References

Arbitron (1991): Television Market Report. The Arbitron Company.
Armstrong, B. (1979): The Electric Church. New York, Thomas Nelson Publisher.
Armstrong, B. (1985/92): The Directory of Religious Broadcasting. Morriston, NJ/Manassas VA, National Religious Broadcasters.
Biener, H. (1992): Aus der Frühzeit der "electronic church". In: Zeitschrift für Religions- und Geistesgeschichte, 44, 345 - 355.
Duke, J.S. (1981): Religious Publishing and Communications. White Plains, NY, Knowledge Industry Publishing.
Elvy, P. (1986): Buying time. The foundations of the Electronic Church. Great Wakering, Essex, McCrimmon Publishing Co.
Fishwick, M. and Browne, R.B. (1987): The God Pumpers. Bowling Green, OH, Bowling Green State University Press.
Fore, W.F. (1987): Television and Religion. The Shaping of Faith, Values, and Culture. Minneapolis, Augsburg Publishing House.
Frankl, R. (1987): Televangelism. The Marketing of Popular Religion. Carbondale, Southern Illinois University Press.
Horsfield, P.G. (1984): Religious Television. The American Experience. New York, Longman.
Lloyd, M. (1988): Pioneers of Prime Time Religion: Jerry Falwell, Rex Humbard, Oral Roberts. Dubuque, IA, Kendabe/Hunt.
Nielsen (1991): Nielsen Station Index. Nielsen Media Research.
Religious Broadcasting. The Official Publication of National Religious Broadcasters, Various Volumes. Parsippany, NJ and Manassas, VA.

Address of the Author

Gisbert Rinschede
Institut für Geographie
Universität Regensburg
93040 Regensburg
GERMANY

BURKHARD HOFMEISTER

From Log Cabin to Edge City

Introduction

"From log cabin to edge city" stands for four centuries of town planning and town building in the United States. Any comprehensive treatment of this topic would have to include the history of building materials and house construction methods, architectural styles, the functions of individual buildings as well as of specific urban localities. This can, of course, not be achieved in a brief paper.

Instead, I should rather like to touch upon a few important aspects of town building in the United States with special regard to the contrast of traditional and modern traits. Modern traits of the nineteenth and twentieth centuries spreading rapidly all over the country have made these cities look rather uniform and monotonous. On the other hand, older traits of the seventeenth and eighteenth centuries that have been more or less well preserved to the present day are apt to underline regional variations in urban morphology.

Colonial Traits

Thus the sun-dried bricks and the construction of roofs with vigas are characteristic of the adobe house of the Southwest. These traits have survived to the present day in the so-called Pueblo Revival Style as it is found in Santa Fe and other towns of the former Spanish-Mexican sphere of influence of the south-western United States.

In the British colonies of the Atlantic coast, wooden structures were predominant. In the very early days settlers lived in simple huts covered with sod which were more primitive than the long houses made of bent young tree trunks covered with strips of bark as they were used by the Powhatan and other Eastern tribes *(Upton 1986, 18f)*. Eventually the New England settlers constructed their saltbox houses and the Virginia settlers their tidewater cottages and similar types of timber houses. Half-timber was generally avoided because of the greater temperature amplitudes causing cracks in the timber frame.

It was the log cabin, however, that was to become the dominant house type throughout the East and the Midwest. It made its first appearance in 1638 in the Swedish colony on the banks of the Delaware River, "but it remained for the Germans to establish log construction firmly in the New World" *(Noble, 1984, 41)*.

The log cabin underwent two simultaneous cycles of development. Made of solid logs in the beginning, it was, not before long, constructed with beams tied to each other in various manners. Since the 1830s, after standardized and mechanically fabricated nails had become available, it developed to the American balloon-frame house made of boards laid in overlapping rows like the tiles of a roof cover.

Under Dutch influence the porch was added to the log cabin. It was usually found in the front. The side porch or Charleston porch, also referred to as a piazza, is a unique feature of the houses in Charleston, SC. It was very likely introduced by British immigrants from Barbados *(Noble, 1984, 62)*. In modern houses the porch has, according to KEIFFER *(1992)*, moved from the front to the back, where it has often been enclosed for privacy. At the same time the family room, now also located at the rear, has become the center of the house.

The British added the fireplace to the log house. Since the early 18th century, instead of the central fireplace, two fireplaces were located at the gable walls, thus enabling the perfect symmetry of houses in terms of the Italian architect Andrea Palladio and making for a house type referred to as the "I-house".

There were also regional differences in street patterns and the layout of open space. In New England towns the meetinghouse was located right next to the "common" or "village green" which was usually surrounded by an irregular street system. In many towns the common survived as open space by virtue of its functioning as cow pasture until the 1830s and as military training grounds in later years.

In the meetinghouse religious and adminstrative functions of the early settlements were combined. After independence, the principle of separation of church and state made two different buildings necessary which, however, used to be located right next to one another as we find it, for instance, in Hadley, MA.

As BOESCH *(1957)* pointed out, the United States during her colonial period was an area of convergence of the grid-pattern town. According to imperial ordinances the Spaniards created a central square or "plaza mayor" that was not only the focal point of the grid pattern of streets but also the pivot for the spatial arrangement of urban functions as well as the social order of residents. The French also applied the grid to urban settlements such as New Orleans or St.Louis. The British only occasionally adopted the grid for places such as New Haven, CN or Philadelphia, PA or Savannah, GA. According to VANCE *(1977)* and FRANTZ *(1987)* the British founders drew upon the French bastides in the cases of Salem, MA, Providence, RI or New Haven, CN, upon the European mercantile town in the case of Philadelphia, PA, and upon the Renaissance town in the cases of Williamsburg, VA and Savannah, GA. Savannah got a unique pattern with 24 squares being integrated into its grid.

The Trustees of the Colony of Georgia were familiar with the so-called "London towns" of the Ulster Plantation, but there was very likely some influence from New Haven and Philadelphia, since Savannah's founder General Oglethorpe had relations to William PENN's son Thomas *(see Fries 1977)*.

The Young Republic

After gaining independence the United States turned, in want of representation and self-expression, to ancient Roman and Greek building traditions. While the Renaissance had a strong influence in the British Isles and, to a certain degree, on the British settlers overseas, Presidents Thomas JEFFERSON and Andrew JACKSON played a major part in the creation of the Roman-inspired Federal Style and the Greek Revival Style respectively. JEFFERSON, being oriented toward Republican Rome. participated in the design of the University of Virginia, of the Capitol Building and L'ENFANT's plan for the City of Washington. Washington's Capitol Building was then copied by the vast majority of the several states. JACKSON and the Democrats found their ideal in Greek democracy and felt great sympathies for Greece's struggle for independence. Thus numerous public and private office buildings came to look like Greek temples, particularly in the area west of the Appalachians along the Ohio River *(Fitch 1968, 90 ff)*. There is, for instance, a conspicuous contrast between the temple-like Main Post Office and the nearby modern multi-storey Federal Building in downtown Denver, CO.

Since British North America, which only in the second half of the 19th century was to become the Dominion of Canada, still remained a part of the British Empire, the Federal and Greek Revival Styles were limited to the United States, thus making for one of the differences between Canadian and U.S. cities *(Goldberg and Mercer 1986)*.

At this point I should like to draw the attention to a very recent development referred to in the literature as New Formalism or Neo-neo-Classicism. One of its representatives is the Japan-based architect Yamasaki. His neoformalist architecture culminated in the temple-like design of the Northern Life Insurance Company Building executed in Minneapolis in 1962-1964.

Urban Preservation

Despite her comparatively short history the United States has made great endeavours during the last decades toward historic preservation. Preservation has been practised on three political levels. The National Park Service as a branch of the U.S. Department of the Interior is in charge of the National Register of Historic Sites, which is kind of a national inventory of sites and buildings to be preserved on the national scale. In the early 1970s the federal government pushed the governments of the several states to elaborate frameworks for historic preservation programs on the state level. Under the condition of completion of such state-wide programs prior to a certain deadline, the respective states were eligible for matching funds from the federal government. Aside from those federal and state programs, many cities got their local Preservation Societies that, by means of revolving funds, buy decaying buildings of historic value and/or located within historic districts, declared as such by historic zoning in order to privatize them and sell them to buyers willing to restore them. The income from such sales will then be used for purchasing more buildings, so that the same procedure could go on.

The objects of historic preservation are of two different kinds. There are many single buildings that might come under the category of industrial archaeology. Examples are the Cannery or Ghirardelly Square on the waterfront of San Francisco Bay or Trolley Square in Salt Lake City. The latter used to be the city's old trolley depot that was no longer used by the transit authority and that was ready to be torn down. It was, however, saved and converted to a leisure park with numerous boutiques, restaurants, and even half a dozen movie theaters. All these objects have become major attractions to tourists and residents alike.

On the other hand there are groups of buildings in the old historic districts often bearing the cultural traits of a particular ethnic group, as for instance, the King William Area in San Antonio, Texas. Probably the largest old town in the former British colonies is Colonial Williamsburg, capital of the then colony of Virginia. More than four hundred houses including the Capitol Building, the Governor's Palace, and the College of William and Mary have been carefully restored to their colonial appearance since 1929 by means of the Rockefeller Foundation. Approximately two thirds of the maintenance costs are provided by the craft shops and restaurants in the restored buildings selling their products and services to the tourists while the lacking third is still donated by the Rockefeller Foundation.

Industrialism and the Skyscraper

The rectangular land survey system established by the Land Ordinance of 1785 was, according to BINDER-JOHNSON *(1976)*, a late adaption of the ancient Roman centuriation system. The section of one square mile was its basic unit. In consequence, the grid became the universal pattern of the land as well as of all newly- founded towns. Open squares, however, were not in high esteem with the exception of the courthouse square at the county seats. Maybe this was due to the fact that most of the new towns came into being during the railroad era and many of them were built around the railroad station rather than around a central square. The functions usually oriented toward the central square of European cities were absorbed by the main street. As HALL *(1966, 163)* put it:

> "The Spanish plaza and the Italian piazza serve both involvement and polychronic functions, whereas the strung-out Main Street so characterstic of the United States reflects not only our structuring of time, but our lack of involvement in others".

The major portion of the 19th century was termed "industrialism" by FITCH (1968). It was a period of preparation of something quite new in American architecture. The construction of factories made two things necessary: wider spans and greater strength. New building materials like iron and steel were used for factories as well as for railroad stations and exhibition halls where large unobstructed floor areas were needed. This innovation caused, according to FITCH, discrepancies between the technical and aesthetic aspects of architecture. I shall refer to this later in this paper.

In 1857 Elisha OTIS developed the passenger elevator. Steel and the electric elevator were the technical prerequisites, the expanding economy with the increasing spatial separation of administrative functions from processing functions was the economic prerequisite for the construction of the skyscraper.

The skyscraper was the first indigenous achievement of American architecture. It may also be considered a symbol of the American way of life or, to be more specific, of the American ideology of growth and progress. Moreover, each company's power was reflected in its office building. It is not suprising that the first skyscraper was the office building of an insurance company. Nor is it surprising that the skyscraper in 1885 made its appearance in Chicago. This city had suffered from a great fire in 1871 and was just in the process of being reconstructed. And this was to a much higher degreee a commercial center than New York City which was more important, but much more multifunctional as compared to Chicago.

The two negative arguments against the skyscraper, that is to say: the damage done to people's health due to lack of light and ventilation in buildings and streets, and the enormous concentration of people and traffic congestion, were put forward during a meeting of the Architectural League in 1894, less than a decade after the first skyscraper had been built. In New York City a *Commission for the Revision of Building Codes* and a private organization called *Committee of Congestion of Population* eagerly discussed height limits and other measures against multi-storey buildings.

In 1892 the 105 m high Pulitzer Building surpassed Trinity Church by ten meters. The Woolworth Building erected in 1910-13 imitating the Victoria Tower of the Houses of Parliament in London was soon called "The Cathedral of Commerce". The Equitable Building, with its 39 storeys and 100,000 sq.m. of rentable office space, occupied a whole block in Manhattan and, at the winter solstice, cast a shadow of 7 1/2 acres. In 1915 the City of New York responded by releasing its zoning ordinance of 1916 that made so-called setbacks or slim towers on wider pedestals obligatory. Soon other cities followed New York's example *(Kaufmann 1970, chapter 3).*

After World War II modern skyscrapers up to over a hundred storeys were allowed to rise straight toward the sky under the condition that ample space on the ground-floor level was provided for the public in the form of arcades or little yards with fountains and some shrubs or trees. The multifunctional megastructures consisting of a number of high-rise buildings and appropriately called "town-in-town" might be considered a variant of this way of constructing skyscrapers in recent years.

As to architectural design, however, Old World traditions were to last till mid-century. Whereas the famous Chicago architect Louis SULLIVAN vehemently argued that new modes of construction require new ways of architectural design and that the skyscraper should reflect "American impulses", the majority of American architects stuck to historical traditions.

The World's Columbian Exposition held in Chicago in 1893 with its 150 buildings constructed under the supervision of Daniel H. BURNHAM and John W.ROOT, many of these buildings had been erected in the Renaissance Revival Style, was particularly responsible for many American architects decorating their skyscrapers with columns, cupolas, and turrets even throughout the 1920s and the 1930s.

In the case of the above mentioned Woolworth Building, its future owner had shown the architect a photograph of the Houses of Parliament in London. European architects soon got excited and participated in skyscraper design. While HOWELL's and HOOD's neogothic design of the Chicago Tribune Tower was executed in 1922 it was the design by the Finnian architect Eliel SAARINEN placed second that was to influence American skyscrapers for many years to come.

Towards the end of the 1920s the Art Deco Style originally developed in Vienna came into high esteem with American architects, New York's Chrysler Building being an outstanding example. This style was soon followed by the so-called Streamline Moderne which even Frank Lloyd WRIGHT, whose basic creed was anti-European, adapted for his administration building of the Johnson Wax Company in Racine, WI (1936/1939).

The Twentieth Century

In contrast to the colonial period and the first 150 years after independence, many urban elements have had their cradle in the United States and have, with a shorter or longer time lag and usually to a much lesser degree, been transferred to other continents. They have obviously been related to the comparatively early and very high degree of private car ownership in the United States. Such urban elements include the motel, the shopping center, the mobile home court, the industrial park, and the business park.

One of the most striking features of almost every large or even medium-sized city was the appearance of so-called commercial strips along major arterial roads. They are characterized by numerous gas stations, auto repair shops, drive-in restaurants, drive-in banks and all kinds of drive-in businesses and, of course, the motel.

The motel dates back to the year 1913 when in Douglas, AZ miners' cottages no longer used for the laborers involved in mining operations were converted into guest rooms for travellers. It was not only the convenient location outside the city center, however, that led to the success of this new type of accommodation, but also the two advantages, associated with it: at least one parking space for each guest room is provided, and the relation between management and guest is rather informal and reduced to registration upon the guest's arrival. Food is usually not served; there may be a restaurant next door under separate management.

Due to these advantages, motels mushroomed during the post-war period, while private car ownership between 1945 and 1965 tripled from 25 to 75 million. Since the 1960s the motel was introduced to the city center as a means of revitalization in the somewhat modified version of the downtown motel.

In more recent years urban expressways connected to the Interstate Highway system have become tough competitors for the commercial strips by diverting through-traffic from local highways. Signs indicating "easy return to expressway" could not really stop the downward trend of the commercial strip that has, to a certain degree, become obsolete.

The shopping center is a completely different type of organization of retail and service functions. Like the commercial strip it caters for the car-driving clientelle, the largest regional shopping centers providing approximately 10,000 parking spaces. The shopping center also dates back to comparatively early times, the first of its kind being the Country Club Plaza in Kansas City, MO, opened in 1925.

Since that time shopping centers have undergone several changes. Firstly, the functions have become so manifold that besides retail outlets and services a modern regional shopping center offers entertainment such as restaurants and movie theaters, sports facilities of various kinds, a hotel for tourists, and public services such as a post office, a fire station, a police station etc. The term shopping center is thus very misleading.

Secondly, older shopping centers used to have a somewhat strip-like arrangement of the various retail and service functions in a number of separate buildings and may be considered kind of an imitation of the commercial strip. Modern shopping centers are of the plaza type with a huge, air-conditioned central building complex surrounded by thousands of car parking spaces.

The shopping center also appeared in the downtown as a means of revitalization in the modified form of shopping gallerias. In some city cores the shopping galleria was located underground, in others it was erected over a former street now cut off for traffic. In some cases it was integrated into the evolving network of skyways that connect downtown retail and office buildings on the first floor level for the convenience of pedestrians who need not cross streets on the street level and are thus protected from vehicular traffic as well as from adverse weather conditions. As a certain contrast, San Antonio's Paseo del Rio or Riverwalk created a "separate pattern one level below downtown San Antonio" *(Attoe and Logan 1989, 143)*.

The mobile home court made its appearance as early as 1929 when seasonally employed laborers were accommodated in trailers. Since then mobile home courts were set up at many construction sites to house laborers for a limited period of time. Since World War II ever growing numbers of Americans, especially newly married couples with small budgets and retired people no longer willing to maintain a big house and garden, moved to mobile home courts. The latter in paricular moved to the sunshine states of California, Arizona, Texas and Florida.

Around 1980 one in twenty dwelling units used to be a mobile home, and at present some ten million Americans are permanent residents of mobile homes.

Many city adminstrators have wrongly argued that people living in a mobile home are a vagrant element of the population and have, by means of zoning regulations, banned mobile home courts from the city proper. This is why clusters of mobile home courts are often found along major arterial roads right outside the city limits.

The industrial park is another element of the urban periphery. The Central Manufacturing District of Chicago, dating back to the first decade of the century, is considered the first industrial park of the United States. At the beginning of World War II there were just about thirty industrial parks in the entire country. Again, this urban element rapidly spread during the post-war period. It is characteristic for the situation in the United States that the vast majority of industrial parks were founded by private railroad companies on their premises no longer used for railroad operations.

Whereas many industrial parks also accommodated service functions, the tide of founding industrial parks was over by 1970. From then office or business parks appeared on the urban periphery. The degree of suburbanization of service functions has now reached high percentages in many U.S. cities. In the extreme case of Atlanta, GA no less than 70% of total office space within the metropolitan area is offered outside the central city.

Free-standing shopping centers and some residential estates often served as foci for new business parks. This development of modern peripheral settlements has been referred to as "urban villages". An urban village is characterized by medium population densities exceeding those of the traditional suburb dominated by single family homes, but considerably lower than those of the central city. It is further characterized by medium numbers of residents in the order of a quarter million. Also in this respect the urban village ranks somewhere between the traditional central city and the traditional suburb. Such city size is considered appropriate for the support of a regional shopping center, a 200-room hotel, and certain cultural functions.

Very often such new urban nuclei referred to as "edge city" by Joel GARREAU *(1991)* are located at intersections of a circulating beltway and a spoke of the Interstate Highway and urban expressway systems. For this reason MOON *(in Janelle)* called them "interchange villages". There may be two reasons for this typical location: firstly, to provide easy access for a great number of customers to the shopping center, and secondly, to enable office workers to easily communicate with downtown offices, for it has been proved that, despite all progress in telecommunication, immediate personal contacts are still vital for many business transactions. The more than two hundred edge cities developing on the outer peripheries of U.S. metropolises are about to become a constituent element of today's American urban landscape.

Conclusion

U.S. cities were, to a high degree, shaped by Old World traditions till about 1880, whether it was by means of cultural transfers by certain immigrant groups, or by deliberate reference to the Eurpean heritage.

The first indigenuos achievement of American architecture was the skyscraper that since 1885 began to transform downtown America. But even then reference was made to Old World traditions inasmuch as American architects decorated their skyscrapers with columns and cupolas.

Since World War I the United States has been the pacemaker as to urban design and planning. U.S. cities have been the first to see the appearance of such new urban elements as the commercial strip, the motel, the shopping center, the mobile home court, the industrial park, and the business park. Since mid-century the USA has made great endeavours to preserve her urban heritage. In an effort to revitalize the urban core, planners have adopted such elements as the motel or shopping center to the downtown, albeit in modified versions. This is why today we often find traditional and modern elements in close vicinity in the downtown areas of U.S. cities.

Zusammenfassung

Bis in die achtziger Jahre des vorigen Jahrhunderts war das Stadtbild in den USA von altweltlichen, teils antiken Traditionen geprägt, sei es aufgrund spontaner Übertragung durch Einwanderergruppen, sei es durch Rückbesinnung auf das europäische Erbe.

Die erste wirklich eigenständige amerikanische Leistung auf dem Gebiet der Architektur war der ab 1885 aufgekommene Wolkenkratzer. Aber selbst er wurde noch bis in die dreißiger Jahre dieses Jahrhunderts mit gotischen oder barocken Stilelementen versehen.

Erst nach der Jahrhundertwende wurden die USA mit neuen städtebaulichen Elementen wie dem Industriepark, dem commercial strip, dem Motel, dem shopping center, dem mobile home court und dem business park weltweit tonangebend. Während sie vor allem die Vorortzonen prägen, weist der Stadtkern noch häufig eine kolonialzeitliche Old Town oder zumindest einzelne historische Bauten und Platzanlagen auf, die sich hier in enger Nachbarschaft zu modernen Elementen wie dem downtown motel oder der shopping galleria finden.

References

Binder-Johnson, H. (1976): Order upon the Land. The U.S. Rectangular Land Survey and the Upper Mississippi Country. New York.
Boesch, H. (1957): Schachbrett-Texturen nordamerikanischer Siedlungen. In: Hermann-Lautensach-Festschrift, Stuttgart, 337-344.
Fitch, J.M. (1966): Vier Jahrhunderte Bauen in USA. Berlin/Frankfurt/Wien, Ullstein-Bauwelt Fundamente 23.
Ford, L.R. (1983): Architecture and the Geography of the American City. In: Geographical Review, 73, 324-340.
Frantz, K. (1987): Die Großstadt Angloamerikas im 18. und 19. Jahrhundert. Wiesbaden/Stuttgart, Erdkundliches Wissen 77.
Fries, S.D. (1977): The Urban Idea in Colonial America. Philadelphia.
Garreau, J. (1991): Edge City. Life on the New Frontier. New York.
Goldberg, M. and Mercer, J. (1986): The Myth of the North American City. Continentalism Challenged. Vancouver.
Goldberger, P. (1984): Wolkenkratzer. Das Hochhaus in Geschichte und Gegenwart. Darmstadt.

Hall, E.T. (1966): The Hidden Dimension. New York.
Hofmeister, B. (1971): Stadt und Kulturraum: Angloamerika. Braunschweig.
Hofmeister, B. (1977): Die Erhaltung historisch wertvoller Bausubstanz in den Städten der USA. In: Die Erde, 108, 129-150.
Hofmeister, B. (1985): Die US-amerikanischen Städte in den achtziger Jahren - Probleme und Entwicklungstendenzen. In: Klagenfurter Geographische Schriften 6, (= Festschrift für Elisabeth Lichtenberger).
Kaufmann, E., ed. (1970): The Rise of an American Architecture. New York.
Keiffer, A. (1992): Bigger, Better and Faster: Technology and the Spatial Reorientation of the American Family Home. In: 27th International Geographical Congress, Proceedings. Washington, D.C., 186-187.
Moon, H. (1992): The Interstate Highway System. In: Janelle, D.G., ed.: Geographical Snapshots of North America. New York/London, 425-427.
Noble, A.G. (1984): Wood, Brick and Stone: The North American Settlement Landscape. Vol. 1 Houses. Amherst:
Upton, D., ed. (1986): America's Architectural Roots. Washington, D.C.
Vance, J.A. (1977): This Scene of Man. The Role and Structure of the City in the Geography of Western Civilization. New York.
Whiffen, M. and Koeper, F. (1981): American Architecture 1607-1976. Cambridge.

Address of the Author

Burkhard Hofmeister
Institut für Geographie
Technische Universität Berlin
Budapester Straße 44/46
10787 Berlin
GERMANY

MICHAEL P. CONZEN

The Moral Tenets of American Urban Form

America has no great capital city, whose direct or indirect influence is felt over the whole extent of the country; this I hold to be one of the first causes of the maintenance of republican institutions in the United States.... Cities may be looked upon as large assemblies of which all the inhabitants are members; their populace exercise a prodigious influence upon the magistrates, and frequently execute their own wishes without the intervention of public officers.

Alexis de TOCQUEVILLE (1835)

The drive to develop large cities and the lessening of the difference between city and country are two of the most important 'trademarks' of our time. North America, this wonderland of modern civilization, has ... run ahead of the Old World with regard to these two tendencies.

Friedrich RATZEL (1876)

Die amerikanischen Städte stehen in viel engerer Abhängigkeit von geographischen Verhältnissen als die Städte Europas. Der Grund dafür liegt teils in der viel grösseren Beweglichkeit der amerikanischen Bevölkerung, teils in dem geringeren Alter der Siedlung.

Albrecht PENCK (1905)

American urbanism as a modern phenomenon - that is, as a set of built environments and as a way of life - has been changing more profoundly in recent decades than perhaps at any time in its earlier development[1]. Urbanized territory is shifting ineluctably from a pattern of largely isolated and *monocentric* fields of local residence and daily interaction toward a continental network of loosely connected but dynamic *polycentric* fields. In this shift, old notions of centrality and peripherality are rendered obsolete or at the very least are being fundamentally redefined. More Americans now live in zones of so-called 'suburbs' today than in conventionally-defined central cities or rural areas. Observers now question whether, historically, America has passed from a long *city* phase and has now entered a *post-city* era (*Boulding 1963; Webber 1968*). In considering whether this is the case it seems worthwhile to look backward in order to look forward, and in particular to examine what common threads of origin and formative character have been woven into the longterm fabric of American urbanism, and whether some defining characteristics are being lost or discarded in the current transition.

There exists no universally accepted model to explain the rise of the distinctive geographical character of American urbanism. A great deal has been written on the geography of American cities, but most of this fits a normative perspective oriented to understanding current spatial structure and interaction. Such work grows out of a tradition of ecological research which presumes that American conditions somehow represent universal modern behavior, and that that behavior is predicated upon functional rationality (*Harris and Ullman 1945*). American geographers have been slow to acknowledge that American urbanism, while developed from European roots, early gained characteristics which set it apart sometimes sharply from those of it parent culture[2], and that this, at its most fundamental, requires understanding in the context of national ideology. Even European attempts to delineate the special geography of the American city have concentrated more on socio-economic, political, and morphological characteristics than on the philosophical system which underlies them (*Hofmeister 1971, 1982; Lichtenberger 1981*).

The twighlight of the geographically discrete, centered city in America

Americans do not build cities anymore. There still are cities in the United States, of course-over 3,000 of them, if one accepts their legal and political status as municipalities, a term which allows more than a few glorified towns and villages also to be included. But Americans certainly are not creating new geographical cities anymore, and it is debatable how many they are even trying to maintain. This proposition concerns 'cities' as culturally complete, functional entities in a traditional, historical sense. In this view, cities are large, corporate communities with extensive, differentiated land use zones unquestionably focused upon a central business and ceremonial core, representing the interests of both the urban residents and those of the surrounding rural territory as spatially discrete members of a broader, regional system of urban places. This definition perhaps still applies to cities in most regions of Europe, notwithstanding the rise and spread of conurbations. But in America the superconurbation that Jean GOTTMANN baptized as *Megalopolis* a quarter-century ago has in the interim become interregional and, in the eyes of many, well-nigh ubiquitous (*Gottmann 1961*). With the new forms have come new names, and today we stagger under the terminological flamboyance of such labels as Peirce LEWIS' *Galactic Metropolis* or Lutz HOLZNER's *Polis Amorphos*, products of the critical counterurbanization Brian BERRY has so adroitly documented (*Lewis 1983; Holzner 1985; Berry 1976*). And if Americans are actively deconstructing their traditional cities as the latest communications revolution redefines the nature and location of production, work roles, and service delivery, one might ask not only what new forms of pseudo-urban settlement will result, but what will be the future character of American urbanism as a way of life. Whether we conclude that it will be an evolutionary modification of current patterns or a radical transformation with unanticipated complexion, it is tempting to enquire, particularly in periods of wrenching change, whether or not there are some fundamental geographical dimensions to the American brand of urbanism that will endure despite the flux, and which perhaps will, and do, guide the course of change in ways not superficially recognized.

To pose a problem of this kind is in some ways to run counter to an orientation long dominant in Anglo-American urban geography. That orientation has been to conflate or put beyond consideration the significance of regional cultures in explaining Western urbanism and urbanization in the interest of generalized process models operative for any advanced non-command economy and society[3]. Levels of economic integration and media-borne cultural exchange are assumed to be so high between, the British Isles, Continental Europe, the United States, Canada, Australia, and New Zealand, for example, that conceptualizations of urban process and form developed with evidence from one of these realms would be considered readily applicable to another. Efforts to explain the contemporary social and land use patterning of Manchester, Birmingham, or Calcutta in the 1960s by resort to BURGESS's and HOYT's models of fundamentally Midwestern American urban ecology (based on 1920s-era Chicago) are enshrined in print. Research in social science-oriented urban geography in Britain and America was long unmindful of, or at best uncomfortable with, the implications that cultural history and modern urban anthropology hold for cross-cultural comparative work.

Happily, things have been changing. No less a figure than BERRY himself announced a conversion of sorts in his *Human Consequences of Urbanization*, recognizing as it did divergent experiences attributable to cultural heritage (*Berry 1973, xii*). The rising interest among human geographers in political economy, structuration theory, and what has been called the 'cultural turn' is enlarging for some the role that national differences in political institutions and social organization play in the urban process. And the appearance in North America of several studies of regional urbanism suggest that cultural differences do matter, and that disregard for them significantly limits, if it does not invalidate, important research findings extrapolated beyond their relevant regional contexts (*Ward and Radford 1983; Agnew et al. 1984; Goldberg and Mercer 1986*). Embedded predilections in Anglo-American urban geography have resisted the premise that American cities have been shaped by fundamentally distinctive social forces in western civilization which are better not confused with or substituted for those operating in European, and specifically British, urban evolution.

So why, then, consider the 'American-ness' of American cities? What makes the topic worthwhile is that the American city has always been regarded as highly dynamic, and that this dynamism is worth emulating. The United States' modern global presence exerts powerful pressures on other nations to examine their own economic and social systems in the light of American practice. Whether advantageous or not, the comparative analysis this inspires cannot be useful without treating the implications of differences in cultural development. It is the more challenging in the case of American urbanism because the influences, while not overtly political, are transmitted through channels enlarged by the many bonds of a common cultural foundation (including language in the case of Britain), and accelerated by the modern imperatives of multinational corporate shaping of a global exchange economy. This exploration, then, is not intended as an antiquarian search for the unique, nor does it denigrate the substantial similarity of values, outlook, and urban living preferences between the United States, Britain and other 'western' cultural realms. Histories interwoven with common threads of mercantilism and industrialism have insured a rich 'interplay of transatlantic orbits' (*Gottmann 1986*). The point is that the communities and urban landscapes of America and its kindred western cultures are not identical and interchangeable, nor are the ever-changing value systems that account for them necessarily recognized with ease.

Geographical perspective on American urbanism

What has been said, then, by geographers and others of the generic character of American cities? Although a single composite picture from the observations of numerous commentators is always open to dispute, the following attempt seeks to include the most-cited features[4]. At the abstract level of cities considered as a network or general grouping in space, the American system of cities is preeminently young. It is a large system, with many members extremely large, and the group as a whole functionally diverse, while at the same time being morphologically rather monotonous. Equally significant, however, is the lack of strong urban primacy, and the relegation of political capital functions to one of the lesser Eastern centers. In modern times the cohesion and importance of relations between cities and their immediate hinterlands within regional subsystems have declined, while at the same time interdependencies have grown among cities occupying the upper levels of the national urban network. These features remind us of several 'baseline' circumstances that have conditioned the system's evolution: the comparative recency of its colonial origins; the highly unified national political framework covering so large a territory; the abundance of natural resources, including vast open land; and the high degree of technological development, especially as applied to the achievement of time-space convergence.

If we can begin with this systemic context, what, then, about the localized character of urban places? Here is a brief checklist of urban qualities. American cities are distinguishable by their generally simple physical layouts, based on repetitive implementation of classical grid-iron concepts. The urban profile is dramatically segmented on the one hand into a 'downtown' core of great building height and density that usually stands on the site of the city's historical kernel, though its oldest fabric has long since disappeared; and on the other hand, a vast penumbra of mostly low-density land use and building patterns, with an overwhelming bias towards single-family residential construction. At the outer edges of the urban mass a broad zone of intermittent development is strewn seemingly at random among vacant land parcels and fields whose days are numbered-a mixture ranging from the mostly built-up semi-order of the suburbs to the anarchic scatter of protoplasmal exurbia. Everywhere the overwhelming influence of the car is seen, most notably in the density of freeways, the ubiquity of drive-in facilities, and the scarcity of mass transit infrastructure. The exceptional density of the urban core and the surrender to the automobile in the rest of the city have produced those classic symbols of American urbanism, the skyscraper (by virtue of the elevator), the motel, the commercial strip, the suburban shopping malls, and the mobile home park. Characteristic of much of the building ethos in American cities is the rapid obsolescence of physical construction and the flimsiness of materials and assembly in the overwhelming majority of structures built with short life-expectancy.

Turning to key aspects of economic and social geography, the American city is distinguishable by the dominance of business in its landscape-the bias of the 'downtown' towards retail and commercial services, the subdued presence of public institutions and activities, and the paucity of in-town open space and pleasant areas. Even beyond the downtown, businesses have become established almost anywhere that can be made profitable, casting doubts on the efficacy of land use zoning laws. Social patterns reflect a heterogeneous mixture of ethnic and racial groups, themselves strongly segregated into more-or-less homogeneous neighborhoods in central city areas, while in the suburban realm wealth differences have re-formed the upwardly mobile into status and life-style-differentiated homogeneous communities. Separated by race, most American urban blacks still inhabit great wedges of the inner city that now reach out sectorally to the outer suburbs. Public housing is grudgingly included among housing options, which its warehouse architecture appropriately reflects. Governmentally, American metropolises specialize in 'balkanized' political jurisdictions, with a plethora of legally independent cities, suburbs, and special governments that range the gamut from parks, to water, sewer, and school provision, flood protection, and judicial districts. Crime and gun-supported violence are considered preeminent city pathologies, health services are almost universally provided by private corporations, and most cultural offerings, with the exception of libraries, are institutionalized for profit, and through the support of private philanthropy.

This is an altogether too sketchy review of the generic characteristics of the American city, and it in no way portrays an articulated vision of how the whole settlement works together. But the emphasis is on American peculiarities, and their externals need not necessarily cohere, as long as they hint at deeper cultural regularities. How, then, have scholars sought to account for those special features of American cities just summarized?

Explaining the geographical dimensions of national urban identity

Unfortunately, very few geographers have concerned themselves with the *identity* of American cities. We have voluminous accounts of urban spatial structure, population movements, historical development, and even morphology, produced in a *normative* tradition in which underlying social assumptions remain implicit but unexamined and comparative context is ignored. Those who have adressed issues of identity have usually done so by counterposing American cities against a generalized European tradition (*Lichtenberger 1981*). Peirce LEWIS, for example, in his galactic tour of urban America, points out that cities there have throughout history and for political reasons been systematically deprived of the most potent of metropolitan functions-as centers of military, political, religious, and educational power-and have been culturally impoverished thereby (*Lewis 1983*). It is not that these functions are absent in cities, but that so much crucial decision-making power was deliberately dispersed to small centers in the hinterlands for safe keeping: state capital towns, remote military bases, small college towns, all well removed from the main arteries of commerce. There have been compensations, though, as the hundreds of small town colleges had students reading Plato and Shakespeare, learning calculus and microbiology far from the distractions of big cities, while little state capitals drew in country lawyers and groomed them for the rigors of national government in Washington.

Another point of view is expressed by those who place American urban evolution in close juxtaposition with European developments, such as David WARD and James VANCE. WARD stresses the common intellectual debates that industrialism and modernization sparked on both sides of the Atlantic, and from this it is hard to tease out 'the American difference' (*Ward and*

Radford 1983). VANCE's position is more distinct, for he is at pains to point out how rapidly American development 'caught up' with European, how ingenious Americans proved to be in the process - and from so early on, how fortunate American cities have been not to inherit limiting traditions, and how superior American urbanism has come to be in providing so many 'options' for individual improvement and material comfort (*Vance 1978*). He ascribes these blessings to the American ability to accomplish goals practically rather than doctrinally. Putting this alongside his spirited defense of urban sprawl, and his view that attacks on "the borrowing of English planning" to stem the process are "shameless and unthinking" and "an alien concern for Americans," one is put in mind of J. Wreford WATSON's characterization of the American "breakaway mind" (*Vance 1977, 359-360; Watson 1979, 154*). For all VANCE's belief in American pragmatism as the cardinal explanation for American differences in urban form, his interpretation relies on a pungent American ideology - economic liberalism.

It was in fact a Dutch geographer in 1962, during a period of growing rejection of ideographic and regional study in North America, who offered the first detailed study of American urban geography couched in the language of cultural analysis. In *American Cities in Perspective*, G. A. WISSINK attempted to explain the specific character and, from a European point of view, wasteful process of urban fringe expansion that Vance and other apologists have so stridently championed (*Wissink 1962*). For WISSINK, the United States offers a unique case study of a cultural system giving rise to a national type of city through the operation of its space-related values, objectives, instruments, and institutions. He outlined four principal American attitudes underlying the urban process: 1) a sentiment favoring a rustic way of life "on one's own," 2) a particular conception of space and distance, 3) an assumption that there is or should be plenty of everything for everybody, and 4) that America is always on the move in time and space. These attitudes are combined with a set of specific instrumentalities - among them technology devoted to mass production, especially of the car, sustained prosperity filtering down to broad segments of the population, great municipal autonomy, and extreme prevalence of economic motivation - and these produce a cultural system "in its space-relatedness" that is young, expansive, optimistic, hugely prosperous, rich in resources, technologically advanced, liberal-democratic, capitalistic-individualistic, and change-oriented.

A decade later Wilbur ZELINSKY developed a more articulated conception of the "central values of American culture" the urban applications of which can easily be derived. Most important is the cultivation of intense, anarchistic individualism, based on a heroic self-image of the lone, self-reliant, upwardly striving character who assumes equal rights and is comtemptuous of tradition and authority. This personality, through such stimulants as the Protestant Ethic and the Success Ethic, can achieve great freedom and material well-being, but only at the price of considerable psychological insecurity. Manifestations of this orientation can be found in attitudes toward government, and how this has shaped American cities. Rampant individualism fears authority and accepts government only as a necessary nuissance to be kept as weak and compartmentalized as possible. The so-called 'balkanization' of local government and inherent duplication of services that entails in a metropolitan setting is a natural outcome. Another manifestaion is an anti-urbanism that derives from problems of crowding and density that call for community solutions that abridge individual freedoms. The flight to the suburbs can be seen classically in this light, as a removal from a thicket of problems housed in a contentious, unappealing environment devoted solely to economic gain, and a retreat to the balm of a simpler, more homogeneous environment closer to nature.

Second in this cultural scheme is the high esteem accorded mobility and change. Americans welcome change and newness. Their sense of process is strong, that of structure weak. Immediate time is valued, historical time is not. "What visible evidence is there," Zelinsky asks, "that New York City has existed continuously for more than 340 years?" (*Zelinsky 1973, 54*). For Americans, time is obstructed by space, so that one goes to great lengths to conserve time by consuming space, hence the 'godliness' of spatial mobility, in which travel becomes the object, never arriving but always on the way. Jean-Paul Sartre summed up the urban outcome succinctly: "For [Europeans] a city is, above all, a past; for [Americans] it is mainly a future; what they like in the city is everything it has not yet become and everything it can be" (*Sartre 1955, 112*).

Third among crucial American traits is a mechanistic world-view. The notion that the world is a simple, mechanical system subject to human control leads to a utilitarian attitude and a belief in efficiency (for the good of the machine). Utilitarianism, of course, denigrates abstract thought and aesthetic experience, and has frequently been invoked to explain the ugliness of vernacular streetscapes in American cities. Utilitarianism is also related to a love of quantification, which in American terms has not only produced the love affair with gridiron street plans but encouraged the affection for giantism that glories in skyscrapers and a predilection for superlatives of all kinds. Finally in ZELINSKY's pantheon of traits there is messianic perfectionism. The belief that Americans have a special mission to realize the dream of human perfectability has produced a certain optimism and enthusiasm about changing existing conditions. While this has most often been applied to the drive for creation of a 'Middle Landscape,' a secular paradise representing, in ZELINSKY's words, "a bucolic mixture of wilderness and urbanity," resulting in overreverence for rural and small town retreats, it has also underlain the many phases of urban reform in which moral degradation could be attacked through manipulation of the physical environment (*Ward 1989*).

WISSINK's attempts to define the American cultural system in relation to the form of American cities and their expanding fringe areas, together with ZELINSKY's discussion of selected aspects of moral philosophy and personal ideology particularly representative of American outlook offer interesting points of connection in the overall search for the 'American-ness' of American cities, but they tend to assume that cultural conditioning rises fully-formed into action. While it would do neither justice to imply they see no historical development of the cultural system, their own formulations do not permit us a sufficiently dynamic view of this central concept. John RADFORD has gone a step further and offered an historical interpretation of the link between ideology and regional urban identity in a brief but stimulating comparison between the emerging moral orders that governed approaches to urbanization in the Canadian province of Ontario and the American South during the nineteenth century in which the transatlantic Victorian ethos developed (*Ward and Radford 1983*). The conservative, deferential, moralistic society of Ontario placed class and community above individualism, reflecting its continued ties with Britain, and represented an evolution in which the technical order may have been American, but towns remained focal points for Victorian British social attitudes. The American South, on the other hand, solidly under the control of rural planter interests found itself before the Civil War increasingly at odds with laissez-faire values and industrial-urban progress in general. Despite the war and its aftermath, the South's distinctive class structure persisted and what urban development occurred was heavily molded by the continuing rural planter 'aristocracy.' In RADFORD's view the rapidly urbanizing American North should be seen as 'hyper-Victorian' in the sense that the openness of society and the general breaking down of old social construction and restraint left competition as the sole sorting mechanism for people and towns alike. The dominant American moral order, therefore, was a universalistic-achievement value orientation which sanctioned competition. Ontario, the closest inheriter of a more 'normal' Victorian ethos, and the American South, upholder of a 'counter-Victorian' ethos, increasingly defined their identities in reaction to the larger, more aggressive, mainstream American one. This regional schematization begs for broader examination.

The rise of an American moral order

The issues raised by these interpretations of the American settlement experience should by now have suggested that in searching for the roots of 'American-ness' in urban patterns it is necessary to establish a framework for examining the prevailing cultural system, for isolating key ideologies working within that system over time to guide the development of specific practices and preferences that resulted in the accumulation of the characteristic forms that distinguish the American city today. Those roots take us back into the nineteenth century, in particular to the period of early nationalism when Americans were struggling to articulate a rationale for independence, a self-conscious policy for peoplehood, and a strategy for their turn at continental colonization. From the early decades of the century through to the Civil War in the 1860s city growth became intertwined with industrialization, and its impact on those who shaped the moral order became more urgent and reciprocal. Before this period American cities were too few and small to represent anything but simple colonial extensions of British urban models. By the end of the nineteenth century most of the cultural dimensions that determined the further development of American urban character were already set. Are there links between what nineteenth century political theorists saw as the central values of their society and the physical characteristics of the cities they created and bequeathed to the modern era? Links occur in three distinct spheres of what ultimately emerged as the American Victorian Consensus: republicanism, perfectionism, and domesticity.

Political independence from Britain and the formulation of a written constitution brought on an intensive effort to set the United States on a course of social development different enough from the experience of Europe to justify the momentous break. The new ideology rejected many English and Continental social and political traditions and rested on the freedom of the individual as critical to the development of mankind. This freedom would be enshrined in property ownership as the bedrock of stability. The greatest potential threat to such freedom would come from the concentration of power, especially as exercised through government but indeed from any single group in the polity. The best defense against this eventuality lay in the civic virtue of the citizenry, thus raising a concern for the idea of 'commonwealth' (*Appleby 1986*). At first, such ideas caused cities to be viewed with suspicion and hostility. To the Founding Fathers, Thomas JEFFERSON most notably, cities were strongholds of the idle rich and havens for the mob-both groups a threat to republican security. Consequently, cities were marginalized from the beginning in the developing apparatus of national government.

As the century progressed, however, republicanism merged with a belief in 'liberal capitalistic individualism' that honored the progress of individuals from rags to riches, even if that occurred in urban settings. And of course it was happening most dramatically in cities. The new nationalism was fiercely competitive with Europe, and many accomplishments in science, arts, and education came in the new nation's cities, where the emphasis was on popular participation and an acceptance of profit as a legitimate goal, even in the erection of institutions geared to public welfare. Whereas in the early nineteenth century property was seen as the means to acquiring liberty, by mid-century this equation was becoming reversed: liberty was seen as a guarantee of gaining property (*Howe 1976*). Alexis de TOCQUEVILLE maintained that general economic equality was the best mechanism for upholding liberty; therefore all efforts should be bent to the preservation of economic equality-too powerful a concentration of wealth could destroy the republic.

As economic equality declined, especially in the cities, the arguments changed and economic *opportunity* became the key. By mid-century and after (the Civil War notwithstanding) the survival of the republic was a fact, so more important were the rising issues concerned with community in the context of more obvious class differences. Thus we see anti-urban thought coming to terms with cities in American life, but as unattractive, if necessary, components of the economic system. Cities might add to wealth, and to individual betterment, but could not be granted broad discretionary powers. In such a light, cities not surprisingly accumulated a host of physical, social, and political problems, a dilemma that Sam Bass WARNER, Jr., has identified as the problem of 'privatism' in urban corporate evolution (*Warner 1967*).

Another important strand in American ideology that emerged in these years was the doctrine of perfectionism. Born of the bourgeois evangelicalism that grew with the rise of the new industrial middle class, this view held that society could be perfected (just as the Utopians claimed the perfectability of Man). Because of this belief, no one individual is locked into a position in life, and therefore all have a duty to improve themselves and others. Many felt that the city could be used as a means of assisting in this process. As Daniel Walker HOWE has noted, "These people were trying, very self-consciously, to humanize the emergent industrial-capitalist order by infusing it with a measure of social responsibility, strict personal morality, and respect for cultural standards. They thought of themselves as preserving certain patrician values while democratizing their application" (*Howe 1976, 12*). Hence HOWE's short list of Victorian moral innovations: prohibition, prisons, and prudery. But more significantly, the American Victorians' chosen methods of social control and social reform, given the pre-modern heritage of violence, centered on various forms of persuasion (in preference to coersion) and this meshed with economic motives to stunt and delay the development of governmental mechanisms to deal with urgent municipal and welfare problems.

And thirdly, in this nexus of Victorian values, was the emergence of a cult of domesticity. Republicanism depends on the public virtue of the citizenry to make the state workable. By the 1830s Americans were already seeing numerous 'men-on-the-make' who might unbalance the basic credo of political stability. The answer was to educate the youth to become decent and responsible citizens while they were on the make. This called for dividing personal life quite precisely into the work sphere and the domestic sphere. If not much virtue could be found in the former, it could be generated with a vengeance in the latter. The home became a haven and a repository of virtue-by persuasion and through the exaltation of motherhood (*Howe 1976, 25-27*). Not only did this aid in saving the psyche of the competitive businessman by supplying him with domestic order and tranquility, it came to assume a central role in the theory of the nation. The implications for urban form and character were, once again, the reinforcement of social values and relegation of civic consciousness-raising to the private sphere (*Hayden 1981*). If this pattern was apparent also in Victorian Britain, its effect was nevertheless mediated there by the survival and strength of historical community institutions and habits of thought, whereas the American pattern was played out on a thinner institutional base. Additionally, the cult of domesticity placed growing pressure on upwardly mobile families to reflect their changing socio-economic status in constant residential mobility and conspicuous consumption, with clear implications for residential homogeneity and segregation (*Ghorra-Gobin 1992, 86f*).

Effects of the moral order on the geography of the city

These appear to be the outlines of a rapidly developing moral order in the first half of the nineteenth century, the structure and power of which set the tone for and defined the limits of public and private initiative in city-building in America. To these fundamental conditions of thought and behavior most of the peculiarities enumerated earlier can, through one set of intermediary relations or another, be traced. There is space for perhaps only one illustration: the workings of the land market as it shaped the morphological development of urban and suburban districts.

Urban property in America, like rural, has been from the outset overwhelmingly freehold, reflecting republican values, thereby facilitating rapid change in ownership and use. Historically, it has also been widely dispersed among a multitude of urban actors. In Boston in 1853 the 50 largest landholders together held less than one percent of the central area of the city. Rarely would an American town in the nineteenth century comparable in size, for example, to Cirenchester, England, have had to depend for its areal expansion on the whims of five or six agrarian land holders around its margins. In most cases, landowners within or at the edge of American cities ran the risk of premature rather than restricted development policies (*Cornick 1938*). The freedom of tenure joined with the rectilinear simplicity of a national cadastral system to encourage very loose forms of urban development.

Checkerboard street-block and plot patterns appealed to the republican mind in search of urban design concepts drawn from politically more attractive classical rather than medieval roots, and endowed with self-evident egalitarian and utilitarian properties. The physical results reinforced the individualistic value system: while early national town plans made provision for courthouse squares because they symbolized the decentralization of governmental power to the level of countless county seats, there were generally no other public spaces set aside. There was no assigned market place, and business was free to colonize the city map wherever individuals saw fit. Small town business districts often did form around the courthouse, though there are numerous examples of such districts abandoning the courthouse in favor of streets leading to wharves and railroad stations. All classes of land use, from shops to factories, residences and institutions, bid for locations within the plan and the outcome, though not indiscriminate, was untidy. Victorian Americans recognized the social disutilities and even the economic inefficiencies of a purely market mechanism in land use ordering, but for the whole of the nineteenth century they could find no way around the enormous rigidities of physical layout and philosophical commitment (*Conzen 1980*).

Urban extension into the periphery was particularly revealing of the subjugation of community efficiency to individual freedom of action. As neighborhoods built up at city's edge, the multitude of landowners on the fringe were at liberty to subdivide their rural property for sale as urban building plots at any time, in any fashion, and without coordination. It was common in Victorian America to leave the responsibility of building homes to the purchasers, thereby sharply separating the process of land division and sale from that of actual building and utility provision. At the scale of the 'plat,' that is, the subdivision plan unit of a single owner, large districts emerged in which 'plats' were strewn about without necessary contiguity or relation to existing roads. Homer HOYT's formidable study of Chicago's land development history showed how extensive such practice was from the city's beginning. This was classic suburban speculation, in which monotonous fragments of prospective residential development cropped up in the grid-iron countryside, each with their own internal layout logic, and succeeded in forming a functional system only by good luck or painful subsequent adjustment (*Hoyt 1933*). Add to this the normal process of scattered house-plot purchases by individual families staking out their claim to the new suburban lifestyle to which their improving incomes gave access, and we conjure up a scene of extreme, superficial, spatial disorder-though set within a generally unimaginative geometry (*Conzen 1990*). Often such a landscape derived from the speculation of streetcar company syndicates who deliberately operated lines at a loss in order to lure new residents to the subdivisions along them.

Subdivisions usually did multiply and fill up the gaps, and likewise homes sprang up one by one to fill the 'plats,' but the process was so casual and could be so episodic over time that industry or commercial intrusions could easily alter the social prospects for neighborhoods overnight. Many a suburban tract displays today a scattering of large, ornate, older homes sharing blocks with younger, meaner housing-testimony to the failed expectations for neighborhood status and the inherent principle of *caveat emptor*. Of course, the first owners of the well-to-do homes would not have stayed long but rather exercised their priviledge of mobility to find other birds of the same feather. Many districts, of course, built-up with more homogeneity than this, and elite families could always control the quality of their residential environments through sheer wealth. But the middle and working classes could depend on less security, and much less environmental quality than they could have expected under even a modicum of coordinated planning.

Sam WARNER blames these shortcomings on privatism: "Privatism encouraged the building of vast new sections of the city in a manner well below contemporary standards of good layout and construction. Privatism suffered and abetted a system of politics which was so weak it could not deal effectively with the economic, physical, and social events that determined the quality of life in the city. In short, the industrial metropolis of 1930 [speaking of Philadelphia in particular, but also generically], like the colonial town, and big city which had preceded it, was a private city and the public dimensions of urban life suffered accordingly" (*Warner 1976, 202*). By privatism, WARNER implies an urban process dependent on essentially private institutions and individual adjustments to achieve productivity and social order. Civility and urbanity had no public defender.

Closing remarks

This essay has tried to put these characteristics into the context of ninetenth century American republican theory and suggest ways in which the dramatic urban-industrial developments of the period put great pressure on the basic assumptions underlying it, but were nevertheless unable to dislodge them. While the political philosophy of Victorian America made great accommodations to the forces of urbanization, the nature of successive waves of urban reform were unable to break out of the 'private' sphere they had been contained within - until the historic collapse of the American economic machine in 1929. By the time of the New Deal government programs, however, the basic cultural mold was set and even the Great Depression could not destroy it.

There are, of course, many other facets of American cultural ideology that have contributed to the 'American-ness' of American cities. Cultural pluralism, for example, is a facet that must be integrated into this picture, although it was relevant for American Victorians only in fact, not in theory. Their views on immigration and acculturation were based on what we now call the doctrine of Anglo-conformity, namely, that the cultural and political institutions of America would transform immigrants into Americans-especially through exposure to freedom. In light of this, no special facilities were deemed necessary for coping with ethno-cultural pluralism, and no formal institutional arrangements either for Americanization or the maintenance of pluralism. How this issue specifically shaped the geography of American cities is only slowly becoming clearer. There is much more for geographers to do in linking their models of urban evolution to changing social philosophies. The few studies that make that link reviewed earlier point in a promising direction for American urban geography. ZELINSKY's implicit challenge to identify and causally connect specific material attributes of American cities to his four general cultural values remains largely to be met, and would benefit from an evolutionary and communal treatment so that origins and transformations can be conceptually distinguished.

This essay has been structured around two premises. First, that urban geography needs not only a vigorous, normative 'social geography' component, but also a multicultural context. This is a plea for an enlarged cultural-historical geography of the American city to place our knowledge of contemporary spatial and environmental structures in the city in a broader framework of continuity and change. The second premise is that the 'American-ness' of American cities resides in that which is peculiarly American about American culture, and that the roots of many key values reach back to early republican ideology. The American city has been built upon a foundation of abundant resources, the primacy of profit, and the sanctity of mobility. Such a combination produces exploitation and discard, rather than humanization and retention. The great dividends have been a phenomenal record of urban growth and economic productivity accomplished in a short time, and the development of technologically advanced forms of domestic life and material comfort for the many who can attain them. The drawbacks have been creation of a physical environment often seriously deficient in spatial coherence, aesthetic interest, and proper upkeep, and also community traditions considerably hampered by the problems of allocating social responsibilities appropriately between the public and private sectors.

In conclusion, it might not be inappropriate to suggest that these last two issues remain very much at the heart of contemporary debate in America, in a setting in which, whatever the balance achieved, the traditional American city - the focused, industrial metropolis many of us have known - is changing out of recognition. In this sense, to the degree to which regional urban traditions elsewhere in the West are subject to similar forces of change, it is worth considering what about American urban culture is *sui generis* and what is common currency. There is unmistakable evidence that the United States may be outgrowing its economic and specialized need for the city as traditionally conceived, and perhaps fortunately the nation still has the space and resources for the new morphology. Perhaps the historical lesson to draw from this examination is that the American city, as a cultural departure from its European parent, lacks a permanent role in its own environmental and social setting. We may be finding that the traditional American city has been as temporary as the heavy industrialization it served, and in being replaced with polynuclear urbanoid landscapes spanning the whole continent, we are seeing a quintessential American reaction to an historically brief settlement form never quite accepted, nor duplicated, in Europe or anywhere else. In the world of urban modelling, it is time to repatriate BURGESS, HOYT, and all the other American conceptions of urban spatial structure, and restrict them to the local community service for which they are best suited - interpreting the spatial outcomes of singular American cultural values.

America's encounter with large-scale industrial urbanism was dictated by an agrarian experience barely comfortable with the earlier merchant cities. That agrarian experience was steeped in republicanism and perfectionism, and the encounter generated domesticity also to create a triumvirate or moral tenets with which to negotiate the rigors of a hyper-concentrated urbanism not native to American soil, and which is now being so willfully rejected by Americans, thanks to the pleasures of technology.

Zusammenfassung

Der vorliegende Artikel ging von zwei Prämissen aus. Erstens, die Stadtgeographie benötigt eine starke, normative sozialgeographische Komponente, die in einen multikulturellen Zusammenhang eingebunden ist. Dies sollte als ein Plädoyer für eine erweiterte kulturgenetische Betrachtung der amerikanischen Stadt verstanden sein. Unser Wissen von den gegenwärtigen räumlichen und sozio-ökonomischen Stadtstrukturen muß in einem weiteren Rahmen der Kontinuität und des Wandels gesehen werden. Die zweite Prämisse geht davon aus, daß das „Amerikanische" der amerikanischen Städte gleichsam in dem typisch „Amerikanischen" der amerikanischen Kultur begründet liegt, und daß die wesentlichen Werte dieser Kultur eng mit der frühen republikanischen Ideologie verwurzelt sind. Die amerikanische Stadt wurde auf einem Fundament errichtet, das sich zusammensetzt aus dem Vorhandensein von üppigen Geldmitteln, dem Primat des Profits und einer unantastbaren, nicht zu hinterfragenden Mobilitätsbereitschaft. Eine solche Kombination von Faktoren führt insgesamt eher zu Verhältnissen der Ausbeutung als zu solchen der Humanisierung, und das Althergebrachte wird eher abgestoßen als beibehalten. Die Früchte dieser Verhältnisse sind ein phänomenales städtisches Wachstum und eine rasante Produktivitätssteigerung. Sie werden, was den technischen Fortschritt betrifft, begleitet von der Bildung hochentwickelter Wohnverhältnisse und einem materiellen Wohlstand, der einem beträchtlichen Teil der Bevölkerung zukommt. Die Schattenseiten dieser Verhältnisse sind verbaute Flächen, die oft nur gering entwickelte räumliche Strukturen und kaum einen inneren Zusammenhang erkennen lassen. Diese Verhältnisse ließen auch Stadtviertel entstehen, die ästhetisch wenig reizvoll und schlecht instandgehalten sind, und die zu einer von Problemen beeinträchtigten Tradition des kommunalen Zusammenlebens führten, bei der die Frage einer angemessenen Verteilung der sozialen Verantwortung zwischen dem privaten und öffentlichen Sektor ungeklärt blieb.

Diese Voraussetzungen scheinen auch heute noch die Debatte in den USA zu bestimmen, in einer Zeit, in der der Typus der traditionellen U.S. amerikanischen Großstadt, d. h. die auf das Zentrum ausgerichtete Industriestadt, im Begriff ist, sich bis zur Unkenntlichkeit zu verändern. Für Städte in anderen Regionen der westlichen Welt, die vielleicht einen ähnlichen Wandel mitmachen könnten, ist es daher durchaus von Interesse zu verstehen, was an der städtischen Kultur der USA und ihrer Entwicklung ausschließlich nur für Amerika gilt und was davon ein sich allgemein abzeichnender Trend ist. Es gibt unverkennbare Anhaltspunkte dafür, daß in den USA an der Stadt, so wie sie traditionell gesehen wird, kein wirtschaftlicher Bedarf mehr besteht. Die USA sind auch in der – vielleicht – glücklichen Lage, in ausreichendem Maße über Land und Ressourcen für eine völlig neue Stadtgestaltung zu verfügen. Die historische Lektion, die wir durch eine solche Überprüfung lernen können, ist, daß der U.S. amerikanischen Stadt, als heute kulturell eigenständigem Ableger ihrer europäischen Eltern, eine beständige Rolle in ihrem sozio-ökonomischen Umfeld fehlt. Wir erkennen vielleicht, daß der Bestand der traditionellen amerikanischen Stadt zeitlich nur befristet war, ähnlich wie bei der Schwerindustrie, der sie diente, und daß diese Großstädte durch mehrkernige, stadtähnliche Landschaften ersetzt werden, die den ganzen Kontinent überziehen. Wir sehen auch eine zutiefst amerikanische Reaktion auf einen historisch gesehen nur kurzlebigen Stadttypus, der weder in Europa noch sonstwo nachgeahmt wurde. In einer Fachwelt, die sich von starren städtischen Modellen leiten läßt, ist es an der Zeit, all die Konzeptionen von Burgess, Hoyt und anderen in Frage zu stellen, und sie auf die lokalen öffentlichen Dienstleistungen zu beschränken, für die sie am besten geeignet sind. Amerikas Einschätzung von der um sich greifenden, großflächigen Verstädterung im Industriezeitalter war von Bewohnern mit einem ländlichen Erfahrungsschatz geprägt, die sich schon mit den frühen, primär auf den Handel ausgerichteten Städten nicht wirklich anfreunden konnten. Diese Erfahrungen waren durchdrungen von einem Streben nach der perfekten Gesellschaft und von republikanischem Ideengut. Diese nicht urbanen Menschen lehnten die großstädtischen Ballungsräume und die um sich greifende Verstädterung mit all ihren Unbilden als etwas Unamerikanisches ab, zogen sich auf ihre vier Wände zurück und lebten ein gutbürgerliches Leben, eine Einstellung, die auch im heutigen Amerika anzutreffen ist und durch den technischen Fortschritt begünstigt wird.

Notes

[1] Urbanism is understood in this essay in terms laid out in *Wheatley 1972*.
[2] Pre-Columbian urbanism in North America will not be considered here, given the lack of evidence that it significantly influenced colonizing Europeans in their establishment of cities on the continent.
[3] This orientation is exemplified by such surveys as *Murphy 1966, Yeates and Garner 1971, King and Golledge 1978,* and *Cadwallader 1985*.
[4] This brief 'portrait' springs from the author's experience. Comprehensive documentation would be impracticable here.

References

Agnew, J., Mercer, J., and Sopher, D. eds. (1984): The City in Cultural Context. Boston: Allen & Unwin.
Appleby, J. (1986): Republicanism in Old and New Contexts. In: William and Mary Quarterly 3rd ser., 43 (1), 20-34.
Berry, B. J. L. (1973): The Human Consequences of Urbanization: Divergent Paths in the Urban Experience of the Twentieth Century. New York: St. Martin's Press.
Berry, B. J. L. (1976): The Counterurbanization Process: Urban America since 1970. In: Berry, B. J. L. (ed.), Urbanization and Counterurbanization. Beverly Hills, CA, Sage.
Borchert, J. R. (1967): American Metropolitan Evolution. In: Geographical Review 57 (3), 301-332.
Boulding, K. E. (1963): The Death of the City: A Frightened Look at Postcivilization. In: Handlin, O., and Burchard, J. (eds.): The Historian and the City. Cambridge, MA, MIT Press.
Cadwallader, M. (1985): Analytical Urban Geography. Englewood Cliffs, NJ: Prentice-Hall.
Conzen, M. P. (1980): The Morphology of Nineteenth Century Cities in the United States. In: Borah, W., Hardoy, J. E., and Stelter, G. E., (eds.): Urbanization in the Americas: The Background in Comparative Perspective. Ottawa: National Museum of Man, History Division, 119-141.
Conzen, M. P. (1981): The American Urban System in the Nineteenth Century. In: Herbert, D. T., and Johnston, R. J. (eds.): Geography and the Urban Environment: Progress in Research and Applications, Vol. 4. New York: John Wiley & Sons, 295-347.
Conzen, M. P. (1990): Town-Plan Analysis in an American Setting: Cadastral Processes in Boston and Omaha, 1630-1930. In: Slater, T. R. (ed.): The Built Form of Western Cities. Leicester, Leicester University Press, 142-170.
Cornick, P. H. (1938): Premature Subdivision and its Consequences. New York, Columbia University Institute of Public Administration.
Ghorra-Gobin, C. (1992): Les Fondements de la ville americaine. In: Géographie et Cultures 1, 81-88.
Goldberg, M. A. and Mercer, J. (1986): The Myth of the North American City: Continentalism Challenged. Vancouver: University of British Columbia Press.

Gottmann, J. (1961): Megalopolis: The Urbanized Northeastern Seaboard of the United States. New York: Twentieth Century Fund.
Gottmann, J. (1986): Transatlantic Orbits: The Interplay in the Evolution of Cities. In: Conzen, M. P. (ed.): World Patterns of Modern Urban Change. Chicago. In: University of Chicago Department of Geography Research Paper 217-218, 457-472.
Hayden, D. (1981): The Grand Domestic Revolution: A History of Feminist Designs for American Homes, Neighborhoods, and Cities. Boston, MIT Press.
Hofmeister, B. (1971): Stadt und Kulturraum Angloamerika. Braunschweig, Friedrich Vieweg u. Sohn.
Hofmeister, B. (1982): Die Stadtstruktur im interkulturellen Vergleich: Geographische Rundschau 34 (11), 482-488.
Holzner, L. (1985): Stadtland USA: Zur Auflösung und Neuordnung der US-amerikanischen Stadt: Geographische Zeitschrift 73 (4), 191-205.
Howe, D. W. (1976): Victorian Culture in America. In Howe, D. W. (ed.): Victorian America. Philadelphia, University of Pennsylvania Press, 3-28.
Hoyt, H. (1933): One Hundred Years of Land Values in Chicago. Chicago: University of Chicago Press.
King, L. J., and Gollege, R. G. (1978): Cities, Space, and Behavior: The Elements of Urban Geography. Englewood Cliffs, NJ, Prentice-Hall.
Lewis, P. F. (1983): The Galactic Metropolis. In: Platt, R. H., and Macinko, George (eds.), Beyond the Urban Fringe: Land Use Issues of Nonmetropolitan America. Minneapolis, University of Minnesota Press, 23-49.
Lichtenberger, E. (1981): Die europäische und die nordamerikanische Stadt: Ein interkultureller Vergleich. In: Österreich in Geschichte und Literatur mit Geographie 25 (4), 224-252.
Murphy, R. E. (1966): The American City: An Urban Geography. New York, McGraw-Hill.
Penck, A. (1905): Amerikanische Städte. In: Österreichische Rundschau 3 (Mai-Juli), 375-390.
Ratzel, F. (1876): Culturbilder aus Nordamerika. Leipzig: F. A. Brockhaus. Published in translation as Sketches of Urban and Cultural Life in North America. New Brunswick, N.J.: Rutgers University Press, 1988, 4.
Sartre, J.-P. (1955): Literary and Philosophical Essays. New York, Criterion Books.
Tocqueville, Alexis de (1835): Democracy in America. London, Saunders and Otley.
Vance, J. E., Jr. (1977): This Scene of Man: The Role and Structure of the City in the Geography of Western Civilization. New York: Harper & Row.
Vance, J. E., Jr. (1978): Metropolitan America: Evolution of an Ideal. In: Enyedi, G., ed., Urban Development in the USA and Hungary. Budapest, Akadémiai Kiadó, 15-44.
Ward, D., and Radford, J. P. (1983): North American Cities in the Victorian Age. Norwich, Eng.: Geo Books, Historical Geography Research Series, 12.
Ward, D. (1989): Poverty, Ethnicity, and the American City, 1840-1925: Changing Conceptions of the Slum and the Ghetto. Cambridge, Eng.: Cambridge University Press.
Warner, S. B., Jr. (1967): Private City: Philadelphia in Three Stages of its Growth. Philadelphia, University of Pennsylvania Press.
Watson, J. W. (1979): Social Geography of the United States. London, Longman.
Webber, M. (1968): The Post-City Age: Daedalus, 97, 1093-1099.
Wheatley, P. (1972): The Concept of Urbanism. In: Ucko, P. J., Tringham, R., and Dimbleby, G. W., (eds.), Man, Settlement, and Urbanism. Cambridge, Mass., Schenkman Publishing Co., 601-637.
Wissink, G.A. (1962): American Cities in Perspective. Assen, Royal Vangorcum.
Yeates, M. E., and Garner, B. (1971): The North American City. New York, Harper and Row.
Zelinsky, W. (1973): A Cultural Geography of the United States. Englewood Cliffs, NJ: Prentice-Hall.

Address of the Author

Michael P. Conzen
Committee on Geographical Studies
The University of Chicago
5828 S. University Avenue
Chicago, IL 60637-1583
USA

Innsbrucker Geographische Studien Bd. 26: Human Geography in North America

LUTZ HOLZNER

American Ideologies and the Building of Compromise-Landscapes in Urban America*

Introduction

American cities are cultural landscapes of a very peculiar kind, quite different from European, Indian or Chinese cities. They are, for instance, not highly concentrated urban settlements, clearly outlined against the surrounding open rural countryside, but they cover amorphously entire regions of the country in a pseudo urban-rural mix. They are not compact and centered around one major urban nucleus, no matter how impressive the skylines of skyscrapers in the old downtowns might appear, but are loosely and centrifugally thinned out and have grown and expanded into their surroundings to form a multi-nucleated, mosaic-like landscape which is neither entirely urban nor entirely rural. The American urban areas are not static and firmly rooted and organized internally, but appear to have been quickly put together in an improvised manner and are continuously expanding like galactic nebula, or like a kaleidoscope in which the many-colored pieces are not only constantly rearranged, but appear to pulsate in a permanent outward expansion. Many older neighborhoods and city districts of central cities are laid waste. They have been abandoned by their former residents and businesses, while newer quarters and neighborhoods, never built for eternity either, might soon be left to decay and abandonment as well, a constant growth and decline without seeming order or continuity. The American urban-land is a patch-work of ghettoes, some of wealth and comfort, and others of poverty and despair, of black and white, of young and old, foreign and native. This American urban-land covers incredibly vast areas, more than the equivalent space of the entire territory of united Germany and Denmark put together. It contains open spaces, woods, parks, and farms and more wildlife including deer, pheasant and fox than in all of France and Germany. The American urban-cultural landscape is truly a compromise of city and country, urban and rural (*Holzner 1990*). The creation and making of this American urban cultural compromise-landscape cannot (and should not) be explained through the alleged inevitability of dictates of modern technology such as the automobile and the telephone, or by the available space in this country, as if technological gadgets or space per se predetermine a people's destiny and behavior. The dispersal of the "city" in America into a very wide, open-spaced geographic organism with a great variety of disparate, more or less interdependent parts and the concomitant rural compromise of today's American urban-land was deliberately planned since the earliest beginnings of U.S. history and continuously pursued over more than 200 years. Long before the invention of the automobile, Charles DICKENS, for example, had written in 1843: "American cities have a very quaint appearance: seeming to bring about a kind of compromise between town and country: as if each had met the other half-way, and shaken hands upon it" (*Dickens 1843, 143*). Much earlier, in 1810, a French

---

* The present paper represents a brief summary of research pursued over the course of several years. It is preceded by publications on this subject (for example *Holzner 1985, 1990, 1993, 1994*). This paper is the first English summation of my research on "Stadtland USA" and contains materials and ideas that will appear in their entirety as Ergänzungsheft (monograph) of Petermanns Geographische Mitteilungen.

visitor to the United States, Felix de BEAUJOUR reported in his book that: "the towns of the United States are not so handsome or splendid as those of Europe, but they are more airy and spacious, and almost all decorated with trees and gardens, which gives them the aspect and agreeableness of the country" (*Beaujour 1814, 75 f*). When William PENN issued orders on how to lay out his city Philadelphia in 1681, he wrote: "Let every house be placed, if the person pleases, in the middle of its plat, as to the breadth way of it, that so there may be ground on each side for gardens or orchards, or fields, that it may be a green country town, which will never be burnt, and always be wholesome" (quoted in: *Morris 1972, 223*).

It was in no way just through historic accidents that American towns evolved the way they did, but by deliberate design by planners, and, more importantly, by politicians and the arbiters of core culture of society, i.e. the elite leaders of America, who were determined to create a new society of democratic men in the former colonies. Two basic ideologies have helped to maintain the urge of Americans to "build their own world" which should "(incorporate) the benefits of city and country alike" (as Ralph Waldo EMERSON put it in 1836): (1) the enlightened-capitalist concept of "possessive individualism" or the myth of the culture of individual property as the perceived basis for democracy, and (2) the American anti-urbanism or the myth of the independent small community of like-minded citizens as the core of democratic self-government and public virtue. In addition to these ideologies, another factor is important: (3) a typically American proclivity to mobility, restlessness and improvised lifestyle which has helped to expedite the pseudo-rural disintegration and shiftiness of the city in the United States from early on. To be sure, technologies of construction, transportation, and communication improved through time and accelerated the building of such vast disintegrated urban-rural landscapes in America, most notably after World War II, but they were not the root causes of these processes, just the ever improving means towards cherished ideological ends, namely the creation of a sprawled-out, not entirely rural and not entirely urban, ghettoized, multi-nucleated cultural landscape of individual property owners, which appears to most Americans as the fulfillment of the age-old "American dream".

The Myth of Individual Property as the Foundation of a Democratic Society (Culture of Property)

18th century thinkers of enlightened England had emphatically elevated the right of individual property as one of the three most basic rights of man. For example, Sir William BLACKSTONE wrote in 1765: "The third absolute right (after life and liberty) inherent in every Englishman, is that of property which consists in the free use, enjoyment and disposal of all his acquisitions, without any control or dimunition, save only by the laws of the land" (quoted in: *Wolf 1981, 84f*). American society until today has also held "these truths to be self-evident, that all men are created equal, that they are endowed by their Creator with certain unalienable Rights, that among these are Life, Liberty and the pursuit of Happiness". The latter words "pursuit of happiness" as the third basic right of man in the Decleration of Independence of 1776 had been chosen by Thomas JEFFERSON to replace an earlier version that read: life, liberty and the pursuit of property". The wording became different, somewhat less outright perhaps, but the meaning remained the same, as pursuit of happiness, now as then, was above all to mean the right to pursue the acquisition of property.

Freedom and pursuit of happiness have always been understood in the United States to mean primarily the right to pursue one's material gains, the freedom to risk and the freedom to win, and, of course, the freedom to lose as well. The 14th Amendment of the U.S. Constitution ratified almost 100 years after Independence on July 28, 1868 refers clearly to the three basic rights as "life, liberty, (and) property". Such ideas had originated with earlier English thinkers of the enlightened era, for example John LOCKE (1632-1704) and later the English economist Adam

SMITH (1723-1790), who wrote in his "Wealth of Nations" 1776 about his belief in the good that lies in the independence of the individual who "intends only his own gain", because: "by pursuing his own interest he frequently promotes that of the society more effectually than when he really intends to promote it". This basic truth was so deply ingrained in English culture, that it had even been expressed in poetic rhyme, as for example by the English poet Alexander POPE (1688-1744) who had written in 1733: "Thus God and Nature link'd the gen'ral frame, And bade Self-love and Social be the same" (Pope 1733, 176).

The founding fathers of the United States, the first republic and democracy in modern time, knew, of course, the writings of England of the enlightened era. They meant to carry these thoughts to fruition and reality in America. They condemned the social and political ills of Europe, most notably the danger of the "urban multitudes" who were believed to be politically irresponsible and subject to manipulation, because they did not own property. John ADAMS (1735-1826) wrote: "very few men who have no property, have any judgment of their own" (C.F. Adams 1850-56, 376). Benjamin FRANKLIN (1706-1790) wrote: "to those who have not landed property the allowing them to vote is an impropriety". It was not until 1860 that non-propertied white males over the age of 21 were granted the right to vote in America (universal white male suffrage). To trust the citizens with participating in the democratic decision-making of the nation, the citizens had to have "a stake in the country", as John ADAMS phrased it. He said: "Power always follows property ... and the balance of power in a society accompanies the balance of property in land". If America was really to become "the land of the free", the land of the nation had to be subdivided and distributed among its citizens. John ADAMS: "The only possible way of preserving the balance of power on the side of equal liberty and public virtue, is to make the acquisition of land easy to every member of society; to make a division of land into small quantities, so that the multitude may be possessed of landed estates ... If the multitude is possessed of real estate, the multitude will take care of the liberty, virtue, and interest of the multitude in all acts of government" (C.F. Adams 1850-56, IX, 376f). Thus, if the political experiment into democracy was to succeed in America, democracy needed a very real geographic foundation. Land had to be "democratized" and made into an "affordable commodity for every man". The Land Ordinance of 1785, one of the first laws to be passed by the U.S. Congress, five years even before final ratification of the U.S. Constitution, divided all land west of the Ohio river, eventually more than three quarters of the present territory of the United States, into a rectangular grid system of surveyed lots, consisting of townships six miles square which were subdivided into smaller subdivisions or sections of one square mile each or 640 acres (Fig. 1).

Both the Land Ordinance (1785) and the North West Ordinance law which followed in 1787 called for the "disposal" (sale) of land ("not under 1 dollar per acre"), and as largest unit no more than one section per buyer. This land division system of the United States has been called the "largest monument to a priorism in all human history" (Boorstin 1965, 245). It was much more than an expedient way of surveying and "disposing of" wilderness land. More importantly, it was "an exercise in metaphysics, as priorism, and prophecy" for a new, largely uncharted society as yet to be built (Boorstin 1965, 243). It was a geographic land system fixed forever in the land cadaster of America with an unmistakingly political intent, or, as J.B. JACKSON put it, it was a "blueprint for a democratic-egalitarian society in the landscape, not just symbol but concrete foundation of a political Utopia, a nation of independent democratic small land-owners" (J.B. Jackson 1970, 4f). This tradition and belief in individual land ownership as the political basis of American democracy has been preserved to the present day and was restrengthened repeatedly through time, as, for example, through the creation of a Corps of Topographical Engineers by Congressional Act in 1838, the Homestead Act 1862, the Servicemen's Readjustment Act (so-called G.I. Bill) of 1944, and the continued subsidization of home ownership through federal and state tax laws which have always favored individual suburban home-ownership over building or rebuilding central cities.

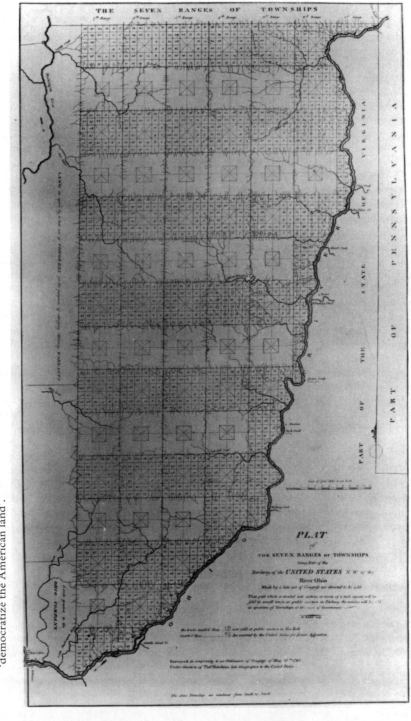

Fig. 1: The first Ranges and Townships. All land west of the Ohio River in the 'Territories' of the United States was laid out in small lots to 'democratize the American land'.

Source: U.S. Library of Congress (unrestricted reproduction).

Anti-Urbanism or the Myth of the Homogeneous Small Community

Another American national myth from early times until the present that has helped to avoid or break up ensuing compact cities in favor of suburban sprawl has been the belief in the homogeneous small community of like-minded citizens as the core of democratic self-government and public virtue. In England, the experience of increasing numbers of rural-urban migrants or landless, rootless masses into the industrializing English cities of the 18th century fostered the idea of the city as the place of wicked business, corruption, lawlessness, and the home of the "criminal classes". Opposite this "brutalizing influence of work in the city, basically the domain of the male world, stood the perceived sacred institution of the family, largely the domain of women and children, who had to be protected against the evils of urban life (*Davidoff 1976; Women and Geography 1984, 49f*). Quite influential were the teachings of the English Evangelical Movement, for instance under William WILBERFORCE (1759-1833), which maintained that the only pleasures allowed a practising Christian were love of nature and family life, premises that were a priori impossible in cities, but could be achieved in the country atmosphere of the suburbs. Here, albeit on a smaller scale, could ordinary citizens imitate the supposed virtuous, free life of the landed aristocracy. These ideas had been directly imported to North America. In the United States, enlightened politicians like Thomas JEFFERSON; Thomas PAINE (1737-1809), John ADAMS or Benjamin FRANKLIN, as well as the national-romanticists of the 19th century, like Ralph Waldo EMERSON (1803-1882), all, of course, educated in English thought and philosophy, demanded the "democratic compromise" between the free country life and the corrupt city through adopting "an urban conception of country", "because man is stronger than the city" (*Emerson: Nature 1836; Self-Reliance 1941*). EMERSON encouraged Americans to "build therefore, your own world" (*1836, 94*), i.e. to create a landscape in America that incorporated "the benefits of city and country alike", where you can "have it both" (*Emerson 1910, 506; Wood 1991, 32*). One of the most outspoken anti-urbanists was Thomas JEFFERSON himself, who coined the phrase: "the country produces more virtuous citizens" (*J.B. Jackson 1970, 1*) and who proclaimed: "I view great cities as pestilential to the morals, the health and the liberties of man. True, they nourish some of the elegant arts, but the useful ones can thrive elsewhere, and less perfection in the others, with more health, virtue and freedom, would be my choise" (quoted in *Glaab 1963, 55*).

It is no historic accident that the first English town founded on the North American continent, Plymouth, Massachusetts (1615), was by design not a compact settlement European-style but a clear forerunner of suburban America, with individual houses on individual lots *(Fig. 2)*.

The New England Village, so highly valued in American folklore, was perceived as the "covenanted community" of like-minded, property-owning citizens, who were willing and able to cooperate as responsible self-governing free men and to determine their own destiny and that of their community. In other words, the English colonial settlers recast the "rich cluster of English-European ideas and attitudes in North America" (as they understood its potential power and the dimensions of its resources), and created in the North American landscape "a concrete embodiment of what had been in Europe a utopian dream (and) on a scale so vast that (eventually) it dwarfed all previous conceptions of possible transformations in human society" (*Smith 1950, 129*). At all times, the layout of American cities, with the exception of the so-called aberration of "the railway-begotten compact industrial city" of the late 19th century (*Wells 1902, 14*), followed this pseudo-rural "suburban", not the "urbane" notion of cities. Anti-urbanism in America flourished throughout the entire 19th and 20th centuries. The populist politician William Jennings BRYAN gave his famous "Cross-of-Gold Speech" in 1896, in which he proclaimed: "burn down your cities (but) leave our farms (intact), and our cities will spring up again as if by magic; but destroy our farms, and the grass will grow in the streets of every city in the country" (*Glaab 1963, 59*). The famous sociologist Adna WEBER wrote 1899: "The rise of the suburbs (in America) ... furnishes the solid base of hope that the evils of city life ... may in part be removed.

Fig. 2: Plymouth, Massachusetts 1630.[1]

[1] This first permanent settlement of English settlers in North America was laid out in a 'suburban' fashion with individual lots and single family dwellings.

Source: Copied from Reps 1965, Fig. 67 (with friendly permission of the author).

If concentrations of population seems desired to continue, it will be modified concentrations which offer the advantage of both city and country life" (*Weber 1899, 91*). In 1902, a certain H.G. WELLS wrote: I hope that "... our railway-begotten giant cities are destined to such a process of dissection and diffusion as to amount almost to obliteration". He wanted to call the new suburban "town provinces" that were emerging everywhere around the unloved compact "dirty" cities "*urban regions*", a term that was indeed introduced not much later into the nomenclature of the Bureau of the Census in 1910 to accomodate for a more realistic counting of urban populations in and around central cities (*Wells 1902, 14*). In 1909-1910, the Building and Housing Commission of Los Angeles called compact cities in the United States "... receptacles for all European evils and the source of all American sins" (*Los Angeles 1909-10, 26*). In a plebiscite in 1910, the people of Los Angeles decided to agree with the Commission's plan to build "not another New York, but a new Los Angeles. Not a great ... mass with a pyramiding of population and squalor in a single center, but a federation of communities coordinated into a metropolis of sunlight and air ... until (the city) meets the country, and until beautiful forms of urban life blend almost imperceptibly into beautiful forms of rural life" (*Fogelson 1967, 287 and 335*). In the 1920s, Henry FORD I. wrote in the Dearborn Independent: "we can only solve the city problem by leaving the city", because the city is "a pestiferous growth" on the American nation (*Burlingame 1955, 7*). In 1943, Frank Lloyd WRIGHT exclaimed: "... Spring man from the trap and cage of the crowded city into the countryside" (*Wright 1943, 548*) and designed a plan of the future American city which he called "Broadacre City, the city of the future, (which) will be everywhere and nowhere, the city which embraces the country and becomes the nation" (*Wright 1958, 119*). The American geographer Brian BERRY concluded 1979 that Americans cannot tolerate compact cities because of "... fundamental predispositions of American culture which is antithetical to urban concentration" (*Berry 1979, 24*). In 1991, Newsweek magazine published a special issue titled "Are Cities Obsolete?" in which the opinion is raised that "the basic problem is that big cities are no longer functional. We don't need them any more" (*Newsweek 1991, 42*).

Roots of the antithetical sentiment towards urban concentrations in America must be sought in the ideology and myth of the wholesome small community, into which a man can retreat, "leaving the troubles of the city behind", in his "desire for the observance of standards of right and seemly conduct in the public places in which one lives and moves, those standards to be consistent with - and supportive of - the values and lifestyles of the particular individual". In his own small community he hopes to be "safe from crime, violence, rebellious youth, racial tension, public immorality, and delinquency" of the city (*Fogelson 1967, 312*). Here, a man believes himself to be among like-minded, away from the "others", the strangers, the different, the dangerous, the people in the city. Ghettoization and small community myth go hand in hand in the United States. In 1906, a town developer offered houses for sale in his new suburban subdivision near Iowa City called Shanandoah. His sales brochure read: "There is no race problem in Shanandoah - no colored people and no foreign population. There are no slums, no tenements, no double houses, and no shacks ... It is neither a village nor a city, being big enough to have all the comforts of the latter, and small enough to enjoy freedom from its drawbacks" (quoted in: *Stilgoe 1988, 296*). Today, such description can no longer be publicized on account of non-discrimination and equal opportunity laws, but the search for "exclusive" neighborhoods and communities, as they are nowadays called, is very much in vogue, perhaps even more so than ever. Many new "safe" communities of suburban America are even walled-in. Only identified residents and their expected visitors are permitted to enter here, the "others" are being kept out.

American National-Psychological Character: Restlessness and Mobility

Land development and speculation as a major part of everyday life calls for risk taking and mobility of body and mind, never really to rest or to sink roots. Americans appear to have been predetermined to the necessary psychological character of restlessness and mobility it takes to pursue, and actually build, the ever expanding, ever changing, improvised, open, pseudo-rural urban-land and to feel happy in such a shifty cultural landscape, full of opportunities and full of risks as well. One of the most ubiquitous (and often described) peculiarities of the U.S. American national character has always been a profound restless mobility of the American people. "The United States are (is) in a constant state of transition. Nothing is final, nothing established to last; a constant mania for change, a perennial quest for innovation seems to drive all classes of society". This statement made in 1848, more than 140 years ago, by a German visitor to the United States, Dr. THÜMMEL of Bamberg, is as valid today as it must have been back then. He continues: "Institutions, which were in force for only fifty years, farm estates that had been under cultivation for only twenty, are considered worn out, and everybody is eager to replace them with different and presumably better ones ... The American is a migratory bird or better a nomad who is not tied to any particular place or residence but feels happy only when moving on. In his youth he leaves behind the land of his birth with indifference and the graves of his fathers with no concern. In his mature years he will, with similar equanimity sell the land he cultivated, together with the cradle of his children and the place of his suffering and joys, to settle anew a thousand miles away and to start a new career" (*Thümmel 1848, 159f*). In 1992, the political commentator Meg GREENFIELD of Newsweek magazine wrote almost verbatim about the American proclivity to newness and change "The opinion of the American majority appears always to hail the new and to grouse and mutter about the old, although the old had, not too long ago, been the new that had been introduced as the greatest improvement of all things" (*Newsweek 1992, 90*).

Americans are the most mobile people on earth. Even after the end of the Western frontier around 1900, 40 to 50 percent of all Americans move every five years, and of these, 10 percent move from one state into another. 1989 alone, 18 percent of the U.S. population moved, that is 45 million people. During the last three decades (1960-1990), a total of 90 percent of all Americans have moved. With a total population of approximately 250 million, this means a constant peoples migration. It can be said without exaggeration that American history has been the history of migrations: immigrations, remigrations, frontier migrations, and constant internal migrations etc. The American national character seems predisposed to constant change and love of newness, as CRÉVECOEUR already put it in 1782, and to a restlessness to leave the troubles behind and building anew in the wilderness. In American tradition, "change" is synonymous with "improvement", "moving on" with "moving up"; quick profit and instant reward counts for happiness. The cliché of the American frontier comes to mind, or is it a cliché? The frontier spirit is not dead in America. It was always nothing out of the ordinary to leave one's home in search for better opportunities elsewhere when conditions seemed less rewarding, or turned somewhat difficult, or simply when the urge to move became too strong. In the early days, farmers would move on when harvests failed, or locust plagues or droughts made life miserable, or a good deal could be struck selling the farm to a newcomer, or gold discoveries promised quick riches elsewhere. During the last half of the 20th century, whole urban districts and central cities have been decimated and abandoned and left to marginal elements of society, the poor, the uneducated, the unskilled, and the minorities. This is not new at all but appears like a red thread leading through the history of the United States. Any attempt to explain the recent accelerated sprawl of urban-land and massive relocations of people in this country would be futile if only economic difficulties were considered without weighing concomitant, long established culture-immanent values and behavior patterns of American society as well. The building of compromise-landscapes in urban America seems preprogrammed through the national character and cultural foundation of American society.

In his novel "*Home as Found*", James Fenimore COOPER has one character explain to a visiting Englishman that Americans should be called "regular movers" with as much justification "as the man who shoes a horse ought to be called a smith, or the man who frames a house a carpenter" (*Cooper 1838*, quoted in: *Lynes 1957-1963, 10*). Charles DICKENS wondered "if Americans ever intended to settle down" (*Dickens 1843-1957, 26*). Another English visitor named Abigail DODGE compared the houses of the Americans with "exaggerated trunks". She observed during her early 19th century visit that Americans engage every May in "spring madness of moving day ... They don't strike roots anywhere. They don't have to tear up anything. A man comes with a cart and horses. There is a stir in one house, - and they are gone; there is a stir in the other house, - they are settled, - and everything is wound up and set to run for another year" (quoted after *Lynes 1957-1963, 12*). In the 20th century, October has joined May for a second annual "move-all" in America. Mobility has spurred America's song writers and poets too.

The image of 'Elsewhere' (*Morrison 1971*) appears in country and western songs, most of which hail the moving on and the new someplace else: "Do you know where hell is, hell is in hello, and heaven's in good-bye", "I was born under a wandering star", "Home was for coming from and dreamin' of going to, which, with any luck at all will never come true", "I'm going far away But I don't know where I will go" etc. (*Raeithel 1981, 5ff*). In his novelette "The Leader of the People", John STEINBECK has a grandfather tell his grandson the story of the great treck of many people he once lead to the West. He calls it "westering": "The westering was as big as God ... it wasn't getting here that mattered, it was movement and westering". And then, one day, they reached California and the ocean "and it was done ... There's no place to go. There's the ocean to stop you. There's a line of old men along the shore hating the ocean because it stopped them" (*Steinbeck 1938, 565*).

Mobility and restlessness call for improvisation of life style and less than permanent edifices for home and business. If one is always prepared to move on, never really growing roots anywhere, so as to be ready to grab a perceived opportunity elsewhere, it cannot be expected that most people would wholeheartedly make long-term and lasting investments which would tie them down permanently. Improvised or temporary arrangements are preferred and investments kept as low as possible so that, when the price is right or the call for moving on is heard, little would stand in the way. The building of compromise landscapes in urban-land USA is, among other things, an expression of this improvisation and urge for newness for the sake of change. "Newness is continuously pursued, obsolescence is planned, and the latest edifices vanish unmourned overnight" (*Lowenthal 1966, 28*). Ralph Waldo EMERSON preached that planned obsolescence is an American virtue. He wrote: "Stone buildings last(ed) too long. Our roads are always changing direction ... our people are not stationary: and so houses must be built that could easily be moved or abandoned" (*Emerson 1893-1912, 12:62*). In his House of Seven Gables, Nathaniel HAWTHORNE wrote 1851: "Our public edifices - our capitols, statehouses, courthouses, city-halls and churches - ought (not) to be built of such permanent materials as stone or brick. It were better that they should crumble to ruin once in twenty years, or thereabouts, as a hint to the people to examine and reform the institutions which they symbolize" (*Hawthorne 1851, 145*).

Conclusion

American cities from earliest times until the present reflect particular sentiments and behavior modes of the American people and their ideologies and values. Americans have built their cities as compromise-landscapes with extreme heterogeneity and mosaic-like scattering of land-use, and with centrifugal sprawl into an ever expanding rural-urban "frontierland", and the constant flux and change that American proclivity to restlessness and mobility continues to promote. Americans have been more mobile-minded and restless than any other society on earth. This is not only and simply explained by the general immigrant nature of America's population per se and the vastness of the land in which to roam, but also by a selection process of particularly mobile-prone personality types, so-called chronic movers (*Morrison 1971*) who actually decided to emigrate to the new world (and who stayed and did not remigrate) versus those home-bound types who could not make such a decision and stayed home in the first place or left America again because they would not fit the migratory bird nature of American life. Recent psychological and behavioral research appears to support the notion of a genetically rooted psychological "propensity to mobility of chronic extrovert neurotic movers" in a majority of Americans (see lit. in: *Holzner 1993*). The profoundly haphazard and fluctuating urban cultural compromise-landscape of American cities seem ample evidence of such an underlying culture-psychological strain of the majority of American people, which, together with supporting national myths such as the "culture of individual property", and the small community as pillars of American democracy mentioned above, may be held at least as responsible for the building of the compromise-landscape in urban America, as technology or the large size of the country have been used in most other assessments of this phenomenon in the past.

Zusammenfassung

"Ideen, gute wie schlechte, sind stärker als allgemein angenommen. Ja, Ideen und Gedankenmodelle beherrschen die Welt" (John Maynard Keynes). Kulturgenetische Unterschiede der urbanen Kulturlandschaften der Erde gehen weitgehend auf zugrunde liegende Geisteshaltungen der jeweiligen Gesellschaft zurück, die die Städte für sich geschaffen hat. Die U.S.-amerikanische Stadt ist aufgelöst, amorph zersiedelt, ein Kompromiß zwischen Stadt und Land, vielkernig und mosaikartig ghettoisiert. Dies ist nicht gradlienig kausal und vorwiegend auf moderne Technologien, wie etwa das Auto oder das Telefon, zurückzuführen, sondern auf Ideen bzw. Ideologien, die seit den Anfängen der Geschichte der USA Gesellschafts- wie Siedlungsplanung der Amerikaner beherrscht haben und während der gesamten zwei Jahrhunderte amerikanischer Geschichte zielgerichtet verfolgt wurden. Drei Aspekte des "American way of life", dieses Komplexes amerikanischer ideologisch fundierter Geisteshaltungen und Wertmuster, werden beschrieben und analysiert: (1) die sogenannte Besitzkultur oder der Mythos des individuellen Grundbesitzes als Grundlage der Demokratie einschließlich der Vorstellung, daß Einfluß in der Gesellschaft immer auf Besitz basiert und daher ausgeglichene Machtverteilung in der demokratischen Gesellschaft immer nur mit einer ausgewogenen Verteilung von Landbesitz der Einzelbürger einhergehen kann. Die Aufteilung des Landes in kleinste handelbare Einheiten durch das Land-Ordinance-Gesetz von 1785 hat die geographische Grundlage für das heutige Stadtland abgegeben. (2) Der zweite Aspekt ist der amerikanische Antiurbanismus oder der Mythos der heilen Kleingemeinde von Gleichgesinnten. Auf diese Geisteshaltung geht weitgehend der Niedergang der amerikanischen Zentralstädte zurück sowie die damit zusammenhängende Auflösung der metropolitanen Großstadtregionen in eine Vielzahl von administrativ eigenständigen Ghetto-Vorort- (oder Außenstadt-) Gemeinden einschließlich der damit verbunden extremen Dezentralisation aller urbanen Funktionen im amerikanischen Stadtland von heute. (3) Zur kulturgenetischen Erklärung des amerikanischen Stadtlandes wird schließlich noch der ausgeprägte Hang der Amerikaner zur Mobilität, Rastlosigkeit und zum Provisorium als Teil eines spezifisch amerikanischen 'Nationalcharakters' herangezogen. Das amerikanische Stadtland ist natürlich das Ergebnis vieler Prozesse und Kräfte, darunter aber ohne Zweifel der weitverbreitete Wille bzw. die Bereitschaft zu Mobilität, Neuerung und Veränderung. Die fast sprichwörtliche Wanderlust, Rastlosigkeit und Veränderungssucht der Amerikaner sind anerkannte Verhaltensmuster in der amerikanischen Gesellschaft und bei der Erklärung der Kulturraumgestaltung in diesem Land als geographisch äußerst relevant anzusehen.

References

Adams, C.F., ed. (1850-1856): The Works of John Adams. 10 vol. Little, Brown and Co., Boston.
Adams, J.S. (1984): The Meaning of Housing in America. In: Annals of the Association of American Geographers, 74, 515-526.
Beaujour, Le Chevalier F. de (1810): engl. transl. 1814, Sketch of the United States of North America at the Commencement of the Nineteenth Century from 1800 to 1810. London.
Berry, B.J.L., ed. (1979): Urbanization and Counter-Urbanization. Urban Affairs Reviews, Vol. 11, London, Sage Publications.
Boorstin, D.J. (1965): The Americans. The National Experience. New York, Vintage Books.
Burlingame, R. (1955): Henry Ford: A Great Life in Brief. New York.
Cooper, J.F. (1838): Home as Found. In: Fenimore Cooper's Works, 32 vols. (1876-84).
Crévecoeur, J.H. John de (1782): "What is an American?", Letters from an American Farmer. In: McGiffort, ed. (1964): The Character of Americans, 36-37, (reprod. original, introduction by L. Lewisohn), London, New York, Thomas Davies.
Davidoff, L. and Newby, H. (1976): Landscape with Figures: Home and Community in English Society. In: Mitchell, J. and Oakley, A., eds.: The Rights and Wrongs of Women. Harmondsworth, Penguin.

Dickens, C. (1843-1957 edition): American Notes and Pictures from Italy. Oxford, London, Oxford Univ. Press.
Emerson, R.W. (1893-1912): The Complete Works of R.W. Emerson. 12 vols., Boston, Century Edition.
Fogelson, R.M. (1967): The Fragmented Metropolis: Los Angeles 1850-1930. Cambridge, MA, Harvard Univ. Press.
Glaab, C.N. (1963): The American City: A Documentary History. Homewood, IL, Dorsey Press.
Hawthorne, N. (1851): The House of the Seven Gables. Boston.
Holzner, L. (1988): Stadtland USA - Zur Auflösung und Neuordnung der US-amerikanischen Stadt. In: Geographische Zeitschrift, 73, 191-205.
Holzner, L. (1990): Stadtland USA - die Kulturlandschaft des American Way of Life. In: Geographische Rundschau, 42, 468-475.
Holzner, L. (1993): I was born under a wandering star: Wanderlust und Veränderungssucht der Amerikaner als geographische Kräfte der Kulturraumgestaltung. In: Die Erde, 124, 169-181.
Holzner, L. (1994): Geisteshaltung und Stadt-Kulturlandschaftsgestaltung: das Beispiel der Vereinigten Staaten. In: Petermanns Geographische Mitteilungen, 138, 51-59.
Jackson, J.B. (1970): Jefferson, Thoreau and After. In: Landscapes, 15, Selected Writings of J.B. Jackson, New York, E. H. Zube.
Los Angeles (1909-1910): Building and Housing Commission Reports, Los Angeles. Los Angeles.
Lowenthal, D. (1966): The American Way of History. Columbia University Forum, 9, 27-32.
Lynes, R. (1957-1963): The Domesticated American. New York, London, Harper and Row.
Morris, A.E.J. (1972): History of Urban Form, London.
Morrison, P.A. (1971): Chronic Movers and the Future Redistribution of Population. In: Demography, 8, 171-184.
Pope, A. (1733): Essays on Man. London.
Raeithel, G. (1981): Go West - Ein psychohistorischer Versuch über die Amerikaner. Nördlingen.
Smith, A. (1776): An Inquiry into the Nature and Causes of the Wealth of Nations. London.
Smith, H.N. (1950): Virgin Land. The American West as Symbol and Myth. Cambridge, MA, Harvard Univ. Press.
Steinbeck, J. (1938): The Leader of the People. In: The Long Valley. New York, Viking Press.
Stilgoe, J. (1988): The Common Landscape of America, 1580-1845. New Haven, CT, Yale Univ. Press.
Thümmel, A.R. (1848): Die Natur und das Leben in den Vereinigten Staaten von Nordamerika in ihrer Licht- und Schattenseite. Erlangen, Palm'sche Verlagsbuchhandlung.
Weber, A.F. (1899): The Growth of Cities in the Nineteenth Century. London, New York, MacMillan.
Wells, H.G. (1902): Anticipations. The Reaction of Mechanical and Scientific Progress on Human Life and Thought. London, Harper and Row.
Wolf, P. (1981): Land in America: Its Value, Use, and Control. New York, Pantheon Books.
Women and Geography Study Group of the IBG (1984): Geography and Gender: An Introduction to Feminist Geography. London, Hutchinson.
Wood, J.S. (1991): Build, Therefore, Your Own World: The New England Village as Settlement Ideal. In: Annals of the Association of American Geographers, 81, 33-50.
Wright, F.L. (1943): An Autobiography. New York, Horizon Press.
Wright, F.L. (1958): The Living City. New York, Horizon Press.

Address of the Author

Lutz Holzner
Department of Geography
University of Wisconsin-Milwaukee
Milwaukee, WI 53201
USA

AXEL BORSDORF

Cities of the Americas: Urban Development in Different Cultural Landscapes

Preliminary Remarks

This paper tries to prove the following thesis:

- Cities are manifestations of civilizations, which represent the very core of cultural identity.
- Anglo-American, Hispanic-American, and Luso-American cities reflect in their beginning the cultural values and norms of their founders.
- The process of urbanization created a dualism between the Anglo-American cities and the others in the New World.
- Urbanization in Anglo-America means city growth, in Latin America a certain development process.
- During the 20th century the North American civilization became so attractive to Latin America, that the South got in danger to lose its own identity.
- Even the search of a new Latin American identity is reflected in the cities. Most models of forming a new national consciousness took their exit from the cities.

Developing the Idea

Throughout history the emergence of early civilizations and the developments of cities were strongly connected. Initially cities served as a focus of religious cults, political organization, trade and industry. Throughout the history of Western civilization the self-image of the society or that of its ruling strata was reflected in the urban morphology. The cultural ideal of most societies are centralized in the cities, where the laws, norms and mores are created and in turn spread to non-urban areas.

The first cities of the continent which was later called the "New World" arose among the civilized realms of Precolumbic America. Cuzco, the capital of the Inca empire, is an example where the city reflects the political ideology of the ruling class. It was designed in the shape of a puma. The puma was the holy animal of the Inca, a symbol of strength, energy, power, and speed, characteristics which formed the coherence of Inca imperial authority. Each anatomical part of the puma served as an important function which nurtured the imperial will. The fort of Sacsayhumán, for instance, formed the symbolic head of the puma. Even today, when a *Cuzqueño* is asked where he lives, the answer is often given in the context of the puma; for instance: *Vivo en las tripas!* ("I live in the intestines!").

The Spaniards, however, superimposed their own ideological symbolization at the expense of those formed by the indigenous culture. The early symbols were destroyed or transformed. Cuzco exemplifies this transformation. The ceremonial centre of the Inca was a square, located between the forelegs and the hind legs of the puma, and open on one side. the Spaniards immediately closed the opening and formed what is now known as the Spanish plaza.

The City in Hispano-America

From the beginning of Spanish colonization the plaza became the most important cultural symbol in the Spanish colonies. In time its symbolic significance was transferred also to Portuguese settlements in America. The design of the plaza was institutionalized by the Spanish crown with a special edict in 1513 *(Wilhelmy and Borsdorf 1984, 66-78)*. The scale of the square in the city-center determined the outlay of the grid patterned city. The Hispanic town was designed like the office of public administration: everybody sent to the colonies by the Spanish crown could easily orientate himself in the well ordered units.

Originally the plaza's principal function was defence like in the Roman "castellum" from where the idea was copied. Partially as a consequence of this early function, the plazas were often the principal battlegrounds in the wars of independence and subsequent rebellions. But for centuries Hispanic-America was a relatively peaceful continent. During this time plaza's main function was that of a tangible manifestation of Spanish imperial power in the colonies. In time these functions became subservient to the more mundane realities of everyday life. The square, a center of celebration, is a center of life and of leisure as well, the scene of religious cult and civil life. Intrigues of all kinds were planned in and about the plaza, news and events were reported there, and the square served as a meeting place for friends. Spain constructed plazas instead of schools for its people. Education and culture were transmitted by the plaza. And there is another difference to the market squares of Europe: trade did not play an important role on the plaza.

The Catholic Church is another cultural symbol of the early European penetration of the New World. Like the Spanish administration system the church, too, is organized in a centralistic matter and needed to concentrate its neophytes in cities. In those regions where the people could not be centralized in cities or Indian reductions the Spaniards introduced the *Sunday market*. This market would draw the Indios once a week to a central place where the Spaniards could indoctrinate them with the "correct" religious and political training.

In this religious context the centrality of a monastery with its closed patio reflects the plaza-structure on another scale. In addition to being the scene of religious meditation, it served as the political setting where church and state decisions were planned and executed.

The motif of the patio with its interior orientation was repeated in the patio house of private citizens. The Hispanic courtyard structure has its origin in a long history which predated Spanish colonization. Nevertheless its inherent inward orientation was a timely and prudent option for the local citizens. It granted a semblance of privacy in an environment dominated by a powerful colonial administration, ever watchful over its citizens.

The City in Luso-America

In contrast to the Spaniards, the Portuguese came to America as merchants and later plantation growers, not as *conquistadores* or colonists. Their first trading settlements were restricted to the coast and consisted of irregular *povoados*, surrounding a small church or chapel. As their wealth and influence spread, the Portuguese integrated the Spanish grid pattern into their settlements, but due to an absence of formal imperial instruction their format was more flexible and diverse. The old plan of the former capital Salvador de Bahia shows this. It also reveals the importance of walls to the Portuguese. Walls were a necessity because the Portuguese, unlike the Spaniards, emphasized a colonial scheme which initially did not include countryside pacification. Under these conditions, security measures providing insurance against outside attack were required. Even the use and structure of the all-important square is diagnostic of the difference between Spanish and Portuguese colonial perceptions. Since Portuguese power was less centralized and under fewer constraints by the crown many *praças* could exist in each urban setting, and they could serve as market squares, too.

Nevertheless, the acceptance of the plaza by the Brazilians shows that the symbol of Spanish colonialism (which the plaza was originally designed for) became the symbol of the essence of the life-style throughout Latin America.

First Luso-American cities were portuary-towns. Unlike the Hispanic towns, situated mostly in flat basin-areas, their location in coastal areas enforced a stricter adaptation to the orography. Many of the Brazilian towns, even in the hinterland, are urban individuals, and reflect the urban morphology of Porto or Lisbon in the home country.

The social infrastructure of colonial society was also reflected by the urban morphology of the city. The hierarchical differences between the upper, middle and lower classes are observed in a clear central-peripheral descent of social quarters. In his model of the Latin American city GORMSEN (*1981*) pointed out, that in colonial times there was a central-peripheral decline of the social-profile from the upper class living in the city center to the lower classes that lived in the peripherial quarters. This profile was reflected by building heights, land-prices and population density. His results form part of the synoptic diagram (*see Fig. 1*).

Development Trends in the 19th Century

The preeminence of imperial symbols in urban morphology was ultimately to prove transitory. The independence movements and subsequent events were profoundly to alter and weaken the earlier patterns. To overcome the Spanish imperial ideology and to subdue colonialism the ideas of the French Revolution were quickly adopted by the emerging nations of Latin America. French urbanistic ideals were copied and began to reshape the urban landscape. The patio house became oldfashioned and was replaced by the European *villa* with its orientation toward a garden. The upper classes moved out of the plaza and constructed their new dwellings along the spacious boulevards, the so-called *paseos, prados* or *alamedas*.

In the later half of the 19th century other economic powers became influential in the economic and cultural life of Latin America. The first of these forces were introduced by the British, who began to exert control over foreign trade, mining, banking, and the transport-sector. Morpholocially the race track was installed and began to compete with the traditionally bullfighting arena in popularity.

However, British influence waned quickly. During the period between the *Monroe Doctrine* (1823) and the *Declaration of Havana* (1940) the aggressive economic policy of the USA overwhelmed the competitors in Latin America. U.S. American businesses began to dominate large parts of the economic sectors. Morphologically the North American influence is seen in the rise of the first tall buildings and skyscrapers. In Buenos Aires and Havana the parliament buildings were constructed as replicas of the House of Congress in Washington, D.C., La Plata, Argentina, and Belo Horizonte, Brazil, new towns of the late 19th century, even copied the street pattern of Washington, D.C.

To follow the question, why the U.S. American influence on Latin America became so powerful it is necessary to investigate the essence of the North American civilization in the same matter as it was done regarding Latin America.

The City in North America

Colonization history in Anglo-America differs clearly from the processes which took place in the Southern half of the continent. The United States are formed by an undirected, agrarian colonization, which were fed by a large potential of population delivered by the agriculture-regions of European countries looking for freedom and wealth in the New World. Tilt wagon and log cabin are symbols of this early colonization process. The wish for independence and liberty connected with the thinking of rural European population created a certain suspicion of the

Fig. 1: Synoptic Diagram of Urban Development in Latin America

Era	1500-1830	1830-1900	1900-1930	1930-1950	1950 - today
Urban Development	Foundation	First process of rapid urbanization	End of first urbanization-phase	Second process of rapid urbanization	Metropolization
Urban layout	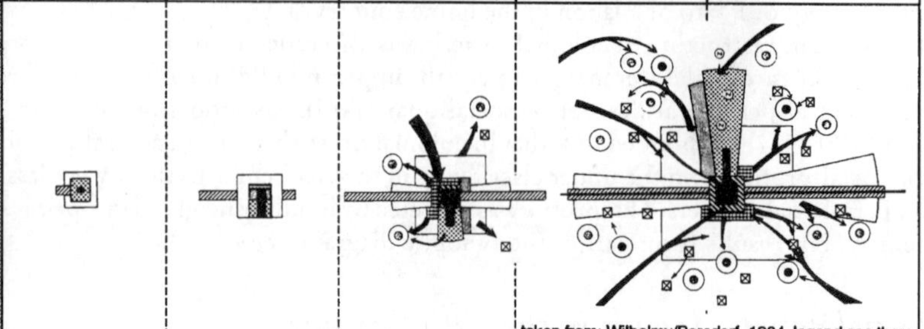				taken from: Wilhelmy/Borsdorf, 1984, legend see there
Urban profile	Plaza / Village	Village	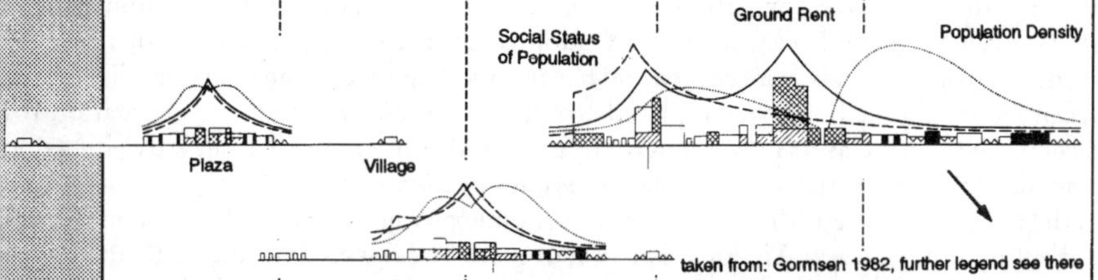 Social Status of Population	Ground Rent	Population Density — taken from: Gormsen 1982, further legend see there
Symbol	Plaza	Alameda	Upper class quarters	Spine, Squatter settlements	Isolated suburbs
Spatial tendency	Centralization	Linearity	First polarization	Polarization	Growing polarization
Urban growth	Natural growth	(European) Immigration	Natural growth	Internal migration, rural exodus	inter- & intraurban migration
Architecture	Renaissance Baroque	Classicism Historism	First tall buildings, first squatters	Bungalows Slums and squatters	Apartment-buildings Squatter consolidation
Foreign affairs	Colony	Creolic Pan-americanism French & british influence	US-american Panameri-canism	Autarkism	US-american interventions, economic imperialism
Economic development	Exploitation	Internal agrarian economy	outward orientated development (hacia afuera)	inward orientated development (hacia adentro)	desarrollismo dependentismo economismo
Socio-political development	Colonial society	Particularism, Conservatism	Particularism, Liberalism	Growth of the middle strata, Populism	Dictatorships, experiments of socialism, re-democratization

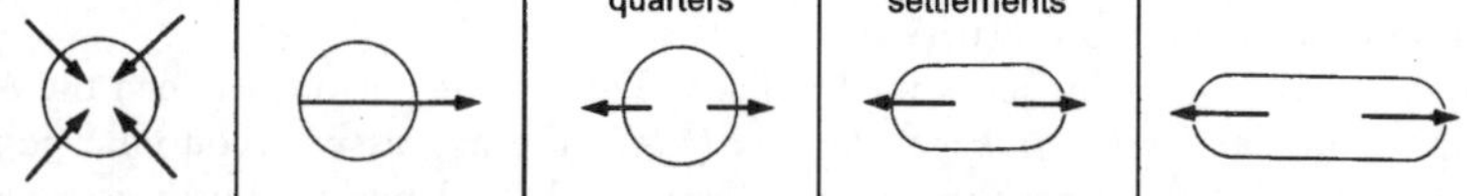

Source: Borsdorf 1995

cities. This is reflected in the outlay of the regional administration system. Central functions are often located in relatively small towns. Not Portland but Salem is the capital of Oregon, not Los Angeles but Sacramento the capital of California, not Chicago but Springfield the capital of Illinois. And in the national context the U.S. American capital is Washington, D.C., which is 27 times smaller than New York. More than twelve state-capitals count fewer than 100,000 inhabitants and about thirty are not the largest cities of their state.

HOLZNER (1989) gave reasons for the tendency of American anti-urbanism, looking at the social and cultural values of the society. He mentioned individualism, attachment and love of nature, mobility, a manifest sense of destiny and the specific values of work ethic which are founded and formed by convinced countrymen like Thomas JEFFERSON. JEFFERSON, who never denied his disapproval of the corrupt cities, was convinced that a non-urban state would create more virtuous citizens than would be possible in urban environments. JEFFERSON did not stand alone with his opinions, he was only the most prominent speaker of the rural oligarchy.

Agrarian orientated representatives, rivalry of political parties, often the influence of members of the leading rural families led to the founding of towns and to the election of capitals in peripheral, neutral locations, which could only hinder their development. Even the administration was divided: one city got the Capitol, the next was the site of the Supreme Court, the third got the state-university. Before the British-American War (1812-1814) Thomas JEFFERSON thought that the United States should be a country without large cities. This was at a time when Latin America already had an urban culture, consolidated in centuries.

Whereas most North American cities were hindered in developing central functions, their trade- and supply-functions grew congruent to the fast process of growth in the United States. At first the towns tended to supply the surrounding rural regions but with the westward expansion they got more and more influence on the interregional trade. *Main street*, the *broadway*, which was broad enough for the transit of tilt-wagons is the symbol of this urban function. Located on the main axis of the city are the most important functions, clearly visible by their two-storey-buildings, the bank, the post-office and the hotel for the meetings of the farmers.

Main street leads to the West, to the future of the country, is the free track for the run for more land, for more expansion. Main street is unlimited. Until today cities grow in a linear manner orientated to this axis. This means a clear difference to the square orientation of the Latin-American cities - and it stands for another type of thinking and a different way of life.

Urbanity in a European or Latin American sense means a dense communication, a bourgeois identity, a responsible connection, and a communal collective spirit. Within a basically antiurban ideology these virtues could not arise. It is not surprising that the bungalow, originally a rural villa, is the most frequent urban house type. The enormous spaciousness of North American cities is not alone a reflection of the land reserve but more a symbol of an individual orientated civilization. The automobile and the urban highway, the telephone and personal computer were only methods to preserve rural habits in the post-industrial age and in huge urban agglomerations.

Moreover, the self-understanding of the Americans is influenced by another experience, the experience of growth. To be able to grow more and more can almost be regarded as an ideology. Firstly the continent form East to West, than the Islands and lastly the third dimension with skyscrapers and the discovery of the moon. The experience of a growth without any resistance, going ahead with a naive faith to the superiority of their own political and ideological system led to the idea of Panamericanism. Firstly the Latin Americans misunderstood this program as bringing them liberty from British dominance. But when they realized more and more the true nature of the U.S. American interpretation of Panamericanism, the North American did not become aware of the disillusion process going on in the Southern hemisphere. They still are convinced they are bringing an "alliance of progress" to the underdeveloped Latins.

The self-consciousness of U.S. American identity has its roots in their understanding of democracy as well. A symbolic element of urban morphology is the Capitol, which in most states is a replica of the main Capitol in Washington, D.C. Designed in classical style it contains ideas of the enlightment as well as imperial Roman thoughts. Latin America copied the tall buildings, the street pattern of Washington and the Capitol - symbols of their misunderstanding of North America. They thought they were importing democracy and wealth, but in fact they were importing imperialism and dependency.

Segregation may be interpreted as another "objectivation" of the North American civilization. Although it was officially understood that North American cities were melting-pots, they originally had their German, Polish, Jewish quarters. Most of these developed in the course of time, only Chinatown, Asian quarters and black ghettos survived. Today social segregation is more important than ethnic segregation. *Fenced cities* are the newest step in the segregation-process. And more: there is a strong tendency to isolate the elderly in their own *retirement areas* or towns. The difference to the Latin American system is easily to be noticed by a comparison of their cemeteries: In the Protestant areas of the United States, cemeteries have no decorations, their green is easy care and they seldom see visitors. The Latin American cemeteries are part of the daily life of the descendants. Many times a year they visit the grave, which in some cases is styled as an urban building, a church or a skyscraper, where they have a party with their ancestors. To a certain degree Americans have the desire to stay eternally young. Strategies to keep health and fitness like jogging, face lifting or weight watching were first invented in the USA. Regarding the actual processes of agewise segregation one could even argue that elder people concentrate in special quarters in order not to disturb the self-image of a "young nation".

The physical mobility of joggers in the city goes hand in hand with the regional mobility of citizens. Mobile homes are another part of urban morphology and another symbol of civilization. But not only the owners of mobile homes change their location frequently during their life. A new job, social mobility and growing wealth is always accompanied by a change of address.

The most significant element of U.S. American cities is the spine or strip where the large supermarkets and fast food restaurants are lined up. These roads run continuously from one city to the other. Seen from the road only the signs of the large supermarkets and restaurants dominate the view. In front of the shops huge parking areas are located. In North America shopping means driving a car. It is characteristic that even the churches brought themselves into a line with the habits of the faithful. Church Street is parallel to the Main Street. The churches of the different denominations compete in the same way as the supermarkets in Main Street: large parking areas and huge advertising signs.

Due to the access to automobiles and the perfect traffic infrastructure the city centers have lost their importance. Shops have closed, window shopping is no longer attractive for the citizens, criminality has spread. The result is the loss of the remaining urbanity North American cities once possessed.

The linear structures of North American cities are repeated in the national urban system, where the large conurbations and megalopolis' are structured like huge linear axes' or stripes. Whereas the semiotic system of early Latin American cities is combined with square structures in the city pattern, the representative buildings and the private houses, a relative compactness, stability and a strong coherence in the citizenship, the U.S. American urban system is represented by linear axes' within the national pattern and the street pattern of each town by an enormous spaciousness, by segregated structures of quarters, and mobility of the citizens.

The North-American Influence on Latin American Cities and the Search for a New Identity

Due to the aura of Panamericanism, Latin America early adapted urbanistic ideas of the USA. Tall building were constructed earlier than in Europe and as was already mentioned, that some Latin American states even copied the Capitol building and the street pattern of Washington, D.C.

Shopping centers grew at the periphery and bungalows became the most attractive private house type and the Latin American cities lost their compactness.

But in the 30s of the present century, opposition to the political, economic and ideological penetration by the USA grew in most Latin American states. These movements became more powerful when the industrialized countries were fixed to their own economical and political problems during the word economic crisis and the Second World War. During this era populistic regimes gained power and kept to a strict anti-imperialistic and anti-American course.

The example of Santo Domingo, where the U.S. Americans formerly had intervened several times, demonstrates the lack of theoretical framework of this populistic ideology. It is the well-known architecture of European totalitarian states we find there, which was only adapted because it seemed to be anti-American. On an economic level the populistic strategy seemed to be more successful. Import-substitution was the goal leading to a rapid industrialization of Latin America. New quarters were constructed for the industrial workers.

But this was the starting signal for the mass of rural population to leave their home regions. An enormous rural exodus began. The migrants found their first homes in the deserted patio houses of the upper classes which were rented room- or bedwise. The inner city slum quarters were later called *conventillos, tugurios* or *vecindades*. Soon landlords started to construct similar buildings to create houses for the migrants, but all these efforts were not sufficient. So in the peripheral areas of the towns squatter settlements grew. In most cases they display a cellular growth pattern, being restricted to less valuable land or properties where ownership was vague or uncontested.

As industrialization increased, special quarters for workers were needed and often constructed. These are variously called *poblaciones* or *urbanizaciones*. In structural terms these developments were manifested in essentially two forms: as terraced houses or as an endless repetition of individual units. Spatially these dwellings are also often disconnected from the urban fringe. As the century matured, this cellular process of growth based on special corporate housing superseded the linear development associated with the incipient industrial spines of the 1930s and the 1950s.

During the course of these events the upper class and its associated economic and social infrastructure was also in transition. In an attempt to remain segregated from the lower classes, the wealthy tended to move to the outskirts of the city. As one might expect, the land-value curve in the profile (*Fig. 1*) follows the outward migration of the wealthy. However, in contrast to the past, the curve of population density no longer correlates to social status and land value. The highest population density now corresponds to the low class areas of the *conventillos* and *poblaciones*. As a result of these processes Latin American cities are characterized by dispersion, disintegration, shapelessness, and discontinuity.

Looking for Solutions in Latin America

In contradiction to its own program Populism in Latin America has enforced Americanization. Contemporary Latin American cities have identical structural problems to their North American equivalents. Polarization, social segregation, spaciousness, financial weakness, and other problems are similar to those of North American cities.

Puerto Rico is an example of a country which consistently followed consequently the way of westernization and Panamericanism. The capital city, San Juan, outside the traditional core, is nowadays dominated by an abundance of tall buildings, subcentres, freeways and large supermarkets - an example of a modern and cosmopolitan metropolis in America.

An alternative in finding a coherent national identity is to stress the long-maligned Latin tradition. It is an attempt reestablish the more cohesive legacy of Hispanic tradition. The restoration of the town centres of Quito or Bogotá are examples. It is not a coincidence that after

Fig. 2: Profiles of European, U.S. American and Latin American Cities

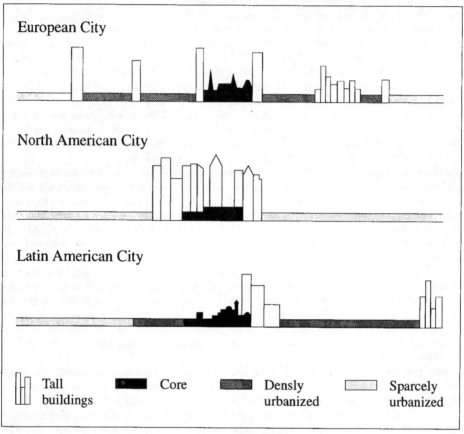

Source: Lichtenberger 1986 and Gormsen 1981, modified and combined

the Columbian earthquake of 1983 the city of Popayán as a focus of Columbian conservatism was rehabilitated in its traditional Iberian form.

The founding of Brasília in 1956 may in some ways be regarded as an effort to overcome old-fashioned habits through urban morphology. The form of the city, resembling a soaring bird or a huge aircraft, is designed to install a new national identity. Development and national consciousness emphasize the national interior in contrast to Rio de Janeiro, the former capital, located in a climate of corruption, leisure and crime. Democracy and idealism were morphologically stressed in an effort to overcome caudillo-leadership and the legacy of corruption. Ostensibly the new social/urban design encompassed the cockpit where the three powers of democracy (legislative, executive and judicial) were installed. Behind the cockpit is the central axis, and the entire entity is supported by the wings where the residential quarters exist. The crucial fuel reserves of an aircraft are located within the wings - and the people in an analogous function are perceived as the energy of the new Brazil.

Brasília had its precedent in the old Inca city of Cuzco, where the urban morphology was seen as a tool to indoctrinate people. Indeed, Brasília displays a multiplicity of elemental designs seen elsewhere: Ebenezer HOWARD's idea of neighborhoods, the Charta of Athens' attempt at functional zonation, the automobile orientation of Los Angeles and the strong ideological fixation of socialist cities within the former Soviet bloc. It is this superimposed dominance of abstract ideas which in reality makes Brasília cold, inhuman, totalitarian and, above all, inappropriate to the realities of Latin American life.

In contrast to the model adopted by the Brazilians, some countries like Cuba, Peru (1969-1975) and Chile (1970-1973) have made great efforts to retrieve the Indian tradition from the precolonial past. In doing so they hoped to establish an identity based on indigenous culture and at the same time unite themselves as a part of the Third Word. It was through these efforts, that the concept of *tercermundismo* was born. The consequences varied. For instance, the decline of Havana is not totally a function of Cuba's ailing economy - it is an intentional policy to strengthen the rural environment at the expense of western urban civilization. This is in keeping with the effort towards establishing a new traditional identity.

In all of these alternatives to find a new Latin American identity through urban politics - the Panamericanism, the Conservatism, the Modernism and the Thirdworldism - there is something in common: They are invented and discussed by members of the upper and middle classes or by university teachers and students. Their development models follow the path from above to below, are therefore top-down-strategies. For a long time they did not realize that there was an alternative, being all day reality in the life of the urban poor, the marginal strata. Their way to survive in the city, to adopt new habits, of human progress is a bottom-up-strategy. But it is another successful path to manage daily life, to obtain an identity and to create urban structures. During the lifetime of a family, single dwellings and whole marginal quarters are consolidated and developed to acceptable buildings and quarters. Informal activities allow them not only to feed themselves, but to modernize and expand their houses, to install infrastructure - and more: to integrate in the urban community. This is not an acculturation process but their own way to search and find a place in the society. It is also a successful way to gain selfconfidence and a cultural identity.

And Anglo-America?

What about Anglo-America? The differences shown in the "Profiles of Cities" (*Fig. 2*) demonstrate more than morphological contrasts. The old core of the town is mostly overbuilt with modern tall buildings which serve as office towers in the quarternary sector. There is a sharp border to the one-story-bungalows which form the mass of the city quarters. In contrast most Latin American cities are still dominated by its old city center surrounding the plaza with its traditional buildings. Towards one end of the town the city functions - not as widespread as in Anglo-America - follow, then densly urbanized quarters of the upper classes and close to the better end of the city, the so-called *barrio alto*, modern apartment-tall-buildings follow. The actual polarization of social strata is to be seen on the other side of the city. Densly urbanized labor quarters and squatter settlements cover the opposite side. It is quite interesting to compare these skylines with the Central-European city. Like in Latin America the core could maintain its traditional morphology, but tall buildings grew in different parts of the city. Some of them contain functions of the quarternary sectors, others are rented for housing purposes.

In contrast to Latin America in North America never took place a change in cultural identity. Linear structures, spaciousness, mobile homes and tall buildings are the logical development in the context of a mobile, fast growing civilization. Segregation has been constitutive since the beginning of urban development and the decline of the city-centre is a logical result of a civilization which is based on the fact that individuals have priority and in which mass-motorization was invented. Therefore it is uncertain if counter-urbanization indicate a cultural crisis. More plausible is that this phenomena may be regarded as the result of a civilization which was based on rural values and design to be anti-urban. Freedom of the individual, trust on the regulative function of the market, social and regional mobility are the main principals on which urbanization in the United States took place. So it is possible, that the development of residential areas may occur even in rural environments. They possess all benefits of urban material infrastructure, but they miss urbanity in a European or Latin American sense. The new American megalopolis allow a compromise between the contrasting lifestyles of urban and rural environments. So it must be questioned if the efforts of citizen movements to change inner urban freeways to communication spaces or to revitalize the downtown areas will be successful. Cities are the material manifestation of ideas, norms and ideologies. And these are anti-urban until today in the United States.

Conclusion

The focus of this paper has been an analysis of Latin and Anglo-American urban morphology as a symbolization of its social and cultural context. Cities in both cultural regions reflect since their beginning the cultural values and norms of their founders, they reflect as well the changes in these principals in the course of time (see Fig. 3). Because of the cultural differences between the anglophone and iberophone regions in the New World there is a dualism, differentiating the Anglo-American urban areas from the Latin American cities. Urbanization in the United States is a process of urban sprawl and city-growth, whereas it occurs as a development process changing the customs and habits of the citizens in Latin America. During the last decades the attraction of North American civilization grew in Latin America and created the danger of an abandonment of cultural values in the Southern regions of the continent. On the other hand processes of searching and finding a new cultural identity are to be noticed in Latin America. Most models of creating a new national consciousness in Latin America originate in the cities.

Zusammenfassung

Sowohl im anglophonen als auch im iberischen Raum der Neuen Welt spiegelt die Physiognomie der Städte die Geisteshaltung der Gesellschaften, die sie hervorgebracht haben. Da sich mehr noch als die sozioökonomischen Strukturen vor allem die kulturellen Normen in den beiden großen Kulturräumen traditionell sehr unterschieden haben, präsentieren sich auch die Stadtstrukturen sehr verschieden. Im traditionell eher städtefeindlichen Milieu der Vereinigten Staaten ist der Urbanisierungsprozeß hauptsächlich durch eine Erweiterung der Stadtfläche, vor allem an den Ausfallstraßen, gekennzeichnet, die Lebensformen der Stadtbewohner sind aber nur in den Kernräumen weniger Städte wirklich urban, der Bungalow ist eher das in die Stadt verpflanzte Landhaus als der Fokus urbanen Lebens. Dagegen sind in beiden großen Kulturräumen Lateinamerikas die Städte Kristallisationspunkte einer urbanen Kultur, die in wachsendem Maße die Gesamtbevölkerung in ihren Normen und Verhaltensweisen prägt. Dennoch übt die nordamerikanische Zivilisation heute eine große Attraktion auf Lateinamerika auf, was sich auch in einer physiognomischen Überprägung der Städte äußert. Letztlich wird damit eine Identifikationskrise in Lateinamerika angezeigt. Es ist aufschlußreich, daß verschiedene Versuche zur Lösung dieser Krise bei der Umgestaltung der gebauten Umwelt in den Städten ansetzen.

Fig. 3: Urban Structures and Trends in the Americas

Latin America	Anglo America
Origins	
plaza	main street
one centralized church	many denominations
patio house (Hispano-America), tall flat-houses (Luso-America)	bungalow
social core-periphery decline	multiple core social structure
compactness	spaciousness
19th and 20th century	
paseo as a magnificent avenue	main street as shopping area
adaptation of tall buildings	invention of tall buildings
rural exodus	social and regional mobility
central slums and marginal settlement	ghetto-formation
cellular growth	linear growth
social polarization	ethnic, later social segregation
moving out of the wealthy	residential areas in rural environments
Results	
high primacy	low primacy
capital city = largest city	capital city often medium sized city
rural-urban dichotomy	rural-urban continuum
centralization	decentralization
metropolization of one city	formation of several metropolitan areas
Trends and Solutions	
Panamericanism, adaptation of the North-American-urbanization process	Persistence of the traditional image of the city
Conservatism: back to the European roots	Decomposition of the urban community: Fenced cities and mobile-home-quarters
Thirdworldism: back to the Indian heritage or forward to Third World structures	Attempts of urban renewal and revitalization of downtown areas
Modernization: search for a new futuristic identity	
Bottom-up-development trends: development of an own lifestyle in self-constructed urban structures	

Source: Borsdorf 1995

References

Arciniegas, G. (1966): Kulturgeschichte Lateinamerikas. München.
Bähr, J. and G. Mertins (1992): The Latin-American City. In: Colloqiuum Geographicum 22, 65-75.
Borsdorf, A. (1994): Die Stadt in Lateinamerika. Kulturelle Identität und urbane Probleme. In: Geographie und Schule, 16, 89, 3-12.
Borsdorf, A. (1989): El modelo y la realidad. La discusión alemana hacia un modelo de la ciudad latinoamericana. In: Revista Interamericana de Planificación, 22, 87/88, 21-29.
Conzen, M. P. (1983): Amerikanische Städte im Wandel. In: Geographische Rundschau, 4, 142-151.
Czerny, M. (1977/78): Las zonas suburbanas de las grandes ciudades en América Latina. In: Revista Interamericana de Planificación 22, 13-20.
Gilbert, A. (1994): The Latin American City. London.
Gormsen, E. (1981): Die Städte im spanischen Amerika. Ein zeit-räumliches Entwicklungsmodell der letzten hundert Jahre. In: Erdkunde, 4, 290-303.
Holzner, L. (1985): Stadtland USA - Zur Auflösung und Neuordnung der US-amerikanischen Stadt. In: Geographische Zeitschrift, 73, 4, 191-205.
Lichtenberger, E. (1975): Die Stadterneuerung in den USA. Berichte zur Raumforschung und Raumordnung, 19, 3-16.
Lichtenberger, E. (1986): Stadtgeographie - Perspektiven. In: Geographische Rundschau 38, 388-394.
Schaeder, R.P., Hardoy, J.E. and Hinzer, N.S., eds. (1978): Urbanization in the Americas from its Beginnings to the Present. Den Haag.
Schnore, L.F. (1965): On the Spatial Structure of Cities in the Two Americas. In: Hauser, P.M. and L.F. Schnore, eds., The Study of Urbanization. New York, 347-398.
Turner, J.F.C. (1976): Housing by People: Towards autonomy in Building Environment. Marion Boyars.
Wilhelmy, H. and A. Borsdorf (1984 and 1985): Die Städte Südamerikas. 2 Vol. Berlin & Stuttgart.
Wright, F.L. (1958): The Living City. New York.

Address of the Author

Axel Borsdorf
Institut für Geographie
Universität Innsbruck
6020 Innsbruck
AUSTRIA

D. W. MEINIG

Forging a National Axis

Problems of Geographical Decision-Making in a Federal State[1]

Quite suddenly, in the mid-nineteenth century the United States assumed a new position and prominence on the map of the world. It was a time of enormous geographical change in the extent, shape, and prospects of the country. Part of this was overt and abrupt: the firm, formal acquisition of a long Pacific frontage upon the division of Oregon and acquisition of California. Other changes were less obvious and more incremental, but no less decisive: the emergence of the railroad as a space-conquering instrument of revolutionary possibilities.
It did not take much imagination to see a strategic interdependence in these two developments: only a radically efficient system of communication and transportation could ensure the integrity of a truly transcontinental republic, and the construction of such a system would demonstrate the remarkable power of the railroad and display to all the world the entrepreneurial genius of the American nation and people. Yet, the basic issue of where to build this essential facility was so momentous, so geographically contentious, that it defied resolution for many years. Let us therefore take a closer look than is usually accorded this topic, to consider what was at stake, what alternatives were considered, and what was finally accomplished in this protracted and provocative struggle to fix the first firm transcontinental axis of the United States.

Concept

The United States now spans the continent from sea to sea as "a magnificent parallelogram" three thousand miles across and half that in breadth, "equal to the whole temperate zone" of North America, and thus "the great idea" so long dreamed of, "an inland communication" from the Atlantic to the Pacific, was "now ripe to be realized." It was worth pondering, Thomas Hart BENTON went on to say, "what a wonderful circumstance in the history of the world" had made it so: "that there should be a nation whose domain is so extensive that she is able to lay down as she chooses, by law, a road across a continent, the whole distance under one flag, and one law." This famous Missouri statesman was quite ready to lay down by law just where and what sort of road this should be. It must be a "great national central highway," he said, linking San Francisco with St. Louis, from where it would connect with routes already opened or in process to form a direct line to the Atlantic and provide ready access to "all the States and cities of this Union." And it should be "a great public highway," open to the people and adapted to the different means of conveyance. "I propose," he said, to reserve a one-mile breadth of land "from the frontier of Missouri to the Pacific Ocean . . . for all sorts of roads - railway, plank, macadamized," as many tracks, independent of one another, as shall be necessary and practical, including a margin given over to "a plain old English road, such as we have been accustomed to all our lives - a road in which the farmer in his wagon or carriage, on horse or on foot, may travel without fear, and without tax - with none to run over him, or make him jump out of the way" (*Benton 1849, 472f*).
Yet, for all his vision and sense of urgency the aged BENTON was more a voice of the past than of the future. His emphasis on a set of parallel roads and on movement by wagons and horseback (sleighs in winter), and his openly expressed doubts about the feasibility of a railroad through the mountains exposed him as only partially attuned to the transformations of the times. For thirty

Fig. 1: Railroads in the USA[1], 1860

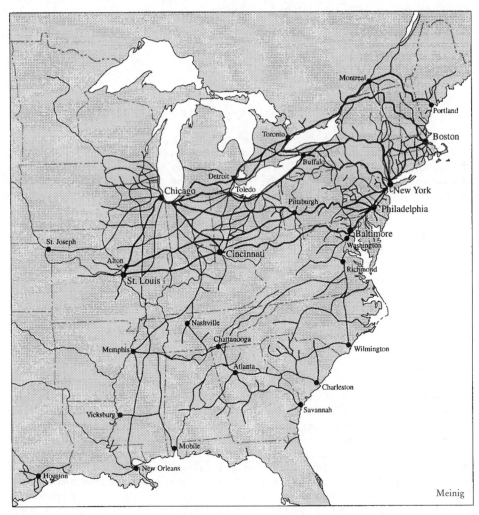

[1] Incipient trunk lines are marked with a heavier line.

years he had presumed to speak for the West and dilate upon its vast potentials. Had he looked as intently eastward he might have discerned more clearly that the means for effecting those vital connections were becoming available at this same moment. For it had taken just twenty years to demonstrate what a radical, transforming instrument the steam-powered railway was. The building of several lines across the corrugated Appalachians, linking the Atlantic seaboard with the Ohio Valley or Lake Erie, confirmed the practicalities of such mountain engineering, the operation of these as single-company linear systems displayed a new dimension of geographic management, and the scheduled daily services set new standards of speed and efficiency in the conquering of distance (*Fig. 1*). Henceforth there need be no doubt that the continents, however broad, lay open to penetration; that all places, however isolated, might be connected; all resources, however difficult of access, might be tapped by the spreading tentacles of the modern world system.

This intersection of profound changes in the shape and position of America and in transport technology was recognized, in some degree, by many different persons. Whereas in 1846 a Senate committee had dismissed Asa WHITNEY's intensely promoted scheme for a railway from Lake Michigan to Puget Sound as "a project too gigantic, and, at least from the present, entirely impracticable," by 1852 relatively few questioned either the necessity or the practicality of such a national project, a railroad to the Pacific became the main theme of commercial conventions, orations, newspapers, and national periodicals, and Pacific railroad bills became a staple of every session of Congress. From this time on the basic questions were not *could* and *should* we build a transcontinental band of iron but *how* and *where* to do so. Historians have examined at length the tangle of political and financial interests involved and exposed some of the reasons why it took twenty years from general recognition of the need to the actual completion of the task. I shall focus attention on the deeply divisive issue of *where* such a connection or connections should be built, and why it took thirteen years and a drastic alteration of geopolitical circumstances to come to a decision.

Objectives

We may begin by noting the objectives, the declared purposes and benefits, of such a line. The most obvious and simple objective was to create a *national trunk line*. Such a link was the essential "chain of union" ensuring "the integrity" of the whole. Inevitably, the famous imperial precedent was called into support: "we know that the Romans - from whom we borrow so many of our ideas, useful or grand - never considered a conquered territory added to the republic or empire until it was perforated by a road." To defend the Pacific Coast was an obvious primary task of empire (concern over British attack was commonly cited), and a railway would also greatly enhance the efficiency and reduce the costs of supplying the many intermediate posts already established along the way to protect emigrants and "keep in check the dangerous Indians." But the purpose here, as in the Roman case, was not only military but to unite "the subjects of the most distant provinces by an easy and familiar intercourse." For an American nation grounded upon popular government not only was such a trunk line "necessary to the unity and promptitude of government, representation, administration, and defense," as the web of railways spread outward from this "great base line of connection... the laws of contact and association... will bind society together in all its parts" until it becomes "coextensive with the boundaries which embrace the American family."

At least as much rhetoric was devoted to the role of the Pacific railroad as a *developmental line*. All advocates stressed its transforming power: "the western wilderness... will start into life under its touch." Whereas the "law of nature" kept population and the commercial economy bound to the river banks,

> "the railroad operates as the river did in olden time... The railroad is the river produced by modern science. We can carry these streams over mountains and across valleys, and they will be followed by towns and cities along the plains. From this great stream rivulets will flow, so that... American civilization will spring up, and the land teem with life" (*Kelley 1862, 1594*).

Most speakers simply pointed to the experience of the eastern states and referred to "the teeming millions who will follow the track of the railroad," confident that "what the Erie Canal has been to the State of New York, a Pacific railroad is destined to be to the whole country."

And a *Pacific* railroad would be more than a national line. It was a decisive part of something far greater that was taking shape: the "last grand revolution in the commercial intercourse of the world" - "the consummation of the great idea which filled the mind of COLUMBUS" - "the American road to India." Such a route was "destined to bear on its long lines that majestic procession of the commerce of the continents of Europe, America, and Asia." The rhetoric was extravagant, but dazzling visions of an *intercontinental trafficway* were connected, however tenuously, to some major discernible developments:

- communication, at a hitherto unimaginable speed, by telegraph, which was already transforming the means and expectations of commercial intelligence; most proposals for a rail included a telegraph line to the Pacific; the laying of a transatlantic cable was soon underway, and plans for a world-girdling network were under avid discussion;
- more substantial was the emergence of the "Atlantic ferry": regular scheduled crossings by fast, iron-hulled, screw-propelled steamships, a system that seemed readily adaptable to the Pacific to capture and expand the Asian trade;
- the rapid push toward consummation of another age-old commercial dream: a canal through the isthmus of Suez. In 1854 DE LESSEPS obtained a concession and formed his company, then assembled an international commission of engineers and naval experts, and in April 1859, he turned the first spadeful of sand to begin excavation of this great ditch.

The Suez route was of course a direct rival of the American prospect, and there was fear that it would be augmented by a British "Asiatic railway from the Mediterranean, by the Persian Gulf and India, to the ports of China." Therefore, it was a contest "between London and New York, between Calcutta and San Francisco, between England and America, by land and by sea ... [for] undisputed command of the commerce of the world." A keen sense of such rivalry (from the French as well as the British) was apparent through all these years of debate. A practical senator from Vermont might dismiss all this talk of overland Asian commerce as illusory, for "nothing but opium or silks" could pay the freight, but a sense of urgent need to secure for the United States a central position within a system that was "to produce a *radical* and *permanent* change" in the routes of world commerce remained a driving force.

Finally, a transcontinental railroad would be a *national symbol of American character*. Such a vast and challenging undertaking was "necessary to the highest destiny of the nation," it would "elevate our national pride, stimulate our national energies and consolidate our national character," and it would put our national virtues on munificent display to all the world. As an early senatorial endorsement phrased it, this "short route to the riches and marvels of the Indies" would soon be thronged with travelers, and

> "This crowd must pass through the heart of our country, witness its improvements, the increase of our population, the activity, the genius, and the happiness of our people, and contemplate the wisdom and the advantage of those free institutions which have produced such glorious effects. It would certainly not be unreasonable to suppose that this intercourse would have an extensive influence upon the opinion and feelings of the civilized world in favor of free institutions" (*Breese 1846, 12f*).

The rehearsal year after year of this compelling set of incentives served to underscore the great paradox: a project of great national importance widely endorsed by public sentiment was repeatedly thwarted by the inability of Congress to act. Although eager to respond to such public interest, support was dispersed among a host of competing routes, and Congress was paralyzed by that lack of focus and the enormity of such a fundamental geographic decision.

The Problem of Route Selection

In the restless search for some sort of formula that would break the deadlock, four desired qualities permeate the discussions: the route must be *practicable, economical, national*, and *equitable*. A major early effort to find a way toward a decision focused on the first two. The act of 1853 authorizing explorations and surveys directed the Secretary of War "to ascertain the most practicable and economical route . . . from the Mississippi River to the Pacific Ocean." The professed hope was that scientists and engineers could assess several alternative routes for their feasibility, calculate the costs of each route, and present the Congress with a route of decisive attractiveness. As the historian William GOETZMANN has observed,

> "It was . . . characteristic of federal policy in the trans-Mississippi West . . . to seek recourse in the disinterested judgment of science. In a sense, this was a way of letting nature itself decide, [placing] the decision beyond the control of mere mortals. . . . Upon such a premise was based the whole idea of the Pacific railroad surveys" (*1959, 262f*).

But that premise was inevitably compromised from the outset. Someone had to nominate the general routes to be investigated, select the leaders and members of the survey parties, and assess the results for presentation to Congress. There was no way of ignoring already vigorously competing interests or of erasing the experiences and biases of those assigned to the task. The Army Topographical Corps and the more than one hundred scientists who participated were for the most part a conscientious force and they produced an immense amount of information in a short time, but they were not devoid of special interests and rivalries; and, indeed, the complete set of thirteen massive volumes includes some surveys sponsored by private promoters, and several of the officers had invested in potential terminal sites.

In simple terms five "transcontinental" routes (the term is not literal in American railway usage but refers to companies and trunk lines extending from the dense web in the eastern half of the nation to the Pacific Coast) were examined, each designated by a particular parallel or parallels of latitude, and each implicitly related to interests focused on a particular city or harbor at either end (*Fig. 2*). We need not review these in detail. Suffice to note that four of the five were declared to be entirely practicable by their investigators (and would eventually have one or more trunk-line railroads). Each had difficulties to surmount, chiefly the double mountain barrier of the Rockies and the Sierra Nevada-Cascades and the climatic conditions: the scarcity of water and timber on portions of the southern routes and the probability of deep snows on the northern routes. Only the 38th parallel prospect (which had been included largely because of Senator BENTON's intense lobbying) was dismissed, as no suitable pass could be found through the complicated mass of the Southern Rockies.

As for "most economical," the figures produced by the leaders of the several surveys were highly uneven in totals and reliability, based as they were on hasty engineering investigations, surmises derived from earlier reconnaissances, estimates about little-known conditions (such as geology, weather, and prospects for water), and the predilections of the investigators. Those ultimately in charge, Captain A. A. HUMPHREYS and Jefferson DAVIS, Secretary of War, grossly adjusted some of these figures (increasing the estimate for the northernmost route by 20 percent and decreasing the 35th parallel route by 44 percent), thereby leaving the whole topic open to severe challenge. Furthermore, cost tended to recede in significance. The nation was not in debt, nor was it going to finance directly the building of such a road but only underwrite bonds and offer land grants from the public domain. And, after all, most would agree that it was important to select the best route, not necessarily the cheapest one.

Such a combination of difficulties and complications doomed this strenuous sprawling search for "nature's decision" to failure. As GOETZMANN concluded:

> "In the end, the effect of the Pacific railroad surveys proved to be almost exactly opposite of their intended purpose as expressed by Congress. They did not furnish a conclusive report on "the most practicable and economical route . . ." Instead, confusion was deepened and competition intensified by the most obvious results of the reconnaissance, which indicated . . . not one but several extremely practicable routes existed, and . . . because of this, the far-western country was possibly more valuable than anyone had previously imagined" (*1959, 295*).

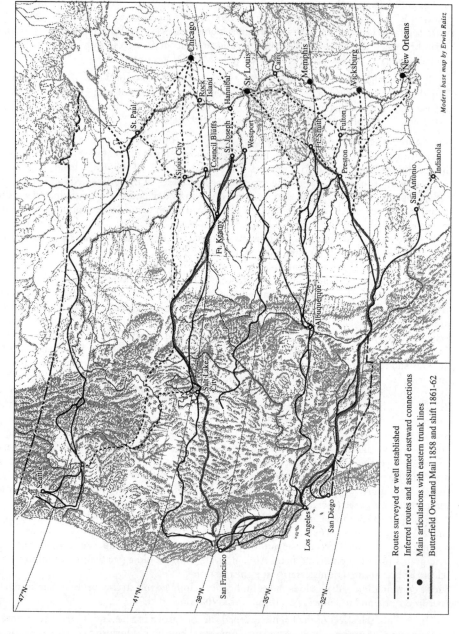

Fig. 2: Pacific Railroad Surveys, 1850s

Thus when Jefferson DAVIS declared to Congress that a comparison "conclusively shows that the route of the 32d parallel is... 'the most practicable and economical route'" because it was not only the shortest and cheapest (by a third) but could be completed much more quickly and would enjoy much less interruption of service once built (*Davis 1855, 29*), he was immediately accused of overweening sectional bias, and he succeeded only in turning the issue back to a contest completely focused on its *national* and *equitable* features.

An early comprehensive journalistic report on transcontinental railroad proposals asserted that "a work so stupendous must be the common work of America, and for this it ought, as nearly as possible, to be *central*" (*DeBow 1849, 20*). Senator BENTON had already propounded that axiom in support of his own San Francisco–St. Louis design: "a central road is the most national in its character, because it accommodates the greatest number, and because it admits of branches to the right and the left with the greatest ease and convenience." Throughout these debates this simplest of designs - "one grand trunk central railroad" (as one bill referred to it) - was repeatedly put forth as a logical and powerful proposition for such a national project.

Once California was acquired there was never great argument about the best Pacific terminus (although Southerners kept a fond eye on San Diego, and Puget Sound had its advocates) because "the bay of San Francisco [was] the finest in the world,... central, and without a rival," and that city would be "the Pacific seat of trade," the great "entrepôt" and "equipoise" to New York. At the outset St. Louis might call on the same kind of geographic logic. Since the days of LEWIS and CLARK it had been the unrivaled gateway to the West, and well-worn trails now led to Santa Fe, Utah, California, and Oregon. Pivotal to all the great waterways of Transappalachia, St. Louis would naturally become a prime objective of railroads in this rapidly developing Interior.

But any such claim was immediately challenged on other grounds. A resolution adopted by a Memphis convention, meeting just a week after a big one in St. Louis, pointed to the "special advantages" for "a national railroad... commencing at San Diego," thence via the Gila River, El Paso, and "terminating at some point on the Mississippi [south of] the mouth of the Ohio." Almost from the first the claim for *sectional equity* was overt and intense. Amendments to specify Memphis, or "not north of Memphis," were countered by those specifying St. Louis, or not south of St. Louis. A Kentuckian's proposal to designate the mouth of the Ohio (Cairo) as the eastern terminus got nowhere, but it openly declared the kind of centrality at issue;

> "[that point] may be said to be the mouth of all the rivers between the Alleghany and Rocky mountains,... [it] is half way from the head to the mouth of the Mississippi, and it is the point on that mighty river where the non-slaveholding and the slaveholding States come together. Thus, sir, it is not only geographically, but *politically, central*" (*Grey 1855, 288*).

By this time, however, developments in the North had further complicated the issue. By 1855 several railroads fanning out of Chicago had reached the Mississippi and extensions across Iowa were underway (*Fig. 1*). Northern interests favoring a trans-Iowa-Platte Valley route thereby emerged as vigorous challengers of St. Louis. Because of a general assumption that Congress could offer land grants only within federal territories (not within states) this issue was often defined in terms of a line commencing from the western boundary of Iowa versus one from the western boundary of Missouri. That differentiation, in turn, was quickly translated into the sectional rivalry between nonslaveholding states (Iowa) and slaveholding (Missouri). Because the designation of any specific point as an eastern terminus proved so inflammatory, recourse was also taken in specifying a band of territory defined by latitudes. However, since "every town on the Mississippi, from St. Paul to the Gulf, is contending for the terminus" any such designation inevitably produced amendments to broaden the eligible band. Thus an attempt in 1855 to fix a terminus between 39° and 40° N (Kansas City to just above St. Joseph) was quickly amended to 37° - 43° N (Cairo-Sioux City) and redefined the next day into two branches diverging from the trunk toward Lake Superior on the north and Memphis on the south. An 1859 bill underwent similar successive attempts at mutation until it reached the (obviously intended) absurdity of 49°

Fig. 3: The Gwin Plan, 1853

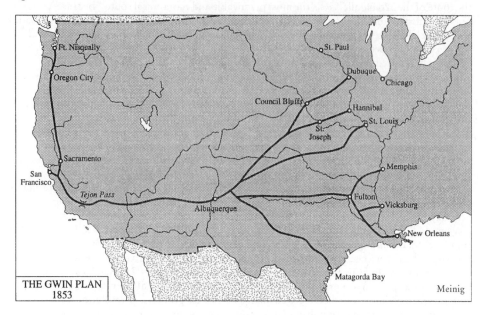

to the mouth of the Mississippi. This eastern terminus issue demonstrated that the selection of a route or routes was not just a national and a sectional issue but one of *regional equity* as well. The first major Pacific railroad bill was obviously designed to meet all these requirements. Presented by William GWIN of California, chairman of the Senate Committee, it proposed a route from San Francisco southeastward in the Central Valley to Tejon Pass to pick up the general line of the 35th parallel route eastward to Albuquerque, from whence the trunk line began to fan into half a dozen branches: to Matagorda Bay in Texas; to Fulton, Arkansas, with branches to Memphis, Vicksburg, and New Orleans; to St. Louis; to St. Joseph and Hannibal; to Dubuque via Council Bluffs (*Fig. 3*). A long branch from the San Joaquin north to Oregon City and Puget Sound completed a vast "horseshoe" system totaling 5,000 miles (*Gwin 1853, 280ff*). GWIN was a Democrat (an emigrant from Mississippi) well attuned to Southern interests and their insistence on a southern trunk line (he would later serve as a Confederate agent in Europe), but the design was obviously the creation of a committee seeking to cater to every regional interest. A flurry of opposition sent it back to committee.

Impasse over the horseshoe design led to a different means to satisfy the same variety of interests (*Fig. 4*). A new committee began with the idea of proposing two trunk lines, a northern and a southern but "concluded that unless we proposed . . . three routes, and gave the chances to the different sections, no bill could pass." The result was a bill authorizing land grants and other aids for the construction of three transcontinental railroads:

- Northern Pacific, from some point on the western boundary of Wisconsin to a port in Oregon or Washington Territory;
- Central Pacific, from Missouri or Iowa to San Francisco Bay;
- Southern Pacific, from Texas to a California port.

Although such a major change in geopolitical strategy generated its own brand of resistance - "Why, sir, as if the difficulty were not enough in the execution of one railroad, . . . we are startled

Fig. 4: Some Abstract Concepts

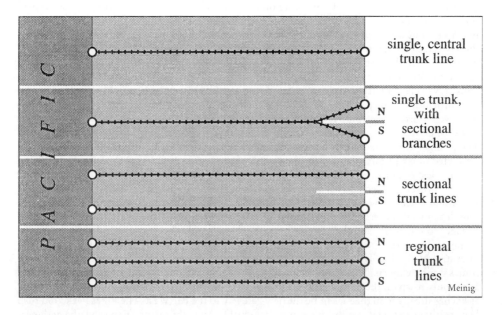

with the enormous proposition to make three" - the Senate actually passed such a bill in 1855 and twice thereafter (1859, 1861), but none of these were endorsed by the other house.
In the House of Representatives the focus was on either one central trunk line with eastern branches or, at most, two trunk lines. Toward the latter 1850s the increasing power of the North in Congress and in the nation led to greater insistence on a single central route. As a senator defending such a proposal argued:

> "it is more central as to the territory of the country; more central to population; more central to the line of emigration; more central to the great business interests of the country."

Even so, chronic geopolitical realities were also taken into account:

> "it is proposed that the line shall have two short branches: one from a slave State, and the other from a free State - one from a northern State, and the other from a southern State - Iowa and Missouri."

However, by this time - 1859 - 1860 - such a limited gesture only infuriated militant Southerners. A similar bill in the Senate the year before had caused Senator IVERSON of Georgia to demand that "the South shall have an equal chance to secure a road within her borders, to insure her benefit whilst the Union lasts, to belong to her when, if ever, the Union is dissolved," and now a Texas congressman bitterly accused the House Committee of designing a bill "for the sole purpose of giving supremacy to one section of the country to the detriment and injury of the other" and threatened secession. Recommitted, the bill reemerged as a proposal for two routes, northern and southern, each with eastern branches to serve contending regional interests; passed by the House in December 1860, differences with the Senate's three-route bill remained unresolved before being overwhelmed by the secession crisis.
In the wake of secession and the onset of the Civil War geopolitical pressures for a Pacific railroad took on new urgency. The need to defend the national territory became more compelling (fears of British intervention in California were now heightened), and the need to "cement the two

coasts of our country, and make the East and the West parts of a well-united nation, easily governed," with no danger of "breaking on the crest of the Rocky Mountains," now seemed starkly apparent.

A central route across the Far West was now the obvious choice because of fresh developments therein as well as the removal of Southern votes in opposition. The new city of Denver was arising near the base of the Rockies to serve the sudden influx of people to nearby mining camps; at the same time, Virginia City emerged atop fabulously rich silver discoveries in the Washoe Mountains of Nevada, directly across the Sierras from the goldfields of California. Meanwhile, the cost and difficulties of dispatching an army to quell the Mormons had underscored the need to improve the arteries of empire. Yet in spite of general agreement on a western extension it took weeks of debate to resolve where it should be attached to the existing eastern network.

The primary controversy was between interests centering at St. Louis and those at Chicago, translated into a terminus at or near the mouth of the Kansas River or the mouth of the Platte. The simplest response was to authorize two branches to serve those alignments. The attempt to do so, however, opened up two more issues: at what point should the branches be joined to the trunk, and exactly which places on the Missouri River should become the terminals. These were interdependent matters in that the point of attachment affected the angle of the branch, the distance to the trunk, and the amount of the land grant and other government aid given to the corporate builders. The original bill in each house set this point at 102° W longitude somewhere in central Nebraska. The initial concept of two branches serving the Kansas and Platte river routes was quickly challenged and eventually amended to include several others. As the first and as yet only town on the middle Missouri River to be reached by a railroad, St. Joseph saw itself as having already won the race to be the new gateway to the Far West. The Pikes Peak gold rush had greatly increased its wagon and stagecoach traffic across the plains. In the end, the designers of the bill gave in not only to St. Joseph but to Leavenworth and Sioux City as well (the latter to appease Dubuque and Minnesota interests). As a result, as one critic of the time observed, "What might have been a great artery . . . became nothing but a sprinkler." With such a lavish sprinkling of the chances for eager capitalists to make a lot of money without putting up much of their own, a Pacific railroad bill was passed by wide margins in both houses and signed into law by President LINCOLN on July 1, 1862.

In summary, the following routes were authorized (*Fig. 5a*): a Union Pacific trunk line from a point on the 100th Meridian between the Republican and Platte rivers, "thence running westerly upon the most direct, central, and practicable route" to the western boundary of the Territory of Nevada," there to meet and connect with the line that the Central Pacific Railroad Company was to construct from a point "at or near San Francisco, or the navigable waters of the Sacramento River, to the eastern boundary of California"; a set of connections with that trunk from Sioux City, Omaha, St. Joseph, and Kansas City; with shorter connections from Atchison and Leavenworth (*Haney 1910, 489 – 498*).

Various incentives relating to construction progress were built into the program and were further adjusted from time to time. Two are of particular note. A provision allowed either the Central Pacific or the Union Pacific to build beyond the California-Nevada line should the other road not have reached that point. And eventually the line from Kansas City (renamed the Kansas Pacific) was allowed to build directly west to Denver and beyond and become the main trunk if it outraced the Union Pacific. The Kansas route represented intensive lobbying by St. Louis gateway interests to offset the ever-more apparent advantages of Chicago. This competition was also affected by the choice of gauge. The original act decreed a uniform width for the entire line but left the choice up to the President. LINCOLN selected five feet (the width of most of the railroads in the South and of a short line in California); whereupon Congress passed a new bill prescribing four feet eight and one-half inches (our standard gauge of today), so as to conform with all the western lines north of St. Louis. The whole system was, by law, to operate "as one connected, continuous line" so that "cars can be run from the Missouri River to the Pacific

Fig. 5 a and b: Union Pacific, as Authorized and Union Pacific and Branches as Built 1871

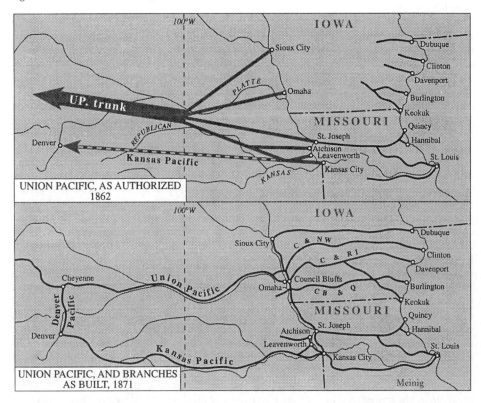

Coast," with grades and curves not exceeding the maximum of the Baltimore & Ohio Railroad (America's first transappalachian trunk line).

Thus after a decade of impassioned, often bitter debate, and only after the federation had partially disintegrated was the central government able to determine where this essential national facility should be built. The difficulties were inherent in both the character of the government and the significance of the choice. The fixing of the nation's communications axis was such a momentous geographical decision as to produce "a trembling anxiety" in the leadership of every state and city"; it was an issue that "so exasperates human passion and so enlists [selfish] human interest" as to paralyze a republican federation. Only by offering a spray of branches to every competing interest could an agreement be reached (the "pork barrel" is a strongly *geographical* dimension of our political system).

Construction and Operations

It was well understood that there was a vast difference between authorization and realization of such an immense project; the original legislation allowed fourteen years for completion. Leland STANFORD turned the first shovelful on the levee at Sacramento in January 1863. Groundbreaking at Omaha did not take place until nearly a year later, and wartime shortages of labor and material as well as chronic problems of financing and adjudication made progress discouragingly slow for some years.

The two companies were faced with starkly different physical conditions in the early stages of construction: the Central Pacific with the formidable, heavily dissected wall of the Sierra Nevada; the Union Pacific with the plains rising almost imperceptibly for nearly five hundred miles to the west with no more than a few shallow streams to cross (*Fig. 6a*). Five routes across the Sierra Nevada were closely examined before the shortest (Emigrant Gap) route was decided upon in late 1865, and it took more than two years of heavy work to cross the mountains. Not until the spring of 1868 did the track reach Reno and the rapid push across Nevada begin. By that time the Union Pacific had surmounted its first physical challenge at the Laramie Range and was building across the Wyoming Basin. As track laying picked up speed, two major decisions faced the converging forces: whether to skirt the Great Salt Lake on the north or the south, and where to meet and to establish the official working junction between the two companies. In spite of the strong urgings of Brigham YOUNG for a route through Salt Lake City and across the broad level salt flats on the south side, the more rugged northern route was chosen, in part because of grave uncertainty about the fluctuating levels of the famous inland sea. Just where the tracks would join was an issue of major financial importance (relating to land grants and per-mile subsidies). The heroic labors of the competing construction crews racing across the deserts would receive great public attention, but the decisive contest was being fought in Washington where the rival lobbyists filed hastily compiled survey and optimistic progress reports to induce government decisions in their favor. Rival survey parties ranged hundreds of miles ahead, those of the Union Pacific into Nevada, those of the Central Pacific to Wyoming, and the accelerating construction crews graded parallel roadbeds more than a hundred miles past one another. The actual meeting point was negotiated privately between the two companies in Washington in April 1869, who agreed to join tracks at Promontory Summit, to transfer forty-seven miles east of that point from the UP to the CP (for a price), and to create a new city adjacent to Ogden as their joint operating terminal. A month later, on May 10, 1869, "the most significant single act of the historical geography of American transportation was accomplished" (*Vance 1986, 312*).

The golden spike set off celebrations all across the land and a gushing torrent of words proclaiming the immense, transforming importance of this long anticipated moment. When the well-traveled and widely read journalist Samuel BOWLES, upon completion of his inspection trip, declared "the Pacific Railroad - open, is a great fact to America, to the world. . . . It is the unrolling of a new map, a revelation of a new empire, the creation of a new civilization," he was confirming, along with many others, that the symbolic objective had been achieved (*Bowles 1869, 5*). Other, more practical objectives were rather more elusive. It would take more than a spiking together of these two flimsy, hastily constructed tracks to wrench world commerce out of its accustomed paths. Pacific steamships continued to focus on Panama and provided such serious competition for transcontinental shipments that the railroad leaders invested heavily in the steamship company and tried to enforce cooperation. Thereafter a slow trickle of teas and silk gave a tantalizing hint of the "colossal" commerce so long anticipated, but "the last grand revolution" in world intercourse was slow to develop.

Viewed as a developmental line, the results were sporadic but more substantial and assured. By 1870 the frontier of colonization was about a hundred miles west of Omaha, and the huge land grant (every other section in a twenty-mile belt) gave the Union Pacific a major means and incentive to extend this salient as far as farming proved feasible. The three main settlement districts farther west, Denver and the Colorado mines, the Mormon oasis, and the Washoe mines around Virginia City, were quickly connected by local branches. As for the vast stretches in between there was only a thin scattering of ranches and small mines and little local freight, and the towns created by the railroads to serve their own operations were the most substantial settlements. Thus Cheyenne, midway along the Union Pacific, became the main division point, with subdivisions breaking at half a dozen points between the Omaha and Ogden terminals

Fig. 6: Profile of Divisions and Subdivisions

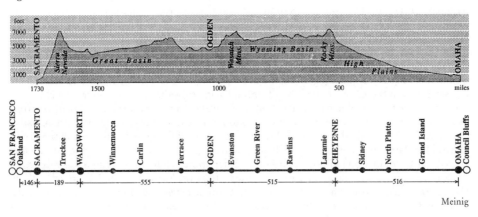

Meinig

(*Fig. 6b*). The larger of these points of crew change, locomotive servicing, and car inspection, with their roundhouses and repair shops, employed hundreds of men, with smaller numbers spaced along the line at various water, coaling, and helper stations. All across western Nebraska, Wyoming, and Nevada the railroads initiated and in large degree set the settlement pattern. Thus the main line was readied to serve as a "great stream" from which "rivulets" would flow and "American civilization ... spring up," although much of this rugged and arid land would never exactly "teem with life."

It is rather paradoxical that the most obvious feature, the physical creation of a railroad to the Pacific, did not in fact result in the primary objective: a national trunk line. When Thomas C. DURANT, the erratic promoter and manager of the Union Pacific, cried out exuberantly after the commemorative spikes were driven, "there is henceforth but one Pacific Railroad of the United States," he might seem to be voicing a common assumption that the "one connected, continuous line" Congress had decreed was now ready for operation. But such was far from the case then (as he well knew) and would never really be the case in any full sense (as he helped ensure). What the public and orators had long envisioned - "unbroken communication by rail across the continent" - made its appearance only in such extravagant displays as the Pullman Hotel Express, a special train created to carry a group of affluent Bostonians (who had helped finance the Union Pacific) on a week-long journey to San Francisco, whereas the routine service was a daily passenger train each way between Omaha and Ogden and another between Ogden and Sacramento (soon with the option of continuing by rail on a subsidiary line to Oakland) and by steamboat to San Francisco. The 1,800-mile journey was scheduled as five and a half days of travel and normally took at least another day because the two trains were not scheduled so as to connect and provide through service (many travelers welcomed the break and the chance to inspect the Mormons).

The fundamental fact was the existence of not "one Pacific Railroad," but two railroads, two separate corporations, authorized by Congress to provide service between Omaha and San Francisco, and any assumption that there would be ready cooperation to obvious mutual advantage was quickly negated. Created and shaped to the interests of powerful leaders, the CP and UP were competitive from the start and remained so long after their tracks were joined. They abandoned the idea of jointly building a new town near Ogden (partly because of Mormon opposition), and they engendered endless problems at the junction they did set up; schedules, transfer time, methods of operating, types of equipment, and, especially, division of rates required constant negotiation. It was soon apparent that the leaders of the Central Pacific saw a much better future in a rapidly developing California than in a debt-ridden elongated line across Nevada, and they created a new instrument, the Southern Pacific, and set out to dominate California and the Southwest. By 1881, through construction and acquisition, they had formed their own "transcontinental" from San Francisco to New Orleans (via the 32d parallel route) as well as a connection at Deming, New Mexico with the new Atchison, Topeka & Santa Fe to Kansas City and thereafter treated their Central Pacific subsidiary as a secondary line.

The Union Pacific, so emblematic in name and fame, was in fact no more than a segment of a trunk line within the emerging continental system, and a very vulnerable one. For years its Omaha-Ogden route generated relatively little local traffic. None of the branches defined in the Pacific railroad legislation was built as originally programmed (*Fig. 5b*). Much the most important area tapped was Colorado, but within a year of the golden spike that lucrative region was reached by the Kansas Pacific, offering an alternative route to the east. Moreover, the KP linked with the Denver Pacific comprised a competitive trunk line from Cheyenne eastward via Kansas City and St. Louis and claimed legal equality of access to transcontinental traffic.

Anyone who traveled across America by rail in the 1870s or was familiar with the actual handling of freight, had a clear - and severe - understanding of just how far the world-famed transcontinental was from being the "one grand trunk central railroad" so long envisioned. At best this band of iron was, quite literally, an articulation, "divided into joints," into four distinct legal and operational segments - Atlantic ports to Chicago, Chicago to the Missouri River, the Missouri to the Salt Lake Valley, the Salt Lake Valley to San Francisco Bay - linked together at three congested, exasperatingly inefficient junctions: Chicago, Council Bluffs - Omaha, Ogden (*Fig. 7*). It took that form because that was the way the United States had decided to create its railroad system: by as many different sets of capitalist entrepreneurs as could survive the vicious competition to build and operate such facilities. Even so, there had still been the option of imposing upon private corporations a requirement that in the national interest this one great trunk railroad be operated (as a keen and sympathetic British observer had admonished) "as a united whole from the Atlantic direct to San Francisco" and not "be permitted to be worked in a disjointed manner." After all, it was widely agreed that building this first Pacific railway was a national task and could be accomplished only by lavish government subsidy. But although such aid was bestowed upon these and many other railroad corporations in great amounts, such intervention was never guided by a rational design for a national transportation infrastructure.

Fig. 7: Transcontinental Articulation

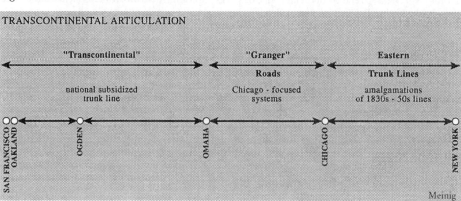

No comprehensive plan for a national network of railroads was ever presented. Yet by fixing a first framework for the western half of the country and thereby profoundly affecting the network already in place in the eastern half, the Pacific railroad issue took on something of the character and significance of such a plan. Obviously the central government intervened here more directly in geographically decisive ways than it had anywhere in the East.

Such intervention was always under challenge. There were recurrent suggestions that the decision on the route of the transcontinental be left to the capitalists who would build the line, on the assumption that entrepreneurial risk takers would select the most economical, practicable, and traffic-generating route - that thereby no particular locality would have any advantage "except that given by nature herself" - but the idea was bitterly denounced in the inflamed political atmosphere of the 1850s. Southerners well understood the almost certain regional consequences of that policy: "Sir, this unequal flow of Government money and Government benefits into the great northern maelstrom has been going on long enough." Even more vehement was the condemnation of an early proposal to let the President of the United States do what Congress seemed unable to do: select an eastern terminal, on the grounds that he was the most likely to respond to what was best for the nation as a whole. Such a radical deference was immediately denounced by senators from the older South: the granting of such "immense influence... in building up one section of the country where it goes, and in injuring that where it does not go" would be a giant step in transforming "a free confederacy of Republican States" into "a consolidated empire." Such a so-called "rape of the Constitution" stood no chance of enactment. The most obvious alternative for such a government was to offer something to every interest. In this bicameral structure it is understandable that a Senate, in which each state had the same number of votes, would be pressured toward *three* Pacific railroads - despite the enormity of such a commitment at the time - as a way of breaking the stalemate, whereas the House, with proportional representation increasingly favoring the North, would tend to hold out for a *single* central trunk line. Had the federal crisis not become so nearly mortal on other grounds, it seems likely that a sectional compromise on a *two*-road program would have been approved, providing for a southern route and a central route (with branches). As it turned out, the Central Pacific–Union Pacific trunk stands as a distinctly *national* creation achieved only on the collapse of the original federation and adapted to provide nominal equity to relentlessly assertive residual *regional* and *local* interests in the North.

This kind of geopolitical problem is so fundamental - and so recurrent in response to new technologies - that I will conclude with a brief look at several other American designs for a national infrastructure.

The first was the *Gallatin Plan of 1808* (Meinig 1993, 313 – 316). Prepared at the request of the Senate by the Secretary of the Treasury, it was comprehensive, covering all the original national territory (the *Louisiana Purchase* had only just been added) (Fig. 8). It was a program of waterways and turnpikes (toll roads) fitted to nature; in general (a) a parallel coastal waterway (with canals across peninsular necks) and turnpikes along the Atlantic seaboard; (b) the great interior waterways of the Ohio and Mississippi; (c) short canal or road connections across the mountains to link Atlantic and interior system; and (d) short canals linking the Great Lakes and the Ohio-Mississippi. It was designed to serve political as well as commercial needs, that is, the military and the mail (there was already great emphasis on the need for efficient communication among all parts of a federal republic). GALLATIN, recognizing geopolitical realities, noted that there would also have to be many local projects "sufficient to equalize the advantages" of those states and districts less directly touched by this design.

The *Gallatin Plan* got pushed aside by the crisis resulting in the War of 1812 with Great Britain. But the experience of that war, the immense difficulties of moving men and armaments and supplies, created a strong focus in the 1820s on a system of *military roads* (Fig. 9) radiating from the national capital: (a) northwest to Buffalo and the Great Lakes; (b) directly west to the Ohio and St. Louis; (c) southwest to New Orleans; and, added in the debates, (d) an interior line

Fig. 8: The Gallatin Plan, 1808

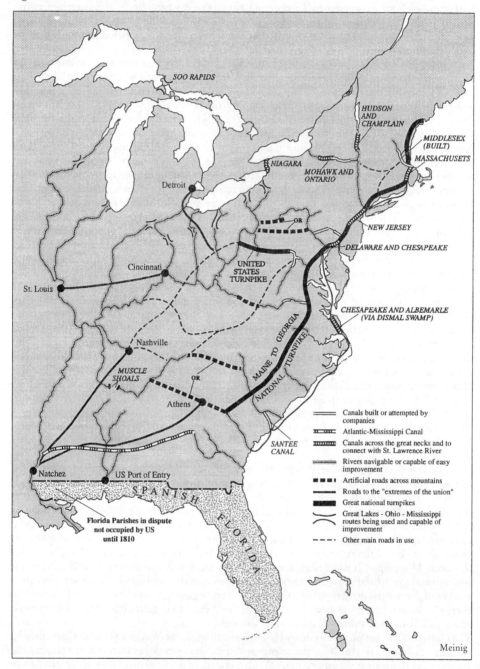

Fig. 9: Military Roads in the USA[1], 1820s

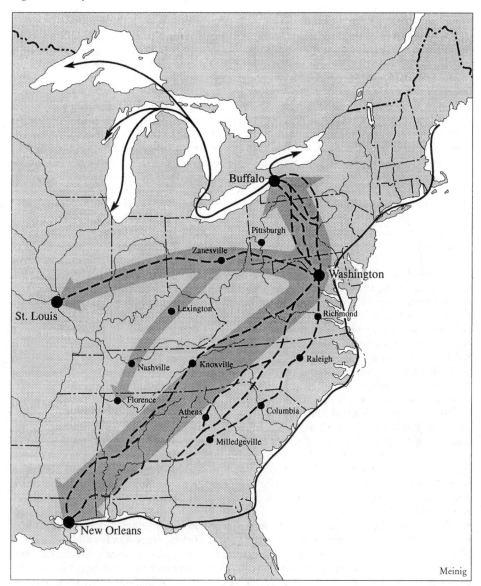

[1]Dashed lines indicate routes actually surveyed.

329

branching to Kentucky and Tennessee (because the United States feared a large regular army, defense depended on state militias, and these interior states having no foreign borders would be major sources). Again, not only military needs but the mail and speedy communication between all states to ensure cohesion of the union were stressed. This plan also foundered on divisive regionalism. European observers were puzzled by this failure. In France all roads radiated from Paris; in the United States there was a determined and successful effort to make sure they did not radiate from Washington. Americans did not want a magnified, powerful, ornamented capital (*Meinig 1993, 339 – 342, 349 – 352*).

Each new form of transportation opens up new opportunities and initiates new geopolitical designs - and struggles. Having looked at the case of the transcontinental railroad, let us jump a century ahead from these military roads of the 1820s to *a highway proposal of the 1920s*. The automobile age emerged with the twentieth century and was accelerated by the First World War. Vehicles were quickly improved but the roads were not. Every modern nation faced an enormous task of building - and an enormous series of geographical decisions on where to build. In the United States, typically, roads were the responsibility of local governments. Gradually, states formed highway departments, and by about 1916 some federal funds were allocated to the states. After the Great War the need for a national system seemed apparent, and the war itself suggested the need for efficient national defense and thereby an excuse for central government initiatives. Accordingly, in 1921 a plan was presented by General John J. PERSHING (the recent leader of American forces in Europe). *Fig. 10* shows only the primary priority; the full plan included many other roads. Note the focus on national borders and entrances; in general it is a very open grid, with a national axis and a northern axis, touching every state - but barely in several cases. This plan, too, was rejected, but the idea was alive and a national network was gradually evolved through state highway departments, with federal money and inducements. (In the meantime, Germany led the way with its Autobahnen.)

And so we move on to another Great War and its aftermath. Studies were undertaken during World War II, but the highway focus was on creating jobs and relieving urban congestion. It gradually became clear that we could not simply upgrade the existing system to create a national expressway network; we would have to build an entirely new system; an enormous, costly task affecting powerful interests - as well as the lives of all Americans.

In 1949 a proposal entitled "Highway Needs of the National Defense" was presented to Congress, but it was not until the 1950s, under President EISENHOWER, that a plan was actually approved. He had invited an old army associate, General Lucius B. CLAY, to chair a committee to draw up a plan. After many modifications, a *"national system of interstate and defense highways"* was approved in 1956 (*Fig. 11*). It was a much denser network, of 41,000 miles (several thousand more would be added by later legislation), binding in every state and taking many years to complete (and we are now faced with enormous tasks of rebuilding it after decades of wear and tear).

Finally, we may take a quick glimpse at another radical transport medium. The *proposed air mail routes of 1918* (*Fig. 12*) show a clear national axis (New York-Chicago-San Francisco); a parallel Washington-St. Louis axis; very limited branches; and an apparent concern for international connections: to Montreal, Key West, and Laredo. We may compare this with the system actually operating (or authorized) in 1926 (*Fig. 13*), which shows a national axis, but, amazingly, no service to Washington (one might infer that Chicago was the national capital).

All of these examples underscore some major features of the American federal case: (a) *fear of centralization* and therefore a tendency to diffuse decision-making to lower levels of state or local government; (b) the inherent difficulties of network decisions because route decisions are place decisions, and every specific project is an exercise in *geographical discrimination,* favoring some places over others. (c) Furthermore, especially in formative times, as in nineteenth-century America, but also with each new mode of transportation, such choices are regarded as *powerful and indelible,* fixing the pattern and the relative opportunities for the future. Therefore, in the

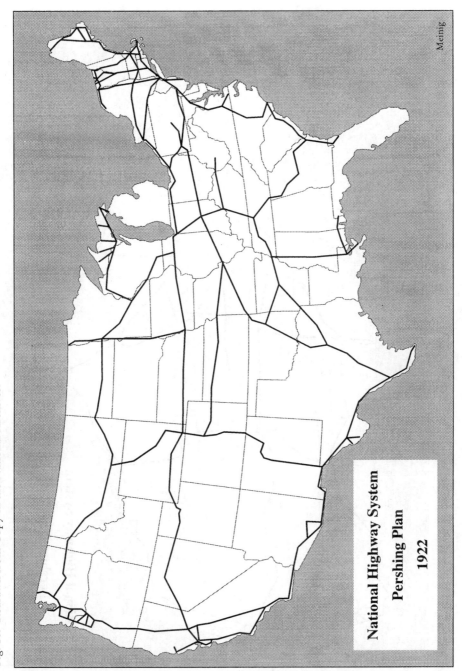

Fig. 10: Redrawn from Copy in the National Archives.

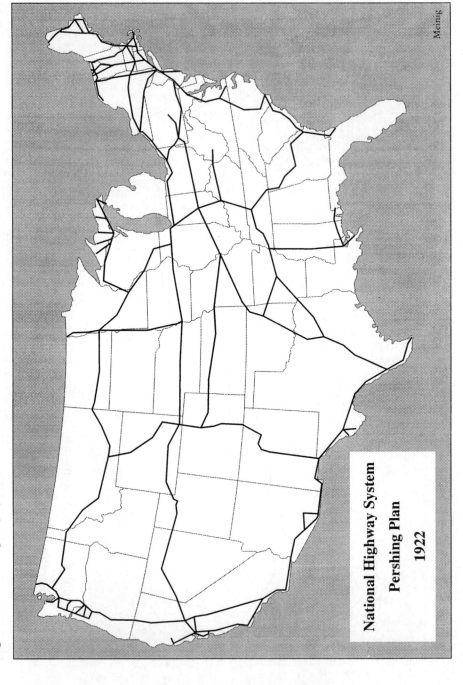

Fig. 11: Interstate Highway System, Eisenhower Plan 1955-1956

Fig. 12: Proposed Air Mail Routes, 1918

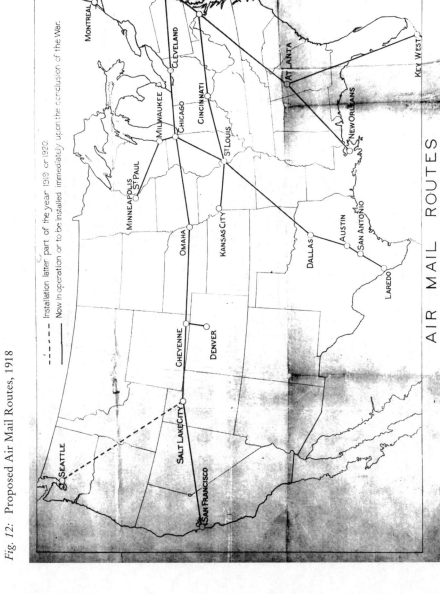

Source: The National Archives.

Fig. 13: Air Mail Routes Operating, Awarded, and Offered as of April 24, 1926

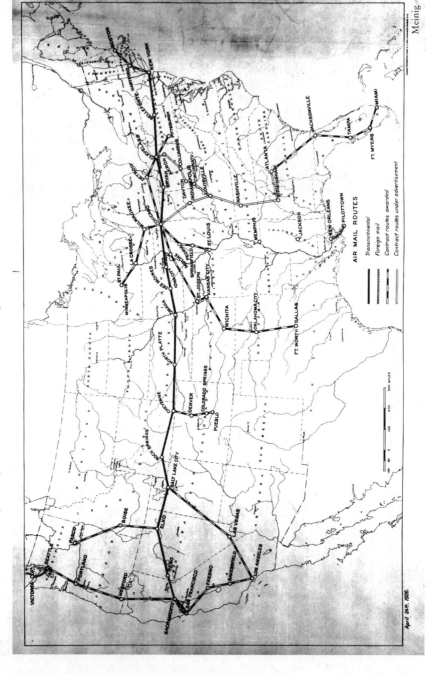

Source: The National Archives.

United States there has been a strong tendency, (d) politically, to turn to the *"pork barrel"*: to give something to everybody; (e) philosophically, to turn to *private enterprise* to make the decisions and to build and operate the network under intense competition. The general result (as with railroads and airlines today) has been great overbuilding, duplication, waste, instability; the offering of some sort of service to most every place, but the lack of a really efficient national transportation system. Setting the national infrastructure is one of the really great geographical topics, and it can only be understood in the geopolitical context of its times.

Summary

Creating the spatial patterns of a national infrastructure is one of the great geographical topics. The emergence of each new form of transportation forces a new round of decision-making about the location of the main arteries, with profound effect upon cities and regions. Such decisions are inherently difficult in a federal republic.

This paper focuses on the problem faced by the United States in determining where to build the first "transcontinental railroad" to the Pacific. This 1850s issue inevitably aroused intense rivalries among major cities and regions. Scientific surveys failed to resolve the matter because several proposed routes were declared to be feasible. Debates over a single trunk line, or two lines (northern and southern), or three lines (northern, central, southern) were not conclusive. Only during the Civil War, after the federation had broken apart, did the North decide upon a central route with a set of branches to connect with the whole span of the existing network. Various features of construction and operation of the Central Pacific-Union Pacific are noted, including their limitations with respect to proclaimed national objectives.

The paper concludes with a brief look at earlier national proposals for a turnpike and canal network, and for a system of military roads, and at post-1920s programs for a national highway system and for airmail service. The general conclusion emphasizes the inherent difficulties in the political exercise of such momentous geographical discrimination, the American fear of centralization and propensity to give something to every major area, resulting in extensive overbuilding, duplication and instability.

Zusammenfassung

Eines der bedeutendsten geographischen Themen ist die Bildung räumlicher Muster der nationalen Infrastruktur. Das Auftreten jeder neuen Transportform zieht eine neue Runde an Entscheidungsfindung über die Lage der Hauptverkehrsadern mit sich, welche tiefgreifende Auswirkungen auf Städte und Regionen haben. Solche Entscheidungen sind in einer föderativ strukturierten Republik von Natur aus schwierig.

Diese Arbeit spezialisiert sich auf jenes Problem, welchem sich die Vereinigten Staaten gegenüber sahen, nämlich der Feststellung, wo die erste "transkontinentale Eisenbahn" zum Pazifik gebaut werden sollte. Diese Frage der 50er Jahre des 19. Jahrhunderts führte unvermeidlicherweise zu Rivalitäten zwischen größeren Städten und Regionen. Wissenschaftliche Untersuchungen scheiterten an der Lösung der Angelegenheit, weil mehrere vorgeschlagene Routen als möglich erklärt wurden. Debatten über eine einzelne Hauptstrecke, oder zwei Strecken (nördlich und südlich), oder drei Strecken (nördlich, zentral, südlich) führten zu keinem Ergebnis. Erst während des Bürgerkrieges, nachdem die Föderation auseinandergebrochen war, entschied sich der Norden für eine zentrale Strecke mit einem Netz an Verzweigungen, um sie mit dem gesamten vorhandenen Netzwerk zu verbinden. Mehrere Merkmale des Baus und des Betriebes der Central Pacific-Union Pacific sind bekannt, welche auch ihre Grenzen in Bezug auf erklärte nationale Einwände beinhalten.

Die Arbeit schließt mit einem kurzen Blick auf frühere nationale Vorschläge für ein Maut- und Kanalnetzwerk und für ein System von Militärstraßen und auf ein Programm nach 1920 für ein nationales Autobahnsystem und für das Luftpostservice. Der allgemeine Abschluß betont die innewohnenden Schwierigkeiten in der politischen Ausführung solcher bedeutsamen geographischen Diskriminisierungen, die amerikanische Angst vor Zentralisation und der Hang etwas jeder größeren Gegend zu geben, welches zu extensiver Überbauung, Duplikaten und Instabilität führt.

Acknowledgement

This essay is adapted primarily from the opening chapter of a book in preparation, *Transcontinental America, 1850 - 1915*, Volume III of *The Shaping of America. A Geographical Perspective on 500 Years of History*. The text and all figures are under copyright to Yale University Press and reproduced here by permission.

Notes

[1] This work is heavily based on the debates in Congress and makes extensive use of quotations to convey something of the imagery and flavor of the rhetoric of the time. Rather than clutter this text with half a hundred references I have identified only a few of greater substance. The source of each quotation will be specified when a slightly different version of this topic is published in book form.

References

Benton, T. (1849): Congressional Globe. 30th Congress, 2d session, July 2.
Bowles, S. (1869): The Pacific Railroad-Open. How to Go: What to See. Guide for Travel to and through Western America. Boston, Fields, Osgood.
Breese, S. (1846): Senate Report on Public Lands, No. 466. 29th Congress, 1st session, July 31.
Davis, J. (1855): Executive Document 78. 33d Congress, 2d session, February 27.
DeBow, J. (1849): Intercommunication between the Atlantic and Pacific Coasts. In: DeBow's Commercial Review, 1 (new series), July, 1 - 37.
Goetzmann, W. (1959): Army Exploration in the American West 1803 - 1863. New Haven, Yale.
Grey, B. (1855): Congressional Globe. 33d Congress, 2d session, January 17.
Gwin, W. (1853): Congressional Globe. 32d Congress, 2d session, January 13.
Haney, L. (1910): A Congressional History of Railways in the United States. Volume II. Madison, WI, Democrat Printing.
Kelley, W. (1862): Congressional Globe, 37th Congress, 2d session, April 9.
Klein, M. (1987): Union Pacific. Birth of a Railroad 1862 - 1893. Garden City, NY, Doubleday.
Meinig, D. (1993): The Shaping of America. A Geographical Perspective on 500 Years of History. Volume II. Continental America, 1800 - 1867. New Haven, Yale.
Russel, R. (1948): Improvement of Communication with the Pacific Coast as an Issue in American Politics 1783 - 1864. Cedar Rapids, IA, Torch Press.
Travelers Official Railway Guide of the United States and Canada. June 1868. Ann Arbor, University Microfilms reprint 1968.
Vance, J. (1986): Capturing the Horizon. The Historical Geography of Transportation. New York, Harper & Row.

Address of the Author

D. W. Meinig
Department of Geography
Syracuse University
Syracuse, NY 13244-1090
USA

Innsbrucker Geographische Studien Bd. 26: Human Geography in North America

> "One of the nice things about being Miss America is it gives you a chance to visit places you never thought people actually lived in, like North and South Dakota and Nebraska."
>
> Kellye CASH (Miss America 1987)

JOHN FRASER HART

The Great American Deserted

Miss America might have been more prescient than many people realized, because large parts of the area that once was stigmatized as *The Great American Desert* are rapidly becoming *The Great American Deserted*. The United States has 282 counties that lost population at each of the last five censuses, between 1940 and 1990 (*Fig. 1*). Five-sixths (235) of these counties are concentrated in an area that extends southward along the 100th Meridian from North Dakota to the Texas Panhandle, and spills over into adjacent states. This paper explores and speculates about some of the geographic and demographic correlatives and consequences of half a century of population loss, with special emphasis on patterns of migration during the 1980s.

Procedure

My universe, or dependent variable, consists of the 235 counties that lost population at each census between 1940 and 1990, plus 150 more counties that lost at every census but one (*Fig. 2*). Most of the "turnaround" counties, which gained only in the 1970s, are in the southeastern part of the region, in an arc from north central Texas to northern Missouri and southern Iowa. Most of the handful of counties that gained in an earlier decade are along the western edge of the region. The geographical patterns within this "Swiss cheese" region are so complex that they are more amenable to statistical aggregation than to cartographic analysis. Maps merely distinguish the poorer counties from the poorest, because most of the counties in the region are in the extreme (whether top or bottom) thirteen percent of the nation with respect to each criterion mapped.

Measuring Migration

I used two techniques, both the natural increase technique and the cohort survival technique, to estimate the net number of people who moved into or out of each county during the 1980s. The natural increase technique is predicated on the truism that people are born, they move, and they die; these three events determine all population change. The *natural increase* is the surplus of births over deaths in any given area. Any difference between the natural increase and the actual change in the population of the area must result from migration. We can calculate the net number of migrants to or from any county by subtracting the number of deaths from the number of births to determine the natural increase, then subtracting the actual population change from the natural increase to determine the net number of migrants.
The annual volumes of the *Vital Statistics of the United States* contain data on the number of births and deaths each year in each county in the United States, both by place of residence and by place of occurrence. Data for place of residence obviously are preferable for the study of migration to and from sparsely populated rural areas that do not have hospitals where births and deaths might occur.

Fig. 1: Counties in the United States that Lost Population at Each and Every Census Between 1940 and 1990.

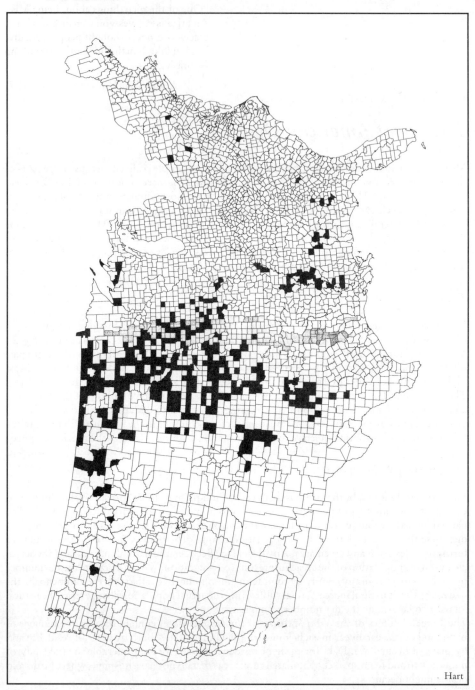

Fig. 2: The Great American Deserted: 235 Counties that Did Not Gain Population at Any Census Between 1940 and 1990 Plus 150 Counties that Gained Population Only Once.

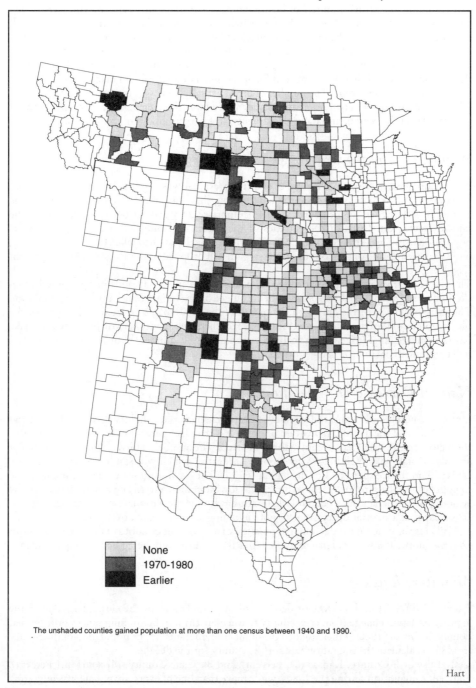

Declining Number of Deaths

The tedium of extracting numbers of births and deaths from twenty separate volumes for 385 counties was alleviated considerably by my growing recognition of a dramatic trend in the birth data. In any given county the numbers of births and deaths will fluctuate from year to year, but it soon became apparent that the year-to-year fluctuations in the number of births actually camouflaged a fairly sharp decline during the 1980s. Five-year totals, which smooth out annual fluctuations, revealed that the number of births declined dramatically in many counties during the second half of the decade. The number of births actually increased in a mere five counties, of which three have large Indian reservations; it dropped more than ten percent in seven-eighths of the counties in the region, and more than twenty-five percent in one-third (Fig. 3).

Women of Child-bearing Age

This phenomenal decrease in the number of births presumably is tied to a decrease in the number of women aged 15 to 44, who comprise a decreasing share of the decreasing population of the region. In 1940, when women aged 15 to 44 comprised 24.3 percent of the population of the United States, four-fifths of the counties of the region had only 20 to 23 percent of their population in this age-sex group; in 1990, when the national share had fallen only to 23.4 percent, more than two-thirds of the counties of the region had dropped to the range of 16 to 19 percent (Fig. 4).

The average county in the region dropped almost one percent per decade during a period when the numbers of people aged 15 to 44 were being bulged by the burgeoning baby boom generation. The sharp decline in births during the latter half of the 1980s may be related to the fact that the oldest women of the baby boom generation have reached menopause, and their biological clocks have stopped ticking. It seems reasonable to assume that the numbers of births in these counties will continue to decline.

Natural Decrease of Population

Unlike the number of births, the number of deaths changed only slightly between the first and second halves of the decade. It went up or down less than five percent in half of the counties of the region, and less than ten percent in three-quarters. The number of births, which was declining sharply, actually dropped below the number of deaths, which was stable, in many counties, especially in the southern half of the region (Fig. 5). These counties suffered a natural decrease in population. The ratio of deaths to births was lowest in the western and northern parts of the region, but only a handful of counties had ratios as low as the national ratio of 55 percent.

It is clear that a natural decrease of population, an excess of deaths over births, was at least partially responsible for the declining population of many of the counties of the *Great American Deserted* in the 1980s. People were dying faster than babies were being born to replace them.

Migration Rates

I subtracted the natural increase or decrease of the population for the entire decade from the actual population change from each county to calculate the number of migrants to or from that county during the 1980s. I then divided the number of migrants by the population of the county in 1980 to calculate the migration rate for the county for the decade.

Only Ellsworth County, Kansas (0.3 percent), and St. Clair County, Missouri (0.1 percent), enjoyed in-migration during the 1980s, while more than one of every six people was migrating

Fig. 3: The Great American Deserted: Births in 1985 - 1989 as a Percentage of Births in 1980 - 1984.

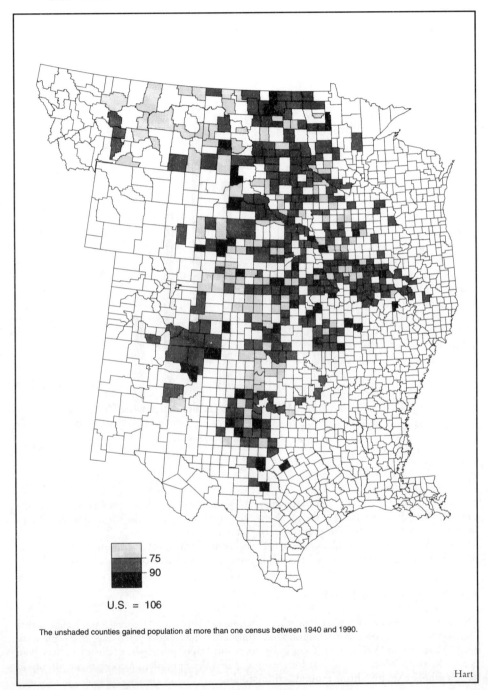

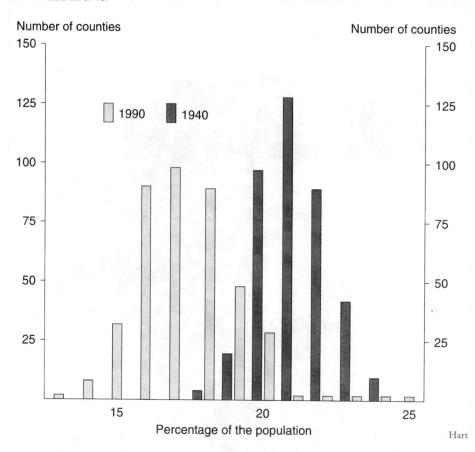

Fig. 4: Frequency Distribution of the Number of Counties in the *Great American Deserted* with Women Aged 15 - 44 as a Specified Percentage of their Total Population in 1990 and in 1940.

out of one-quarter of the counties in the region (*Fig. 6*). Out-migration rates were highest along the 100th Meridian, especially at the northern and southern ends, but they exceeded ten percent in more than two-thirds of the counties in the region.

The demographic outlook is bleak indeed for a region in which more than one of every ten people migrated from counties that have been losing population for half a century or more.

Percentage 65 and Over

Out-migration rates were lowest in northern Missouri and in eastern Nebraska and Kansas, areas that also have the greatest concentration of counties in which a high percentage of people were aged 65 and over in 1990 (*Fig. 7*). Their low rates of out-migration may reflect the fact that there is no one left to leave, and popular lore maintains that their population consists mainly of old people who are simply sitting around waiting to die.

Fig. 5: The Great American Deserted: Deaths in 1985 - 1989 as a Percentage of Births in 1985 - 1989.

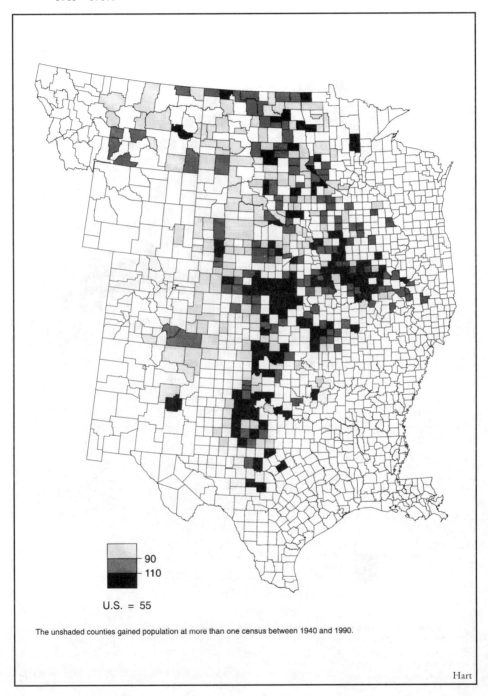

Fig. 6: The Great American Deserted: Migrants Between 1980 and 1990 as a Percentage of the 1980 Population.

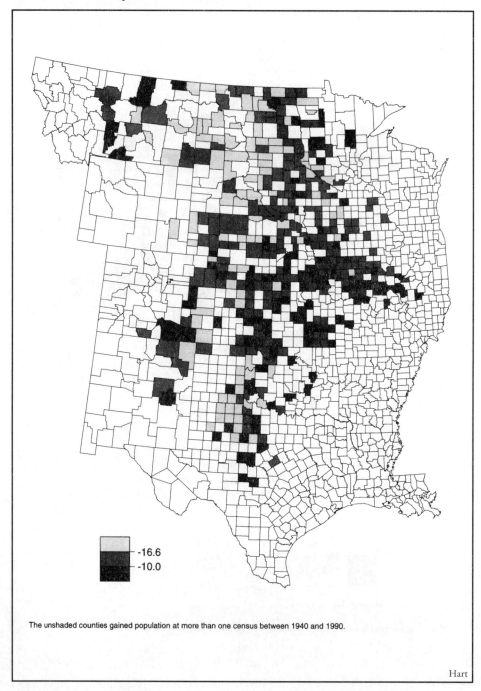

Fig. 7: Percentage of the Population Aged 65 and Over in 1990.

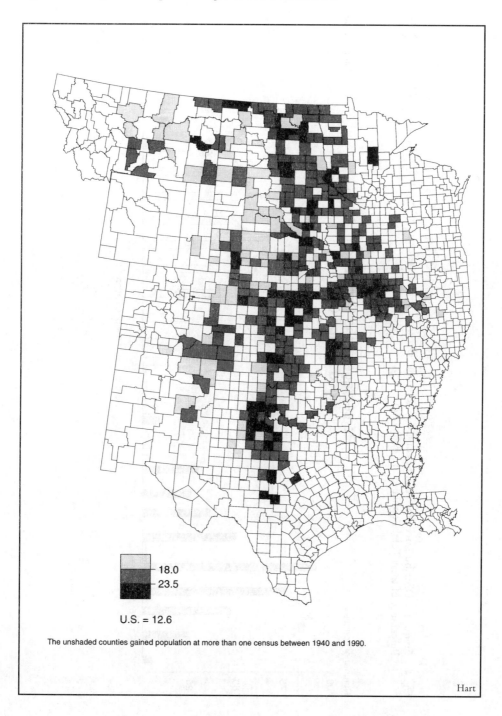

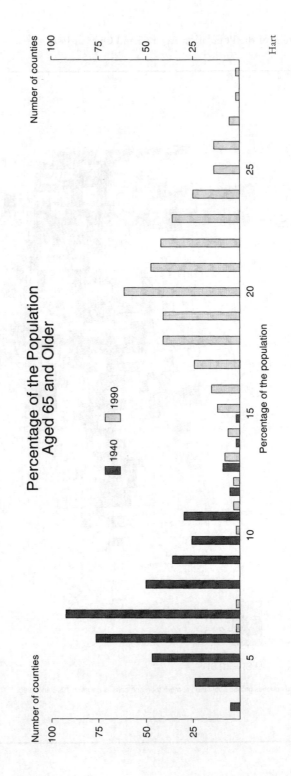

Fig. 8: Frequency Distribution of the Number of Counties in the *Great American Deserted* with Persons Aged 65 and Over as a Specified Percentage of their Total Population in 1940 and in 1990.

Tab. 1: Age Specific Migration Budgets for Three Nebraska Counties, 1980-1990.

Age cohort in 1990	Burt		Furnas		Otoe	
	Gain	Loss	Gain	Loss	Gain	Loss
0 – 4	518	...	287	...	951	...
5 – 9	633	...	394	...	1,110	...
10 – 14	5	...	...	24	27	...
15 – 19	...	100	...	90	...	165
20 – 24	...	373	...	252	...	558
25 – 29	...	288	...	179	...	406
30 – 34	22	...	...	27	47	...
35 – 39	...	18	...	24	18	...
40 – 44	...	5	...	24	...	53
45 – 49	...	41	...	19	...	1
50 – 54	...	14	...	34	...	67
55 – 59	...	42	...	36	...	34
60 – 64	...	77	...	39	...	87
65 – 69	...	114	...	33	...	99
70 – 74	...	109	...	64	...	158
75 – 79	...	145	...	75	...	222
80 – 84	...	170	...	158	...	302
85 +	...	627	...	536	...	932
Total	1,178	2,123	681	1,614	2,153	3,084
Net change	– 945		– 933		– 931	

Source: calculated by the author.

The population of the *Great American Deserted* is aging far more rapidly than the population of the nation as a whole. In 1940 most of the counties of the region were fairly close to the national percentage of 6.8 percent of the population aged 65 or older, but by 1990, when the national figure had risen to 12.6 percent, most of the counties of the region had climbed to the range of 18 to 22 percent (*Fig. 8*). Counties in which one of every five persons is aged 65 or over may represent the end of the line demographically.

Migration Budgets

Who are the people who are leaving? I used cohort survival analysis to calculate age-specific migration budgets for each county in the region. An age cohort consists of those people who were born in a five-year period. Its members are ten years older when a census is taken ten years later, and their number can change only by migration or by death.

Sample age-specific migration budgets for three Nebraska counties that lost approximately the same number of people during the 1980s reveal that population change is heavily concentrated in three age brackets (*Tab. 1*). Children aged 0 - 9 are classified technically as in-migrants, because they had not been born when the census was taken ten years earlier; comparison of the cohorts aged 0 - 4 and 5 - 9 shows the effect of the sharply declining number of births in all three counties. Heavy losses in the cohorts aged 20 - 24 and 25 - 29 reveal that these cohorts experienced the

Fig. 9: Cohort Survival Ratios for Burt, Furnas, and Otoe Counties (Nebraska), 1980 - 1990.

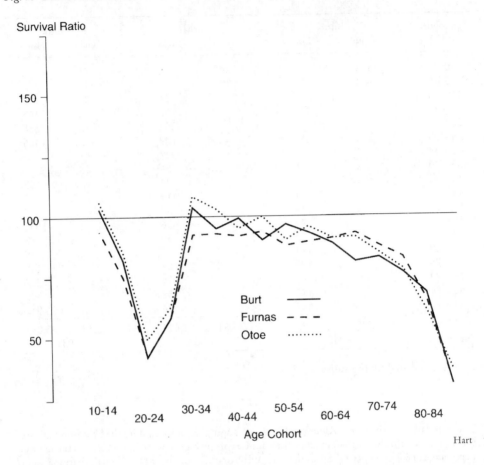

greatest out-migration. Death apparently plays a minor role in reducing the size of cohorts below the age of 60, but after that age it becomes an increasingly important factor in population change. In all other age cohorts the numbers for gain or loss were less by an order of magnitude, which indicates the highly age-selective nature of migration. Most people seem to stay put between the ages of 30 and 60.

Cohort Survival Ratios

I divided the number of people in each cohort in 1990 by the number of people in that same cohort in 1980 to calculate age-specific cohort survival ratios for each county. A ratio above 100 indicates in-migration, and a ratio below 100 indicates out-migration. The graph of survival ratios for the three Nebraska counties shows a blank for the two cohorts under 10 (who had not been born in 1980), a sharp drop when those aged 20 to 29 migrate from the county, relative stability between the ages of 30 and 65, a gentle decline between 65 and 80, and a sharp drop thereafter (*Fig. 9*).

Cohort Aged 20 - 24

One of the striking features of this graph is the similarity between the curves for all three counties. Such similarity is the norm, because the survival ratio profiles for most of the counties in the region are generally similar. The graph of median survival ratios for all counties shows that every cohort in the median county suffered out-migration during the 1980s, with the heaviest losses in the cohort aged 20 to 24 (Fig. 10). In the median county almost half of these young people departed for college, for military service, or for the bright lights of the big city.

Many counties in the northern part of the region lost more than sixty percent of their young people aged 20 to 24, and only northern Missouri, eastern Kansas, and Oklahoma had significant numbers of counties that lost less than forty percent (Fig. 11).

Cohort Aged 30 - 34

Some out-migration of the cohort aged 20 - 24 probably is not only inevitable, but desirable. No one can complain when high school graduates go away to college or to a stint in the military, but

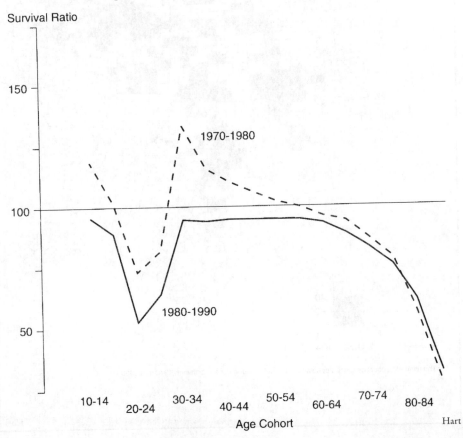

Fig. 10: Median Cohort Survival Ratios for the Counties that Gained Population in the 1970s and then Lost Population in the 1980s.

Fig. 11: The Great American Deserted: Survival Ratio for the Cohort Aged 20 - 24 in 1990.

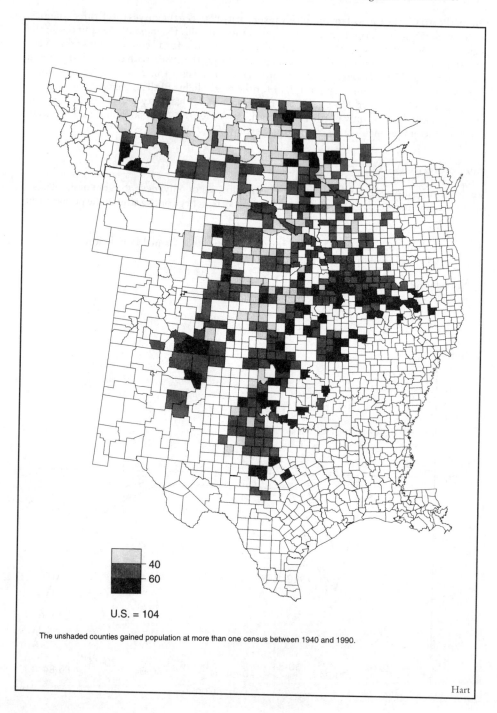

The unshaded counties gained population at more than one census between 1940 and 1990.

Fig. 12: The Great American Deserted: Survival Ratio for the Cohort Aged 30 - 34 in 1990.

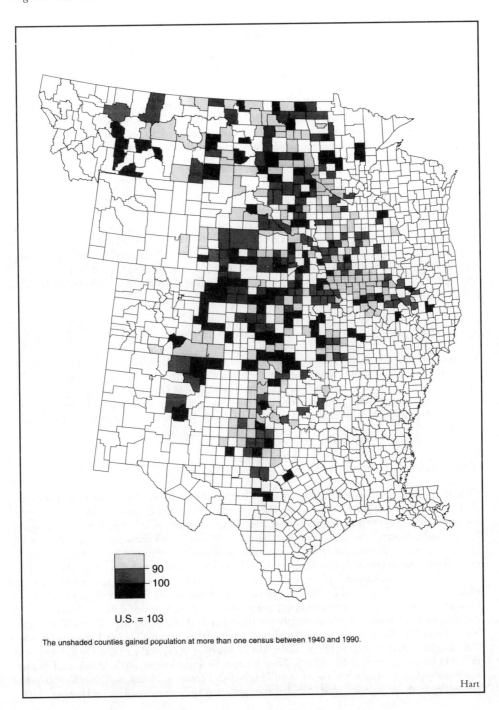

a county that cannot regain some of its young people, that cannot convince them to return home after they have finished college or military service, is a county that seems doomed to continue to lose population unless it can identify some new source of in-migrants. For that reason, the migration behavior of the cohort aged 30 - 34 is a major determinant of population change. The survival ratio for this cohort reflects the ability of a county to attract back home some of the young people who had left ten years earlier, and most counties in the region fared very poorly indeed during the 1980s. Even those that did relatively well were merely the least worst of a pretty sorry lot in this regard.

The heaviest losers not only were unable to entice back those who had already left, but they even lost more than one-tenth of those who had not left earlier (*Fig. 12*). Kansas and adjacent states did comparatively well, but there were ominous concentrations of heavy losers in North Dakota and southwestern Minnesota, along the Iowa-Missouri line, and on the rolling plains of Texas and western Oklahoma.

The "Turnaround" Counties

The importance of the migration behavior of the cohort aged 30 - 34 for population change is highlighted by comparing the median survival ratio profiles for the 1970s and the 1980s for the "turnaround" counties, those that gained population during the 1970s and then lost again during the 1980s (*Fig. 2*). The median turnaround county enjoyed in-migration of people aged 30 to 54 during the 1970s, when it was gaining population, but it lost people in all cohorts during the 1980s, when it was losing (*Fig. 10*).

Cohort Aged 10 - 14

The survival rates for most cohorts seem to vary quite independently of the survival rates for all other cohorts, with a single exception: the survival rates for the cohort aged 10 - 14 are fairly closely related to the survival rates for the cohort aged 30 - 34 (*Fig. 10*). Children aged 10 - 14 presumably are too young to migrate on their own, and a comparison of survival rates suggests that they migrate with the members of the cohort aged 30 - 34, who are the right age to be their parents.

The Older Cohorts

One of the advantages of doing things by hand, instead of feeding data into a machine, is the fact that you are forced to think about what you are doing at each step of the way, and you become aware of nuances in the data that are almost impossible to detect once they have been processed. For example, in many counties the cohorts aged 55 - 59 and 60 - 64 show faint, very faint, signs of a slight uptick in survival ratios. The actual numbers are very small, rarely more than a percentage point or two and a dozen people or so, but they suggest two things. First, a few people seem to be going back to the old home place to retire, no matter how bleak and uninviting that place might seem to an outsider. Second, apparently people in this region really do live longer than people in other parts of the country, and it does not just seem that they live longer.

Although it has not been nearly so widely publicized as the baby boom after World War II, the First World War also enjoyed its own small postwar baby boomlet in the early 1920s, which was followed by a sharp decline in births during the Depression years of the 1930s. The babies born in the 1920s started to turn 65 in 1985. They seem to be living longer, so the number of deaths has remained fairly stable, but they too will inevitably become statistics, and after they die the percentage of the population aged 65 and over might actually decrease until around the year 2010,

when the first members of the post-World War II baby boom start to reach this age.
The possibility that a few older people may be retiring to some of the counties in the *Great American Deserted*, and the possibility that old people in the region might live longer, have some sobering implications for public policy. How can a county with a dwindling population provide adequate care and services for an elderly population that might be increasing at an even more rapid rate than we realize?

Conclusion

The *Great American Deserted* is a belt of counties that extends from North Dakota to the Texas Panhandle and spills over into adjacent states. These counties have lost population at each census since 1940, and the rate of loss may actually be increasing. More than half of the young people in these counties migrate elsewhere around the time they attain the age of discretion, and only a handful ever return. Those young adults who do come back are the principal migrants to these counties, and their numbers have never been large enough to counter the massive out-migration of young people in their early 20s. Why should a college graduate want to move to one of these counties? (*Fig. 13 - 16*)

The principal determinant of population growth in these counties has been the surplus of births over deaths, but this surplus began to disappear in the latter half of the 1980s, when the oldest members of the baby boom generation began to approach the end of their child-bearing years, and many counties in the region actually experienced a natural decrease in population during the latter half of the decade.

The number of deaths in these counties remained fairly constant during the 1980s, even though half a century of out-migration has left a residual population of increasingly elderly people who seem to be living longer than their predecessors. Both the number and the percentage of people aged 65 and over may decrease slightly when those born during the post-World War I baby boomlet are replaced by those born during the baby bubble of the Depression years, but both the number and the percentage will start to increase once again around the year 2010, when those born during the post-World War II baby boom begin to reach the age of 65.

Cohort survival analysis is a useful complement and perhaps even a corrective to calculating the percentage of the population that is in any given age group, which is the traditional approach in analyses of population composition, because the percentage of the population in any age group is affected by the numbers of people in all other age groups, but the number of people in an age cohort can be changed only by the migration or the death of the members of that specific cohort.

Zusammenfassung

Die *Great American Deserted* besteht aus einem Band von Bezirken, das sich von Nord Dakota bis zum Texas "Pandhandle" erstreckt und sich bis in die angrenzenden Staaten ausbreitet. Diese Bezirke haben seit 1940 bei jeder Volkszählung an Bevölkerung verloren. Das Ausmaß dieses Bevölkerungsrückgangs dürfte im Steigen sein. Mehr als die Hälfte der jungen Bevölkerung dieser Bezirke ziehen weg, wenn sie das Alter erreichen, in dem sie nach eigenem Ermessen handeln, und nur wenige von ihnen kommen zurück. Jene jungen Erwachsenen, die zurückkehren, sind im wesentlichen die einzigen Zuwanderer in diesen Bezirken. Ihre Zahl ist noch nie groß genug gewesen, um der massiven Auswanderung von jungen Leuten in ihren frühen 20er Jahren entgegenzuwirken. Warum sollte ein Universitätsabgänger in einen dieser Bezirke ziehen wollen?

Der ausschlaggebende Faktor des Bevölkerungszuwachses in diesen Bezirken ist der Geburtenüberschuß. Dieser Überschuß begann aber in der zweiten Hälfte der 80er Jahre zu verschwinden, als für die ältesten Mitglieder der "Baby Boom" Generation das Ende ihres gebärfähigen Alters

Fig. 13: Suitcase Farmers Travel from Farm to Farm in Camper Vans and Need No Farmhouses.

Fig. 14: Abandoned Farmsteads Are Not Uncommon.

Fig. 15: Massive Farm Machines Have Reduced Farm Labor Requirements.

Fig. 16: Lost Springs (Wyoming) Grew from Five People in 1960 to Seven in 1970 - a 40% increase.

zu nahen begann. Viele Bezirke in der Region erfuhren damals einen natürlichen Bevölkerungsrückgang.

Die Zahl der Todesfälle in diesen Bezirken verblieb in den 80er Jahren ziemlich gleich, obwohl ein halbes Jahrhundert an Auswanderung eine Wohnbevölkerung mit zunehmend älteren Personen zurückgelassen hat, die länger als ihre Vorfahren zu leben scheinen. Sowohl die absolute Zahl als auch der Anteil der Personen von 65 Jahren und älter könnte leicht sinken, wenn jene, die in der Zeit des "Baby Booms" nach dem 1. Weltkrieg geboren wurden von jenen ersetzt werden, die während der Phase der Depressionsjahre zur Welt kamen. Um das Jahr 2010 wird sowohl die absolute Zahl als auch der Anteil der älteren Bevölkerung wieder steigen, wenn jene, die während des "Baby Booms" nach dem 2. Weltkrieg geboren wurden, das Alter von 65 Jahren erreichen werden.

Bei jeder Bevölkerungsprognose ist eine Gruppenüberlebensanalyse eine nützliche Ergänzung und sie wirkt möglicherweise sogar korrigierend bei der Berechnung des Bevölkerungsanteils jeder gegebenen Altersgruppe. Dies ist der traditionelle Ansatz für Analysen der Bevölkerungszusammensetzung, da der Anteil der Bevölkerung in jeder Altersgruppe von der Zahl der Personen in allen anderen Altersgruppen beeinflußt wird, aber die Zahl der Personen in einer Altersgruppe nur durch die Abwanderung oder den Tod eines der Mitglieder dieser spezifischen Gruppe verändert werden kann.

Acknowledgments

I greatly appreciate the advice and encouragement I have received from J. Clark ARCHER and Katherine M. KLINK; the data that have been made available to me by Sue JOHNSON of the Minnesota Department of Health; the help in obtaining unpublished data that I have received from Mabel G. SMITH of the U. S. National Center for Health Statistics and from Wendy TREADWELL and Doug REDWELL of the University of Minnesota Machine-Readable Data Center; the extraordinary help I have received from Julia F. WALLACE and her colleagues in the Government Publications Library at the University of Minnesota; the customary expert draftsmanship of Mui D. LE and Alan WILLIS; and the kindness with which Helga LEITNER translated my summary into German.

Address of the Author

John Fraser Hart
Department of Geography
University of Minnesota
Minneapolis, MN 55455,
USA

ALVAR W. CARLSON

Sources of Overseas Tourists (Pleasure Arrivals) to the United States, 1950-1989

Introduction

International tourism has become a major industry in the world's merging economies. Yet only a small percentage, an estimated 8 percent, of the world's 5.2 billion people had traveled by 1990 beyond the borders of their country of residence. Most of these travelers were international tourists who revealed to a considerable extent the global increases in leisure and discretionary incomes which, when spent on travel, contribute to the growth in tourism and the redistribution of wealth (*Matley 1976, 1*). In response to this growth, countries have increasingly needed tourism infrastructures that provide accessibility, accommodations and attractions. As a result, additional air routes and facilities have linked countries with the sources of not only their traditional tourists, but also their relatively new and developing sources. While Europe as a region is the world's leading destination for tourists, the U.S. as a country has become the world's leading destination. This study analyzes America's growth as a destination for international tourists in the four decades between 1950 and 1989 to determine, in particular, not only its major sources, but also its emerging sources, which have implications in determining future tourism policies.

American Policy on International Tourism

Like most countries, the United States has welcomed the increasing number of foreign tourists. After World War II, international tourism was recognized by the federal government as a fairly significant industry, but not as important as the country's domestic tourism, and therefore did not receive strong support for growth. It was not until the postwar decline of the long established industries, especially manufacturing and heavy industry, and the concurrent growth of the service economy that the potential of international tourism became more fully realized. Meanwhile, technological advancements permitted major changes, including faster transportation and communication systems, that could increasingly tie together countries of the world. It was also apparent that the increasing annual outflow of American tourists to foreign destinations, compared to the considerably smaller number of foreign arrivals, contributed to an ongoing and frustrating imbalance of payments. As a result, the U.S. government became more aggressive in formulating policies that sought to promote and increase international tourism.
Following President Eisenhower's proclamation "Visit the USA Year" in 1960, Congress passed the International Travel Act in 1961 to encourage travel to the United States, but little was accomplished. It was not until 1975 that two international events re-focused the country's lagging attention on international tourism:

- the Helsinki Accord that committed America and other countries to greater cooperation in tourism, and
- the establishment of the World Tourism Organization (WTO) to be based in Madrid, Spain with the motto "Tourism: Passport to Peace." The United States endorsed this motto and became a supporting member. The pursuit of international peace had become intertwined

with promotions for international tourism and the intention of bringing foreign travelers together with their hosts and having all benefit socially, culturally, politically and economically from their experiences.

Realizing both the economic potential and goodwill from tourism, Congress passed in 1981 the National Tourism Policy Act that established the U.S. Travel and Tourism Administration (USTTA). This new agency replaced the U.S. Travel Service that lacked a strong mandate to promote international tourism. The USTTA was given directives to develop more international tourism that would lead to economic growth within the country, a reduction in America's foreign travel deficits, and a better image of America in foreign countries. Since then, the promotion of rural tourism within America has been added to the agency's responsibilities. To make travel to the United States easier, the 1986 Immigration Reform and Control Act instituted a visa waiver pilot program for tourists from 8 countries: Japan and 7 in Europe. (This pilot program was extended to 21 countries in 1992: New Zealand, Japan, and 19 in Europe). America is now firmly committed to encouraging more international tourists.

Data Sources

Both the WTO and the USTTA compile data on international tourism to America. Using data gathered before its inception in 1975 and thereafter, the WTO claims the country's international tourist arrivals increased from 38.7 million in the 1950s, to 64.7 million in the 1960s, to 159.9 million in the 1970s, and to 266.4 million in the 1980s. It reports more than 175 million tourists already for the first four years of the 1990s (Paci 1994). Since 1981, the WTO has used data provided by the USTTA, which employs the WTO's definition of a tourist as a temporary visitor who stays for at least 24 hours in the country visited with the purpose of "...1) leisure, recreation, holiday, health, study, religion and sport; 2) business, family, mission, meeting...." (Edgell 1993, 9). Travelers who stay under 24 hours, including those on cruises, are classified as excursionists and excluded in their tourist data. Therefore, both agencies reported, for instance, 36.6 million international tourist arrivals for 1989.

Meanwhile, the U.S. Department of Justice's Immigration and Naturalization Service (INS) has compiled data on all arriving nonimmigrant temporary visitors who have needed visas for entry into the country. Until 1986, all foreign residents who sought a nonimmigrant visa had to obtain it at an overseas U.S. Consulate where the intent of the temporary visit is determined. Exceptions to this procedure now include the residents of the 21 countries participating in the visa waiver program. Upon entry to the U.S., travelers were also required to complete INS Form 1-94

Tab. 1: Nonimmigrant Overseas Arrivals to America, 1950 - 1989.[1]

All Categories (thousands)	1980s	1970s	1960s	1950s
	94,356	40,252	13,117	3,929
% Pleasure Arrivals	73.0	72.4	60.7	52.5
% Business Arrivals	16.0	12.4	12.5	16.3
% Other Arrivals	11.0	15.2	26.8	31.2

[1] No data for July-September, 1979 and fiscal year 1980. These arrivals exclude Canada and Mexico. No data is given for July – September, 1979 and fiscal year 1980

Source: U.S. Department of Justice, Immigration and Naturalization Service, Statistical Yearbook(s) of the Immigration and Naturalization Service (Washington, D.C.: Government Printing Office, 1950 - 1989).

(Arrival/Departure Record), which is used by immigration inspectors to record the class of admission and port of entry.

This procedure allows the INS, therefore, to classify the purpose of entry for all visitors. As a result, the INS has long had a class, since the Immigration Act of 1924, for those visitors who enter solely for pleasure, visiting friends or relatives and attractions, and are called tourists. There have been no annual restrictions or quotas on their numbers. Other classes have included temporary visitors for business, students, foreign government officials, and transit aliens. Twenty classes were in use by 1989 when the INS counted a total of 16.2 million nonimmigrant arrivals. Of this number, 12.1 million were for pleasure, 2.6 million for business, and less than half of a million for any of the 18 remaining categories. Since 1950, pleasure arrivals have constituted the largest class (*Tab. 1*). It is important to point out here that the INS data exclude millions of Canadian and Mexican temporary visitors, largely border crossers. Both Canadians and Mexicans routinely do not need visas or to complete INS Form 1-94 and are granted expedited entry. Canadian visitors for pleasure may stay for 6 months without needing nonimmigrant visas. Mexicans can obtain border crossing cards that allow them unrestricted admission for pleasure within 25 miles of any Southwestern border for no longer than 72 hours. The INS acknowledges that the count of border crossers varies considerably among the ports of entry.

Consequently, WTO and USTTA data on tourists are not comparable with those of the INS. Whereas WTO data show nearly 530 million tourist arrivals during 1950-1989, the INS data on nonimmigrant visitors for pleasure, exclusive of Canadians and Mexicans, totaled only 108 million (*Paci, 1994*). WTO's data include, by its definition of a tourist, those overseas nonimmigrant visitors who come to conduct commercial transactions or business, students, and estimated numbers of corresponding Canadians and Mexicans. The inclusion of business travelers and students is based on the assumption that they are tourists during some of their stay. For instance, USTTA tourist arrivals from Austria in 1989 totaled 106,097, but the INS counted 87,711 pleasure arrivals. USTAA's figure includes the 87,711 temporary visitors for pleasure as well as 17,535 temporary visitors for business, 833 students, and 18 spouses and children of students.

Previous analyses of international tourists have used WTO and USTTA data, which provide higher numbers than those compiled by the INS. Foreign travelers who come to America for business or study and do not have pleasure as their main objective are in fact directed or assigned, according to their purpose, to certain destinations. Therefore, an unknown number of them may not become involved in any touristic activities. Consequently, this study considers only the international visitors who come merely for pleasure or as true tourists. After all, "tourism in its purest sense is travel for pleasure...." (*Rafferty 1993, 1*). Furthermore, to eliminate questionable data on Canada and Mexico, only the sources of overseas arrivals are analyzed. Unfortunately, no INS data exist for the July-September quarter of 1979 and fiscal year 1980.

America's Overseas Visitors for Pleasure (Tourists)

Europe as a region has been the dominant source of America's overseas nonimmigrant visitors for pleasure, henceforth referred to simply as overseas tourists, except for the decade of the 1950s when the nearby Caribbean was the leading source (*Tab. 2*). Since 1960, more than 40 percent of the overseas tourists have been Europeans, mostly western Europeans. Western Europe's persistence can be attributed to its developed economies that produce high discretionary incomes and leisure and to its many historical as well as cultural linkages with America. Many of these tourists, too, speak English, which removes a possible language barrier. In addition, the entry of major American air carriers into the European market has provided Europeans with greater accessibility to America at very competitive fares. Five of America's top sources of overseas tourists came from Europe in the decades of the 1970s and 1980s: United Kingdom, Germany, France, Italy, and the Netherlands (*Tab. 3*). In total, 24 European countries were the sources of at least 10,000 tourists to America during both decades of the 1970s and 1980s. The number of

Tab. 2: Sources of Overseas Tourists (Pleasure Arrivals) to America, 1950 - 1989.[1] (Excludes Canada and Mexico)

	Europe	Asia	Africa	Oceania	Caribbean	Central America	South America	Total
No. of Tourists (thousands)								
1980s	29,967	19,851	962	2,805	5,607	2,217	7,497	68,906
1970s	12,393	6,645	327	1,543	3,197	1,267	3,776	29,150
1960s	3,746	588	93	348	1,369	458	1,359	7,962
1950s	630	73	20	62	779	127	374	2,064
% of World's Origins								
1980s	43.5	28.8	1.4	4.1	8.1	3.2	10.9	
1970s	42.5	22.8	1.1	5.3	11.0	4.3	13.0	
1960s	47.0	7.4	1.2	4.4	17.2	5.8	17.0	
1950s	30.5	3.5	1.0	3.0	37.7	6.2	18.1	

[1] No data for July-September, 1979 and fiscal year 1980. Source: U.S. Department of Justice, Immigration and Naturalization Service, Statistical Yearbook(s) of the Immigration and Naturalization Service (Washington, D.C.: Government Printing Office, 1950 - 1989).

Tab. 3: Ranked Sources of Overseas Tourists (Pleasure Arrivals) to America, 1970 - 1989.[1] (Excludes Canada and Mexico)

Rank	1980s	1970s
1	Japan	Japan
2	United Kingdom	United Kingdom
3	Germany	Germany
4	France	France
5	Bahamas	Venezuela
6	Italy	Bahamas
7	Venezuela	Australia
8	Australia	Italy
9	Brazil	Netherlands
10	Netherlands	Colombia

[1] No data for July-September, 1979 and fiscal year 1980. Source: U.S. Department of Justice, Immigration and Naturalization Service, Statistical Yearbook(s) of the Immigration and Naturalization Service (Washington, D.C.: Government Printing Office, 1970 - 1989).

Tab. 4: Leading Sources of Overseas Tourists (Pleasure Arrivals) to America, 1970 - 1979. (Minimum of 10,000 Arrivals. Excludes Canada and Mexico)

	10-99	Number of Tourists (in thousands) 100-299	300-499	500-999	>1 million
Europe [4]	Czechoslovakia, Hungary, Iceland[3], Luxembourg[3], Romania[3], Soviet Union	Austria, Belgium, Denmark, Finland, Greece, Ireland, Norway, Poland, Portugal, Yugoslavia	Spain, Sweden	Italy, Netherlands, Switzerland	France (1.4), Germany (2.6), UK (3.7)
Percent	1.3	14.2	6.3	16.2	61.7
Other	0.3				
Asia [4]	China[6], Indonesia[3], Iraq[3], Jordan, Korea, Kuwait[3], Lebanon, Malaysia[3], Pakistan, Saudi Arabia[3], Singapore[3], Syria[3], Thailand, Turkey	Hong Kong, India, Iran, Philippines	Israel		Japan (5)
Percent	7.3	12.0	5.2		74,7
Other	0.8				
Africa [4]	Egypt[3], Ghana[3], Kenya[3], Liberia[3], Morocco[3], Nigeria[3]	South Africa			
Percent	34.6	40.5			
Other	24.9				
Oceania [4]	French Polynesia[1], Fiji[3]	Pacific Islands Trust Territory	New Zealand	Australia	
Percent	3.9	6.7	25.3	61.8	
Other	2.3				
Caribbean [4]	Antigua, Barbados, British Virgin Islands, Cayman Islands[3], Cuba[3], Dominica, Grenada[2], Guadeloupe[2], Martinque[3], St. Lucia, St. Kitts[5], Turks and Caicos Islands[3]	Bermuda, Haiti, Netherlands Antilles, Trinidad & Tobago		Bahamas, Dominican Republic, Jamaica	
Percent	12.7	21.4		64.0	
Other	1.9				
Central America [4]	Belize	Costa Rica, El Salvador, Guatemala, Honduras, Nicaragua, Panama			
Percent	3.1	96.9			

	Number of Tourists (in thousands)				
	10-99	100-299	300-499	500-999	> 1 million
South America [4]	Bolivia, Guyana, Paraguay[3], Suriname[3], Uruguay[3]	Chile, Ecuador, Peru		Argentina, Brazil, Colombia	Venezuela (1.1)
Percent	4.9	14.9		45.6	
Other	0.1				30.0

[1] No data for 1970. [2] No data for 1971. [3] No data for 1970-71. [4] No data for July-September, 1979. [5] No data for 1979. [6] Mainland China and Taiwan. Source: U.S. Department of Justice, Immigration and Naturalization Service, Statistical Yearbook(s) of the Immigration and Naturalization Service (Washington, D.C.: Government Printing Office, 1970-1979).

Tab. 5: Leading Sources of Overseas Tourists (Pleasure Arrivals) to America, 1980-1989. (Minimum of 10,000 Arrivals. Excludes Canada and Mexico)

	Number of Tourists (in thousands)				
	10-99	100-299	300-499	500-999	> 1 million
Europe [1]	Czechoslovakia, Iceland, Luxembourg[2], Romania, Soviet Union	Hungary, Portugal, Yugoslavia	Denmark, Finland, Greece, Poland	Austria, Belgium, Ireland, Norway, Spain	France (3.1), Germany (5.5)[8], Italy (1.9), Netherlands (1.3), Sweden (1.1), Switzerland (1.3) UK (10.1)
Percent	0.9	1.7	5.0	10.9	81.4
Other	0.1				
Asia [1]	Bangladesh[2], Kuwait, Sri Lanka, Syria, Cyprus[7], Vietnam[5], Iraq[4], United Arab Emirates[4]	Indonesia, Iran, Jordan, Lebanon, Malaysia, Pakistan, Saudi Arabia, Singapore, Thailand, Turkey	Hong Kong, Korea	China[9], India, Israel, Philippines	Japan (13.9)
Percent	1.2	8.7	4.4	15.2	70.1
Other	0.4				
Africa [1]	Algeria[4], Ethiopia, Ghana[4], Kenya[4], Liberia [6], Morocco, Senegal[2], Zimbabwe[4]	Egypt, Nigeria, South Africa			
Percent	17.7	64.2			
Other	18.1				

	Number of Tourists (in thousands)				
	10-99	100-299	300-499	500-999	> 1 million
Oceania [1]	Fiji[6], French Polynesia[4], Pacific Islands Trust Territory[4], Western Samoa[4]			New Zealand	Australia (1.8)
Percent	3.2			30.2	64.6
Other	2.0				
Caribbean [1]	Antigua, Bermuda[4], Cayman Islands[4], Cuba[5], Grenada[4], Guadeloupe[4], Martinque[4], St. Kitts & Nevis, St. Lucia[3], St. Vincent & Grenadines[4], Turks and Caicos Islands[4]	Barbados, Dominica, Netherlands Antilles	Dominican Republic	Haiti, Jamaica, Trinidad & Tobago	Bahamas (2.0)
Percent	7.4	10.3	8.1	37.3	35.0
Other	1.9				
Central America [1]	Belize	Nicaragua	Costa Rica, El Salvador, Honduras, Panama	Guatemala	
Percent	3.2	7.2	62.5	27.1	
South America [1]	Guyana, Paraguay, Suriname	Bolivia, Uruguay	Chile, Ecuador	Argentina, Peru	Brazil (1.6), Colombia (1.3), Venezuela (1.9)
Percent	2.7	3.0	10.5	20.0	63.8

[1] No data for 1980. [2] No data for 1986. [3] No data for 1986 and 1989. [4] No data for 1986 - 89. [5] No data for 1987 - 88. [6] No data for 1987 - 89. [7] No data for 1989. [8] Includes East Germany. [9] Mainland China and Taiwan.. Source: U.S. Department of Justice, Immigration and Naturalization Service, Statistical Yearbook(s) of the Immigration and Naturalization Service (Washington, D.C.: Government Printing Office, 1980 - 1989).

tourists from nearly each of these countries more than doubled in the 1980s. As a result, 14 countries moved into categories of higher numbers of tourists (*Tab. 4 and 5*).

Europe has been a persistent and rapidly growing source, but Asia's strong emergence since 1970 as the second leading source of overseas tourists has not been less than phenomenal. Providing only 3.5 percent in the 1950s it climbed to the position of being the source of nearly 29 percent in the 1980s. Japanese tourists alone numbered nearly 14 million, not only the highest number for any single country in the 1980s, but their number amounted to more than the populations of most American states including Hawaii, a major destination. Japanese tourism nearly tripled in the 1980s over that of the 1970s, both decades that found Japan ranking at the top of the overseas sources and contributing more than 70 percent of Asia's tourists (*Tab. 3*). Other Asian tourists have come mainly from China, India, Israel, and the Philippines. Whereas 20 Asian countries were the sources of at least 10,000 tourists in the 1970s, the number increased to 25 countries in the 1980s when Asian arrivals more than tripled over those of the 1970s.

While Europe and Asia now account for two-thirds of America's overseas tourists, arrivals from the world's other 5 regions increased, too, in absolute numbers, but mostly percentages declined (*Tab. 2*). South America and the Caribbean are, in particular, the other major sources. If Central America were added to these two regions, Latin America as a whole was the source of 20 percent of all overseas tourists, leaving Oceania and Africa combined accounting for the remaining 5 percent.

Tabl. 4 and 5 show 94 countries of the world's 166 countries with populations of 150,000 or more, excluding Canada and Mexico, were sources of a minimum of 10,000 overseas tourists in the 1970s and 104 countries out of 170 countries were similar sources in the 1980s. The ten additions were primarily developing countries found in Africa and Asia. In fact, most countries listed under the category of 10-99,000 overseas tourists for the 1980s had developing economies that were beginning to generate growing numbers of arrivals. Notable exceptions were the small and developed countries of Iceland, Luxembourg, and Kuwait.

In the late 1970s, 16 of the 94 countries listed on *Tab. 4* were rated by the United Nations as being "more developed" because of their 1979 per capita GNPs of at least 7,260 US$[1]. They contributed 12.6 million overseas tourists to America or 43.3 percent of the decade's total. Japan, United Kingdom, and Germany were the three leading sources (*Tab. 3*). Meanwhile, the twelve "less developed" countries with 1979 per capita GNPs of 560 US$ or less on *Tab. 4* were the sources of only 771,300 tourists or 2.6 percent (*World Population Data Sheet 1981*)[2]. The leading sources were India, Honduras, and Haiti. An average of 240,000 tourists originated in each of the remaining 66 countries, which together sent 15.8 million visitors or 54.1 percent.

What becomes significant is that of the 104 countries in the 1980s, the 11 "more developed" countries with 1989 per capita GNPs of 16,990 US$ or over on *Tab. 5* provided more tourists, a total of 20.9 million, but only 30.4 percent of the decade's total[3]. The three leading "more developed" sources were Japan, France, and Switzerland (*Tab. 5*). Eighteen "less developed" countries with 1989 per capita GNPs of 750 US$ or less on *Tab. 5* were the sources of 3.1 million tourists or 4.5 percent for the decade (*World Population Data Sheet 1991*)[4]. China, India, and Haiti led the group. In this decade, the remaining 75 countries contributed an average of 598,000 tourists, amounting to 48.9 million visitors or 65.1 percent. These comparisons of overseas arrivals by decade reveal that not only have more "less developed" countries, notably China, become sources, but that more countries are sources and generally more tourists are coming from all of the sources. This indicates a trend toward democratization of international tourism, a process that has already occurred in many countries in regard to domestic tourism.

Critics may argue that countries with small populations may inherently not become major sources of overseas tourists in contrast to countries with large populations that have greater possibilities of being included in *Tab. 4 and 5*. Interestingly enough, some countries with 1980s populations of under 10 million, such as Sweden and Switzerland, were each the source of more than 1 million tourists during the decade. "Less developed" India, on the other hand, had a population of 860 million by 1989. It was the source of an increasing number of tourists in the 1980s, but yet a relatively small number (632,000) for the size of its population. Then, too, there is "less developed" Haiti that had a population of approximately 6 million and was at the same time the source of 527,000 tourists. Undoubtedly, other variables besides economic conditions, such as the ability to obtain visas and proximity, are important in the decision-making processes of whether residents of foreign countries will travel overseas and where.

Changing foreign immigration to America since the passage of the 1965 Immigration and Nationality Act Amendments may be another variable in determining overseas travel, especially from the emerging sources. The Amendments, which eliminated origins quotas that had long favored Europeans, opened America to many new and large sources of immigrants. Consequently, Asian and Latin American immigrants accounted for 75 percent of all immigrants (4.4 million) in the 1970s and 85 percent of the 6.3 million immigrants of the 1980s (*Carlson, 1994a*). For example, Haiti and India appeared for the first time in each decade on the list of sources of at least 50,000 immigrants. Haiti was the source of 186,000 immigrants while India contributed 418,000 immigrants during the two decades (*Carlson 1994a, b*). Relatives and friends of these Asian and Latin American immigrants are very likely to become tourists and to develop new patterns of travel to America.

Conclusions

The United States has witnessed since 1950 a rapid growth in the arrival of overseas visitors whose purpose is solely for pleasure. This brief analysis of their origins contributes not only to an understanding of the regional associations and global interactions created by overseas tourism, but also clues to economic development. Undoubtedly, America, as do many major tourist destinations, attracts most of its tourists from the highly developed countries, which are commonly acknowledged in the tourism literature. What is not identified are the emerging sources. America needs to be aware of these new sources in assessing and developing touristic strategies as well as in promoting an appreciation of the tourists' different cultural backgrounds.

Surely, many more millions of overseas residents will choose the United States for their destination as growing economies provide additional discretionary income, airlines expand global routes and carry larger passenger loads, and political harmony unites the world. In order to fully study and understand this further growth of international tourism, the United States needs to establish an enumerating system that provides unquestionable tourism data, which will enhance comparisons of methods and findings. American geographers, too, need to recognize the spatial significance of international tourism. It is disturbing to find that leading economic geography textbooks, for example, still lack material on international tourism, probably because it has not been a traditional subject for the discipline (*Carlson 1980, 156*)[5].

Zusammenfassung

Die Vereinigten Staaten haben seit 1950 einen rapiden Zuwachs an Ankünften von Freizeittouristen aus Übersee verzeichnet. Diese kurze Analyse über ihre Herkunft trägt nicht nur zum Verständnis der regionalen Verbindungen und der globalen Wechselwirkungen bei, die durch den Tourismus aus Übersee hervorgerufen werden, sondern bringt auch Ideen zur wirtschaftlichen Entwicklung ein. Amerika, wie viele andere Haupttouristenziele, zieht ohne Zweifel meist Touristen aus hochentwickelten Ländern an, was im allgemeinen von der Fremdenverkehrsliteratur auch bestätigt wird. Dabei werden aber die neuen möglichen Länder meist nicht festgehalten. Amerika muß sich diese neuen Quellen vor Augen halten, indem es sowohl Tourismusstrategien festsetzt und entwickelt als auch mit der Anerkennung der unterschiedlichen kulturellen Hintergründe der Touristen wirbt.

Sicher werden noch Millionen von Überseebewohner die Vereinigten Staaten als ihr Reiseziel wählen, da die wachsende Wirtschaft zusätzlich verfügbares Einkommen ermöglicht, Luftlinien ihre globalen Flugrouten ausweiten und mehr Passagiere transportieren und politische Harmonie die Welt vereint. Um das weitere Wachstum des internationalen Tourismus zu untersuchen und zu verstehen, müssen die Vereinigten Staaten ein Zählsystem errichten, welches unumstrittene Tourismuszahlen zur Verfügung stellt und so Vergleiche der Methoden und Ergebnisse erleichtert. Amerikanische Geographen müssen ebenfalls die räumliche Bedeutung des internationalen Tourismus erkennen. Es ist nicht verständlich, daß zum Beispiel führende US-amerikanische Lehrbücher der Wirtschaftsgeographie immer noch kein Material über internationalen Tourismus beinhalten, wahrscheinlich deshalb, weil Fragen wie diese kein traditionelles wirtschaftsgeographisches Thema sind (*Carlson 1980, 156*)[5].

Notes

[1] The 16 "more developed" countries (1979): Austria, Australia, Belgium, Denmark, Finland, France, Germany, Iceland, Japan, Kuwait, Luxembourg, Netherlands, Norway, Saudi Arabia, Sweden, Switzerland.
[2] The 12 "less developed" countries (1979): Bolivia, China, Dominica, Egypt, Ghana, Haiti, Honduras, India, Indonesia, Kenya, Liberia, Pakistan.
[3] The 11 "more developed" countries (1989): Denmark, Finland, France, Iceland, Japan, Kuwait, Luxembourg, Norway, Sweden, Switzerland, United Arab Emirates.
[4] "The 18 "less developed" countries (1989): Bangladesh, Bolivia, China, Egypt, Ethiopia, Ghana, Guyana, Haiti, India, Indonesia, Kenya, Liberia, Nigeria, Pakistan, Senegal, Sri Lanka, Western Samoa, Zimbabwe.
[5] For example, see A. deSouza and F. Stutz (1994): The World Economy: Resources, Location, Trade, and Development. New York, Macmillan.

References

Carlson, A. (1994a): America's New Immigration: Characteristics, Destinations, and Impact, 1970-1989. In: The Social Science Journal, 31 (3), 213-236.
Carlson, A. (1994b): Caribbean Immigration to the U.S., 1965-1989. In: Caribbean Affairs, 7 (1), 142-160.
Carlson, A. (1980): Geographical Research on International and Domestic Tourism. In: Journal of Cultural Geography, 1 (1), 149-160.
Edgell, D. (1993): World Tourism at the Millennium. Department of Commerce, U.S. Travel and Tourism Administration, Washington, D.C, Government Printing Office.
Matley, I. (1976): The Geography of International Tourism. In: Association of American Geographers, Washington, D.C.
Paci, E. (1994): World Tourism Organization, Market Research, July 25, Madrid, Spain.
Rafferty, M. (1993): A Geography of World Tourism. Englewood Cliffs, NJ, Prentice Hall.
World Population Data Sheet (1981): Population Reference Bureau, Washington, D.C.
World Population Data Sheet (1991): Population Reference Bureau, Washington, D.C.

Address of the Author

Alvar W. Carlson
Department of Geography
Bowling Green State University
Bowling Green, OH 43403
USA